WALTER STARKIE

For Charlotte

Walter Starkie
1894–1976

An Odyssey

JACQUELINE HURTLEY

FOUR COURTS PRESS

Set in 10.5 on 12.5 Ehrhardt for
FOUR COURTS PRESS
7 Malpas Street, Dublin 8, Ireland
www.fourcourtspress.ie
and in North America for
FOUR COURTS PRESS
c/o ISBS, 920 N.E. 58th Avenue, Suite 300, Portland, OR 97213.

ISBN 978-1-84682-363-3

Printed in England by
Antony Rowe Ltd, Chippenham, Wilts.

Contents

Illustrations

CREDITS

España. Ministerio de Educatión, Cultura y Deporte. Archivo General de la Administración, Fondo Medios de Communicación Social del Estado, signatura F-03834-040-011: 22; María Victoria Alfaro Drake: 21; William Chislett: 28; Louis De Goor: 15; Elaine Evans: 25; Billie Heller: 26, 27; *Irish Independent*: 17; Diana Murray: 18; the John Murray Collection: 1, 2, 4, 13, 14, 16, 19, 20, 23; J. Richardson, *Enid Starkie* (London, John Murray, 1973): 9; Special Collections Research Center, Southern Illinois University Carbondale – J.B. Pond Correspondence and Papers, 1928–32: 11; E. Starkie, *A lady's child* (London, Faber & Faber, 1941): 3, 5, 6, 7, 10; The Enid Starkie Papers, Bodleian Library, University of Oxford, and Alma Starkie: 8, 12, 24

Abbreviations

JBP, SIUC	J.B. Pond Correspondence and Papers, 1928–1932, Southern Illinois University, Carbondale
LLSD	Lord Lloyd's Spanish Diary
OHP, UCLA	Oral History Program, University of California Los Angeles
RIA	Royal Irish Academy
RIAM	Royal Irish Academy of Music
SCRC, UCL	Special Collections Research Center, University of Chicago Library
SRL, UKAN	Spencer Research Library, University of Kansas
SRL, UKAN, RVC	Spencer Research Library, University of Kansas, Robert Vosper Correspondence
TCD	Trinity College Dublin
TNA, BC	The National Archives of the UK, British Council Files
UCD	University College Dublin
ULL, GLS	University of Liverpool Library, Special Collections and Archives, Gypsy Lore Society
WJM	William Joseph Myles Starkie

Note

Readers wishing to consult the GLS material should note that the first numbers which follows the reference GLS are to be cited in Roman numerals.

Acknowledgments

The biography that follows could not have been produced without the interest, cooperation and support of many people to whom I am greatly indebted. A number of their names are mentioned in the Interviews and Correspondents list in the Bibliography but I also wish to acknowledge here the generous disposition over many years of W.F. Starkie's daughter, Alma, and thank her most sincerely for her cooperation. I also thank other members of the Starkie family: W.F. Starkie's sister Muriel, grandsons Michael and Patrick, his sister-in-law, Nenelle Bonetti, his nieces Pamela Bacon and Gillian E. Leonard for speaking to me and providing me with material. Over several years I was afforded the opportunity to consult the correspondence and papers relating to Starkie's John Murray publications as well as being provided with a privileged space and ever kindly welcome at 50 Albemarle Street by Virginia Murray. John R. Murray was always ready to assist and Diana Murray graciously contributed to the enterprise by allowing me to interview her.

I gratefully acknowledge research scholarships awarded by (what was) the Spanish Ministerio de Educación y Ciencia and the Generalitat de Catalunya as well as a travel grant from the European Society for the Study of English (ESSE). The Ministerio grant enabled me to explore some of the material held in the Enid Starkie Papers as well as files in the BBC Written Archives Centre. Grants from the Generalitat de Catalunya afforded me the possibility of consulting holdings in the United States. On a first visit I was able to see material at the Humanities Research Center at the University of Texas, Austin, from where I travelled to the University of Southern Illinois, Carbondale. On a second journey I consulted the script of the Bernard Galm interview with Walter Starkie carried out under the auspices of the Oral History Program at UCLA and accessed material in the University Archive. The ESSE bursary financed travel and accomodation in Budapest, from where I was able to travel into Romania.

I am most grateful to staff in libraries and archives in Ireland, England, Italy, Spain, Canada and the United States for their professionalism and patience. I thank Charles Benson, Bernard Meehan and Ruth Potterton at TCD as well as Lydia Ferguson, the latter for most generous efforts on my behalf; Seamus Helferty at UCD was also exceptionally helpful as were Mairéad Delaney at the Abbey Theatre and Brigid Dolan at the Royal Irish Academy. The staff at the National Library of Ireland were splendidly efficient and kept me in good spirits during long hours poring over microfilm; Leslie Guider merits special mention for diligence in dealing with reams of photocopies and, moreover, with a twinkle in his eye. Ian Lee introduced me to material at RTÉ Written Archives and Brian Lynch was selfless in making me familiar with Walter Starkie material there. I also thank Niall Matthews for bringing my attention to Cathal Shannon Snr's interview with W.F. Starkie and going out of his way to facilitate access to it. I am grateful to Philip Shields at RIAM for providing me with assistance over years and also, more recently, to Laoise Doherty. I am most grateful to Mary Clapinson as then Keeper of Western Manuscripts and Judith Priestman, both at the Bodleian Library, for enabling initial access to Starkie family correspondence in the Enid Starkie Papers. Colin Harris was also most helpful at that juncture in Room 132 and has continued to be so. I am greatly indebted to Maureen Watry for meticulous assistance with Gypsy Lore Society material in the Archive at the University of Liverpool, where I was also rendered splendid service by Mícheál Ó hAodha. Joan Murrell was most helpful with YMCA material when it was housed at George Williams College in London. Staff at the British Library in Bloomsbury and at the Newspaper Library in Colindale have always been most efficient and helpful as have staff at The National Archives at Kew, The National Archives of Ireland and at the BBC Written Archives Centre. I also acknowledge the valuable assistance of British Council Records Management Officer Peter Bloor as well as that of staff at the British Institute in Madrid. I appreciate the interest expressed in the project by Ireland's Ambassador to Spain, Justin Harman, and thank him for material provided as well as for the time he gave me. J.B. Lawson, former librarian at Shrewsbury School, was exceptionally helpful when I visited the school in the 1990s; more recently, I am indebted to Mike Morrogh for answering my queries. I also acknowledge the help of staff at the Archivo General de la Administración in Alcalá de Henares, at the Biblioteca de Catalunya in Barcelona as well as in the library at the Universitat de Barcelona. My gratitude to José Manuel Calderón, archivist at the Fundación Casa de Alba in Madrid for facilitating materials. Lorenzo Maté at the Abadía de Santo Domingo de Silos afforded me great assistance in tracking down records of Walter Starkie's sojourns at the abbey and I thank him most sincerely.

Apart from the individuals in libraries and archives mentioned above or in particular footnotes in the text on account of help with specific materials, I wish to express deep gratitude to those who have seen me through the Walter Starkie 'chase' over more years than I (and surely they!) care to remember. Doireann MacDermott was the supervisor of my PhD and generously took on the reading of yet another manuscript. I am most grateful for the time she spent with me once again and for her careful commentary. I have also been very fortunate in receiving pondered feedback and criticism over a number of years from John Barnes, who defied antipodian distance in getting through to me. Josephine Barnes was always supportive and I learnt much from her; I deeply regret that she cannot contemplate the finished product. There are others, too, who lent great support along the way and whose loss I also lament: Frank and Ethel Hurtley, Elena Catena, Nena Pérez de Nanclares, Sally Smith, Enriqueta Comín and Antolín Moren.

Finally, I wish to record my thanks to Terence Brown, Andrew Carpenter, Valentine Cunningham, Terence P. Dolan, Tadhg Foley, Nigel Glendinning, Dermot Keogh, Declan Kiberd, Edna Longley, José-Carlos Mainer, W.J. McCormack, Christopher Murray and David Staines for listening to me and providing encouragement as well as the benefit of their knowledge. I am further indebted to Valentine Cunningham,

Dermot Keogh and José-Carlos Mainer for kindly supporting my application for research grants. I also thank Christine O'Doherty for sharing her work on W.J.M. Starkie with me and am grateful both to her and Dick O'Doherty for their hospitality. My gratitude, too, to Éibhear Walshe for helping me reach Rosscarbery. I also thank David Pierce for interest shown at an early stage in the research. I am grateful to Fernando Alonso, Olga Borderas, Elizabeth Butler Cullingford, Antonio de Toro, Angela Downing, Katherine Duncan-Jones, Fernando Galván, Yolanda Gamboa, Gian-Antonio Giacopelo, Justin Grant, Heidi Grünewald, Michael Holroyd, Rosemary Hone, Mihaela Irimia, Helen Kirrane, Enric Lluch i Martin, John London, Simon Luterbacher, Franco and Flavia Marenco, Susan McClary, Maureen Murphy, Barbro Norbelie, Anna Pastorino, Luigi Pastorino, Roberto Pastorino, Rosa Pérez, Hermann and Erika Real, Ferenc Takács, Jaime Vandor, Loreto Vilar and Sara Wilbourne, all of whom helped in a variety of ways.

I gratefully acknowledge a grant-in-aid facilitating publication from the Research Committee in the Facultat de Filologia at the Universitat de Barcelona (UB). I also wish to express most sincere thanks to the Head of the Departament de Filologia Anglesa i Alemanya at the UB, Isabel Verdaguer, who, together with the Faculty Head of Studies, Ana Moya, and Coordinator of the English Section in Literature, Enric Monforte, succeeded in affording me a sabbatical semester, which enabled me to complete the manuscript. I am deeply grateful to Mercedes Padial for painstaking assistance with the lay-out of the manuscript. I thank my colleague Brian Mott for his company in Hungary and Romania and all colleagues and friends in the Facultat de Filologia for their interest and support. A number of members of IASIL have shown interest, provided encouragement and friendship over a number of years. Michael Kenneally, Rhona Richman Kenneally, Wolfgang and Hannelore Zach have constantly been supportive. I thank them all. Long-standing friends have sustained me and I thank them most heartily for their support and understanding: Sarah Brook, Sandra Carroll, Mary Carroll, Mary Collins, Pauline Ernest, Susan Fernyhough, John Fernyhough, David Fulton, Barbara Marcus, Gloria Montero, Liz Russell and Alex Smith. Particular thanks to Kathleen Firth for helping me not to lose my sense of humour.

Last but certainly not least, I thank the readers at Four Courts Press who provided valuable comments and criticism of an earlier version of the manuscript.

I recall Michael Adams with gratitude for so warmly welcoming the prospect of a biography on Walter Starkie. Whilst bemoaning his absence, I gratefully acknowledge the ongoing warmth, and professional cool, of Martin Fanning.

Correspondence and other unpublished material cited in the text appears courtesy of the following individuals, bodies and institutions, to whom I am most grateful: Alma Starkie; Ampleforth Abbey; Archivio Centrale dello Stato; Archivo General de la Administración; Archivo Manuel de Falla; BBC Written Archives Centre; Biblioteca de Asturias Ramón Pérez de Ayala; Biblioteca de Catalunya; Biblioteca Marucelliana; Bodleian Library; British Institute of Florence; British Council; California State University, Dominguez Hills; Casa-Museo Unamuno; Cleveland Museum of Art Archives; Daniel Harmsworth; Fundación Casa de Alba; Harry

Ransom Center, University of Texas at Austin; Harvard University Archives; Michael Starkie; Monasterio de Santo Domingo de Silos; National University of Ireland Galway; RTÉ Written Archives; Special Collections, University of Houston Libraries; Special Collections Research Center, Southern Illinois University Carbondale; Special Collections Research Center, University of Chicago Library; Spencer Research Library, University of Kansas; the Athenaeum; the Board of the Abbey Theatre; the Board of the National Library of Ireland; The Board of Trinity College Dublin; The British Library; the John Murray Collection; the National Archives of the UK; the Royal Irish Academy; the Trustees of the St John's College Robert Graves Trust; Trinity College Archives, Trinity College, Hartford, Connecticut; University of California Los Angeles University Archives; University of Liverpool Library, Gypsy Lore Society Archive; University of Reading Special Collections, Chatto & Windus Archives, Random House Group Ltd; University of Reading Special Collections, Records of Macmillan & Co. Ltd; Uppsala universitetsbibliotek; Westminster Diocesan Archives.

Every effort has been made to obtain permission to quote from unpublished materials. The author will rectify any omission in future publications if further information on the copyright holder is received.

Words are tricky things, … they're much more tricky than violins.

M. Ondatjee, *The English patient*

Little Friend of all the World … what he loved was the game for its own sake.

R. Kipling, *Kim*

'Murphy, all life is figure and ground.'
'But a wandering to find home,' said Murphy.

S. Beckett, *Murphy*

Introduction

Nation, Narration, Nomadism

Nations, like narratives, … only fully realise their horizons in the mind's eye. […]
… a particular ambivalence … haunts the idea of the nation, the language of
those who write it and the lives of those who live it. It is an ambivalence that
emerges from a growing awareness that … the cultural temporality of the nation
inscribes a much more transitional social reality.[1]

The insight of Parsi critic Homi Bhabha into a sense of ambivalence regarding nation
and narration is pertinent, as is the concept of nomadism, in pondering the eighty-two
years of a life that began in Victorian Dublin and ended in post-Franco Madrid. In the
four score years in between, apart from Ireland, where this existential narrative begins,
it is mainland Britain and, more particularly, the metropolitan south-east of England
which come into the picture, as do France, Italy, Spain, Portugal, Greece, Germany,
Hungary, Egypt, India, Iran, Armenia, Bulgaria, Macedonia, Rumania, Serbia,
Turkey, North Africa, Abyssinia, Canada and the United States. No mean series of
destinations for a sufferer of chronic asthma. The list might suggest a restless
existence; it certainly conveys one that was not characterized by repose, but neither
was the *fin de siècle* in which Walter Fitzwilliam Starkie descended upon Dublin.
Indeed, there was a rallying of social and political organization, propelled by a sense
of determination, which came to forcefully threaten and eventually undermine a
status quo established for well-nigh a century.

   The nationalist consciousness that had been gathering momentum in Ireland since
the late eighteenth century would grow over the nineteenth in the wake of the sacrifice
of Wolfe Tone, already bent on '[breaking] the connection with England.'[2] The creation
of the Gaelic Athletic Association in 1884 and the Gaelic League in 1893 were both
symptomatic of the organization and determination alluded to above and specifically
geared towards constructing a de-Anglicized Irish identity. As Douglas Hyde, one of
the founding fathers of the League, asserted in his address to the Irish National Literary
Society in 1892, it was now time to produce good Irishmen instead of poor imitations
of Englishmen.[3] Thus, the dominant discourse of the nation as established under the
Union of Great Britain and Ireland in 1801 came to increasingly lose its hold and would
be radically challenged by those Republicans-made-martyrs to the cause of an
independent Ireland in 1916, when W.F. Starkie was twenty-one years of age. A little
over five years later, the young man would be taking his Italian bride to a country that
was to begin re-fashioning itself with the signing of the Anglo-Irish Treaty in

1 H.K. Bhabha, 'Introduction: narrating the nation' in H.K. Bhabha (ed.), *Nation and narration*
(London, 1994), p. 1. 2 K. Curtis, *P.S. O'Hegarty (1879–1955). Sinn Féin Fenian* (London, 2010), p.
9. 3 D. Hyde, 'The necessity for de-Anglicising Ireland' (1892) in M. Storey (ed.), *Poetry and Ireland
since 1800: a source book* (London, 1988), pp 83–4.

December 1921 and was to increasingly become something of a foreign country to his ilk over the 1930s. Thus, wandering, already his wont as the First World War drew to a close, became a feature of his wide-ranging activity in the 1920s and established itself as a way of life come the 1930s with the rise of Eamon de Valera's star.

The biography that follows focuses on those eighty-two years of existence, honing in on childhood, youth and the professional life over the 1920s, 30s, 40s as well as into the 50s when W.F. Starkie left Western Europe to take up residence in the United States, where he remained until the 1970s. Memory of him today tends to rest on the travel books he published in the 1930s, two of which carry the notion of raggle-taggle in the title, thus the reputation which tends to surface when his name is aired. In Spain, he is also particularly remembered for the position he occupied as British Council Representative from 1940 until 1954, that is, over the first decade, and into the second, of General Franco's regime. However, in spite of the official post he held in Spain with the Council, his professorship of Spanish at Trinity College Dublin and the responsibility he bore as a government-appointed Director of Dublin's Abbey Theatre alongside W.B. Yeats and Lady Gregory, the raff and rabble reputation has lingered, a lingering which the subject himself only partially contributed to. This first biographical study of W.F. Starkie is published, then, as the liminal label lingers on, indeed, appears securely rooted. I do not ignore the raggle-taggle component; I could only do so at my peril as the Gypsy pursuit concentrated much of Starkie's energy as well as that of those who remember or have written about him, but I am interested in exploring the roving in the context of changing times, of borders redrawn, both at home and abroad. Therefore, I seek to move beyond the rogue-bound repute with a view to providing a wider picture of a life lived in nations subject to moments of intense political activity and transformation: a partitioned Ireland in the wake of the Anglo-Irish Treaty of 1921, fascist Italy of the 1920s, 30s and into the 40s, the 'One, Great and Free' Spain of General Franco following the Civil War, together with the experience of the subject's sallies into other shifting territories: Hungary, Roumania, Germany, Abyssinia and Portugal in the period between the World Wars.

Performance is a fundamental notion in considering the life of W.F. Starkie. A talent for playing a part, registered by his sister Enid when recollecting her childhood,[4] might account for her brother's facility in donning identities. However, Julie Ann Stevens's reflections on 'particular notions of Irish national character' constructed in the nineteenth century could also be brought to bear here. Hence, the 'malleability, duality and extremeness' recorded by Thomas Crofton Croker in both the landscape and people of 'the south of Ireland' or the '[w]avering between extremes'[5] that so fascinated the Trinity College Dublin divine Charles Robert Maturin and led to his creation of Melmoth, the wanderer, in his eponymous novel of 1820. Similarly, Lady Morgan and Sheridan Le Fanu 'are enthralled by their characters' "shifting faces", faces that slip in and out of different masks.'[6] Thus, Stevens concludes: 'Irish novelists

---

4 E. Starkie, *A lady's child* (London, 1941), p. 96. Enid Starkie became Reader in French at Somerville College Oxford, where, apart from her teaching and research activity, she acquired a degree of notoriety on account of a flamboyance made manifest in her dress, speech and behaviour.   **5** J.A. Stevens, *The Irish scene in Somerville and Ross* (Dublin, 2007), p. 135.   **6** Stevens specifically cites Lady Morgan's

note how the extreme conditions of Irish life affect characterization. Emphasis rests on a trembling or wavering position that can manifest itself as a masking/unmasking process' and, in the case of Melmoth, manifests itself as 'ambivalence'.[7] The present biography does not, initially, approach W.F. Starkie as a fictional character; it is bent, rather, on tracing identity through historical records relating to the life. However, it might well be argued that the lifespan in question comes to make manifest the shifting quality, the masking/unmasking process and ambivalence alluded to in the Irish fiction in English cited above. And, certainly, as Starkie became an adult, he witnessed his place of birth becoming dislodged from the meanings that had defined its identity and shaped generations of Starkies. From 1916 on, the territory beneath his feet increasingly made its troubled nature felt for those who, materially, like himself, had led the least troubled of lives. Finally, apart from relating W.F. Starkie's 'spirit of performance'[8] to nineteenth century Irish literature in English, it will be seen that the observations of Russian critic Mikhail Bakhtin regarding the rogue, clown and fool in the novel also prove pertinent in assessing the range of roles acted out by the biographical subject in an increasingly totalitarian Europe of the 1930s and 40s.[9]

* * *

[O]f all the major literary genres [biography] is probably the most political – the one most likely to influence how a nation and its history are defined and to be forced into serving the dominant point of view.[10]

In *Reflections on biography*, Paula Backscheider uses the expression to push the envelope to refer to biographies which extend the current limits of performance, which challenge established boundaries: 'There are biographies that "push the envelope." Tom Wolfe made the phrase familiar, as he used it to refer to the limits of a particular aircraft's performance and the pilot's daredevil probing of these outer limits.'[11] An early instance of 'daredevil probing of … outer limits' in relation to biographical form would be Virginia Woolf's *Orlando* (1928). The text is disruptive of the biographical subject as established, of the way in which s/he had been narrated, foregrounding, even flaunting, and stimulatingly exploring 'how', as Norman Denzin has insisted: 'persons are created in texts and other systems of discourse.'[12] Paul de Man's piece on 'Autobiography as defacement' might be cited here too since W.F. Starkie's travel books claimed to be based on his own experiences and, beyond these, two of his texts foreground the notion in the sub-title: *The waveless plain. An Italian autobiography* (1938) and *Scholars and Gypsies. An autobiography* (1963). As Michael Benton has explained, de Man's point is that 'autobiographies are texts that generate fictions or figurative images rather than the self-knowledge they purport to seek.'[13] These fictions or figurative images are regarded by

Florence Macarthy (1818) and Le Fanu's *Uncle Silas* (1864) in this connection.   7 Stevens, *The Irish scene*, pp 146, 147.   8 J. Yeats cited by R. Tracy, 'Foreword' in Stevens, *The Irish scene*, p. xi.   9 M.M. Bakhtin, *The dialogic imagination*, trans. M. Holquist (Austin, 1981), pp 158–67.   10 P.R. Backscheider, *Reflections on biography* (Oxford, 1999), p. 216.   11 Ibid., p. 164.   12 N.K. Denzin, *Interpretive biography* (Newbury Park, 1989), p. 23.   13 M. Benton, *Literary biography. An introduction*

the American critic as 'de-facement',[14] masks, which conceal the subject, who becomes a figure of rhetoric. Also worth bearing in mind here is de Man's claim that the autobiographical project 'may itself produce and determine the life and … whatever the writer *does* is in fact governed by the technical demands of self-portraiture and thus determined, in all its aspects, by the resources of his medium.'[15] Taking de Man's observations into consideration, the subject of this biography as reflected in his autobiographical writings might be conceived of as less than real and I take on that neither can the strictures of form outlined by the American critic be ignored. Therefore, the autobiographical texts are not necessarily as reliable as might be anticipated for providing information on the biographical subject. On the other hand, if the subject's life writing is taken as relaying 'the real', the potentially distorting filter of memory cannot be overlooked either. Thus, I am aware that the autobiographical writings of W.F. Starkie and his sister Enid, which I have drawn on as a source of knowledge for the childhood and youth, are prone to possess the above-mentioned slips and slants. Recourse to them in this biographical enterprise is undertaken for their potential as documents of perception into lived experience within a period though also with a consciousness of their potential for limited insight.

In *Orlando*, 'the first duty of a biographer' is outlined as the following procedure: 'to plod, without looking to right or left, in the indelible footprints of truth,' and there is further elaboration on this dutiful task: 'unenticed by flowers; regardless of shade; on and on methodically till we fall plump into the grave and write *finis* on the tombstone above our heads.' Woolf's satirical text dispenses with interests later described as 'highly restricted',[16] abandons a method which subjects, in order to pursue a revolutionary form, one which will enable the biographer to follow the 'flowers', wherever they might be blooming, or wilting, and to explore the 'shade'. The present biography is more modest in its endeavour, making no claim to revolutionary form, but in working to produce a life of a much mythologized subject, the biography has entailed wandering widely, exploring and analysing the 'shade', where truths, or further fictions, have surfaced. In his *Literary biography*, Benton refers to the narratological concepts of *histoire* and *récit*, distinguishing the former, defined as: 'the chronological sequence of events', from the latter: 'the text's representation of events.'[17] Observing the distinction, it is clear that the chronological sequence in Starkie's life, began in 1894 and ended in 1976. These biological facts have, on occasion, been erroneously recorded, but were registered according to the law of the land and can, therefore, be verified. However, what sets the biographer peering in the shade in the case of W.F. Starkie is not the *histoire* but the *récit*, that is, the representation of events, as well as character, to be found in texts authored by the subject himself and in narratives produced by others.

A chronological sequence has purposely been adopted in reconstructing the decades of W.F. Starkie's lifespan. It is hoped that the reader will not feels s/he is being

---

(Oxford, 2009), p. 133. **14** P. de Man, 'Autobiography as de-facement', *Modern Language Notes*, 94:5 (Dec. 1979), 919–30 at 930. **15** Ibid., 920. The italics are in the original. **16** V. Woolf, *Orlando. A biography* (Oxford 1998), pp 40, 58. **17** M. Benton, *Literary biography*, p. 86.

subjected to plodding through the years but by means of the contextualization, is acquiring a greater sense than has been established to date with reference to the historical and political *milieux* in which the biographical subject moved and which contributed to determining decisions at particular junctures. It also aims to provide further insight into the workings of politics and culture in Europe in the period between the two World Wars, during the Second World War, and into the 1950s. It might be claimed that the contextualization constitutes a notable nudge of the envelope as Starkie has rarely been situated within the wider historical and political contexts of his time.[18] References to him have constructed a '*character*',[19] an 'eccentric',[20] predominantly encasing him within the myths of picaresque professor, scholar gypsy, versatile vagabond, pilgrim or the fellow with a fiddle.[21] While recognizing these diverse identities as roles wrought out of 'Walter's wardrobe', the biography that follows seeks to challenge the mushrooming myths, to deconstruct the sustained image of 'that merry wanderer'[22] and to unravel the 'complex' character registered in recent scholarship.[23] It makes no claim to producing a definitive version of the man or matters.[24] It does, however, provide another (hi)story.

18 James Whiston's entry on W.F. Starkie in the *Oxford dictionary of national biography* contributes to redressing the imbalance. 19 I. Gibson, 'Prólogo' in W. Starkie, *Aventuras de un irlandés en España*, trans. A. Espina (Madrid, 2006), p. 10. The italics are in the original. 20 D. Callahan, 'The early reception of Miguel de Unamuno in England, 1907–1939', *Modern Language Review*, 100: Supplement (2005). *http://www.mhra.org.uk/ojs/index.php/MLR/article/viewfile/21/31*, p.391, accessed 11 August 2011. 21 In this connection, see Ian Gibson's prologue to the reprint of the Spanish translation of *Spanish raggle taggle* (W. Starkie, *Aventuras de un irlandés en España*, trans. Antonio Espina (Madrid, 2006), pp 9–13) and I. Gibson, 'El hispanista andarín y juglar' in the reprint of the Spanish translation of *The road to Santiago. Pilgrims of St James* (W. Starkie, *El camino de Santiago. Las peregrinaciones al sepulcro del apóstol*, trans. Amando Lázaro Ros (2nd ed. Palencia, 2010), pp 5–8). For comment on Espina's translation, which carries a series of omissions and adaptations, see J. Hurtley, 'The writer, the translator and strategic location: adapting the adventures' in L. Pegenaute, et al. (eds), *La traducción del futuro: mediación lingüística y cultural en el siglo 21*, vol. 1 (Barcelona, 2008), pp 27–34. More recently, two Spanish publications have highlighted Starkie's irresistible personality: I. Pérez de Villanueva-Tovar, *La Residencia de Estudiantes, 1910–1936. Grupo universitario y residencia de señoritas* (Madrid, 2011), p. 500; A. Rivero Taravillo, *Luis Cernuda. Años de exilio (1938–1963)*, vol. 2 (Barcelona, 2011), p. 332. 22 W. Shakespeare, *A midsummer night's dream* (Oxford, 2008), p. 155. 23 I. Pérez de Villanueva-Tovar, *La Residencia*, p. 500; A. Rivero Taravillo, *Luis Cernuda*, p. 332; C. Wills, *That neutral island* (London, 2007), p. 347. Wills appears to confuse W.F. Starkie as designer of 'Irish educational reforms' with his father, W.J.M. Starkie. (C. Wills, *Neutral island*, p. 348.) 24 The release of British government documents over the current century may contribute to further knowledge: witness, for instance, the changing portrait of Arthur Ransome following the declassification of 'a portion of papers' by MI5 in 2005 (R. Chambers, *The last Englishman. The double life of Arthur Ransome* (London, 2010), pp 157, 368). Further to the matter of additional sources of information, the sale and purchase of a so-called Walter Starkie Archive by the Durán auction rooms in Madrid in 1987 and 1996, carried through by Durán on behalf of an anonymous vendor and anonymous purchaser, should be mentioned. Judging from the description in the catalogues, the archive carried correspondence and papers of historical interest in relation to Spain between the wars and following the Civil War. To my knowledge, the where-abouts of the archive is unknown. (See: 'La subasta del archivo de Walter Starkie', *El País*, 12 Dec. 1987, p. 22, and *Durán. Libros y manuscritos. Subasta número 210*. Madrid, 1987 (enero); 'L'arxiu de l'his-panista Walter Starkie es ven', *Avui*, 16 Feb. 1996, p. 37, and *Durán. Subastas de arte, libros y manuscritos. Subasta número 313*. Madrid, 1996 (diciembre).)

Prologue

In the Service of Majesty

A southern or western Irish Petty Sessions Court can teach many things, often useful, still more often entertaining.[1]

Through the years of the Union of Great Britain and Ireland, Walter Fitzwilliam Starkie's forebears sustained a worthy record of service to the British crown. The fictional world of Somerville and Ross's stories, narrated by Major Sinclair Yeates, RM, evokes the task of his father's father, William Robert Starkie. Born in Cork in 1825, he went up to Trinity College Dublin[2] at the age of seventeen.[3] In the wake of the Famine decade, Protestant William Robert Starkie, Esq., JP, married Catholic Frances Maria, Fanny, youngest daughter of the deceased Michael Power of Waterford, in his twenty-fifth year.[4] Four years later he became a Resident Magistrate, a post he was qualified for as a member of the ruling class[5] and which he occupied for over forty years in the counties of Mayo, Cork and Sligo. Thus the RM exercised his authority during the intense Fenian agitation of the 1860s and was in a position to acquire a first-hand awareness of an increasing challenge to the power of the Union. Two of his sons, Robert Fitzwilliam and William Joseph Myles, also became British civil servants.

In 1879, at the age of twenty-three, Robert Fitzwilliam was appointed a 3rd Sub-Inspector in the Royal Irish Constabulary, having spent six months as a private in the 19th Hussars and two-and-a-half years as a clerk in the National Bank of Ireland. He became an Adjutant at the Phoenix Park Depot between 1891 and 1893 and occupied the post of Private Secretary to the Inspector General over the next two years. He then followed in his father's footsteps, qualifying as a Resident Magistrate 3rd class in 1895, 2nd class in 1902 and 1st class in 1913.[6] In 1916, he would be made a Companion of

---

1 E.OE. Somerville, 'Preface' in E.OE. Somerville & M. Ross, *The Irish R.M.* (7th ed. London, 2000), page not numbered. 2 Henceforth TCD. 3 G.D. Burtchaell & T.U. Sadleir (eds), *Alumni Dublinenses. A register of the students, graduates, professors and provosts of Trinity College in the University of Dublin (1593–1860)* (Dublin, 1935), p. 776. The undergraduate is listed as Starkey [*sic*], William. There appears to be no record of his graduation. 4 'Marriages', *Cork Examiner*, 30 Oct.1850, page not numbered. The marriage took place in Dublin on the 29th. 5 P. Bonsall, *The Irish RMs. The resident magistrates in the British administration in Ireland* (Dublin, 1998), p. 16. 6 For full details of dates of service and positions occupied on Commissions of Enquiry at Dublin Castle and chairmanships, see J. Herlihy, *Royal Irish Constabulary officers. A biographical dictionary and genealogical guide, 1816–1922* (Dublin, 2005), p. 291. With reference to 'some evidence to suggest that family connections were of assistance in getting public employment', E. O'Halpin has cited 'R.M. [*sic*] Starkie, a resident magistrate [who] repeatedly pressed his claims to higher office with the support of his brother W.J.[M.] Starkie, the head of the Board of National Education' (E. O'Halpin, *The decline of the Union. British government in Ireland, 1892–1920* (Dublin, 1987), pp 95–6).

the Order of the Bath. His brother, William Joseph Myles,[7] was born in 1860 when the family resided in County Sligo, initially a less demanding post for his father's profession than that of Cork.[8] They occupied a house at Rosses Point, 'Elsinore', evocative of Shakespeare's *Hamlet* and the English Literature to which WJM, future Resident Commissioner of Education, devoted much of his own energies, whilst also seeking to channel those of Irish children towards the canonical works of the English bard. Further hours were spent in his study annotating Aristophanes and translating the Greek dramatist's texts into Elizabethan English. Brought up a Catholic,[9] he had been educated at Clongowes Wood College in County Kildare before attending Shrewsbury, the English public school where he was the only Catholic pupil, yet he became Head Boy. He pursued an academic career, graduating from Cambridge with a first-class degree in Classics, going on to do an MA and being awarded an Hon. D.Litt. at TCD, where he became a Fellow and tutor.[10] He also established a lifelong friendship with the Professor of Ancient History and Greek enthusiast, twenty-one years his senior, the Reverend John Pentland Mahaffy. Perhaps most remembered today outside Ireland as Oscar Wilde's flamboyant tutor at TCD, Mahaffy would be knighted by the British monarchy but acquired particular notoriety in Ireland for his disparaging response to the Irish language in spite of, in the words of his biographers, 'his admiration and affection for [the] country [being] deep and strong'.[11] His colleague and friend WJM would also be awarded British recognition, rising to to the rank of Right Honourable.

In the early 1890s, WJM was teaching at Alexandra College, the Church of Ireland school for girls in the city of Dublin, where he met his future wife, May Caroline Walsh, then one of his pupils. The couple were married in July 1893 and in August of the following year their first son was born, Walter Fitzwilliam, named after his great grandfather, Walter Starkie, Esq., a captain in the 82nd Regiment of Foot (South Lancashire Regiment), a veteran of the Peninsular Wars, 'for which he obtained the medal and seven clasps, and who had a miraculous escape in 1816 from the wreck of the *Boadicea* which sank ... when returning from the Battle of Waterloo.'[12] Walter's second forename commemorated the first-born of William Robert Starkie and his wife. Robert Fitzwilliam had died in 1855 at the age of four as a consequence of water on the brain[13] and his two forenames had been given to the second son of Walter Fitzwilliam's grandparents on his father's side. WJM and May Caroline's first and only son to survive inherited names charged with particular meanings: a first which ressonated distinguished service to the nation-state abroad, one which might be trans-

7 Henceforth, the abbreviation WJM will be used when referring to Walter Fitzwilliam Starkie's father, William Joseph Myles Starkie. 8 P. Bonsall, *The Irish RMs*, p. 23. 9 On possible reasons for WJM and his sisters Fannie and Edyth being baptized Catholics, see C.T. O'Doherty, 'William Joseph Myles Starkie (1860–1920). The last Resident Commissioner of National Education in Ireland' (DPhil. thesis, May 1997), p. 9. 10 J.E. Auden (ed.), *Shrewsbury school register* (Shrewsbury, 1928), p. 251; J.A. Venn, *Alumni Cantabrigienses, Part 2: 1752–1900* (Cambridge, 1954), vi, p. 16; 'William Myles [*sic*] Joseph Starkie', *Hermathena*, 19:43 (1922), pp v–viii. 11 W.B. Stanford & R.B. McDowell, *Mahaffy. A biography of an Anglo-Irishman* (London, 1971), p. 116. 12 J. Herlihy, *Royal Irish Constabulary Officers*, p. 291. 13 *Cork Examiner*, 25 May 1855, page not numbered.

1 W.R. Starkie and family at Rosses Point, Co. Sligo, ready for an outing.

mitted as a challenge for the descendant who came to bear it, and a second which the child's uncle, his father's elder brother, had borne before him and who faithfully served in the British administration at home in Ireland, perhaps ever conscious of his own elder brother who had been denied the opportunity to follow in his father's footsteps.

Therefore, the summons to service under the Union had been honoured by three generations of the Starkies before Walter Fitzwilliam[14] and their dedication was rewarded by the trappings of the *patria* and her institutions: medal, clasps, the Order of the Bath and the distinction of Right Honourable. Their heir would have to find his way in a new order and in the wake of his father's premature death but the widow of the Right Honourable[15] remained: to hold the fort and fly the flag.

14 Henceforth, Walter Fitzwilliam Starkie will be referred to as Walter Starkie, the full name by which he is most widely known.   15 Mary Caroline Starkie continued to identify herself in public life as Mrs W.J.M. Starkie thirty years on from the death of her husband. See, for instance, her contribution as Vice-President of the Royal Irish Academy of Music (henceforth RIAM): Mrs W.J.M. Starkie, 'The Royal Irish Academy of Music' in A. Fleischman (ed.), *Music in Ireland: a symposium* (Cork, 1952), pp 104–12.

PART I

The Welding of a West Briton

'I'm always telling my brother Alan ... that he shouldn't encourage the waltzes, polkas and all those English dances here in the country. I declare to God he's becoming more of a West Briton every day.'

'What's a West Briton, Maggie? I suppose I'm one myself.'

'Sure of course you are! But we forgive you, for how could you be otherwise? You know less about your country than if you were a foreigner. Your parents have never given you the opportunity of understanding our struggle for our country's right to be free and independent.'

W. Starkie, *Scholars and Gypsies* (London, 1963), p. 46.

Ballybrack to Bray via Galway

HARROW HOUSE AND HEGEL, 1894–7

… it is solely by risking life that freedom is attained; […] The individual who has not staked his life may … be recognised as a Person; but he has not attained the truth of … recognition as an independent self-consciousness […] The one is independent whose essential nature is to be for itself, the other is dependent whose essence is life or existence for another. The former is the Master, … the latter the Bondsman.[1]

Harrow House on Church Road, Ballybrack, County Dublin, might well have been acknowledged as a suitable abode for the son of a Resident Magistrate seeking to establish his social standing in 1890s Dublin. Throughout his career William Joseph Myles Starkie appears to have looked to consolidating his social rank by inhabiting noteworthy houses. Thus, Harrow House, his first family home, would be followed by a number of splendid properties in and around Dublin to be occupied by Mrs W.J.M. Starkie and himself, their ever-growing family, and an assortment of staff. They ranged from the semi-rurally located, Georgian grace of both Harrow House and Somerset (the latter in Blackrock), to the assured Edwardian substance of the last, Melfort, in Shrewsbury Road, within the Dublin suburb of Ballsbridge: 'reminiscent of North Oxford',[2] passing through the sober city-Georgian of Fitzwilliam Place and the 'elevation and harmony'[3] of Undercliff[4] in Strathmore Road, Killiney.

Writing about his life almost seventy years on, Walter Starkie would begin with his 'earliest memories',[5] rooted in Harrow House, where he was born on 9 August 1894. Walter was the first of six children conceived by May Caroline, eldest daughter of the Dublin solicitor Cornelius Walsh, whose people hailed from County Kerry,[6] and the only son of WJM and herself to survive. In the first paragraph of his autobiographical

1 G.W.F. Hegel, 'Independence and dependence of self-consciousness. Lordship and bondage' in *The phenomenology of mind*, trans. J.B. Baillie (London, 1910), pp 180, 182. 2 D. Guinness, *Georgian Dublin* (London, 1988), p. 9. 3 D.G. Rossetti, cited by F. O'Dwyer, *The architecture of Deane and Woodward* (Cork, 1997), p. 468. 4 O'Dwyer refers to the Killiney house as 'Undercliffe', perhaps following Enid Starkie in *A lady's child* (London, 1941), whom he cites (F. O'Dwyer, *The architecture*, pp 467, 471, 598 (note 72)). See also a photograph of the house, p. 469. Walter Starkie (not referred to by O'Dwyer) also remembers Undercliffe [*sic*] in *Scholars and Gypsies* (London, 1963), perhaps following his sister's recollection. However, as it stands today, the house carries the name 'Undercliff', i.e., the name according to an announcement about the designing of the house, together with five others, in *The Dublin Builder* in 1861 (P. Pearson, *Between the mountains and the sea: Dun Laoghaire – Rathdown County* (Dublin, 1998), p. 72). The house shall be referred to here as 'Undercliff'. 5 W. Starkie, *Scholars*, p. 3. 6 May C. Starkie wrote of visiting her grandparents with her brother at Coolnaleen in Co. Kerry ('Holiday in Kerry of May and John', ES Bodl.).

text, Starkie immediately recalls what would have been the more enchanting and, undoubtedly, freer territory for the child, the garden. The beeches and sycamores, still standing today, would have contribute to the garden's appeal and the 'fine view of the Dublin mountains',[7] visible from the dining- and drawing-rooms, with the pinnacles of the Church of Ireland temple steadily rising on the left midst lush vegetation, would have created a sense of the enduring in both nature and the spirit. The vista might have been considered a fortifying one for the paterfamilias who was a practising Catholic throughout his life and would have become a Jesuit, a believer who, according to his eldest daughter, 'was singularly free from religious bigotry.'[8]

The son's evocation of Harrow House is juxtaposed to that of the beings closest to the child on his coming into the world: mother and father, or father and mother, as they are presented in Starkie's autobiographical volume. As in the poem 'Autobiography' by fellow Irishman Louis MacNeice, the order is not insignificant. Initially, 'Pater' is qualified as: 'mysterious', moreover, superlatively so: '[t]he most mysterious being in the world',[9] yet he rapidly acquires the dour dimension captured by V.L. O'Connor in his caricature of the future Resident Commissioner.[10] Thus, he is represented as a man who reduced his male offspring to the level of spectator on his life and who maintained his domineering position through a reign of fear. Of a morning the son: 'would walk down with him to the gate and watch him collect his mail from the post-box in the tree before setting out' but the habit appears to have been void of any verbal or physical contact, as was the father's reappearance in the home when he would be seen at close quarters, as close as 'the end of my bed', though the proximity appears not to have fostered any fond exchange either. A man of: 'booming voice'; of 'threats' when the child showed fear; 'a man of wrath', and who, moreover, some sixty years on, still strongly 'centre[d]'[11] his son's recollection.

In contrast to the father's despotic demeanour, the mother provided access to fantasy at bedtime, through the reading of *Alice in Wonderland* and *Arabian nights* favourites, such as 'Sinbad the sailor'; to the world of the spirit through the reciting aloud of night prayers; to security, as she tucked the child in, accompanied by the spontaneity of animals. Therefore, many years on, Starkie will remember his 'two friends Mick, the Irish terrier, and Puss' though the departure of mother and pets from the child's bedroom would signal the coming of 'anxieties'.[12] However, May Caroline is far removed from the carefree yellow and aura of 'gentle, gently, gentleness', characteristic of the mother as recalled in MacNeice's poem. The solicitor's eldest daughter firmly followed the Professor's path in the education of her first-born. Indeed, her iconoclastic daughter, Walter's wayward sister Enid, resolutely not 'a lady's child',[13] affirmed: 'as long as [my father] was alive, [my mother] saw everything through him'[14] and, as her son recalled, she also acted according to his dictates,

---

7 W. Starkie, *Scholars*, p. 3.   8 E. Starkie, *Lady's child*, p. 327.   9 W. Starkie, *Scholars*, p. 3.
10 V.L. O'Connor, *A book of caricatures* (Dublin: Tempest [1916]).   11 W. Starkie, *Scholars*, pp 3, 4, 5.
12 W. Starkie, *Scholars*, p. 5.   13 Note the title and further content in E. Starkie's family memoir (E. Starkie, *Lady's child*).   14 E. Starkie, *Lady's child*, p. 41. It may be argued that May Caroline continued to '[see] everything through him' beyond her husband's death since she went on identifying herself as his wife (Mrs W.J.M. Starkie) rather than his widow. For comment on May C. Starkie as 'emissary of [the] ideological values [of] the patriarchal family', see E. Grubgeld, *Anglo-Irish autobiography. Class,*

2 Harrow House, Ballybrack, Co. Dublin, home to William Joseph
Myles and May Caroline Starkie when W.F. Starkie was born.

never questioning or doubting: 'My mother ... carried out [my father's] precepts to
the letter and devoted the morning to my instruction'.[15]

The binaries rendered in the autobiographer's presentation of his parents are
broken by the introduction of Dalkey neighbour, Fellow and colleague of WJM at
TCD, Henry Stewart Macran. As lecturer in Mental and Moral Philosophy at Trinity,
Macran is remembered, like his teacher before him, John Pentland Mahaffy, as a
'Master', while the childhood memory of the former is one of fear-cum-fondness,
ultimately not unlike the relationship experienced with the father. Narrator of his life,
Starkie recalled his father's becoming: 'an affectionate parent', though no illustration
substantiates the claim. He is repeatedly portrayed as an ambitious overseer, who
dictated and placed demands on rather than listened to or enquired of his offspring.
In contrast, Macran displays a patience, gentleness and understanding when dealing
with the little one. It is the outsider – initially perceived by the child as an 'evil
genie' when he throws pebbles up at the boy's window; unkindly converted into a
'Bogey Man'[16] by an unsympathetic nurse – who is sensitive to the infant's vulnerability, embracing him fondly, relieving his fears through the balm of music and
subsequently soothing him through stories built around garden flowers, insects and

gender and the forms of narrative (New York, 2004), pp 80, 81. 15 W. Starkie, *Scholars*, p. 5. See also:
C.T. O'Doherty, 'William Joseph Myles Starkie', pp 34–6. 16 W. Starkie, *Scholars*, pp 5, 4. 17 W.
Starkie, *Scholars*, pp 4–5. As Starkie recalls, Macran's playing a melody from Humperdinck's 'Hansel
and Gretel' on the piano brought relief to the child on the night he was startled by the impact of the

3 W.J.M. Starkie, *c*.1920.

birds.[17] Indeed, Starkie's recollection of Macran bears witness to K.C. Bailey's account: 'He was ... kindly, large-hearted, tolerant ..., ... unselfish, understanding'[18] and Ulick O'Connor's claim that he was: 'a man of the sweetest possible nature'.[19]

Starkie identifies Macran and his father as 'Hegelians',[20] a not-unusual philo-

pebbles on his window. The adult Starkie's taste for Wagner might also be partially derived from Macran's. According to Mahaffy, Macran 'idolized' the composer 'as he did Hegel'. (W. Starkie, *Scholars*, p. 63.) Also cited by W.B. Stanford and R.B. MacDowell, *Mahaffy*, p. 59.   **18** K.C. Bailey, *A history of Trinity College Dublin, 1892–1945* (Dublin, 1947), p. 237.   **19** U. O'Connor, *Oliver St John Gogarty* (London, 1981), p. 33. O'Connor has also defined Macran as 'a man incapable of unkindness' (Author's interview with U. O'Connor, Dublin, 3 Apr. 2002). Further information on Macran is provided in R.B. MacDowell & D.A. Webb, *Trinity College Dublin, 1592–1952. An academic history* (Cambridge, 1982), pp 458–9, as well as in J. Knowlson, *Damned to fame. The life of Samuel Beckett* (London, 1996), p. 211.   **20** W. Starkie, *Scholars*, p. 5. O'Connor claims that Macran was 'the foremost living authority on Hegel' at this time (U. O'Connor, *Oliver*, p. 17). Macran produced translations and annotations for two of Hegel's texts: *Hegel's doctrine of formal logic. Being a translation of the first section of the subjective logic*. With introduction and notes by H.S. Macran (Oxford, 1912); *Hegel's logic of world*

sophical following at the end of the nineteenth century within the western Academy.[21] What aspects of Hegel's philosophy might warrant the classification at this juncture is not made clear but Starkie will again refer to Hegel in connection with Macran as lecturer at Trinity, identifying the German philosopher as: 'the Master Mind, who had inspired [Macran's] life' and describing the lecturer as: '[drawing] us [those present in the lecture room] upwards after him into the higher regions of Hegel's Absolute Idealism.'[22] It is worth pondering what aspects of the philosopher's theories would appeal to Macran, to WJM and, more particularly, to the latter. Within the context of Hegel's political philosophy, they would have been the German's emphasis on the sovereignty of Reason in the universe, the conviction that only the Whole is real and the spiritual dimension of this Whole or Absolute, together with the recognition of national genius and World Historical Individuals,[23] all of which became the son's legacy. Finally, Hegel's essay on Lordship and Bondage[24] lends light to an understanding of the power dynamic at work, initially between father and son and, subsequently, in assessing the latter's positioning in relation to his 'elders and betters'.

QUEEN'S COLLEGE GALWAY, 1897–9

The year 1897 was one of no mean achievement in WJM's academic career: his edition of Aristophanes' *The wasps* was published and following the resignation of Sir Thomas Moffett, he was appointed President of Queen's College Galway. Consequently, his son came to experience the first of a number of domestic upheavals in his childhood (an experience he would put forward in his autobiography as possibly accounting for '[t]he streak of nomadism in [his] character'),[25] though none of the moves were to be as far-reaching as this one: from the east to the west coast of the island. The boy would also feel the impact of another important change: after 18 August he would no longer be an only child. Enid Mary, the '*esprit fort*'[26] of her father's eye, the bane of her mother and French governess Léonie Cora's lives, was the first of four sisters to join Walter as he grew towards adolescence: Muriel followed Enid in 1898; Ida Florence Maud, who came to be known as Chou-Chou, in 1902, and Nancy in 1909.[27] Galway would also constitute an unfortunate experience for Walter in that it was there that he began to develop chronic bronchial asthma, an ailment that hampered him throughout his life.

A Fellow and Tutor of TCD since 1890, WJM resigned in order to be able to

and idea, being a translation of the second and third parts of the subjective logic, with an introduction on idealism limited and absolute (Oxford, 1929). **21** See: B. Russell, *A history of western philosophy* (London 1984), p. 701. **22** W. Starkie, *Scholars*, p. 119. See: B. Russell, *A history*, p. 702; P. Singer, *Hegel* (Oxford, 1983), pp 91, 93–5, 104–8, and L.W. Lancaster, *Masters of political thought* (London, 1978), p. 25, for Hegel's absolute and idealism. **23** See: L.W. Lancaster, *Masters*, pp 19–70 and B. Russell, *A history* (1984), p. 709. **24** G.W.F. Hegel, 'Independence', pp 175–88. **25** W. Starkie, *Scholars*, p. 5. **26** E. Starkie, *Lady's child*, p. 41. **27** A second son, Humphrey William Robert, was born in 1915 but died in infancy (IT, 'Births', 9 Aug. 1915, p. 1; 'Deaths', 31 Aug. 1915, p. 1). Ida's pet name, Chou-Chou, derived from governess Mlle Cora referring to her as 'le petit chou' (E. Starkie, *Lady's child*, p. 84).

take up the Presidency of Queen's College, Galway. He has been classified as 'one of the Brazen Guts'[28] of the period since he not only occupied the Presidency but simultaneously held the Chair in History, English Literature and Mental Science. However, this was no less than his predecessor Sir Thomas W. Moffett, who had combined the two posts for twenty years when WJM was appointed, though Moffett had been some twenty years older when taking on the double load.[29] In 1896, the year before he retired and the younger man took over, Moffett was knighted, the crowning glory of a long career of distinction and dedicated service to the Queen's College. His performance would provide a moral and professional challenge to his successor[30] and WJM was going to meet it with mettle, supported by a zealous, and no less ambitious, wife.

It appears to be difficult to find records of WJM's activity as President at Galway,[31] however, a comment in a letter from Mary T. Redington to her sister Fanny on 13 September 1898 provides some insight into his appearance and behaviour at the time. Redington mentions having received a visit the previous day from Mr Starkey [*sic*] of Queen's College, who had cycled to her home with a view to repaying some money. In spite of being qualified to meet the moral and intellectual challenge provided by his predecessor in the post, the letter conveys a picture of a socially awkward man, of set expression, not at ease with his body, and certainly not disposed to being contradicted: 'What an ungainly man in appearance and manner and so like ... a fish. I am sure he is a very honest man but what a contrast to the suave Dr Moffat [sic]. By the bye, *he would have it* that Nicholas Comryn had died at Lagos, West Africa, the other day!'[32]

Starkie's memories of life in Galway, between Walter's third and fifth years, are brief. However, there is fond recollection of boating expeditions on Lough Corrib and picnics to Menlough Castle[33] as well as some stereotypical representation through reference to the City of the Tribes and red petticoats in the Claddagh district. As regards the experience of everyday living, the sense of spaciousness is recalled and there is a memory of mother '[presiding]' at afternoon tea in 'a stately drawing-room in the College',[34] a glimpse of the sense of decorum and ceremony so characteristic of Mrs. W.J.M. Starkie, as highlighted by her eldest daughter some forty years on.[35] This

---

28 A. Keaveney, 'Classics in Victorian Galway' in T. Foley (ed.), *From Queen's College to National University. Essays on the academic history of QCG/UCG/NUI, Galway* (Dublin 1999), p. 330.   **29** T. Foley & F. Bateman, 'English, history and philosophy' in T. Foley (ed.), *From Queen's College*, p. 390. **30** See T. Foley & F. Bateman, 'English' in T. Foley (ed.), *From Queen's College*, p. 394, for reference to evidence from the many testimonials which accompanied Moffett's application for the Chair he held from 1863 until his retirement.   **31** See: A Keaveney, 'Classics', p. 330. I am grateful to Séamus MacMathúna for providing preliminary data on W.J.M. Starkie in 1991.   **32** Mary T. Redington to her sister Fanny, dated 13 Sept. [1898] in the Wilson Lynch Papers, National University of Ireland, Galway, LE6/D170. The underlining is in the original by means of which, I understand, the letter writer seeks to convey the President's determined reluctance to entertain any other version of the event but his own. The dots in the first sentence of the quote indicate a piece of the text that is illegible in the original. **33** Starkie refers to Menloe [sic] Castle. It is referred to as Menlough Castle in M. Bence-Jones, *A guide to Irish country houses* (London, 1990), pp 204–5, and as Menlo in P. Melvin, 'The Galway tribes as landowners and gentry' in G. Moran (ed.), *Galway. History and society. Interdiciplinary essays on the history of an Irish county* (Dublin, 1996), p. 326, *passim*.   **34** W. Starkie, *Scholars*, p. 6.

4 W.F. Starkie and sister Enid, Galway, *c*.1900.

vignette of the President's wife performing her role in highly decorous manner, in spite of her youth, in a no-less refined setting, is juxtaposed to the mention of Greely, the old porter, in his den, recalled by the ageing autobiographer as the small boy's 'favourite spot'. Indeed, he records a sense of liberation on being released from the drawing-room company and, furthermore, Greely is remembered as being responsible for introducing the President's son to 'the first wandering fiddler I ever met, a queer scarecrow of a man with a straggly grey beard, and a wild eye, who travelled from fair to fair. Greely called him "an oul' boozer" and said he was a tinker.' Following the fiddler's departure, Starkie recalls joining him again under a tree, where the musician played for the boy. Finally, the fiddler puts in a further appearance, when Walter accompanied his parents to the fair at nearby Athenry to buy a pony. He lagged behind them in the crowd and was drawn towards the sound of a melodeon and a fiddle, only to discover 'the same old fiddler ... performing to a crowd in a shebeen'. The player is now described as having adopted the guise of more conventional citizen for performance at the fair: 'He was dressed in a brown suit of homespun with tan shoes, his beard was trimmed, and he wore a broad-brimmed black hat.'[36]

The account of the boy's attachment to Greely and his encounter with the fiddler

---

35 E. Starkie, *Lady's child*, p. 43 (the account of mother joining the children in the nursery or schoolroom for tea), passim. Starkie identifies his mother's 'rigid principles' as belonging to the '*fin de siècle* Anglo-Irish ascendancy' (W. Starkie, *Scholars*, p. 11).   36 W. Starkie, *Scholars*, pp 6, 7.

5 May Caroline Starkie
(née Walsh, *c.*1893).

at an early age are worth pondering since they are not insignificant in terms of a
pattern that repeats itself in Starkie's account of his life in the autobiographical
volume, but also elsewhere, and from sources other than his own. The lifestyle and
values that Starkie was born into and brought up with were those of the upper middle-
class in Ireland, the protestant Ascendancy, even though both parents professed
Roman Catholicism, and it is the lifestyle and values of the Anglo-Irish that constitute
a point of reference throughout his life. Yet, in his childhood he was drawn to and
sought the company of those at the bottom of the social ladder or beyond it, thus the
porter, jarvey, gardener, cook, wandering fiddler (generally representative of the
underprivileged Catholic majority in Ireland) and those on the margins of the
mainstream in later life, most memorably (European) Gypsies. In his travel writing of
the 30s, we shall see him crossing the boundaries of class by adopting unconventional
garb and keeping the company of a waiter or a man by the wayside; however, this will
never be with a view to siding with the other but, on the one hand, with the intention
of hearing other opinions, but also for the exhilaration of spontaneous company, in
which one was not subjected to the dictates of propriety.

In 1899 the boy would have his first taste or, rather, smell (since the child was struck
by 'the all-pervading stench of horse dung') of London when he went to stay with

Grandma Starkie, that is, his father's mother, resident in Haverstock Hill with her youngest daughter, the painter Edyth Starkie, 'the romantic member of the family', according to her brother. Little is remembered of this first visit to the metropolis, which may well have taken place in the summer as Starkie records Walter being 'barely five years of age.' Apart from the odour, the impact of city noise is highlighted, a feature which must have been singularly striking after the hush of Harrow House and quiet of Queen's. In spite of unwelcome smell and sound, however, the visit was a rewarding experience since Aunt Edyth spoilt her nephew and was found to be 'full of mischief', an unexpected pleasure given her brother of the earnest brow, the boy's 'austere father'.[37]

FITZWILLIAM PLACE, DUBLIN, 1899–1900

> I see [WJM] Starkie has got poor [C.T. Redington's] place, I dare say he will suit but I fear the work of anxiety shortened our dear friend's days – …[38]

George Morris's ominous remark following the appointment of WJM to the post of Resident Commissioner in the wake of the death of 'strong Home Ruler'[39] the Right Honourable Christopher T. Redington on 4 February 1899 augured what undoubtedly represented 38-year-old WJM's greatest professional challenge to date. However, the post that he now left Galway to take up, scarcely two years after becoming President at Queen's, would be a taxing one for him up until the time of his own premature death in 1920, just the year following that of his friend and TCD colleague John Pentland Mahaffy.

Redington, who had been appointed Resident Commissioner of National Education in 1894, held an Oxford degree and had been Vice-President of the Senate of the Royal University. He had little administrative experience, a lack which, judging from the article in the *Freeman's Journal* on the occasion of his death, was not remedied during the five years he held the post: 'rigour was not his strong point … he was rather a popular than a strong administrator.'[40] Certainly, Redington had not inherited an efficient Education Office in the wake of Sir Patrick Keenan's idiosyncratic procedures,[41] so that the metaphor employed on inviting WJM to take up the post seems not to have been a case of hyperbole:

> I was informed by the Government that I had been specially selected to undertake a very critical task, although I was not a candidate for the vacant position, and had only recently gone to Galway. They had heard on the highest

---

37 W. Starkie, *Scholars*, pp 6, 7, 17, 18.   **38** George Morris to Major John Wilson Lynch, 25 Feb. 1899 (Wilson Lynch Papers, National University of Ireland, Galway, LE6/D/109). See also a letter from Edmund Dease to WJM: 'I was not aware that poor Redington's break down in health was caused by the worry he had to go through – though I am not surprised now to hear it …' Cited by C.T. O'Doherty, 'William Joseph Myles Starkie', p. 60.   **39** FJ, 6 Feb. 1889, page not numbered.   **40** Ibid. Cited by C. O'Doherty, 'William Joseph Myles Starkie', pp 49–50.   **41** See C.T. O'Doherty, 'William Joseph Myles Starkie', pp 59–60.

authority that the Education Office was an 'Augean Stable'; the system of education was antiquated; some of the higher officials were incompetent, and in the absence of a *strong supervising hand* 'things were in a very bad way.' They could not conceal it from me that they were asking me to fill what was perhaps the most difficult position in their gift; but I was assured that I could count on their confidence and support in my efforts to reform the system of administration.[42]

With a view to maintaining a denominational balance, the post of Resident Commissioner of National Education was occupied alternately by Catholics and Protestants. Redington professed Roman Catholicism so that it was now the turn of the other creed and there was a Protestant candidate,[43] but, as John Henry Bernard (a Trinity Fellow since 1884, appointed Vice-Warden of Alexandra College in the year that WJM married May Caroline[44] and on the Board of Education as a Commissioner since 1897)[45] had observed in a letter to his friend and colleague at Trinity, days before the latter's appointment: 'I do not know whether the Government will appoint a Roman Catholic or Presbyterian or one of us … It is undoubtedly the turn of the "Protestant" side. But I do not hear that any very desirable person of any Protestant persuasion is coming forward.'[46] Presumably the Protestant candidate did not possess the qualities which made WJM a 'very desirable person' for the post, according to the criteria of Bernard who, alternatively, viewed anarchy in the offing: 'I should be very glad of your appointment. It is all important that the Resident Commissioner be a man of strict impartiality and of unimpeachable veracity, and a gentleman. If these conditions are not fulfilled, there will be chaos.'[47]

In spite of WJM's protestation some four years on, as he looked back nostalgically to his Galway post as 'a position of literary [*sic*] ease [which] I valued',[48] it may be argued that just as he constituted a 'very desirable person' for the post (for the reasons outlined by Bernard, together with his family credentials: the father's having been a Resident Magistrate and WJM's elder brother Robert Fitzgerald then rendering the same service), there is reason to believe that the rise in status and salary would not have been disregarded. If the then President of Queen's University Galway were doubtful about accepting the post (though there is no evidence that he was; rather to the contrary, he appears to have canvassed for it),[49] his wife would have been inclined to encourage him to accept it, in spite of the upheaval. Her son recalled: 'the harassed face of [his] mother as she began again the weary task of taking the inventory and of

42 W.J.M. Starkie, *Statement of evidence given by W.J.M. Starkie, Resident Commissioner to the [IRELAND] Vice-regal Committee on National Education* (s.i., 1913), p. 1; my italics. The Augean Stable metaphor is used by O'Doherty as the title of her second chapter and cited within it. See: C.T. O'Doherty, 'William Joseph Myles Starkie', pp 45–87. 43 See C.T. O'Doherty, 'William Joseph Myles Starkie', pp 63–5. 44 See *Alexandra College Magazine*, 111 (Dec. 1893), 117–18. 45 See C.T. O'Doherty, 'William Joseph Myles Starkie', p. 51, n. 17. 46 John H. Bernard to W.J.M. Starkie, 12 Feb. [1899], TCD, W.J.M. Starkie Papers, SP 9209, Box 1, no. 19. 47 Ibid. 48 W.J.M. Starkie to G. Wyndham, 10 Mar. 1903, TCD, W.J.M. Starkie Papers, SP, 9210c. The letter was not sent. Cited by C.T. O'Doherty, 'William Joseph Myles Starkie', p. 66. 49 C.T. O'Doherty, 'William Joseph Myles Starkie', pp 67–8.

packing [his] father's large classical library into wooden cases'[50] for the return journey eastwards, but it is also worth bearing in mind here his sister's perception of their mother in terms of her '[admiring] success'.[51] Therefore, WJM's appointment would no doubt have delighted her and, to boot, his salary would have been almost double the amount he had earned as President of the university.[52] Moreover, the siblings had now been joined by a further sister, Muriel, so the question of income would not be a negligible consideration in terms of domestic finance. A suitable family house would now have to be found. Before settling in Killiney in 1901, the Starkies took up residence at number 11 Fitzwilliam Place,[53] 'a fashionable part of Dublin'[54] and within walking distance of the Resident Commissioner's workplace, Tyrone House, across the Liffey river in Marlborough Street.

Starkie's memories of Fitzwilliam Place are fundamentally two. Closely situated in relation to the back and front of the house, they are of ceremonial strain and colonial connection: Queen Victoria's visit to Dublin in the spring of 1900[55] and the marching Dublin Fusiliers, en route for the Boer War. The area is recalled and the narrow balcony of the Georgian façade, on which the children were perched, decked out in celebration to honour the Queen on what became her final visit to Ireland. A festive occasion is evoked and the five- (almost six-) year-old's awe on contemplating the accompanying soldiers:

> At the Leeson Street entrance of our street a majestic city gateway had been erected in honour of Her Majesty's visit, and from our balcony we had a clear view of the royal procession. The whole street was decorated with flags and bunting, and we children sat on the balcony which was draped with flags and brocade. So fascinated was I by the troops marching that the arrival of the Queen in her open carriage came rather as an anticlimax.

The other memory to surface through the flotsam and jetsam of the years is, as Starkie qualified it, 'a musical one', though it is also visual. The boy's bedroom was situated at the back of the house, overlooking Dublin's Grand Canal as it runs from the late eighteenth century Eustace Bridge towards Macartney Bridge, and from there he heard and saw the Queen's servants resolutely en route to serve their country:

---

50 W. Starkie, *Scholars*, pp 7–8.   **51** E. Starkie, *Lady's child*, p. 178.   **52** As President at Queen's College Galway, W.J.M. Starkie's salary was £800 a year; his accommodation, fuel and light were also provided. As Resident Commissioner, his salary would rise to £1,500 per year (C.T. O'Doherty, 'William Joseph Myles Starkie', pp 40–1; 66).   **53** W. Starkie recorded that his father rented 'one of the big old houses in Fitzwilliam Place' (W. Starkie, *Scholars*, p. 8) but doesn't supply the number of the house. W.J.M.'s correspondence at TCD reveals that he was resident at number 11 between 1900 and 1901. See, for instance, W.J.M. Starkie to A. Purser at the Education Office, 22 Aug. 1900, and W.J.M. Starkie to A. Purser, 17 Oct. 1901 (TCD, W.J.M. Starkie Papers, SP 9210).   **54** P. Bonsall, *The Irish RMs*, p. 154.   **55** Queen Victoria visited Ireland from 4 to 26 Apr. 1900 (K. Barry (ed.), *James Joyce. Occasional critical and political writing* (Oxford, 2000), p. 317, n. 47). Starkie states it was autumn (W. Starkie, *Scholars*, p. 8).

In the early morning of that autumn [*sic*] I used to be awakened occasionally by the sound of military music ... and from the windows I saw the red-coated soldiers of the Dublin Fusiliers marching by to the tune of *The girl I left behind me*, one of the songs my mother used to sing. It was their song of farewell, for they were marching to the boat on their way to the South African War.[56]

Given Mrs Starkie's patriotic fervour, as evidenced in her fondness for the Union Jack[57] and 1916 pamphlet,[58] she would not have led her son into any sort of critical enquiry as to the value of soldierly sacrifice. Indeed, the interrogative form of her title for the pamphlet (which carries no question mark) is misleading, given that no enquiry is engaged in. The author proceeds to pronounce exaltedly on dedication to one's country:

> ... the same spirit governs the great war of 1914 as governed the war of 1815, and every war back to the struggle between Athens and Sparta; the inspiring motive has always been love of one's country, Patriotism [sic]. In every cataclysm from the beginning of the world, some different working out of this divine instinct has been the cause of the struggle of nations and men, for it is a passion strong as religious faith with which it is bound up, and able to transport men to the sublimest heights of self-sacrifice.[59]

But not all citizens in Ireland shared the convictions of the author (and her husband) as to the *patria* they loved and would be prepared to lay down their lives for, as Easter 1916 would demonstrate. In his reminiscences, her son endearingly recalled Victoria as: '[t]he little old lady ... [acknowledging] the plaudits of the multitude' but such applause became increasingly anachronistic as the boy grew up and reached adulthood, over years that came to register the decline of the Union, of so much that his parents' lives had signified in terms of national identity and citizenship.

On 4 March 1899, the month following WJM's appointment as Resident Commissioner, the first issue of Arthur Griffith's *United Irishman* appeared. It had carried a direct challenge to the notion of patriotism to be promoted by May C. Starkie seventeen years on, asserting a rival tradition: 'Lest there might be a doubt in any mind, we will say that we accept the nationalism of '98, '48 and '67 as the true nation-alism and Grattan's cry "Live Ireland – perish the Empire!" as the watch-word of patriotism.'[60] Not surprisingly, as F.S.L. Lyons recorded, Griffith mustered little sympathy for the monarch, producing a *realpolitik* response, far removed from the pomp and pageant experienced by master Walter. Thus, the future co-founder of Sinn

---

56 W. Starkie, *Scholars*, p. 8.   **57** Author's interview with Muriel Horsford (née Starkie), Gerrards Cross, England, 13 Feb. 1990. Mrs Horsford recalled the ubiquitous presence of Union Jacks in her childhood, at her mother's garden parties, for instance.   **58** May C. Starkie, *What is patriotism. The teaching of patriotism* (Dublin, 1916), published by HMSO under the auspices of the Commissioners of National Education and with the approval, therefore, of the author's husband.   **59** May C. Starkie, *What is patriotism*, p. 3. For further comment on the pamphlet, see Chapter 3, below.   **60** Cited in F.S.L. Lyons, *Ireland since the Famine* (London, 1985), p. 248.

Féin had emitted: 'scathing comments on Queen Victoria's last visit to the country in 1900, when she came, or was sent, over, as the *United Irishman* truly enough remarked, "in her dotage … to seek recruits for her battered army".'[61] But the five-year-old boy on the balcony with his beady eye on the bunting, captivated by Victoria's troops, safe in his bed, or gazing down from the bedroom sash at the Boer-bound soldiers marching by, was blissfully unaware of the mounting tide of mutiny.

UNDERCLIFF, KILLINEY, CO. DUBLIN, 1901–6

> The hill of Killiney, Cill-inghen-Leinin (the Church of the daughters of Leinin), adjoins Dalkey, and rises boldly from the sea to a height of 500 feet, extending along the shore towards Bray for nearly two miles. […] From the summit of the hill the eye commands the entire outline of the Bay of Dublin, and of the lovely Bay of Killiney which sweeps in one unbroken curve along its southern base, and thence to the bold headland of Bray.[62]

Undercliff was one of six houses referred to in an announcement in the *Dublin Builder* in 1861. The architects Thomas Deane and Benjamin Woodward were designing 'six new dwelling houses for different parties, among whom is Mr Joseph Robinson, the eminent concert singer. The foundations have been laid out.'[63] Undercliff was acquired by Joseph Robinson's brother, Francis, and has been qualified unequivocally as Woodward's work as well as 'the apparent prototype from which the others were derived.'[64] This development of Killiney in the 1860s was to transform what had been 'a barren hilly stretch of coastline into Dublin's most fashionable suburb.'[65] It was into this desirable area, and to a house the view from which reflected WJM's taste for dramatic landscapes,[66] that the recently-appointed Resident Commissioner now transported his family, in time for Christmas 1901. According to his son, the following five years constituted: 'the happiest … of my father's life'.[67] Strikingly, he will never comment on the happiest in his own.

When reminiscing about the Undercliff years, the eldest Starkie offspring recalls them in terms of enchantment. The house holds a commanding position over the bay and its two turrets and, at that time, ivy-clad walls awarded it an air of fairy tale. As a child, Enid found the turrets 'fascinating'[68] and for her brother the house possessed 'all the mystery of a fairy castle.'[69] The sister's evocation of her childhood years in

61 F.S.L. Lyons, *Ireland*, p. 250. 62 *Thom's official directory of the United Kingdom of Great Britain and Ireland: for the year 1903* (Dublin, 1903), pp 1707–8. 63 Cited by P. Pearson, *Between*, p. 72. 64 F. O'Dwyer, *The architecture*, p. 467. 65 Ibid., p. 466. Pearson also qualifies Killiney as 'firmly established as one of Dublin's most favoured residential quarters' by the middle of the nineteenth century. P. Pearson, *Between*, pp 54–5. Kevin Kearns refers to the flight of 'the "respectable" classes to the suburbs in the second half of the nineteenth century [as] entire districts [of Dublin] fell into tenement "slumdom".' (K.C. Kearns, *Dublin tenement life. An oral history* (Dublin, 2006), p. 1). W.J.M. Starkie's predecessor in the post of Resident Commissioner of National Education, C.T. Redington, was resident in Killiney when he died in 1899. See his obituary in FJ, 6 Feb. 1899, page not numbered. 66 See: Chapter 2, below. 67 W. Starkie, *Scholars*, p. 8. 68 E. Starkie, *Lady's child*, p. 22. 69 W.

Killiney are pervaded by a sense of nostalgia for a paradise lost, a *'paradis perfumé'*.[70] Her memory of the house, the garden, the surrounding area and the climate are utopian in thrust, evincing a land of abundance and sensuousness, all permeated by the ubiquitous sound of the sea, lulling in summer, raging in winter, providing a path to the fantastic. Starkie's description does not linger so longingly, indeed, he dispenses with Undercliff, garden and all, in an eight-line paragraph.[71] However, brother and sister both record an enthusiasm for one of their mother's sisters: Helen. The two siblings were bewitched by her beauty, charm, vivid imagination, spontaneity, and waywardness, much of which was savoured against the backcloth of Undercliff.

Enid gives a captivating account of how Auntie Helen entered into her childhood imaginary world, 'a large bunch of bluebells in her arms', matching her blue eyes, to reveal herself as Enid's longed-for 'Queen of the Fairies'.[72] Helen evinces sensuousness too, to which Enid is granted greater access given her female status.[73] Thus, she evokes Helen's 'Edwardian girl's room' at her home in Crosthwaite Park, Kingstown (present-day Dun Laoghaire), decorated in pale colours with muslin curtains, frills and bows and alludes to her exotic undergarments, far more daring, like her make-up, than her eldest sister May Caroline's decent duds and attitude of duty-bound disapproval. Like the children's mother, Auntie Helen would tell fairy stories, but the *Arabian nights* as narrated by Auntie Helen in no way resembled the rigorous reading of the bedtime story as delivered by her sister. Helen reinvented the *Nights*, Grimm and Hans Christian Anderson, telling them 'all her own way', just as when she played her rôle of Fairy Queen, blurring the boundaries of reality and fantasy. She introduced 'real food and drink' into playing dolls' tea party and pulled the hairpins out of her lady-like chignon dramatically when the children cried: '"Rapunzel, Rapunzel, let down your long hair!"' Moreover, when playing dolls' tea party, the awe-striking aunt is reported as defiantly borrowing minute coffee cups that had been brought back from Persia by WJM and treasured in a drawing-room cabinet. In spite of what Enid qualifies as 'a scrupulous and even intransigent standard of truth and honour' in her aunt, Helen's iconoclastic bent and indulgent lifestyle throw into relief the note of *gravitas* earnestly fostered in the Starkie household. May Caroline's sister Ida is also remembered for her Rabelaisian wit, which Enid believed her brother Walter and youngest sister, Nancy, to have inherited 'to a marked degree.'[74] She is memorable, too, for having challenged her daunting brother-in-law. Auntie Elsie, the youngest of the Walsh sisters, was the least familiar to the children: Enid focuses on her in an unsympathetic way overall and her brother limits himself to simply mentioning her name as one of his mother's sisters.

Starkie, *Scholars*, p. 9.   **70** E. Starkie, *Lady's child*, p. 35. The stanza with which Enid Starkie ends the opening chapter of her autobiography, devoted to Undercliff, is from 'Moesta Errabunda' in Baudelaire's *Les fleurs du mal* (C. Baudelaire, *Les fleurs du mal* (Paris, 1961), pp 69–70). For comment on the accounts of happy (idealized) childhood in Anglo-Irish autobiography, see S. Deane, 'Autobiography and memoirs, 1890–1988' in S. Deane (ed.), *The Field Day anthology of Irish writing*, 3 vols (Derry, 1991), iii, pp 380–3, and D. Kiberd, *Inventing Ireland* (London, 1995), pp 101–4.   **71** W. Starkie, *Scholars*, pp 8–9.   **72** E. Starkie, *Lady's child*, p. 68.   **73** The brother registers his sense of deprivation. See W. Starkie, *Scholars*, pp 12–13.   **74** E. Starkie, *Lady's child*, pp 73, 72, 63.

6 Helen Walsh, 'Auntie Helen'.

A characteristic note in Enid's account of life at Undercliff is the mingling of fantasy and reality: Woodward's Ruskinian-influenced Undercliff lent itself to the world of fairy tale and the presence of Auntie Helen served to reinforce for Enid what she came to experience as the more vivid life, that is, that which she lived in the realm of her imagination. Walter did not share the intimate bonding with Auntie Helen experienced by his sister, yet a bent towards fantasy is manifest throughout his life, further stimulated in his childhood and youth through contact with his aunt on his father's side, the painter Edyth Starkie; her husband Arthur Rackham, the illustrator; the Irish writer in English James Stephens and through his own contact with ordinary folk, such as Shamus [*sic*] the tinker. His account of this period focuses, in terms of action, on adventure: boys' mischief, 'men's company' and travels with his father as well as his first experience at school. However, another important strand in his experience over the Killiney years is his encounter with folklore through people for whom it constituted part of the cultural fabric of daily life.

Like many boys growing up in the railway age and, moreover, living in a house overlooking the Dublin, Wicklow and Wexford railway line, the Resident Commissioner's son acquired a taste for trains. Starkie recalls Walter developing 'a craze for locomotives'[75] and aspiring to become an engine-driver. Two or three years the boy's junior, doctor-to-be Robert Collis remembers looking up to his elder, impressed by his knowledge, his experience, and being desirous of working by his side:

75 W. Starkie, *Scholars*, p. 13.

'on one occasion he actually brought his steam-engine down to the beach to show me. I thought him a wonderful fellow: he knew so much about trains. Once he had travelled from Killiney to Dalkey on a real engine. He said he was going to be an engine-driver, and I begged to be allowed to be his stoker.'[76] Walter may not have told Robert that another neighbour, Kit Hone, who lived next door to the Starkies at Temple Hill,[77] had given the Starkie boy 'his fine brass steam-engine and tender which was bigger than any model [Walter] had ever seen'.[78] Moreover, Kit helped his neighbour to construct a model railway at the bottom of the garden at Undercliff (to be destroyed by cottage-dweller Paddy Dowling, whose action would ignite a 'class war') and the Hone brothers, Joe, Pat and Kit, taught Walter to play cricket, enabling him to join the team in a county match on one or two occasions. Enid provides a further glimpse of Walter engaged in another pursuit typical of boys: playing with an air gun, which, she claims, her brother was anxious to try out on her or to threaten her with.[79] However, Walter's playmates were not exclusively drawn from his family or class, as Starkie's account of the relationship with cottage-dweller Paddy Dowling reveals.

The Dowling children appear to have been several, but some sixty years on, Starkie particularly remembered the eldest, Paddy, some three or four years Walter's senior, of whom wildness and an unkempt quality were characteristic, as they had been in the wandering fiddler in Galway. He recalls an uneven relationship with Paddy: 'relations varied from vigilant neutrality or non-belligerency to frontier skirmishes and even open warfare', but admits to being attracted to his neighbour's physical distinction and accomplishments as well as the opportunity for adventure that he provided: 'he was a handsome youth, and I envied him his muscles and his great skill in climbing trees and finding birds' nests. [...] ... secret expeditions with Paddy Dowling appealed to my sense of adventure.'[80] Enid mentions another group of children, the Doolans, the offspring of a railwayman, whose cottage was situated below the garden wall of Undercliff. Her brother's peer, Mickey Doolan, would climb over the garden wall to fight with his neighbour, but would become someone to be ignored when greeting his playmate near church, as Enid recalls: 'I can remember Walter's blushing embarrassment and discomforture [sic] as we went to Mass on Sundays with our parents and Mickey Doolan used to shout derisively at him from the corner as our family moved in stately procession along the road, "Hullo! Waalther [sic]!"'[81] Enid's description, highlights the Starkies' sense of their social rank and when speaking of Paddy Dowling, Starkie explains that his parents were opposed to their offspring mixing with 'the cottage children beyond the wall.'[82] This led the adult son to express regret

---

76 R. Collis, *The silver fleece. An autobiography* (London, 1937), p. 7.   **77** E. Starkie, *Lady's child*, p. 30. The family of painter Nathaniel Hone were friends of the Starkies, parents and offspring, throughout their lives. See correspondence from E. Starkie to Joseph Hone and Vera Hone (Joseph Maunsell Hone Papers, UCD Archive) and W.F. Starkie's letter to V. Hone on the occasion of J.M. Hone's death, 16 April 1959, reproduced in J.M. Hone, *Memories of W.B. Yeats, Lady Gregory, J.M. Synge and other essays* (Dublin 2007), pp 7–9. I am grateful to Juliet Roopnarinesingh for providing me with a copy of Hone's *Memories* and putting me in touch with Rosemary Hone.   **78** W. Starkie, *Scholars*, p. 13.   **79** E. Starkie, *Lady's child*, pp 31, 32.   **80** W. Starkie, *Scholars*, p. 13.   **81** E. Starkie, *Lady's child*, p. 21.   **82** W. Starkie, *Scholars*, p. 14. See also Enid's account of her mother's reaction to Muriel on her daughter's

regarding his underprivileged status in not having had the opportunity of access to what he perceived as experiences which would have equipped him more fully for later life:

> Even today after three score years I still feel a pang of regret that my early years were not spent in the untamed school of nature, learning how to live like an animal, strengthening my muscles like Paddy Dowling, so as to be able to stand my ground when attacked, and picking up what the Spaniards call *gramática parda* – the earthy folk-culture which has been handed on through the ages. If my parents had only trained me first in the outdoor school of nature, following the traditional methods of peasant, tinker or caravan-dwelling Gypsy, before teaching me to read or write, my mind, trained already to observe, would have been more alert than those minds reared for a sedentary existence.[83]

There are three other instances of Walter's breaking the boundaries of class during the Killiney years: through his association with a cottage-dwelling family called Homan, his conversation with old Tim, a coachman, and in his renewed contact with the Galway tinker.

The Homans lived 'in a group of cottages along the beach, a little distance from Undercliffe' and earned their living by fishing for mackerel and herring. Starkie recalls spending 'many hours' with the father of the family: 'a bronzed old man of the sea, who occasionally took me out fishing and told me stories of the waifs and strays who camped in caves along the coast ... [and] tales ... of the Wreckers along the coast who used to light false flares and lure the ships on to the rocks.' Old Homan, by Killiney beach, became a source of oral story-telling, as H.S. Macran was at Harrow House and Auntie Helen up at Undercliff in her re-fashioning of the *Arabian nights* and other classic tales. Moreover, through Homan Walter acquired 'the taste for cave life', one Starkie declared on writing his autobiography that had lasted all his life and which he would delight in satisfying on the *Sacro Monte* in Granada in later years. Old Tim was the coachman of the horse-drawn landau which took Laurence A. Waldron, a Commissioner of the Board of Education, WJM and the Resident Commissioner's son on a tour of national school inspection through Counties Cork and Kerry in 1904. While WJM and Waldron were engaged in the inspection exercise, ten-year-old Walter became enthralled by the coachman's story-telling, bewitched by both the content of the narrative as well as the story-teller's manner:

> ... old Tim ... thrilled me by his tales of ghosts, goblins and tinkers of which he had a limitless store. Grey-haired, red-faced, with a beard and mutton-chop whiskers, his voice fascinated me by its musical rise and fall, and he knew the secret of keeping me in suspense as he described the haunted houses we had passed on our journey towards Bantry.

exchanging new dolls' houses for 'a couple of wretched and filthy dolls' belonging to the Doolan girls (E. Starkie, *Lady's child*, pp 21–2). **83** W. Starkie, *Scholars*, p. 14.

Furthermore, Tim put Walter to rights about the exploits of Saint Finbar in Cork and proved a mine of information about the *shee*. Finally, he took the boy to the Puck Fair in Killorglin where Shamus the tinker reappeared: 'now wilder and more unkempt',[84] and who again played the fiddle while also becoming a source of lore, telling a story about a hunchback from his native Tipperary.

Less pleasurable for the boy over this period, would be encounters with his father's friends, when Walter's progress would be subjected to the lofty expectations of two highly successful men, formidable presences in Dublin on the stock exchange and in the academy: the bachelor stockbroker and British MP, Board of Education Commissioner Laurence A. Waldron, together with the TCD Professor and clergyman John Pentland Mahaffy. Walter's father, firmly established as Resident Commisioner of Education, completed the taxing trinity. WJM may have come to further appreciate the qualities of Killiney through his acquaintance with the Ballybrack-born, Dublin stockbroker and fellow member of the Royal Irish Yacht Club, Waldron, known as 'Larky' in the Starkie family circle and referred to by the children as 'the moving mountain'[85] given his 'immodest bulk'.[86] 'Marino' in Killiney was one of Waldron's residences from 1899 until his death in 1923.[87] His Killiney home dated from the early 1830s but was largely rebuilt at the beginning of the twentieth century in the Arts and Crafts style[88] and, Starkie recalled, was furnished with Chippendale furniture, rare china and housed first editions. Waldron's weighty presence was met by the children while the family was resident in Killiney:[89] down on the beach, where 'the men' would gather for an early-morning swim, or as a guest at Undercliff for lunch. Enid remembered her father lunching with Larky 'every Saturday of his life'[90] and presumably it is these lunches which her brother was to recall being allowed to join.[91] Walter was literally put in his place on these occasions: 'at a little side table whence I could spy out the land',[92] and from where he would gather crumbs from the table of the rich man and his distinguished guests, a gathering of classical companions: Professor of Latin, Greek and Ancient History at Trinity and one of the foundation members of the British Academy, Robert Yelverton Tyrrell, as well as Mahaffy, WJM and their host, who had shown 'a marked aptitude in classics'[93] at The Oratory in Birmingham, together with the throat and nose specialist Robert Woods and some of Waldron's 'practical, bridge-playing pals from the Royal Irish Yacht Club.'[94] Walter became a more central feature after desert, pounced on by the

84 W. Starkie, *Scholars*, pp 14, 9, 21, 22.   85 E. Starkie, *Lady's child*, p. 30. Starkie labels him 'Dublin's fattest man' (W. Starkie, *Scholars*, p. 15).   86 J.M. Hone, 'Great householder: Rt Hon. Laurence Waldron' in *Memories*, p. 168. In his entry on Waldron in the *Dictionary of Irish biography*, David Murphy records that Waldron was 'known as eccentric', whose friends, among whom figured Oliver St John Gogarty, George Moore and J.M. Synge, 'knew him as Larkey [*sic*]', D. Murphy, 'Waldron, L.A.' in J. McGuire & J. Quinn (eds), *Dictionary of Irish biography* (Cambridge, 2009), vol. 9, p. 698.   87 See Waldron's obituary, IT, 29 Dec. 1923, p. 8.   88 P. Pearson, *Between*, p. 70.   89 According to Joseph Hone, WJM and Waldron were 'old friends' (J.M. Hone, 'Great householder', p. 167).   90 E. Starkie, *Lady's child*, p. 30.   91 Though Starkie refers to the lunches as taking place on Sundays. W. Starkie, 'Sir John Pentland Mahaffy, 1839–1919' in D.A. Webb (ed.), *Of one company. Biographical studies of famous Trinity men* (Dublin, 1951), p. 90; W. Starkie, *Scholars*, p. 15.   92 W. Starkie, 'Sir John', p. 90. The additional information contained here draws on W. Starkie, *Scholars*, pp 15–16.   93 IT, 29 Dec. 1923, p. 8.   94 W. Starkie, 'Sir John', p. 91.

host (qualified by the adult Starkie as possessing 'sadistic and ogre-like tendencies')⁹⁵ with a view to providing entertainment for the company gathered there by means of subjecting the boy to a test of his command of mental arithmetic. When not performing as required, the victim would be exposed to public humiliation:

> A series of questions were fired at me in quick succession, I blushed, paused, stumbled and gave the wrong answer, whereat the booming voice [this time Waldron's, not his father's] announced to the company that I was no credit to the Resident Commissioner of National Education, that I had lost my originality in growing older, that I had adenoids which needed extirpation at the hands of the celebrated Robert Woods there present.⁹⁶

Midst such distressing circumstances, however, Starkie recalls Mahaffy coming to the schoolboy's rescue and 'always [taking] up the cudgels on my behalf against my father'.⁹⁷ Unfortunately only Waldron and the boy's father were present when Walter went along on the national school inspection to Cork and Kerry in 1904 so that the ten-year-old had no means of escape except arrival at the schools:

> While we drove along through the countryside, my father and Mr. Waldron, in the intervals of arguing on different matters, fired questions at me, and the latter tried to stimulate my faculties of observation by asking me the names of birds, animals, plants and flowers. I was relieved when we halted at schools, for I was then left to my own devices.

But not all Starkie's recollection of his father at Killiney is harsh. He remembers sailing with him in a light craft christened 'Water-Wagtail' though his account is hardly an enthusiastic one. He notes his father's 'calmness in an emergency',⁹⁸ recording an occasion when he lost control at sea, leading to Walter being thrown overboard. However, the father summoned sufficient *sang froid* to haul his son back up, by the hair.

During this period, Walter was educated at home, a prim Miss Allen coming from Bray to teach him over the morning hours in the dining-room.⁹⁹ However, it appears that her charge was becoming 'too undisciplined,¹ as were the other three children,² therefore, the parents decided to send their son to day-boarding school and looked to French governesses to discipline the girls. Aravon School in nearby Bray was chosen for Walter, the school, founded in 1862, which Roger Casement and J.M. Synge had

95 W. Starkie, *Scholars* p. 16. He also qualifies Waldron as 'tyrannical' and 'a tormentor' (W. Starkie, *Scholars*, p. 17). **96** W. Starkie, 'Sir John', p. 92. **97** W. Starkie 'Sir John', p. 92. In this essay on Mahaffy, Starkie explains that he always used to call the former his godfather (W. Starkie, 'Sir John', p. 92). In their biography, Stanford and McDowell refer to Starkie as Mahaffy's 'godson' (W.B. Stanford and R.B. MacDowell, *Mahaffy*, p. 58) but Enid questioned her brother's classifying him thus in a letter following the publication of his autobiography in 1963 (E. Starkie to W. Starkie, 11 Oct. 1963, ES Bodl.). **98** W. Starkie, *Scholars*, pp 20–21, 9. **99** Details of Miss Allen are supplied by Enid (E. Starkie, *Lady's child*, pp 33–4). **1** W. Starkie, *Scholars*, p. 25. **2** E. Starkie, *Lady's child*, p. 81.

7 W.F. Starkie with sisters (left to right) Enid,
Ida ('Chou-Chou') and Muriel, c.1905.

attended.[3] Aravon 'laid great emphasis on Church of Ireland teaching' and an 'Imperialistic atmosphere' was fostered there by the English headmaster.[4] Starkie recalls going willingly to school though he provides no information about school life. What appears to have been most memorable are the pranks played on the train journey, particularly on the journey home between Bray and Killiney when, according to the assessment of the elderly autobiographer: 'we made confounded nuisances of ourselves'. He illustrates the 'adventures' the lad and other neighbouring children from Killiney, the White boys, engaged in on the homeward-bound train: 'We shouted, we let off squibs and slap-bangs in the carriage, frightening the lives out of the old ladies, we flung trailers from the window of one compartment to the window of the next carriage and floated balloons.'[5] The old ladies might have been inclined to overlook the boys' high jinks but the captains of industry and other city men of note were less tolerant. As Enid recalls: 'The line from Dublin to Greystones was patronized by pompous, important men, stockbrokers, lawyers and company directors, and they sent a joint letter of protest to the station master at Killiney, who complained to the fathers of the boys in question'.[6] Starkie claims that Walter's 'contacts' at Killiney station, 'the bearded old station-master ... and Ned the signalman', served to

3 Author's interview with Mrs Patricia O'Malley, Joint Principal of Aravon School, Bray, 15 July 1994.
4 C. Mansfield, *The Aravon story* (Dalkey, no date [1975]), pp 2, 13. 5 W. Starkie, *Scholars*, p. 26.
6 E. Starkie, *Lady's child*, p. 83.

protect him from the onslaught of complaints. However, Pater must have been distinctly displeased, just as he was disappointed by Walter's inability 'to make the grade ... at Aravon',[7] pronounced at the end of his son's short sojourn at the school, accelerated by Walter being kicked on the head in a playground fight. The injury resulted in him being invalided home and subsequently suffering an acute attack of what had already become a chronic complaint, bronchial asthma.

As stated above, Starkie provides no information in his autobiography as to life at Aravon or the teachers and boys Walter found there. However, Robert Collis does give an account of the formidable headmaster, Richard Hastings Bookey, who was already the Principal when Walter became a day-boarder.[8] Collis's recollection is pertinent in depicting Walter's exposure at the impressionable age of ten to a representation-cum-caricature of British superiority in manners and morals: 'The headmaster was an Englishman who, if he had worn top boots, would have completely resembled the traditional John Bull. [...] He was thick-set, stout, had a red face and scaly, hairy hands. He had an almost pathetic belief in British honour. He avowed that an Englishman never told a lie.'[9]

Walter's contact with Englishmen over the Killiney years included the artist and illustrator Arthur Rackham, 'prim, precise and very English in manner, in spite of his bohemianism and his elfish kinks',[10] whom his father's sister, Edyth, had married in 1903. Enid recalls Edyth staying with the family at Undercliff: 'I remember seeing her standing at her easel in the garden ... and painting. I remember, too, that she used to colour pictures for us in our book of fairy stories.'[11] However, Enid appears not to have been graced with visits to London as a child; the visit to the metropolis was Walter's privilege. His first visit in 1899 was followed by another in 1902 when his aunt introduced him to Rackham, to whom she was already engaged. Starkie remembers the enjoyment of going off with his uncle-to-be on 'a painting expedition'[12] to Kensington Gardens where, at a time when Rackham was engaged in producing the illustrations for *Peter Pan in Kensington Gardens*,[13] the boy was bewitched:

> ... the painter ... would people my imagination with elves, gnomes and leprechauns. He would make me gaze fixedly at one of the majestic trees with massive trunk and tell me about Grimm's fairy tales ... and about the little men who blew their horns in elfland. He would say that under the roots of that tree the little men had their dinner and churned the butter they extracted from the sap of the tree. He would also make me see queer animals and birds in the branches of the tree and a little magic door below the trunk, which was the entrance to Fairyland. He used also to tell me stories of the primitive religion of man which, in his opinion, was the cult of the tree; ...[14]

7 W. Starkie, *Scholars*, p. 26. 8 R.H. Bookey was Headmaster of Aravon from 1894 to 1924. (C. Mansfield, *The Aravon*, p. [8].) 9 R. Collis, *The Silver*, p. 9. Mansfield provides another view of Bookey (C. Mansfield, *The Aravon*, pp 5, [7], 9). 10 W. Starkie, *Scholars*, p. 19. 11 E. Starkie, *Lady's child*, p. 59. 12 W. Starkie, *Scholars*, p. 18. 13 J. Hamilton, *Arthur Rackham. A life with illustration* (London, 1990), p. 72. 14 W. Starkie, *Scholars*, p. 19. Rackham goes on to dwell on the punishment administered to those who injured trees which, Hamilton observes, is taken out of J.G. Frazer's *The*

Walter would be brought back to the real with a bump on arrival at his grandmother's house. His father's mother, Frances Mary, would interrogate her grandchild in a manner that recalls her son's examination of his male offspring on arrival home from Trinity. Both adults turned what was potentially pleasurable into a toiling geared towards adult success:

> ... the old lady would *catechise* me upon all that I had seen during the morning. She would test my powers of observation and deduce from my answers whether I should in my future life follow the path of William (my father) or my Uncle Robert.
> ... my father wanted me to follow in his footsteps and become eventually a classical scholar, and for this reason he gave my mother no peace until she had taught me to read and write. Every evening when he arrived home from college he would *catechise* me searchingly and make me spell words and would watch the progress of my writing.[15]

Not long before the family moved nearer to the city of Dublin, Mlle Léonie Cora arrived at Undercliff, eager to impose '*bon ordre*' in the wake of a Mlle Bordeaux, taken on for the girls when Walter was sent to Aravon. Enid observed that the old French governess was 'too old and feeble to have any authority over us',[16] but her successor was neither old nor lacking in spirit. Starkie asserts that she swiftly became 'dictator of the whole household', using 'tactics [that] resembled Napoleon's by their lightning rapidity and ruthless efficiency'.[17] Mlle Cora had a taste for the theatre, the opera as well as music so that the family's move to a residence nearer Dublin would favour her stimulating a taste in the children for cultural activities available in the city. Thus, trains and caves moved into the realm of memory for Walter.

Finally, the Killiney years also carry memories of another royal visit to Dublin, that of King Edward VII and Queen Alexandra in July 1903. On this occasion the (almost) nine-year-old was positioned in Phoenix Park for the review, 'which was the climax'. Some sixty years on, Starkie recalled the royal visit producing 'a wave of popular enthusiasm'[18] and portrayed a compassionate monarch, set on administering justice and anxious to satisfy Ireland's needs. The style in which the episode is narrated is reminiscent of other prose publications of Starkie's where historical events or political policies are rendered in a conversational mode, a style which also evokes the paternalistic discourse of colonialism contained in popular nineteenth-century boys' adventure stories. Thus:

> The King was prepared to meet the Irish half-way and, sympathizing as he did with poverty, he wished to give practical help to the distressed country. 'What do

golden bough, 'which clearly Rackham was reading'. (J. Hamilton, *Arthur Rackham*, p. 72.) When Enid asks her father about the nature of fairies, he refers her to Frazer's work (E. Starkie, *Lady's child*, p. 166) and W. Starkie cites Volume I of Frazer's work in a footnote to his first travel book (W. Starkie, *Raggle-taggle* (London, 1940), p. 369). **15** W. Starkie, *Scholars*, pp 19, 5. My italics. **16** E. Starkie, *Lady's child*, pp 84, 83. **17** W. Starkie, *Scholars*, p. 29. **18** W. Starkie, *Scholars*, p. 20.

the Irish want?' the King asked. 'Education and security in their land,' the Chief Secretary replied. 'I shall come to Ireland,' was His Majesty's reply, 'with an Education Bill in one hand and a Land Bill in the other.'[19]

When speaking of her mother, Enid recalls that to see her at a party was to see her at her best and she recognizes that her mother and sisters all knew how to entertain 'in the grand manner.' With WJM's improved salary as Resident Commissioner, his taste for social life and his wife's eagerness to play hostess: 'many were the parties given at Killiney. In the summer there were tennis and garden parties; in the winter bridge and dinner parties', all of which were a source of excitement for the children as the house was decorated with flowers in pots and vases, the best silver and glass set out on the French-embroidered linen tablecloth, 'the ice-pudding packed in its pail of ice'. Enid recalls delicious strains of 'hot soup with sherry in it, roast chicken or duck',[20] among other savoury fragrances. The family employed a French *chef* over a period but a *penchant* for stealing bottles of wine led to his being dismissed and may have been the reason for WJM securing the key to the cellar in his pocket. Around this time, the beloved Lizzie O'Beirne, cook, constant and caring, appears to have taken over command in the kitchen, the good and faithful servant until beyond WJM's death. She, like the recently arrived French governess, would now accompany the family to Somerset in Stradbrook, near Blackrock, where the Starkie lifestyle was to be on an even grander scale.

---

19 W. Starkie, *Scholars*, p. 20. The dialogue as presented in Starkie's text may have drawn on Sir Sidney Lee's biography of Edward VII (S. Lee, *King Edward VII. A biography*, ii (London, 1927), p. 167).
20 E. Starkie, *Lady's child*, pp 42, 43.

2

Stephen's Green to Shrewsbury via a Wild Coast of Mayo

[W]hen I was eleven years of age, began the five Sybaritic years of my father's life, years of the Edwardian era, which as I recall them today seem to belong to another world.[1]

Starkie explains the fourth experience of moving house as a consequence of WJM's professional commitments and the children's schooling. However, the move may also be attributed to the Resident Commissioner's social and political ambitions, supported by his wife's delight in success. The bow-ended Georgian house, Somerset, was one of the first to be built in the area and possessed the distinction of having been the summer set or seat of Lord Mayo in the 1790s.[2] The aristocratic association would no doubt suit WJM, who confessed towards the end of his life to being 'a lover of power'. The 'large' property with 'finely proportioned rooms',[3] a winter-garden, conservatory and generous grounds would provide the Resident Commissioner's wife with ample scope for creating elegant surroundings for both family life and grander social events.

The positioning of Somerset, near the village of Stradbrook, just over a mile from Blackrock, Co. Dublin, did not provide a sea view unless one leaned far out of the dormer windows in the bedrooms situated 'at the top of a narrow little staircase',[4] where the Starkie girls slept in the company of governess Léonie Cora. However, there was some compensation for the loss of the sea: the children had two large fields in which to play, as well as the grounds, although their presence there might be restricted according to who was being entertained. Somerset provided a sense of rural life with cows grazing in one of the fields, a donkey occupying space there too. There was stabling in a large yard where cows and donkey would be given shelter as well as hens and ducks. Pigs completed the farmyard feature but these are barely mentioned by Enid,[5] and not at all by Walter. What brother and sister both highlight, however, is the grand lifestyle adopted by the family over this period: Walter recalls 'lavish days'[6] and Enid a life: 'of great luxury and extravagance',[7] indeed, to such a degree that it would come to undermine the family's financial solvency.

Somerset is cherished by Enid as a land of great abundance, from the size of particular rooms in the property: the 'spacious' dining room and 'colossal cavern' of a kitchen to the 'large' fruit and vegetable garden and circular flower beds outside, passing through the 'enormous' built-in dressers in the kitchen and, again, 'enormous'

---

1 W. Starkie, *Scholars*, p. 31. 2 P. Pearson, *Between*, p. 204. 3 E. Starkie, *Lady's child*, pp 39, 85.
4 E. Starkie, *Lady's child*, pp 39, 85, 87. 5 The reference records repulsion towards the sow and her litter (E. Starkie, *Lady's child*, p. 91). 6 W. Starkie, *Scholars*, p. 73. 7 E. Starkie, *Lady's child*, p. 92.

stone troughs in the laundry. She also recalls the cornucopia of everyday plenty. In the dairy stood 'pans always filled with foaming milk, ... smaller pans for the cream ... and tubs for the eggs' and in the dining room, both quality, 'Mrs Beaton [*sic*] cookery', and quantity, 'lashings of everything at every meal', were savoured. Wine was never lacking at dinner and 'hot-house fruit, grapes and peaches' were also to hand. Moreover, the splendid fare enjoyed at home was also afforded relations and friends, Walter not even being deprived when he went off to public school in England. Tuck reached him weekly from home: Enid observes that the Co. Meath cook, Lizzie, 'imagined that English food had no nourishment in it, so she sent ... large, rich, home-made cakes, soda bread, jam, fresh eggs from our hens, butter, sausages, bacon and fruit from the garden.'[8]

The room at Somerset recalled in greatest detail by Enid is the drawing-room, its décor assessed as a projection of the 'great charm and grace' of her mother's character. An exception to the Edwardian style was an Italian presence: 'two beautiful semi-circular tables of Italian satin-wood, light golden wood inlaid with garlands and flowers in delicate pastel shades', though Enid claims that they did not rupture the harmony of the room; not so the naked bronze statues of Narcissus and a Satyr brought back from Naples by WJM which flaunted their nakedness on pedestals, coming to constitute a cultural affront to the lower orders: Enid remembers them as '[outraging] modest Irish maids'. Finally, a 'little curio table with a glass top'[9] was another non-Edwardian piece of furniture, its *raison d'être* the display of WJM's acknowledged merit and standing in the form of gold medals and a gold key with which the Resident Commissioner had on one occasion opened an elementary school.

The senses of colour and smell were seductively indulged at Somerset through the array of flowers and plants displayed both inside and outside the house as well as between the two, in the winter-garden and conservatory. According to Enid, palms and flowering plants were a constant feature of the interior while the scent, emanating from the purple and blue of heliotrope and periwinkle perfumed the territory of the garden and, at the end of the vinery, the portion maintained at a higher temperature, accommodated tropical plants. Here Enid particularly focuses on: 'a tank covered with exotic water lilies [and] lotus flowers.' In front of the house, set in the lawn, there were flower-beds 'filled with rich plants': the tobacco-plant spreading its sweet smell at evening and the 'rich velvet calices'[10] of the salpiglossis, seductive to sight and touch. The high hedge of sweet peas enclosing the tennis court lent a riot of colour. Enid recalls her mother's pride in her garden. Indeed, her John Singer Sargent-like presence can be visualized, instructing the gardeners, arranging her drawing-room flowers, showing off her prize-winning chrysanthemums in the autumn or presiding over tea, exquisitely served with silver tray and cake stand, under the ash tree in the summertime. May Caroline would also contribute to the creation of sweet sound at Somerset: the source a Schiedmayer grand piano, a gift from WJM to his wife when the family took up residence at Somerset.

8 E. Starkie, *Lady's child*, pp 85, 86, 88, 86, 87, 92, 93, 127. 9 E. Starkie, *Lady's child*, pp 86, 85, 86.
10 E. Starkie, *Lady's child*, pp 85, 88.

And Somerset signified a stream of parties and social whirl. Walter particularly recalls the Christmas festivities of 1910, the 'grand finale of our Edwardian lavish days'[11] while Enid remembers 'constant parties':[12] tennis and croquet parties in the summer, garden parties designed to exhibit the herbaceous borders at their most becoming, bridge parties in the winter as well as fancy-dress parties. WJM and his wife would attend dinners for which May Caroline would be groomed by the Grafton Street hairdresser Charles Bundina.[13] Enid's recollection of her parents preened for presentation at Dublin Castle provides some idea of the quality of splendour in the social life experienced by the Resident Commissioner and his wife: 'my mother in her court dress with a beautiful blue turquoise velvet train, fastened from her shoulders, and with three feathers in her hair; my father in white knee breeches, silk stockings, buckled shoes, gold braided tunic and feathered cocked hat like that of an admiral.'[14]

The maintenance of the *quasi* regal lifestyle adopted at Somerset was provided by a range of staff: the much-loved Co. Meath cook Lizzie O'Beirne; maids, sardonically remembered by Enid over twenty years on serving at Sunday lunch: 'dressed in their silver-grey shantung dresses, their little white muslin aprons and their mob caps, looking exactly as if they had tripped out of a musical comedy';[15] a butler and head gardener, aided by two others. Léonie Cora, the Parisian governess, increasingly became a force to be reckoned with over the Somerset years. Relentlessly hostile to Enid, who defined her as: 'the tyrant of my existence', she was proficient in administering the '*gifle*' and ready to recommend a '*fessée*'[16] in the case of the eldest girl but was ever supportive and increasingly seductive, as well as surrendering, according to the recollection of her male charge. 'Mademoiselle' would be responsible for fostering a response to religion, music, the theatre and opera in the Starkies' only son as well as stimulating his awakening sexual appetite with her *fin-de siècle* follies and titillating tales.

Léonie Cora was brought into the family in the wake of the arrival and swift departure of the enfeebled Mlle Bordeaux. The latter's substitute was brimming with energy and decisiveness. The authority she wielded became absolute, both in domestic arrangements concerning the children, from clothing to food, and in the schoolroom, where the French language and the culture of Léonie Cora's *patrie* prevailed. Indeed, in his memorable recollection of her, Starkie recognized that the power she exercised in the family steadily increased and was not to be contested by her employer since it allowed him to pursue his classical scholarship, rather as in the case of (and Starkie himself introduces the comparison) the *paterfamilias* of Jane Austen's *Pride and prejudice*, ever content to forfeit parental responsibility in favour of withdrawal to his

11 W. Starkie, *Scholars*, p. 73.   12 E. Starkie, *Lady's child*, p. 93.   13 Enid refers to Budina [*sic*] as of Austrian descent and resident in Blackrock (E. Starkie, *Lady's child*, p. 93). *Thom's directory* (1903) lists a Charles Bundina 'court hairdresser' with addresses at 63 Grafton St and 2B Main St, Blackrock (p. 1812).   14 E. Starkie, *Lady's child*, p. 93.   15 E. Starkie, *Lady's child*, p. 124. Walter mentions a housemaid, Ellie, and a parlourmaid, Kate Hyde (W. Starkie, *Scholars*, p. 29). May Caroline had been waited on by a French maid, Marthe, while the family were resident in Killiney but it is not clear from Enid's account that Marthe accompanied her mistress to Somerset (E. Starkie, *Lady's child*, p. 81). 16 E. Starkie, *Lady's child*, pp 115, 109, 112.

library: 'Mademoiselle Cora's influence over our family grew day by day, and as my father had a "Mr Bennett [*sic*] complex"[,] he welcomed anyone with a personality strong enough to keep his volatile children in check and prevent them from worrying him, when he wanted to get on with his Aristophanes.'[17] Starkie's memories of the governess's physique complement Enid's. She is remembered by the siblings as small and plump with a sallow complexion and black hair.[18] However, while her male charge recalls her eyes as 'fiery,[19] expressive of the governess's spirited nature, his sister describes them in a meaner manner, as regards both size and colour, and in an alliterative sequence of predominantly strong stresses, thus conveying Mademoiselle's bullying behaviour: 'small brown beady eyes like boot buttons'. Starkie's sister also elaborates further on Mademoiselle's black hair. Straight, long and thin, it was usually worn coiled in a round *chignon* on the top of her head, made substantial by means of 'a pad of artificial hair'. Nevertheless, her least favourite charge observes that she was ever disposed to letting it down and would then adopt a schoolgirl pose: 'on the pretext that she had one of her *migraines* and could not bear the weight of [her *chignon*] ... [s]he wore [her hair] in two long straggly plaits, very thin at the tails, and tied with two large pink bows.' However, Mademoiselle's body was gendered as a woman and further rendered fashionably feminine by her coquettish determination to create a small waist and 'opulent bosom',[20] achieved by means of rigorous tight-lacing,[21] her *gorge* further accentuated by tight-fitting blouses.

In an article published in 1943,[22] Enid observed that Léonie Cora had dreamed in her youth of joining the Opéra-Comique.[23] The governess's ambition may have derived from the influence of the man she claimed to have been her piano teacher, Raoul Pugno (1852–1914). Professor of Harmony at the Paris Conservatoire between 1892 and 1896 and of pianoforte from 1896 to 1901, Pugno wrote four comic operas[24] and was perhaps responsible for inspiring a taste for the genre in his pupil. Whether or not, a distinct sense of the histrionic is acquired through Mademoiselle's bearing. Starkie remembers her becoming excited 'on an average of every three minutes'[25] and, more specifically, Enid recalls her being a dramatically poor loser at croquet: 'Many were the croquet mallets which Mademoiselle broke as the result of her defeats and new mallets were constantly being bought'.[26] But the dramatic thrust was not confined to the Edwardian pastime, rather it was essential to life as conceived of by this conscientiously Catholic and 'ardently patriotic Frenchwoman'.[27] Enid asserted: 'Mademoiselle had a feeling for the drama of life and a sense of the pageantry fitting to each festivity and each holiday of the year.' Thus, in the month of May, a

---

17 W. Starkie, *Scholars*, p. 34. **18** E. Starkie, *Lady's child*, p. 100; W. Starkie, *Scholars*, pp 28, 30. **19** W. Starkie, *Scholars*, p. 28. **20** E. Starkie, *Lady's child*, p. 100. **21** Enid reflects that Mademoiselle Cora 'must have been the last person in Europe to tight-lace' (E. Starkie, *Lady's child*, p. 100). **22** E. Starkie, 'Nostalgie de Paris d'une Irlandaise', *Aguedal*, May 1943. Typed manuscript dedicated to Josep Carner by E. Starkie (Biblioteca de Catalunya, Arxiu Josep Carner, Inventari 179, MS 4865). **23** Since Enid uses the hyphen, I presume she is referring to the Parisian theatre where comic opera was performed (E. Starkie, 'Nostalgie', cited in J. Richardson, *Enid Starkie*, p. 17). **24** M. Kennedy (ed.), *The concise Oxford dictionary of music* (Oxford, 1996), p. 582. **25** W. Starkie, *Scholars*, p. 28. **26** E. Starkie, *Lady's child*, p. 99. **27** W. Starkie, *Scholars*, p.35.

little altar of Mary was set up; in December, 'a large Bethlehem crib' occupied the schoolroom. The governess's enthusiasm for pageantry had the opportunity to express itself on a grander scale in July 1907 when, on the occasion of the International Exhibition in Dublin, Edward VII and Queen Alexandra made their last visit to the city and were programmed to drive past the gate of Somerset en route for Herbert Park, the exhibition site in Ballsbridge.[28] Mademoiselle threw herself into producing a triumphal arch with '*Vive l'Entente Cordiale*' wired across it and surrounded by flowers. When the King and Queen eventually passed, Mademoiselle gave full vent to her emotions. Enid remembers her with tears running down her face, shouting: '*Vive la France, vive l'Angleterre, vive l'Entente Cordiale!*' It seems that Mademoiselle had great hopes for Edward VII, relying on him, 'the greatest living ruler in the world', to win back Alsace and Lorraine for France. Moreover, his beard and manners would lead her to pronounce him '*un Français tout craché*'![29]

But there appears to have been a more disturbing dimension to Léonie Cora's character. A sadistic strain may be detected in different episodes recorded by Enid though the eldest child, male, and three years Enid's senior, appears to have been spared such distress. Indeed, the adult Starkie speaks of 'a strong bond' established between Mademoiselle and himself, assessing her favourably, as: 'a guiding spirit, encouraging me to persevere and strengthening my will.'[30] Whereas Mademoiselle became exclusively responsible for the girls' education, the boy, who had been receiving tuition from an ex-National school teacher, James Waldron, as well as French classes from the governess, was now sent to school again, this time in the city. In his autobiographical volume Starkie mentions that he was sent to a day school in St Stephen's Green but does not refer to it by name; it is Enid who provides the precision, stating that it was called Strangways.[31] In the year of Starkie's birth, a Leonard R. Strangways, MA, TCD, was already running a private school at 74 & 75 Stephen's Green South, that is almost next door to where WJM's brother, Robert FitzWilliam Starkie, was resident when he was a District Inspector in the Royal Irish Constabulary and Private Secretary to Sir Andrew Reed, Inspector General of the RIC at Dublin Castle. Perhaps Walter was sent to Strangways following a recommendation from his uncle, on familiar terms with his neighbour, or perhaps WJM knew Leonard Strangways as a Trinity graduate. However, although Strangways was still running the school on Stephen's Green in 1906, the year the Starkies left Killiney for Stradbrook, by 1907, W.J. Chetwode Crawley, LLD, DCL, was the director of the private school at 74 & 75 St Stephen's Green South as well as being the principal of the King's Service Academy at 3 & 4 Ely Place. One W.S. Chetwode Crawley, MA (Camb.) (WJ's brother?), a barrister, was the headmaster of the school at 74 & 75 St Stephen's Green South in 1907 and it is also possible that the Resident Commissioner knew this member of the Chetwode Crawley family from his Cambridge days. Starkie mentions Walter receiving 'a grudging compliment from Mr Chetwode Crawley, the

28 B. Siggins, *The great white fair. The Herbert Park exhibition of 1907* (Dublin, 2007).   29 E. Starkie, *Lady's child*, pp 101, 107, 108.   30 W. Starkie, *Scholars*, p. 34. And later: 'In me she encouraged independence and the desire to strike out by myself' (W. Starkie, *Scholars*, p. 35).   31 E. Starkie, *Lady's child*, p. 115.

headmaster, for [his] mathematics,'[32] on one occasion, but his relation to the school was one of absence rather than attendance. From the single allusion to Mr Chetwode Crawley, the headmaster does not appear to have been generous in his encouragement so the boy would not find him a motivating source and although he was dogged over this period by asthma attacks, preventing him from attending school, he also took to playing truant: '[wandering] in Stephen's Green or along the quays looking at the books in the stalls',[33] occasionally aided and abetted by Léonie Cora.[34] But wandering did not yet concentrate as much of Walter's energies as in later life. The schoolboy's major pursuit and passion at this time, forcefully inspired by Léonie Cora, became music and, more particularly, the violin.

When Mademoiselle joined the Starkie family, it was understood that she was 'a good musician'.[35] Enid, an accomplished pianist, suspected that the governess had been the pupil of a pupil of the pianist, organist and composer of French and Italian descent, Pugno, however, she recognized some talent in the governess's playing, in spite of a tendency to 'tread' the keys. On the other hand, her brother claims Walter was 'fascinated … by her piano playing',[36] ready to be soothed, following French grammar and dictation, by her rendering of the work of another composer of comic opera, Cécile Chaminade, as well as by Chopin, on an instrument which until Mademoiselle's arrival had bored him. Starkie accounts for the passion for the violin by reference to a concert which the boy attended at the Theatre Royal in Dublin with Léonie Cora in October 1905.[37] Perhaps the eleven-year-old experienced a degree of empathy, if not awe, towards the fourteen-year-old performer, the Russian-born Mischa Elman (1891–1967). In any event, over fifty years on, Starkie would still remember three of the pieces he played: Lalo's *Symphonie Espagnole*, Saint-Saëns' *Rondo Capriccioso* and the 'Nocturne in E flat' by Chopin-Sarasate and qualified the experience as 'a revelation', leading the lad to return home 'in a daze'. Starkie records Léonie Cora also becoming 'deeply moved' and, characteristically prescriptive, she subsequently ordained that her charge should start learning the violin without further ado, herself undertaking to instruct him in musical theory. Thus began a battle between the boy's (and Mademoiselle's) increasing passion for the instrument and Pater's ambition for his son to follow in his footsteps as a classical scholar. Notwithstanding WJM's opposition, *Grove's dictionary of music* now became the aspiring violinist's 'favourite reading' though he claims to have read 'every book I could find on music and

32 W. Starkie, *Scholars*, p. 54. **33** E. Starkie, *Lady's child*, p. 115. **34** Enid explains: 'I remember that when my father and mother were away from home [Walter] used to come to the schoolroom to beg Mademoiselle to write a letter to the headmaster saying that he had been absent from school on account of ill health and she always granted his request' (E. Starkie, *Lady's child*, p. 115). **35** E. Starkie, *Lady's child*, p. 101. **36** W. Starkie, *Scholars*, p. 30. **37** W. Starkie, 'Intermezzo' (1956) in R. Pine and C. Acton (eds), *To talent alone. The Royal Irish Academy of Music, 1848–1998* (Dublin, 1998), p. 291. Starkie claims he attended the concert in 1907 but a note in Pine and Acton explains that Elman performed at the Theatre Royal in Dublin two years earlier. This information would contribute to establishing the fact that Léonie Cora began her employment with the Starkie family in 1905. The Pine and Acton 'Intermezzo' is Starkie's article (save some paragraph changes) 'Random memories of the Academy' in *The Royal Irish Academy of Music, 1906–1956. Centenary souvenir* (Dublin, October 1956), pp 25–33.

musicians, especially violinists'[38] and Mademoiselle took it upon herself to cultivate contacts with virtuosi such as Pablo de Sarasate and Eugène Ysaÿe.[39] Intrepid, she wrote a letter on the boy's behalf to the former, who replied with a dedicated photograph. She also led her charge to hear Ysaÿe at the Rotunda Theatre in Dublin, further applying herself on the former's behalf. Starkie recalls her forceful tactics: 'she pushed her way into the artist's room and presented me to the massive Belgian virtuoso who towered over me like a colossus.'[40]

While he was a pupil at Strangways, Walter attended violin lessons, theory classes and orchestra practices at RIAM in Westland Row in the afternoons. Thus, he spent the day in Dublin, having lunch at the café whose 'Chinese-like pagoda' James Stephens would be unable to identify on the Friday of Easter week[41] and which would be immortalized by Joyce in *Ulysses*:[42] the DBC. Starkie records that the boy now began to acquire a sense of separation from his sisters in the schoolroom, coming to forge a more independent existence in the city. In recalling his days as a pupil at RIAM Starkie highlights the piano teacher of Italian origin, a man of prodigious energy and temperament, who significantly marked the development of the Academy and musical life in Dublin between 1882 and 1928, Michele Esposito, '[t]he personality above all others who is stamped on my mind'[43] and whose company the former pupil continued to keep as an adult in Dublin's musical circles. Mademoiselle's cultural influence was not limited to music. Her passion for theatre and opera was also impressed upon Walter, precisely around the time of the development of Ireland's National Theatre, the Abbey. Indeed, the twelve-year-old was in the audience in January 1907, on the opening night of Synge's *The playboy of the western world*, to witness what the adult would come to qualify as: '[t]he most exciting theatrical experience of my youth' even though he could scarcely hear the actors above the 'milling mob'. The experience also served to foreground the political differences that the Starkies would become increasingly exposed to as the century advanced: a group of students from Trinity College Dublin singing 'God Save the King' in response to the pit's rendering of Thomas Davis's challenging 'The West's Asleep'.[44] However, Mademoiselle's taste, like that of her employer, was more disposed towards the traditional literary canon and, again like Starkie's father, she was 'a great believer in the educational value of Shakespeare'.[45] WJM, a future President of the British Empire Shakespeare Society and promoter of the study of Shakespeare in the National Schools in Ireland in his role as Resident Commissioner, customarily read Shakespeare's plays at home on Sunday evenings.[46]

---

38 W. Starkie, *Scholars*, pp 40, 54. He adds that the *Grove's* in question was the first edition of 1889.
39 Sarasate died in 1908 so Léonie Cora must have written soon after 'the passion' for the violin began. Kennedy records that Pugno '[f]requently played in duo' with Ysaÿe so the governess may have known the latter through Pugno (M. Kennedy (ed.), *The concise Oxford dictionary of music*, p. 582).   40 W. Starkie, *Scholars*, p. 41.   41 J. Stephens, *The insurrection in Dublin* (Gerrards Cross, 1992), p. 59. 42 J. Joyce, *Ulysses*, p. 238, passim.   43 W. Starkie in R. Pine and C. Acton, *To talent*, p. 291.   44 W. Starkie, *Scholars*, pp 37, 38.   45 E. Starkie, *Lady's child*, p. 102.   46 WJM's practice may have been influenced by the National Home Reading Union. Founded in 1889, the Union was particularly aimed at middle or working-class readers 'who might be taught the "right" way and a kind of reading to assist them in cultivating a civilized mind [but] the actual membership often consisted of the educated middle and sometimes upper classes' (Susann Liebich, 'Educating adult readers: the National Home Reading

Therefore, he would not object to Mademoiselle accompanying his offspring to Shakespeare performances in Dublin even though, as the adult Starkie recalled, Mademoiselle's response was emotional rather than analytical: 'To see *Othello* with her was a shattering experience, … Iago was a "*scélérat*" from the start – "*un sale type*". Of Desdemona, "*quelle pureté d'âme, pauvre petite!*" When we came to the fourth act and Othello's downfall Mademoiselle became inarticulate, her tears began to flow and they continued uninterruptedly up to the end of the play.' Walter also acquired his first taste of Wagnerian opera through the governess's insistence that he take himself to see *Tannhäuser* at the Theatre Royal in Dublin where the Moody-Manners Opera Company were performing with the Irish bass Joseph O'Mara and English soprano Fanny Moody in the leading roles. Starkie registers the experience as opening 'a new world'[47] to him at the age of thirteen, that of music and drama. At a more informal level, there were amateur dramatics at Somerset, plays being acted out by members of the family, with Mademoiselle participating and relations as well as friends also being roped in.

Enid recalls that Mademoiselle and Mrs Starkie produced a French stage adaptation of *Cinderella* in which Enid played the part of Cinderella with her brother in the role of Prince Charming. Sporting robes his father had worn in Persia, Enid remembered Walter as 'like a young Sultan from the *Arabian nights*', while she was no less elaborate:

> like a figure from an eighteenth century illustration for Perrault's *Tales* in a dress with panniers and powdered hair dressed high on my head by Budina [*sic*], … the front panel of my frock consisted of a white satin table centre, with bunches of roses painted by hand on it, one of the atrocious gifts sent periodically to my father from convents up and down the country.

Mrs Starkie would play the parts of Fairy Godmother and the Queen in the ballroom scene while Mademoiselle was one of the ugly sisters together with one of the Hone children from nearby Temple Hill, Olive. Muriel, who had difficulty remembering her words, was parked as a page. In describing the performance, Enid confesses that she ruined Walter's moment of glory, the long speech in which he '[celebrated] the loveliness of the little slipper and [expressed] his resolve to wed none but its owner' since she forgot to change out of 'the disgraceful old pair of slippers gaping at the toes.' Thus, Walter found himself holding up a far from lovely little slipper and becoming the laughing stock of the evening. Enid was mortified, remembering as she wrote almost forty years on that her brother 'was very proud of his acting and [as was the case with his mother] liked success.' However, his reputation would be redeemed in the next family production: scenes from Shaw's *John Bull's Other Island*, when, according to Enid's account, Walter delivered a memorable Stage Irishman performance:

Union in Australasia, 1892–1898.' A paper read at the 2008 SHARP conference. The quote is taken from the abstract at http://ah.brookes.ac.uk/conference/presentation/educating_adult_readers/, accessed: 18 April 2012). **47** W. Starkie, *Scholars*, pp 36, 42.

My chief memory of the play is Walter's magnificent acting of the part of Barney Doran, especially his delivery of the long speech describing the drive in the car with Haffigan's pig. ... in a suit and bowler-hat borrowed from Rankin, the gardener, he gave a magnificent impersonation of what Rankin would have been had he been Barney Doran. His interpretation of the part was perhaps too common, but the audience did not care about such niceties and they roared with laughter at every word which came from his lips.[48]

Léonie Cora was also responsible for discovering the spiritual world to Walter, shocked that he had not received 'any systematic religious instruction'.[49] Thus, she further prescribed that he be prepared for his First Communion and Confirmation. Her insistence led to him being sent to the Convent of Mercy in Carysfort Park near Blackrock where, as Starkie fondly recalled, an elderly nun, Sister Michael, not only taught the boy catechism but spoke at length of the saints. Hence, at the age of twelve, decidedly later than his peers, Walter made his First Communion. Another, more earthy experience for the adolescent was the erotic and Mademoiselle would intervene here too. When writing of her childhood, Enid concludes that Mademoiselle was 'a little in love' with Walter and remembers: 'how excited [Léonie Cora] used to become and how red in the face when he came to schoolroom tea ... she used to giggle a great deal.' She also recalls that Walter would sing to Mademoiselle 'a French music hall song whose refrain began, "*Viens poupoule!* ...",' the popular song of 1902 by the French *chanteur comique* Mayol, which would send Mademoiselle into 'paroxysms of wild laughter'.[50] Since the governess's account is unavailable, whether she was 'a little in love' with her charge cannot be ascertained. However, the adult Starkie refers to two incidents which suggest that Mademoiselle found the schoolboy attractive. The first alludes to her behaviour on his return home from seeing Wagner's *Tannhaüser*. As instructed, Walter dutifully went to her room to report on his impressions of the opera, finding Mademoiselle reading in bed, apparently having decked herself out to appeal to the boy's age group as his contemporary: 'her hair ... in plaits ... gave her the air of a coquettish young girl.' In Starkie's account, the emotional pitch rises as Mademoiselle cross-examines Walter on his feelings and responses. The encounter is depicted through the adult's recollection as coming to a climax with the governess embracing the boy passionately, the narrative carrying an echo of Stephen Dedalus's experience at the close of Chapter 2 of Joyce's *A portrait of the artist as a young man*. The second episode is set in Co. Wicklow in the summer of 1908 when the Resident Commissioner and his wife were engaged 'on a long tour of [school] inspection in the south of Ireland' and the children were packed off with Mademoiselle to a farmhouse, remembered by Enid as being situated at the foot of the Sugar-Loaf. Whereas the first episode left the boy feeling 'dumbfounded', in Wicklow he records encountering a transformation in the starched and straight-laced governess, suggesting that he fell

---

48 E. Starkie, *Lady's child*, pp 95, 96. 49 W. Starkie, *Scholars*, p. 32. 50 E. Starkie, *Lady's child*, p. 115. Walter's account of the siblings' sojourn in Wicklow in the summer of 1908 has Mademoiselle singing the music-hall refrain: 'She sang loudly in her metallic French voice *Viens Pou-Poule, Viens*, as she moved about unpacking the trunks' (W. Starkie, *Scholars*, p. 44).

prey to her seductive qualities: 'In Wicklow her health improved and she shed her aggressive manner, her sallow complexion and tightly corsetted appearance. I then suddenly saw her in a detached way, not as my sisters' governess but as a woman, and I became physically aware of her vivacious temperament and charm.' However, Mademoiselle's antics came to cause her charge more embarrassment than satisfaction, as when she turned up for Sunday mass: 'dressed like a little girl of ten years of age in a skirt to her knees, showing lace-edged drawers, bare legs and diminutive socks. Her long wispy black hair hung down her back and she had put on one of Enid's straw hats. She skipped out of the trap with all the juvenile mincing graces.'[51] The Resident Commissioner's son was not amused and depicts himself in his autobiographical narrative as taking on the rôle of head of the household, scolding Mademoiselle for behaving in an inappropriate manner. Mademoiselle, in turn, is recorded as feeling mortified.

The body also came to complicate the relationship between father and son at this stage in the boy's development. Walter received a beating on Pater's discovering his tracings of naked statues of Hermes and Aphrodite from books in the scholar's library, his son's efforts interpreted as 'grossly obscene'. Immediately following the incident, having been struck on back, legs and shoulders with 'a big stick', Starkie records the boy seeking consolation for his physical and emotional pain by cycling into the Wicklow mountains, grieved that he should be punished for showing an interest in the naked bodies of male and female when the drawing room at Somerset exhibited 'two aggressively naked statues, of Narcissus and a Satyr in Pompeian bronze, on pedestals'. Music also provided a balm at this juncture. WJM's colleague Dr Mahaffy introduced the downhearted adolescent to the Professor of Music, Ebenezer Prout, an encounter that enabled the boy to hear a young tenor and soprano brought over to Dublin by Prout to sing the Bach Cantatas. Henry Macran was also at the concert and is recalled as encouraging his former neighbour to resist his father's prejudice towards music: 'Don't let him browbeat you! ... Music is as necessary as classics in life!'[52] A further gesture of kindness that contributed to alleviating Walter's pain was delivered by Mahaffy. The professor took Walter to his rooms and gave him a violin produced by Jacobus Steiner of Absom while taking advantage of the opportunity to qualify Macran's claim as to the importance of music, lending support to the conviction of Walter's father regarding the boy's classical studies. However, Mahaffy did provide his friend and colleague's son with further musical stimulus, introducing him to the conductor-associate of Wagner, Hans Richter, on the occasion of his leading the Hallé Orchestra in Dublin in 1908. The period coincided with Walter's receiving violin instruction at RIAM from the leader of the orchestra at the first performance of 'The Ring' in 1876, Adolf Wilhelmj.[53]

---

51 W. Starkie, *Scholars*, pp 42, 44. 52 W. Starkie, *Scholars*, pp 53, 55. 53 Starkie explains that Wilhelmj delivered 'the senior violin classes' and refers to Patrick Delany as his 'teacher [who was] entrusted with the teaching of all the aspiring boy fiddlers.' (W. Starkie, 'Intermezzo' in R. Pine and C. Acton, *To talent*, pp 292. See also 'Musical notes. Irish musician's who's who', IT, 18 Jan. 1937, p. 4, where it is claimed that Starkie also studied under Michael Zacharewitsch in both Dublin and London.

As a result of Mahaffy's kindness, so Starkie explains, WJM invited his fellow Trinity lecturer to join him on a schools inspection visit in Donegal and Antrim. Mahaffy himself was no stranger to inspecting schools, having been asked by the Endowed School commissioners to make an inspection of the Irish grammar schools in 1879,[54] but he would be especially delighted to visit Donegal, where his father hailed from. Walter was allowed to join the two Trinity men, who were also accompanied by WJM's secretary from the Office of Education, Andrew Bonaparte Wyse, and one of the Chief Inspectors, John McNeill.[55] The group travelled in style, in a 1907 Darracq, chauffered, as Starkie recalled over fifty years on, by one James Mulligan, 'a tall, lanky, red-haired Dubliner with a rich brogue', next to whom the most junior member of the company was perched. The 'primitive state of the roads' in Co. Donegal did not make for a smooth journey in spite of the splendid vehicle. However, the journey enabled Walter to discover an Ireland unknown to him. The 'roaming symposium' travelled up to the Inishowen Peninsula, reaching Malin Head, a territory where, Starkie observes, 'many of the people did not seem to speak English at all and answered us in Irish' and where '[t]he bleak-grey cliffs of the Bloody Foreland buffeted by the Atlantic struck [him] as the most awe-inspiring landscape [he] had ever seen'. Mount Errigal was another piece of breath-taking landscape viewed en route, with the advantage of contemplation over a few days' stay in Gweedore where, Starkie tells, the boy won the favour of 'the prettiest little postmistress in all Ireland', aided by the chauffeur's 'Harlequinesque resourcefulness.'[56] In recalling the days spent on the schools inspection tour in 1908, Starkie also remembers that the two Trinity scholars would indulge their enthusiasm for classical studies over dinner and throughout the evening, causing weariness in the schoolboy, thus leading him to seek escape. He records him going down to 'the little fishing harbour' in Buncrana, where he listened to fishermen telling 'yarns of the sea and tales of the McSwineys'.[57]

The year 1908 marked the end of Walter's growing up exclusively in Ireland albeit with occasional visits to London. In the summer term of 1909 he was sent to public school in England, to Shrewsbury, where Pater had blazed the trail in the 1870s, rising to Head Boy in 1879. In the month of May, having taken leave of Cécile Jephson, a violincellist whom he had met at RIAM and with whom, according to Enid, '[Walter] was in love in those days',[58] the boy was seen off at Kingstown by Mlle Cora together with his sisters Enid, Muriel and Chou-Chou, from where he took the mailboat bound for Holyhead. Once in England, he would follow his father's advice, visiting the Roman walls of Chester while he waited for a rail connection to Shrewsbury. The visit prompted reflection on the benefits of 'a superior civilization' and the expression of regret that Ireland had not been equally graced: 'The Romans, alas, had never taken it into their heads to invade our neighbouring island',[59] a disappointment that may well have been felt by the adolescent but which undoubtedly originated in the conviction of his classical scholar-father whose 'championing of the Classics' was a consequence

54 W.B. Stanford & R.B. McDowell, *Mahaffy*, p. 47.   55 On WJM's visits to schools 'all over Ireland', see J. Coolahan with Patrick F. O'Donovan, *A history of Ireland's School Inspectorate, 1831–2008* (Dublin, 2009), p. 73.   56 W. Starkie, *Scholars*, pp 58, 59, 60.   57 W. Starkie, *Scholars*, p. 59.   58 E. Starkie, *Lady's child*, p. 126.   59 W. Starkie, *Scholars*, p. 65.

of his belief that 'Greek and Latin ... were the repositories of the spirit which informs civilization'.[60]

In Old Salopian Desmond Coke's *The bending of a twig* (1900), Thomas Marsh, Victorian father, is determined that his son should not dream but '*do* something'. The parent's resolve informs his decision to send son Lycidas to 'one of the great English Public Schools': 'Shrewsbury's ... on a hill now, towering above the town and river. Just the very place: new buildings, old traditions. What could possibly be better? Shrewsbury's the place for him.'[61] Enid recalls Walter reading the novel before his departure for England with a view to finding out about life at Shrewsbury. There was also a further source of information in another colleague of WJM's at TCD, also an Old Salopian who, like the Resident Commissioner, had been Head Boy and who sometimes lunched with the Starkies: Robert Tate,[62] elected to classical Fellowship at TCD, the year before Walter went up.[63] Both WJM and Tate had been at Shrewsbury under the Headship of the Reverend Henry Whitehead Moss, a 'brilliant old Salopian scholar',[64] who had retired following forty-two years of service in 1908, the year before Walter became a pupil. Over the nineteenth century three 'scholars and teachers of the highest order',[65] Samuel Butler, Benjamin Hall Kennedy and Moss, gained a pre-eminence for the school in classical learning, many of the pupils opting to go up to Cambridge. Over the thirty-year-period before WJM was sent there: 'thirty-seven Shrewsbury men obtained a first-class in the Classical Tripos'[66] and Walter's father would follow, graduating in 1883.[67] As Headmaster in the 1880s, Moss had overseen the relocation of the school from its then 'cramped and confined'[68] position in the town to a spacious area above the River Severn some three miles from the Market Place and known as Kingsland. Thus, Walter would benefit from a far more open setting. Furthermore, the boy would no longer be discriminated against on the grounds of his Catholicism, unlike his father in the 1870s. It had then been necessary for WJM to be registered as a dayboy while his son was able to lodge in the house of E.B. Moser, MA, late Scholar of St John's College, Cambridge, a fellow under-graduate of the future Resident Commisioner's in the 1880s.

As the junior member of his study of three boys, Walter was immediately intro-duced to the practice of fagging. He was required to take the eldest boy his shaving water, to clean his shoes and be ready to act as messenger. On the evening of his arrival the new boy was elected hall crier in the house, a post which involved making announcements at mealtimes, beginning traditionally with an 'Oyez! Oyez! Oyez!' and always ending with the pro-monarchical proclamation: 'God save the King and down with the Radicals'.[69] Enid recalls that her brother was 'very nervous'[70] at the prospect

60 'William Myles [*sic*] Joseph Starkie', *Hermathena*, 19:43 (1922), vi, vii. **61** D.F.T. Coke, *The bending of a twig* (London, 1925), pp 19, 20, 22. **62** E. Starkie, *Lady's child*, p. 126; J.E. Auden (ed.), *Shrewsbury School register* (Shrewsbury, 1928), pp 305–6. **63** W. Starkie, *Scholars*, p. 108; J.E. Auden (ed.), *Shrewsbury School*, p. 306. **64** J.M. West, *Shrewsbury* (London, 1937), p. 82. **65** Ibid., p. 40. **66** G.W. Fisher, *Annals of Shrewsbury School* (London, 1899), cited in J.M. West, *Shrewsbury*, p. 65. **67** J.E. Auden (ed.), *Shrewsbury School*, p. 251. **68** J.M. West, *Shrewsbury*, p. 93. **69** J.M. West, *Shrewsbury*, pp 59–60; W. Starkie, *Scholars*, p. 67. Shrewsbury's royalist commitment is also reflected in the school's two 'Evening prayers', dating from the sixteenth century and which, according to West, were still recited every Sunday into the 1930s (J.M. West, *Shrewsbury*, pp 25–6). **70** E. Starkie, *Lady's*

of having to sing in the dormitories at night, dreading that his efforts might not please and that he would be the butt of wet sponges and hair brushes. Starkie records Walter's 'misgiving' in connection with hall-singing, having heard stories from Old Salopians in Dublin 'about being howled down' and forced 'to drink a mug of salt water'. Thus, armed by friends with 'some *risqué* French-English songs', Walter prepared to meet his ordeal. However, the adult autobiographer recalls the shy new boy doubting his ability to put the songs over effectively and therefore opting for a safer option. 'The Vicar of Bray' was his choice and spared him the sponge, hairbrush or mug of salt water though, as Starkie observes, it was a less entertaining option for his audience: 'my song passed muster and did not cause a ripple of interest'. Out on the sports field, Walter's chronic asthma did not enable him to shine or even hold his own. Starkie remarks on the boy's having felt an inferiority complex because of his 'lack of proficiency in football, cricket and athletics' and realizing that he should look to obtaining 'the games passport'[71] with a view to acceptance among his peers. Aware of his physical limitations, he took on the role of goal-keeper and with a degree of dedication came to acquire an expertise that led to him being included in teams when Shrewsbury was playing against other public schools.

Part of the rationale for sending the fourteen-year-old to Shrewsbury was, as the son declares, to break his 'obstinate and long-sustained determination to study the violin and be educated musically.'[72] In their history of Shrewsbury School going back to the 1880s, Von Monté and Milns West observed the lack of emphasis awarded music, the subject 'never [having] taken a very prominent place in the School programme'.[73] Thus, WJM might rest assured that his offspring would not be distracted by what had become the latter's passion. However, unpredictably, the boy's enthusiasm for music and his aptitude for the violin increased given the professional guidance of Hubert Salt, first violin in the Hallé Orchestra,[74] and through his contact and friendship with 'the Men',[75] two young assistant masters whose arrival at Shrewsbury coincided with Walter's in 1909. Malcolm White and Evelyn Southwell were graduates of Cambridge and Oxford, respectively, and both were accomplished musicians: White on the violin, Southwell on the piano.[76] White had also acquired a reputation as a singer while Southwell was a first-class oarsman and professed a 'love of French literature and the French nation'.[77] Doubtless, Southwell's familiarity with musical comedy and his devotion to France and her culture would have attracted the new boy in the wake of Mlle Cora's instruction; on the other hand, with his sense of fun he would have been drawn to White's 'keen sense of humour'[78] and, of course, his proficiency on the violin. Starkie recalls sharing music with both men on Sunday evenings in White or Southwell's rooms before an audience of masters and boys:

child, p. 126.   71 W. Starkie, *Scholars*, pp 67, 71.   72 Ibid., p. 64.   73 W.J. Von Monté & J. Milns West, *Shrewsbury School: the last fifty years* (Shrewsbury, 1932), p. 77.   74 W. Starkie, *Scholars*, p. 70. 75 The title derived from each addressing the other as 'Man'. See H.E. Howson (ed.), *Two men: a memoir* (Oxford, 1919), p. 1.   76 Having commented on the lack of emphasis on music at Shrewsbury, Von Monté and Milns West add: 'but for a few years before the War a Musical Society existed giving a concert in the summer term' (W.J. Von Monté & J. Milns West, *Shrewsbury School*, p. 77). White and Southwell enthusiastically contributed to the Society.   77 H.E. Howson (ed.), *Two men*, p. 2.   78 Ibid.

8 W.F. Starkie engaging in one of his hobbies as a young man.

'playing the [Bach] concertos and sonatas for two violins, and the works of Vivaldi and Purcell.' Indeed, in recollection, Starkie asserts that the 'friendship' and 'close associ-ation' with those two young, gifted and enthusiastic teachers 'meant more [to the adolescent Walter] than anything else in the world'.[79]

Walter's experience of homesickness during his first term was perhaps quickened by the arrival of the weekly hampers lovingly prepared by the Starkie household's devoted cook, Lizzie. However, rather than portraying a pining for the wholesome fare of home, Starkie depicts Walter particularly missing his music. Playing his instrument wasn't allowed in free time on Sundays but following the boy's comment to 'one of the assistant masters' (perhaps White or Southwell though Starkie doesn't specify), he was granted permission to play his violin on condition that he produced 'good music … never [descending] to waltzes, foxtrots or other frivolous dances.'[80] His violin classes were programmed for 6:30a.m. so as not to interfere with the school syllabus but Starkie recalls rising an hour or thirty minutes beforehand so that he could get into school as soon as the doors were opened and practise in peace. His autobiography registers the adolescent's growing sense of self-confidence as well as his awareness of improvement in his technique and the school magazine bears witness to his talent as revealed in school concerts in 1910, 1911 and 1912, the latter two years when Walter played solos being particularly complimentary.[81] However, the boy's talent had already been noted at the beginning of his years at Shrewsbury, the summer term of 1909 witnessing the debut of the Shrewsbury School Musical Society, which produced a first concert on 23 July at 8:30p.m., to which Walter contributed. *The Salopian* declared: '... the Society's first concert was a decided success. [...] ... the duets for two violins ... were both remarkably well executed. Starkie is a violinist of great promise, and he was most ably supported by Longworth as second violin.'[82] Further witness to Walter's musical distinction are the prizes he was awarded in 1910, presented to him by the Headmaster's wife, Mrs Alington, sister of the Headmaster of Eton, Dr Edward Lyttleton.[83]

With regard to Walter's progress in other subjects, he appears to have acquired particular distinction in French, already obtaining the Dukes Prize in 1910[84] and coming top of the class for French in the Lent Term, when in the Lower Division of the Fifth Form with A.F. Chance, MA, in a class of nine boys. However, his performance in Classics was a lesser achievement with him only occupying sixth place. This pattern continued in the Summer Term: while in 'Lower Remove' with E.B. Moser in 1911, he again obtained first place for French and now managed third for Classics in a class of six boys, a slight improvement on his earlier performance. In the 'Upper Remove' he maintained his position in French but obtained lower ratings in Classics. Walter's father would have been disappointed by his son's failure to achieve equal distinction in the Classics but Walter's obtaining the 'Head Master's English Literature Prize', twice in 1911 and again in 1912,[85] may have provided some consolation.

Of the approximately fifteen pages devoted to Shrewsbury in Starkie's account of his schooldays in England, the master who occupies the most space and is awarded the greatest enthusiasm is the Reverend Cyril Argentine Alington, MA, late Fellow of All Souls' College, Oxford, appointed Headmaster at Shrewsbury in 1908 at the age of

81 'The School Concert, 16 Dec. 1909', *The Salopian*, 29:17 (29 Jan. 1910), no. 202, 336–8 at 337; 'The Concert [December 1910]', *The Salopian*, 30:5 (4 Feb. 1911), no. 130, 69–70 at 69; 'The Concert [December 1911]', *The Salopian*, 32:7 (3 Feb. 1912), no. 237, 90–1 at 90.   82 'The School Concert', *The Salopian*, 29:10 (July 1909), no. 195, 269–70 at 270.   83 'Prizes. Lent term: Music prizes – Given by the Hon. Mrs Alington', *Shrewsbury School Prize List* (summer 1910), p. 35; 'Prizes. Summer term: Music prizes – Given by the Hon. Mrs Alington', *Shrewsbury School Prize List* (Michaelmas 1910), p. 35.   84 The Dukes Prizes were two, 'founded in accordance with the Will of the late Mr E.R. Dukes, of Christ Church, Oxford', *Shrewsbury School Prize List* (summer 1910), p. 35.   85 'Prizes: Head Master's English Literature Prizes ... Junior – W.F. Starkie', *Shrewsbury School Prize List* (Michaelmas term, 1911), p. 38; 'Prizes. Head Master's English Literature Prizes ... Junior – W.F. Starkie', *Shrewsbury School Prize List* (summer term, 1911), p. 36; 'Prizes. Head Master's English Literature Prizes – Junior – W.F. Starkie' (*Shrewsbury School Prize List* (Lent term, 1912), p. 38; 'Prizes. Head Master's English Literature Prizes – Sixth form – ...W.F. Starkie', *Shrewsbury School Prize List* (Michaelmas term, 1912), p. 46; 'Prizes. Head Master's English Literature Prizes – Sixth form – ... W.F. Starkie' (*Shrewsbury School Prize List*) (summer term, 1912), p. 39.

twenty-four, following the departure of Moss, and Walter's master in the sixth form.[86] Starkie remembers him as 'handsome, nervy and temperamental'[87] and recalls already being drawn during his first term at Shrewsbury by Alington's rhetoric in defence of reform in the public schools. His account reveals Alington as an exacting task master, whether it was on the football pitch or in the classroom. The headmaster's own teaching was complemented by visits from distinguished men, scholars or celebrities in their particular fields of expertise. Thus, Walter was able to hear the Cambridge classical scholar J.E.B. Mayor; the Catholic Chaplain-to-be at Oxford, the Reverend Ronald Knox, sometime Classics master at Shrewsbury, and the Catholic tenor Gervase Elwes, a personal friend of Alington's, among others.

Starkie records the headmaster's classes over Walter's last term at Shrewsbury as '[t]he most inspiring'[88] he received during his almost three years at the public school. The classes in question made use of the daily *Times*. Each boy in the Upper Sixth was provided with a copy of the newspaper of the day and the class focussed on page 5, which frequently carried the 'Imperial and Foreign Intelligence' section, largely taken up in Walter's last term at Shrewsbury with news of the Balkans. War was threatening in the autumn of 1912 and the First Balkan War broke out in the month of October: 'the Ottoman Empire [fighting] a loose alliance of Balkan states, which included Bulgaria, Greece, Montenegro and Serbia.'[89] The countries of the Balkan League were rising up against the imperial nation, Turkey. As the *Times* declared in a leader: 'it was inevitable that, sooner or later, the Turk would have to fight to retain his hold on the remains of his Empire in Europe'.[90] The news coverage of those months of autumn into winter of 1912 repeatedly focused on issues related to colonial rule and exploitation whether in connection with the war in the Balkans, the Franco-Spanish Treaty dealing with new frontiers in Morocco, [91] the Putumayo atrocities exposed by Sir Roger Casement,[92] the question of the responsibility of the British Directors of the Peruvian Amazon Company being enquired into by a Select Committee,[93] and the

---

86 Alington would be headmaster at Shrewsbury until 1916 when he took up the position at Eton, where he remained as headmaster until 1933. He was also Chaplain to the King from 1921 until 1933 (*Who was who, 5, 1951–60* (London, 1961)). 87 W. Starkie, *Scholars*, p. 69. 88 Ibid., p. 78. 89 See R.C. Hall, *The Balkan wars, 1912–1913: prelude to the First World War* (London, 2000), p. 1. 90 'War begun in the Balkans', TT, 9 Oct. 1912, p. 7. 91 'France and Spain in Morocco', TT, 28 Oct. 1912, p. 5; 'The Spaniards in Morocco. Policy and prospects', TT, 19 Nov. 1912, p. 7; 'Franco-Spanish treaty. A new era in Morocco', TT, 2 Dec. 1912, p. 6; 'The Franco-Spanish treaty. The Conservative Party view', TT, 14 Dec. 1912, p. 7. 92 In his autobiography, Starkie recalls Casement lunching with the family at Somerset in 1910, together with the Belfast antiquarian and historian Francis Joseph Biggar. He registers the impact Casement had on the adolescent: 'his personality cast a glamour upon me. He seemed to me then an heroic figure who had exposed with unflinching courage the most appalling human abominations known to man in the Putumayo rubber region in Brazil' (W. Starkie, *Scholars*, p. 138). 93 'The Putumayo atrocities', TT, 9 Oct. 1912, p. 10; TT, 11 Oct. 1912, p. 10; 23 Oct. 1912, p. 10; 'The Putumayo atrocities. Evidence of Sir Roger Casement. Position of British directors', TT, 14 Nov. 1912, p. 7; 'The Putumayo atrocities. Evidence as to Barbadian labour', TT, 19 Nov. 1912, p. 7; 'The Putumayo atrocities. Attitude of the British directors', TT, 21 Nov. 1912, p. 12; 'The Putumayo atrocities', TT, 28 Nov. 1912, p. 4; 'The Putumayo atrocities. Position of British company directors', TT, 5 Dec. 1912, p. 4; 'The Putumayo atrocities. Expenditure of the company on rifles', TT, 18 Dec. 1912, p. 11.

debates around the Irish Home Rule Bill, reported on daily. In early September, the *Times* had announced that it would be carrying the reports of a Special Correspondent in Ulster, 'commissioned to investigate the state of feeling and the political conditions in view of the coming demonstrations against Home Rule.'[94] Before the end of the month, the 'Solemn League and Covenant' had been signed by a significant number of those who were opposed to Home Rule,[95] accentuating the disagreement between those who wished to maintain the *status quo*, led by Sir Edward Carson, 'the unyielding advocate of Ulster Unionism in 1912',[96] and those who were supporting Ireland's struggle for autonomy, with John Redmond at the helm, to be assessed by Starkie in the context of the First World War as 'a noble Christian gentleman whose patriotism had soared above the narrow limits of nationality.'[97]

Therefore, the international political contexts of Walter's last term at public school in England were dominated by a lexicon of instability: 'unrest', 'tension', 'danger', 'crisis', the 'threat of war', 'the passion for war' and an 'ominous coarse of events' before the eventual 'outbreak of war' in Central and Eastern Europe together with voices of doom sounding nearer home as the Westminster parliament struggled to pass a Home Rule Bill for the third time. Speaking at the Exhibition Buildings in York on 16 November 1912 at an event organized by the local Liberal Association, Redmond both appealed to and challenged his audience by reference to events in the Balkans:

> Your hearts are stirred, and rightly stirred, by the spectacle of Bulgaria, Servia [*sic*] and little Montenegro fighting for their liberty, fighting for an ideal, and your national heart goes out to them. Can you not believe that the little island of Ireland has also a soul and an ideal? Can you not sympathise with, aye, and honour in us what you sympathise with and honour in every other part of the world. This is a question of the reconciliation of the Irish race.[98]

But the views expressed by Carson and Timothy Healy, future Governor-General of the Irish Free State, during the debate on Clause 29 of the Bill in early December 1912, illustrate the radically different perspectives and the difficulty of reconciliation.[99] During those latter months of 1912, the *Times* would also carry a letter from Walter's father, refuting the accusation by Nationalist MP John Dillon that a recent manifesto of the Commissioners of National Education signified opposition to the Home Rule Bill. WJM was characteristically tenacious and outspoken.[1]

94 'Ulster and Home Rule', TT, 7 Sept. 1912, p. 6.   **95** 'Ulster and the Covenant', TT, 15 Nov. 1912, p. 6; 'Signatures to the Ulster Covenant', 22 Nov. 1912, p. 8. See also http://www.proni.gov.uk/index/ search_the_archives/ulster_covenant.htm, accessed 20 April 2012.   **96** A. Jackson, *Sir Edward Carson* (Dublin, 1993), p. 6.   **97** W. Starkie, *Scholars*, p. 130. See C.A. Alington's critical comment on Carson, cited by W. Starkie, *Scholars*, p. 80, and further information on John Redmond in P. Bew, *John Redmond* (Dublin, 1996).   **98** 'Mr Redmond on Home Rule. Solidarity of the Coalition', TT, 18 Nov. 1912, p. 8. **99** 'Parliament. House of Commons. Home Rule Bill. Appeals on constitutional questions', TT, 5 Dec. 1912, p. 10.   **1** 'Irish Education under Home Rule. Dr Starkie's reply to Mr. Dillon', TT, 18 Sept. 1912, p. 8. The Resident Commissioner's outspokenness did not jeapordize, indeed, may have favoured, his being nominated to serve on the Advisory Committee of the Imperial Education Conference and he was present at its first meeting at the offices of the Board of Education in London on 18 Nov. 1912 (TT,

Also revealed in the pages of the *Times* during the period is the growing challenge to British Government representatives in Ireland, which was becoming manifest around the country. When the Conservative MP George Wyndham was lecturing in Limerick on the night of 10 October 1912, speaking in favour of the Unionist policy which, he claimed, would foster Ireland's material prosperity, his words were not met by unanimous approval and his departure was disrupted:

> There were a few interruptions during the meeting, and afterwards a crowd which had gathered outside the hall caused a disturbance. Stones were thrown by gangs of boys at the secretary of the meeting and at some of those who had attended, and they had to seek refuge in the Post Office. The motor car in which a gentleman was leaving the hall was damaged, and the windows of the Protestant Young Men's Association and other buildings were broken. The disorder was becoming serious when the police charged with batons and dispersed the crowd. No one was injured.[2]

The following month, when Lord Lieutenant of Ireland Lord Aberdeen and his wife attended a conference in the Rotunda in Dublin on behalf of the Roman Catholic Boys' Brigade, they were subjected to a hostile reception: 'some young men … sang "God Save Ireland", shouted "Down with Aberdeen!" and cheered for an Irish Republic.' The report further informed that a Fr Gaynor subsequently thanked the Aberdeens for having attended and expressed his regret that 'a few foolish and irresponsible boys' had created a disturbance. Aberdeen was cavalier in his reply, claiming that: 'after forty years of public life he knew too much to pay serious attention to such interruptions.' The report ends with reference to Lord and Lady being 'loudly cheered'[3] on leaving the hall. However, in less than four years those 'gangs of boys' in Limerick and the young men cheering in support of an Irish Republic in the Rotunda would be provided with the opportunity of lending their support to the proclamation of an Irish Republic. It was then that the government Lord Aberdeen represented would be driven to pay very serious attention to what was no longer a question of occasional interruptions.

Another news item that filled the pages of the *Times* over the months of September to December 1912 but which appears not to have merited C.A. Alington's attention, or memorably struck his pupil, was another struggle on the home front: women's suffrage, a struggle which would challenge the conservative energies of Walter's mother during her son's years at public school in England. Over the autumn to winter months of 1912, the *Times* carried several reports relating to Suffragist activity, most of which highlight the persistent challenge to the Establishment represented by militants. A number of the articles relate to incidents in England, such as the attacks on pillar boxes and destruction of letters,[4] but acts of protest in Dublin were also

'Imperial education. Meeting of the Advisory Committee', 19 Nov. 1912, p. 7).   2 'Unionist policy for Ireland. Mr. Wyndham at Limerick', TT, 11 Oct. 1912, p. 8.   3 'Lord and Lady Aberdeen. A hostile demonstration in Dublin', TT, 26 Nov. 1912, p. 15.   4 'Attacks on pillar boxes in London. Destruction of letters. Supposed suffragist outrage. Outrages in the Midlands', TT, 29 Nov. 1912, p. 8; 'Destruction

recorded. In September, Mrs Mary Leigh, one of two English suffragists who had been sentenced to five years penal servitude in August for the 'outrage' at the Theatre Royal in Dublin on the occasion of Mr Asquith's visit to the city, was released from Mountjoy Prison given her state of health.[5] In early November, suffragists broke windows of the Custom House[6] and at the end of the month 'Votes for Women' was daubed in white paint on hall doors in Elgin Road, Clyde Road and Herbert Park in the residential suburb of Ballsbridge,[7] where the Starkies were resident by 1912 and from where the Resident Commissioner's spouse continued her campaigning for women not to be granted the vote.

When remembering the 'constant parties' held at Somerset, Enid mentions her mother's annual chrysanthemum show in the autumn when head gardener Rankin's beautiful blooms were exhibited, highlighting 'one year'[8] when her mother charged an entrance fee to the show, the proceeds going to the Anti-Suffrage League. Enid recalls the colourful cakes ready for tea, 'decorated with the Anti-Suffrage colours' and registers the indignation she experienced:

> Even at that time, small child that I was, my feminist instincts were outraged and I protested to my mother. She answered that she saw no reason why a woman should need a vote, since she could always influence public affairs through her husband, that she had in this way more power than she could ever hope to achieve with suffrage.[9]

As *A lady's child* reveals, mother and daughter disagreed on a number of issues and women's rights was undoubtedly a fundamental bone of contention. In mid-December 1912, the *Times* quoted a text signed by The Dowager Lady Ancaster, Lady Haversham, Lady Charnwood and Mrs Bischoffsheim, writing as representatives of the Mayfair and St George's Branch of the National League for Opposing Woman Suffrage, urging 'all those who wish to prevent … amendments [to the Franchise Bill] being carried to come forward without delay with subscriptions (either large or small) and with energetic work to meet this great emergency.'[10] By this time Walter and Enid's mother had been devoting her energies to the anti-suffrage cause for three years. The first annual meeting of the Dublin Branch of the Women's National Anti-Suffrage League was held in the Molesworth Hall on 25 January 1910 and presided

---

of letters by suffragists', TT, 30 Nov. 1912, p. 6; 'Woman suffrage. Further destruction of letters', TT, 16 Dec. 1912, p. 4; 'Renewed attacks on letter boxes. Three women arrested', TT, 18 Dec. 1912, p. 8. **5** 'Mrs. Leigh released. A hunger strike of forty-four days', TT, 21 Sept. 1912, p. 6. **6** 'The suffragist outrages. Four women charged', TT, 7 Nov. 1912, p. 2. **7** 'Hall doors painted by suffragists', TT, 3 Dec. 1912, p. 8. **8** E. Starkie, *Lady's child*, p. 93. **9** E. Starkie, *Lady's child*, p. 94. Mrs Starkie's view echoes one of the *dicta* of the National League for Opposing Woman Suffrage: 'Women do not need to vote; they are represented without voting. Political agreement is the rule in a household, whether of husband and wife, father and daughter, mother and son, or brother and sister; the vote of the man represents, therefore, the party political wishes of the woman. It does this with economy of time, trouble and cost. Why change? Women are represented.' ('Advertisement of the League', *Anti-Suffrage Review* (Feb. 1914), p. 9). **10** 'The League for Opposing Woman Suffrage', TT, 16 Dec. 1912, p. 4.

over by Mrs Bernard, wife of the Archbishop J.H. Bernard, Dean of St Patrick's and colleague of WJM's. The Honorary Secretary read the report for the past year, referring to 'the steady, if quiet, progress'[11] and it was at this initial gathering that 'Mrs Starkie' read a paper entitled 'A Consultative Chamber'.[12] The Resident Commissioner's wife subsequently figures in the *Anti-Suffrage Review* as having delivered papers at the AGMs in 1911 and 1912. She read her 'A Forward Policy for the National League Opposing Woman Suffrage' at the annual meeting of the Dublin Branch of the League in February 1911, arguing: 'Feminine unrest is the logical outcome of the higher education and opening up of professions to women' and going on to outline what she understood to be 'eminently women's work', that is, the tasks that women had traditionally been concerned with: 'To look after the young, the old, the infirm, to teach and raise the fallen'. What was required, therefore, was 'more women guardians, women inspectors, both sanitary and educational; ... women on educational committees and on municipal councils.'[13] In the April 1912 issue of *The Anti-Suffrage Review*, 'Mrs Starkie' is reported as having read 'an interesting paper' on 'The Forward Policy of the [Anti-Suffrage] League'[14] and in September 1912, her 'Irish Women and the Vote' was awarded a full-page spread, an article which the author, May C. Starkie, claimed was written 'to protest against the suggestion that Irish women should be enfranchised under the Home Rule Bill' and which concludes: 'our high birth rate and also the fact that we are mainly an agricultural country, whose women have neither the time nor the opportunity for studying political questions, ought to constitute a final argument against imposing on us further responsibilities and duties, even had we shown ourselves willing to undertake them.'[15]

At the AGM of 1913, 'Mrs Starkie' was present but does not appear to have delivered a paper.[16] By this time (27 May), her eighteen-year-old son was back in Dublin.

MELFORT, BALLSBRIDGE, CO. DUBLIN, 1911–20

The weather during the week-end has been very severe throughout the country ... keen frost and heavy falls of snow. [...] Snow has fallen over the greater part of Ireland. In some places it is reported to be six inches in depth. After a night of severe frost in Dublin, snow fell for a short time yesterday morning but later in the day, showers of rain washed away all traces of it on the streets.[17]

The month of December 1912 began with weather that did not augur a smooth crossing from Holyhead to the port of Kingstown when Walter was to travel home as

11 'Women's Anti-Suffrage League. Meeting in Dublin', IT, 26 Jan. 1910, p. 6.   12 No copy of the paper appears to remain.   13 'Our Branch Newsletter. Dublin', *Anti-Suffrage Review*, 29 (Apr. 1911), 76.   14 'Our Branch Newsletter. Dublin', *Anti-Suffrage Review*, 41 (Apr. 1912), 79. No further information on the content of the paper is provided.   15 May C. Starkie, 'Irish women and the vote', *Anti-Suffrage Review*, 47 (Sept. 1912), 216.   16 'Branch News. Dublin', *Anti-Suffrage Review*, 57 (July 1913), 157.   17 'A wintry week-end. Frost and snow throughout the country', TT, 2 Dec. 1912, p. 6.

a pupil of Shrewsbury School for the last time. His father's financial straits prevented his son from staying on at public school in England until the end of the school year (July 1913) and so the boy, become a somewhat dandy fellow while at Shrewsbury,[18] would find himself back in Dublin and with the family now residing nearer to the centre of the city. Enid remembers Melfort as a larger house than Somerset but with grounds that seemed 'cramped'[19] by comparison with the rural spread of the family's former residence. However, there were compensations: one of the two tennis courts at the back of the house was reserved for the children and there were cousins close by to play with. Thus, Enid recalls tennis taking over from croquet, her sister Muriel and herself practising with their cousins and neighbours at number 16 Shrewsbury Road, Cyril and Ruth Hoey, the son and daughter of Mrs Starkie's sister Ida and her husband Charles.

The weather report in *The Times*, quoted above, writes of 'the country', still one under the Union, though Walter's perception of Irish difference would be 'brought home' to him by James Stephens following his return to Dublin in 1912. Already during the Christmas holidays of 1910, Walter, then 'a youth from an English public school accustomed to plod through a Greek tragedy word by word in class and learn by heart passages from Shakespeare', had been bewitched by Synge's *Deirdre of the sorrows*. Performed at the Abbey with Molly Allgood in the rôle of Deirdre, Starkie recalls the sixteen-year-old receiving it as revelation:

> I can remember no play that produced so deep an impression upon me as *Deirdre of the Sorrows*. I still see clearly in my mind's eye the wild young princess gathering up her rich robes and jewels, and I hear her voice saying prophetically: 'I will dress like Emer in Dundealgan, or Maeve in her house in Connaught. If Conchubor 'll make me queen, I'll have the right of a queen who is a master, … […] I will not be a child or plaything; I'll put on my robes that are the richest, for I will not be brought down to Emain as Cuchulain brings his horse to the yoke, or Conall Cearneach puts his shield upon his arm; and maybe from this day I will turn the men of Ireland like a wind blowing on the heath.'[20]

Deirdre's determination constitutes an affirmation of her human dignity, of her right to assert her independent authority. In words included in the same pronouncement by Deirdre, and which are, strikingly, omitted by Starkie in quoting from the play, her right to choose is asserted: 'If Conchubor make me a queen, I'll have the right of a queen who is a master, *taking her own choice and making a stir to the edges of the seas*.'[21] Walter had been drilled at home to conform: by his father, the dutiful public servant; by his mother, whose 'rigid principles belonged to the *fin de siècle* Anglo-Irish ascendancy'[22] and subsequently he was subjected to the stern rule of Mlle Cora, who commandeered the school room with her firm sense of '*le devoir*'. And a strong notion

---

18 E. Starkie, *Lady's child*, p. 128.   19 E. Starkie, *Lady's child*, p. 169.   20 W. Starkie, *Scholars*, pp 82–3.   21 J. M. Synge, 'Deirdre of the Sorrows', *Collected plays* (London, 1952), p. 223. My italics. 22 W. Starkie, *Scholars*, p. 11.

of duty, of responsibility to the *status quo*, was reinforced by the adolescent's charismatic teacher at Shrewsbury, the Revd C.A. Alington. Apart from the context of formal teaching in the sixth-form classroom, when the headmaster's ideological convictions had been impressed on the boys through the comparisons he drew between Classical heroes and events and what he interpreted as their latter-day counterparts,[23] his chapel homilies were also used for didactic purposes and on these occasions he came, increasingly, to adopt the fable form. On 26 November 1912, Confirmation Sunday Evening of that year, at which Walter would have been present, the Headmaster delivered 'A Fable', centred on 'a bitter dispute going on in the Grate; the Paper, the Wood and the Coal were all quarrelling, for each maintained that he was the most important part of the fire.' The moral of the tale is summed up in a 'little song' sung by the Grate, which conveys a lesson for the Christian and the British citizen of the Empire of self-denial and cooperation for the greater good:

> Thou hast made us all, Paper and Coal and Wood,
> Lo, we have heard thy call; lo, we have understood.
> Paper that flares and goes, Wood that crackles in flame,
> Coal that abides and glows, surely their end is the same.
> All that we have we give, giving we know not why,
> Nor for ourselves we live, and not to ourselves we die.
> Not to ourselves we die, fulfilling our Lord's desire;
> Coal, Wood, Paper and I, we have made our Master's fire.[24]

Alington's views on duty are outlined in his first published text, *A schoolmaster's apology*, where he outlined his radical opposition to the progressive ideas of Maria Montessori, then taking hold in pedagogical circles:

> It seems to me worse than nonsense, in fact disastrous folly, to suggest that what is most needed by the average modern child is encouragement to follow its own inclination. Enough encouragement of that kind is provided by the conditions of modern society, and a school which makes a child do what is uncongenial from a sense of duty is, at the moment, *playing a* more valuable *part*.[25]

The theatrical metaphor on which the above sentence ends is echoed in Starkie's autobiography when paying tribute to the boy's former teacher: 'Dr Alington was the only headmaster or teacher I have ever known who possessed the power of portraying in Time [*sic*] and Space [*sic*] for an intelligent youth of eighteen years the historic stage upon which he would shortly be obliged to *act* his *part*.'[26] Walter's encounter with James Stephens would challenge the former's Anglocentric upbringing and public school grooming and might have led him to play a different part to the one his elders

---

23 W. Starkie, *Scholars*, p. 79. 24 C. Alington, 'A fable' in *Fables and fancies* (London, [n.d.]), pp 1, 2. 25 C.A. Alington, *A schoolmaster's apology* (London, 1914), p. 21. My italics. 26 W. Starkie, *Scholars*, p. 78. My italics.

and betters had traced for him but the discourses had delved deep and would be reinforced during his tertiary education at TCD under the authority of, among others, the imposing personalities and servants of Empire, Major Robert Tate, Commanding Officer of the Officers' Training Corps within the university from the founding of the Corps in 1910 until 1922, and the Reverend John Pentland Mahaffy, both of whom received knighthoods. Thus, by the time Starkie graduated from TCD and the First World War had ended, he was fully fledged for a life of service to the Empire.

3

Dublin to Genoa via London

In those days in Dublin there was one 'grande Dame' who gathered all the intellectuals, whether Hellenists like Dr Mahaffy, Tyrrell or my father, or Irish national bards like W.B. Yeats or George Russell, A.E. In [the] salon of Lady Ardilaun, amid all the celebrities there was one figure that monopolised all my attention: a strange little dwarf of a man ... James Stephens was his name, and he symbolised for me the spirit of my country and the ceaseless quest for something which had been denied to all of us who had grown up in the deadening influences of the end of the nineteenth century.[1]

In December 1912 Walter's final report from Alington at Shrewsbury recommended that he be sent to London to play the violin for an expert, who would map out his future. Other masters (Salt and White are mentioned) suggested he should be sent to France or Germany[2] while Sir Alfred Lyttelton, Mrs Alington's brother, whose advice was also sought, proposed that Walter should go to London and play for Sir Henry Wood. None of this advice was heeded by his father. Plans were made for the youth to go up to TCD in October 1913 to study Classics, but, Starkie recalls, James Stephens 'solemnly' told Walter: 'You are not made for that university world. You should break away from it altogether'.[3]

Enid remembers her brother playing the violin at her mother's musical 'At Homes' at Melfort, sometimes alone and at other times accompanying the RIAM pianist Edith Boxwell. She also recalls the distinguished player Annie Lord performing and the presence of '[m]any famous men', naming W.B. Yeats, his brother, Jack, Oliver St John Gogarty and Æ in particular, as well as the artist Sarah Purser, also describing the idiosyncratic postioning of James Stephens in their midst: 'sitting on a pouff, looking for all the world like one of his own leprechauns on a toadstool',[4] though she has little else to say about him. In contrast, her brother appears to have struck up a close relationship with the author of the highly popular romances *The charwoman's daughter* and *The crock of gold*, both published in the year Walter left Shrewsbury. Indeed, almost forty years on, Starkie mutinously declared that those two texts: 'meant more to [him] than the world of classical scholarship in which [he] had passed [his] youth.'[5] The eighteen-year-old appears to have been seduced by Stephens' knowledge of Irish folk culture as well as by finding himself challenged in the mould that had been set for

1 W. Starkie, 'Sir John', p. 95. Much of the information contained in Starkie's 1951 tribute to Mahaffy is repeated in Chapter 5 of *Scholars* though Lady Ardilaun's 'salon' is not cited, nor is the reference to 'my country', the 'quest' and 'the deadening influences' of the late nineteenth century as registered here, experienced by those growing up in Ireland at the *fin de siècle*. 2 W. Starkie, *Scholars*, p. 80. 3 W. Starkie, *Scholars*, pp 86, 87. 4 E. Starkie, *Lady's child*, p. 179. 5 W. Starkie, 'Sir John', p. 95.

him. Stephens introduced Walter to 'the intensely Irish yet cosmopolitan'[6] Stephen
MacKenna, translator of Plotinus, collector of Irish folk music, and one for whom 'the
Irish language was nearest his heart'.[7] Hone recalls 'the flow of [MacKenna's] miraculous speech' and lists Stephens among others, all of whom succumbed to: 'the
fascination of his presence, the spell of his voice, his gaiety, wit and fire'. He also cites
from J.C. Squire's obituary, in which the poet claimed:

> Sitting with [MacKenna], one forgot the contemporary world, and explored all
> the abysses of time and space – or rather he did – for nobody wanted to interrupt
> him, when with the firelight illuminating his sensitive brow, he talked, as it were
> to himself, in the loveliest imagery, about the bewilderment of the human soul in
> the mysterious universe.[8]

Such twilight company, so far removed from the rigour of public school in England,
bewitched Walter, who now found himself drawn towards the mystery, magic and
music of '[his] own country'.[9] Furthermore, the young man listened to Stephens
meditating on the minstrel life and in those months between school and university
would often wander through the streets of Dublin with this latter-day Demophon as
mentor, perhaps contributing to the formation of a lifestyle Walter came to adopt
abroad, most intensely over the 1930s.

But Walter wasn't totally led astray in this period between school and university.
There was the discipline of his musical instruction at RIAM where, in spring of 1913,
he would receive extra instruction from Achille Simonetti as he practised to master the
Wieniawski Violin Concerto for the Irish music festival, the Feis Ceoil. At the same
time he was also working ('slaving', as he recalled it)[10] at Classics, French, English and
Mathematics for the Junior Exhibition examination at Trinity College, monitored by
the Resident Commissioner, still an exacting task master. His daughter perceived that
her father 'in his heart of hearts … did not really consider music the equal of
learning'[11] and his son remembers him citing the conviction of Professor of Music at
TCD, Percy Buck: 'the study of music tends to make youths languid, self-indulgent
and devoid of will-power',[12] a view which further substantiated WJM's scepticism. In
the event, Walter's efforts were rewarded on both counts: he won the first prize and
senior gold medal in the Feis, with his musical talent being additionally recognized at

6 Walter Starkie, *Scholars*, p. 88. See also: W. Starkie, 'Afterword' in J. Stephens, *Deirdre* (New York,
1962), p. 152.   7 J.M. Hone, *Memories*, p. 14. Walter's friend and neighbour in Killiney, J.M. Hone,
recalls being introduced to MacKenna by the latter's friend, J.M. Synge, when Hone was editing the
English-language journal *The Shanachie*, defined on the cover as 'An Irish Illustrated Quarterly'. The
journal published contributions by Æ, a number of Synge's travel essays and provide support for the
beleaguered playwright in the wake of the *Playboy* riots in 1907. Reproductions of the front covers of
Volume II, Number Three (March 1907) and Volume II, Number Four (Summer 1907) of *The
Shanachie* can be viewed in J.M. Hone, *Memories*, p. 12, and N. Grene (ed.), *J.M. Synge. Travelling
Ireland. Essays, 1898–1908* (Dublin, 2009), p. xliii. For comment on George Roberts' essay on Synge as
'A national dramatist', following the *Playboy* riots, in March 1907, see N. Grene (ed.), *J.M. Synge*, p. xlv.
8 J.M. Hone, *Memories*, pp 13, 15.   9 W. Starkie, *Scholars*, p. 87.   10 W. Starkie, *Scholars*, p. 90.
11 E. Starkie, *Lady's child*, p. 242.   12 W. Starkie, *Scholars*, p. 90.

RIAM where he was distinguished with the Vandeleur Scholarship;[13] he also secured a place at TCD for the forthcoming academic year, 1913–14.

Starkie recalled the period Walter spent back in Dublin before war was declared in 1914 as belonging to 'a dreamlike existence', describing the city as one of 'feasting and gaiety'.[14] As the Dublin Lockout came to demonstrate in 1913, not all was so carefree but Starkie's autobiographical narrative does not focus on the labour unrest.[15] Indeed, the owner of the Dublin United Tramway Company, William Martin Murphy, is never mentioned while James Larkin and the Lockout are only alluded to.[16] His memories of the year are coloured by the Anglo-Irish social calendar and recreational pursuits, thus: 'polo matches in Phoenix Park between the Irish and the visiting team of the Duke of Westminster, racing at Baldoyle, Leopardstown and Punchestown, cricket in the College Park and out at Woodbrook, Sir Stanley Cochrane's 'extensive demesne'[17] near Bray. Also remembered are the concerts of classical music given by the London Symphony Orchestra under the direction of Hamilton Harty, held in an auditorium built by Cochrane in the grounds of his impressive property. When recalling the entertainment available in the city of Dublin, Starkie alludes to the only cinema then in existence, situated close to TCD in Grafton Street, referring at greater length to six theatres, which, he declares, 'played to packed houses': the Gaiety, the Theatre Royal, the Empire, the Tivoli, the Queens and the Abbey.[18] Ireland's National Theatre was frequented by the young man about town every Friday night, his regular attendance enabled by his friend John F. Larchet, a former pupil of Michele Esposito at RIAM and Director of Music at the Abbey Theatre from 1907.

With regard to university life, Starkie remembers the 1913–14 academic year as 'memorable for its processions, or "Rags" [*sic*],' a transgressive celebration soon to be sacrificed following the departure of students for the Front and to be replaced by what is summed up in the remove of memory as: 'the grim years of political trouble in Ireland after 1916'.[19] In the recollection of undergraduate days at TCD, the Professor of Ancient History and Hellenist John Pentland Mahaffy and the Kipling-inspired Old Salopian Major Robert Tate are afforded the greater protagonism. Most attention is fondly and awesomely paid to the former, long-standing Fellow and Provost from November 1914 until his death in 1919, adopted by Walter as his godfather,[20] 'a

13 For further information on the Vandeleur Scholarship, see Pine and Acton, *To talent*, pp 110–12, passim. See also 'Musical Notes. Irish musician's who's who', IT, 18 Jan. 1937, p. 4, where Starkie's winning the Arthur Darley Prize in 1913 is also noted. 14 W. Starkie, *Scholars*, p. 105. 15 For further information on the lockout, see P. Yeates, *Lockout: Dublin 1913* (Dublin, 2001). 16 I am presuming that the mention of 'the General Strike of 1913' (W. Starkie, *Scholars*, p. 107) refers to the Lockout. The labour unrest around the Lockout would no doubt have been commented on over meals the Starkies shared with Laurence Waldron, 'a director of the Tramway and Canal Companies' (J.M. Hone, *Memories*, p. 174). In mentioning James Larkin, Starkie admits to having been 'fascinated by [his] leonine figure and personality' (W. Starkie, *Scholars*, p. 134). 17 W. Starkie, *Scholars*, p. 105. Starkie produced an entry on Sir Stanley H. Cochrane, Bart (among others) in A. Eaglefield-Hull (ed.), *A dictionary of modern music and musicians* (London, 1924), p. 97. Professor William [*sic*] Starkie figures, together with Mr Hamilton Harty and Dr J.F. Larchet, as a member of the national committee and one of the sub-editors for Ireland (A. Eaglefield-Hull (ed.), *A dictionary*, p. ix). 18 W. Starkie, *Scholars*, p. 106. 19 Ibid., p. 107. 20 'I used always to call [Dr Mahaffy] Godfather.' (W. Starkie, 'Sir John', p. 92.) In his autobiographical volume Walter will refer to Mahaffy simply as 'my godfather' (W. Starkie,

sparkling writer and a brilliant conversationalist'[21] in English, but whose views on the Irish language and culture would brook him little sympathy among the growing tide of nationalist sympathizers. Starkie narrates a variety of anecdotes in connection with 'the Master' or 'the General', as addressed by Laurence Waldron, but does not touch upon the latter's notorious confrontation with the College Gaelic Society in Walter's second year.[22]

In June 1914, old boy Starkie crossed over to England at the invitation of his former headmaster to give a violin recital at Shrewsbury School. He took the mailboat from Kingstown on the night of 28 June and recalls hearing of the assassination on the previous day of the Archduke Franz Ferdinand and his wife at Sarajevo when he changed trains at Chester. The undergraduate stayed with his old housemaster Freddy Prior but Starkie claims that Walter no longer felt so close to him since he had come to 'shed the public school mentality'. He portrays Walter as alienated from the institutional ethos, recording him feeling 'disconcerted' on finding 'such complacent unconcern on Ireland'.[23] Lying on a rug watching cricket matches over the long summer afternoons, as he had done when a pupil, he reflected on how blissfully and enviably unaware his English peers were: 'the Test Match would draw its crowds to Lords, and county cricket would continue peacefully, as though all the world was at peace'.[24] The gifted violinist returned to Dublin at the beginning of July and travelled down to Co. Cork to join the rest of the family for a holiday in Kilbrittain, at the foot of the Old Head of Kinsale. Starkie recalls that the family, accompanied by two Inspectors of Education who sallied forth on tours of schools with the Resident Commissioner, made 'a merry party' since they had a wing of the hotel almost entirely to themselves. None the less, over the holiday WJM became 'seriously worried at the political state of the country, and the daily disturbances that took place between the Nationalist Volunteers of the South and West and the Ulster Volunteers of Sir Edward Carson'.[25] Thus, the return to Dublin on the last Sunday of the month of July was filled with a sense of anxiety.

Early August found the young man at a recruiting depot, ready to enlist but he would be rejected on health grounds. Having been attested, he was given a khaki armlet with a red crown on it to show that he had been through the procedure and to prevent his being presented with a white feather. He contemplated going over to England to volunteer for national service but Pater insisted that his son's duty was to stay in Dublin and devote his energies to completing his degree. Therefore, Walter stayed at home for the duration in the company of his father, now eager to follow the movements of the troops on the large-scale maps erected on the doors of his study,

Scholars, p. 54). As has been noted, the kinship was disputed by Enid in a letter to her brother following the publication of *Scholars* (E. Starkie to W. Starkie, 11 Oct. 1963, ES Bodl.). **21** K.C. Bailey, *A history*, p. 4. **22** The Society were eager to have the founder and headmaster of the nationalist-inspired boys' school St Enda's, Patrick Pearse, speak at their meeting but Mahaffy opposed the proposal on ideological grounds within the context of the war since he understood Pearse to be 'a supporter of the anti-recruiting agitation' afoot in Ireland and was therefore viewed by the Provost as holding 'traitorous views' (W.B. Stanford & R.B. MacDowell, *Mahaffy*, p. 223). **23** W. Starkie, *Scholars*, pp 124, 125. **24** W. Starkie, *Scholars*, p. 126. The observation carries an echo of George Orwell's impressions as recorded

aided by his daughters Muriel and Chou-Chou together with Mrs Starkie. The latter is remembered by her son as throwing herself into war work at a Red Cross depot: 'rolling bandages and making dressings for the front'.[26] Enid noted that her mother also helped to organize a club for soldiers' wives and sat on a committee of the Alexandra College Guild, which opened a hostal for young girls who had travelled up to Dublin from rural areas in order to work in munitions factories.[27]

At TCD, Starkie remembers a 'quasi-monastic atmosphere' with so many students and members of staff at the front. The year 1915 did bring some joy: the second-year undergraduate was nominated third scholar in classics, following his friends Hal Mack and R.H. Micks. However, there was much sadness to be endured: the deaths of so many of his contemporaries, among them his oldest school friend Paddy Toibin, killed at Suvla Bay in the Dardanelles, whom Walter had seen off at the North Wall when the Pals Batallion of the Dublin Fusiliers and other Irish troops departed. Starkie specifies that on 15 August 1915 eight of Walter's 'dearest friends' from school in Dublin and from Shrewsbury lost their lives. Among the Shrewsbury casualties on the Somme figured the beloved masters, 'the Men', with whom the public schoolboy had spent so many happy hours.[28] 1916 would witness the sacrifice of numerous Irish lives in the Battle of the Somme but before the devastation of that year, Starkie records 'bitter feeling'[29] already growing in Ireland over 1914 and 1915 given the loss of life at the front, together with 'the broken pledges of the British Premier'[30] and what he records as the lack of recognition in the British press for the Irish regiments, whose 'families ... had sent their sons to fight in France and on the far-flung frontiers of the British Commonwealth.'[31] There was also sadness experienced within the Starkie family in 1915, not mentioned by Starkie in his autobiography but recorded by Enid in hers. The birth of a sixth child caused great rejoicing given that it was another boy. Humphrey William Robert was born the day before Walter's twenty-first birthday, on Sunday, 8 August.[32] His christening was to coincide with Walter's coming-of-age party but the child was delicate from birth and soon became seriously ill. Enid was sent to fetch the priest so that the child could be baptized and, as she explains, she acted as godmother. The child died on Sunday, 29 August.[33] Walter and his father accompanied the body to Glasnevin cemetery, where WJM would join his last-born some five years on.

By early 1916 some 146,000 Irishmen were mobilized in the Great War.[34] The year following the passing of the Starkies' second son marked the tercentenary of William Shakespeare's death and in spite of the war it was seen that the occasion 'should ...

on his return to England from Spain during the Civil War (G. Orwell, *Homage to Catalonia* (London, 1938), p. 314 (not numbered). **25** W. Starkie, *Scholars*, p. 127. **26** Ibid., p. 131. **27** E. Starkie, *Lady's child*, p. 200. **28** 'Evelyn H.L. Southwell, 2nd Lieut. 13th Bn. Rifle Brigade, Master'; 'Malcolm Graham White, Lieut. 6th Bn. Rifle Brigade, Master.' *Shrewsbury, Royal School, Old Salopian Club. Shrewsbury Roll of Service September 1915* (Shrewsbury [1915]). **29** W. Starkie, *Scholars*, pp 136, 133, 132. **30** Ibid., p. 132. Asquith's assurance that Kitchener, the Secretary of State for War, would sanction the formation of an Irish Army Corps, delivered at a dinner in the Provost's House in late September 1914, at which Walter's father was present, was not honoured. Kitchener issued an order that the Irish troops were to be dispersed. **31** W. Starkie, *Scholars*, p. 133. **32** 'Births', IT, 9 Aug. 1915. **33** 'Deaths', IT, 31 Aug. 1915. **34** S. Hegarty and F. O'Toole, *The Irish Times book of the 1916 rising*

not … be allowed to pass unobserved'. WJM, sometime President of the British Empire Shakespeare Society,[35] was one of a number of distinguished men (for the most part) of the empire who contributed to a tribute of biblical bulk paid to 'the genius of the greatest Englishman'.[36] The Resident Commissioner was accustomed by this time to appearing in print, either in scholarly articles, through his meticulous editions of works by the Greek playwright Aristophanes, in the published versions of his public lectures or by means of letters to the press. As has been seen, his wife's voice had been heard in anti-suffrage circles and in 1916 May C. Starkie authored a sixteen-page booklet composed of two essays on 'Patriotism' [sic].[37] Enid remembers that her mother 'used … to read papers at certain societies on educational theories.' Such papers, like the texts included in the publication on patriotism, may be seen as complementing the task of the Commissioners of National Education, under whose auspices the booklet was published. They may also have been the foundation of the Resident Commissioner's wife being dubbed in Trollope guise 'an educational Mrs Proudie'.[38]

The overall thrust of May C. Starkie's two pieces included in the booklet may be interpreted as constituting a contribution to the drive for more Irish volunteers for the front while seeking to sustain support for Great Britain. In the first piece, patriotism is defined, seen as a spiritual essence which transcends time and wars: 'the same spirit governs the great war of 1914 as governed the war of 1815, and every war back to the struggle between Athens and Sparta; the inspiring motive has always been love of one's country, Patriotism', and is further assessed as a 'divine instinct …, a passion strong as religious faith with which it is bound up, and able to transport men to the sublimest heights of self-sacrifice'.[39] Taking the city-state of Athens as inspirational (not least because of size), it becomes clear that the author is seeking to extol the land of Ireland and her distinguished historical record, but is calling on her not to disassociate herself from the imperial whole. In words that echo, to some degree, the moral of Alington's 'Fable' and evoke Renan on the nation,[40] it is claimed: 'nations, like individuals, have souls, and in great crises are able to merge their differences, and to evolve one resultant Will made up of the sum of the heroism and self-denial of the units, working together for the survival of the ideal of the whole.' And the sanction of Christianity is brought to bear: 'Do unto others as you would wish them to do unto you,' the piece drawing to a close with a challenge to the Irish people to make their contribution at the present time, preaching that the 'good and noble' means

(Dublin 2006), p. 5.   **35** Founded in 1901, the Society aimed 'to diffuse widely among our fellow-countrymen, both in Great Britain and in all parts of the Empire, a knowledge and love of the greatest dramatic poet the world has ever known, whose work encarnates all the noblest and most splendid qualities of the British race' (C. Kahn, 'Remembering Shakespeare imperially: the 1916 tercentenary', *Shakespeare Quarterly*, 52:4 (Winter, 2001), 456–78 at 459.   **36** I. Gollancz (ed.), *A book of homage to Shakespeare* (Oxford, Humphrey Milford), p. vii. W.J.M. Starkie focussed on 'The wit and humour of Shakespeare', pp 212–26. See C. Kahn, 'Remembering' on *Homage* as 'cultural performance' (C. Kahn, 'Remembering', p. 457).   **37** M.C. Starkie, *What is patriotism. The teaching of patriotism* (Dublin, 1916).   **38** E. Starkie, *Lady's child*, p. 178. The Trollopian label is attributed to a critic of the Resident Commissioner's, delivered in a newspaper article according to Enid Starkie though she does not supply the precise source.   **39** M.C. Starkie, *Patriotism*, pp 3, 4.   **40** E. Renan, 'What is a nation?' [Qu' est-ce qu' une nation ?] (1882) in H.K. Bhabha (ed.), *Nation*, pp 8–22.

9 W.F. Starkie with siblings Muriel (standing), Enid, Nancy and Ida ('Chou-Chou') (left to right, seated); the babe-in-arms is Humphrey William Robert, Dublin, August 1915.

commitment to the national war effort. Mrs Starkie's appeal ends with a quote of almost two pages from Thucydides' *Funeral oration of Pericles*, the last sentence beginning with the pronouncement: 'For heroes have the whole earth for their tomb.'[41] Such sentiment may have provided scant consolation in the wake of the heavy casualties suffered in the Battle of the Somme 1916, thousands of whom were Irishmen. The second, shorter contribution in the booklet is aimed at engaging (in Althusserian terms) the Ideological State Apparatus of the School in creating a patriotic following, while acknowledging that those other ISAs, the Church and the Family, are also influential in this connection.[42] The essay contains references to the classics: Plato, Aristotle, Tacitus and Quintilian, but also to Christianity and to English thinkers on education: Locke and Milton, arguing that the child must be interpellated at a tender age in order to produce the stuff of heroes:

> it is clear that the early school days, when character is malleable, easily moulded, are the seasons for receiving ideas of Patriotism and social service, and for responding to the cause of self-sacrifice. The little seed of loyalty, which can grow to a strong, healthy tree, is sown in the school. From the idea of loyalty to the school, pride in its success, the endeavour of each pupil to raise the standard, will come the larger idea of loyalty to his country, and the wish to serve her, and so out of the school-boy the hero is made.

41 M.C. Starkie, *Patriotism*, pp 6, 11. 42 Further to the concept of ISAs, see Louis Althusser, *Lenin and philosophy, and other essays* (London, 1971).

The article ends with a request to the schools to perform a very specific function, that of lending support in the light of the consequences of the war so far and bolstering the ongoing effort:

> to encourage the giving freely of sympathy and help to those who have suffered fighting for those at home; to assist in making others ready to do their part; to inculcate temperance and thrift; to develop each one so as to be fit to serve his country in whatever capacity she may determine when she calls upon him.[43]

* * *

Easter Monday of 1916 in Dublin has been remembered as 'a lovely day for an outing.'[44] For those with gardens, the day might have lent itself to open-air pause or pottering. The Resident Commissioner took to his Shrewsbury Road plot to occupy himself in scholarly mode. His eldest daughter recalls her father poised before the printed page, reading *Pliny's letters* while her brother's memory of the day is of the milkman delivering the news that 'the rebellion' had occurred and 'the Sinn Feiners had seized Harcourt Street Station'.[45] Walter was then in his third year at TCD. His cousin and neighbour in Shrewsbury Road, Cyril Hoey, was also an undergraduate at Dublin University and had joined the Officers Training Corps in the College, intending to volunteer for service in the Royal Flying Corps. Cyril now donned khaki and on a borrowed motorcycle 'acted as dispatch rider between Trinity College and the outside world'. Enid's recollection of her cousin's behaviour expresses some scepticism and a degree of impatience with the sixteen-year-old's antics, claiming that for Cyril the events were in the nature of 'an exciting game'.[46] The sense of a boy's adventure story is certainly present in her sibling's account of the week, over which he found his bicycle 'a godsend', enabling him 'to follow the progress of the fighting in the various zones of the city'. Starkie registers relishing what became a challenge to the twenty-one-year-old's powers of invention as he made his way back and forth: 'bypassing the cordons, barricades and sentry spots'.[47]

In her narrative of the week of the 'Rebellion' [*sic*], Enid makes the point that in Ballsbridge the family was at a safe remove from the fray, only hearing 'the sound of firing from the centre of the city and the heavy thud of the high explosive from the gunboats shelling Liberty Hall'.[48] However, some action also struck the neighbourhood when troops who had docked at Kingstown then started marching into the city and came to a halt at the end of Shrewsbury Road. Starkie recalls that at midday Enid 'rushed in from the garden'[49] with the news that a soldier had been shot at the end of the road and a boy had come to the gate asking for water. Enid does not record the soldier's injury or the boy's request, but simply recalls that 'the owners of the houses round brought [the soldiers] mugs of hot tea and sandwiches'.[50] Her brother only mentions 'a number of people racing down Shrewsbury Road with tumblers and buckets of water.'[51] What both do agree on is how disconcerted the soldiers were. Enid

43 Ibid., pp 15, 16 (not numbered).   44 S. Hegarty & F. O'Toole, *The Irish Times book*, p. 39.   45 W. Starkie, *Scholars*, p. 140.   46 E. Starkie, *Lady's child*, p. 202.   47 W. Starkie, *Scholars*, p. 148.   48 E. Starkie, *Lady's child*, p. 202.   49 W. Starkie, *Scholars*, p. 146.   50 E. Starkie, *Lady's child*, p. 202. 51 W. Starkie, *Scholars*, p. 147.

remarks: 'They were surprised when they saw us and heard us talking English, for they had been told on embarkation that they were going to Kut [-El-Amara] to relieve General Townshend.'[52] Her brother supplies a fuller account, commenting on the state of the men, who had already marched five kilometres on their way from Kingstown towards the city, while fearing for their rural innocence. His narrative of the same period focuses on scenes of looting in Sackville Street, recorded as proceeding in 'riotous good humour'; on two particular deaths: that of journalist and pacifist Francis Sheehy-Skeffington, depicted as 'fearless', a 'true-hearted idealist', together with that of cricketer F.H. Browning, a member of the veterans corps, and on members of Sinn Féin. Starkie's representation well nigh half a century on of the supporters of Sinn Féin over the almost twenty pages he dedicates to Easter Week 1916 and its aftermath is to dismiss them as quixotic: 'dreamers'. He refers to 'a conscious cult of heroism' among Sinn Feiners in 1916 and their belief that they could create afresh 'a pure Gaelic Catholic civilization'. He also mentions an interview with one of the rebel officers in custody, whose remark provides grist to the mill of the argument claiming for the wrong-headedness of the movement. The latter is introduced as representative of 'the young Irish intellectual minority who had joined the Sinn Fein [*sic*] movement after 1914,' who comes to claim in the interview that they were not badly led, but misled. Further illustration of the tragic consequences brought about by the rising will be the re-appearance of Wicklow-born Maggie Donovan. Met a short time after the end of the 'Rebellion', she had been in the College of Surgeons with Countess Markiewicz but managed to escape just before the surrender. The description renders her a shadow of her former self, as if her strength had been sapped: 'She seemed to have become smaller physically, and all her vivacity and vitality had evaporated.' Maggie herself is quoted as lamenting: 'I'm sick to death with all the tragedies I've seen.'[53] All told, then, in the autobiographical volume published in the decade of the fiftieth anniversary of Easter 1916, solemnly celebrated in de Valera's Dublin, no support was expressed for the Rising and Sinn Féin are dismissed as visionaries who generated deception and destruction.

The year in which Walter graduated from TCD did not bode well for the family fortunes. The 'climax' of WJM's financial concerns was prompted by a letter from the bank which informed the Resident Commissioner of Education that his overdraft had attained 'perilous dimensions'.[54] His reaction was characteristically drastic: he contemplated moving out of Melfort and over to London, having Enid leave Oxford, where she had just begun an undergraduate degree, to transfer to TCD, and sending Muriel '*au pair*' to Paris. However, the lease on Melfort held until December 1920 so the family remained in Shrewsbury Road. Mrs Starkie wrote to her eldest daughter, impressing upon her that she should leave Oxford and obtain a job as a secretary or clerk in a government office in England until she married. It was Emily Penrose, classical scholar and the Principal of Somerville College, who persuaded Enid's father to allow his daughter to continue her degree at Oxford, where her scholarship partially

---

52 E. Starkie, *Lady's child*, p. 202. **53** W. Starkie, *Scholars*, pp 147, 149, 152, 151. **54** W. Starkie, *Scholars*, p. 158. Running into debt already appears to have been characteristic of WJM when he was a much younger man, as an undergraduate at Trinity College Cambridge (E. Starkie, *Lady's child*, p. 12).

covered her fees, arguing that an Oxford degree would subsequently enable Enid to obtain a lucrative post. Muriel stayed at home and, together with Chou-Chou, would go on to win 'a record number of prizes' at RIAM before the year was out. Muriel distinguished herself on the violin and Chou-Chou on the violincello as well as in string quartet, trio and duet, all of which provided some solace for their father, who appears to have been working at a feverish pace both with regard to his educational work as well as in making his contribution to the war effort. Walter remembers him 'touring every part of the country, visiting even the smallest schools in the out-of-the-way parishes, presiding not only over the National and Intermediate Boards but also at war committees such as the Strength of Britain and the Registration Council, and giving interviews to the Press.'[55] It is over this period, too, that Starkie situates the decline in his father's health: he rapidly lost over a stone in weight, symptomatic of the diabetes that was to be the cause of his death in 1920. In the meantime, he denied himself and appealed to the rest of the family to follow suit. Enid's account provides some idea of her father's extravagant lifestyle, now radically abandoned in pursuit of thrift. Her picture of his survival in reduced circumstances in the wake of lordly excess also conveys the pity she felt on witnessing his pinching self-denial:

> He bought no more new clothes until the last months of his life, when his salary was increased. [...] He also gave up his wines, his cigars, his delicacies [,] ... that lavish spending of money which I had always associated with him, that regard-lessness, contempt almost, of money. The expensive pencils, by the dozen, the bundles of knives, the enormous sticks of sealing-wax, all the things which had made his writing-table a joy to behold, all these things were now no more. There was something pathetic in seeing him with a cheap pencil jealously guarded in his pocket. In a few days he seemed to turn ascetic. For the rest of his life he spent almost nothing on himself.[56]

In spite of the family's financial setback, Walter graduated at TCD in 1917, obtaining, according to Starkie's account 'a second place in Classics, Senior Moderatorship, first class and gold medal; and second place, Senior Moderatorship, first class and gold medal in History and Political Science'.[57] He was also awarded the Brooke Prize, given to the candidate who comes second in the double final. Starkie recalls the Resident Commissioner expressing his satisfaction with his son's achievements by inviting him to lunch in the Fellows' luncheon-room at TCD with a number of his distinguished colleagues: Provost Mahaffy, another future provost, Edward J. Gwynn, Walter's tutor Ernest Henry Alton, Hegel-scholar Henry Macran and William Alexander Goligher, who occupied the Chair of Ancient History in the wake of R.Y. Tyrrell and Mahaffy

---

55 W. Starkie, *Scholars*, pp 164, 159.   56 E. Starkie, *Lady's child*, p. 256.   57 W. Starkie, *Scholars*, pp 163–4. See also: Trinity College, *A catalogue of graduates of the University of Dublin vol. 5, containing the names of those who proceeded to degrees from the September commencements of the year 1917 to the spring commencements of the year 1931* (Dublin, 1931). 'Starkie (Walter Fitwilliam)' is listed as having obtained his 'B.A., *Hiem.*' in 1917.

and was to be providing guidance to the Resident Commissioner's heir until into the 1930s.[58] Over his last year at TCD, Walter witnessed the proceedings of the Irish Convention, set up by Lloyd George in the hope that a solution might be found for 'the Irish question' by bringing together some hundred Irishmen, representatives of both northern and southern unionists, the Irish parliamentary party, the churches, the Irish peers, labour, the chambers of commerce and local authorities. The sessions were held in the Regent House of TCD and Mahaffy was invited to take part in the Convention, one of a group of 'fifteen members nominated by the government, ... well-known Irishmen of widely varying views'.[59] Starkie recalls that over the period, when Mahaffy wanted to consult some matter with WJM, he would give the young man 'special messages and typewritten statements' which he was instructed to deliver to his father 'without fail'.[60] Thus, the youth came to exercise a function similar to that which he had carried out as a boy in Killiney or Blackrock when he functioned as 'liaison officer'[61] between the downstairs world of the grown-ups and the schoolroom above. It is a practice which would also become a characteristic feature of his life's employment.

Having obtained his degree, the graduate sought to obtain 'a war job' through the intercession of his father's friends: the Chief Secretary for Ireland between 1916 and 1918 and Unionist politician Henry Edward Duke, Sir Horace Plunkett and Walter Long, the Minister for Colonial Affairs. The young hopeful had his sights set on the Foreign Office, where there would be scope for his knowledge of French and some German, but Long came up with a temporary vacancy in the Upper Division of the Dominions and Colonial Office. Thus, Walter set out for London, where he was met by his uncle, Arthur Rackham. On the day following his arrival, the candidate was faced with the ordeal of an interview at the Dominions and Colonial Office in Downing Street but his father's friends again came to the rescue. He found himself in the office of T.C. MacNaghten, who had been a fellow undergraduate of WJM's at Cambridge. Walter came through the interview successfully and began his employment as a temporary clerk in the Upper Division immediately. His 'special work'[62] was on prisoners of war and was under Lord Newton, though Starkie recalls seeing little of his superior.

Initially the embryonic civil servant lived at a hotel on the Cromwell Road, the Stuart, 'a modern and well-furnished hotel patronized by men and women working in government departments'. Subsequently he befriended Arthur J. Dawe, an Oxford graduate who had been gassed at the front in France and invalided home, having lent his writing talent to reporting from Verdun for the *Times*. He, too, was employed as a temporary clerk in the Dominions and Colonial Office and the two young men moved into a flat in Ashburnham Mansions in Chelsea. The company of others with whom Walter worked in the Dominions and Colonial Office is also recorded as an enjoyable experience. Together with 'a few kindred spirits in the office', a Rabelais study circle

58 See the author's acknowledgments in *Spanish raggle-taggle, Don Gypsy* and *The waveless plain*. 59 W.B. Stanford & R.B. McDowell, *Mahaffy*, p. 233. For further information on the convention, see R.B. McDowell, *The Irish convention, 1917–18* (London, 1970). 60 W. Starkie, *Scholars*, p. 160. 61 E. Starkie, *Lady's child*, p. 97. See also pp 43, 106, 124. 62 W. Starkie, *Scholars*, pp 165, 168.

was formed, consisting of 'readings of "The Great Laughter" from time to time after
a cosy dinner washed down by a few bottles of claret.'[63] Starkie also remembers in
passing the two Under-secretaries: Henry Lambert, who dealt with Dominion
questions, and Mr Grindle, who dealt with Colonial, as well as George Fiddes, the
Parliamentary Secretary. However, much more space is allotted to Marie Motto,
founder in 1903 of the Marie Motto Quartet,[64] whose home became a refuge for, as
Starkie recalls, 'many wanderers like myself', as well as providing consolation in the
month of March 1918 when the news of German advances caused much pessimism.
Starkie explains that it was through Motto that Walter became 'intimately

---

[63] W. Starkie, *Scholars*, p. 168.   [64] S. McVeigh, '"As the sound on the sea-shore": Women violinists in
London's concert life around 1900' in E. Hornby & D. Maw (eds), *Essays on the history of English music
in honour of John Caldwell: sources, style, performance, historiography* (Woodbridge, 2010), p. 252.

acquainted'[65] with Westminster Cathedral and Brompton Oratory and recalls that he would go with the Italian-born violinist to hear the boys' choir directed by Richard Terry.

Walter also enjoyed a wider social life in London. When first in the capital for his interview, Arthur Rackham had taken his nephew to the Café Royal, where he had met the painter Augustus John, and later, with Dawe, he dined there, coming to frequent the company of the poet Sherard Vines and Hugh Kingsmill [Lunn], son of Sir Henry Lunn. Hugh Kingsmill shared his enthusiasm for James Joyce with the young man from Ireland and forwarded the episodes from *Ulysses* currently being published in the *Little Review* to the two junior clerks. Thus, the Irish mock-epic took over from the Rabelais-centred routs at the Dominions and Colonial Office. Over this period in London, particularly in the months of April and May, Starkie speaks of spending 'many happy hours'[66] at the home of Cecil and Emilie Alberta Harmsworth with whom he shared a friendship that spanned their lifetimes.[67] The Harmsworth London home at that time, situated in Montagu Square[68] with its central swathe of green vegetation from end to end, enclosed in railings, would have been evocative for Walter of Georgian squares in Dublin, not least Fitzwilliam Square, adjacent to Fitzwilliam Place, where the Starkies had lived on their return to Dublin from Galway in 1899. Therefore, the setting would not feel altogether, if at all, alien and at number 28 he would find himself in the company of people whose mind set was familiar to him, Cecil: 'Anglo-Irish by birth and upbringing', and Emilie: 'daughter of the Church of Ireland Rector of Finglas.' Walter's parents counted among their friends and acquaintances in Dublin Westminster MPs such as Laurence Waldron, but now Walter was closer than ever before to the seat of colonial power, not only through the Dominions and Colonial office post he was occupying but through those whom he met at the Harmsworths' home and within the House of Commons itself. The opportunity to frequent Cecil's company, whose 'long experience in the House of Commons had given him a profound knowledge of English politics' and who, more recently, 'had made a special study of foreign affairs', as well as to come into contact with a wide range of men who were at the forefront of the day's political events and developments must have represented a stimulating experience for the twenty-three-year-old graduate, possessed of a youthful curiosity and thirst for adventure. His autobiography registers the intensity and variety of his initiation into the corridors of power:

> The house was always thronged with politicians, journalists, war correspondents, and officers on leave from the war fronts. Sometimes my hostess would invite me to the House of Commons … for as Cecil Harmsworth had to be in the House

---

65 W. Starkie, *Scholars*, pp 168, 169. **66** W. Starkie, *Scholars*, p. 176. **67** Cecil was the younger brother of the press barons Lord Northcliffe and Lord Rothermere, a graduate of TCD and a Liberal MP. In 1918 he held the government post of Parliamentary Secretary for Foreign Affairs in Lloyd George's government. Starkie dedicated his first travel book, *Raggle-taggle*, to C. and E. Harmsworth. (See 'Harmsworth, Alfred Charles William' in J. McGuire & J. Quinn (eds), *Dictionary of Irish biography*, vol. 4, pp 464–5). **68** The building is no longer standing. The properties that numbers 27 to 29 occupied have been replaced by a block of flats.

at the evening sessions[,] he used to reserve a private dining-room for his guests
... stolid politicians and press pundits [as well as] some of the younger intellectuals and eccentrics.[69]

At the Harmsworth residence in Henley-on-Thames, Magdalen House, Walter met
Alfred, Harold and Cecil's Irish mother, the formidable Geraldine Harmsworth (née
Maffett), in May 1918. Starkie recalls her asking Walter to play Scottish and Irish
melodies on his violin after dinner and his diverting the company with 'The Coolin',
'The Londonderry Air' and 'Avenging and Bright'. Thus, Walter, frustrated in his
desire to pursue a musical career with his violin, was beginning, at the behest of the
Harmsworth family, to perform the role of entertainer, a role which he would play
with some frequency over his future career. As he was to discover, it would facilitate
access to a wide range of circles, both at home and abroad.

   In spite of the excitement and stimulation of London life, Walter also experienced
'the gloom' of the period as a consequence of developments in the war in March and
its destruction, visible in the West End of London. Moreover, his health was poor. On
two occasions he was laid up with asthma: the first when he was resident at the Stuart
and was diagnosed with influenza; the second in late June when he suffered 'severe
asthmatic attacks'. The senior clerk, MacNaghten recommended that he hand in his
resignation. In recalling the period, Starkie alludes to '[t]he general hostile attitude in
official circles in London towards Irishmen of military age' and mentions a letter from
Walter's father who impressed upon his son that he should go back to Ireland, arguing
that his Irish roots, Catholicism and the fact that he had not been in the forces would
all work against him in England. Furthermore, Pater now envisaged his son studying
law in Dublin and being able to carry out historical research at TCD as well as boosting
his income with occasional journalism. Walter speaks of consulting with Marie Motto,
his 'staunch' Italian friend in London, whose advice echoed James Stephens's some
five years earlier, namely, that the young man should strike out independently in order
to find himself: 'You should make a complete break-away from your father's influence.
Indeed it would be still wiser to exile yourself from your whole family. [...] ... you
need to win your freedom in the world and be yourself, ... open the windows of your
soul to all the winds that blow.'[70] The twice-proferred advice was not heeded.

   The day following Marie Motto's counsel, Starkie recalls a chance encounter
between Walter and a man 'in Mooney's hostelry in the Strand', one who, like the
young graduate, had not been fit enough for the forces but was working with the
YMCA in Egypt. His account of the activities he was involved in, 'running huts and
concerts',[71] led Walter to the headquarters of the association in Tottenham Court
Road where he volunteered for service in the Middle East and Egypt, North or South
Italy, or France. Before the end of July, he returned to Dublin. Starkie records that
Walter was pleased to find that his father approved of the YMCA project. Thus, in
August he travelled back to London, having been notified that he should join a

69 W. Starkie, *Scholars*, pp 176, 177.   **70** W. Starkie, *Scholars*, pp 170, 184.   **71** W. Starkie, *Scholars*,
p. 185.

fortnight's course of instruction at the YMCA Centre at Mildmay Park. The Mildmay Park complex was acquired by the association in 1917 with a view to training candidates. An article in the *Red Triangle Bulletin* explained:

> To Mildmay Park will come for a fortnight's training our workers for overseas and home camps. [...] The students will be shown how to keep accounts and play games as well as how to run camp meetings or conduct a course of lectures and classes. [...] Mr Procter[72] summed up the hope in all our minds when he said that Mildmay, as a YMCA centre, would be 'a training camp and an armoury from which the Lord's heroes will go forth mighty in the battle for many years to come.'[73]

It was in the latter part of the year in which Walter spent a number of months in London, 1918, that an agreement was forged between the War Office and the YMCA. Sir Arthur K. Yapp recorded that as soon as the War broke out, the YMCA had offered the War Office its services for the Expeditionary Force,[74] but it was not until 29 August 1918 that, as Colonel Lord Gorell, Deputy-Director of Staff Duties (Education) between late August 1918 and late May 1920, later explained: 'the educational scheme of the Army was officially inaugurated and a new department set up at the War Office charged with its organisation and control.'[75] An Order of 24 September 1918 recognized the importance of education at that time and during demobilization and provided for 'an establishment of organizing officers.'[76] Hence, Walter's fortuitous meeting at Mooney's was indeed fortunate since it took place at a time when the YMCA together with the War Office were re-fashioning themselves with a view to answering to the needs of the troops who were coming to the end of their period of service at the front. Moreover, with his asthma in mind, Italy was one of the warmer climes that Walter had volunteered for and the War Office Scheme was to be implemented in Italy, together with France and Great Britain, 'with the least delay possible'.[77] Therefore, Walter's placement would suit his health, his desire to be at a remove from the controlling family and, more particularly, Pater, the need to earn a living and answer to his youthful thirst for adventure. And the young graduate was a promising candidate for those employing him. He was able to place the benefits of a privileged education at home, at public school and at university, together with his musical talent, in the service of reconstruction.

Apart from the professionals with whom Walter came into contact over his fortnight's training at Mildmay, ranging from Basil Yeaxlee, Henry Hadow and Percy Scholes to J.O. Dobson and a Major Cameron of the War Office who, together, guided the new recruit in his educational work with the British Expeditionary Force in Italy,

72 The Reverend C.J. Procter, vicar of Islington.   73 [Unsigned], 'The Opening of Mildmay', *The Red Triangle Bulletin*, 7 (14 Sept. 1917), 2.   74 A.K. Yapp, *In the service of youth* (London, 1927), p. 67.   75 Lord Gorell, *Education and the army. An essay in reconstruction* (London, 1921), pp 44–5.   76 B.A.Y. [*sic*], 'Sir Henry Hadow Goes to the War Office', *The Red Triangle*, 2:2 (Oct. 1918), 65. For further information on the Order of 24 September 1918, see Lord Gorell, *Education*, pp 45–8.   77 Lord Gorell, *Education*, p. 48.

Starkie mentions Walter's befriending two fellow 'workers'. William Gee was the son of an Irish mother and English father, who took Walter out to Clapham to a *ceilidh* and introduced him to his family. Gee's mother is identified by her daughter as 'the Sinn Feiner of the family'[78] and in recalling 'that one evening in Clapham', Starkie claims Walter 'heard more scarifying sedition talked, and learnt of more fanatical plans for future warfare against England than [he] had ever heard in Dublin.'[79] Robert Benzley is remembered as a 'strange vagabond character' who told Walter 'the story of his wanderings', which 'fascinated'[80] the young man. Benzley appears to have been something of a gambler with a taste for amateur theatricals. Starkie explains the story of a bet which Benzley took on whereby, for ten thousand pounds sterling, he travelled the world in extravagant garb, pushing a pram, and with a tin mask on his face.

The taste and ability for a range of performance: Walter's own rollicking rendering of Barney Doran in the family circle's *John Bull's other island* and the outlandish act carried out by Benzley, registered in a degree of detail by Starkie in his autobiography, is worth bearing in mind in assessing the latter's personality. Moreover, the matter of the mask is worth pondering. Benzley is the second 'man in a mask' whom Walter came into contact with as he moved towards adult life; the first, one of the beloved 'Men' at Shrewsbury.[81] Walter spoke, metaphorically, of adopting a mask while he was at Shrewsbury: the outsider seeking acceptance. This practice, taste or opting for disguise might be borne in mind as the years of Walter's adult life come to the fore with a view to approaching an understanding of how he spent the time of his life, and why.

---

78 W. Starkie, *Scholars*, p. 190. 79 W. Starkie, *Scholars*, pp 190, 191. 80 W. Starkie, *Scholars*, p. 189, 190. 81 In the volume of tribute, published in the wake of the deaths of both Southwell and White on the Somme, one of the 'stories' remembered about Malcolm White was his travelling in a domino mask. H.E. Howson, *Two men*, p. 15.

PART II

Courting Carnival

'The *Commedia dell' Arte* was a play in which the author did not write the dialogue; he only wrote out the argument, gave a sketch of the scene, and left the actor to improvise the rest.'

W. Starkie, 'The *Commedia dell'Arte* and the Roman comedy' (Dublin, 1924), p. 333.

4

Italia

'We'll send you to Italy,' said the chief, 'and we'll use you as a hut-worker, teacher of languages, lecturer, and above all, fiddler.' 'Call me camp-follower, sir,' said I, '... there's no title I'd rather have.'[1]

Walter's YMCA posting provided the twenty-four-year-old with a sense of purpose at a moment when, Starkie claims, the youth was 'sunk in despondency'. He left Dublin for Italy on Friday, 11 October 1918. By this time, as the war drew to its close, he was well aware of the destruction wrought by the conflict and the suffering generated, given the numbers of the European dead, of Irishmen who had lost their lives, and of his own peers: 'classmates in Dublin, members of the Pals Battalion who fell in Gallipoli, ... others ... known at Shrewsbury.' Now, as he prepared for his departure, the horror was brought close to home, closer than when the RMS *Lusitania* went down off the Old Head of Kinsale in May 1915. On the morning of 10 October, RMS *Leinster* was torpedoed by a German U-Boat: 'off the Kish lightship, a little way out from Kingstown'.[2] The majority of those on board were killed, over five hundred passengers and crew,[3] among them staff employed on the mail-boat with whom Walter had struck up friendships during the crossings between Kingstown and Holyhead over the years of his schooldays and subsequently. His parents' 'dear friends',[4] Sir Lucas and Lady White King, would also lose one of their twin sons, fifteen-year-old Alfred Curzon White King, on his way back to public school in England.[5]

The new recruit travelled to Genoa via sea and rail: across the Channel from Southampton, by train to Paris, and on another train to the Italian frontier via Modane, where 'papers were scrutinized and ... luggage searched', but where spirits were also revived. The ageing autobiographer recalled the 'tasty *ragout* [and] a bottle of Beaune at the *auberge*' as well as the fire that provided warmth until the Italian train was due to leave. The journey through the Mont Cenis Pass was barely scenic given the enveloping mist and snow but splendid sunshine greeted the travellers at Bardonecchia where the compartment in which Walter was travelling was invaded by 'young Italian soldiers belonging to a regiment of Alpini',[6] who provided him with the opportunity of practising his Italian. Both the young soldiers and an elderly lawyer from Turin travelling in the same compartment are referred to as expressing pro-British sentiments: the former hailing the English [*sic*] in the immediate context of the war as their allies and the latter recalling the British who aided Italy in her *Risorgimento*.

1 W. Starkie, *The waveless plain* (London, 1938) p. 12. 2 W. Starkie, *Scholars*, pp 12, 216, 195. 3 See: *www.rmsleinster.com*, accessed 25 April 2012. 4 W. Starkie, *Scholars*, p. 195. 5 P. Lecane, *Torpedoed! The RMS Leinster disaster* (Penzance, 2005), p. 44. 6 W. Starkie, *Scholars*, pp 196, 197.

The YMCA office in Genoa was housed in the Hotel Londres, where the new recruit met the man in charge, Alan Rodie, 'a British Shipping Agent', whose daughter carried out secretarial duties. The new arrival was housed in a spacious flat on Via Acquarone, run as a boarding house for the YMCA. Starkie recalls Walter performing a variety of tasks at this early juncture, among them night shifts serving tea and coffee to the many sick and wounded from the northern front who passed through Brignole Station. He was also given responsibility for the library set up on the ground floor of the Villa Acquasola in Piazza Corvetto, though volunteer helpers were soon forthcoming. A few doors away from his lodgings, the young man also found help in an Italian family, the Sommarugas, whose second daughter, Helvezia, offered her services at the Villa Acquasola. Her assistance came to be regarded as indispensable and she managed to mobilize further aid, bringing in girlfriends to help in the library, some of whom went on to organize a tea room for British soldiers. Upstairs rooms at the Villa were converted into classrooms and the graduate soon found himself giving classes to soldiers 'in French, Italian and even Spanish' as well as being 'besieged by *Signorine* ... eager to learn the English language'.[7] He also cooperated with other YMCA centres in the city and played his violin for hospital patients, a task, as Starkie recalls, Walter had already performed in Ireland. Other British residents in Genoa also cooperated with his labours.

The range of the camp-follower's activity would be widened following a visit to Genoa by the Head of the YMCA Education Scheme, J.O. Dobson. Dobson was able to organize lecturers and preachers being sent out from England and Starkie claims to have personally arranged talks from the Reverend Geoffrey Anketell Studdert Kennedy (more familiarly known as 'Woodbine Willy/Willie' given his practice of sharing the popular cigarettes with the troops), a graduate of TCD in Classics and Divinity in 1904, and Dr George William Hudson Shaw, another Church of England clergyman and public lecturer. Dobson also recommended that the new recruit's work be extended beyond Genoa: 'to the army centres in the north of Italy near the front' and that following the Armistice, not only classes should be provided for the troops, but also 'lectures, plays, concerts and especially concert parties [,] which would mobilise and use the talent available in the army, the YMCA and the Red Cross.'[8] Thus, before the end of October 1918, together with YMCA and Red Cross colleagues, the twenty-four-year-old recruit was travelling to bases of the British Expeditionary Force, at Arquata, Scrivia, Novi and Tortona. His 'peregrinations as fiddler and lecturer' would lead to him becoming something of a talent spotter, ever keeping 'a watchful eye on the men who offered to take part in ... informal sing-songs and recitals'.[9] Eventually 'The Riviera Concert Party' would be born, a troupe created by the camp-follower, which exploited the variety of amateur talent as well as including some professional entertainers.

7 W. Starkie, *Scholars*, pp 198, 202. 8 Ibid., pp 203, 204. In both *The waveless plain* (1938) and *Scholars and Gypsies* (1963), Starkie refers to a letter received from J.O. Dobson on the day the camp-follower was demobilized in 1919. He quotes the letter at some length in the former work, Dobson complimenting Starkie on his 'wonderful music', referring to the 'many pleasant hours' spent in Starkie's company and recognizing 'how much men are made happier by you' (W. Starkie, *Waveless*, p. 154). 9 W. Starkie, *Scholars*, p. 225.

Walter celebrated Halloween 1918 at the Sommaruga home, where spirits were high given the positive developments for the allies on different fronts. Starkie recalls spending the afternoon of 1 November, 'All Saints' Day', visiting British sick and wounded in the wards of the eleventh General Hospital, set up in the Grand Hotel Miramare, and on the 2nd, 'All Souls' Day', he remembers following other Genoans to the *Campo Santo*. On 3 November he was woken by the sound of sirens hailing the Italian victory of Vittorio Veneto and the entry of the troops into Trento and Trieste. There were celebrations at his lodgings in Via Acquarone and the festivities continued over the morning, the teacher's English Literature class being interrupted by a crowd of young people carrying Italian banners, the colours of the allies, and desirous of '[saluting] the British flag'. YMCA worker Walter addressed them from the terrace overlooking Piazza Corvetto. The technique he chose to adopt as a consequence of his 'ignorance and pedestrian Italian' demonstrates the young man's resourcefulness. Starkie explains in his autobiographical volume that he had been reading D'Annunzio's plays *La nave* [The Ship] and *La facciola soto il moggio* [The Torch under the Bushel] and he now exploited the Italian author's 'dramatic method of turning his speeches into a dialogue with the audience.' It might be said that his own comment on the choice of strategy also reflects a degree of cynicism alongside a clear awareness of the manipulative method: 'I found little difficulty in uttering the usual platitudes expected from citizens of an allied country, especially when I put them in the form of questions to the public which my chorus would answer for them.'[10]

Once Walter had arrived at the office on the morning of 3 November, Starkie recalls him having received instructions from General Broadbent, RAMC, to go with his violin to Red Cross Hospital Number One in the afternoon, where a celebration to mark the victory of Vittorio Veneto was planned. The afternoon would find the violinist at the hospital, performing on a stage draped in the Italian Tricolour on which he played a rousing selection: Sarasate's 'Zigeunerweisen' (in all likelihood the final *Allegro molto vivace* section) and Hubay's 'Hejre Kati', before going on to 'our [*sic*] war tunes … [playing] them one after another [and] introducing them with a few Italian words of comment.'[11] It was here too that a 'Signorina Italia' was requested to perform, a young Red Cross nurse who came on stage and sat at the piano. She sang the '*Canzone dell' Alpino*', displaying in Starkie's memory: 'a beautiful high soprano voice', a match for her fairy tale appearance, as recalled by her admirer: 'pink and white complexion and golden hair' that, moreover: 'glittered in the lights of the hall'.[12] The nurse was Italia Augusta Porchietti, one of the daughters of Colonel Alberto Porchietti,[13] currently Director of the Red Cross Hospital in Genoa, and his wife

10 W. Starkie, *Scholars*, pp 208–9, 211.   11 W. Starkie, *Scholars*, p. 212. In *The waveless plain*, where much of the Italian material which appears in the latter part of *Scholars and Gypsies* originally appeared, Starkie cites the war tunes 'Tipperary', 'Pack up your troubles', 'Hold your hand out, naughty boy' and 'The long, long trail' (W. Starkie, *Waveless*, p. 9).   12 W. Starkie, *Scholars*, p. 212. In *The waveless plain*, Italia is described as 'lovely' (p. 9) and in *Scholars and Gypsies*, both voice and girl are 'beautiful' (p. 212). In the former text, Italia is also described as having sung the '*Canzone del Grappa*' and '*Le campane di San Giusto*' (p. 9).   13 For further information on Alberto Porchietti, see the entry under his name in D. Petriella & S. Sosa Miatello, *Diccionario biográfico Italo-Argentino*. http://www.dante.edu.ar/web/

Delfina, all of whom Walter was to meet on the Sunday following the Armistice. In the meantime, the sirens from ships in the port were again ringing out on the morning of the 11th, announcing the end of the war. Starkie strikes a melancholic note in his account of the announcement of the end of hostilities, given the loss of life, but also recalls the three days and nights of celebration in Genoa. He records Walter celebrating with members of his troupe and a 'bohemian friend', one Alan Smith 'of the British military mission', remembered as sporting disguise: 'always dressed in civilian clothes and [who] roved through the Italian cities collecting information'. The carnivalesque celebration would lead to the *chianti*ful violinist playing from the dizzy heights of an equestrian statue of Garibaldi, surrounded by a cheering crowd calling out: '*Viva l'Inghilterra!*'[14] The ubiquitous frenzy prompted the fiddler to play patriotic anthems: 'God Save the King', '*La Marsellaise*' and the '*Inno di Garibaldi*', events drawing to a close in the early hours with the exhausted player coming to rest in the Cathedral of San Lorenzo.

The remaining weeks spent in Genoa brought Italia and her northern beau closer together. On the afternoon of Sunday, 13 November, Walter went out to the family's villa at Capo Santa Chiara, the first of a number of times before he left Genoa. He was introduced to Italia's parents and her sisters Eva and [Valen]Tina, the former already married to Mario Bonetti, a captain in the Italian navy. While the women of the household were engaged in domestic tasks, the young man found himself in the company of the Colonel, his son-in-law Mario, together with an unnamed ex-mayor of Genoa, identified as a fervent Mazzini supporter. Over the evening Italia's father spoke about his native Pinerolo in Piemonte, his education at the University of Turin and the admiration he had acquired for Carducci. After years of '[wandering] from one side of the world to another', the Colonel had bought land by the River Plata in Buenos Aires where he founded a school, the 'International College'. His wife reminisced about her Neapolitan grandfather, Domenico Landi, and her father, Domenico, who had joined Garibaldi's cause. The Colonel explained that the whole family had travelled back to Italy when the World War broke out in order to offer their services to the 'beloved fatherland'.[15]

Following a 'star performance' of the camp-follower's troupe in Genoa in January 1919, the Riviera Concert Party took to the road. A tour of northern Italy was arranged by the military authorities and the soldiers chosen to participate by the leader of the troupe were to be released from their duties. In spite of the order from GHQ, Walter ran into what Starkie sums up as a 'barrage of red tape and army ignorance' in the shape of authorities on the ground who argued that the men could not be spared 'owing to the stress of demobilization'.[16] However, the situation was eventually resolved, the troupe being provided with a lorry to transport themselves and their equipment so that they were able to set out for the town of Arcole. There were mishaps: the lorry breaking down and a local quartermaster sergeant in Trissino taking offence at the mimicking of army types but entertainment was delivered and,

dic/p.pdf, accessed 25 April 2012. 14 W. Starkie, *Scholars*, p. 213. 15 W. Starkie, *Scholars*, p. 220. 16 W. Starkie, *Scholars*, pp 225, 226.

according to Starkie's report, widely enjoyed in a number of towns and camps in the Venetian province over those early months of 1919. Apart from Arcole and Trissino, the latter 'the billeting site for divisional HQs' in 1918, Starkie mentions Arzignano, Montecchio Maggiore, 'one of several billeting areas' in the Valle dell'Agno, Schio, the Abbazia di Praglia near Padua, occupied by the Army Wing and Camouflage School of the British Expeditionary Force in 1918,[17] and Montebello Vicentino. Of the many incidents and episodes experienced by Walter over the period, one in particular caused a lasting impact.

After giving a recital in a YMCA hut near Montebello, Starkie explains that Walter was approached by five Austrian prisoners, currently employed 'in rough jobs in the camps by the British Army authorities until their repatriation', who turned out to be Hungarian Gypsies. Through a spokesman, addressing the troupe leader in a medley of Italian and German, they made known their desire to make themselves violins out of any wood that might be spared. The camp-follower 'scrounged a number of empty packing-cases of Woodbine, Ruby Queens, Cup ties and other rationed cigarettes' from the quartermaster-sergeant at nearby Tavernalle, produced some strings and resin of his own, and the Gypsies themselves managed to find hair for the bows, coming to produce a music which, according to Starkie's account, bewitched the YMCA worker: 'their fiddles worked a potent spell when throbbing under the devilish fingers of the Romanichals. Such glamour the five cast over me that I would stand and stare at them time and time again like one in a trance.'[18] Starkie registers Walter's being particularly struck by the playing of one of the men, recalled as having taught the Vandeleur prizewinner and eager amateur a number of Magyar tunes, the haunting effect of a *lassú* still potent as the autobiographer wrote in recollection some forty years on.[19] Starkie claims that Walter and Farkas became brothers, but more than the brotherly bond, blessed in blood, it was the impact of Farkas's music that came to haunt the former YMCA worker over the following decade, by which time he had been absorbed into the academy. It becomes emblematic of the desire to escape. Thus, Starkie confesses: 'In the middle of a serious lecture to a university class, the diabolical Gypsy tunes of Farkas would steal into my brain and make my body tingle for longing to be away.'[20]

Before a further tour with the Riviera Concert Party covering Treviso, Asolo, Padua and with a final session in Venice, after which, not surprisingly, Walter collapsed with exhaustion, he was invited to visit the Italian armies in the mountains and provide concerts for their entertainment. The occasion is recorded as not only providing him with the opportunity to become acquainted with regiments of *alpini*, found to possess 'discipline and efficiency' and to display 'a charming spirit of *camaraderie* between officers and men',[21] but also enabling him to collect a large repertory of songs, such as

---

17 F. Mackay, *Battleground Europe. Touring the Italian front, 1917–1918. British, American, French and German forces in northern Italy* (Barnsley, 2002), pp 98, 92, 88–9.   **18** W. Starkie (1963), pp 231, 232.   **19** The *lassú* is reproduced in W. Starkie, *Scholars*, p. 233. Starkie's encounter with the Hungarian gypsies is limited to a quote from his diary in *The waveless plain*: 'Montebello. – Strange meeting with Hungarian prisoners who turned out to be Gypsy fiddlers' (W. Starkie, *Waveless*, p. 77).   **20** W. Starkie, *Scholars*, p. 234.   **21** W. Starkie, *Scholars*, pp 236–7.

the well-known '*Sul ponte di Bassano*' and the '*Canzone del Grappa*'. He became further acquainted with the territory as he took part in concerts with the *alpini* in Treviso, Bassano, Schio and Udine and reached the summit of Mount Grappa, the victorious defence of which, 'with timely help from a French division', had enabled the 'much-needed [myth]'[22] that the kingdom had been saved.[23] Driving through the 'blackened ruins' of towns and villages on the Asiago Plateau, Walter would also be struck by what Starkie recalled as 'the destruction caused by modern war',[24] though twenty-five years earlier, he had merely attributed the devastation to the more abstract, or the monster, 'War',[25] that is, not awarding the modern variety with further destructive powers, as is the case in the 1960s text. The troupe leader's collapse in Venice, led to his being taken to the American military hospital in Vicenza, from where he was sent to Sirmio on Lake Garda to convalesce. Back in Vicenza, he found himself 'on light duty' and, thus, with plenty of time to spare. It was spent 'rambling' with Italian friends.[26] At this juncture Starkie also records Walter's encounter with the Neopolitan Paolo Merello, whose barnstorming *commedia dell'arte* company would, like the encounter with the Hungarian gypsies, command an impact on Starkie's future development, both academically and ideologically.[27]

The camp-follower was not left to ramble in Vicenza for long. The army authorities appointed him language teacher for French, Italian and Spanish in an army school established at Montebello, projected as 'a model institution organised under the auspices of the War Office and Lord Gorell to enable the officers and men of the British forces in Italy to prepare themselves for civil[ian] life in Great Britain.'[28] Starkie recalls that the army school was set up in a large country house, at a few miles' distance from Montebello, claiming that it soon came to be regarded by those involved in the project as 'a miniature Urbino'.[29] Classes were delivered in the mornings; the afternoons were taken up with football matches or sightseeing in Padua, Montecchio Maggiore, Verona or Venice and in the evenings rehearsals took place for concert pieces or plays which would provide entertainment on Saturday nights, an amateur theatre having been set up in one of the estate's stable buildings.

Apart from teaching others, Walter's own political education was broadened during the months he spent in Italy. The early months of 1919 found him witnessing the rise to national and international fame of both Gabriele D'Annunzio, in the year of the Fiume expedition, and Benito Mussolini, who launched his Fascist movement that spring. In *The waveless plain*, Starkie recalls the enthusiasm expressed by a young Italian, present at the meeting presided over by Mussolini in Milan on 23 March when

22 M. Thompson, *The white war. Life and death on the Italian front, 1915–1919* (London, 2008), p. 322. 23 See M. Thompson, *White war*, pp 355–60 for further information on the battle of Mount Grappa. Starkie's text reflects the myth commented on by Thompson: 'It was the heroic defence of Mount Grappa that prepared the way to the final victory' (W. Starkie, *Scholars*, p. 238). 24 W. Starkie, *Scholars*, p. 236. 25 W. Starkie, *Waveless*, p. 80. 26 W. Starkie, *Scholars*, p. 240. 27 See Chapter 5, below. 28 See Chapter 6, below, for further information on Starkie's contact with with Lord Gorell in the 1930s. W. Starkie, *Scholars*, p. 250. Starkie's teaching activity appears not to have been limited to language classes. When he speaks of the interested response of his soldier pupils, he refers to classes covering historical and artistic information. 29 W. Starkie, *Waveless*, p. 102.

the first *Fascio* was formed. He quotes the young man's enthusiasm for the new movement and his perception of Mussolini's rhetoric as antidote to the spread of communism among urban workers: 'All my companions are joining the new movement. Mussolini's speech is the best answer to those in the factories who are calling out "Viva Lenin!" Every one of us is ready to go back to the trenches if necessary.'[30] In his 1930s text, Starkie will also refer to Walter's presence in Venice on the Day of St Mark, 25 April, in 1919, and his hearing D'Annunzio address the crowd in the square from the *loggetta* of Sansovino. In the wake of the indignant withdrawal of Italy's Vittorio Orlando from the Paris Peace Conference on 21 April,[31] given President Wilson's refusal to deliver Fiume to Italy, the poet 'urged the Venetians to take up arms again and redeem what was theirs'.[32] As was the case with Arthur Symons and Harold Nicolson on hearing D'Annunzio on other occasions,[33] Starkie's recollection evokes the seductive impact of D'Annunzio's voice, filtered through images that evoke his passion for the violin and his Irish roots. He registers the effect on both Walter and the crowd: 'Little by little, I began to sink under the fascination of the voice [...] He played upon the emotions of the crowd as a violinist upon a Stradivarius. The eyes of the thousands were fixed upon him as though hypnotised by his power, and his voice like that of a *shanachie* bewitched their ears.'[34] However, in spite of D'Annunzio's mesmerizing oratory,[35] Starkie notes that ultimately the poet chose 'the lonely path to anarchy' and 'dwindled into a lonely eccentric' while Mussolini is credited with '[galvinizing] the youth of Italy into activity' and producing a 'dynamic New [*sic*] Italy',[36] a nation which Starkie would become increasingly familiar with over the 1920s and into the 30s.

Whether Walter was influenced by tales told of *Magna Graecia* by his father's friend and colleague John Pentland Mahaffy[37] or by his reading of George Gissing's *By the Ionian Sea. Notes of a ramble in Southern Italy* (1901), following demobilization he too undertook a 'ramble', 'a solitary journey to the wild south'.[38] He sometimes followed in Gissing's footsteps and, like the erstwhile wanderer, could certainly claim to 'a love of classical antiquity' as well as being content to 'dream [him]self into that old world ... of the Greeks and Romans'.[39] Gissing had set out from Naples by boat and on his

---

30 Ibid., p. 120. When charting the incident in *Scholars and Gypsies*, Starkie quotes the young Italian as declaring: 'All *ex-combattenti* are joining the new movement' (W. Starkie, *Scholars*, p. 260).   31 For information on the development of the Paris Peace Conference, see: http://.history. sandiego.edu/GEN/ww1/1919League2.html, accessed 27 April 2012.   32 J. Woodhouse, *Gabriele D'Annunzio. Defiant archangel* (Oxford 1998), p. 318.   33 Ibid., pp 16, 318.   34 W. Starkie, *Waveless*, p. 125; W. Starkie, *Scholars*, p. 263. In the former text, Starkie speaks of 24 April as the Day of St Mark and in the latter, Starkie refers to the 24 March as the Day of St Mark. As is noted by Woodhouse, St Mark's Day is celebrated on 25 April (J. Woodhouse, *Gabriele D'Annunzio*, p. 318).   35 Qualified by Woodhouse as a 'jingoistic speech' (J. Woodhouse, *Gabriele D'Annunzio*, p. 319).   36 W. Starkie, *Scholars*, pp 265, 267, 266, 267.   37 W. Starkie, *Scholars*, p. 294.   38 G. Gissing, *By the Ionian Sea. Notes of a ramble in southern Italy* (Oxford, 2004), p. 5.   39 G. Gissing, *Ionian Sea*, pp 2, 5. One striking aspect in which Starkie's text differs from Gissing's is in the former's 'catholicization' of the account, as, for instance, in the reference to Cotrone, where Starkie refers to the shrine of the Madonna of the Cape (W. Starkie, *Waveless*, p. 206). He also refrains from the criticism found in Gissing's text with regard to the 'pillage' wrought by a bishop of Cotrone on the temple of Hera (G. Gissing, *Ionian Sea*, pp 47, 48).

return Walter travelled back up to Genoa via the city in the Gulf; however, his journey south was on a troop train. Starkie describes it as 'long and tedious',[40] aggravated by congested quarters, heat and dirt. The men Walter was travelling with were destined for Egypt but he parted company with them in Taranto, the Apulian town which marked the last stage of his YMCA commitment. Once there, he discarded his uniform and abandoned the militarized lifestyle of months for a 'spell of wandering'.[41] His desire to rove, to roam[42] may have been inspired by tales of yore but Starkie also speaks of Walter's '[longing] to postpone the return to a life of duty day by day'.[43] Thus, the young man ignored his father's call to return to Ireland as soon as possible to take up a career in law.[44] Starkie also records the youth's feeling reluctant at the thought of returning to a destabilized country[45] where jobs were sparse and in which he would feel alien:

> The letters I received from my own country did not fill me with optimistic thoughts on the future of the Emerald Isle. They gave a dismal catalogue of calamities … The more I thought of Ireland[,] the less I relished the prospect of returning to Dublin and swelling the ranks of lean job-hunters. [...] I should find myself out of touch with the young generation that had grown up, filled with thoughts of liberating Ireland. I was born with the old régime [*sic*] in my bones, and I should assist as a passive spectator at the barricades just as I had done in the tragic Easter week in 1916, when a handful of young poets and desperate revolutionaries had roused a slumbering nation.[46]

Neither would he be returning to the affluence he had enjoyed in his childhood and adolescence. Having run up an overdraft of 'some thousands of pounds' and with 'large outstanding accounts with many tradespeople'[47] to be settled, the family now lived in reduced circumstances. With a view to remedying the situation, a severe regime had been imposed by WJM,[48] but to little avail. As daughter Enid observed, the Starkies were never to recover from having lived so lavishly beyond their means. Thus, in spite of her impoverished life as an undergraduate in Oxford, the Resident Commissioner's eldest daughter found her existence there 'particularly restful … with the escape it afforded from incessant talk of money',[49] her mother's struggle to keep up appearances and her father's self-imposed reclusion 'through poverty'.[50]

40 W. Starkie, *Scholars*, p. 275.   41 W. Starkie, *Waveless*, p. 155.   42 Starkie uses the synonyms of "wander" in the account of his change from camp follower to minstrel in the summer of 1919. See: W. Starkie, *Waveless*, Chapter 11, pp 147–58.   43 W. Starkie, *Waveless*, p. 151. In the 1960s memoir, Starkie ends the sentence on 'return'.   44 In both *The waveless plain* and *Scholars and Gypsies*, Starkie quotes from one of his father's letters in which he laid out plans for his son's future (W. Starkie, *Waveless*, p. 152; *Scholars*, p. 277).   45 In the general election of 24–8 December 1918, Sinn Féin won 73 of Ireland's 105 seats (D. Ferriter, *The transformation of Ireland, 1900–2000* (London, 2005), p. 183).   46 W. Starkie, *Waveless*, p. 152.   47 E. Starkie, *Lady's child*, p. 254.   48 Enid provides a poignant account of her father's pinching and saving (E. Starkie, *Lady's child*, p. 256), quoted earlier, p. 68.   49 E. Starkie, *Lady's child*, p. 265.   50 E. Starkie, *Lady's child*, p. 256. Enid Starkie devotes Chapter 1, Part 4, of her autobiography to the 'Financial crisis' experienced by the Starkie family during the First World War and up to her father's death in 1920.

Therefore, Walter's opting for postponing his return to Ireland might well have had as much to do with the sorry personal and political circumstances awaiting him as with the struggle between what Starkie came to express as the tension between his Don Quixote and Sancho Panza personalities.

Having chosen to follow his fiddle, Walter took advantage of contacts he had made in Taranto prior to being demobilized. He refers to a violin recital he gave 'to an audience of cultivated amateurs' in the 'palatial house' of a Taranto family. Present in the audience was a music critic who wrote for the Rome newspaper *Il Messaggero* and who produced a flattering article that 'the village Paganini' subsequently carried round with him with a view to promoting his profile. However, the weeks ahead were not spent in palatial dwellings or fine concert halls but trudging along dusty roads stretching out from Taranto to small towns in the vicinity: Massafra, Palagiano and Mottola. In the daytime the rover would make his way, taking advantage of the shade provided by olive trees when the sun was at its height and nourishing himself on the local fare: 'At cottages by the way I would buy some bread and ricotta ... As for wine, there was always plenty – a delicious, fragrant Calabrian wine.'[51] In the evenings he would go to a local café and pull out his fiddle, being rewarded by a meal in the café at Massafra, where the host accompanied the vagrant on his mandolin. It may have been the disapproval of the youth's wandering, expressed by the local figure of authority in Massafra, schoolmaster Don Riccardo, who questioned why such a young man should be living the life of 'a vagabond',[52] which prompted Walter to start moving further south. Before leaving Taranto, however, he paid tribute to Gissing by going in pursuit of the Galaesus, 'the river beloved by Horace',[53] as the novelist had done in 1897: 'I walked the three miles under the broiling heat of the June sun to discover the spirit of Gissing'.[54] Starkie's text further evokes Gissing's through reference to the purple dye-yielding murex shells found in the region as well as to the fishermen and peasants, the pattern of whose lives is viewed by both authors as quintessentially echoing that of their forebears.[55]

Starkie claims that Walter was bent on walking across the heel of Italy, from Taranto to Brindisi, and set out to fulfil his desire. Sore feet delayed him near Francavilla but relief was provided by a peasant couple, the wife rubbing his feet with oil obtained from the crypt of St Nicholas in Bari. It is after Walter has visited Bari himself that Starkie records his coming across a gypsy encampment in the plain, an encounter that is evocative of the impact generated on the camp-follower by the Hungarian gypsies met at Montebello Vicentino. Although the second group of gypsies are not musicians, Walter finds in their company a sense of release, a liberation from the constraints of convention and this episode, like the earlier one with the Hungarians, will leave him with a lingering sense of longing: 'How could I find words to describe my feelings of ease and freedom, as I rested by the smouldering fires, surrounded by those dark-eyed vagabonds? [...] ... ever since, I have felt at certain moments a longing to be away on

51 W. Starkie, *Scholars* (1963), pp 155, 156. **52** W. Starkie, *Waveless* (1938), p. 165. **53** Starkie identifies the river as Gissing does (G. Gissing, *Ionian Sea*, p. 31; W. Starkie, *Waveless*, p. 161). **54** W. Starkie, *Waveless*, p. 161. **55** See Chapter 4 in G. Gissing's *By the Ionian Sea* and Chapter 12 in W. Starkie's *The waveless plain*.

the plain, near the tents of the wandering folk.'[56] Starkie records that it was among these gypsies that Walter spent his first night in a gypsy camp, a night which is also romantically recalled as a liberating experience: 'I have never felt so deeply the thrill of Nature's freedom as I did on that night of initiation into the mystery of the Gypsy camp-fires.'[57] With a message from the Gypsy Chief's wife for her sister Carlotta requesting that Walter be introduced to Cesare, considered to be 'the finest mandolinist and harmonica player in the kingdom',[58] the traveller headed for Brindisi.

In the port town the young man meets up with Carlotta, an early instance of the witch-like females who inhabit Starkie's travel narratives of the 1930s: 'She was a fat, sallow-faced woman, dressed in a tattered red gown [with] a yellow handkerchief ... [o]n her head ... in Romany fashion ... long earrings of gold, ... her bodice ... studded with various little amulets', and with Cesare, *il gobbo*. Starkie claims that the hunchback and Walter became 'confederates', the latter learning from Cesare 'the tricks of the itinerant musician's trade [and] how to endure with equanimity the sordidness of poverty'.[59] Initially, they travelled back to Taranto and from there headed down 'on an extended ramble'[60] through Calabria to Reggio, passing through a host of places: Amendolara, Corigliano and the convent there of Santa Maria del Patire, Rossano, Metaponto and Cotrone, the town where Gissing had also spent some time during his visit to the region a quarter of a century earlier.[61] In Cotrone, Cesare took his new acquaintance to lodgings run by one Leda, 'a villainous-looking old woman', where Walter re-encounters the chief of the Gypsy tribe he had met near Brindisi, now named Adamo, and was introduced to, among others, Aldo and Susanna. Cesare promoted the former as a versatile performer: 'he can do anything with his fingers or his body: ... card tricks, conjuring tricks, juggling, somersaults, cart-wheels, and there isn't in all Southern Italy his equal at imitating the twittering of birds, the lowing of oxen, or the braying of an ass' while Susanna is summed up as 'a whore on holiday'. Through the archness of Leda and Cesare, Walter finds himself, not for the last time, having to draw on his 'meagre reserves of money', on that first occasion with a view to financing both his own and Cesare's lodgings as well as providing some wine for the company over their meal. Before leaving Cotrone, remembering the reminiscences of Mahaffy,[62] and again following in Gissing's footsteps,[63] Walter visits the Lacinian promontory, where, 'in lonely majesty, stands the single column of the temple of Hera, ... once ... one of Greece's most hallowed shrines,' a visit which leads him to reflect nostalgically on 'the sad majesty of that Greek world which ha[s] faded away.'[64]

56 W. Starkie, *Waveless*, pp 179, 181; W. Starkie, *Scholars*, pp 283, 284.   57 W. Starkie, *Waveless*, p. 181; W. Starkie, *Scholars*, p. 284.   58 W. Starkie, *Scholars*, p. 284. The assessment is that of the wife of the gypsy chief.   59 W. Starkie, *Scholars*, p. 288.   60 Ibid., p. 191.   61 G. Gissing, *Ionian Sea*, chapters 7 to 11, pp 44–81. In *Scholars and Gypsies*, Starkie concludes that Gissing was prejudiced against Cotrone as a consequence of being stricken down there by malaria (W. Starkie, *Scholars*, p. 291). In the same publication he makes no mention of Metaponto but claims in *The waveless plain* that he '[tramped] all the way from the station to see [the] venerable columns' of the Table of the Paladins (W. Starkie, *Waveless*, p. 193).   62 W. Starkie, *Scholars*, pp 291, 292, 296, 294.   63 G. Gissing, *Ionian Sea*, pp 46–7.   64 W. Starkie, *Scholars*, pp 294, 295.

From then on, along the route to Reggio, Cesare and Walter are joined by Aldo and Susanna. Having met up with the young couple in Cutro, where Adamo and company were camped, Cesare and Walter set out with them for Catanzaro where, according to Cesare: 'there was plenty of money'. The Cesare and Walter duo stop off to play in the seaside resort of Catanzaro Marina before travelling up to the mountain town, where Aldo had gone ahead with Susanna to prepare the ground for their performance, the first of a number in Catanzaro as well as in other town and villages on the road to Reggio. In the town at the tip of the mainland, the northern nomad parts company with all three, particularly motivated to move on by Aldo's 'tyrannical'[65] behaviour, yet regretting the farewell to Cesare.

Sicily was to be the last stage in the traveller's solitary ramble south. Gissing's journey ended in the stronghold of Reggio Calabria, 'a gateway of *Magna Graecia*'[66] but Walter is presented as crossing over the Strait by steamer, eager to continue his pursuit of antiquity: 'the cities consecrated by ancient Greece'.[67] Following a day in Messina, the route points south, as far as Syracuse, via Taormina and Catania, before inclining westwards, inland to Castrogiovanni, and towards the south again, to Girgenti and Porto Empedocle; the last port of call, Palermo, in the north-west of the island. The attraction in Taormina was the ruins of the Greek theatre but it also became significant as a consequence of Walter striking up new friendships there, two Danish sisters who are reported as regarding the young traveller as 'an incorrigible nomad'.[68] In Catania Walter visits the house where Vincenzo Bellini was born and pays a visit on Giovanni Verga. Starkie recalls that Verga queried Walter about '*la verde Erinne*' and is portrayed as 'listening silently and gravely' to the latter's explanations while 'gazing at me all the time with his large, sad eyes.'[69] The statue of Aphrodite Anadyomene, the Greek theatre, the Great Harbour and the Latomie were sources of interest in Syracuse but while in the city Walter doesn't limit himself to the pursuit of high culture.[70] Starkie explains that the young man took to playing 'wandering minstrel', frequenting the neighbourhood of the cathedral in the mornings, where he came to know the 'vagabond fraternity', and later in the day going to 'the deep quarries from which the city was built.' He speaks of Walter playing his violin in the 'Latomia del Paradiso', a cave (one of the favourite haunts of Walter's childhood) with the appearance of a human ear, through which the sound from his violin 'swelled in volume like an organ'. In Syracuse, too, he makes the acquaintance of fishermen who provide him with the opportunity of witnessing the killing of the tunny fish. Castrogiovanni signifies a visit to 'the grim citadel', the Fortress of Enna, seen in the company of two blind musicians, befriended on the way from Syracuse, together with their guide. On the Rock of Ceres near Manfred's Castle, Walter has his violin stolen and fears that he would never recover it given his appearance of 'down-at-heel vagabond, outside the pale of the law'. The violin was recovered courtesy of the Mafia

---

65 W. Starkie, *Scholars*, pp 296, 298. 66 G. Gissing, *Ionian Sea*, p. 124. 67 W. Starkie, *Scholars*, p. 303. 68 W. Starkie, *Waveless*, p. 224. 69 W. Starkie, *Scholars*, p. 305. The italics are in the original. In *The waveless plain*, Starkie qualifies the explanations supplied by Walter as 'timid' (W. Starkie, *Waveless*, p. 236). 70 A fuller account of places and people in Syracuse is provided in chapter 18 and into chapter 19 of *The waveless plain* than in Chapter 13 of *Scholars and Gypsies*.

and Walter continued on his way to Girgenti, where, as Starkie recalls, he was able to experience the rapture of antiquity:

> to stand upon the hills of Girgenti and gaze down over the trees at the long line of temples silhouetted against the sea, is to see in a flash a complete vision of Greek antiquity. … the view of Girgenti's row of temples, rising out of the landscape like a magic city, becomes the epitome of all that one has ever dreamed about ancient Greece. At night the temple of Concord in the light of the moon becomes the most beautiful Greek monument in the world.

The modern harbour of Girgenti, Porto Empedocle, provides a radical contrast to the majesty of ancient civilization. The 'mean, miserable industrial town' is represented in Dickensian mode, the product of 'modern barbarians, following their instincts of greed', while the workers employed in the sulphur mines are viewed as a 'wretched hang-dog crew',[71] evocative of Stephen Blackpool and his ilk in *Hard times*.

Palermo's Golden Shell, 'the fertile valley stretching like a vast garden behind the city into the mountains', provided sweet relief in the wake of such desolation as did the cloister of the twelfth-century church of San Giovanni degli Eremiti, which became Walter's 'favourite resting-place' in the city. In *The waveless plain*, Starkie gives an account of Walter's visiting the Convent of the Capuchins while in Palermo, but he would also play entertainer. 'One evening', having been playing for four hours and with little more than three lire to show for his efforts, the solo violinist comes across Cesare, the hunchback, now performing with a story-teller, 'a lanky[,] squint-eyed individual'. Walter joins forces with them, returning to a low-life existence, '[thinking] only of the day and never of the morrow', the trio coming to spend some days together 'roaming Palermo' as 'musical picaroons'. Starkie explains that the young man's wandering life was brought to a close following a sleepless night which brought to the fore Walter's 'real life from which [he] had escaped'. At the *poste restante* on the following morning, he collected anxious letters from home together with one from Italia Porchietti, taking him to task for not having written since Taranto. That night he embarked for Naples, his 'truant minstrel'[72] days at an end – at least for the present.

Walter travelled back to Genoa via Rome, managing to catch fleeting views of the Claudian acqueduct, the Forum, the Castello San Angelo and the dome of St Peter's from his third-class railway carriage. Starkie's description of Capo Santa Chiara on the sunlit afternoon on which Walter went out to the Porchietti villa evokes an idyllic setting against which the reunion with Italia is staged, something of a match for the view from his childhood 'Undercliff': 'the air was clear and my eye took in the full panorama of graceful coast outline; the Ligurian mountains and hills studded with cypress trees and dotted with white villas; the distant purple headland of Portofino rounding off the landscape.'[73] In a scene perhaps worthy of opera, Starkie recalls strains of Scarlatti reaching Walter's ears, the voice of Italia, whose singing Starkie

71 W. Starkie, *Scholars*, pp 305–6, 307, 308, 309, 310.   72 W. Starkie, *Scholars*, pp 310, 311, 312, 313, 314.   73 W. Starkie, *Waveless*, p. 290.

portrays the young man responding to by playing Dvořák's ballade, one of her favourite pieces.

Walter was also reunited with Italia's parents, Don Alberto and Donna Delfina. The energetic, fifty-seven-year-old Colonel had enrolled in the Faculty of Medicine at the University of Genoa and spoke with enthusiasm of finding himself among students of nineteen or twenty years of age, convinced that 'we older men must learn and draw our strength ... from the young' and noting 'a new spirit in the air', that is, as is explained: 'the Fascist Movement of Benito Mussolini.'[74] The conversation between the young man and his future in-laws serves to highlight criticism of the government of left-wing sympathizer Francesco Saverio Nitti and, more emphatically, to convey an anti-Communist discourse. Thus, the Colonel is represented as sighing, raising his hands with a gesture of despair and delivering the following apocalyptic assessment of the current political situation: 'Things are going from bad to worse, ... We are in the hands of Bolshevists. Soon they will seize all the factories and plunder the country in the name of Socialism'.[75] He alludes to the 'epidemic of strikes' which had gripped the country but has no criticism to make of the workers, whom he sees as having no alternative in the light of soaring prices. His wife also speaks out in defence of the workers and attributes current social unrest to socialist machinations: 'It isn't the workers who cause the strikes but the Socialist committees of action who try to foment political disturbances in the name of the Russian Millenium. Our country at present is the victim of international Bolshevik agents.'[76] Walter's contribution to the conversation is to inform that on his travels he met members of the Association of Ex-Servicemen (*Associazione dei Combattenti*) who were 'determined to oppose the Bolsheviks and all those who insult the men who defended their country in the War'[77] but he queries whether they will be strong enough. The Colonel's reply carries conviction as to the support that Mussolini commanded: 'The ex-servicemen will follow Mussolini to a man because their best members already belong to the *Fasci di Combattimento*, but to them you must add the great mass of generous youth who have allied themselves with their elder brothers of the Fasci. They are gradually uniting their forces and preparing for the big struggle in the near future.'[78]

Walter was soon to be allying himself to the struggle in question and his efforts were to be sustained over the following two decades. In the short term, however, his active commitment to Italia was a personal one, to Don Alberto and Donna Delfina's daughter. As recorded by the autobiographer, on the day following his return to Genoa, Walter and Italia Augusta (three years his senior), became engaged.[79] Sometime later,[80] the twenty-five-year-old *fidanzato* left for an Ireland plunged into

---

74 W. Starkie, *Waveless*, p. 292.   **75** W. Starkie, *Scholars*, p. 291.   **76** W. Starkie, *Waveless*, p. 291.
77 W. Starkie, *Scholars*, p. 293.   **78** W. Starkie, *Waveless*, p. 293 and W. Starkie, *Scholars*, p. 316. In the latter text, the first sentence reads: 'like a man', as opposed to: 'to a man' and Alberto's words end in the first sentence at the word 'youth'.   **79** Starkie speaks of the purchase of rings in Genoa, engraved with the couple's names and the date of the engagement, which were presented to Italia and himself by his future mother-in-law. Starkie's daughter does not possess the rings nor does she have a record of the date of the engagement (telephone conversation with Alma Starkie, 13 February 2010). **80** No dates are supplied in either *The waveless plain* or *Scholars and Gypsies* with regard to exactly when

the War of Independence, a country bent on becoming increasingly less like the one where the allegiance of the Starkie family had lain for generations, struggling to free itself from the wisdom which had welded the West Briton. Sinn Féin's manifesto for the December 1918 election had stressed Ireland's difference and the strength of her resistance to British rule, highlighting: 'our unbroken tradition of nationhood, ... a unity in a national name which has never been challenged, ... our possession of a distinctive national culture and social order, ... the moral courage and dignity of our people in the face of alien aggression.'[81] Another Ireland was coming into her own. It was hardly the homecoming the young man would have expected or, indeed, hoped for.

Starkie travelled back up to Genoa from Sicily or when he left Genoa for Ireland. Indeed, no date is supplied in the whole of his account of the period he spent travelling south apart from the reference to the month of June (1919) when he walked in the wake of Gissing to see the river Galaesus. His sister speaks of his being away 'almost a year' (E. Starkie, *Lady's child*, p. 281). 81 D. Ferriter, *The transformation*, p. 183.

5

Troubled Territories and Novel Nations

> How I cursed my return to my native land! Out in Italy there was the same chaos;
> there were bombs and shooting, but there was hope. I knew that the university
> students out there had joined with the ex-servicemen to create a new movement
> of national solidarity, and I had profound faith in their ideals. In my own country
> I was torn by agonizing doubts.[1]

Having taken his leave of Italia in Genoa in order to make his way back to Dublin,
Starkie alludes to Walter's experiencing a sense of 'despairing uncertainty'.[2] He might
have prolonged his stay in Capo Santa Chiara but in the anxious correspondence from
his family, there was an earnest request for him to return in haste given his father's
poor state of health. Moreover, the family must have been disturbed, when not
alarmed, by 'the enormity of the political change',[3] in the wake of the establishing of
an Irish parliament, Dáil Éireann, on 21 January 1919, and with Eamon de Valera
having taken up the presidency in April.

In a letter to his son in Italy, WJM had recommended that he study for the Bar and
this was the path which Starkie embarked on at TCD in the autumn of 1919, though,
as Enid recalls, her brother began 'in a desultory and half-hearted manner'.[4] Starkie
records finding the College 'transformed',[5] the lecture halls accommodating a motley
crowd of men in the wake of demobilization, perhaps contributing to his sense of
alienation. The Resident Commissioner, now 'acutely anxious both on health and
financial grounds', must have been prey to some dismay, perceiving his only son to be
in 'his most lotus-eating mood' when the diligent civil servant would see that the
moment required resolve. Enid also observed her sibling's restlessness, registering
surprise at the neglect of his beloved instrument: 'He ... wandered from amusement
to amusement and did not even practise his violin seriously.'[6] However, as the eldest
offspring, and certainly qualified to earn a living, the youth took on a number of tasks:
coaching students for the university examinations, lending himself to some lecturing
at TCD, as well as teaching at Earlsfort House School. The Resident Commissioner's
close colleague and friend the Reverend Mahaffy died in April 1919 while R.Y.
Tyrrell had passed away in 1914. However, the young man was not without elders,
members of staff at TCD, WJM's contemporaries, who were ready to offer him
counsel as he struggled to adjust to his family's straitened circumstances and to finding
a suitable career path. It was William Alexander Goligher, Professor of Ancient
History in the wake of Mahaffy and Tyrrell, remembered by Enid as 'always [giving]

---

1 W. Starkie, *Waveless*, p. 298. 2 W. Starkie, *Waveless*, p. 294. 3 D. Ferriter, *The transformation*, p.
185. 4 E. Starkie, *Lady's child*, p. 281. 5 W. Starkie, *Waveless*, p. 295. 6 E. Starkie, *Lady's child*, p.
282. 7 E. Starkie, *Lady's child*, p. 282. The role of Goligher as provider of 'kind advice' is registered
in Starkie's 'Preface' to *Spanish raggle-taggle* (W. Starkie, *Spanish raggle-taggle* (London, 1934), p. x). In

the family the wisest and most far-seeing advice',[7] who suggested that her brother turn his talent for modern languages to the study of Spanish. The recommendation led to Starkie developing his career in this direction, going on to produce a PhD on the Spanish Nobel Prize-winning playwright Jacinto Benavente and subsequently occupying the first Chair of Spanish at TCD.[8] But before these achievements took place, there was another death in the family to contend with.

Both the Starkie siblings remember the year of their father's death as particularly dark: Enid placing the event in the context of 'the "Troubled Times" in Ireland';[9] her brother summing 1920 up as 'mournful'. Starkie also records the personal grieving in the public context of 'murders and burnings', which, he observes, 'had increased tenfold through 1920.' The Royal Irish Constabulary recruits had been arriving in Ireland since the month of March and the 'sinister brutality' of the Black and Tans was registered in *The waveless plain* as was the indignation felt towards 'England's politicians for using such a dastardly weapon against Ireland.'[10] However, in the same autobiographical volume, the account of Bloody Sunday in 1920 particularly highlights the assassination of fourteen British officers by the IRA on 21 November, making no mention of the killing of twelve civilians later the same day by British auxiliaries who, Alvin Jackson has claimed, were 'bent on indiscriminate revenge'.[11] Enid also recalls that there was 'great sadness in the country' in the final year of her father's life as well as 'an undercurrent of sadness and anxiety in our home',[12] which would come to a climax with the death of the Resident Commissioner in the summer.

On 2 April 1920, the Dublin physician William Boxwell diagnosed WJM as suffering from diabetes but urged him to seek a second opinion.[13] Enid recalls that his brother Robert tried to persuade him to travel to London to consult a specialist as insulin was beginning to be used in England but her father refused, making, in his daughter's opinion: 'a tragically mistaken effort at economy' though it seems that her father was also sceptical with regard to 'the power of doctors to cure disease'.[14] The Resident Commissioner was on edge, too, given Sinn Féin attacks on British officials. Enid's claim that he commanded 'universal respect' because of 'his widespread reputation for perfect justice and integrity' seems to be somewhat undermined, however, by her additional claim that it was 'generally believed' that her father would not be spared:

> There had been many casualties among civil servants, for many had been murdered. It was generally believed that my father figured on the list of those to

the 'Acknowledgements' to *Don Gypsy* and *The waveless plain*, the Professor of Ancient History is thanked together with Starkie's publisher, John Grey Murray, for 'kind advice' (W. Starkie, *Don Gypsy* (London, 1936), p. x) and 'much kind advice' (W. Starkie, *Waveless*, p. xi), respectively. 8 The French Department at TCD '[boasts] the oldest chair of French in the world (1776)'. http://www.tcd.ie/French, accessed, 9 May 2012. The College also possesses 'the world's oldest tradition of university level Italian Studies, dating back to 1776', http://www.tcd.ie/Italian, accessed 9 May 2012. When Starkie was appointed to the Chair of Spanish in 1926, the *Irish Times* reported that the University authorities at TCD were 'following precedents of the eighteenth century when, as early as 1778, some provision was made for the teaching of Spanish as well as of Italian' (IT, 9 Mar. 1926, p. 13). 9 E. Starkie, *Lady's child*, p. 299. 10 W. Starkie, *Waveless*, pp 307, 298, 299. 11 A. Jackson cited in D. Ferriter, *The transformation*, p. 235. 12 E. Starkie, *Lady's child*, p. 299. 13 Information provided in WJM's diary (J. Richardson, *Enid Starkie*, p. 43). 14 E. Starkie, *Lady's child*, p. 306.

be murdered … his life was in a certain amount of danger, and he used to say that he often woke at night thinking he heard sounds outside which indicated that the house was being surrounded and the Sinn Feiners had come to kidnap him or to murder him. Tyrone House, the Education Office, had … been attacked some weeks previously, and this had very greatly shaken him.[15]

WJM himself recorded in his diary for 16 April 1920 that he was woken at 6 a.m. by the song of a thrush though he had interpreted it as 'the whistle of a Sinn Feiner about to attack the house'.[16] Notwithstanding the Resident Commissioner's fading strength and perhaps motivated by his state of anxiety, on 26 June, the family (initially WJM with Muriel, Nancy, the cook Lizzie O'Beirne and the girls' governess) drove to the north east of the country to stay in Cushendun in the Glens of Antrim, in 'a typical Irish country house of the eighteenth century'.[17] Cushendun House was let to the family by Ronald McNeill, later Baron Cushendun, Conservative MP at the time for the Canterbury Division of Kent. The Starkies had stayed at the house in the summer of 1916 for ten weeks and, according to Enid, were delighted to be back even though it was 'bitterly cold'.[18] WJM's eldest daughter joined the family in the glory of having obtained a first-class degree with distinction at Oxford, a piece of news that would bring Enid's father great relief with regard to her future and lead him to publicize his satisfaction by sending a notice to the *Irish Times*.[19]

As on the family's previous sojourn in the north, WJM combined the period of recreation with visiting schools in the neighbourhood but Enid, who accompanied him on a few occasions, was able to appreciate that he was no longer fit enough to carry out the task: 'visibly the effort was too much for him … he was often absent-minded and tired'.[20] After days of poor health, which, nonetheless, did not prevent him from paying official visits to National Schools, he became unconscious and died in the early hours of 21 July[21] when, as Enid notes, his son 'was still in Dublin with his friends'.[22] The Resident Commissioner's first-born arrived over the morning to join his sister at their father's bedside. Enid recalls the moment: 'Walter came up and stood by the bed, with tears flowing down his cheeks. I had not seen him cry since I was a tiny child, and he apologised for weeping before me. We stood arm in arm together, … but we could say nothing to one another.' At this point May Caroline Starkie is depicted by Enid as a mostly silent figure, even aloof, through her husband's dying and at his death. The eldest daughter admits to not knowing how to address her mother since, she claims, they had 'never spoken of deep feelings'. Thus, the sister's linking arms with her brother is singled out as 'the first human contact' she had experienced since her father's passing. As was the case when the infant Humphrey William Robert died, it was Lizzie O'Beirne, 'who could always be trusted to do the right thing',[23] who then

15 E. Starkie, *Lady's child*, p. 313. **16** Cited by J. Richardson, *Enid Starkie*, p. 44. **17** E. Starkie, *Lady's child*, p. 246. **18** E. Starkie, *Lady's child*, p. 321. **19** J. Richardson, *Enid Starkie*, p. 45. **20** E. Starkie, *Lady's child*, p. 315. **21** 'Obituary. The Right Hon. W.J.M. Starkie', IT, 22 July 1920, pp 4–5. **22** E. Starkie, *Lady's child*, p. 317. In the B. Galm interview, Starkie explains that he was involved in examinations (B. Galm interview with W. Starkie, OHP, UCLA, 1970–1). **23** E. Starkie, *Lady's child*, pp 324, 318, 324, 321.

supervised the necessary arrangements. Following the local priest having administered extreme unction, she had recited the prayers for the dying and, following WJM's last breath, it was she who pronounced prayers for the dead and closed the eyes of her 'Master'.[24] The eldest daughter's subsequent recollection of her father lying in his satin-lined coffin, dressed in clean but 'shabby, darned, and faded pyjamas'[25] is poignant. The shabby, darned and faded were qualities that had become familiar of late to the family of the last Resident Commissioner of National Education and may be regarded as providing a measure of the impoverishment that lay ahead for his widow, their children and, indeed, the regime he had so rigorously and devotedly served for almost twenty years and which had been upheld by his no less loyal forebears. Obituaries paid tribute to the Right Honourable W.J.M. Starkie as 'a highly capable administrator with gifts of initiative, rapidity of judgment',[26] with valuable moral qualities: 'sincere, free from self-interest, and eminently fair as a fighter … almost invincible in controversy … ever on the look-out for truth', 'most instructive and inspiring'[27] as a lecturer and a man of 'brilliant and trenchant wit.'[28] The challenge for his only son was formidable.

Enid used the metaphor of 'a ship sailing in a storm without a captain'[29] to describe the family's position in the wake of her father's death. The 'storm' in the household was predominantly financial and drastic measures had to be adopted, not least removal from the Edwardian ease of Melfort. The family moved with Lizzie O'Beirne to more modest accommodation within walking distance of Shrewsbury Road, a property in a terrace of town houses, situated in Anglesea Road, at the Donnybook end of the thoroughfare, number 129. The situation seems to have been one of dire straits. There was no pension for the Commissioner's widow and the only fund available was a life insurance premium.[30] Enid recalls her mother's brother John, who took to 'repeating on every occasion he came to the house, "There will be precious little money, May, to live on, precious little!"'[31] Enid now left home to take up a post as assistant mistress at Lingholt School in the Surrey village of Hindhead in England, but would not tarry in being awarded a Gilchrist Studentship, which enabled her to work for a doctorate at the Sorbonne, the first step in a career which led her to a Readership in French at Somerville College Oxford. Her brother abandoned his father's project of reading for the Bar and toyed with the idea of working with the YMCA again, this time in Germany. An offer came from Mr Sparling, proprietor of the Bohemian Picture House in Dublin, where, for a salary of £20 per week, he would 'lead the small

24 E. Starkie, *Lady's child*, p. 326. Enid refers to Lizzie seated by the kitchen fire, praying for the repose of the soul of the 'Master, poor man' following his funeral at the Pro-Cathedral in Dublin. **25** E. Starkie, *Lady's child*, p. 324. **26** 'Rt Hon. William Joseph Myles Starkie, P.C., LL.D.', *Westminster Gazette*, cited in the *Irish Book Lover*, 12 (October–November 1920), p. 44. **27** 'William Myles [sic] Joseph Starkie', *Hermathena*, 19:43 (1922), v, vi, vii. **28** 'Obituary. The Right Hon. W.J.M. Starkie.' IT, 22 July 1920, p. 4. **29** E. Starkie, *Lady's child*, p. 328. **30** J. Richardson, *Enid Starkie*, pp 50, 284 (note 8). It seems that some government funds were made available to the widow: 'Mrs W.J.M. Starkie has received a grant from the Civil List in recognition of her late husband's services to classical scholarship and literature, and to the cause of education in Ireland' (J.E. Auden (ed.), 'Obituary of Old Salopians', *Shrewsbury, Royal School, Old Salopian Club Year Book* (London, 1922), p. 47). **31** E. Starkie, *Lady's child*, p. 328.

orchestra and play solos'.[32] Anxious to earn funds in order to finance his return to Italy in December 1920, the twenty-six-year-old was tempted to accept. However, he records being approached by his former tutor at TCD, Dr E.H. Alton (a Latinist and Fellow of the College since 1905),[33] who told him of the University Board's intention to invite him to do some lecturing in Latin and French the following Michaelmas term, with the possibility of a more secure future ahead. In a style that becomes a characteristic feature of Starkie's travel writing in the 1930s, he cites, re-creates, Alton's words to him: '[T]here is a probability that the Board will introduce shortly a series of new University lectureships in various subjects, one of which will be Romance languages. With your preparation in French, Italian and Spanish, and your teaching experience abroad in army education, you will be the most likely candidate to receive a university post.'[34]

Whether Alton expressed himself precisely thus is debatable. However, Starkie went on to obtain a Fellowship in Modern Languages in 1924, a post which, according to a source cited by Webb and McDowell, appears to have been among those tailored to a particular candidate:

> There is no doubt that on a few occasions the qualifications were so framed that it was unlikely that more than one candidate would materialise; in 1924 when Walter Starkie (who was a competent violinist) was elected to the Fellowship in Modern Languages, a cynical commentator suggested that the only qualification for candidature that had been omitted was 'must be able to play the fiddle'.[35]

Undoubtedly Starkie had the support of former colleagues of his father who held positions of authority at TCD. Not least among them was the Provost, the Most Reverend and Right Honourable John Henry Bernard, DD, former Dean of St Patrick's Cathedral, elected archbishop of Dublin in 1915, a position he had occupied until his appointment as Provost. Former colleague of WJM at Alexandra College, Bernard had wrested the provostship from him in 1919 when the Resident Commissioner was contemplating the possibility of occupying the post as a solution to his pressing financial straits.[36] WJM had noted in his diary his perception of being at a disadvantage as a candidate, in spite of professional and personal qualifications, given his Catholicism: 'There is no doubt that Catholics cannot look for preferment in Trin[ity]: no case could be stronger than mine – I am popular with them, I am not a priest's man, and I am known, in addition to being a scholar, an administrator, and a fighting man.'[37] Therefore, it is conceivable that apart from considerations with regard to the widow and family's straitened circumstances, Bernard might have been moved

---

32 W. Starkie, 'Autobiography part 2', TCD MS 9187, p. 40. 33 Obituary of Ernest Henry Alton in the *Proceedings of the Royal Irish Academy*, 54, App. 1 (1951–2), 6–7. 34 Ibid., p. 41. At a TCD Board meeting in May: 'It was resolved that the Board hereby define, as full time Professorships, in pursuance of their resolution of November 1st 1919, the following Chairs: Applied Chemistry, Geology, Zoology, Bacteriology, Romance Languages, German, Engineering' (TCD Register, Board Meeting, 1 May 1920, TCD MUN/V/5/22, p. 34). 35 R.B. MacDowell & D.A. Webb, *Trinity College Dublin* (Cambridge, 1982), p. 436. 36 J. Richardson, *Enid Starkie*, pp 41–2. 37 Ibid., p. 41.

by the desire to provide for the son since the father had been denied what he sought towards the end of his life by his contemporary.[38]

Joanna Richardson claims that in the wake of the death of the Resident Commissioner, Enid sought 'a dominant figure to replace the father she had lost';[39] it is possible that her brother was infused with a similar desire or need. What is certainly revealed over the 1920s is Starkie's pursuit of strong leadership and a sense of belonging. His feeling of loss when deprived of his uniform in the wake of demobilization in Italy in 1919 already illustrates the extent to which he craved a secure identity. Thus, the change into 'civies' did not signify liberation but a sense of disorientation; being outside the body of soldiers or group, going it alone, is equal to a world of gloom: 'The thought of getting out of uniform gave me the uneasy feeling of being thrust into an outer world of darkness to fend for myself.'[40] In mulling over the question of life without a uniform, T.E. Lawrence's thoughts in *The seven pillars of wisdom* are brought to bear, a text that is the first in a list of four to which Starkie expresses indebtedness in the 'Acknowledgements' to *The waveless plain*.[41] The passage he quotes begins: '[T]he secret of uniform [is] to make a crowd solid, dignified, impersonal: to give it the singleness and tautness of an upstanding man.'[42] However, Lawrence goes on to deliver an indictment of both the uniform, viewing it as representing the wearer's slavery, and the wearer himself, since, in the author's view, the latter has sacrificed his selfhood:

> This death's livery which walled its bearers from ordinary life, [*sic*] was sign that they had sold their wills and bodies to the State: and contracted themselves into a service not the less abject for that its beginning was voluntary. [...] ...the soldier assigned his owner the twenty-four hours' use of his body; and sole conduct of his mind and passions. [...] His affections must be hired pieces on the chessboard of the king.[43]

The charge is also cited by Starkie, apparently unaware of the incongruence of Lawrence's observations to his argument. The fact that he limits himself to only referring to the opening sentence when citing Lawrence some twenty-five years on suggests that he had become aware of the irrelevance of the later assertions to his purpose or that he no longer wished to highlight the portrayal of abject service.

As shootings took place in the city by both day and night, Starkie draws a forlorn portrait of Walter at TCD in 1920: '[a]lone' in his 'gloomy college rooms looking out on College Green', attempting to temper his solitude and the surrounding penumbra

---

38 J.H. Bernard was born in another imperial outpost, India, in the same year as W.J.M. Starkie, 1860. His family hailed from Kerry, the county of May Caroline Starkie's forebears.   39 J. Richardson, *Enid Starkie*, p. 49.   40 W. Starkie, *Waveless*, p. 150.   41 The following three are: E.J. Dillon's *The peace conference* (1919), John Ruskin's *Verona and other lectures* (1894) and George Gissing's *By the Ionian Sea* (1905).   42 T.E. Lawrence, *Seven pillars of wisdom. A triumph*, 2 vols (London, 1939), p. 662, cited in W. Starkie, *Waveless*, p. 150. Starkie (mis)quotes the sentence in *Scholars and Gypsies*, adding: 'sequence' before 'singleness and tautness of an upstanding man' (W. Starkie, *Scholars*, p. 276).   43 T.E. Lawrence, *Seven pillars*, pp 662–3, cited in W. Starkie, *Waveless*, pp 150–1.

with dreams of 'an ideal life' with Italia 'under sunny Italian skies'. Italia now wrote regularly to her fiancé from Milan, where she was taking singing lessons at the conservatory. Her letters spoke of 'chaos and misgovernment' in Italy but, as Starkie was well aware, daily life in Dublin was plagued by instability, a situation which is attributed to Britain's uneven or desperate response: 'day by day we watched the ever-vacillating British policy in Ireland, weak at one moment, too drastic at another'.[44] However, the young man could now conceive of an academic career at TCD and as Ireland's partitioned future was coming into being,[45] he went back to Genoa to make arrangements for his marriage, planned for the following summer. Starkie records a feeling of relief in relation to the period spent in Italy in late 1920, there is certainly a sense of the carefree in his account. The *promessi sposi* moved beyond Genoa and Capo Santa Chiara, taking the coast road to the towns of Recco and Camogli. They also travelled further afield: to Santa Margherita, Paraggi and Portofino as well as going up into the mountains, to the village of Zoagli, where Walter is portrayed as playing 'all the Italian and Sicilian tunes' he could muster while Italia sang the '*Canzone del Piave*' and '*Monte Grappa*', the local women represented in this, again, opera-like vignette working on their traditional brocades. Beyond romance, Starkie also records a political reality in the country: '[e]verybody' was speaking of 'the Fascist revolution' and, thus, Walter is depicted as making his first acquaintance with 'the young student Black Shirts'.[46]

According to the announcement in the *Irish Times*, Starkie's marriage to Italia took place in Genoa on 10 August 1921,[47] the day following the groom's twenty-seventh birthday. The couple then left Italy for a honeymoon in Spain, partly, or wholly, financed by Lady Ardilaun.[48] They travelled by rail from Italy into France, descending via Bourdeaux into Spain where they covered the country from north to south on third-class kilometric tickets. As Starkie recollected some forty years on, they became acquainted with a number of cities: Madrid, Salamanca, Burgos, Jerez, Granada, Seville, Córdoba, Valencia, Barcelona and with representative writers of the time: the prominent Basque novelist and philosopher Miguel de Unamuno, with whom Alberto

---

44 W. Starkie, *Waveless*, pp 301–2, 302, 301.   45 The Government of Ireland Act was passed on 23 December 1920 and the Anglo-Irish Treaty would be signed on 6 December 1921.   46 W. Starkie, *Waveless*, pp 314, 312.   47 'Marriages', IT, 30 Aug. 1921, p. 1. No details are supplied as to where the marriage took place, apart from 'at Genoa'. Starkie provides no details of a marriage ceremony in *The waveless plain, Scholars and Gypsies* or in the interview he held with with Bernard Galm at UCLA, nor does his sister in *A lady's child*. Given the Starkie family's lack of means in the wake of WJM's death, coupled with Italia not being a practising Catholic, there appears not to have been a wedding in church or a reception of any magnitude. In the interview with Galm, Starkie does specify that Italia's family accompanied the couple. Neither was the marriage registered at the British Consulate in Genoa. It might also be noted that in the opening paragraph of Chapter 23 of *Spanish raggle-taggle* the narrator refers to spending three months of his honeymoon in Burgos in 1921 and recalls being present in July [*sic*] of that year when, with his wife, the couple 'saw the national hero of Spain [El Cid] laid to rest in the Cathedral' (W. Starkie, *Spanish*, p. 251).   48 In the interview with Bernard Galm, Starkie explains that Lady Ardilaun gave him a substantial gift following his playing at a concert at the Chapel Royal in Dublin which she had invited him to take part in. Starkie played the violin and the organist of the Chapel Royal, William Hopkins, the organ (B. Galm interview with Walter Starkie, OHP, UCLA, 1970–1).

Porchietti appears to have been acquainted,[49] and the Andalusian Brothers (Álvarez) Quintero as well as the composer Manuel de Falla.[50] In Burgos, where University of Toulouse professor Ernest Merimée had been running summer courses geared towards foreigners since the beginning of the century,[51] they followed a course in Spanish and also attended classes in Spanish language and history at the University of Madrid. The time spent in the Spanish capital provided them with the opportunity to visit the Prado Museum and the *Biblioteca Nacional* as well to travel to the nearby Escorial Palace. In October, the couple travelled to Ireland via London, where they went to the theatre.[52] The crossing from Holyhead to Dublin was rough, it was raining on arrival and they were taken to Ballsbridge in a shabby taxi via 'a series of slum districts'. The Irish spouse came to detect 'the chill of disillusion'[53] on his Italian bride's face following her exposure to Irish weather and, more distressingly, the city's poverty, reflected in the less than elegant vehicle as well as in the 'dilapidated tenements'.[54] However, Starkie claims that Italia didn't tarry in adapting herself to Irish life though it appears she was never to become enamoured of it. In the event Dublin was to become her home for the following well-nigh twenty years, the first two of which were spent under her mother-in-law's roof and in a land sunk in strife.

Mr and Mrs Walter Starkie arrived in Dublin some two months before the signing of the Anglo-Irish Treaty. The agreement would transform the island at which the couple disembarked, and which Mr W. Starkie had lived in since birth, into the twenty-six counties of the Irish Free State (Saorstát Éireann), an entity with Dominion status, and the six counties of Northern Ireland, both contained within the United Kingdom of Great Britain and Ireland. In the wake of the signing of the Treaty in autumn of 1921 and into 1922 there was much unmapped territory to be negotiated by Irish citizens. The Starkie family's safe haven had been undermined and it now behoved Unionist institutions and bodies that the Starkies had served through generations or been associated with to forge adjustments. Undoubtedly it was a time of uncertainty. As columnist Nickevo remarked in the *Irish Times* regarding the impact on TCD: 'with the passing of the Union with Great Britain ... Trinity College has been launched into an uncharted sea'.[55] On the domestic front, the widow of WJM would have her son and daughter-in-law living with her in the most modest home she

---

49 So Starkie claims in the interview with B. Galm (OHP, UCLA, 1970–1). For further information on Starkie's correspondence with Unamuno, see below.   50 On his return from Spain, Starkie sent a postcard of Dublin's Westmoreland Street to Falla on which he thanked the composer for the unforgettable time spent in his home: 'Je n'oublierai jamais cette soirée magnifique à votre maison et ses nocturnes, surtout celle de la 'Generalife' (W. Starkie to M. de Falla, 14 Oct. 1921, Archivo Manuel de Falla, Granada, 7652.001.02.GIF).   51 'Los actos conmemorativos del cincuentenario de los Cursos de Verano para Extranjeros comenzaron ayer en nuestra ciudad.' *Diario de Burgos*, 20 July 1958, p. 1. In the interview with B. Galm, Starkie states that Unamuno was delivering a course in Burgos in the summer of 1921 (B. Galm interview with W. Starkie, OHP, UCLA, 1970–1).   52 Starkie mentions a Galsworthy play but doesn't specify the title or where it was performed (W. Starkie, *Waveless*, p. 316).   53 W. Starkie, *Waveless*, p. 317.   54 Referring to an article in the *Irish Press* in 1936, Kevin Kearns has noted that by the decade of the 1930s 'Dublin's dilapidated tenements were deemed the "worst slums in Europe"' (K.C. Kearns, *Dublin tenement life*, p. 1).   55 Nickevo [Robert M. Smyllie], 'Irishmen of Today – 3. The Provost of Trinity College', IT, 11 Feb. 1922, p. 7.

had occupied since her marriage twenty-eight years earlier, together with her three
younger daughters: Muriel, Chou-Chou and Nancy, the youngest, then in her twelfth
year. Both 'Mrs W.J.M. Starkie' and her daughters had to become acquainted with
another woman in the household whose roots, Italian and raised in Buenos Aires, were
far removed from their own and they were obliged to share their daily life with her.
The only son and brother had acquired the responsibility of a wife, apart from the
duty already fallen to him towards his widowed mother and fatherless sisters, and he
now set to working towards an MA and PhD in order to qualify him for tenure at
TCD. Finally, Italia found herself facing a number of challenges: as the wife of a
young and struggling academic, with whom she had initially communicated in
French,[56] adjustment to the damp northern clime and learning to perform in English
as daughter-in-law, sister-in-law and (house)wife. English was a language with which
she was much less familiar than with French but she was ever eager to learn. However,
some of her fellow citizens were increasingly coming to deny and ignore the imperial
tongue, choosing rather to communicate in Irish,[57] a language which her husband's
family were not acquainted with and neither did they seek to be. On the academic
front, TCD had to refashion itself within the new order. As Nickevo further signalled:
'Trinity College has burned its boats, or, rather, they have been burned by the British
Government, and henceforward its destinies will be involved inextricably in the
fortunes of the Irish Free State'.[58] However, with Provost John Henry Bernard at the
helm, a sense of 'good omen' was expressed by the columnist together with confidence
in the former Archbishop's capacity not to alienate either of the parties involved:
'Nobody could be better fitted than he to uphold the traditions of dignity and
independence which have been handed down through generations of Trinity men.
Nobody is likely to display greater tolerance towards those from whom he differs, or
to recognise more clearly the need for a new outlook in a new time.'[59] But before the
end of the decade Bernard was dead.

Writing to Unamuno in Salamanca from 'this distracted country' during the
Christmas break of 1921, Starkie expressed his delight in having seen Spain, 'the land
of my dreams'.[60] On his return to Ireland, he wasted no time in working towards
advancing his academic career in the field of Spanish literature. By November he was
lecturing in this connection at TCD, his MA having been conferred *stipendi i conditione*
in the month of June.[61] Over December, 'Mr Walter Starkie, MA'[62] delivered three
public lectures at the Regent House, on the campus of TCD, the first of which dealt

---

56 Author's interview with Alma Starkie, 4 Nov. 2011. The daughter of Walter and Italia Starkie
remembers reading the correspondence in French between her parents, which had been preserved by
the family, though it is unclear where it is today.   57 See in this connection, albeit with particular
reference to the de Valera era, H. Hamilton, *The speckled people* (London, 2003).   58 Nickevo [Robert
M. Smyllie], 'Irishmen of Today – 3. John Henry Bernard', IT, 11 Feb. 1922, p. 8.   59 Ibid.   60 W.
Starkie to M. de Unamuno, 29 Dec. 1921, Casa-Museo Unamuno, Salamanca (henceforth CMU), CMU
46/78, 2.   61 That is, as a condition of service, meaning years of service. Starkie was appointed
Lecturer in Languages with a tenure of three years in 1920 (TCD Register, Board Meeting, 15 Oct.
1920, TCD MUN/V/5/22, p. 55). The MA was agreed by the Board in 1921 (TCD Register, Board
Meeting, 18 June 1921, TCD MUN/V/5/22, p. 141).   62 'Trinity College Lectures', IT, 28 Nov.
1921, p. 4.

with the novel in Spain, the second with poetry and the third drew on the lecturer's impressions of the country.[63] He would not deliver a public lecture on the Spanish theatre until April 1923 when he spoke of '[s]ome tendencies of modern Spanish drama' before the British Drama League in the theatre of the Royal Academy for Dramatic Art in London.[64] Indicative of the contacts that Starkie had forged at the diplomatic level by this time is the presence at the lecture of Spain's Ambassador to Great Britain, Alfonso Merry del Val[65] (brother of Cardinal Rafael Merry del Val), who presided.

When addressing Unamuno, 'Maestro' [Master],[66] at the close of 1921, Starkie referred to himself as 'a young man starting off on Life's [sic] fretful course' and remarked on his personal good fortune in having met a 'great man who [would] shine afar as a beacon for him'.[68] In the absence of the forceful father (a copy of whose last article was sent by Starkie to Unamuno),[69] the son may be seen to be casting around for an anchor and guide. Given the manner in which he addressed Unamuno, he would appear to have found the necessary inspiration in this Spanish contemporary of the former Resident Commissioner of Education, whom he interpreted as 'an expression of the Spanish *hidalguía* [chivalry] that is not ashamed of "belonging to the country which produced Tertullian and St Augustine".'[70] In mid-October, Starkie had already written to Unamuno, reporting that he was reading his books. He also informed the writer that his wife Italia had found *La tía Tula* [Aunt Tula], 'charming'[71] and expressed his personal admiration for the *Novelas ejemplares* [Exemplary novels].[72] He claimed that he had ordered the rest of the Basque author's output so as to familiarize

---

63 All three lectures were announced in the *Irish Times*, 'Trinity College Lectures', IT, 28 Nov. 1921, p. 4, and subsequently reported on in the paper on the day following each of them: 'Modern Renaissance in Spain. The Spanish Novel', IT, 2 Dec. 1921, p. 4; 'Renaissance in Spain. Modern Poetry', IT, 9 Dec. 1921, p. 4; 'Impressions of Spain. Mr. Starkie's last lecture', IT, 14 Dec. 1921, p. 3. 64 IT, 7 Apr. 1923, p. 9. 65 Alfonso Merry del Val y Zulueta (henceforth Merry del Val) was Spain's Ambassador to Great Britain from 1913 until the coming of the Second Republic in 1931. Salvador de Madariaga qualified the ambassador as 'a very stupid man' with the caveat that he was 'very much liked in Britain both because he spoke perfect English and because he was stupid, a feature the British do not dislike in a foreign Ambassador.' (S. de Madariaga, *Morning without noon. Memoirs* (Farnborough, 1974), p. 141.) See also: S. de Madariaga, 'El marques de Merry del Val (1864–1943)' in *Españoles de mi tiempo* (Barcelona, 1974), pp 37–45. 66 Starkie began his letter: 'Dear Maestro [Master]' (W. Starkie to M. de Unamuno, 29 Dec. 1921, CMU 46/78, 2). 68 Ibid. On a postcard sent to Unamuno from Madrid and signed by both Starkie and his wife, Starkie thanked Unamuno for 'the two wonderful days' spent in his company (Italia de Starkie and Walter Starkie to M. de Unamuno, 7 Sept. 1921, CMU 46/78, 4). 69 'An Aristotelian analysis of "The Comic", illustrated from Aristophanes, Rabelais, Shakespeare, and Molière', *Hermathena*, 19 (1920), 26–51. Starkie dedicated the article to 'Professor Unamuno', inscribing it with the words from Virgil's *Aeneid* (Book One, line 462), 'Sunt lacrimae rerum et mentem mortalia tangunt'. The article is signed Walter Starkie and dated 31 Jan. [*sic*] 1921. It was sent to Unamuno with a letter dated 29 Dec. 1921, as is clear from a postscript added to the letter: 'I enclose an article by my father which might interest you. It was one of the last lectures he gave' (CMU 46/78, 2). 70 W. Starkie to M. de Unamuno, 29 Dec. 1921 (CMU 46/78, 2). Starkie is quoting from Unamuno's *Del sentimiento trágico de la vida* [The tragic sense of life]. The letter is written in English. 71 W. Starkie to M. de Unamuno, 17 Oct. 1921 (CMU 46/78, 1). Starkie wrote in Spanish on a postcard which shows the Bank of Ireland in Dublin. The translation in the text above is my own. 72 Starkie was referring to Unamuno's *Tres novelas ejemplares y un prólogo* [Three exemplary novels and a prologue] (1920).

himself in depth with the magnitude of Unamuno's work and with a view to writing about it thoroughly.[73] At the end of the year, he stated that he had been 'working diligently' through Unamuno's texts and had 'studied a good number'[74] though he was having trouble obtaining some of them. He remarked that he was particularly interested in obtaining *La vida de Don Quijote y Sancho* [The life of Don Quixote and Sancho] and requested that Unamuno might send it to him, as he had offered to do so. Starkie also explained that he had devoted one of his public lectures to Unamuno and included *El* [sic] *sentimiento trágico de la vida*: 'among the works to be studied in the Spanish literature course at the University'[75] together with *La tía Tula* and several essays.

Starkie was not alone in searching for guidance at this time. The *Irish Times* registered a sense of loss and need more widely, in generational terms. In the wake of Viscount Bryce's death in January 1922, the passing of men of Bryce's ilk was lamented in the Unionist newspaper: 'One by one the great Victorians are leaving us, and how can we replace them? … the scholar-statesman is disappearing into tradition […] The new democracy brings many blessings but it does not produce men of this stamp.'[76] Therefore, as the decade began, there was a sense of personal void for Starkie given the loss of his father, of beloved peers, of the two unforgettable Shrewsbury Men, White and Southwell, as well as many Irishmen at the front, and of an affluent way of life in Victorian and Edwardian Ireland. In the wake of the premature passing of Lord Northcliffe, the Co. Dublin-born and most notorious of the brothers Harmsworth, the *Irish Times* highlighted how '[u]ntiringly and urgently he [had] preached Ireland's need of the Empire and the Empire's need of Ireland.'[77] By contrast, Italy rang of regeneration to Starkie's ears and his new wife might have been perceived as embodying her own country's rousing energy. According to her husband's account, Italia appears not to have been intimidated by the prospect of a meaner material existence in Ireland[78] or perhaps this seemed preferable to being unmarried in Italy at thirty-one. In any event, she was to prove a tower of strength in practical terms, both domestic and scholarly, as her husband blazed the academic trail in Spanish over the early 1920s. While Ireland struggled to redefine itself in two distinct entities, the young couple, possibly influenced by the political persuasion of Italia's parents, apart from any personal conviction they may have held, became fired with enthusiasm for Italy's forceful new leader, who defended a single, strong nation. They

---

73 W. Starkie to M. de Unamuno, 17 Oct. 1921 (CMU 46/78, 1). **74** W. Starkie to M. de Unamuno, 29 Dec. 1921 (CMU 46/78, 2). **75** Ibid. **76** IT, 23 Jan. 1922, p. 4. The Starkie family was familiar with Bryce's 'stamp'. He had signed in favour of WJM's application to become a member of the Athenaeum Club in London in 1902. The Resident Commisioner was proposed by the late Wilfred Ward, Esq., FSA, and seconded by the Archbishop of Dublin (The Athenaeum, Certificate of Candidate for Ballot, entered in the Candidates Book: 23 May 1902; elected: 15 May 1916). **77** 'Death of Lord Northcliffe', IT, 15 Aug. 1922, p. 4. **78** In *The waveless plain*, Starkie depicts Italia braving the prospect of poverty energetically: ' "What matter if we shall be paupers? … We are young and we both can work"' (W. Starkie, *Waveless*, p. 311). In *Scholars and Gypsies*, when taking her leave of her fiancé on his return to Ireland in the summer of 1919, Italia is represented as declaring: ' "Remember we are both young: we can live on nothing. I will give you plenty of courage"' (W. Starkie, *Scholars*, p. 317).

returned to Italy in the summer of 1922[79] and by the autumn Walter was reporting in the *Irish Times* in defence of the totalitarian politics which he would actively engage with over the 1920s and throughout the 30s.

The first of two articles, both of which were published in Saturday editions of the *Irish Times*, appeared in October and presented the observations of one who had been in Italy 'this year', seen 'a country emerging in its strength from the contest with communism and noted 'a great improvement...since the victory of the Fascisti'.[80] The united nation ('The greatness of the Fascist movement is that it is unifying the country'[81]) is projected as a hive of industry ('Work in the factories and ports throbs feverishly'), led by a man of 'acute political instinct and ...high patriotism',[82] Benito Mussolini. Voice is also given to Dr Lantini, 'the political secretary of the Fascisti of Liguria',[83] who responds to enquiry as to 'the true aims of [Fascism]', which are summed up as regeneration of the nation, the elimination of profiteers and the bringing down of prices, while also projected as '[upholding] the immortal idea of Fatherland.'[84] The second article appeared a fortnight later and expressed a degree of surprise as to how quickly events had evolved in Italy. The article is informative as regards Fascist policy in relation to land distribution, Italy's discontent following the treaties wrought at the end of the First World War and her distrust of the League of Nations. It also seeks to dispel misunderstanding 'in our countries' (presumably Northern Ireland/Britain and the Dominion) as regards the Italian Fascists who, it is (wrongly) claimed, are imagined to be 'inverted Socialists, or ...animated by a fiercer Imperialism and desire for conquest.'[85] Finally, in the context of recent events, it displays a triumphal air though ends on a note of *gravitas* together with a sense of utopian promise: 'On [Mussolini's] shoulders rests the responsibility for the movement he has led: young Italy looks to him now to open up vistas of an "Eldorado".'[86]

While coming out as a fellow traveller in the context of the October March on Rome, Starkie was also seeking to establish himself in the academic world and the early 20s reveal him going through the motions that would fit him to compete for a post: producing an MA dissertation, a PhD thesis, publishing a book, articles or a review in pertinent publications and delivering public lectures. New year greetings were sent to Unamuno in December 1922 on behalf of the young academic and his wife[87] but come

---

79 Starkie was also in Switzerland in the summer of 1922. It was agreed by the Board of TCD in May that he would represent the university at the Conference of Swiss and British Universities at Basel on 22 and 23 August 1922 (TCD MUN/V/5/22, Minutes of the Board Meeting, 11 May 1922, p. 252). In the interview with B. Galm, Starkie recorded that he had been a member of the International Centre of Fascist Studies in Lausanne since 1922–3 (B. Galm interview with W. Starkie, OHP, UCLA, 1970–1). 80 W[alter]. F[itzwilliam]. S[tarkie]., 'With the Fascisti in Italy', IT, 21 Oct. 1922, p. 9. 81 Ibid., p. 10. 82 Ibid., pp 9, 10. 83 Ferruccio Lantini was listed by university lecturer, journalist and literary critic Camillo Pellizzi as among those 'strong-willed, eager men, men of the people chosen from among our very best youth in the name of national necessity' (C. Pellizzi, 'Fascism's problems and realities' (1924), trans. Maria G. Stampino and Jeffrey T. Schnapp in J.T. Schnapp (ed.), *A primer of Italian fascism* (Lincoln, 2000), p. 100). 84 Ibid., p. 10. 85 W[alter]. F[itzwilliam]. S[tarkie]., 'The New Italy', IT, 4 Nov. 1922, p. 10. 86 Ibid. 87 The greeting is written in Spanish in Italia's hand on the visiting card of Mr and Mrs Walter Starkie who: 'greet the master, wishing him a thousand occasions of

1923, Starkie, now lecturer in Spanish as well as French language and literature at TCD, turned to producing a book on Jacinto Benavente. In January, he addressed Macmillan, mentioning his awareness that the publisher had produced works by his father on Aristophanes and explaining that he was writing a book on the Spanish playwright, 'winner of the Nobel Prize for 1922'.[88] He also stated that the text was destined to become his PhD thesis: 'I intend to present it for the degree of Litt.D. in Dublin University.'[89] The awarding of the Nobel Prize for Literature to the Spanish playwright determined the course of Starkie's critical energies in relation to Spanish literature over 1923, both before General Miguel Primo de Rivera's *coup* in September, following it, and into 1924, arguably encouraged by the Spanish Ambassador Merry del Val, to whom the Oxford University Press publication, *Jacinto Benavente*, was dedicated. In January 1923, articles on Benavente by Starkie appeared in the *Times Literary Supplement* and in the *Contemporary Review*.[90] In December Starkie lectured before the recently founded Anglo-Spanish Society in London.[92] The Marquis Merry del Val again presided.

In the presentation speech delivered by Per Hallström, Chairman of the Nobel Committee, at the Nobel Award Ceremony in December 1922, the 'most distinctive quality' of Benavente's writing was summed up as 'grace', assessed as 'such a rare value, especially in our own times'.[93] The Chairman described the Spanish author's plays as thoroughly Establishment: 'middle-class', 'mainly' dealing with 'the life of the upper classes', 'not [seeking] to harrow the spectator', and he identified Benavente's purpose as 'a solution of conflicts that is harmonious even in melancholy and sorrow' a 'harmony ... usually gained by resignation'.[94] Hallström also affirmed that in the last instance Benavente upholds 'the spiritual value' and towards the end of his speech the Chairman enlarged upon the quality of grace (highlighted as he began speaking) as the outstanding quality in the Spaniard's writing, relating it to the classics. Thus, Benavente's work as assessed by Hallström in its formal grace, bowing to the classics, representation of the bourgeoisie and void of any challenge to the middle-class spectator, in the absence of conflict, upholding of spiritual values and comfort through resignation would make Benavente (already a supporter of the Spanish conservative politician Antonio Maura earlier on in the century)[95] sympathetic to both his middle-class audience (potentially on edge in the wake of revolution in Russia) and to the Primo de Rivera dictatorship.[96] Whether led away from his enthusiasm for Unamuno towards Benavente by the Spanish Ambassador Merry del Val, or not, the

happiness in the new year' (Mr and Mrs W. Starkie to M. de Unamuno, Dec. 1922, CMU 46/78, 3). My translation.   88 W. Starkie to 'Dear Sir', Macmillan and Co. Ltd, 4 Jan. 1922 [*sic*] (University of Reading Archive, Records of Macmillan & Co. Ltd, MAC STA). In the letter Starkie refers to having produced an article on Benavente for 'this month's *Contemporary Review*.' The article appeared in January 1923 – see details in note 90, below.   89 Ibid.   90 W. Starkie, 'Jacinto Benavente and the Modern Spanish Drama', *TLS*, 11 Jan. 1923, p. 27; 'Jacinto Benvente, Winner of the Nobel Prize', *Contemporary Review*, 123 (January–June), 1923, 93–100.   92 The Anglo-Spanish Society was founded by Spain's Ambassador to Great Britain, the Marquis Merry del Val.   93 http://nobelprize.org/ nobel_prizes/literature/laureates/1922/press.html, accessed 12 June 2010.   94 Ibid.   95 R. Villares & J. Moreno Luzón, *Restauración y dictadura* (Barcelona, 2009), p. 429.   96 Primo de Rivera counted on Benavente's support when contemplating setting up a newspaper which would be a mouthpiece of

values contained in Benavente's writing could have also held an appeal for Starkie. Certainly his 1924 book on Benavente displays an essentialist and hackneyed view of Spain, one which resists change, insistently foregrounding tradition. The following provides illustration:

> The Spaniard worships life with passion and death with passion, and his soul has not changed since the days when the Knight of the Sorrowful Countenance [Don Quixote] rode out to vanquish chivalry, only to raise up a nobler ideal. [...] All Spanish writers who start their careers by trying to be European, inevitably, sooner or later, return to the national tradition. [...] The traditional Spanish nature can never be driven out even with a fork [*sic*]. [...] In examining Benavente's crowded stage we shall see pass before our eyes all the types of modern life, and we shall watch the struggle between the new growth of modern twentieth-century civilization superimposed on top of [*sic*] a deep layer of old traditions that have never died out and that give a characteristic flavour to the Spanish character.[97]

Apart from devoting himself to familiarizing the British with Benavente, Starkie sought to improve his professional profile on home ground by applying for membership of the Royal Irish Academy. His application was submitted in January 1923 and supported by a number of distinguished scholars, ranging from the protestant clergy, thus the Reverend H.J. Lawlor and the Most Reverend and Right Honourable J.H. Bernard, Provost of TCD, E.J. Gwynn, a future Provost of TCD, and the naturalist and historian R. Lloyd Praeger.[98] His presence would also begin to be noted outside strictly academic circles through his involvement with George Russell (Æ)'s new initiative, the second edition of the *Irish Statesman*,[99] the weekly journal which set out to address 'all living in Ireland, north and south, as one people.'[1] As Nicholas Allen has remarked, the journal was unique in Ireland, both when it began publication in September 1923 and throughout its almost seven full years of existence, in that it brought together political commentary and cultural analysis. Starkie's contributions began in 1924 and were primarily cultural: music, drama and book reviews.[2]

---

the new regime (C. Seco Serrano & J. Tusell, *La España de Alfonso XIII: el estado y la política (1902–31). Historia de España Menéndez Pidal, 38,* 2 vols (Madrid, 1995), ii, p. 218). **97** W. Starkie, *Jacinto Benavente* (Oxford, 1924), pp 9, 16, 20, 21. In connection with the use of English in this passage, see later comment in this chapter in relation to Starkie's *Pirandello* (1926). **98** Apart from those mentioned above, Starkie's application was also signed by O.J. Bergin, R.I. Best, R.A.S. Macalister and T.F. O'Rahilly. He was elected on 16 Mar. 1923 (Royal Irish Academy, henceforth RIA, Certificate of Candidate, Members' Certificates file, 1920 – , Mc – Z). **99** For details with regard to the first edition of the journal, see N. Allen, *George Russell (Æ) and the new Ireland, 1905–30* (Dublin, 2003), p. 139. **1** G. Russell, 'A confession of faith', IS, 15 Sept. 1923, p. 3. Cited in N. Allen, *George Russell*, p. 144. **2** According to Allen, Starkie interviewed Mussolini for the journal. He also claims that it was Starkie's wife, 'an Italian fascist herself, who helped organize it.' (N. Allen, *George Russell*, p. 176.) No interview by Starkie was published in the journal but an account of an interview Starkie held with Mussolini was supplied over ten years on in *The waveless plain*, where it is stated that the interview in question was arranged '[t]hrough the kindness of the Marchese della Torretta, Italian Ambassador in London' (W. Starkie, *Waveless*, pp 387–402). Francis Hackett produced a text in the *Irish Statesman*, published over

The year 1923 was eventful both at home and abroad. Walter and Italia's first child, a son, named Landi after his maternal grandfather, was born in Italy in the month of July.[3] In September General Miguel Primo de Rivera carried out a coup in Spain that would lead to a period of dictatorship, with the King's consent, which lasted up until the end of the decade, some seven years over which Starkie repeatedly visited the country and where he would be distinguished with the '*Orden Civil de Alfonso XII*' [Civil Order of King Alfonso XII]. It was in 1923, too, that the '*Comité Hispano-Inglés*' [The Hispano-English Committee] was set up by the Duke of Alba and Britain's then Ambassador to Spain, Sir Esme Howard, with a view to organizing lectures for a select audience in Madrid.[4] Indeed, the following three years were to prove particularly intense as Starkie consolidated his position at TCD and became increasingly visible within Dublin society and abroad. He delivered public lectures, steadily attended concerts produced under the auspices of the Royal Dublin Society in Ballsbridge as well as going to those organized by other bodies and at different Dublin venues. He was in the audience for performances at the Abbey[5] and other Dublin theatres, participated in activities related to the Cumann na nGaedheal government in power, authored the book on the Spanish playwright Benavente, another on the Italian Pirandello, and forged contacts in the cultural and political realm in Spain and Italy.

Starkie contributed over a hundred pieces to Russell's *Irish Statesman* between May 1924 and the last issue, which appeared in April 1930.[6] The sum total of his contributions in 1924 was only five, perhaps because of other commitments,[7] but they would grow as the 20s advanced: eleven in 1925; nineteen in 1926; thirty-one in 1927, thirty-seven in 1928, though 1929 signals a drop with only eight, falling to two in 1930 when the journal folded. The majority of Starkie's contributions are concerned with music though there are some theatre and book reviews or articles, not infrequently relating to Spain. His first piece, in the month of May, was a review of Sacheverell Sitwell's *Southern Baroque art*, which focuses on the art of Spain and Italy as well as turning to

---

two weeks, based on an interview he had been granted with Mussolini ('Mussolini, Red and Black', IS, 12 Mar. 1927, 7–8; 'Mussolini, Red and Black (cont.)', IS, 19 Mar. 1927, 31–2).   **3** The dates of the birth and death of 'Landi William Starkie' on his gravestone at the British Cemetery in Madrid are: 10 July 1923–10 Sept. 1982. He was registered at Ampleforth Abbey in York as Landi Humphrey Starkie, i.e., his middle name evoking not Walter Starkie's father, William J.M. Starkie, but his parents' last-born, who died shortly after birth (see Chapter 3, above) (Ampleforth Abbey Archive).   **4** For further information on the setting up of the *Comité* and the lectures delivered over the 1920s, see A. Sinclair, ' "Telling it like it was"? The "Residencia de Estudiantes" and its image', *Bulletin of Spanish Studies*, 81:6 (2004), 739–63 and Á. Ribagorda, 'El Comité Hispano-Inglés y la Sociedad de Cursos y Conferencias de la Residencia de Estudiantes', *Cuadernos de Historia Contemporánea*, 30 (2008), 273–91.   **5** R. Hogan & M.J. O'Neill (eds), *Joseph Holloway's Irish theatre*, 3 vols (Dixon, CA, 1968), i, p. 39, passim.   **6** See Appendix.   **7** 'In 1924 [Starkie] contributed the majority of entries on Irish subjects to Dent's [*A*] [D]*ictionary of* [*modern*] *music and musicians*, including those relating to Stanley Cochrane, James Culwick, Esposito, H. Plunket Greene, Harty, Larchet, Levey, John McCormack, Edward Martyn, Joseph O'Mara, Annie Patterson, Joseph Robinson, Ethel Sharpe and Sir Robert Stewart' (R. Pine & C. Acton, *To talent*, p. 296). Starkie figures (as Professor William [*sic*] Starkie), together with Mr Hamilton Harty and Dr J.F. Larchet, as a sub-editor for the *Dictionary*. The three sub-editors constituted the National Committee for Ireland.

Mexico. All told, the assessment is positive and this tends to be the tenor of Starkie's reviewing. The Sitwell review also carries trite turns of phrase that come to be customary in Starkie's writing, thus: 'these days of steel and stress', and the concept of the mask will be worked in, introduced here in a statement smacking of the purple prose which comes to litter his writing on occasion: 'From Naples we dash to the Escurial [*sic*] of Philip [II] and thence to Mexico in dazzling inconsistency, but we are never allowed to wear the mask of boredom'.[8] Starkie's further contributions to the *Irish Statesman* in 1924 did not appear until October and November, but from early on in the year he had been busy pronouncing and publishing, particularly on matters Italian, though he also produced an article for the *Contemporary Review* on the work of the contemporary Spanish playwright Gregorio Martínez Sierra.[9] Sporting his MA, he read a paper to the Royal Irish Academy in February, devoted to the *commedia dell' arte*, and as the year advanced he was intent on publishing a book on modern Italian drama. He wrote to G.A. Whitworth at Chatto and Windus in late August, anxious to know 'definitely before the autumn'[10] whether the manuscript he had deposited with him would be accepted for publication. Whitworth replied within a fortnight, flattering the author that his 'Three Dramatists of Modern Italy' was 'clearly a most interesting and ex[h]austive study of the subject', but arguing that publication was not possible since 'the public for a book on Italian dramatists is not sufficiently large to warrant us embarking on the venture.'[11] Whitworth's reader's report recognized that while Starkie was 'soaked in his subject', he was not 'a very original or illuminating writer', further claiming: 'One has an uneasy feeling that all the best critical remarks … are quotations from other people'.[12] The report concluded: 'it is necessary to state that the book [*sic*] itself is not in any sense inspired'.[13] A book carrying the title of the manuscript given over to Whitworth at Chatto & Windus was never published but Starkie managed some mileage from the text through other publications in that same year: an article on 'Il Teatro Grotesco' in the *Dublin Magazine*[14] and another on 'Luigi Chiarelli' in the *Irish Statesman*.[15] Two years on, he would publish his book-length study devoted to Luigi Pirandello, which alludes to the work of Grotesque playwrights Enrico Annibale Butti and Roberto Bracco.[16]

At a TCD Board Meeting on 16 June 1924, 'Walter Fitzwilliam Starkie, MA' was elected to Fellowship, being admitted by the Provost, J.H. Bernard, the following day.[17]

8 W. Starkie, '*Southern Baroque Art*. By Sacheverell Sitwell (Grant Richards. London. 20/-)', IS, 10 May 1924, 274/276 at 274.   **9** See bibliography. Martínez Sierra's *The two shepherds* was performed at the Abbey Theatre in the month of August (IT, 26 Aug. 1924, p. 3).   **10** W. Starkie to G.A. Whitworth, 27 Aug. 1924, University of Reading Archive, Chatto & Windus Ltd Archive, Chatto & Windus letters file, 1915–25: So–Sy, CW 20/5.   **11** G.A. Whitworth to W. Starkie, 9 Sept. 1924 (University of Reading Archive, Chatto and Windus letterbook CW A/109, p. 84).   **12** Report on '"Three Dramatists of Modern Italy: Butti, Bracco, Pirandello." By Walter Starkie, Fellow of Trinity College Dublin' (University of Reading Archive, Chatto & Windus Papers, Reader Report 829).   **13** Ibid.   **14** See Bibliography (Articles).   **15** See Appendix.   **16** For comment on Italian Grotesque theatre and, more particularly, Chiarelli, see M. Vena, 'Introduction: Twentieth Century Italian Grotesque Theater' in *Italian grotesque theatre* (Madison, 2001), pp 11–21.   **17** TCD MUN/V/5/23, p. 92. Starkie's election was reported in the *Irish Times*, 17 June 1924, pp 7–8; see also p. 9, and the *Irish Times*, 18 June 1924, p. 7. The Fellowship was in Modern Languages (R.B. MacDowell & D.A. Webb, *Trinity College Dublin*, p.

The lecture on the *commedia dell'arte* read to the Royal Irish Academy in February had been published in the Academy *Proceedings* in April[18] and at some time following the publication of the paper, Starkie sent a copy to his father's contemporary, the *Times* drama critic A[rthur]. B[ingham]. Walkley, 'once a Government official in Dublin'.[19] In the *Times* of 17 September, under a column headed 'Entertainments', 'A.B.W.' extolled TCD, presenting it as an oasis of calm through the ages and playing down the consequence of recent social and political upheaval in the country:

> Whenever I read the daily budget of news from Dublin, with its distracting alarums [*sic*] and excursions, I like to think of Trinity College. It has stood firm and serene through centuries of violent ups and downs in Irish history, and there it stands still. Perhaps at a distance (whether of space or time) we are apt to exaggerate the extent of political and social upheavals, and forget that they leave the fundamental elements of human life unaffected. [...] We hear of angry disputes in the Dail [*sic*] and of exciting affrays around Mountjoy Prison, but Trinity College presents a little nook of 'still life' among all the 'battle pieces.' The Sacred Lamp still burns brightly there, and learning and literature placidly pursue their steady course, unharmed.[20]

Walkley made sardonic reference to current political divisions in the Irish Free State (to the advantage of Cumann na nGaedheal), going on to portray academic work being carried out at TCD *au-dessus de la mêlée*, thus further substantiating an ivory tower representation of the academic institution and, more particularly, of the research pursuit of 'Mr Walter Starkie, FCTD': 'Ireland, after all, is something besides a cockpit of rival politicians and a carnival of "gunmen." While Mr Cosgrave is keeping order in the Dail [*sic*] and Mr. De Valera is issuing more and more manifestoes, scholars at Trinity College are unconcernedly investigating the history of the *Commedia dell'Arte*.'[21] In an editorial piece two days later, the *Irish Times* informed on the piece produced by 'A.B.W.', expressing approval of Walkley's assessment of TCD's resistance: 'The tribute is well deserved. Trinity College has "carried on" in the same high and calm temper from the days when James II sacked its plate until now. It held a term examination when British troops were camping in the quadrangle in Easter Week of 1916.' Nonetheless, the article in the *Irish Times* also took advantage of Walkley's idealized memory of TCD to challenge it, highlighting 'anxieties'[22] besetting the institution in the wake of partition.

Starkie's name would again surface in the *Irish Statesman* in October. He contributed an article on Luigi Chiarelli at the beginning of the month, following *The*

---

436). **18** W. Starkie (1924). See Bibliography (Articles). **19** '"A.B.W." and T.C.D.', IT, 19 Sept. 1924, p.4. The connection of A[rthur]. B[ingham]. Walkley (1855–1926) with TCD was of long standing. He had been programmed to give a session on 'The First Principles of the Theatre' on 15 December 1908 in a lecture series organized at TCD over the 1908–09 academic year following correspondence between Cecil Harmsworth and Provost Anthony Traill (C. Harmsworth to Anthony Traill, 12 Feb. 1908; a typed and handwritten sheet headed 'Lecturers in Journalism' (Daniel Harmsworth)). **20** A[rthur]. B[ingham]. W[alkley]., 'The Commedia dell'Arte. Trin. Coll. Dub. Prepared Impromptus.' TT, 17 Sept. 1924, p. 8. **21** Ibid. **22** '"A.B.W." and TCD', IT, 19 Sept. 1924, p. 4.

mask and the face [*La maschera e il volto*] having been performed at the Gaiety Theatre in Dublin.[23] Some of the material contained in the article, with slight modifications, would be recycled for Starkie's book on Pirandello two years later. On the whole, the changes introduced into the 1926 book are minor and relate to the use of English rather than matters of content but in spite of some of the awkward stylistic features being rectified in the later text, the book provides a number of instances of an English which is not that of a native speaker of the language. In their history of TCD, McDowell and Webb state that it was rumoured that Starkie's wife, Italia, had intervened in some of his popular travel writing in the 30s.[24] Arguably, her hand might already be located in his writing of a more serious or academic nature in the 1920s, particularly, though not exclusively, that which dealt with Italy.[25]

The Minutes of the TCD Board Meeting of late October 1924 record that Starkie had written explaining that he had received an invitation to lecture in Madrid 'under the auspices of the Anglo-Spanish Association [*sic*].' In his letter, Starkie further expressed his desire to stay on in Spain 'a sufficient time to carry out research in the writings of [Pedro] Alarcón and Ramón de la Cruz' of whose works he hoped to publish editions.[26] He also requested 'some financial aid'[27] to enable him to prolong his stay and was granted £75 from the Madden Fund.[28] When the Board met on 10 December, Starkie must have already left for Spain since, having approved the favourable report of 'The Examiners',[29] his Litt.D degree was awarded 'stip cond', that is, as was the case with his MA, as a condition of service, and, on this occasion, 'in absentiâ'.[30] According to correspondence from Ambassador Merry del Val in London to the Duke of Alba in Madrid, Starkie himself had approached the Ambassador, suggesting that he would be disposed to delivering a variety of lectures in Madrid:

> I could give lectures in English or in Spanish on the various dramatic movements since Shakespeare. I have made a special study of the modern dramatic tendencies in England considered from a European point of view and have drawn parallels with Spanish, Italian and French literature. With regard to Shakespeare I have special lectures arranged also.[31]

The Ambassador recommended Starkie to the Duke, arguing that he knew him well and describing him as knowledgeable, exceptionally pleasant, of moderate, calm ideas,

---

23 The play had been performed in London in May (IT, 29 May 1924, p. 5). 24 '[T]he supposed amatory adventures retailed by Walter Starkie ('Don Gualtero') in his books (some of them rumoured to have been inserted by his wife to liven up the narrative' (R.B. McDowell & D.A. Webb, *Trinity College Dublin*, p. 431). 25 See also the following chapter for further reference to Italia's possible intervention in articles relating to fascism, signed by Starkie and published in the *Irish Independent* in 1938. 26 The editions in question did not come to fruition. 27 TCD MUN/V/5/23, Board Meeting: 24 Oct. 1924, p. 112. 28 Thomas Rudmose-Brown, Professor of Romance Languages from 1909 (K.C. Bailey, *A history*, p. 200), had been less fortunate in his application earlier in the year for a grant to enable him to spend a month in Italy to improve his knowledge of Italian (TCD MUN/V/5/23, Board Meeting, 23 Feb. 1924, p. 60). 29 The Minutes do not specify the identity of the examiners. 30 TCD MUN/V/5/23, Board Meeting, 10 Dec. 1924, p. 130. 31 Cited in A. Merry del Val to the Duke of Alba, 13 Feb. 1924 (Archivo Duques de Alba, Madrid: Fondo Don Jacobo, henceforth ADDA, FDJ).

very familiar with the literature of England as well as with Spain's. The Ambassador also added that the willing lecturer commanded Spanish, a fact that he could bear witness to as he had heard him deliver lectures in the language.[32] Starkie further specified in his letter to the Ambassador that he would be free to go to Spain between 14 June and 10 October. In the event his two lectures, which were announced as dealing with English Contemporary Theatre, were delivered just before Christmas: on 22 and 23 December.[33] Under the heading 'Characteristics of the English Theatre', the first lecture dealt with 'Realistic drama'. The card announcing the lecture[34] indicated that the lecturer would refer to the work of seven playwrights: T.W. Robertson, H.A. Jones, Wilde, Pinero, St John Hankin, Galsworthy and J.M. Barrie. The publication reveals that Starkie may have referred to a number of others, and not only English: the range is wide, going back to Greek and Roman comedy and forward to the contemporary Spanish theatre of Benavente and Martínez Sierra. In terms of content, however, the lecture is limited to cursory comment rather than analysis of any substance. The second lecture was announced as dealing with nine playwrights: first of all Bernard Shaw and Granville Barker, with reference to the influence of Ibsen; authors classified under 'Irish Renaissance': W.B. Yeats, J.M. Synge, Edward Martyn, Lady Gregory, Lennox Robinson and, finally, two authors placed under the heading 'English poetic theatre': John Drinkwater and James Elroy Flecker. These two, together with Gordon Bottomby, are merely mentioned towards the end of the lecture, which focussed essentially on the Irish playwrights in English, as Alison Sinclair has remarked.[35] Sinclair is struck that lectures dwelling, apparently, from the title, on contemporary English theatre should have spent a considerable amount of time and space on the Irish. However, it may be argued that this was precisely the point, that is, to draw Irish drama in English into the English fold. In this connection, it is perhaps significant that Yeats and Lady Gregory's nationalistic *Cathleen Ni Houlihan* is not referred to. Further to the matter of English or Irish identity, it is also pertinent to note that at the beginning of his first lecture Starkie identifies himself as coming from Ireland, but not that he is Irish.[36]

Italia may have travelled to Italy for Christmas 1924 to be with her father, widowed since January,[37] and her unmarried sister [Valen]Tina. If she remained in Ireland, her husband wasn't with her. Starkie appears to have stayed on in Spain into the new year. He wrote to the Duke of Alba from the *Residencia de Estudiantes* in Madrid on 2 January 1925, thanking him for his 'generous gift of the collections of reproductions of the treasures of art in the Palacio de Liria' and referring to 'that night', when he was able to contemplate such 'glories'. He also expressed his gratitude to the Duke for

32 A. Merry del Val to the Duke of Alba, 13 Feb. 1924 ((ADDA, FDJ). 33 The lectures were published in the first issue of *Residencia*, the journal of the *Residencia de Estudiantes*, in 1926. See Bibliography, p. 320. 34 ADDA, FDJ. 35 A. Sinclair, '"Telling it like it was?"', p. 756. 36 Starkie read his lectures in Spanish. The published version reads: 'Irlanda – de donde procedo – ...' [Ireland – where I come from/where I hail from]. My translation. (W. Starkie, 'El teatro ingles contemporáneo' [The contemporary English theatre], *Residencia*, 1:1 (enero-abril 1926), 42–53 at 42). 37 Starkie provides an account of his mother-in-law's passing in Chapter 25 of *The waveless plain* (W. Starkie, *Waveless*, pp 347–53.

the kindness shown him, further claiming that his visit had 'opened [his] eyes to all kind [*sic*] of impressions' and assuring the Spanish aristocrat: 'I shall return to England [*sic*] immensely richer in every way.' Finally, he enquired when he might visit the Duke so that he could give him a copy of his book on Benavente and obtain his 'autograph'[38] in the book he had received from him as a gift.

In its 'zealous pages'[39] of January 1925, the *Catholic Bulletin* pronounced that as a TCD lecturer, Starkie was far from being a valid representative of the Irish nation abroad: 'A Madrid audience will hear little indeed about [the] real Ireland and its true people from any of the "rats" that betake themselves to the Elizabethan Academy.' The conviction was further expressed that no-one educated 'first at a day school under Protestant control in Dublin, and then at a thoroughly Protestant boarding school in England' could provide a portrait of 'the real Irish nation':[40]

> Mr Starkie lectured for the hyphenated [Anglo-Spanish] Imperialists ... and was, of course, well reported by cablegram in the London *Times*. We need hardly say that the Irish Literary Movement means to Mr Starkie what it means to TCD, to Plunkett House, and to the *Irish Statesman*: Irish Literature means Pollexfen Yeats, Shaw, George Moore, Lennox Robinson, Stephens, and the rest of the Associated Aesthetes, the Mutual Boosters, ...[41]

However, in contrast to the rabid response registered in the *Catholic Bulletin*, Starkie's fortunes now began to flourish in the Spanish cultural realm. In early January 1925, José Manuel Rodríguez Carracido, a member of the Spanish Royal Academy [Real Academia Española], addressed the Duke of Alba, informing him that on the previous day the name of Walter Fitzwilliam Starkie had been proposed as a Corresponding Member of the Academy by the linguist Ramón Menéndez Pidal, the Secretary Emilio Cotarelo y Mori and himself.[42] By the end of the month, the candidate had been nominated. The news reached TCD in February and was reported in the *Irish Times*, which also vindicated Starkie's performance at the *Residencia de Estudiantes*: 'His recent lectures in Madrid are said to have made a deep impression upon the Academicians.'[43] Both the *Irish Times* and the *Irish Independent*[44] carried favourable reviews of Starkie's book on Benavente in the same month, the former noting that the study of the Spanish playwright's works had been published at 'an opportune moment' since 'Dublin playgoers have had their interest stimulated by the recent

38 W. Starkie to the Duke of Alba, 2 Jan. 1924 [*sic*], ADDA, FDJ.   39 T. Brown, *Ireland. A social and cultural history* (London, 2004), p. 52.   40 *Catholic Bulletin and Book Review*, 15:1, Jan. 1925, pp 16, 15. 41 Ibid., p. 15.   42 J.M. [Rodríguez] Carracido to the Duke of Alba, 4 Jan. 1925, ADDA, FDJ. According to the 'Libro de Actas' [Book of Proceedings] at the *Real Academia Española* [Spanish Royal Academy], Starkie's name was put forward on 3 January 1925 by R. Menéndez Pidal, J.M. Rodríguez Carracido and Gabriel Maura. At a meeting of the Board on 29 January 1925, Starkie was nominated 'Miembro Correspondiente Extranjero en Irlanda por unanimidad' [Unanimously nominated Corresponding Member for Ireland] (Archivo de la Real Academia Española, Expediente 60/21; Libro de Actas no. 43, p. 327).   43 'Trinity College Dublin.' IT, 17 Feb. 1925, p. 6.   44 'Jacinto Benavente', IT, 6 Feb. 1925, p. 3; G. O'B., 'A notable Spanish writer', II, 9 Feb. 1925, p. 5.

production of "The School of Princesses" by the Drama League, "The Passion Flower", "No Smoking" and "His Widow's Husband".'[45]

Starkie's contributions to the *Irish Statesman* doubled in 1925 though the greater number appeared in August, October and November, nine of the eleven articles being concert reviews. In late April, Starkie read a second paper at the Royal Irish Academy on the *commedia dell'arte*, tracing the form through the seventeenth and eighteenth centuries before going on to consider Goldoni's contribution.[46] He next appeared in print in late May: a report from Madrid on the contemporary Spanish theatre, which familiarized readers of the *Irish Statesman* with a number of theatres in the Spanish capital as well as mentioning the Nobel winner Benavente together with his contemporary Manuel Linares Rivas; a significant amount of space was also devoted to the dramatist and theatre impresario Gregorio Martínez Sierra.[47] In the meantime, Italia appears not to have been locked into domesticity. She obtained some publicity for Italy by means of a photograph in the *Irish Independent* in late April showing 'Mrs Walter Starkie' in the costume of a traditional Italian dancer, complete with tambourine, alongside Mr Arthur Duff, 'of the Army School of Music', dressed as 'a Fascist'.[48] The caption explained that she would be wearing the national costume of her country at the Nine Arts Ball on the following night.

Three of Starkie's 1925 contributions to the *Irish Statesman* are book reviews, published in the 'Literature and Life' section of the journal. Two relate to publications produced by Oxford University Press that year, one focussed on Spain: Aubrey Bell's book on the Spanish monk *Fray Luis de León (a study of the Spanish Renaissance)* and one on Italy: A.G. Whyte's text on the Italian statesman Count Cavour, *The early life and letters of Cavour, 1810–1848*. The remaining review, entitled 'Wagner's message to-day', dealt with G. Ainslie Hight's critical biography of Wagner, published by Arrowsmith. Starkie is complementary with regard to Bell's publication, judging it to be 'extremely interesting';[49] Hight is recognized as 'a critic of long standing in the Wagnerian world'[50] and Whyte's merit lies in being the first to reveal Cavour's 'personal character … to English readers',[51] but space is also taken advantage of in the three reviews to make particular points of pertinence to contemporary Ireland. The piece on Bell's *Fray Luis de León* is prefaced by a sub-title, under 'Spain and the Renaissance', that is, 'Universities and the nation', which is followed by a quote from Wordsworth referring to 'that glorious time' when learning possessed a unifying thrust, appealing across the boundary of class to both peasant and king. Starkie is

45 'Jacinto Benavente', IT, 6 Feb. 1925, p. 6.   **46** W. Starkie (1925) – see Bibliography (Articles). The paper 'Carlo Goldoni and the *Commedia dell'Arte*' was read on 27 April 1925 and published in the *Proceedings of the Royal Irish Academy* some four months later, on 24 August.   **47** W. Starkie, 'The present condition of the Spanish theatre' (1925) (see Appendix).   **48** 'Dublin's Art Ball', II, 30 Apr. 1925, p. 3. Duff was a graduate of TCD in music and became 'the first Irish-born bandmaster to hold commissioned rank in the Irish Free State Army' (*www.arthurduff.com*, accessed 30 Sept. 2010).   **49** W. Starkie, 'Universities and the nation' (1925), p. 691 (see Appendix).   **50** 'Wagner's message today', p. 787 (see Appendix).   **51** W. Starkie, 'The early life and letters of Cavour' (1925), p. 240 (see Appendix).

interested in pondering the place of the University in the new Ireland: 'Nowadays in our own island, with its new laws, its budding institutions, people are seeking to mobilise all the forces of the country, whether material or intellectual.' Thus, he argues that it is interesting to look back at 'the enormous part played by the University in the national life of Spain'. In his final paragraph, he will mention Fray Luis and the famous anecdote that quotes him as declaring: 'As we were saying yesterday' when he embarked on his classes following five years' imprisonment by the Inquisition. The reviewer will conclude by referring to the monk's 'good sense and knowledge of his nation's needs'.[52] Therefore, it may be argued that Starkie is seeking to convey that Fray Luis's cool judgment and sense of continuity signal a lesson for the university in contemporary Ireland, making a point akin to A.B. Walkley's perception of academic activity at TCD in 1924, following receipt of Starkie's article on the *commedia dell'arte*, that is, the value of remaining steady, unruffled, focussed on the task in hand, in spite of the surrounding storm.

In the review of Whyte's biography of Wagner, Starkie refers to Nietzsche's *The case of Wagner*, producing two quotes from the text, the second of which (like the first) is not commented on but which acquires particular significance in the context of political developments in the inter-war period and Starkie's own, apparently growing, enthusiasm for (dictatorial) performance. Hence, Nietzsche, as cited by Starkie: 'Victor Hugo and Richard Wagner both prove one and the same thing that in declining civilizations, wherever the mob is allowed to decide, genuineness becomes superfluous, prejudicial, unfavourable. The actor alone can still kindle enthusiasm. And thus it is his golden age which is now dawning.'[53] Finally, in the Cavour review, reference will be made to 'a long essay on Ireland' which the Italian statesman produced between 1842 and 1843. Starkie informs: 'The first half of the essay is a historical sketch of England's government of Ireland; the second part studies the question of a separate government for Ireland, which [Daniel] O'Connell was then claiming. He examines the taxation, commerce, industry, emigration, and gives his opinion that Ireland is better off under the Union.' The reviewer observes that Whyte has 'some interesting remarks' in relation to the pamphlet, among them the observation that Cavour 'looked at the Irish question from a purely economic point of view, and attached no weight to the claims of national sentiment.' However, Whyte's recognition of 'the lovable and human side that Cavour undoubtedly possessed', further supported by 'the sympathetic description given by Panzini in his short history of Italy, *La vera istoria dei tre colori* [The true story of the three colours], published a few months ago'[54] would seem to tip the balance in favour of Cavour and, ultimately, on the side of Unionism.

Among the remaining contributions, there is encouragement for young performers and recognition for violinist Jascha Heifetz's 'peerless technique'[55] together with comment on recitals by John McCormack at the Theatre Royal in the month of

---

52 W. Starkie, 'Universities and the nation' (1925), pp 690, 691 (see Appendix).   53 W. Starkie, 'Wagner's message today' (1925), p. 788 (see Appendix).   54 W. Starkie, 'The early life and letters of Cavour' (1925), pp 241–2 (see Appendix).   55 W. Starkie, 'Jascha Heifetz' (1925), p. 306 (see Appendix).

August, a singer who, as Starkie claimed in his first review of a McCormack performance, had become 'a musical symbol in the world of the Irish spirit'.[56] In spite of the *Irish Statesman* reflecting a rise in the number of reviews supplied by Starkie in 1925, he appears to have spent some three to four months away from Dublin. In his article from Madrid in May on contemporary Spanish theatre, he refers to having spent two months in the Spanish capital, a period that may go back to December 1924 when he lectured and, conceivably, one which stretched into February, or it may refer to late December into late January together with the month of May. Certainly, his first *Irish Statesman* contribution of the year, as noted above, was not published until late March. There were no contributions to the journal in June, nor were there any in July, September or December. In September, Starkie was in Venice from where he reported for the *Irish Independent* on the music festival of the International Society for Contemporary Music. Starkie's article reveals elements that become characteristic of his journalism and travel writing in the 1930s: a populist strain and resistance to modernity. The opening paragraphs of the article focus on the recreational aspects of the week: not rising early, the celebrities spending late mornings at the Restaurant Florian, 'sipping their Vermouth', people meeting for tea in the afternoon and 'at night for coffee, when the band plays in the piazza', before singling out three composers with whom 'the musical [*sic*] critic', as Starkie styles himself here, held 'conversations': Arnold Schönberg, Gian Francesco Malipiero and Igor Stravinsky. Starkie expresses defeat before Schönberg's 'Serenata Opus 24', declaring: 'after looking through the score before the night's performance, it was impossible to grasp the significance of such a work. It is all so weird, apparently so disconnected, as if it were a book wherein the full stops and punctuations [*sic*] had been omitted.' This latter observation will lead him to compare the musical score to Joyce's ground-breaking literary text, published in Paris three years earlier. He then attempts to explain what is heard in the movement of Schönberg's 'Serenata' entitled 'scena di danza', going on to construct a sequence intended to be evocative of the linguistic disruption found in *Ulysses*:

> At first there is just the beginning of waltz rhythm, suddenly dissolved by shrill harmonies and whistles on the clarionet – the mandoline twangs petulantly, the guitar strums monotonously, the violin plays spicatto a jerky little bit of phrase which is broken off by the entrance of the gruff bass clarionet. We could imagine it in language thus: 'Jazz dance nigger minstrels frilly petticoats red lips Guinness corks popping railway engine 11.30p.m. train Killiney-Westland Row Bay of Naples mandoline serenade headache Eno's nightmare.'

Starkie also records the impact on the singer, whose voice, he claims, was drowned by the strident sound: 'Josef Schwarz, who has a magnificent voice, struggled like a Siegfried with the powers of destruction. But even his Titan voice was overwhelmed and jazz-tortured dissonance triumphed.' Moreover, the audience is described as

---

56 Walter Starr [*sic*], 'Mr John McCormack's recital. A great singer's evolution' (1925) (see Appendix).

yawning. Thus, Starkie will reflect: 'It is difficult to see where this music of Schönberg will lead us', going on to represent an idealized notion of human nature threatened by mechanization: '[W]ill such music satisfy human nature with its romance and soul-hunger, or will it not rather symbolise a civilisation of Robots, who have no nerves?' Less space is devoted to Stravinsky. The critic notes 'with pleasure' that the 'romantic' quality of the Rusian composer's piece would appeal to a larger audience, leading him to pose another rhetorical question, one which highlights the importance of the past: 'Have he and his followers come to realise that music can never withdraw itself altogether from the path of tradition marked out by Bach, Mozart, Beethoven, Wagner, Debussy, in successive generations?' Malipiero constitutes a contrast to the two experimental composers, his 'Le Stagioni Italiche' being suitably patriotic: 'a work symbolising Italy and its genius',[57] as the music critic remarks.

Starkie may have stayed on in Italy following the Venice gathering. The chapter which follows the account of the September 1925 festival in *The waveless plain* begins: 'I embarked at Cività Vecchia for La Maddalena, *en route* for Caprera to make a pilgrimage to the tomb of Garibaldi.'[58] However, no dates are mentioned and the following chapter refers to 1927. Therefore, where exactly Starkie was is unclear: if not in September 1925 (since he was certainly in Italy for part of the month), in February (if not in Madrid); in June, July (perhaps in Italy) and December (in Italy again?). Come mid-December, however, he was in London, lecturing to the Anglo-Spanish Society on Ramón de la Cruz and Spanish Drama in the Eighteenth Century.[59] Webb and McDowell recognize Starkie's talent as a lecturer but remark on what became his notorious absenteeism at TCD: 'he was a stimulating lecturer – when he lectured, for his absences were frequent and at times prolonged.'[60] It will be recalled that as a schoolboy Starkie pleaded with Mlle Cora to cover for him when he played truant from school; that he tarried in Italy after completing his YMCA posting, and these instances from his school days and youth might be connected to his Gypsy jaunts in the 30s, indicating, all told, a dissatisfaction with a life conceived of as drab duty and, consequently, the pursuit of a freer and potentially more stimulating existence. Certainly, Starkie projected himself romantically, as escaping from the humdrum and grey mediocrity of industrialized society. The play of identities may be detected in the signature to one of Starkie's contributions to the *Irish Statesman* in 1925: his review of John McCormack's second concert in the month of August, which is signed 'Walter Starr'[61] but attributed to Walter Starkie in the index to the publication. Earlier in the year, too, when reporting from Madrid in May on the state of the contemporary Spanish theatre, there was no recourse to a pseudonym but the contributor did refer to himself, as it were, outside himself, in a variety of ways. 'The present writer' might not be regarded as uncommon usage but the six other instances

---

57 W. Starkie, 'Glorious Musical Pageant', II, 17 Sept. 1925, pp 7–8. See also W. Starkie, *Waveless*, Chapter 27, where some of the material in the 1925 newspaper article is recycled. 58 W. Starkie, *Waveless*, p. 377. 59 'Spanish Drama', IT, 15 Dec. 1925, p. 6. The lecture took place on 16 December and was chaired by the Spanish Ambassador Merry del Val. 60 R.B. MacDowell & D.A. Webb, *A history*, p. 458. 61 W. Starkie , 'Mr John McCormack's recital. A great singer's evolution' (1925), p. 692 (see Appendix).

come to suggest a taste for (dis)guise. Thus, the author of the article is referred to as: 'The critic who goes from these islands to Madrid'; 'the Irish enthusiast of drama'; 'the man from the North'; 'our critic'; 'the Spanish student, who at last sees in action those scenes through which he has often plodded wearily, grammar in hand' and 'the stranger visiting Madrid.'[62]

Dublin's radio station 2RN was launched on New Year's Day 1926, the event being celebrated with a message from the Minister for Posts and Telegraphs, J.J. Walsh, and an inaugural speech from the founder of the Gaelic League, Douglas Hyde. Both the message and the speech emphasized the Free State's distinct identity. Walsh spoke of Ireland's 'separate culture and consciousness'[63] and Hyde chose to open the new broadcasting station, as he declared: 'in our own national language' with the prescription: 'The people of Ireland must understand that our nation is an exception, a nation that has its own rich language and will make its official business through Irish.' Indeed, Hyde would go on to assert: 'The time has arrived, almost, when no young man without Irish can call himself an Irishman – for there will be no Irishmen (the other side of the border being an exception) who will not have some knowledge of their own national language.'[64] The latter claim would have an alienating effect on the likes of Walter Starkie whose Anglo- and Eurocentric-based culture would not accommodate with any ease the exclusion which Hyde's words might signify. However, for the time being, Starkie was able to make his mark in the new medium in English, or Spanish, a task he achieved on a weekly basis. Over the first year of 2RN, the TCD lecturer delivered a series of half-hour lectures on Spanish music with musical illustrations[65] but also began to occupy a fifteen-minute slot each week devoted to the teaching of Spanish, one, moreover, which he would continue to occupy over the 20s.[66]

The year 1926 also marked a culminating point in Starkie's university career to date. The Minutes of the TCD Board Meeting of 11 January record the Provost's proposal to create a professorship of Spanish, destined to be occupied by 'Dr Starkie'.[67] The improvement in Starkie's salary came into effect in the last week of February[68] and

---

62 W. Starkie, 'The present condition of the Spanish theatre' (1925), pp 367, 368 (see Appendix). 63 Message of J.J. Walsh, Minister for Posts and Telegraphs, '2RN Tonight. Official Opening of Dublin Station. Minister's Message', IT, 1 Jan. 1926, p. 5. 64 Cited in R. Pine, *2RN and the origins of Irish radio* (Dublin, 2002), pp 187–8. 65 The first lecture on Spanish music, 'with musical illustrations', was delivered on 10 May 1926, at 8:30p.m.; the second on 7 June 1926, again at 8:30p.m.; the final lecture in the series took place on 21 June 1926, at the same time ('Broadcasting Today', IT, 10 May 1926, p. 9; IT, 7 June 1926, p. 9; IT, 21 June 1926, p. 9). 66 The first Spanish lesson was broadcast on 27 April 1926 at 7:45p.m., IT, 27 Apr. 1926, p. 7. Classes were also given in French and German by a Mademoiselle M.T. Guidicelli and a Miss O. Von Wenckstern, respectively. 67 '[...] The Provost proposed that the Registrar be instructed to draw up for the next meeting a decree creating a Professorship of Spanish in favour of Dr Starkie, at a salary of £100 a year, for a period of five years' (TCD MUN/V/5/23, p. 220). The draft of the decree was approved by the Board at the following Board Meeting on 16 January 1926 (TCD MUN/V/5/23, p. 222). The University Council's approval of the draft decree 'establishing a Professorship of Spanish in favour of Dr Starkie' was expressed at the Council Meeting of 10 February 1926, as recorded in the Minutes of the Board Meeting of 13 February 1926 (TCD MUN/V/5/23, p. 234). 68 'Dr Starkie's salary as Professor of Spanish is to be paid from the day the Decree was signed by the Visitors, viz. 22 February, 1926' (Minutes of the Board Meeting,

further bounty was provided with his being granted the lease of the 'Curator's House', situated in the grounds of TCD's Botanic Gardens,[69] which became his family home for the next twenty years. Thus, the couple with their two-and-a-half-year-old son, Landi, and a new baby expected in September, were able to live independently of Walter's mother, who continued to live a fifteen-minute walk away, in Anglesea Road.[70]

On the same day as the Board Meeting at which the Provost put forward his proposal with regard to a professorship of Spanish, Starkie represented TCD at the Requiem Mass celebrated at Dublin's Pro-Cathedral for Queen Margherita of Savoy, the late Italian Queen Mother. The *Irish Times* reported that '[o]ver two hundred Italians were present', which included 'about fifteen members of the Fascist organisation in Dublin.'[71] Starkie would come to be more closely associated with Fascism as the year, and decade, progressed. In the meantime, apart from his university commitments, he was attending concerts and plays, and producing reviews for the *Irish Statesman*. His only contribution for the month of January reviewed two recitals given by the Hungarian-born violinist Jelly D'Arányi at the Royal Dublin Society's hall in Ballsbridge on the evening of the 11th. Starkie comments on a 'rhythmic power' in her playing, going on to produce an extravagant assessment of her performance, perhaps influenced by the Fascist presence at the morning mass: 'Miss D'Arányi always seems to say to us those words of D'Annunzio: "Marciare non Marcire"; but she translates them, "rush on madly after me into a new sunny world instead of becoming steadfast and cobweb-ridden in your murky, mildewy world of the past".'[72]

The *Irish Times* of 12 February 1926 recorded the riotous reaction to O'Casey's *The plough and the stars* on the opening night at the Abbey Theatre. The headlines to the article provide a vivid sense of the mayhem that ensued: 'Abbey Theatre scene. An attempt to stop Mr O'Casey's new play. Fight on stage. Actresses struck by man from audience. Women ejected.'[73] However, Starkie's review of the play in the *Irish Statesman* the following day carries no reference to riot, indeed, according to theatre critic 'W.S', on the night that he saw the play: 'Mr. O'Casey held his audience spellbound' and he projects the play as a global pacifist piece, thus de-contextualizing its specific political pertinence to Easter 1916 in Dublin:

6 March 1926, TCD MUN/V/5/23, p. 240). **69** 'Agreement to Lease of the Curator's House attached to the Trinity College Botanic Gardens to Walter Fitzwilliam Starkie, Esq. F.T.C.D.[,] on a yearly tenancy at a rent of sixty pounds a year. The rent is to be paid quarterly by deduction from his salary on the quarter days of March, June, September and December. The tenancy is to begin on the 1 March 1926, …' (Minutes of the Board Meeting, 6 Mar. 1926, TCD MUN/V/5/23, p. 240). The house was demolished when the Gardens were cleared, the land coming to accommodate a hotel. Under Starkie's tenancy, the house came to be known as 'Botanic House'. It was occupied by the Starkies until into the 1940s when Starkie stayed on at the head of the British Council in Spain. See Chapter 7, below. **70** *Thom's official directory of Great Britain and Ireland for the year 1926* (Dublin, 1926), p. 2207, lists 'Starkie, Walter Fitzwilliam, M.A., F.T.C.D.', as resident at 129 Anglesea Rd, Ballsbridge, and at 68 Lower Leeson St. Therefore, the Starkies may have rented a property in the city before the lease of the 'Curator's House' was made available to them. **71** 'Queen Margherita's Funeral. Impressive Ceremony at the Pantheon', IT, 12 Jan. 1926, p. 6. **72** 'Miss Jelly D'Aranyi [*sic*]' (1926), p. 624 (see Appendix). **73** IT, 12 Feb. 1926, p. 7.

Mr O'Casey ... leaves us at the end before the darkened stage with nothing but misery in our hearts. 'Oh, the senselessness of it all!' What can humanity over the whole world obtain by torturing itself on the rack of war? Let the war be in Ireland or in France or in Russia, it is all the same senseless war dictated by *narrow nationalist ideas*, and we remember the Covey's words: 'There's no such thing as an Irishman or an Englishman, or a German or a Turk; we're all only human bein's'.[74]

It would be left to Liam O'Flaherty in a Letter to the Editor of the *Irish Statesman*, dated two days after Starkie's review, in which the writer identified himself as 'not a Nationalist in the political sense',[75] but who took it upon himself to contest the qualification of 'narrow nationalist ideas' and the forfeiting of the historically and politically specific in Starkie's review by paying homage to 'the courage of Pearse and Connolly and their comrades'.[76]

On the last Saturday in February, Starkie attended a concert featuring the German-born Elena Gerhardt and the Hungarian Léner Quartet. Starkie both organized and attended another concert in the Examination Hall at TCD on the night before St Patrick's Day: a male choir of twenty-five voices composed of members of Cambridge University and conducted by A.H. Mann, organist to the University of Cambridge.[77] Starkie's review of the concert at the end of the month drew attention to music as providing 'an unrivalled opportunity for drawing closer the ties that bind the different universities.' One might also infer the different countries and, more specifically on this occasion, England and Ireland, though Starkie's article seems bent on only mentioning Irish institutions within the twenty-six counties in this connection: 'I imagined Trinity College giving concerts with the National University, and University College, Cork, visiting Dublin to engage in tournaments of song. Football and athletics unite the various universities and clubs, why not music?' However, his assessment of the performance on the night of the 16th is full of praise.

Starkie was busy as a performer himself in the month of March. He played 'the "Spanish Suite" and a Kreisler group' on the violin at a concert organized in aid of the Sandford centenary fête on the night of the 24th[78] and on the following afternoon was among the soloists taking part in a 'Musical and dramatic performance' at the Abbey Theatre in aid of the Sunshine Home at Stillorgan.[79] Yet another commitment was a speech, albeit 'brief', at the end of 'the final meeting of the session of the French Society', following a programme of music, in which Starkie acknowledged the artists who had performed 'and spoke of the dominating position that France holds today in

74 W. Starkie, 'The plough and the stars' (1926), p. 716 (see Appendix). My italics. 75 Liam O'Flaherty to the Editor of the IS, dated 15 Feb. 1926, IS, 20 Feb. 1926, p. 739. 76 Ibid. O'Flaherty's letter makes no reference to Starkie's review. He does reveal the degree to which he was incensed by Yeats's 'protest against the protest of the audience' on the Thursday previous to his writing. 77 W. Starkie, 'The Cambridge Concert' (1926), p. 74 (see Appendix). See the advertisement for the concert under 'Public Amusements' in IT, 13 Mar. 1926, p. 6, where 'Dr Starkie' figures as 'Hon[orary]. Organiser' from whom tickets could be obtained. 78 'Sandford Centenary Fête Concert', IT, 25 Mar. 1926, p. 9. 79 'Sunshine Home Stillorgan', IT, 13 Mar. 1926, p. 6.

music and the other arts'.[80] In between these commitments and his university activity, the theatre goer also managed to see the Dublin Drama League's performance of Shaw's *Heartbreak House* at the Abbey. Here, too, the reviewer was not stinting in his praise of either the play, claiming that it contained the best of Shaw: 'because there is no thesis to be proved', or the production: 'Rarely have I seen on the Abbey stage a play produced with such care, such subtle suggestion. Mr Lennox Robinson must be congratulated on his art as a producer.'[81] As noted above, towards the end of the month of April, Starkie gave the first of his fifteen-minute Spanish lessons on 2RN but his energies were not exclusively devoted to Spanish literature and culture or travel to Spain at this juncture. In early April, he headed for Italy where, in the week of the 11th, he delivered a course of four lectures at the British Institute in Florence,[82] then run by Fascist apologist Harold E. Goad.[83] Starkie's lectures dealt with 'the modern dramatic movement in England and Ireland'[84] and were delivered in Italian. He travelled to Florence with a letter of introduction to scholar Carlo Placci from the Italian Ambassador to Great Britain (1922 to 1927), Pietro Paolo Tomasi, Marchese della Torretta, in which the Ambassador described the Irish professor as a valuable scholar of Italian literature, a sincere friend of Italy and a fervent supporter of closer literary relations between Italy and England.[85]

Before leaving for Florence, Starkie submitted his only contribution to the *Irish Statesman* for the month of April, a review of Ernest Boyd's *Studies from ten literatures*. The review opens with a characteristic purple thrust, which may carry a playful, or not so playful, reference to an identity in formation over the 1920s, that of the keen-sighted observer (apparently) wandering without purpose over the troubled territories he would tread, nonplussed by the political puzzle. The reviewer declares: 'The literature of contemporary Europe resembles a labyrinth wherein the lynx-eyed critic wanders aimlessly through countless conflicting paths without ever solving the enigma.' The image of the rambling critic in the maze of Modernism might be interpreted as the expression of a sense of displacement on the part of Starkie himself, whose opening paragraph reiterates an apocalyptic sense of disorientation and division within the present: 'Nowadays we have outlived all systems: ... all is chaos: man has

80 'French Society. An enjoyable concert', IT, 25 Mar. 1926, p. 9.   81 W. Starkie, '*Heartbreak house*' (1926), p. 45 (see Appendix).   82 'The British Institue of Florence, established in 1917, and granted a Royal Charter in 1923, was the first of the British cultural institutes to operate overseas and served as a model for the establishment of the British Council in 1934.' http://www.britishinstitute.it/ en/aboutus/asp, accessed 16 Oct. 2010.   83 Goad's pamphlet *What is fascism? An explanation of its essential principles* was published in Florence in English in 1929.   84 'The Modern Dramatic Movement', IT, 8 Apr. 1926, p. 6. The information in the *Irish Times* further specifies: First lecture: 'Forerunners'; second lecture: 'Bernard Shaw'; third lecture: 'Abbey Theatre'; fourth lecture: 'Postwar Drama in England.' The annual report of the British Institute of Florence noted that 'Prof. Starkie' lectured on 'Contemporary British Drama' (*Annual report 1925–1926*, The British Institute of Florence Archive, BRI:1:F:ii:4, p. 6). I am grateful to Alyson Price at the Institute in Florence for her aid in obtaining information and material both from the Institute and the Fondo Placci.   85 Torretta [Pietro Paolo Tomasi, Marchese della Torretta] to Signor Carlo Placci, London, 6 April 1926. The original Italian reads: 'Il Prof. Starkie, valoroso cultore della literature italiana ed amico sincero del nostro paese, è un caldo fautore di più intime relazioni letterarie fra l'Italia e l'Inghilterra' (Fondo Placci, Biblioteca Marucelliana, Florence, C.P1.901.1). My translation.

destroyed the Walhalla of his old beliefs, and his mind is torn this way and that by conflicting passionate opinions.' Similarly, the reviewer finds cohesion lacking in Boyd's text, which is assessed as a consequence of the author's 'Modernist idea', making the 'short isolated articles' void of any 'bond of union'.[86]

On 5 May 1926, the Spanish Ambassador to Britain, Alfonso Merry del Val, addressed a letter to the Vice-Chancellor of the University of Dublin, Lord Glenavy, expressing the satisfaction of the Spanish Government with the founding of a Chair in Spanish and Starkie's appointment as the first occupant:

> The Government of His Majesty the King of Spain having been informed of the foundation of a Chair of Spanish at Trinity College, Dublin University, and the appointment thereto of Professor Dr Walter Starkie who has specialised in the study of Spanish literature, I have been requested to express the satisfaction with which they have received the news and to beg you to make the appreciation known to the Authorities of the said College.[87]

Five days later, Starkie broadcast the first of three half-hour lectures on Spanish music[88] and later in the month, in the Graduates' Memorial Hall, he delivered the lecture he had given at the Anglo-Spanish Society in London in December 1925 on 'Ramón de la Cruz and Spanish Drama in the Eighteenth Century',[89] now illustrated 'by lantern slides'[90] and open to the Dublin public. He also continued with his Spanish lessons on 2RN and reviewing in the *Irish Statesman* though, as in April, he was only to contribute one review over the month of May. The review in question was dedicated to the recent celebration of the Feis Ceoil [Festival of Music][91] and refers to a singer and players who participated as well as to 'two great forces in music in England', Professor Granville Bantock and Mr Robert Radford, from whom, Starkie claims: '[i]t was very gratifying to our sense of national pride to receive ... words of praise and encouragement.'[92] The text also reveals an ongoing preoccupation with unity in the post-Partition period, whether it be that which is achieved by the celebration of the festival itself: 'because it *brings* people of all the provinces *together*'; that of players and audience: 'how much of the singer's art and inspiration may not be due to the subtle influences that *unite* him to those unheard voices in the audience'; the conjunction of music-lovers: 'The man from the North meets the man from the South and the West: ... All *join together* without losing the great charm of their local peculiarities' or the creation of an orchestra: 'which will *unite* all the best players in Dublin *without excluding* anyone'.[93] Starkie's review on the Feis appeared in the *Irish Statesman*

---

86 W. Starkie, 'Literature and life. Tendencies of contemporary literature' (1926), p. 126 (see Appendix).   87 A. Merry del Val to Lord Glenavy, 5 May 1926, TCD MUN/V/5/23, p. 255. See also 'Spanish in Dublin University', IT, 18 May 1926, p. 9, where the letter was reproduced. 88 'Broadcasting Today. Dublin 2RN 397 metres. 8.30: Lecture on Spanish Music by Dr Walter Starkie, with musical illustrations', IT, 10 May 1926, p. 9.   89 'Trinity College Dublin', IT, 21 May 1926, p. 8.   90 Ibid.   91 W. Starkie, 'The Feis Ceoil' (1926) (see Appendix).   92 Ibid., p. 263. 93 Ibid., pp 263, 264. My italics. With regard to the non-sectarian nature of the Feis, see Charles Oldham and W.P. Geoghegan's comments in 1897 and 1914, respectively, cited in R. Pine & C. Acton

on the 15 May, the day before the founding of an organization that would work against the understanding of unity stated by the reviewer, altering the political landscape in the latter, ailing, years of the Cumann na nGaedheal government, before setting about radically transforming it in the 1930s, that is, Eamon de Valera's Fianna Fáil (Warriors of Fál, or Ireland).[94] As the leader declared at 'a largely attended meeting'[95] in early August on the Mall, Waterford, while Starkie was in the throes of the Horse Show in Dublin[96] (the gatherings and locations highlight significant differences with regard to class and culture), the main purpose of his party was 'to reunite the Irish Ireland forces'.[97]

In June, the two remaining half-hour lectures in the series of three on Spanish music were broadcast[98] but neither over this month nor in July did Starkie contribute any reviews to the *Irish Statesman*. However, he was certainly on campus at the beginning and end of the month as he attended Senate Meetings at TCD on the 5th and 29th.[99] Following the latter, four honorary degrees were conferred on 'men of great distinction',[1] among whom figured Dr Nathan Söderblom, the archbishop of Upsala and primate of Sweden. In his capacity as Public Orator at the investiture, Sir Robert Tate, highlighted Söderblom's service 'in the cause of the reunion of Christendom, which [had] made him a figure of European importance'.[2] The ceremony was followed by a garden party in '[p]erfect weather', hosted in the Fellows' Garden by the Provost and Mrs Bernard, who offered their guests '[t]ea, ices, straw-berries and cream, ... served in a large marquee' while '[t]he band of the 1st (St Matthias') Company of the Boys' Brigade was stationed on the lawn.'[3] Starkie was at the garden party with his mother and wife and may have had the opportunity to speak to the Swedish primate but, in any event, he had attended the two lectures (of three) which the archbishop had delivered on 'The Scholar, the Ascetic and the Hero of Religion'.[4] At the investiture, in his capacity as Public Orator, Sir Robert Tate had further stated that Dr Söderblom had 'laboured for the ideal described in St Paul's phrase as "one body and one Spirit; one Lord, one faith, one baptism".'[5] Undoubtedly, the ecumenical ideal was one which would appeal to Starkie in his pursuit of unity. Moreover, a conversation he shared with the archbishop on the 28th appears to have made an impact on him, as he explained in a letter addressed to His Grace on the day of the investiture. Having expressed his enjoyment of Dr Söderblom's lectures, he added: 'the conversation I had yesterday morning was a great boon to me. I shall not

(eds), *To talent*, p. 220.   **94** The translation of the title of de Valera's party is taken from T. Brown, *Ireland*, p. 36.   **95** 'Mr de Valera. The objects of his party', IT, 2 Aug. 1926, p. 6.   **96** 'Some of the Foreign Visitors for the Dublin Horse Show', IT, 2 Aug. 1926, p. 7. Starkie figures in a photograph which shows 'Three members of the Reception Committee'.   **97** Ibid.   **98** 'Broadcasting Today. Dublin 2RN 397 Metres. 8.30 – Lecture on Spanish Music, with illustrations on the violin (2nd of series), Walter Starkie, LL.D.', IT, 7 June 1926, p. 9; 'Broadcasting Today. Dublin 2RN 397 Metres. 8.30 – Lecture with musical illustrations (3rd of series), Dr Walter Starkie', IT, 21 June 1926, p. 9.   **99** 'Dublin University. A Degree Established', IT, 7 June 1926, p. 9; 'Meeting of the Senate. Honorary Degrees', IT, 30 June 1926, p. 7.   **1** 'Meeting of the Senate. Honorary Degrees', IT, 30 June 1926, p. 7.   **2** 'University of Dublin', IT, 30 June 1926, p. 5.   **3** Ibid.   **4** "The Archbishop of Upsala [*sic*]', IT, 22 June 1926, p. 6. The final lecture would be delivered on the 30th.   **5** 'University of Dublin', IT, 30 June 1926, p. 5.

soon forget it.'[6] Whether the archbishop invited the TCD professor to Sweden at this point is unclear but Starkie also stated in his letter that it would be a great pleasure for him to lecture there, arguing: 'There are many points in Spanish literature[,] both ancient and modern[,] that would be interesting[,] I think[,] to the great mystical people of the North.'[7] In late September Starkie would be en route for Stockholm but before his departure he had much to occupy him: his book on Pirandello would be out before the end of the year and the manuscript might have still required completion, modification or proof reading; there were reviews for the *Irish Statesman* to submit, Spanish lessons on 2RN to be broadcast, attendance at the Horse Show and, not least, the birth of a second child to adjust to.

Starkie's last and longest contribution to the *Irish Statesman*, in the month of August 1926, was a review of Luigi Villari's *The Fascist experiment* (1926), which followed on from the author's earlier tome *The awakening of Italy* (1924).[8] It served to introduce Villari to *Irish Statesman* readers as well as to promote him as a spokesman of authority on present-day Italy. The reviewer identified him as the 'son of the famous historian, the late Senator Pasquale', adding that he had 'served in the Italian Diplomatic Service in various parts of the world' as well as having been 'attached to the League of Nations'.[9] Starkie may have met Villari, almost twenty years his senior, through Harold Goad since Commendatore Luigi Villari was on the Governing Board of the British Institute in Florence.[10] However, he was not unknown as an author in Britain and had already penetrated Establishment circles in the Edwardian period: T. Fisher Unwin had published his *Fire and sword in the Caucasus* in 1906 and his name had already been put forward for membership of the London Athenaeum Club in 1902.[11] More recently, Villari had been sent to London, where the discovery of anti-Fascist propaganda led to his settling in the city in 1926 with a view to leading a counterattack, '[taking] orders directly and only from the Duce'.[12] Therefore, it is also possible that the names of Starkie and his wife were passed on to Villari by the Italian consulate in Dublin. It was not unusual to find material on Italian Fascism in the *Irish Statesman*. Already in 1923 there were contributions dated in Florence from the corporatist Odon Por,[13] and the Editor himself, possessed of a 'deep aversion to popular democracy ... developed during the civil war',[14] had reviewed Por's book, *Fascism* (1923), for which he had produced the English-language introduction, in the

---

6 W. Starkie to the Most Reverend Dr Söderblom, archbishop of Upsala and Primate of Sweden, 29 June 1926 (Uppsala universitetsbibliothek, Nathan Söderbloms samling. Brev från utlänningar). 7 Ibid. 8 Both volumes were published in London: the first by Methuen, the second by Faber and Gwyer. 9 W. Starkie, 'The Fascist experiment' (1926) (see Appendix). 10 See: List of the Board of Governors in alphabetical order, *Annual report of the British Institute of Florence, 1925–1926* (The British Institute of Florence Archive, BRI :1 : F : ii : 4, page not numbered). 11 Villari's membership of the Athenaeum was proposed by the Honourable Arthur D. Elliott, seconded by Bernard Mallet Esq., C.B., and supported by, among others, Sidney Lee, Lord Bryce and Henry Newbolt ('Certificate of Candidate for Ballot', Date of entry 24 Apr. 1902. Elected 10 Apr. 1916 (The Athenaeum)). 12 C. Baldoli, *Exporting fascism. Italian fascists and Britain's Italians in the 1930s* (Oxford, 2003), p. 10. 13 See: 'Fighting Unemployment in Italy', IS, 1 Dec. 1923, pp 364–6; 8 Dec. 1923, pp 398, 400; 15 Dec. 1923, p. 429. 14 N. Allen, *George Russell*, p. 124.

first issue of the journal.[15] Starkie's wife, Italia, may have contributed to the review,[16] but the style, whether his or hers, is profusely purple, as illustrated in the following instance:

> The ponderous weight of history hangs heavy [sic] over Italy like a cloud laden with thunder – the dusky multitudes of pedants, like hordes of locusts, have overwhelmed the beauty of its art and literature. In the Renaissance, when a new world came to birth, like Boticelli's Venus from her shell, poetry and painting led men's minds aloft into the sunlight by the golden ladder of dreams.

Style apart, the main thrust of the review resides in its will to facilitate understanding of a movement which is 'deeply ... misunderstood in foreign countries', to clarify what Fascism signifies (anti-Bolshevism and anti-Socialism; 'sane, idealistic patriotism') and to explain it in context ('The Italians have always ... welcomed the dictator, the "condottiere" who is able to appeal to their sense of the heroic') while seeking to allay fears with regard to Fascism's becoming a panacea ('Nobody would seriously hold that Fascism should be tried in other countries'). Fascist Syndicalism is also explained, with workers represented as showing consideration to the interests of other classes and strikes in Italy having been reduced to a minimum, which might have held an appeal to captains of industry in the wake of the General Strike in Britain in May 1926. In his penultimate paragraph, Starkie claimed that Gentile's educational reform 'should be of great interest to us in Ireland' and expressed particular interest in the introduction of choral singing into elementary schools. Finally, he highlighted the current 'faith and devotion to the nation' found in Italy, 'a nation of young men full of ideals'.[17] Significant numbers of Starkie's peers in Ireland had 'ideals' too and many of them would not be long in voting for de Valera.

September 1926 began and ended for Starkie with major events: the birth of his daughter, Alma, on the 3rd,[18] and another journey abroad, northwards now, to countries he had never visited: Sweden, Norway and Denmark.[19] The youngest of the Starkie siblings, Nancy, had been living with her brother Walter and Italia for two months when Alma was born. She described Botanic House for the benefit of her sister Enid in Oxford: 'a beautiful little house, and very nicely furnished', where evenings were spent listening to 'Cortot, Bauer, Lamonde and Prokofieff and many others' thanks to a Duo-Art Piano, on loan to Walter from music critic Percy Scholes.[20] A fortnight later, Nancy also remarked on her sister-in-law's striking energy, qualifying Italia as 'perfectly wonderful, when you think that the very day the girl was born[,] she brushed down the stairs ... and tyedied [sic] everywhere.'[21] Starkie carried

---

15 Ibid., pp 154–5. 16 There are two instances of an incorrect use of English: 'Just as the first article of Mazzini's creed was to combat *against* materialism, ...'; 'Marciare non marcire' – 'March on, [*do*] not lag behind and rot.' (W. Starkie, 'The Fascist experiment', p. 686 (see Appendix).) The errors are in italics. 17 W. Starkie, 'Literature and life. The Fascist experiment' (1926), p. 686 (see Appendix). 18 'Births: September 3 1926 at Ivanhoe, Landsdowne Rd, to Italia ...' IT, 4 Sept. 1926, p. 1. 19 N. Starkie to E. Starkie, 15 Oct. 1926: 'Walter arrived back from Sweden, Norway, Denmark yesterday' (ES, Bodl.). 20 N. Starkie to E. Starkie, 1 Sept. 1926 (ES, Bodl.). 21 N. Starkie to E.

on with his Spanish lessons on the air in what became his usual Tuesday slot over the first fortnight of September[22] and also broadcast a half-hour 'Lecture with musical illustrations', dedicated to 'Old Naples'.[23] He also managed to go to the Abbey on the 6th to see Lennox Robinson's 'The Big House', a play he reviewed for the *Irish Statesman*, particularly focussing on the character of Kate Alcock and her father and further singling out Kate's indictment of the attitude of her class, which was quoted: 'We were ashamed of everything, ashamed of our birth, ashamed of our good education, ashamed of our religion, ashamed that we dined in the evenings and that we dressed for dinner, and, after all, our shame didn't save us or we wouldn't be sitting here on the remnants of our furniture.' Following the quote, Starkie will also censure the failure of the Ascendancy to fall short of the role assigned to them, all but taking up the gauntlet on their behalf: 'No, they have not *played* their *part*. In the future they can become again formidable if they care to make themselves so, if they give up their poor attempt to pretend they are not different.'[24] Thus, he will end the particular paragraph of his review with Kate's exultant vindication of her class: 'We must glory in our difference, be as proud of it as they are of theirs.'[25] A Letter to the Editor, published in the *Irish Statesman* the following month, would make reference to Starkie's 'praise' of Kate Alcock's 'last explanatory speech', which constituted in the correspondent's view: 'the one really unconvincing part of a most interesting play', claiming: 'Surely what is wrong with that dwindling class is their aloofness, their difference. The whole play seems to point out this, … then at the last the moral is contradicted in a most illogical way.'[26]

Italia went home from the nursing home on 16 September, accompanied by a nurse who stayed with her for a fortnight. By this time, Nancy was living with her mother in Anglesea Road and it seems that neither mother-in-law nor sister-in-law was going to be providing support at Botanic House. Indeed, Nancy remarked in the light of Walter's departure: 'Italia … will be very lonely.'[27] It was on the evening of the following day that Starkie left for Sweden.[28] The *Irish Times* had announced earlier in the week that Professor Walter Starkie, FTCD, had been invited by the Olaus Petri Foundation at the University of Upsala to deliver a course of lectures at the end of the month on 'Modern Interpretations of Don Quixote', 'Calderón and the Spanish Mystic Drama' and 'Miguel de Unamuno'. The article further explained that he would deliver 'lectures on Spanish literature and on the Abbey Theatre under the auspices of the Anglo-Swedish Society, at Stockholm, Gothenburg, Lund and other cities',[29] adding that he would also be lecturing at the University of Copenhagen. Starkie was away for almost a month, arriving back in Dublin on 14 October. When Nancy wrote to her sister Enid on the day following his return, she stated that Walter

---

Starkie, 17 Sept. 1926 (ES, Bodl.).   **22** 'Broadcasting', IT, 7/14 Sept. 1926, p. 2, on both occasions. Starkie's lessons were also broadcast in his absence: 'Broadcasting', IT, 21/28 Sept. 1926, p. 3, on both occasions; 5/12 Oct. 1926, p. 3, on both occasions.   **23** 'Broadcasting', IT, 13 Sept. 1926, p. 2.   **24** My italics.   **25** W. Starkie, 'Mr Lennox Robinson's new play. "The big house"' (1926), pp 14, 15 (see Appendix).   **26** N. Campbell to the Editor of the *Irish Statesman*, 9 Oct. 1926, p. 107.   **27** N. Starkie to E. Starkie, 17 Sept. 1926 (ES, Bodl.).   **28** Ibid.   **29** 'Dr Walter Starkie', IT, 13 Sept. 1926, p. 3.

looked 'flourishing' and reported 'a splendid success'.[30] Italia was 'very well' too though from what Nancy explained to her sister, their brother was returning to a far from peaceful home: 'Italia's house is a house of chaos, no quiet[,] only chase, chase, chase, after one baby, then for the other, then after the nurse, or after the cat ... She cannot even sit down for her meals.' However, the children, nurse and cat are not held responsible for the chaos. Italia is considered by her sister-in-law to be the culprit: 'She makes every one [*sic*] nervy and tired [and] cannot manage servants.'[31] Nancy further criticized Italia, claiming, for instance, that she was spoiling her children, and also finding that she lacked balance in her domestic economy: 'She is so sparing with money in some ways, then she is so extravagant in others. But when she buys things, which is seldom, she pays exhorbitant price[s]. This summer she bought Landi two little shantung suits at £2.2s.0d, and she could have made them for 10/-.'[32]

Starkie wrote to Dr Söderblom to thank him for 'all [his] kindness and hospitality' on the day he returned to Dublin.[33] On the following evening, he occupied a forty-minute slot on 2RN in which he spoke of a subject that was going to figure prominently in his pursuits from the end of the decade of the 20s and into the 30s: 'Gypsies and their Music.'[34] In the last week of October, he shared a two-hour slot on 2RN with the Station Orchestra and actor Frank Fay, entitled '400 BC calling'. Starkie's contribution consisted in telling 'Greek stories'.[36] Neither did he tarry in his labours as a reviewer. On the 16th, he was at the Theatre Royal to hear Fritz Kreisler's recital and before the end of the month attended the opening of the Dublin Drama League's new season with its performance of Pirandello's 'The Pleasure of Honesty' at the Abbey.[37]

In spite of Pirandello's 'The Pleasure of Honesty' being, in Starkie's view, 'one of the weaker works of the author',[38] his review at the end of October of the Dublin Drama League production might have served to whet appetites for more Pirandello fare and Starkie was to provide it before the year was out. In the mid-November issue of the *Irish Statesman*, *Luigi Pirandello* headed an advertisement for thirteen publications brought out by the London publisher J.M. Dent and Sons. The blurb announced: 'Professor Starkie has written an illuminating examination from all points of view of the extraordinary literary personality of Pirandello' and highlighted the final chapter 'in this important book',[39] which was devoted to Pirandello and George Bernard Shaw in the year that Shaw had been awarded the Nobel Prize for

---

30 N. Starkie to E. Starkie, 15 Oct. 1926 (ES, Bodl.). I have found no other source of information to confirm that Starkie also visited Norway at this time, as his sister claims. 31 Ibid. 32 N. Starkie to E. Starkie, 1 Nov. 1926. See also N. Starkie to E. Starkie, 17 Sept. 1926, for further censorious comment from Nancy on what she perceived as Italia's extravagance. (ES, Bodl.) 33 W. Starkie to N. Söderblom, 14 Oct. 1926 (Uppsala universitetsbibliotek, Nathan Söderbloms samling. Brev från utlänningar). 34 'Broadcasting', IT, 15 Oct. 1926, p. 9. 36 'Broadcasting', IT, 25 Oct. 1926, p. 9. 37 In his review, Starkie doesn't state the date of the performance of 'The Pleasure of Honesty' which he attended but it must have been on Sunday, the 17th or the 24th: 'The Dublin Drama League ... produced Pirandello's *Henry IV* (in 1924) and *The Pleasure of Honesty* (in 1926) at the Abbey on Sunday nights' (A. Roche, *Contemporary Irish drama. From Beckett to McGuinness* (Dublin, 1994), p. 292, n. 43). 38 W. Starkie, 'Pirandello at the Abbey' (1926), p. 182 (see Appendix). 39 IS, 13 Nov. 1926, p. 233.

Literature.[40] In the meantime, Pirandello was being performed in Dublin, a playwright who, as Starkie explained: 'holds the attention of Europe; in nearly every country his plays are performed to crowded houses, and the word "Pirandellian" has become as expressive as "Shavian".' Starkie's review presented a Pirandello who was 'one of the greatest champions of the modern movement in art', contrasting him in style to D'Annunzio and linking him to the *commedia dell'arte*. Early on in the review, Starkie had noted the recognition of '[a] full house in the theatre', who 'welcomed enthusiastically the efforts of a society that is doing noble service in bringing before the Dublin public modern plays of international reputation'. In similar terms to his comments on the creation of a Dublin audience for music,[41] Starkie also alluded to the fact that a theatre audience of quality and devotion was being forged in the city: 'Thus Dublin is gradually producing a cultivated, theatre-loving public which is able to appreciate not only the splendid efforts of its own theatre but also the new movements in other countries'.[42]

Over November, Starkie continued to broadcast his weekly Spanish lessons over the Dublin airwaves but before his first lesson of the month, on the 2nd, he broadcast a programme which echoed his September–October visit to northern climes. The programme was devoted to 'Sweden and Its Music', on the night of the 1st.[43] He also contributed three reviews to the *Irish Statesman* over the month, dealing with a variety of concerts and musical events. Come mid-November, Starkie lectured on the French playwright François de Curel, Sir Robert Tate presiding.[44] The news item in the *Irish Times* informed that Starkie was translating one of De Curel's plays, 'La fille sauvage' for production at the Abbey Theatre in March 1927.[45] The highlight of November, however, was the publication of Starkie's own work on Pirandello, which was reviewed by L[ennox]. R[obinson]. in the *Irish Statesman* in the month of December.[46] Robinson's review speaks of Pirandello as 'the most arresting figure in the dramatic world today' and provides a potted history of the reception of the Italian dramatist in Ireland, referring to the Dublin Drama League's productions of *Six characters in search of an author* in the spring of 1923 and *Henry IV* in 1924, noting, moreover, that in both cases the plays had not then been produced in England. Hence, Robinson claimed: 'It is … very fitting and an honour to Irish letters that the first book in English on Pirandello should be by an Irishman, who is Fellow of Dublin University and Vice-President of the Dublin Drama League.' The review is complimentary throughout. Robinson observes that Pirandello's six volumes of poetry are excluded from the volume, but makes no further comment on the omission, ending his review

---

40 The news of the Prize being awarded to G.B. Shaw was reported in the *Irish Times*, 12 Nov. 1926, p. 7, i.e., the day before the J.M. Dent and Sons advertisement appeared in the *Irish Statesman*. **41** See: W. Starkie, 'Music and Life. Elena Gerhardt and the Lener [*sic*] Quartet'; 'The Feis Ceoil'; 'Musical events of the Week'; 'Music of the week. Mr Duffy's recital. Colonel Brase as conductor. Royal Dublin Society. The recital of Miss Myra Hess' (1926) (see Appendix). **42** W. Starkie, 'Pirandello at the Abbey' (1926), p. 182 (see Appendix). **43** 'Broadcasting', IT, 1 Nov. 1926, p. 5. **44** 'Francois [*sic*] de Curel. Dr Starkie's lecture on the French playwright', IT, 18 Nov. 1926, p. 5. **45** I have no knowledge of the translation or any performance of it. **46** 'Reviews', IS, 11 Dec. 1926: L[ennox]. R[obinson]., '*Luigi Pirandello*. Walter Starkie (Dent 7/6 net.)', pp 328–9.

on a wholly positive note: 'no student of drama can afford to overlook Dr Starkie's most excellent book.'[47] Undoubtedly, Starkie's text possessed the merit of making the Italian playwright known, or further familiar, to readers of English both in Ireland and beyond. However, the superlative qualification pronounced by Robinson may be questioned in the light of a text which, stylistically, reflects Starkie's bent for fustian, prolixity, and what may have been his wife's awkward use of English. With regard to content, the text moves steadily (perhaps Italia's tempo)[48] through Pirandello's production, situating him within the contemporary context in Italy (where material is drawn on which figured in Starkie's 1924 review in the *Irish Statesman* on Luigi Chiarelli) before highlighting his Sicilian roots and moving on to deal with him as novelist, short-story writer and, finally, as a playwright. However, although the text moves methodically through Pirandello's works, there is more plot summary than argument and the occasion for analysis is forfeited in favour of propaganda, a tendency that may be detected in Starkie's writing from the time of his book on Benavente in 1924 to the text devoted to the pilgrim route to Santiago some thirty years on, passing through his books and journalism of the 1920s and 30s.

In the 'Preface' to *Luigi Pirandello*, dated at TCD in July 1926, the author claims that he had fallen 'under the spell of Pirandello' four years earlier and then began writing the text but had since revised some of his impressions and modified his viewpoint. Apparently these changes are mentioned in an attempt to account for 'contradictions and repetitions in the book', which the author then seeks to justify: 'I console myself ... by reflecting that it is well-nigh impossible to review Pirandello without contradicting or repeating oneself, especially as many of his works seem to be modern variations on the same theme'.[49] The study of the Sicilian author begins with D'Annunzio's much quoted (not least by Starkie himself) 'Marciare non Marcire', which is represented in visionary, purple-tinged terms, as: 'revealing in a flash the spirit of the young writers of that New Italy which is spreading its wings in the golden sunlight[,] conscious of its great destiny.' Thus, as the text proper begins, its filofascist positioning is made clear and will be reiterated as the text develops as, for instance, in Chapter 3, where: 'the great political unifying work done by the Risorgimento' is represented as having been 'carried to such a pitch of perfection by Mussolini and Fascism'. A task of political unification would have its appeal for Starkie, whose sense of 'things [falling] apart' would be borne out in the wake of the Rising of 1916, the Civil and Anglo-Irish Wars at the turn of the decade in Ireland, World War in Europe, the General Strike in England and attempts on the lives of Mussolini and the King of Spain in 1926. Indeed, as the text begins, the 'restless' or 'feverish spirit of the times' is ascribed to causes that convey an apocalyptic picture in the wake of industrial-ization: 'the increase of material civilization, the electrifying of the modern world, the whizzing and whirling of its cogwheels[,] which allow no truce, no rest, as man dashes

47 Ibid., pp 328, 329. **48** In a diary entry for 18 May 1935, i.e., some nine years on, Signe Toksvig registers being at Bray motor races with Italia and her children, among others. She describes 'Mrs S.' as 'quite lovely and quite intelligent, but with something schoolmistressed about her' (L. Pihl (ed.), *Signe Toksvig's Irish diaries, 1926–37* (Dublin, 1994), p. 317). **49** 'Preface' in W. Starkie, *Luigi Pirandello* (London, 1926), p. vii.

on grotesquely in a mad race.' In a later chapter, the twentieth century will be referred to as both 'soul-tormented' and reducing men to mechanical function. Thus, Serafino Gubbio in Pirandello's *Quaderni di Serafino Gubbio Operatore* [*Shoot! The notebooks of Serafino Gubbio, cinematograph operator*] (1925), like Dickens's Stephen Blackpool in *Hard times* (1854), becomes 'a [H]and and nothing else.' The indictment of mechanized civilization relates to Pirandello's position in his works but no critical or analytical view towards the writer's position is voiced. There are echoes of Samuel Butler and William Morris in what is described as: 'the horror of our civilization, where man has become a mere cog-wheel in a gigantic engine. [...] The development of the machine is the revolution bringing in man's servitude and helplessness. [...] Pirandello...cannot help comparing our present feverish age with former ages when Individuality [*sic*] had freer play.'[50] The sense of nostalgia for the authority and class structures of the past, a feature, as will be seen, in Starkie's 1930s writings, may also be detected here in references to the loss of '[c]onsistency', seen 'not [to be] a virtue nowadays when there is no austere Inquisitor in black to point the finger of reminder', and in the character of Donna Caterina Auriti-Laurentano in Pirandello's *I vecchi e i giovani* [The old and the young] (1913), described as possessing 'all the pride and steadfastness of the feudal aristocrat'.[51] The past is seen as offering a certainty which the present, 'an age of indecision and continual doubting', has forfeited. Moreover, both the theoretical and the experimental are assessed in negative terms: 'The drama of Europe since the War is a mass of discordant visions: there is no unity to be found anywhere. Writers are no longer driven by great impulses to create with their own life-blood immortal works: all art, whether in drama, music, painting, limits itself to theory or to the fruitless quest of originality.'[52]

Apart from focussing on Pirandello's fiction and drama, there are particular features of the text that are striking. In terms of content, the frequent references to the *commedia dell'arte*, seen to have been influential on Pirandello, the presence and impact of masks, and acting a part[53] are all aspects of the playwright's work which acquire a further significance in Starkie's own life, being acted out both in the immediate Free State structure in Ireland and in the wider context of Anglo-Italian relations. In this latter connection, the fascist propagandist and member of the Board of Governors of the British Institute in Florence, Luigi Villari, son of senator Pasquale Villari the president of the Dante Alighieri Society from 1896 to 1903, should not be ignored. His labours in London between 1926 and 1934 may be related to the conviction of Giuseppe Bastianini, 'a former *squadrista* from Perugia, secretary of *Fasci* Abroad between 1923 and 1926 and ambassador to London from 1939', who had argued in a memorandum to representatives in France and Britain in 1924: 'that Fascists abroad had to create social links with local citizens, especially journalists, politicians, industrialists and

---

50 W. Starkie, *Pirandello*, pp 11, 63, 11, 102, 114, 114–15.   **51** Ibid., pp 17; 258. Starkie would dedicate a book to Cardinal Cisneros, Spain's [as the title of the book has it] *Grand inquisitor* (W. Starkie, *Grand inquisitor. Being an account of Cardinal Ximenez de Cisneros and his times* (London, 1940). See Chapter 7, below.   **52** W. Starkie, *Pirandello*, pp 16, 17.   **53** W. Starkie, *Pirandello*: on the *commedia dell'arte*, see pp 19, 32, 44, 45, 64, 108, 137, 147, 156, 160, 225, 246, 259; on masks, see pp 109, 137, 173, 208, 214, 267; on acting a part, see pp 197–8, 208, 224.

intellectuals' with a view to bringing them over to fascist 'style and thought'. Following a visit to London in the summer of 1925, Villari reported to Mussolini on what he deemed to be 'a "poisonous" anti-Fascist campaign'. It was then that the Commendatore was sent to London, where 'his propaganda technique involved letters and articles in British newspapers, the publication of books, and a well-developed social "diplomatic" net among the various British clubs'.[54] Hence a letter he addressed to the Editor of the *Irish Statesman* in 1927, contesting the representation of the Fascist state by one 'Politicus'[55] (conceivably a Starkie mask with a view to enabling Villari's response) may be more fully appreciated, as may his ongoing membership of the Athenaeum Club and Walter Starkie's 1926 publication on an Italian playwright who had thrown in his hand with Mussolini in 1924 and was afforded recognition and material facilities in fascist Italy.[56]

As regards form, Starkie's text is plagued by a failure to supply necessary source references or to be consistent with regard to the translation, or not, of text from the Italian,[57] but the most striking feature is the incorrect use of English, which is ubiquitous.[58] Starkie's book is dated in Florence in April 1926, that is, the occasion on which he visited Florence to lecture at the British Institute. It will be remembered that he also lectured in Sweden between September and October of 1926 and earlier on, the year in which he occupied the first Chair of Spanish at TCD, he also produced an article on the Spanish contemporary philosopher Ortega y Gasset in the *Contemporary Review*.[59] Therefore, Starkie had not had much time at his disposal for producing a book in 1926 or, indeed, in the years from 1922 on, when, as stated in the 'Preface', he had begun writing. The book is dedicated to the memory of his mother-in-law, Delfina Landi Porchietti,[60] a supporter of fascism herself, and this, together with her daughter's own conviction and what she might have envisaged as her patriotic contribution, could have led her to participate in the writing of a text signed by her husband.

Before the year was out, in the first fortnight of December, Starkie contributed two reviews to the *Irish Statesman*, not re-appearing as a reviewer in the journal until mid-January 1927. Nancy remarked in a letter to her sister Enid that their sibling was off to Brussels at Christmas time.[61] Therefore, Italia would be spending another Christmas without her husband, now accompanied by two offspring. A week before the festivities, the Free State Minister of Justice, Kevin O'Higgins, spoke out in favour

54 C. Baldoli, *Exporting fascism*, pp 9, 10. 55 Politicus, 'The Fascist State', IS, 25 June 1927, p. 375; L. Villari to The Editor of *The Irish Statesman*, IS, 7 July 1927, p. 422. 56 See: R. Matthaei, *Luigi Pirandello*, trans. S. & E. Young (New York, 1973), pp 15–16; G. Giudice, *Pirandello: a biography*, trans. A. Hamilton (London, 1975), Chapter 7, pp 142–65; S. Bassnett-McGuire, *Luigi Pirandello* ((London, 1983), pp 10–12. Pirandello's *Teatro d'Arte*, founded in Rome in 1925, is twice mentioned in Starkie's book on the Sicilian playwright (W. Starkie, *Pirandello*, pp 238, 246). 57 W. Starkie, *Pirandello*: on the failure to supply necessary source references, see pp 41, 231, 160; as regards translation, or not, from the Italian see p. 71. 58 W. Starkie, *Pirandello*: the following pages provide some of the instances of incorrect usage: 47, 92, 94, 112, 116, 117, 119, 120, 126–7, 128, 131, 132, 140, 142, 144, 152, 153, 158, 159, 161, 162, 163, 170, 174, 178, 179, 185, 186, 193, 201, 245 254, 264, 265, 267. 59 See Bibiography, p. 320. 60 Her gravestone places her husband's surname first: Delfina Porchietti Landi. 61 N. Starkie to E. Starkie, 1 Nov. 1926. (ES Bodl.)

of establishing 'some form of friendly association with Great Britain', declaring it to be a necessary condition for securing 'the unity of Ireland'.[62] Starkie would doubtless have sympathized, both on the grounds of an association he felt part of and given the principle of unity. However, such sympathies were becoming increasingly less popular in the Dominion and in a matter of months O'Higgins's voice would be drastically silenced.

* * *

In her diary entry for 10 January 1927, Lady Gregory noted that she had received a letter from Lennox Robinson, who had broached the subject of a new Director for the Abbey Theatre. She stated that Yeats and herself favoured Starkie over other possible Catholic candidates, T.C. Murray and Daniel Corkery, whose names had followed the younger man's in Robinson's letter. Apart from Starkie's docile quality – Lady Gregory qualified the candidate as 'very tractable' while expressing her conviction that he wouldn't 'give us any trouble'[63] – there was the imperative to have someone in sympathy with Yeats, Robinson and herself: 'We must "have someone we can talk freely to and before".'[64] Thus, Lady Gregory considered that the thirty-two-year-old brought together a series of elements that recommended him for the post. Furthermore, he was, she reasoned: 'the obvious choice from the point of view of mental qualifications, he is young, very interested in the theatre, has just published his book on Pirandello, is Professor in TCD in Italian [*sic*][65] and Spanish,… *But* he isn't a very good Catholic.'[66] Starkie was appointed and remained in the post until 1942.[67]

In 1927 and 1928, Starkie was to publish more reviews in the *Irish Statesman* than in any of the three preceding years, thus ensuring a greater visibility for 'the splendid educational work'[68] being performed by the RDS, the ongoing consolidation of links

---

62 'Association with Britain', IT, 18 Dec. 1926, p. 7.   **63** In a letter to her husband, George Yeats commented on Starkie's tendency 'to agree with everything anyone says' (G. Yeats to W.B. Yeats, 29 Feb. 1932 in A. Saddlemyer (ed.), *W.B. Yeats and George Yeats. The letters* (Oxford, 2011), p. 298.   **64** In the same diary entry, Gregory notes that the Minister of Finance, Ernest Blythe, 'wants a Catholic'; D.J. Murphy (ed.), *Lady Gregory's journals*, ii, p. 161. I understand that the text in inverted commas in Lady Gregory's diary entry is citing Robinson's letter to her.   **65** Starkie was Professor of Spanish and Lecturer in Italian. The possibility of him being nominated Professor of Italian together with Spanish was broached at the TCD Board Meeting when the proposal for a professorship of Spanish was put forward but a majority (7 votes to 5) voted against the post also including Italian (TCD MUN/V/5/23, 11 Jan. 1926, p. 220).   **66** D.J. Murphy (ed.), *Lady Gregory's journals*, ii, p. 161. The italics are in the original.   **67** Starkie's resignation dates from the AGM of the National Theatre Society Ltd, held at the Abbey Theatre, Dublin, on Thursday, 17 September 1942, Ernest Blythe presiding. The argument was wielded that the government-appointed Director 'had not attended any meeting of the Board for a very considerable time prior to the AGM held on 26 June 1941 [when] it had been agreed … that he should not … be re-elected'. At the September AGM, Starkie stated that he was 'unable at present to attend meetings of the Board' (Starkie was holding the post of British Council Representative in Madrid by this time) and, therefore, expressed his desire to tender his resignation (National Theatre Society Ltd, Abbey Minute Book, Acc 3961/NFC 98 (16)).   **68** W. Starkie, 'RDS. The Philharmonic Trio' (1927), p. 506 (see Appendix). In conection with the RDS's educational task, see also W. Starkie, 'Sir Hamilton Harty's Orchestra' (1927), p. 626 (see Appendix).

with British (musical) culture and the reinforcing of a European range of reference in
an Ireland with League of Nations ambitions.[69] Back from Brussels, where his lecture
had been chaired by 'Monsieur Jaspar' and attended by, among others, an acquaintance of Archbishop Söderblom's, 'Monsieur Hymans',[70] Starkie initiated his new
year attendance at recitals and concerts. In February, he also began to deliver a series
of six lectures devoted to the life and works of Beethoven in this centenary year of the
composer's death. The sessions were held at his home, Botanic House, and from the
report on the first of the lectures in the *Musical Times*, it can be seen that the lecturer
adopted the procedure adopted in his 2RN lectures related to music, that is, the combi-
nation of verbal delivery with musical illustration: 'Dr Walter Starkie … pointed out
Beethoven's great capacity for work, as evidenced by his sketch books, and gave an
account of his triumphs at Vienna'. Several illustrations, including the 'Appassionata'
Sonata, were played by the lecturer.'[71] Come March, Starkie went to 'an exceedingly
interesting concert'[72] on the 13th, an attempt to recreate the Dublin Orchestral Society
by members of staff at the RIAM and personal friends of the reviewer,
Commendatore Esposito and John F. Larchet. Starkie's last review in March was
devoted to the two concerts held at the RDS on the 17th, dedicated to Irish composers
and Irish players, when 'close on five thousand people applauded the music of
Irishmen', a review that constituted his most political to date. The text gave prece-
dence to 'two big works' performed by composers knighted by the British
Establishment: Charles Villiers Stanford and Hamilton Harty. The former's 'Overture
to an Irish Comedy' and the latter's 'Irish Rhapsody for Orchestra Number 1 in D
Minor, Opus 78' were conducted for the St Patrick's Day celebration by J.F. Larchet.
Latched on to the remarks regarding the variety of performers is Starkie's reference
to 'so sincere an artist as Mr Seamus Clandillon', whose songs (not named) were set
by his wife and were 'as near as possible to the original Folk.' While recognising the
impact on the audience: 'a deep effect … owing to [the singer's] simple and unaffected
way of singing', the reviewer claimed that Mr Clandillon's songs did not constitute art.
Thus, he entreated:

> Let us realize that music springs from the folk melodies and dances, but they are
> only as it were, the rough material for fashioning the world of art. Before the
> structure rises[,] it is necessary for the composer, whose musical soul has been
> excited by that melody, to work with all the resources of modern European
> harmony and then[,] when his work is finished[,] the musicians must draw near

69 See M. Kennedy, *Ireland and the League of Nations, 1919–1946. International relations, diplomacy and politics* (Dublin, 1996), Chapter 2, pp 43–72.   **70** W. Starkie to N. Söderblom, 5 [8?] Jan. 1927 (Uppsala universitetsbibliothek, Nathan Söderbloms samling. Brev från utlänningar). What Starkie lectured on is unclear. No references have been found other than the correspondence of his sister Nancy to their sibling Enid, mentioned above, and Starkie's letter to Söderblom cited here in which no further infor-mation is supplied. It may be presumed that M. Jaspar was Henri Jaspar (1870–1939) of the Belgian Catholic Party, PM of Belgium from 1926 to 1931, and M. Hymans was Paul Hymans (1865–1941) of the Belgian Liberal Party, Minister of Justice from 1926 to 1927 and Foreign Secretary between 1927 and 1935.   **71** 'Music in Ireland. Dublin', *Musical Times*, 68:1010, 1 Apr. 1927, p. 366.   **72** W. Starkie, 'The Dublin Orchestral Society' (1927), p. 40 (see Appendix).

in loving cooperation and carve and chisel in tones the work that before only existed in plaster.[73]

Therefore, the reviewer's final comment on Mr Clandillon's songs might be interpreted, at best, as condescending, if not as the dismissal of a country bumpkin's efforts: 'It was most interesting to hear the pure, unadulterated folk song as a contrast to music that has passed through European minds.'[74] However, the most ideologically charged content in the review, in terms of a wider strategic pertinence within the immediate context of Fianna Fáil's radical challenge to the Free State order and Cumann na nGhaedheal's declining fortunes, follows the opening acknowledgement of the role played by the RDS in graciously providing the St Patrick's Day opportunity to the public 'to welcome its composers and performers' for which, the reviewer claims, the institution 'deserves deep gratitude'. Irishmen are represented as fiercely individualistic while a plea is made on behalf of other voices and in favour of working together. Thus, the musical *milieu* functions as a metaphor for a state of political intolerance, valiant resistance being prescribed and superlative success posited as the product of steadfast cooperation:

> Every Irishman among us is a furious individualist who tries to sing his own song to the detriment of everyone else. The result of our furious individualism is that we decry many of our fellow-countrymen who are trying to sing their song. [...] We must fight bravely to withstand these blasting influences. In no art is this courage more necessary than in music where all that is greatest depends on the perseverance and perfection of team work.[75]

In the meantime, hope is drawn from the numbers who attended the two concerts at the RDS on St Patrick's Day. The principle of pulling together is similarly voiced in Starkie's review on the 1927 Feis Ceoil whereby a harmonious entity might be forged, thus overriding the 'furious', now 'fierce' individualism (a gloss on oppositional political persuasions):

> In Ireland we are all fierce individualists, and in music as in athletics we prefer the solo efforts. The Feis Ceoil, however, is educative, and it attempts to make us all combine to create a big collective mass of harmony. I heard one adjudicator remark sadly on several occasions last week: 'here are splendid solo violinists and 'cellists; why don't you meet together and form quartets?'[76]

---

73 W. Starkie, 'Irish composers and Irish players' (1927), pp 68, 70, 68 (see Appendix).   74 Ibid., p. 70. The reviewer's comments would be followed in the month of November by Dr Donal O'Sullivan's 'scathing review of a collection of Irish songs, and the compilers, Mr and Mrs Seamus Clandillon, brought a libel action against the reviewer, the editor and the paper' (H. Summerfield, *The myriad-minded man: a biography of George William Russell 'AE', 1867–1935* (Gerrards Cross, 1975), p. 245. Cited by N. Allen, *George Russell*, p. 228). The costs of the court case were to be crippling for the *Irish Statesman*.   75 W. Starkie, 'Irish composers and Irish players', p. 68 (see Appendix).   76 W. Starkie, 'The Feis Ceoil' (1927), p. 227 (see Appendix).

The Feis Ceoil review also speaks out in favour of 'the close bond uniting stage and audience' and satirizes, in Swiftian vein, disagreement being expressed in the audience by a show of different coloured flags in order to make a point about the Irish not being 'a nation of flag-wavers', which, the reviewer forcibly (hopefully?) asserts, would be 'utterly unlike the true Irishman'.[77]

Starkie made no contributions to the *Irish Statesman* in the month of April. In May, he reviewed the Civil Service Musical Society's second annual concert. As was the case in the St Patrick's Day programme at the RDS, the outstanding pieces performed were authored by composers whose careers had developed in England. The reviewer declared: 'Of all the choral items of the evening the most striking performance was in Charles Wood's setting of "He has a secret to tell thee", for male voices, and "Quick, we have but a second", by Stanford.'[78] Just as hope was expressed with regard to the future of music in Ireland given the numbers who attended the RDS St Patrick's Day concerts, in his June review of the Dublin Wireless Orchestral Concert, Starkie highlighted the radio concerts as contributing 'a great deal to advance the cause of music in Ireland', even envisaging 'the great awakening of Ireland's musical life.' He also noted in his review 'the power of wireless', its potential to defeat distance: 'Imagine the ethereal music of Mozart wafted through the air and reaching the confines of the West.'[79] Of course, it would not only be 'the ethereal music of Mozart' which would reach the remoter Western seabord but all the music and messages on 2RN, whatever ideas they might be emitting. It is interesting to note, therefore, that at a time when de Valera increasingly occupied more space in the media and would be working towards setting up a daily newspaper, Starkie's presence on the Dublin airwaves became more audible: his Spanish classes remained a regular feature on Tuesdays but he would also contribute to a variety of other programmes related to music, broadcasting at what might be considered peak listening times on a Friday and Saturday evening.[80] Moreover, the Starkie name also multiplies in Dublin in daily reportage either through Starkie's own activities and appearances at Trinity, in public lectures, at social gatherings, from balls to funerals, or through an increased involvement in government-related events; through the performance of his sister Ida (Chou-Chou) as a cellist;[81] sister Nancy, a bridesmaid on the occasion of Ida's marriage to Civic Guard Michael O'Reilly;[82] his mother, recorded as attending the annual conference of the Alexandra College Guild[83] or present at the executive committee meeting of the Feis Ceoil,[84] as well as his father, being remembered among 'a world-famous band of critics, historians, philologists and archaeologists',[85] envisaged as a gift to Classical scholarship by TCD.

---

77 Ibid., p. 228.   78 W. Starkie, 'The Civil Service Musical Society' (1927), p. 212 (see Appendix). 79 Ibid.   80 E.g., 'Broadcasting Today. 8:00 – Dr Walter Starkie and Station Orchestra. Norway and its music', IT, 20 May 1927, p. 3; 'Broadcasting Today. 8.20 – talk, Finland and its music. Dr W. Starkie, with violin illustrations,' IT, 12 Aug. 1927, p. 3; 'Broadcasting Today. 7:00 – talk on music with violin illustrations). Dr W. Starkie', IT, 16 Sept. 1927, p. 5.   81 'Broadcasting. 8.40: Ida Starkie (cello solos)', IT, 12 Jan. 1927, p. 3.   82 'Marriage of Miss Ida Starkie', IT, 9 May 1927, p. 7.   83 Caption under photograph: 'The annual conference of the Alexandra College Guild was resumed at the College last Saturday', IT, 11 May 1927, p. 11.   84 'The Feis Ceoil', IT, 24 Oct. 1927, p. 4.   85 'The New Vice-

But powerful as broadcasting or the press might be, Starkie's energies and appeal were not exclusively devoted to radio listeners or readers of the daily press and neither was his pedagogical prowess limited to instruction in the Spanish language. Following the publication of his book on Pirandello, somewhat negatively reviewed in the *Irish Times* in the month of January,[86] Starkie turned to Machiavelli in the year of the fourth centenary of his death, perhaps prompted by Luigi Villari. A lecture on Niccolo Machiavelli by Professor Walter Starkie, Litt. D., FTCD, was announced in the *Irish Times* on Friday, 4 March, and took place on the following Wednesday, the 9th, in the Graduates Memorial Hall at Trinity College at 4p.m., the public being admitted free and without ticket. The lecture appears to have also been delivered for the Catholic Central Library Committee at the Hall, 18 Lower Leeson Street in Dublin, an occasion taken advantage of by the *Catholic Bulletin* to lampoon Starkie's ubiquitous energies, referring to him as 'the one and only Walter Fitzwilliam Starkie ... By himself alone, he is an Academic Orchestra. [...] He is heard of everywhere from Seville to Stockholm', going on to adopt its characteristically vituperative voice on the Anglican inheritance of TCD:

> There is no doubt that Machiavelli, who died in 1527, when Henry VIII got religious scruples and decided to promote a Divorce, was rightly commemorated within the Elizabethan Academy: for Machiavelli elevated lying and fraud, hypocrisy and deceit, thieving and thuggery into an intellectual system, and provided a scientific exposition of the statecraft and the savagery of the two Tudor Monarchs with whom 'Our Church and Our University' are so closely allied.[87]

An editorial piece in the *Irish Statesman* on the first Saturday in March (published between the initial announcement of Starkie's Machiavelli lecture at TCD on Friday, the 4th, and the second one, on the day of the lecture) proclaimed that fascism was 'developing into the most ambitious attempt to remake a nation on new lines that Europe has witnessed for centuries.'[88] The issue of the following week then carried the first of two pieces by Francis Hackett, focussing on a forty-minute interview the Irish writer had held with Mussolini. However, overall, the text projected a negative view of Il Duce, assessed as 'a centre of egoism', qualified as 'the hero of one of those terrific dramas of upstart genius of which Italy has often been the theatre'[89] and, finally, felt to be: 'a dangerous, unscrupulous and malignant force'.[90] It may partly have been such negative publicity, together with Starkie's close contact with Villari as well as his own, and Italia's, desire to correct the unfavourable portrait, which led to the

---

Provost. Retirement of Dr L.C. Purser', IT, 26 Oct. 1927, p. 7. **86** '[T]he book as a whole suffers heavily from constant repetition and redundancy. Lucidity often is sacrificed.' I say 'somewhat negatively reviewed' above as the review concludes: 'Professor Starkie has written an illuminating work on a perplexing character' ('Books of the week', IT, 21 Jan. 1927, p. 3). **87** 'Professor [*sic*] Fitzwilliam Starkie on Machiavelli', *Catholic Bulletin and Book Review*, 17:4, Apr. 1927, pp 343–44. **88** IS, 5 Mar. 1927, p. 613. **89** F. Hackett, 'Mussolini, Red and Black', IS, 12 Mar. 1927 p. 8. **90** F. Hackett, 'Mussolini, Red and Black (cont.)', IS, 19 Mar. 1927, p. 32.

TCD professor being afforded an interview with the dictator on Monday, 11 July 1927, that is, as it turned out, the day following the assassination of the Free State minister Kevin O'Higgins.

According to his own recollection some ten years on, Starkie received the news of O'Higgins's death in Rome, on the eve of his interview with Mussolini at the Palazzo Chigi. He appears to have been in the Italian capital for the summer, staying at an apartment loaned by his 'friend'[91] Villari. At one point in his account of the interview, Starkie alludes to having been conversing with Mussolini for forty minutes, precisely the period of time cited by Francis Hackett in his encounter,[92] and Starkie's account of his own interview in manuscript certainly evoked Hackett's, even appearing to be seeking to remedy impressions conveyed by the Irish writer. For instance, Hackett declared: 'Mussolini is a fencer. His own words occurred to me, "good strategy is calculation and audacity," and I made up my mind that in this fencing match it was best to be tactless.'[93] He also spoke of the Italian dictator striking him as histrionic. Starkie's text reads: 'During the forty minutes that we had been conversing I noticed no traces of the theatrical.'[94] And the text had continued: 'With me he was in no necessity of fencing with words, and so the conversation was carried on by him in a pleasant manner.'[95] The implication is that Mussolini was less at ease with Hackett. However the sentence was removed from the published text of *The waveless plain*, which appeared ten years after Hackett's interview.

Chapter 29 of *The waveless plain* provides an account of Starkie's interview with Mussolini as well as reference to another 'friend' of the interviewer, Senator Giovanni Gentile, 'not only the philosopher of the Movement [*sic*], but the great reformer in education', further assessed as 'the personification of philosophic [*sic*] calm', and to Edmondo Rossoni, 'the great authority of the Corporative State'. Starkie identifies himself at the beginning of the chapter as 'a friend of Italy', anxious to improve the profile of 'the Leader', whose message, he claims, has been distorted through 'ceaseless propaganda against the Dictator in newspapers, books, cinema and radio'. Thus, Starkie produced a text that conveys an exclusively favourable portrait of a patriarch, 'Father of his country', an account which covers Mussolini from face ('his large dark eyes … sparkled when his voice became animated'; 'a most lively and winning countenance') to fingers ('As I looked at his broad white hands with well-padded fingers, I said to myself that he had the touch of the violinist, the natural *vibrato*, which is a source of power when added to his supreme mastery of rhythms') and manifests the interviewer's fascination in a manner evocative of Lemuel Gulliver's before the Master Houyhnhnm ('I was hypnotized'; 'I found myself gazing'). The impact of Machiavelli and Nietzsche on Mussolini are also recorded and the inter-viewer expresses his desire 'to lead up to the great state-religious question', a cue for Mussolini to point back to Manzoni's Catholic identity, Mazzini's being 'deeply

---

91 W. Starkie, *Waveless*, p. 387.   **92** W. Starkie, *Waveless*, p. 396; F. Hackett, 'Mussolini, Red and Black', IS, 19 Mar. 1927, p. 31.   **93** F. Hackett, 'Mussolini, Red and Black', IS, 12 Mar. 1927, pp 7–8.   **94** W. Starkie, *Waveless*, p. 396.   **95** W. Starkie, Manuscript of *The waveless plain* (MS 11/645, JMC). On Mussolini and fencing, see also W. Starkie, *Waveless*, p. 392.

religious', and, at this delicate juncture with regard to relations between Church and State, for him to recognize the Church's authority: 'I believe that the only universal idea now existing in Rome is that represented by the Vatican. There are in the world over 400,000,000 men who look to Rome from all parts of the earth. That is a source of pride for us Italians.'[96]

As Starkie's interview with Mussolini began, the Italian premier had communicated his awareness of O'Higgins's death and expressed admiration of him. Given his sojourn in Italy, Starkie did not attend the funeral of the Free State Minister but his name appeared among those who expressed their condolences to the widow.[97] He renewed his contributions to the *Irish Statesman* in August and the months leading up to the end of the year indicate an intensified contribution to the journal. Before the end of 1927, Starkie produced seventeen reviews, chalking up 4 in November and as many as six in December, more than he had ever published in any one month since his first contributions in 1924. The first review in August carried comment on a John McCormack recital in the wake of the Dublin Horse Show, an event that would enable Starkie to convey national cohesion by means of the singer between Anglo- and Irish-Ireland and to reiterate the notion of evolution. Thus, he begins: 'It was fitting that after our great week of festivities we should all throng to hear the voice of our national bard' and before the reviewer turns to comment on the recital proper, space is devoted to constructing a joint sense of community around 'our music',[98] together with a vindication of it. Moreover, whereas he had earlier argued for the necessity for Irish music to be filtered through 'European minds',[99] now there appears a change of direction: a looking to the impact of Irish folk music on Europe, rather than asserting the need for Ireland to Europeanize her output in order to rise to the appropriate rank, coupled with a (newly acquired) consciousness of neglect with regard to indigenous production and a vindication of determination and constancy in the pursuit of quality:

> so far [the ...] songs of the people ... have not exercised great dominating influence on the music of Europe. Too little do we study these folk songs of ours, for by no other means are we going to *evolve* here in our country a school of Irish composers. We have all the rough materials, but we have not yet acquired the steadfast qualities which enable men to raise the artistic structure. [...] Ireland is a small country amidst the nations but she has a very big message of art and culture to give to the world.[1]

However, having underlined the importance of Irish folk music, Starkie dwells on McCormack's rendering of songs by European composers while highlighting the

---

96 W. Starkie, *Waveless*, pp 402, 404, 388, 396, 395, 398.   97 'Sympathy with Mrs Higgins', IT, 14 July 1927, p. 5. Starkie appears thus: 'Walter Starkie, Masone', that is, he is recorded as being resident in the Ligurian village where his mother-in-law had died in 1924, not in Rome.   98 W. Starkie, 'John McCormack' (1927), p. 545 (see Appendix).   99 See above Starkie's remarks on Seamus Clandillon's performance at the RDS on St Patrick's Day 1927 ('Irish composers and Irish players' (see Appendix).).   1 W. Starkie, 'John McCormack' (1927), pp 545–6 (see Appendix). My italics. The notion of evolution will be reiterated in relation to McCormack's development, as will be seen in further references to the singer's performance.

singer's simplicity, his command of diction and, particularly, the emotional experience, even capable of disarming the critic at his post: 'I am sure McCormack wept as he sang "To the children" by Rachmaninoff, and few of us in the audience were dry-eyed. On such occasions the musical [*sic*] critic ceases to rap, casts away his pedant's gown and becomes a human being.'² Another song that produced a similar effect was 'Christ went up into the hills' by Hageman. Finally, the reviewer will point to what he considered '[t]he most perfect moment in the whole recital', McCormack's singing of Brahms's 'Mainacht', observing that the German composer's song illustrated 'the wonderful *evolution* that has taken place in McCormack's art' and whose 'greatness' was constituted through the achievement of 'the exact *balance* of tone and expression'.³ Oh (a sub-text might read) that such national equilibrium could also be afforded and through the same gradual and poised means! Starkie evoked the notions of evolution and balance in relation to McCormack's artistic achievement again, a month later, when commenting on the artist's performance at an inaugural recital for 'Civic Week' in Dublin. Once more, McCormack becomes the pivot who unites us, the nation, most immediately as audience:⁴ 'It was most appropriate to commence our week's festivities with a recital given by our great national singer, John McCormack.' He has become 'a symbol of Irish song' yet alongside the national dimension he has achieved international status: 'he possesses in his bones the very essence of the Irish folk song ..., but he is also the great cosmopolitan artist whose musical idiom is under-stood in Paris or Rome as well as in London or New York ... he has *evolved* from the opera to the "lieder" singer, and thus his extraordinary technical command of voice is *balanced* by his intellect.' As in the earlier review in August, Starkie focussed on McCormack's performance of European composers: his rendering of arias by Handel and Bach, songs by Chausson, Strauss and Bantock. In contrast to the earlier occasion, however, he refers to McCormack's distinct rendering of 'a group of Irish folk songs', of which no details are supplied though the authors of the arrangements are cited: Herbert Hughes, Dr [*sic*] Larchet and Vincent O'Brien. Interestingly, he registers the rapport established between singer and audience when the Irish folk songs were performed in the second half of the programme, 'many encores in response to an enthusiastic audience'⁵ taking place.

Starkie's last review in August and the first in September were both devoted to the theatre: Arthur Power's play *The Drapier Letters*, written seven years earlier (when, the reader is reminded, 'the stage had not yet begun to mirror the sadness and despair of revolutionary days')⁶ but only just performed at the Abbey, and Yeats's 'graceful and pliant'⁷ version of Sophocles's *Oedipus at Colonus*. While recognizing 'many excellent dramatic qualities'⁸ in Power's play, Starkie records little enthusiasm for the author's

2 Ibid., p. 546.   3 Ibid. My italics.   4 With regard to the nation united as audience under the Cumann na nGaedheal government in the 1920s, see P. Reynolds, *Modernism, drama and the audience for Irish spectacle* (Cambridge, 2007), Chapter 5.   5 W. Starkie, 'Civic Week. Music Notes. John McCormack. Comendatore [*sic*] Esposito' (1927), p. 64 (see Appendix).   6 W. Starkie, 'New play at the Abbey. "The Drapier Letters" ' (1927), p. 597 (see Appendix).   7 W. Starkie, '*Oedipus at Colonus* at the Abbey Theatre' (1927), p. 40 (see Appendix).   8 W. Starkie, 'New play at the Abbey Theatre' (1927), p. 597 (see Appendix).

first attempt at writing for the theatre. His review of Yeats's rendering of the Greek original carries more compliments, both on account of Yeats' English prose and Lennox Robinson's production, considered 'a great triumph', though there is criticism of the choruses and with regard to some of the casting. In assessing Yeats' task, Starkie sees the translator as approaching Sophocles 'through the paths of folk drama and folk poetry' and claims that the version succeeds in '[calling] up before us the image of the Athenian national soul.' A parallelism is then drawn between 'the healthy and vigorous simplicity of the rustics of Attica, with their heroes of the past allied to the vivid, active mind of the rising urban population' and '[w]e in Ireland, living in a small agricultural country' whose 'poets ceaselessly search through the woods and valleys for the spirit of their former heroes.' Subsequently, the reviewer's witnessing of the audience's response at the Abbey Theatre on the night of the 12 November 1927 will convey their contemplation of a 'soulful' experience which drew them together in awe, creating a unified response and, thus, a shared sense of identity: 'the audience…were profoundly moved [and] sat in solemn silence as though listening to the performance of some great ritual.'9

In later September and early October, Starkie contributed a number of reviews dealing with musical events during Dublin's Civic Week, a period presented as constituting a balm to a politically taxed Free State: 'a country that has just emerged wearily from the Second General Election within a few months'.10 The 24 September issue of the *Irish Statesman* carried three contributions by Starkie: a book review, dealing with three Beethoven publications (which might well have proved useful in the lectures delivered earlier in the year at Botanic House), reviews on a recital by John McCormack (referred to above) and a concert by Commendatore Esposito, who is recognized as '[having] done more than anyone else for music in our city for the last forty-five years.'11 Starkie comments further on Civic Week events in the 1 October issue: a review of the Children's Concert, given by Dr Larchet and his Orchestra at the Theatre Royal on 20 September, and another on the concert provided by the Dublin Philharmonic Orchestra on the 24th, at which Beethoven's choral symphony was performed. In his review of the Children's Concert, Starkie hails the success of the Civic Week venture, recording that all the concerts were well attended and claiming that the events have served to stimulate 'the musical consciousness of our city.'12 In noting the success of the Beethoven choral symphony, Starkie expresses the opinion that part of the success was a consequence of two double basses from Belfast and two from Manchester's Hallé Orchestra. Whereas on earlier occasions (before the death of Kevin O'Higgins), the reviewer might have commented on the quality imports, he now vindicates indigenous worth: 'It struck me as strange that at a concert given during the Civic Week of our capital city the authorities had to import bass players from other countries. Surely in this city so rich in theatres we have plenty of double bass players able to uphold the traditions of Irish musicianship?'13 The

9 W. Starkie, '*Oedipus at Colonus* at the Abbey Theatre' (1927), p. 40 (see Appendix). 10 W. Starkie, 'Civic Week music. Children's concert' (1927), p. 86 (see Appendix). 11 W. Starkie, 'Civic Week music notes. Comendatore [*sic*] Esposito' (1927), p. 64 (see Appendix). 12 W. Starkie, 'Civic Week music. Children's concert' (1927), p. 86 (see Appendix). 13 W. Starkie, 'Civic Week music. Dublin

performance of Colonel Brase, represented as a conductor-cum-dictator, '[having] the strength of personality to compel the exact obedience of his players', is praised and attention is given by means of specific reference to 'the choral works of our own composers': Stanford, Larchet, Weaving, Hewson, Molyneux Palmer, Harold White and Joze. Thus, the reviewer used his final paragraph to highlight Irish composition and its promise as well as to appeal to his readers to engage in exploiting home talent in building the nation: 'The conclusion of the concert made us all feel that Dublin need never feel pessimistic about its musical future. We have the building materials, let us construct a noble edifice.'[15]

Musical events apart, Starkie produced three book reviews in the month of December, all of which were related to Spain: Nina Larrey Duryea's *Mallorca the magnificent*,[16] *Virgin Spain* by Waldo Frank together with J. Meier-Graefe's *The Spanish journey*[17] and Janet H. Perry's edition of Juan Valdés's *Diálogo de las lenguas* [The dialogue of languages].[18] No critical comment is made on Perry's edition of Valdés and little on the Larrey Duryea book on Mallorca. The third review, while dealing to some degree with the texts published by the American novelist and scholar Waldo Frank and German art critic Julius Meier-Graefe, dwells at greater length on 'the spirit of Spain', as announced in the title of the review, one which resists 'this machine-mad age of ours.' Indeed, in the post-First World War wasteland, 'these days of crumbling traditions', the reviewer will assert: 'it is good to look on Spain preserving inviolate many of the customs handed down the centuries'. Before touching on the texts to be reviewed, Starkie devotes three paragraphs to considering the significance of Spain in the present and reviewing her history from the time of the Moorish occupation and subsequent expulsion in the fifteenth century. Spanish colonialism is presented as a spiritual exercise as well as a material one, and thus it is justified: 'The Spanish will to world [*sic*] domination was a sublime gesture because it was not limited to wordly glory: there were warriors fighting for guerdons in the realm of the spirit.' The juxtaposition of 'men of indomitable will and limitless powers of action', such as Cortes and Pizarro, to 'spiritual warriors', such as Fray Luis de León, St Teresa and St John of the Cross, illustrates that 'beside the contemplative seer stands the fierce man of action' and constitutes, furthermore, a 'country of contrasts'.[19] Finally, the importance of Castile is highlighted in its unification of the whole country, a point that will be undermined by Frank's book, which underlines Spain's Arab and Jewish inheritance. However, Starkie does not enter into debate about Spanish identity but does criticize what he perceives to be a lack of unity in Frank's text, later expressing his disagreement with the author, both in the realm of art and with regard to 'the spirit of Spain'. He also takes exception to Meier-Graefe's rejection of Velázquez though he registers finding 'charming pages' on the different

Philharmonic Society' (1927), p. 87 (see Appendix).   **15** Ibid.   **16** W. Starkie, '*Mallorca the Magnificent*. By Nina Larrey Duryea. (London. Faber and Gwyer)' (1927) (see Appendix).   **17** W. Starkie, 'Literature and life. The spirit of Spain' (1927), pp 371–3 (see Appendix).   **18** W. Starkie, '*Diálogo de las lenguas*. By Juan de Valdés. Edited with Introduction and Appendices by Janet H. Perry, M.A. (University of London Press)' (1927), p. 378 (see Appendix).   **19** W. Starkie, 'Literature and life. The spirit of Spain' (1927), p. 371 (see Appendix).

regions making up the country. Starkie's review ends with a visionary view of Spain, which underlines the transcendence of the past within the present and expresses resistence to modernity, convictions Starkie reiterated in his writing on Spain in the following decade:

> The spirit of ancient Spain looks on eternally, so that any traveller to that country finds himself at once in communication with the phantoms of the past. I remember once when wandering over the parched uplands watching Fray Luis de León on his mule riding pensively through the twilight towards Salamanca. At another time I heard the Gargantuan laughter of the Arch Priest of Hita carousing with the old woman Trotaconventos and two Arab dancers. In the still evenings at the 'posada' in Cinco Casas I chatted with the inn keeper and Simón Carrasco: in the distance over the plain, beyond a clump of cypress trees, I saw a ghostly rider followed by his squire on a mule. No modern mechanical age can ever dissipate these visions: the spirit of the knight of the sorrowful countenance lives on in the most futuristic of Spaniards.[20]

Following these moments of vision, it is surprising to find the reviewer declaring: 'Today Spain is at the beginning of a great material awakening' though the remaining part of the sentence returns to the country's 'spirit' which, it is claimed: 'lives on in the great nations beyond the sea that make up the Spanish world'.[21] The declaration with regard to Spain's 'great material awakening' is sudden and comes over as forced, seemingly bearing no relation to the earlier sequence of what constitutes the final paragraph of the text. Therefore, it might be queried what reason, or request, motivated the introduction of the idea and, indeed, some of the earlier historical evocation, which bears little or no relation to the book reviews apparently under scrutiny. Starkie might have suddenly been possessed by a consciousness of Spain's 'great material awakening'; on the other hand, were the latter to be the case, who would have supplied the request or cue? Events in 1928 and the part Starkie played in them may point to possibilities.

The Remembrance Day celebrations of November 1927 sharply highlighted the political division in the Free State. On Monday, 7 November, the *Irish Times* devoted its customary page of photographs to providing a record of Remembrance Day services in Dublin. One showed members of the British Legion marching from Molesworth Street to St Patrick's Cathedral for the special service, another captured the (female) relatives of men who fell in the war en route, while ex-servicemen marching to mass at the Pro-Cathedral were also shown. On Armistice Day, no Arts lectures were delivered at TCD between 10a.m. and 12 midday and the university's great bell was tolled eleven times at 11a.m. The *Irish Times* recorded that 'the largest crowd ever seen at a Remembrance Day ceremony in Dublin'[22] gathered at the Cenotaph in the Phoenix Park and also noted that a '[r]ecord number of poppies were worn'.[23] However, the Fianna Fáil meeting in College Green on the night of the 8th

20 Ibid., p. 373.   21 Ibid.   22 IT, 12 Nov. 1927, p. 6 (photo page).   23 'Quiet night in Dublin.

had not lacked support. Sean Lemass and de Valera, together with others, addressed the crowd, the Free State parliamentarian Seán T. O'Kelly asserting, according to the account: 'they were there to demonstrate that Ireland was no colony, and that the Irish people would be no party to anything that flavoured of British imperialism' and de Valera proclaiming, as reported: 'Until complete freedom was gained, England's flag in this country was the flag of the enemy, and ought to be dealt with as such'.[24]

Over the autumn and winter months of 1927, Starkie became yet more of a presence within Dublin society. Apart from being regularly heard over the radio: his weekly Spanish lessons on 2RN; visible at recitals and concerts as well as at the theatre; in print through his reviews in the *Irish Statesman*, he presided over a free public lecture in late October on Irish minstrelsy[25] and on the first Friday of November, he was present to lend his support at the sessional opening of the TCD Classical Society.[26] At the end of the month, a further instance of Starkie's growing involvement with the Free State government at an official level would be made manifest when the *Dublin Gazette* announced that he had been appointed a member of the Censorship of Films Appeal Board in place of Senator Gogarty, who had resigned.[27] However, intense activity in Dublin did not lead to his severing links with the British metropolis. In the month of April his application for membership of his father's London club, the Athenaeum, had been submitted, his candidature being proposed by the archbishop of Dublin and seconded by his father's contemporary, the Old Salopian and editor of *Punch*, Owen Seaman,[28] a supporter of the Resident Commissioner's application for membership a quarter of a century earlier.[29] Perhaps the TCD Professor of Spanish was already looking towards transfer from Ireland to England. The Alfonso XIII Chair in Spanish was endowed at the University of Oxford in 1927 and Starkie was to present his candidature for the post in 1928. Indeed, his lecturing once again at the *Residencia de Estudiantes* in Madrid might be considered part of the grooming for election.[30] In the meantime, however, he was at his teaching post in Dublin and his contributions to the *Irish Statesman* provide evidence of his presence in the country over the first quarter of the new year.

1927 drew to a close with de Valera's departure for the United States in pursuit of funds for the founding of a daily newspaper.[31] Less than a month later President Cosgrave would also cross the Atlantic, going on to Canada from the US, and his new year tour began to be commented on in the December press. Starkie figured on the

Record number of poppies worn', IT, 12 Nov. 1927, p. 9.   **24** 'The Union Jack denounced', IT, 9 Nov. 1927, p. 7.   **25** 'Irish minstrelsy', IT, 27 Oct. 1927, p. 4.   **26** 'The Emperor Augustus. His place in history of religion. Classical Society Paper', IT, 5 Nov. 1927, p. 6.   **27** *Dublín Gazette*, 29 Nov. 1927. **28** 'Certificate of Candidate for Ballot' of Professor Walter Fitzwilliam Starkie, F.T.C.D., M.A., Litt.D. Dublin, M.R.I.A., No. 11644, Date of entry: 27 April 1927 (The Athenaeum). I am grateful to Sarah J. Dodgson, Librarian at The Athenaeum in 1994 for help in locating documents and for photocopies supplied.   **29** Another supporter of both father and son in their applications for membership was Horace Plunkett.   **30** L[uis]. C[alvo]., 'Una conversación acerca del teatro moderno. Mr. Walter Starkie' [A conversation about the modern theatre. Mr Walter Starkie], *ABC*, 12 Apr. 1928, p. 10. Calvo became theatre critic of the Madrid newspaper *ABC* in 1926 (J. Burns, *Papa spy* (London, 2009), p. 158). For further information on Luis Calvo, see J. Burns, *Papa spy*, pp 158–61, passim.   **31** 'Mr De Valera off to America. Raising money for a new paper', IT, 13 Dec. 1927, p. 7.

committee organizing a 'banquet'[32] for the President prior to his departure and was present at Clery's restaurant in Dublin on the night of the 5 January together with Italia.[33] However, he also appears to have had time to attend the New Year's Day recital given by John McCormack before 'a crowded audience stacked on the stage as well as in the theatre itself'. In his comment on the recital, Starkie claimed that the singer's voice 'rang out as a paean to peace among us'.[34] Again a review was exploited as a means of conveying a political point. There are not so many instances of the device in the reviews over 1928 but Starkie did take advantage of his comments on the 1928 Feis Ceoil to drive home the idea of unity and the need for stability in institutions in order for achievements to succeed. His review praised both the RDS and Feis Ceoil for their staying power and for the manner in which they had proceeded. With regard to form, it will be seen that Starkie's expression echoes A.B.Walkley's words on scholars at TCD when alluding to Starkie's article on the *commedia dell' arte* in 1924: 'I can think of no two greater educative institutions in music in the world than the Feis and the Royal Dublin Society: both pursue their course serenely, taking no account of political upheavals or passing difficulties, and thus they are able to point to great achievements.'[35] The myth of Ireland as a land of 'fierce individualists' is again introduced, now juxtaposed to what the music festival signifies in terms of contrast, and an ensemble procedure is prescribed: 'The Feis Ceoil … is educative, and it attempts to try [sic] to make us *unite* in harmony. We should, therefore, do our best to organise quartets and trios.'[36] However, the prescription was subsequently undermined by the reviewer's going on to draw attention to the many interesting musical personalities that the festival had yielded, accompanied by his claim: 'it is here that such a festival performs the greatest good in our musical life'.[37] Another instance of the idea of unity is expressed in Starkie's review of the Dublin Philharmonic Orchestra's concert in the month of March when the conductor, Colonel Fritz Brase, whose 'commanding'[38] personality had already been singled out by Starkie in January, was assessed as largely having achieved success through the bond established between himself and cellist Ida Starkie, the reviewer's sister. The central work of what was considered a 'memorable'[39] concert was Tchaikovsky's Pathetic Symphony but the Elgar concerto for violincello and orchestra was also introduced. Having hailed his sister's playing, Starkie concluded: 'A great deal of the success of the performance was due to the *unanimity* that existed between soloist and conductor and Miss Starkie found in Colonel Brase a tower of strength'.[40]

March was not the first occasion in 1928 when Elgar had been performed. In February, violinist Albert Sammons had played the violin concerto of 'that most essentially British composer'.[41] Elgar's presence in the Dublin Philharmonic concert and Sammon's recital are revealing of a not-unsubstantial British presence in the

---

32 'Mr Cosgrave's tour', IT, 30 Dec. 1927, p. 5. 33 'President Cosgrave honoured', IT, 6 January 1928, pp 7, 8. 34 W. Starkie, 'Music of the week. John McCormack' (1928), p. 422 (see Appendix). 35 W. Starkie, 'The Feis Ceoil' (1928), p. 229 (see Appendix). 36 Ibid., p. 230. My italics. 37 Ibid. 38 W. Starkie, 'Music notes. The Dublin Philharmonic Society' (1928), p. 480 (see Appendix). 39 W. Starkie, 'Music notes. Dublin Philharmonic Orchestra' (1928), p. 12 (see Appendix). 40 Ibid. My italics. 41 W. Starkie, 'RDS. Albert Sammons' (1928), p. 540 (see Appendix).

musical activities reviewed by Starkie over the first quarter of 1928. All told, he reviewed 18 concerts or recitals produced by Irish, British or international players: 7 Irish, 6 of international provenance and only 4 British. However, the British 'penetrated' Irish activities, as was seen above in the Dublin Philharmonic concert, and it would also be the case when the Abbey Theatre Ballet School was set up and Miss Culwick's Choir gave a concert.[42]

Starkie's last contribution to the *Irish Statesman* in March reviewed a performance of Racine's *Andromaque* at the Peacock Theatre, produced by his colleague at TCD and Beckett's mentor Thomas Rudmose-Brown, 'in collaboration with Miss [Sarah] Purser',[43] for the Dublin University Modern Languages' Society. Starkie's comments on individual performances were largely positive, the star turn in the reviewer's view being the French *lecteur*, Beckett's future friend and co-translator of Joyce's 'Anna Livia Plurabelle', Alfred Péron, and he concluded that the production constituted 'a credit'[44] to the Society. In the latter part of the month, he set off for Madrid, leaving Italia with four-and-a-half-year-old Landi and toddler Alma in a snow-bound Dublin.[45] Italia de Starkie's Italian classes continued on 2RN, as did Dr W. Starkie's Spanish ones, albeit in his absence. Husband and father did not return until late April when, as a Director of the Abbey, he was met by what Christopher Murray has suggested might now be viewed as 'no more than a storm in a Hibernian teacup',[46] that is, the uproar surrounding the rejection for performance at the national theatre of O'Casey's First World War-inspired play, *The Silver Tassie*.

Starkie's lecture entitled 'Three Turning Points of the Modern Theatre: Ibsen, Shaw and Pirandello' took place at the Madrid *Residencia de Estudiantes* on Friday, 30 March, with the Duke of Alba in the chair. The *Irish Times* reported that the lecture was attended by 'most of the literary personalities of the Spanish capital' and further provided the lecturer's subsequent itinerary: 'Holy Week' in Seville, on to Jérez, 'the great wine centre'[47] (and birthplace of Spain's first twentieth-century dictator, General Miguel Primo de Rivera), before returning to Dublin via Madrid, where he would interview Primo de Rivera. In February, the *Daily Express* was advertising its publication of a series of articles by the first Governor-General of the Free State, Timothy Healy (which included one on de Valera)[48] and it was the Beaverbrook newspaper that published Starkie's piece on the General. It was dated in Madrid on Friday, 13 April, and apart from the text carried the reproduction of a handwritten message from the General. The interview reads as a public relations exercise, seeking

---

42 W. Starkie, 'Music notes. Abbey Theatre Ballets. Miss Culwick's Choir' (1928), p. 501 (see Appendix). When Ninette de Valois inaugurated the School of Ballet at the Abbey she took over to Dublin some of her pupils who 'cooperated', as Starkie's review explains, with the Dublin pupils. When Miss Culwick's Choir performed at the Metropolitan Hall, Starkie remarked that Miss Culwick had been 'very fortunate in securing the services of the most artistic singer England has today', for whom he reserved his greatest praise: Dorothy Silk.   43 'Racine in Dublin', under 'An Irishman's Diary', IT, 6 March 1928, p. 4.   44 W. Starkie, ' "Andromaque" at the Peacock Theatre' (1928), p. 35 (see Appendix).   45 'Heavy snow in Dublin', IT, 13 March 1928, p. 7. The snow fell on Monday, the 12th, and was the heaviest snowfall in Dublin in the month of March for ten years.   46 C. Murray, *Seán O'Casey. Writer at work. A biography* (Dublin, 2006), p. 201.   47 'An Irishman in Madrid', IT, 4 April 1928, p. 11.   48 Advertisement in the IT, 3 Feb. 1928, p. 3.

to convey a portrait of a responsible ruler who is also projected as an accessible human being and in no way constituting a threat to British trading interests. The interview with the Spanish dictator was not carried out in isolation. As the *Daily Express* reported, the General was also visited on 13 April by British Admiral of the Fleet Earl Beatty and Air Vice-Marshal Sir Sefton Brancker[49] and further support is lent to the favourable portrayal of Primo de Rivera by editorial comment in the paper on the same day.[50] The headline to Starkie's piece reads 'Dictator's call to religion' in capital letters. However, apart from the claim that 'a stronger religious feeling' is needed in the contemporary world as an antidote to 'rampant ... egoism and indifference', highlighted early on, there is no further consideration of religion or ethics. The article mainly focuses on the quality of this 'soldier of Spain': 'a good simple man, full of humanity', who, readers are informed, was motivated by an 'imperious call to duty' on contemplating his country in a state of 'hopeless misgovernment and chaos'. It also provides information on the current state of the country, where 'peace and prosperity' now reign instead of 'anarchy', where '[t]he people are content and the work of reconstruction proceeds steadily'.[51] There is also some comment on the condition of industrial relations in the country, on Spain's foreign policy with regard to the League of Nations, Morocco and Tangiers, and confirmation of Spain's favourable disposition with regard to Anglo–Spanish relations.

On the Monday following the publication of the interview with Primo de Rivera, a further article signed by Starkie was published, pondering the current status of bullfights in Spain and conveying 'English [*sic*] Professor's impressions of a fantastic sight'.[52] The professor assured *Daily Express* readers that football was currently more popular in the country than bullfighting 'because every year the country is evolving nearer to the goal of modern civilisation'.[53] Interestingly, there is no adverse comment on 'modern civilisation' here, as tends to be the case in Starkie's writing, which suggests that the object of this particular exercise was to convey the idea of Spain's embracing modernity, thus lending further support to the 'awakening' of the country, as expressed in an article in the *Irish Statesman* some four months earlier.[54] However, Starkie's description of the bullfighter conveys the cult of personality, characteristic of his production in the 1920s and 30s, highlighting the seductive quality of the bullfighter's appearance and technique while the cruelty of the event is played down.[55]

On the day before Starkie's interview with General Primo de Rivera, the Dublin professor was introduced to readers of the Madrid monarchist daily *ABC* as 'the distinguished Irish [*sic*] literary critic' and as a director of the Abbey Theatre, identified in turn as 'the most progressive stage in the United Kingdom [*sic*]'. Now the interviewee, Starkie makes reference to contemporary theatre in France, Italy, Germany, Spain and mentions Hungary, Russia, as well as Elmer Rice and Eugene O'Neill in the United States. An 'eminent London critic', John Palmer, is also referred

49 'Earl Beatty's visit', DE, 14 Apr. 1928, p. 11.   **50** 'The Dictator's Message', DE, 14 Apr. 1928, p. 10.   **51** W. Starkie, 'Dictator's call to religion', DE, 14 Apr. 1928, p. 11.   **52** W. Starkie, 'Is Spain growing tired of bullfights?', DE, 16 Apr. 1928, p. 9.   **53** Ibid.   **54** W. Starkie, 'Literature and life. The spirit of Spain' (1927), pp 371–3 (see Appendix). See also the editorial 'Awakening Spain', IT, 10 July 1928, p. 6.   **55** W. Starkie, 'Is Spain growing tired of bullfights?', DE, 16 Apr. 1928, p. 9.

to but no specific mention is made of the theatre in England. Indeed, having been introduced as Irish, Starkie comes over as bent on asserting the nation's separate identity, dismissing 'England, an insular country', and promoting the recently founded Free State, which he becomes something of a spokesperson for, as may be appreciated in his pronouncements: 'We're a new country ... In Ireland ... we're not guided by the English compass. We think independently and are not tied to tradition.'[56]

Starkie travelled back to Ireland in the latter part of April and wrote to Yeats on his return, explaining that he had been in Spain 'for the past two months'.[57] He claimed that at the time of writing to his fellow Abbey director he had read O'Casey's *The Silver Tassie* 'several times very carefully'[58] and had also re-read the playwright's three published plays. He then provided his views on the controversial text, assessing it both initially and at the end of his letter as innovative: 'a new departure ... [O'Casey] is groping after a new drama outside the conventional stage; at any moment he may make a great discovery'.[59] In Starkie's view, *The Silver Tassie* certainly conveyed no 'great discovery': he found the characters lacking and although he was able to qualify the first act as 'masterly' and could imagine some appeal being created through the 'weird verse-chanting' in Act 2, he claimed that the play went downhill from that point on, both these comments echoing Yeats's own assessment in a letter to O'Casey over ten days earlier.[60] In spite of his reservations, however, Starkie came out in defence of the play being produced in Dublin, arguing that, ultimately, judgment should lie with the audience: 'I feel that the author is experimenting in a new world of drama; for this reason I feel strongly that the Abbey Theatre should produce the play. Seán [*sic*][61] O'Casey has given us so many fine works that we ought to leave the final decision with the audience that has laughed and wept with him.'[62] Starkie's argument appears not to have carried any weight, indeed, went unheeded, since Lady Gregory wrote to O'Casey without consulting the junior director.[63]

Starkie's sole contribution to the *Irish Statesman* in the month of May was his review of the Feis Ceoil, commented on above. No reviews appeared in June, July, August or September though there was comment from Starkie on fourteen musical events in Dublin between October and December as well as a piece on musical publications. Both Walter and Italia de Starkie continued with their Spanish and Italian classes on 2RN and Dr Starkie also delivered a half-hour 'Illustrated Lecture Recital'

---

56 L[uis].C[alvo]., 'Una conversación', p. 10. 57 W. Starkie to W.B. Yeats, 30 Apr. 1928, reproduced under 'Correspondence. The Abbey Directors and Mr Sean O'Casey', IS, 9 June 1928, pp 271–2. Starkie wrote up his views of the play on 4 June and, following Yeats' instructions, backdated his letter to 30 April (C. Murray, *Seán O'Casey*, p. 201). 58 W. Starkie to W.B. Yeats, 30 Apr. 1928, IS, 9 June 1928, p. 271. 59 Ibid., pp 271, 272. 60 W.B. Yeats to S. O'Casey, 20 Apr. 1928, reproduced under 'Correspondence. The Abbey Directors and Mr Sean O'Casey', IS, 9 June 1928, pp 268, 269. 61 Christopher Murray has noted that O'Casey 'did not use the accented "a" [in his forename] and it never appears on his title pages.' (C. Murray, *Seán O'Casey*, p. 451.) Starkie consistently accents the 'a' in O'Casey's forename throughout his letter to W.B. Yeats, presumably aimed at highlighting the Protestant playwright's 'authentic Irishness'. 62 W. Starkie to W.B. Yeats, 30 Apr. 1928, 'Correspondence. The Abbey Directors and Mr Sean O'Casey', IS, 9 June 1928, p. 272. 63 O'Casey's play was first produced in London on 11 Oct. 1929 (C. Murray, *Seán O'Casey*, pp 207–9).

early in June.[64] Later in the month a twenty-five minute 'Lecture Recital', which became a series, was devoted to musical composers.[65] The couple also attended a number of social events, sometimes accompanied by other members of the Starkie family. Thus they were present, together with Mrs W.J.M. Starkie, at the Provost's garden party at TCD on 12 June, at which the 'now rarely heard strains of "God Save the King" heralded the entrance of the Governor-General',[66] James McNeill. Muriel Starkie was with her brother and sister-in-law at the Dublin University Boat Club Dance at the Metropole Ballroom on Friday, 15 June.[67] Towards the end of the month, the widow of the late Resident Commissioner of Education presided over the meeting of the Central Branch of the British Legion (Women's Section) and was also present at the unveiling of a portrait of the late Provost and teacher at Alexandra College, John Henry Bernard, in early July.[68] Her son was present at the conferring of degrees at TCD on Saturday, 30 June, was broadcasting his Spanish lessons throughout July and August and was particularly busy in early August with the members of the Union of Graduates in Music, assembled in Dublin for their annual conference. They attended a reception at TCD on the 2nd at the invitation of the President of the Union, C.H. Kitson, Professor of Music in Dublin University, and Starkie himself, Registrar of the School of Music at TCD. The Professor of Spanish was also with the officers who represented France at the Dublin Horse Show and took them to the Leopardstown Races on the 4th. His presence was repeatedly registered in reports from the Horse Show in the week of the 6th, accompanied by his sister, Muriel, or by Italia together with his mother.[69] Professor and Mrs Starkie were also listed '[a]mong those noticed in the Members' Enclosure'[70] at the Phoenix Park Races on Saturday, the 11th. On the previous night, Professor Starkie had accompanied his sister Muriel to the British Legion Ball.[71] The social whirl continued at the end of the month with the presence of a host of journalists, in Dublin for the conference of the Institute of Journalists. Following the morning session on Monday, 27 August, a state reception was held at the Mansion House, followed by a luncheon offered to the delegates by the Free State Government. The *Irish Times* reported that 390 people were present, among them Dr [*sic*] and Mrs W. Starkie. Desmond FitzGerald, Minister for Defence in the Free State Government, presided in the absence of President Cosgrave, who was in Paris for the signing of the Kellogg-Briand Pact. Following the signing of the Pact, the American Secretary of State, Jack B. Kellogg, travelled to the Irish Free State. Kellogg was given the Freedom of the City of Dublin and, among other events, a reception and dance

64 'Broadcasting Today. 8.50 – Dr W. Starkie: illustrated lecture recital', IT, 8 June 1928, p. 13. 65 'Broadcasting Today. 9:45 – Dr W. Starkie: lecture recital, musical composers', IT, 22 June 1928, p. 3. See also 'Broadcasting Today. 9.10 – Dr W. Starkie: illustrated lecture recital, musical composers', IT, 7 July 1928, p. 5. 66 'The Provost's garden party', IT, 13 June 1928, p. 6. On the *Irish Times* nostalgically recording occasions when the British national anthem was sung in Dublin over the 1920s, see M. O'Brien, *The Irish Times* (Dublin, 2008), p. 66. 67 'Trinity Week dance. An enjoyable event', IT, 16 June 1928, p. 9. 68 'Late Dr Bernard', IT, 2 July 1928, p. 5. 69 'Some visitors to the Horse Show', IT, 9 Aug. 1928, p. 6; 'Ladies Day at the Horse Show', IT, 10 Aug. 1928, p. 6; 'Visitors at the Horse Show', 11 Aug. 1928, p. 6. 70 'Phoenix Park races. Large attendance of English visitors', IT, 13 Aug. 1928, p. 4. 71 'Last night's dances. British Legion ball. Brilliant function at the Plaza', IT, 11 Aug. 1928, p. 7.

were given at the United States Legation on the night of 31 August. The Starkies were on the guest list.[72]

* * *

Salvador de Madariaga explains his success in becoming the first occupant of the King Alfonso XIII Chair of Spanish at the University of Oxford in 1928 on two counts: 'a scarcity of Hispanists at the time in Britain; [*sic*] and the feeling that my books had fostered that I should be a good professor'.[73] His claim with regard to the lack of Hispanists is debatable since, apart from Starkie, Edgar Allison-Peers and J.B. Trend had already embarked on their careers in Spanish Studies. However, Madariaga undoubtedly constituted a more spectacular first occupant of the post given his established international profile following service at the League of Nations. Apart from an accumulation of social engagements, as illustrated above, 1928 was also busy for Starkie academically since he presented his candidature for the Oxford Chair and might well have felt confident about obtaining it since he was supported by the Duke of Alba, the Spanish Ambassador to Britain, Alfonso Merry del Val, and the Spanish Academy philologist Ramón Menéndez Pidal. Writing to his sister Enid over twenty years later, he recalled: 'I was led to believe that I was the favoured candidate'[74] and stated that according to his father's friend, civil servant and organizer of the British Empire Exhibition of 1924 to 1925, Sir Lawrence Weaver, and British Library librarian Henry Thomas, he lost the Chair to Madariaga by only one vote. This first disappointment was to be followed by two more, in 1931 and 1953, when Starkie would again put himself forward as a candidate for the Oxford Chair.

Another dimension of Starkie's political activity at this juncture is reflected in his membership of the Governing Body of the Lausanne-based International Centre of Fascist Studies (Centre International d'Études sur le Fascisme – CINEF), the President of which was Swiss resident and sometime librarian at the University of Nijmegen Herman de Vries de Heekelingen;[75] the Secretary-General was the English convert to Catholicism and member of the Italian Fascist party J.S. Barnes. The latter's *The universal aspects of fascism* was published in 1928, the year in which the first volume of *The Yearbook of the International Centre of Fascist Studies* appeared, which contained twelve contributions, among them pieces by Barnes, Odon Por, Starkie's Italian fascist friend Luigi Villari and the professor himself.[76] In the title,

72 'Reception at U.S. Legation', IT, 1 Sept. 1928, p. 6.   73 S. de Madariaga, *Morning*, p. 125.   74 W. Starkie to E. Starkie, 1 July 1952 (ES, Bodl.).   75 In the 'Biographical notes' to *A survey of Fascism. The Yearbook of the International Centre of Fascist Studies*, vol. 1 (London, 1928), Vries de Heekelingen is represented as 'D.Litt. Professor of Paleography and Diplomatics at the University of Nijmegen, 1923– 1927', and 'Corresponding Member of the Royal Academy of Fine Arts and Historical Sciences of Toledo' (p. 237). See also Graham Jefcoate, '"A difficult modernity": The library of the Catholic University of Nijmegen, 1923–1968'. De Vries de Heekelingen had been dismissed from his post as librarian at Nijmegen in 1927. http://dare.ubn.kun.nl/dspace/bitstream/2066/90906/1/90906.pdf, accessed 14 March 2012.   76 Roger Griffiths states that Starkie and Professor Edmund Gardner were 'foundation members of the CINEF in 1927.' (R. Griffiths, *Fellow travellers of the right. British enthusiasts for Nazi Germany, 1933–1939* (London, 2010), p. 19.) Thomas Linehan has assessed the CINEF

Starkie's article posed the provocative question 'Whither is Ireland heading – Is it Fascism?', which was followed by 'Thoughts on the Irish Free State.' The text provided few '[t]houghts' about Ireland's possible path to fascism, in spite of references to Gentile, D'Annunzio, Odon Por and the assertion: 'it is quite possible that Ireland may come to assimilate a great deal of fascist political doctrine, properly understood'.[77] Moreover, what a proper understanding of fascist political doctrine might signify is never clarified. The article's main thrust appears to be to lend support to what Gearóid O'Tuathaigh has qualified as 'the responsible, cautious and virtuous state apparatus constructed by decent Mr Cosgrave and his ministers during the difficult 1920s', a state apparatus, as O'Tuathaigh further claims, 'under very effective, if very often discreet or hidden, British control'.[78] Thus, the Free State government representatives are projected by Starkie as 'the revolutionaries of Ireland' who, having 'achieved their purpose … [,] turned their attention to the task of setting up a firm government for the country'.[79] In effect, the Cosgrave administration were the pro-Treaty supporters, clearly not representative of all 'the revolutionaries of Ireland' if, indeed, any. In spite of the provocative gambit to Starkie's article, it appears to have been geared, rather, to promoting Cumann na nGaedheal's initiatives and efforts over the five-year period of 'reconstruction' between 1923 and 1928 with Kevin O'Higgins's death in 1927 represented as '[marking] the end of the chapter of revolution.'[80]

Writing to his father's good friend, Sir Lawrence Weaver,[81] in mid-October 1928, Starkie apologized for his tardy reply to a 'kind letter'[82] received from the former, stating that he had been away from Dublin, though without making any reference as to where his absence had taken him. Before the end of the month he would again be reviewing for the *Irish Statesman* and there would be a number of contributions from him before the end of the year, reviewing concerts and recitals by players of international repute.[83] His energies were also deployed in organizing a lecture tour in the United States, to take place in the first quarter of 1929. Hence, it would appear that his correspondence with Sir Lawrence Weaver at this point was related to his planning for America. In late September, Starkie had already addressed Professor of Fine Arts Arthur Kingsley Porter to enquire whether he might deliver a lecture at Harvard, as TCD professors Mahaffy and Tyrrell had done before him[84] and in October he wrote to Weaver thanking him for 'such an informative letter,' explaining that he had been

as 'little more than a propaganda vehicle for Mussolini and Italian fascism' (T. Linehan, *British Fascism, 1918–1939. Parties, ideology and cultures* (Manchester, 2000), p. 128. In correspondence with his sister Enid, Starkie asserted that he became a delegate to the Fascist Studies Centre at Lausanne in 1922–3 (W. Starkie to E. Starkie, 18 June 1938, ES Bodl.).   77 W. Starkie, 'Whither is Ireland heading – Is it fascism? Thoughts on the Irish Free State', in *A survey of Fascism*, p. 232.   78 G. O'Tuathaigh, 'The age of de Valera and newsreel' in L. Dodd (ed.), *Nationalisms visions and revisions* (Dublin, 1999), pp 26, 24.   79 W. Starkie, 'Whither is Ireland heading', p. 224.   80 Ibid., pp 225, 226.   81 W. Starkie to E. Starkie, 20 Feb. 1953 (ES Bodl.).   82 W. Starkie to Sir Lawrence Weaver, 15 Oct. 1928 (Walter Starkie Correspondence, 1928–1932, VFM 602, Special Collections Research Center Southern Illinois University Carbondale. Henceforth JBP SIUC).   83 See Appendix.   84 W. Starkie to A. Kingsley Porter, 26 Sept. 1928 (Arthur Kingsley Porter Papers, Harvard University Archive, HUG 1706.102/Box 11/FOLDER "S", May–December 1928).

'rather in the dark concerning U.S.A.' He expressed concern about finding a suitable agent with a view to organizing a lecture tour, arguing that he feared being unable to cover expenses: 'unless I get general lecturing to do.'[85]

Starkie crossed the Atlantic in the wake of President Cosgrave's visit, between January and February 1928, which had been followed later in the year by that of the editor of the *Irish Statesman*, on whom a Doctor's Degree in Literature was conferred at Yale.[86] Starkie spoke to Russell about the agent who had represented him in America. Æ had found James B. Pond, son of the Major of the same name who had founded the Lecture Bureau in 1873, 'altogether admirable in every way'. Thus Starkie approached Pond through another 'friend',[87] the New York judge Richard Campbell, one of the American investors in the *Irish Statesman*.[88] In the meantime, Starkie asked Weaver, who knew Pond 'so well',[89] to write to the New York impresario recommending the Dublin professor. Finally, he outlined the content of his lectures, which connected with his areas of interest and political pursuits in relation to Spain and Italy and to his day-to-day activity and literary range of reference in contemporary Ireland:

(1) Personalities of Modern Spain (Primo de Rivera, Benavente, Blasco Ibáñez, etc.) and the life of the country;
(2) Personalities of Modern Italy (Mussolini, D'Annunzio, Pirandello, etc.) and life in the country under Fascism;
(3) Personalities of Modern Ireland (Yeats, Russell, Stephens, etc.).[90]

He further explained that the lectures would be illustrated by anecdotes and records of interviews with the selected personalities.

Financial considerations may have led Starkie to contemplate an American lecture tour. Apart from his immediate family, Italia and the two children, his mother had few resources of her own and came to depend particularly on her eldest children, Walter and Enid. Certainly, when he first wrote to Pond, Starkie explained that he wanted to secure 'as much lecturing in the universities, Women's Clubs, Societies, Libraries, etc., as possible',[91] though he may also have been politically motivated, eager to proselytize in America to as many as possible on 'the awakening of Spain' under Primo de Rivera, the achievements of fascist Italy and the success of the Irish Free State. It is possible, too, that his trip was partially financed by each of the interested parties. The lure of the Manhattan skyline together with tales of American plenty might also be taken into consideration in assessing the thirty-four-year-old professor's drive to absent himself from Dublin in early 1929.

The Pond Bureau produced publicity promoting Starkie's 'American–Canadian Lecture Tour', programmed for 1 February to the 20 April 1929: 'Here is a noted

85 W. Starkie to Sir Lawrence Weaver, 15 Oct. 1928 (JBP SIUC).   86 'An Irishman's Diary: AE's Degree in America', IT, 13 July 1928, p. 5.   87 W. Starkie to Sir Lawrence Weaver, 15 Oct. 1928 (JBP SIUC).   88 N. Allen, *George Russell*, p. 140. See also correspondence between J.S. Cullinan and R. Campbell in the J.S. Cullinan Papers, University of Houston Libraries.   89 W. Starkie to Sir Lawrence Weaver, 15 Oct. 1928 (JBP SIUC).   90 Ibid.   91 W. Starkie to J.B. Pond, 22 Oct. 1928 (JBP SIUC).

SPECIAL ANNOUNCEMENT

James B. Pond presents for an American-Canadian
Lecture Tour · February 1st to April 20th, 1929

Dr. WALTER STARKIE

One of the Most Picturesque Figures
in Present Day Ireland

Fellow of Trinity College, Dublin

Member of the Royal Irish Academy

Professor of Spanish Language and
Literature, University of Dublin

Lecturer in Italian Language and
Literature, University of Dublin

Corresponding Member, Royal Spanish Academy

Knight of the Order of Alfonso XII
(Conferred on him by the King of Spain for merit in Literature and Scholarship)

Director of the Abbey Theatre, Dublin

Author of "Luigi Pirandello" (Dutton); "Jacinto Benavente"
(Oxford Press); "Literary Personalities in Modern Spain,"
"The One Act Play in Spain," etc.

DR. WALTER STARKIE is in many respects the most interesting, versatile, and paradoxical man in Ireland. Here is a noted scholar who is bohemian at heart and has roamed with the gypsies throughout Europe, an ardent Irish Nationalist whose interests and activities are cosmopolitan and who is as well-known in the cultural and political centers of Rome, Florence, Madrid, Upsala, and London as in Dublin, a talented violinist with an uncommon knowledge of the history of music who has elected to teach in a university, a Director of the Irish National Theatre which produces only Irish plays, who is the greatest foreign authority on the Spanish and Italian drama and has been knighted by the King of Spain for his services to literature!

Still in his early thirties, such achievements and honors would do credit to a man twice his age. Withal his brilliant record sits lightly on his broad shoulders and does not suppress the charm, wit, and affability which induced the Free State Government to appoint him Chairman of the Reception Committee to welcome distinguished guests to Ireland. In this capacity and in his travels he has met the most celebrated men of the day. His genial personality enables him to make friends easily and his thorough acquaintance with contemporary dramatic, literary, and political movements goes beyond books and reports to the very men who are making history.

In his lectures he looks at modern Europe through its salient figures, introducing them to his audiences as he himself knows them, relating what they have confided to him of their deeds, plans, and aspirations. An Irishman who is at the same time a European envoy to America, our generation will have few opportunities to meet and hear a more fascinating and likable person than Walter Starkie.

Write or wire for Terms and Available
Dates at once to

THE POND BUREAU
25 West 43d St.   New York, N.Y.

> **AVAILABLE**
> **THIS SEASON**
> **ONLY ! !**
> ──────
> **BOOK NOW**

11 J.B. Pond Bureau flyer advertising W.F. Starkie's
first American lecture tour, 1929.

scholar who is bohemian at heart and has roamed with the gypsies throughout Europe, an ardent Irish Nationalist whose interests and activities are cosmopolitan.' Apart from highlighting the lecturer's fellowship, professorship of Spanish and lectureship in Italian at TCD, his membership of the Royal Irish Academy, corresponding membership of the Spanish Royal Academy and directorship of the Abbey Theatre, Pond was also able to announce his knighthood [*sic*] of the Order of Alfonso XII, conferred on him in 1928, for merit in literature and scholarship. Apart from the academic profile, it is interesting to see Starkie already portrayed in the guise of bohemian and one who has roamed with gypsies, aspects of this 'most interesting, versatile and paradoxical man',[92] which might be more readily associated with his 1930s profile, though his first recorded journey in pursuit of gypsies was made in July 1929. However, perhaps most striking in the list of Starkie's attributes is the identification of him as 'an ardent Irish Nationalist', whereby such nationalism is presented as being no less the domain of those associated with Cumann na nGaedheal than with the followers of Fianna Fáil, albeit, in Starkie's case as represented here, one which is deliberately qualified by cosmopolitan interests and activities. In this connection, it is pertinent to assess Starkie's lecture tour in the wake of de Valera's visit to the United States a year earlier and, independently of whatever the professor was lecturing on, it no doubt constituted an opportunity to reinforce the views and convictions expressed by W.T. Cosgrave and George Russell as to the good of the Free State order in their own visits to the United States in 1928.

In letters to Pond in November and December, Starkie quoted a range of scholars and others in positions of authority in church, state and business with whom Pond might establish contact with a view to arranging talks. The eager lecturer had already drawn on his network of family and friends: uncle Arthur Rackham was writing to 'various influential people' and 'using his influence to help [him]'[93] while 'the Harmsworth family' were providing 'strong backing in [the] USA and Canada'. Cecil Harmsworth gave Starkie letters of introduction to Martin Vogel, 'former assistant secretary to the Treasury, USA', to Colonel David Flynn, President of the First National Bank in Princeton, New Jersey, and a friend of President Wilson, to the prominent manuscript collector R.B. Adam at Buffalo, to the *Daily Mail* correspondent in New York, to the Prime Minister of Canada, Mackenzie-King, the Governor General of Canada, Lord Willingdon, and to Sir Alexander Currie, Principal of McGill University in Montreal. Another friend, Shane Leslie, provided letters for, among others, Governor Al Smith, for his sister-in-law, married to congressman W. Bourke Cockran, for Mr Archer Huntington, 'the great Maecenas of Spanish Studies', and he recommended Starkie to the Catholic University of America, while yet another, R.D. Blumenfeld, editor and part proprietor of the *Daily Express* had contacted the newspaper's New York correspondent on Starkie's behalf. A 'great friend', Dr Michael O'Doherty, the archbishop of Manila, had already written in 1927 to 'various institutions' in the United States 'recommending them strongly to invite [Starkie] out to lecture.' Starkie's relationship with the Spanish and Italian ambassadors in London was also brought to bear: Merry del Val produced 'a very strong letter'[94] for the Spanish Ambassador at Washington and the Italian Ambassador wrote

92 'Special Announcement' – a sheet of publicity announcing W. Starkie's American-Canadian Lecture Tour: 1 February to 20 April 1929 (JBP SIUC).   93 W. Starkie to J.B. Pond, 21 Nov. 1928 (JBP SIUC). 94 W. Starkie to J.B. Pond, 22 Dec. 1928 (JBP SIUC).

to his counterpart there on Starkie's behalf. The Swedish Minister in London was also forthcoming. When Starkie was writing to Pond in November 1928, he reported that Dr Nicholas Murray Butler was arranging lectures for him at Columbia, as was Professor J.M.D. Ford at Harvard. The American Minister in Dublin, Frederick A. Sterling, gave Starkie a letter of introduction to A. Lawrence Lowell, President of Harvard, together with 'a good many letters to useful people for lectures … like Mrs Boyd Horniman [*sic*]',[95] the latter in connection with lectures for women's clubs. Starkie also cited other contacts in the field of education: David R. Robertson was the Assistant Director of the American Council of Education in Washington, DC, and, apart from being a 'friend', was 'very interested' in Starkie's lectures in America, while the Institute of International Education in New York, founded and initially directed by Dr Stephen Duggan 'wanted to arrange a tour of the universities in USA' for the TCD professor as he had been 'strongly recommended to them'.[96] Finally, the business world was also called upon to accommodate Starkie. The lecturer had already used a Duo-Art instrument in 'a good many illustrated music lectures' over the 20s and the Aeolian Company had given him one of their instruments. Furthermore, he was 'one of the contributors to the World Series of Educational Music rolls for Duo-Art'.[97] Therefore, the Directors of Aeolian London now wrote to Franklin Dunham, the Educational Director of the Aeolian Corporation in New York from 1923,[98] on Starkie's behalf. Another powerful captain of industry was Texan J.S. Cullinan, supporter of the *Irish Statesman*. He arranged for Starkie to deliver a course of three lectures on modern Spain at the Rice Institute on the understanding that they would be published in the Rice Institute Pamphlets, designed to be: 'the new institution's contribution to the world of scholarship, showcasing the work of [the] faculty as well as other scholars of high reputation'.[99] A number of sheets in Starkie's hand in the James B. Pond papers at the Morris Library suggest that there were a host of other contacts, among them Padraic Colum, who fixed up '3 or 4 engagements';[1] Reverend Father L.J. Kelly, Provincial of the Society of Jesus, Maryland, New York Province; the Reverend Charles L. O'Donnell, Congregation of the Holy Cross, Notre Dame, Indiana; Charles Merz, on the editorial staff of *New York World*, a contact facilitated by Francis Hackett; Professors Baker and Cross at Yale, both of whom knew Starkie through Æ, and Professor Arthur Kingsley Porter, whom Starkie expected to be travelling with.[2]   On Saturday, 19 January, Starkie's review of Ernst Von Dohnányi's

95 W. Starkie to J.B. Pond, 21 Nov. 1928. Starkie may have heard Mrs Borden Harriman's name over the telephone and interpreted it as 'Boyd Horniman'. He refers to Mrs Borden Harriman by name in a later letter to Pond before his departure (W. Starkie to J.B. Pond, 10 Jan. 1929 (JBP SIUC)).   96 W. Starkie to J.B. Pond, 22 Dec. 1928 (JBP SIUC). Starkie states at this point that he had written to the Institute of International Education explaining that he had made other arrangements. However, the IIE would be the first American institution to receive Starkie when he embarked on a career in the United States following his retirement from the British Council in 1954 (*Annual Report of the Institute of International Education* (1956), p. 32).   97 W. Starkie to J.B. Pond, 22 Dec. 1928 (JBP SIUC). 98 *Presto*, 13 Oct. 1923, p. 5.   99 *http://ricehistorycorner.com/2010/12/06/the-rice-institute-pamphlets/*, accessed 19 May 2012.   1 'List of people interested', sheets in Starkie's hand (JBP SIUC). 2 In reply to Starkie's letter of 26 Sept. 1928, Kingsley Porter expressed his hope that Starkie might travel across the Atlantic with his wife and himself: 'We are sailing by the way from Liverpool on the

recitals at the RDS on Monday the 14th was published.[3] As the journal was circulating in Dublin, the reviewer sailed out of Liverpool on the White Star liner, RMS *Cedric*, scheduled to arrive in New York on the 28th. He arrived on an 'ice-blown day', feeling 'very small fry' and 'grasped [Pond's] hand of greeting.'[4] James B. Pond had spelt out his conditions in correspondence with his client in the month of December.[5] He had committed himself to booking lectures for Starkie at the best fees obtainable fifty per cent of which would be for himself. All travelling expenses incurred in the United States would be covered by Pond and he would also cover the outward journey, from Ireland to the United States. Advertising, promoting, booking and managing the tour would be at his expense as was all necessary printing and advertising material. The lecturer was required to pay his own hotel bills and personal incidentals of travel. Pond calculated that 'the normal fees'[6] for lectures would be 150 or 200 dollars and thought it likely that 250 or 300 dollars might be obtained. Indeed, Starkie had informed the agent that J.S. Cullinan had stated that his honorarium for the lectures at Rice would be 300 dollars though this amount was projected as emolument for a course of three lectures.[7]

Starkie was programmed to deliver the lectures on personalities of modern Spain, modern Italy and modern Ireland as well as lectures illustrated by lantern slides and violin playing on Venice and Spain in the eighteenth century. Pond also advertised as 'A Unique Lecture and Concert' Starkie's 'The Gypsies and Their Music', a lecture and concert 'founded on Dr Starkie's wanderings as a fiddler among the gypsies'.[8] Thus, what has been established as Starkie's gypsy cult, particularly in evidence through his travel books in the 1930s, appears to have been rooted to some degree in a lecture subject for public consumption both during and prior to his first American tour at the end of the 20s. Correspondence with Pond reveals, on the one hand, that Starkie was keen to deliver the gypsy lecture, which he had already delivered in January 1929 and also, at least according to the lecturer's reports, that it was popular.[9] In this connection, it is also pertinent to bear in mind the relevant gypsy contacts Starkie made on his first American visit. Future employee of the American Embassy in London during the Second World War and subsequently a highly successful publisher, Victor Weybright met Starkie on the latter's first visit to New York in 1929. In an obituary dedicated to Starkie, Weybright recalled that he was invited to meet the visitor:

Cedric January 19 as she calls at Cobh. I am hoping you may happen to be taking the same steamer. That would be a great pleasure for us.' (A. Kingsley Porter to W. Starkie, 26 Nov. 1928 (Arthur Kingsley Porter Papers, Harvard University Archive, HUG 1706.102/Box 11/FOLDER "S", May–December 1928)).   3 W. Starkie, 'RDS. Dohnányi' (1929), p. 401 (see Appendix).   4 W. Starkie to J.B. Pond, 12 May 1929 (JBP SIUC).   5 J.B. Pond to W. Starkie, 11 Dec. 1928 (JBP SIUC).   6 Ibid.   7 W. Starkie to J.B. Pond, 22 Dec. 1928 (JBP SIUC).   8 'Here is a fascinating man' – a sheet of publicity announcing W. Starkie's second [?] lecture tour of the United States (JBP SIUC).   9 'I hope you will be able to book the Gypsy lecture in some places as I enjoy giving it.' (W. Starkie to J.B. Pond, 10 Jan. 1929); 'I must tell you that I think I may get some other engagements at Chicago as all these ladies are very enthusiastic about gypsies.' (W. Starkie to J.B. Pond, 14 Mar. 1929, JBP SIUC).

at the apartment of Elizabeth Robbins Pennell, widow of Joseph Pennell the
etcher, and a niece and biographer of Charles Godfrey Leland ... the prime
mover in founding the G[ypsy] L[ore] S[ociety] in 1888. [...] Among those
present were Irving Brown, a pioneer scholar-gypsy, then Professor of Romance
languages at Columbia University, and Richardson Wright, editor of *House &
Garden* and an occasional contributor to the Journal on Gypsies [*sic*] and other
nomadic travellers in the USA.[10]

Starkie may have spent the month of February lecturing in and around New York
city and state. However, writing to Pond (now familiarly addressed as 'Bim') from
Dublin on Sunday, 12 May, to thank the tour manager for his welcome, kindness and
encouragement, Starkie didn't mention any of the institutions or groups he had
lectured for. He did recall evenings spent with Pond in the company of, among others,
two writers and travellers into other cultures, William Seabrook and Upton Close,
both of whom may also have been influential in Starkie's subsequent pursuit of the
pariah, together with Pond himself, who had travelled widely and possessed a taste for
adventure.[11] In the above-mentioned obituary, Weybright also recalled how he had
introduced the visitor to clandestine drinking establishments in the East-coast capital
in 1929 and described the impact exercised in one of them by the deceptively dressed
fiddler:

> This was during the prohibition era in America; so after Mrs Pennell's gentle
> soirée, I volunteered to introduce Walter to a few nearby speak-easies. The first
> illegal bar we visited was run by an Italian, and within a half-hour of our arrival
> on the premises and a few glasses of wine, Walter was playing his violin to the
> enchantment of all present. I discovered later that the speak-easy proprietor
> thought Walter was an opera star of some sort because of his addiction to rather
> formal dark garb.[12]

As Starkie wrote to Pond in May, he was nostalgic, imagining the impresario being that
very evening 'at the Deauville guzzling pink clover clubs ... or else in that other night
club[,] dancing the "blues" in the intervals of whisky sours'.[13] Hence he expressed his
longing to be back in New York the following year.

Before Starkie struck the mid-west in 1929, Pond had sent out a promotion piece
explaining that 'the witty Irish lecturer' would be available in March.[14] While on the
road that month, Starkie wrote to the manager, telling him that he had enjoyed

---

10 V. Weybright, 'Walter Fitzwilliam Starkie', *Journal of the Gypsy Lore Society* (henceforth JGLS),
Fourth Series, 1:3 (1977), 155, 156. I am grateful to Virginia Murray for bringing my attention to
Weybright's obituary and for providing me with a photocopy. See also V. Weybright, *The making of a
publisher. A life in the twentieth century book revolution* (New York, 1967), p. 12.   11 http://sdrc.lib.
uiowa.edu/traveling-culture/chau1/pdf/pondja/4/brochur, accessed 26 Dec. 2010.   12 V.
Weybright, 'Walter Fitzwilliam Starkie', p. 156.   13 W. Starkie to J.B. Pond, 12 May 1929 (JBP SIUC).
14 A sheet of publicity headed 'An unusually interesting visitor to America arrives shortly' [no date]
(JBP SIUC).

Philadelphia greatly, stating that he had never talked and played in such a lovely hall
as the Academy of Music. On 16 March, he attended the St Patrick's banquet
organized by the Irish Fellowship Club at Palmer House in Chicago, at which Michael
Mac White, the Free State Minister to the United States, was present and delivered a
speech.[15] Writing to Pond two days before the event, Starkie joked: 'I suppose I'll say
a few words of home truths about Irishmen!'[16] By the end of the month, the lecturer
had performed in St Louis and experienced 'adventures' in San Antonio and New
Orleans, reporting that the latter two places far surpassed any others he had visited,
New Orleans being singled out as 'the peach of them all!'[17] In early April a course of
two lectures was programmed for North Western University and, mid-month, Starkie
lectured at Harvard on 'Venice in the Eighteenth Century', a lecture illustrated by
lantern slides and violin selections of old music, which was open to the public.[18] He
stayed on in America until 27 April and told Pond that he would be able to book him
up until that day: 'in the hope that there may be a rush of engagements to round of
[*sic*] my trip'.[19]

In correspondence with J.B. Pond in May, July and October 1929, Starkie leaves no
doubt as to his eagerness to return to the United States in 1930 while also reiterating
his interest in delivering as many lectures as might be programmed for him during his
new year tour. By July he was delighted with the response and eager for more: 'I am
very pleased to see the bookings are rolling up for next year: I hope you are able to fit
three lectures per day if necessary.'[20] Come October, he was calculating that he would
be able to cross the Atlantic again about the 12 or 13 March 1930. In the meantime,
since his return from America, he had travelled to France, Italy, Hungary and
Roumania.[20a] Writing to Pond on 19 July from his father-in-law's home in Genoa in a
heat of 105° fahrenheit, the tireless traveller explained that he had 'just returned from
a vagabondage through Provence',[21] staying at Les Baux, Arles, Aigües Mortes and
Les-Saintes-Maries-de-la-Mer, and was about to leave for Hungary and Romania: 'to
live with gypsies and gather material.'[22] Both these experiences, the French,
Hungarian and Roumanian would shape the content of two travel books: his first,
Raggle-taggle. Adventures with a fiddle in Hungary and Roumania (1933), and one which
might have been published in the 1940s had the author not taken up the post of British
Council Representative in Spain in 1940, that is, *In Sara's tents* (1953).

Writing from Dublin in May 1929, Starkie referred to being back in 'this
"distressful country"'[23] but, as indicated above, he wasn't there for long before going
abroad for some two months[24] and, therefore, not in the city to contemplate for long

15 'Envoy speaks as Chicago Irish honor St Patrick', *Chicago Sunday Tribune*, 17 Mar. 1929, Part 1, p.
6. **16** W. Starkie to J.B. Pond, 14 Mar. 1929 (JBP SIUC). **17** W. Starkie to J.B. Pond, 29 Mar. 1929
(JBP SIUC). **18** 'Lecture by Dr Walter Starkie', *Harvard University Gazette*, 24:30, 13 Apr. 1929, p.
130. **19** W. Starkie to J.B. Pond, 29 Mar. 1929 (JBP SIUC). **20** W. Starkie to J.B. Pond, 19 July 1929
(JBP SIUC). **20a** Roumania is spelt with a "u" throughout the text following the form adopted in the
subtitle of Starkie's *Raggle-taggle* (1933). **21** W. Starkie to J.B. Pond, 19 July 1929 (JBP SIUC). **22**
Ibid. Starkie's *In Sara's tents* (1953) focussed on the gypsy pilgrimage to the shrine of their patron at
Saintes-Maries-de-la-Mer. **23** W. Starkie to J.B. Pond, 12 May 1929 (JBP SIUC). **24** He noted in
his letter to Pond from Genoa that his father-in-law's address there should be used for any correspondence until 10 Sept. 1929 (W. Starkie to J.B. Pond, 19 July 1929 JBP SIUC).

what the *Irish Statesman* recognized as 'the evidence everywhere of the magnitude and profundity of feeling evoked by the centenary of Catholic Emancipation'.[25] In June, two paragraphs Starkie had produced on Belgian Jean Du Chastain, successor to Commendatore Esposito as Senior Professor of Piano at the RIAM, were published in the *Irish Statesman*.[26] The piece in question was the reviewer's only contribution to the journal following his return from the United States and was to be followed by only five more: one in August and the remaining four over November and December. In October, Starkie was back at TCD, though finding it 'hard to knuckle to again' after 'a wonderful time in Hungary and Roumania in every way' which, none the less, had been 'gruelling'[27] at times. On the same day he was writing to Pond following his summer adventures, the *Irish Times* reported that the TCD professor had been awarded the title of Knight of the Order of the Crown of Italy: 'in recognition of his writings on Italian literature',[28] the cross of the decoration being presented to him by the Italian Consul-General, Commendatore Silenzi. In early November, Starkie delivered a 'Special Lecture' at the RDS with music and lantern illustrations, entitled 'Recent Rambles among the Gypsies of Southern Europe'[29] and before the year was out, he was again delivering a Gypsy-inspired lecture, on this occasion at a meeting of the Dublin Literary Society. Professor William Magennis presided at the lecture, which had an occult emphasis: 'Gypsy Sorcery and Witchcraft.'[30] Three days earlier in the month of December, the, by now, versatile performer, had contributed to an event at the High School in aid of the Athletic Fund: a concert together with episodes from *The Acharnians* of Aristophanes in Greek. Dr Walter Starkie and Mr Sealy Jeffares contributed, together with the school choir and others.[31]

Terence Brown has diagnosed the 1920s in the Free State as 'a dispiriting decade from the social and cultural point of view', though he recognizes that the state did succeed in '[establishing] and [protecting] democratic institutions'.[32] As has been seen, Starkie made his contribution within the Free State on a number of fronts: academic (TCD, RIA), cultural (RDS, RIAM, the Abbey Theatre, 2RN, the *Irish Statesman*) and political (The Film Censorship Board, Consul for Chile, government appointee on the Abbey Theatre Board). As the son of a family who had strongly identified with imperial Britain, and continued to, he would undoubtedly have found certain social and cultural developments over the decade 'dispiriting' while, at a personal level, the reduced circumstances of the Starkie family were hardly heartening. However, the decade was not devoid of spiriting qualities for him: he acquired a fellowship at TCD, a Chair, frequently attended recitals, concerts, nights at the theatre, experienced the new domain of broadcasting at first hand and increasingly came to frequent government circles, being awarded responsibilities within the structure of the state.[33]

---

25 'The proof of national character', under 'Notes and comments', IS, 29 June 1929, p. 323. 26 W. Starkie, 'Monsieur Jean Du Chastain' (1929), p. 313 (see Appendix). 27 W. Starkie to J.B. Pond, 22 Oct. 1929 (JBP SIUC). 28 'Professor W.F. Starkie, FTCD', IT, 22 Oct. 1929, p. 6. 29 'RDS Special Lecture', IT, 8 Nov. 1929, p. 8. 30 'Gypsy Sorcery and Witchcraft. Dr Starkie's Lecture', IT, 14 Dec. 1929, p. 7. 31 'The High School, Dublin', IT, 5 Dec. 1929, p. 8. 32 T. Brown, *Ireland*, p. 125. 33 Among other distinctions listed on the publicity flyer headed 'Here is a Fascinating Man' and produced by J.B. Pond in connection with Starkie's lectures in the USA, the lecturer is identified as 'A prominent

Should he have felt dispirited in Ireland, he was able to experience 'parallel lives' in Italy, in Spain and, as the decade came to a close, he discovered the United States, Canada, Hungary and Romania. These latter discoveries might particularly have led him to feel he was approaching the crest of a wave. America was an intense experience with what became a challenging regime of lectures but it also constituted a liberating and financially rewarding one. Overall the sojourn had been invigorating, even intoxicating, and he was bent on going back. His summer experiences in Hungary and Romania yielded '800 pages of impressions'[34] and in May he had already turned to producing a book.

figure in the present government, … a member of the Advisory Board of Broadcasting and Chairman of the Free State Reception Committee' (JBP SIUC) (The flyer carries no date).   **34** W. Starkie to J.B. Pond, 22 Oct. 1929 (JBP SIUC).

PART III

On with the Motley

'Motley's the only wear.'
W. Shakespeare, *As You Like It* (Act II, scene vii)

6

Exile and Cunning: Walter the Wanderer

I will not serve that in which I no longer believe, whether it call itself my home, my fatherland, or my church: and I will try to express myself in some mode of life or art as freely as I can and as wholly as I can, using for my defence the only arms that I allow myself to use: silence, exile and cunning.[1]

So pronounces Stephen Dedalus in conversation with his fellow undergraduate and friend Cranly in Joyce's *A portrait of the artist as a young man* (1916). Stephen's resolve was never Walter Starkie's: the former rebelled against the authority of family, nation and religion while the latter laboured to uphold those institutions within the Dominion as nearly as he had known them under the Union. As the Free State moved towards greater independence after 1932 and a new constitution was created in 1937, Starkie continued to channel his energies towards the fatherland which his parents and forebears had served, '[t]he imperial British state',[2] albeit not exclusively. His energies were also concentrated into specific interests and pursuits, which might provide financial reward (school fees coming to occupy an additional feature in the domestic economy) but which were also compatible with larger British concerns in the field of foreign policy, as conceived of by particular groups or individuals, if not by the government in power. Thus, his travel books *Raggle-taggle* (1933), *Spanish raggle-taggle* (1934) and *Don Gypsy* (1936), the autobiographical *The waveless plain* (1938), his biography of Cardinal Cisneros, *Grand Inquisitor* (1940), as well as his journalism over the period, all illustrate what became a life of service to given political projects within a Europe increasingly polarized between the radical right and left.

Stephen Dedalus opted for 'silence, exile and cunning'. Starkie would be resident in the Free State until 1940 but as the decade of the 30s advanced, his existence might be conceived of as one of exile, in Paul Ilie's conception of 'inner exile',[3] as the country he had been born into and grown up in was increasingly becoming the place of (s/he who had been) the Other, the (imperial) One now displaced. Thus he would come to spend an increasing amount of time away from it and become skilful in refashioning himself in the guise which, it may be argued, his identity has been fixed in the popular imagination, that of wandering minstrel, gypsy scholar, latter-day wayfarer. Unlike Dedalus, however, he would not choose silence. This might be explained as a consequence of an ebullient personality, no longer subject to paternal stricture after the death of WJM. Furthermore, as in life, so in 'literature': the 1930s publications develop in a prolix manner but one which, none the less, reveals construction in an ideological vein. The texts cover time past and present, introducing a host of person-

1 J. Joyce, *A portrait of the artist as a young man* (London, 2000), p. 208.   2 J. Joyce, *Ulysses*, p. 20.
3 P. Ilie, *Literature and inner exile: authoritarian Spain, 1939–1945* (Baltimore, 1980).

alities from across the social board, but they also speak volumes within the context of political propaganda in the 1930s, a neglected feature in considerations of the author's output.

As the decade approached, a transformation of certain sights and sounds in Dublin became indicative of further change on the horizon. The removal of the statue of Queen Victoria from its position in front of Leinster House in Dublin was mooted, giving rise to comment by a number of correspondents in the *Irish Statesman*, among them O. Grattan Esmonde, whose earnest request that the statue of the monarch might be deposited within the walls of the university where Starkie was a member of staff was not unreasonable given the College's foundation and historical allegiance to the British crown.[4] It was precisely in 1929, too, that TCD had been prevented from affirming her allegiance when, on the occasion of a visit to the institution for the college sports by the Governor General James McNeill, the College maintained that 'God Save the King' rather than the 'The Soldier's Song' should be played even though McNeill was not opposed to the Irish anthem being chosen. In the event, neither was played since McNeill was recommended by the government not to attend. The determination to revive the Irish language was reflected in legislation over the 1920s, proficiency being 'compulsory for entrance to the civil service from 1925 onwards'.[5] Thus, over the decade of the 20s Starkie witnessed the dismantling of the country he was born into, had grown up in, and the nation which was coming into being beyond the walls of the institutions he frequented, particularly TCD and the RDS, became increasingly alienating for him and his ilk. His wife had not known Ireland under the Union so had no experience of either the country or the Starkie family's fortunes in more bountiful times. It is possible that she may have found WJM's commanding personality, akin to her father's, and, therefore, to her taste, but she only experienced the family's penury in the wake of his passing. The Starkies' plunge into relative poverty constituted only one of a number of circumstances that contributed to her dissatisfaction with her lot in spite of the determination she is recorded (by her husband) as having expressed when the couple first met to join forces with her spouse with a view to raising their prospects. Not least among the circumstances that Italia might have found alienating in the Free State was 'the wonderfully staged triumphalism of the celebrations marking the centenary of Catholic emancipation in 1929',[6] and there would be more to come, on a 'grander'[7] scale, in 1932 when the Eucharistic Congress took place in Dublin.[8] Italia's father hailed from the free-thinking region of Piemonte and it seems that the Porchietti family were not practising Catholics.[9] Therefore, it may be surmised that the triumphalist and

4 O. Grattan Esmonde to the Editor of the *Irish Statesman*, 'The Old Lady must go', IS, 28 Dec. 1929, p. 336. 5 D. Ferriter, *The transformation*, p. 350. 6 Ibid., p. 334. 7 G. McIntosh, 'Acts of "national communion": the centenary celebrations for Catholic Emancipation, the forerunner of the Eucharistic Congress' in J. Augusteijn (ed.), *Ireland in the 1930s. New perspectives* (Dublin, 1999), p. 83. 8 R. O'Dwyer, *The Eucharistic Congress, Dublin 1932* (Dublin, 2009). 9 Alberto Porchietti's grandaughter Nenelle has described her grandfather as 'a freethinker' (author's interview with Nenelle Bonetti, daughter of Eva Porchietti and Mario Bonetti, Torino, 27 Sept. 1994). In the chapter in *The waveless plain* in which Starkie refers to his father-in-law's passing he has a repentant Don Alberto declare: 'We

ubiquitous manifestations of Catholic piety whereby the Free State 'deliberately [identified] itself as a Catholic state'[10] in 1929, and again in 1932 in the wake of de Valera's triumph at the polls, would have held little appeal.

Not surprisingly, January 1930 found Starkie laid up with a temperature and asthma, as he informed Pond.[11] He had chalked up a good amount of travelling over 1929: in Spain, France, Italy, Hungary and Roumania as well as across the Atlantic, and in France, Hungary and Roumania, he had sometimes been roughing it. The pace would have been challenging for someone who didn't suffer from chronic asthma. Moreover, apart from his commitments at TCD and with the Abbey Theatre, he had also been lecturing through Gerald Christy's agency in England and was finding that his talk on gypsies generated a wide appeal: 'My gypsy lecture is going like "hot cakes".' Before the end of January he was busy writing at some length to Pond, referring to a number of places and institutions (St Louis, Buffalo, D'Youville, Smith, Vassar and Wellesley) where lectures might be given over his second lecture tour in the United States, and he expressed satisfaction that his manager had already been able to arrange 'a good many engagements' for March and April 1930. He was eager for Pond to set up as many as possible since, as he explained: 'I need to be very busy ... I shall need to make money.'[14] Starkie's preoccupation with earning as much as possible may not only have been related to his own immediate family but to the financial straits his mother continued to find herself in. Writing to sister Enid from her mother's Anglesea Road address in May 1930, Nancy complained about the expense her sister Muriel and husband were putting their mother to and mentioned an overdraft of 'very nearly £1,400'.[15] Thus, brother Walter's lecture on gypsies might become the goose that could lay the golden egg. However, its popular appeal made it inappropriate for wide consumption in Dublin and thereabouts, presumably given the lecturer's professorial position at TCD. He told Pond: 'It is a little difficult for me to have my talk over here' while insisting on his need to earn money. Thus he had contracted 'an immense number of engagements for next season' through Gerald Christy and '[had] been working very hard lately at [his] book on gypsies'[17] with a view to completing it before he embarked on his lecture tour in the United States. In early March he lectured before the Alpha Club in Belfast on 'Hungarian Gypsies'[18] but there is no further record of his lecturing on gypsies in the Free State following his 'Special Lecture' at the RDS in November 1929 when he gave an account of his recent rambling among the gypsies of southern Europe.[19]

Garibaldians, in the past, were too extreme: we did not think enough of the great masses who must be given spiritual manna which will enable them to live' (W. Starkie, *Waveless*, p. 410). **10** G. McIntosh, 'Acts of "national communion",' p. 91. **11** However, in correspondence connected with his Visiting Professorship at Chicago in the summer of 1930 three days prior to the letter to Pond quoted above, Starkie declared that he had 'returned from Spain a few days ago.' (W. Starkie to David H. Stevens, Associate Dean of Faculties, 28 Jan. 1930. (Presidents' Papers *c*.1925–1945, Box 108, Folder 7, Special Collections Research Center, University of Chicago Library, henceforth SCRC, UCL). **14** W. Starkie to J.B. Pond, 31 Jan. 1930 (JBP SIUC). **15** N. Starkie to E. Starkie, 3 May 1930 (ES Bodl.). **17** W. Starkie to J.B. Pond, 31 Jan. 1930 (JBP SIUC). **18** 'News from all Ireland: Gypsies', IT, 7 Mar. 1930, p. 8. **19** 'Among the Gypsies. Lecture by Dr Starkie', II, 9 Nov. 1929, p. 6.

When writing to Pond in later January, Starkie spoke of having booked a second-class passage on the Cunard liner *Aquitania*, which would be leaving Southampton on 12 March and arriving in New York on the 18th. He planned to be in America until 18 April, when he would sail back on the French *Ile de France*. However, his plans must have changed, perhaps as a result of having been invited to take up a Visiting Professorship at the University of Chicago in the summer of 1930. Nancy informed Enid in April that their brother was due to sail on Easter Sunday, 20th April, and he may have stayed in the United States from late April until the month of August, travelling up to lecture in Canada in September before sailing back to Britain. Before leaving Ireland, he contributed two reviews to the ailing *Irish Statesman*.

In June, Starkie was in the United States and on Monday, the 16th, received an honorary degree at Trinity College, Hartford, Connecticut.[20] He had met the President of the College, the Reverend R.B. Ogilby, on the White Star liner, the *Cedric*, when he crossed the Atlantic for his first lecture tour in 1929. Once he had settled at the University of Chicago three days after the conferring of the degree, he wrote to thank Ogilby for his 'wonderful kindness' and was already feeling nostalgia for 'the green shades of Hartford' and 'rather lonely' on the 'huge'[21] campus at Chicago.

Starkie took up the Visiting Professorship at Chicago over the Summer Quarter of 1930. The professorship was financed by means of a fund set up through contributions of $200 presented by a number of businessmen who supported the Irish Fellowship Club, at least some of whom, if not all, would have met Starkie at the St Patrick's celebration he had attended in Chicago in 1929. Among the sponsors were E.A. Cudahy, Jr, a descendant of Michael Cudahy, who emigrated to the United States at the age of eight in 1849 and built up a meat-packing business, multi-millionaire Edward Hines and F.J. Lewis, a builder and real estate magnate.[22] The Visiting Professor's remit included the delivery of 'one full course [in Spanish literature], eight public lectures on the Quadrangles, and an equal number downtown'.[23] Thus he had

---

20 'Virum tam iucundum quam eruditum, dulce disserentem, dulce psallentem, dulce canentem, dulce ridentem, ad te duco Gualterum Starkie.' Taken from the Latin oration at the conferring of an honorary degree on Walter Starkie at the one hundred and fourth Commencement, Trinity College, Hartford, CT, 16 June 1930 (Walter Starkie File, Trinity College Archives, Trinity College, Hartford, CT). For an account of the day's proceedings, see the *Hartford Courant*, 17 June 1930, pp 1, 10. I am grateful to Peter J. Knapp, Trinity College Hartford Archivist, for help in locating the relevant papers and supplying me with copies.   21 W. Starkie to the Revd R.B. Ogilby, 19 June 1930 (Walter Starkie File, Trinity College Archives, Trinity College, Hartford, CT).   22 'The following contributions have been received to a fund for bringing Professor Walter Starkie, of the University of Dublin, to the University of Chicago as a Visiting Professor: F.J. Lewis, $200; John J. O'Brien, $200; Edward Hines, $200; and E.A. Cudahy, Jr., $200' (SCRC, UCL, Board of Trustees Minutes, 19, Jan.-Dec. 1929, p. 351. Dated: 12 Dec. 1929). I am grateful to John McHugh for facilitating information on the Chicago sponsors of the Visiting Professorship which Starkie was awarded.   23 D.H. Stevens to Mr John Dollard, Faculty Exchange, 30 Dec. 1929 (SCRC, UCL, Presidents' Papers *c.*1925–1945, Box 108, Folder 7.) The university public lectures and radio lectures which were delivered by Starkie ranged from Italy and Spain in the eighteenth century, covering literature, art and music; contemporary Italian and Spanish theatre, to Irish folk music and the Irish National Theatre, passing through 'Life with the Gypsies' and 'Gypsy sorcery and witchcraft'. (*University of Chicago Weekly Calendar*. The lectures are listed for the following days: 25 June 1930; 2 July 1930; 7 July 1930; 9 July 1930; 14 July 1930; 16 July 1930; 21 July 1930; 28 July

little time for correspondence, as he explained to Pond in the first of two letters from Chicago addressed to the New York agent, explaining that he had been 'very busy', was having 'a very hectic time' with 'at least 3 invitations every night and the weekends out at Lake Forest and Wisconsin, etc.' He informed on the popularity of his public lectures: 'crowded every week, averaging over 1,000 people'. He also referred to going out to the opera at Ravinia Park 'nearly every night' and mentioned the Valencian soprano Lucrecia Bori in this connection, identifying her as 'a friend of mine'.[24] He wrote to Pond again in the last week of his professorship, reporting that he was 'deluged with letters about the various gypsy lectures'[25] and stating that the lectures on the Hungarian, Roumanian and Spanish Gypsies were the most popular. He told Pond of his plans following completion of his commitment in Chicago: he would be travelling to Santa Fé on the 29th in order to see the Indian candlelight dancers on the 31st, from where he would travel to Los Angeles, San Diego and San Francisco, his only regret being that Pond had not been able to arrange any lectures for him in California. However, he may have managed to secure some subsequently.[26] In the meantime, Alberto Porchietti had passed away. Starkie stages the Colonel's death at the end of the chapter devoted to 'The Duce' in *The waveless plain*, recalling that he was in Capo Santa Chiara with the family in the summer of 1930, yet he couldn't have been at his father-in-law's side when he died on 10 August[27] as he wrote to Pond from Chicago on the 11th. Moreover, he delivered a public lecture on 'Contemporary Spanish Theater' on Wednesday, the 6th, in the Leon Mandel Assembly Hall at 4.30p.m., and another on the following Wednesday, the 13th, on 'Irish Folk Music' at the same time and place. Thus, the ideas attributed to Don Alberto in support of the Lateran Treaty, of the social role of religion and in favour of European unity[28] may have been expressed by Italia's father but the son-in-law could not have heard them personally in Capo Santa Chiara in August 1930.

Starkie travelled up to Canada in the month of September, where he spoke of Gypsies. On the 18th, *The Gazette* in Montreal announced his imminent arrival from New York to deliver a lecture entitled 'Roaming with the Gypsies, their Romance and their Music', a subject which, the lecturer claimed, was 'dearest to his heart'.[29] Starkie's 'friend',[30] John Barrett, Director of the Montreal daily, *The Gazette*, had organized the event with the assistance of the city editor J.S. Slattery. The lecturer was introduced at Victoria Hall that night by Colonel Wilfred Bovey, Director of the

1930; 30 July 1930; 6 Aug. 1930; 13 Aug. 1930; 18 Aug. 1930; 20 Aug. 1930). **24** W. Starkie to J.B. Pond, 11 Aug. 1930 (JBP SIUC). **25** W. Starkie to J.B. Pond, 26[?] Aug. 1930 (JBP SIUC). **26** Announcing Starkie's lecture in Montreal on 18 September, *The Gazette* reported that Starkie had been on a lecture tour in California, 'including a stay at Hollywood', following his Visiting Professorship at the University of Chicago ('Irish Professor to give lecture on gypsy romance', TG, 18 Sept. 1930, p. 8). **27** The tombstone carries the following inscription: Carlo Alberto Porcietti [*sic*] (8 Apr. 1862–10 Aug. 1930). He is buried together with his wife, Delfina Porchietti Landi (7 June 1867–12 January 1924), and his daughter, Eva Bonetti Porchietti (7 July 1894–2 Feb. 1958), her husband, Ammiraglio Mario Bonetti (3 Mar. 1888–19 Feb. 1961) and two of their children: Orazio Bonetti (8 Mar. 1922–7 Aug. 1943) and Alma Serena Bonetti (19 July 1919–29 Mar. 1921) (Cimitero di Apparizione, Comune di Genova, Italy). **28** W. Starkie, *Waveless*, pp 410–12. **29** 'Irish Professor to give lecture on gypsy romance', TG, 18 Sept. 1930, p. 8. **30** W. Starkie to J.B. Pond, 4 Oct. 1930 (JBP SIUC).

Department of Extra-Mural Relations at McGill University, under whose auspices the lecture was given. On the 19th, *The Gazette* reported that Starkie had held his 'very enthusiastic' audience, of some 1,100 people according to Starkie,[31] for more than two hours 'while he described in vivid terms and illustrated with his violin some facets of the soul of the gypsy'. The report claimed that 'the kernel of Dr Starkie's talk' was the association of the gypsies with humanity's will to be free. As had become customary in Starkie's lectures by this time, the violin formed an integral part of his delivery. On this occasion he played 'several gypsy selections' as well as what had become a *pièce de résistance*: Sarasate's 'Zigeunerweisen'. The *Gazette* reporter was struck by Starkie's prowess as well as by the passion he exhibited: 'In addition to being a violinist of considerable technical ability, he endowed his playing with a curious warmth and fire that lifted it completely out of the ordinary ... his playing of Sarasate's "Zigeunerweisen"...was totally different from the usual concert rendering, infinitely more exciting and interesting.'[32]

By early October, Starkie was back in Dublin. Writing to 'Bim' early on in the month, he reported that he had travelled home 'on the Duchess boat', possibly SS *Duchess of York* (or one of her sister ships),[33] operated by the Canadian Pacific Steamship Company. He explained that he had not been afforded a fee for his lecture at McGill but his passage home in first-class accommodation was provided and he had 'made whoopee all the way across'[34] in the company of doctors belonging to the British Medical Association.[35] His letter was mostly taken up with requests that Pond contact different people in order to arrange lectures for 1931: Barrett at *The Gazette* in Montreal, through whom there was also a possibility of setting up a lecture in Toronto; a Kevin Kelly in Chicago, who was interested in a lecture on Irish folk music, and Franklin Dunham at the National Broadcasting Company in New York, who had suggested Pond contact him to organize lectures for the musical supervisors in the schools. Starkie also insisted on the funds which had been destined to promoting his Canadian lecture and himself: the city editor of *The Gazette*, J.S. Slattery, had spent $300 in publicity. Perhaps Pond was not disposed to disembursing further funds in this connection. In any event, Starkie didn't hear from him in October and wrote to the impresario again in early November, expressing his surprise at not having received news since his return while claiming that he had written to Pond 'several times'[36] and enquiring about his new circulars.

By October, Starkie had taken up his teaching again at TCD and as President of the Dublin University Modern Language Society was in the chair for the opening meeting

---

31 Ibid.   32 'Mystery of gypsy life is unfolded', TG, 19 Sept. 1930, p. 13.   33 SS *Duchess of Bedford*, SS *Duchess of Atholl* and SS *Duchess of Richmond*. The *Duchess of York* was employed on the Liverpool–Quebec–Montreal route over the summer period. http://www.theshipslist.com/ships/lines/cp.html, accessed: 29 Dec. 2010.   34 W. Starkie to J.B. Pond, 4 Oct. 1930 (JBP SIUC).   35 The doctors in question had gathered at Winnipeg in late August for their annual meeting (*Canadian Medical Association Journal. Association Notes*, 72 (1 Feb. 1955), p. 229). http://www.ncbi.nlm.nih.gov/pmc/articles/PMC1825574/pdf/canmedaj00702, accessed: 29 Dec. 2010.   36 W. Starkie to J.B. Pond, 7 Nov. 1930 (JBP SIUC). A handwritten note on the first page of Starkie's letter indicates that the letter was answered on 18 Dec. 1930.

at 3p.m. on 28 October in the Regent House, as well as contributing as a speaker.[37] In the November and December letters addressed to Pond, Starkie referred to the lecturing he had contracted through Gerald Christy's agency in England. In October he spoke of over twenty engagements to be carried out before the end of the year and which meant that he had to 'rush over every week-end to London and fly to various places.'[38] By November, they had become 'close on 30' and he remarked that he was still 'doing well' with the gypsy lecture.[39] By the end of 1930 it might be said that the lecturer had become something of a nomad himself: spending a considerable amount of time away from home, indeed, increasingly so, and his visiting professorship at Chicago had further prevented him from being by his wife's side when her father died. In December he was honouring his father's peers at St Patrick's Cathedral, where two memorials to the late Archbishop Bernard and the late Earl of Iveagh were unveiled and dedicated as well as two tablets in memory of the late Earl and Countess of Iveagh.[40] As for Italia, she honoured her maternal duties, though in her sister-in-law Nancy's view she pushed her son excessively and ruled him with a rod of iron.[41] It seems that she had experienced enough of Irish life by what would soon be ten years on from taking up residence in Dublin following her marriage. Her husband became a fully-fledged member of the London Athenaeum in 1931; if he could obtain a Chair in England, she would be able to walk away from what, according to her sister-in-law Nancy, she '[hated]':[42] the people, religion and politics of Ireland. Oxford was again to offer the possibility with the current occupant, Salvador de Madariaga, being appointed the Spanish Republic's Ambassador in Washington.

When Spain's Second Republic was declared on 14 April 1931, Starkie was in the United States, though details are lacking as to the length and extent of this his third and last American lecture tour organized by J.B. Pond.[43] A note addressed by the lecturer to a Miss Hardman at the Pond Bureau at the end of April, requesting he be sent a cheque to cover payment owing to him, mentioned his having lectured at the select Porter's boarding school for girls in Farmington, Connecticut, on the 16th and, on the following day, he had returned to lecture at Trinity College Hartford.[44] By the

37 'Dublin University Modern Language Society', IT, 28 Oct. 1930, p. 6.   38 W. Starkie to J.B. Pond, 4 Oct. 1930 (JBP SIUC).   39 W. Starkie to J.B. Pond, 7 Nov. 1930 (JBP SIUC).   40 'St Patrick's Cathedral. Two memorials unveiled', IT, 12 Dec. 1930, p. 6.   41 'Italia is inclined to force [Landi] too much, and she is frightfully severe with him' (N. Starkie to E. Starkie, 13 Apr. 1930, ES Bodl.). 42 'Italia would love him to get the Oxford Chair. She does not like living over here. She hates the people, the religion and the politics' (N. Starkie to E. Starkie, 13 Aug. 1931 (ES Bodl.)).   43 A letter addressed to the President of Trinity College Hartford, CT, in March 1934 on behalf of Alber and Wickes, Inc., an organization that occupied itself with 'booking transcontinental tours for famous speakers, dramatic and concert artists', queried whether the College might be interested in a lecture by Dr Walter Starkie on 'modern Europe through its salient figures'. It was explained that the tour would be taking place 'in the fall of 1934 and the winter of 1935', but appears not to have materialized (Monica H. Greely to Mr R.B. Ogilby, 20 Feb. 1934, Trinity College Archives, CT, Hartford). Starkie's engagement with another company suggests that he may have experienced a disagreement with Pond. A letter from Starkie to Pond in 1930 already indicates that Pond had accused Starkie of breaking his word in connection with an Abbey Theatre visit to the US, an accusation Starkie vehemently rejected. (W. Starkie to J.B. Pond, 9 Jan. 1930 [incomplete] (JBP SIUC).   44 W. Starkie to Miss Hardman, 30

12 May C. Starkie (left) with her daughter Muriel (centre), daughter-in-law Italia (right) and grandchildren Landi and Alma, Dublin, *c*.1930.

time he was writing to the New York office, the Spain which had fêted him over the 1920s had disappeared: King Alfonso XIII had abdicated and gone into exile; Alfonso Merry del Val had resigned his post as Spain's Ambassador to Great Britain. However, Starkie's contact with Spain would continue energetically, the Spanish publications and journalism he produced over the decade constituting, for the most part, support for the displaced Establishment. In this connection, Starkie struck some new territory: in the summer of 1931 he travelled to Spain, to the Benedictine Monastery of Santo Domingo de Silos in the province of Burgos, where he would initiate a lasting friendship with one of the monks, Fray Justo Pérez de Urbel.

Early 1931 reveals Starkie on the social circuit in Dublin. On the afternoon of 16 February, together with his mother and Italia, he attended the opening of an exhibition of pictures by the wife of Major Kirkwood, the secretary of the Irish Polo Club, and daughter of Senator Andrew Jameson.[45] He would also be performing social tasks in May which were academically related, such as looking after a Frenchman who was programmed to deliver a lecture at TCD,[46] though some such tasks might have a pointedly political purpose. A case in point is a tea party at the Shelbourne, offered by Commendatore Piero Toni, Royal Italian Consul-General in the Free State, to the

Apr. 1931 (JBP SIUC).   **45** 'Art at Home', IT, 17 Feb. 1931, p. 4.   **46** 'Dublin University Lecture', IT, 23 May 1931, p. 6.

students who had been attending the Italian classes given by Dr O. Delle Piane since November 1930, 'under the supervision of Sir Robert Tate and Dr Walter Starkie.'[47] Professor and Mrs Starkie were present as well as Sir Robert Tate, among others.[48] In June, Professor Starkie and his wife were at the dinner party given by the Governor-General of the Irish Free State and Mrs McNeill at the Viceregal Lodge.[49] June was a busy month given the celebrations held to mark the bi-centenary of the Royal Dublin Society. Starkie occupied the presidency of the 'Section for the General Purposes of the Society' and contributed an article to the commemorative volume of the bi-centenary[50] in which he contrasted the conservative membership of the past with the 'completely democratic' present, even going so far as to claim that in the RDS of 1931 'young anarchists and mad idealists' were to be found alongside 'the fierce conservatives'[51] of yesteryear. There are also echoes of Starkie's references to the work of the RDS in the articles he contributed to the *Irish Statesman*. Thus, he also took advantage of the space to promote the present-day institution as one that sought to cross boundaries and unite: 'drawing its strength from every sphere of influence in Ireland. Every class and creed was to be represented here; there should be no distinction of religion or politics; the society, in fact, should be a meeting-place, and of all Ireland, whether North or South.'[52] And as the regime in Italy approached its tenth anniversary, the last sentence of the article was used by Starkie to evoke it, bringing to the fore, yet again, 'the famous Italian slogan: *Marciare non marcire*', which, the author declared: 'might be taken as the motto of the Royal Dublin Society in all its long career'![53]

There was also a family social occasion in the month of June: Landi Starkie made his first communion in the chapel of the convent of St Mary Magdalen in Donnybrook. In a letter to her sister Enid in Oxford, Nancy described what she witnessed on arrival at the chapel with her mother: 'We entered and saw fat Walter kneeling on Landi's left, looking very amused, and Italia, crying, on his right.'[54] Nancy further explained in her letter that she had been at 'the period ball' the night before and had only slept for two hours. Perhaps her brother had been at the same ball and had also experienced a short night, or no night, which might contribute to explaining his amused expression as well as Italia's tears, or perhaps Landi's mother didn't want her son to be a (Catholic) communicant. As Enid's youngest sister informed her, some time before the event, Nancy had been approached by a local priest, Father Fennelly, who enquired whether Landi had ever been baptized since he had heard rumours to the contrary and was most concerned. Nancy reported to Enid that she had answered in the affirmative, then: 'fled home to write to Italia and tell her'.[55] Italia replied but did not dispel the doubt. It was in the same letter that Nancy addressed to her sister Enid that she spoke of Italia's contempt for Irish people, religion and politics. Judging from Italia's reply to Nancy's letter regarding Fr Fennelly's enquiry, she appears to have been at the end of her tether, the survival of her marriage seen to be dependent

47 'Italian classes. Course to be held in Trinity College', IT, 7 Nov. 1930, p. 4. **48** 'Italian classes in Dublin. Tea party to students', IT, 29 May 1931, p. 4. **49** Under 'Court and personal', IT, 19 June 1931, p. 6. **50** W. Starkie, 'What the Royal Dublin Society has done for music' in *Royal Dublin Society bi-centenary souvenir* (Dublin, 1931), pp 60–5. **51** Ibid., p. 63. **52** Ibid. **53** Ibid., p. 65. **54** N. Starkie to E. Starkie, 13 Aug. 1931 (ES Bodl.). **55** Ibid.

on her husband's obtaining the Oxford chair. Nancy relayed Italia's reply to Enid: 'She writes back to say that if Walter gains Oxford, it will be possible for them to go on living together, but if he continues in TCD[,] she will probably go and live in Italy.'[56]

The decade Italia had endured in Dublin had no doubt been challenging as her husband struggled to establish himself academically as well as to answer to the responsibility of three of his father's daughters, his sisters Muriel, Chou-Chou and Nancy, and their mother. There was also the strain of living in her mother-in-law's home in straitened circumstances in the early period of her married life, followed by residence in Trinity's Botanic House. The location may be considered as having been ideal, set in TCD's leafy Botanic Gardens, but one niece recalled from childhood visits that the profusion of trees and green created a 'gloomy' atmosphere, she was afraid to go upstairs, and the house was 'damp',[57] while another has described it as 'a terrible little house',[58] with such a degree of damp that mushrooms flourished under the floorboards. The damp within coupled with the Dublin damp without, Italia's frequently single parenting, given Walter's increasingly prolonged absences, and her isolation from his sisters and mother, appears to have led to something of a crisis in the marriage, certainly as experienced by Italia. Her husband was away in the United States again in spring 1931 but March also brought some good news: the election of the candidate Walter Fitwilliam Starkie to membership of The Athenaeum in London.[59] Italia might have constructed this as a promising move towards the family's establishing themselves in England, as a good omen. Perhaps the Oxford chair would be for Professor Starkie this time.

In August 1931, Italia went down to County Wicklow with her children to stay at a guest house in Jack's Hole. Her husband was in Spain. He appears to have spent some time at the home of the Basque painter Ignacio Zuloaga, 'Santiago Etxea', in the town of Zumaia in the Basque Country,[60] to have travelled to Loiola, where he visited the house of the founder of the Jesuit order, Ignatius, and to the village of Ezkioga, where villagers were claiming they had seen apparitions of the Virgin Mother of God,[61] before taking up residence at Santo Domingo de Silos in the first fortnight of August,

---

56 Ibid.   **57** Author's interview with Pamela Bacon (née Horsford), daughter of Muriel Horsford (née Starkie), High Wycombe, 22 Nov. 1995.   **58** Author's interview with Gillian Leonard (née O'Reilly), daughter of Ada (Chou-Chou) O'Reilly (née Starkie), Brighton, 11 Nov. 1995.   **59** Certificate of Candidate for Ballot: Walter Fitzwilliam Starkie. Entry: 27 Apr. 1927. Elected: 11 Mar. 1931 (The Athenaeum).   **60** The gathering (*tertulia*) Starkie describes at Zuloaga's home in the introductory essay to his translation of Pérez de Ayala's *Tigre Juan* may be considered to be inspired in his 1931 visit since the essay is dated Salas de los Infantes, Castile, August 1931. The essay was presumably written, or partially so, when he was staying at the Monastery of Santo Domingo de Silos subsequently. The address as supplied to his family, cited by Nancy in inverted commas when writing to her sister Enid is: 'Real Monasterio de Santo Domingo de Silos por Salas de los Infantes (Provincia de Burgos' [*sic*] (N. Cooper to E. Starkie, 13 Aug. 1931 (ES Bodl.). The introductory essay was published in R. Pérez de Ayala, *Tiger Juan*, trans. W. Starkie (London 1933), pp 11–38.   **61** Starkie recorded his journeys to Loiola and Ezkioga in his first Spanish travel book, *Spanish raggle-taggle*, where the Spanish forms of the place-names are used: chapters 10 (Loyola [*sic*]); 11, 12 and 13 (Ezquioga [*sic*]). The text of the 1934 publication begins with a departure for Spain for a sojourn until the month of October. Reference is made to being at the Gare d'Orsay in Paris on the night of 2 July, but no year is supplied.

from where he wrote to his mother and sister. Nancy situated her sister Enid as to her brother's whereabouts: 'It is a very famous Benedictine Monastery in the wilds of Castile, far from the rail-road' and delivered an account of their brother's daily schedule: 'He is living a complete monastic life, working in the library, going to mass in the mornings at 8 o'clock, and compline in the evening. He gives lectures for the monks.'[62] This first August of the Republic was also the first occasion that Starkie visited the Monastery. The Gatehouse Book carries his signature[63] and reveals that a number of distinguished visitors, with whom he would develop ties and further bonds, over the decade ahead, had preceded him since the years of the First World War and over the 20s: the Duke of Alba, the linguist and literary historian Ramón Menéndez Pidal, the Asturian novelist Ramón Pérez de Ayala, already the Spanish Republic's Ambassador in London,[64] and the Basque painter Ignacio Zuloaga. A number of supporters of General Franco's cause would also frequent the monastery during the Civil War, not least among them Pablo Merry del Val, the son of the Marquis Merry del Val, Spain's Ambassador in London until King Alfonso XIII's abdication. As Head of Press and Propaganda in Salamanca, 'the capital of General Franco's Nationalists',[65] the son of the former ambassador would welcome Starkie to the occupied territory in 1938.

The monks' timetable was not one for the faint-hearted: rising at 3.30a.m., praying for eight hours in the choir and carrying out daily chores all the year round without any form of heating. Fortunately Starkie was there in August when it would have been pleasantly cool and, in any event, there is no evidence to suggest that the visitor rose before daybreak. One of the charms of the monastery, apart from the eleventh century cloister, the splendid library, the Gregorian chant and ubiquitous sense of serenity, was Fray Justo Pérez de Urbel, who had acquired a reputation as a 'historian, writer and poet'[66] by the 1930s and whose company was sought by a range of Spanish writers, from the poets of the so-called 1927 Generation, Rafael Alberti, Pedro Salinas and Gerardo Diego, to the philosopher and novelist Miguel de Unamuno. Starkie made the learned monk's acquaintance in that first summer of the Republic and before the end of the month, Pérez de Urbel, a monk with a strongly material consciousness of the press as possessing a 'formidable power in the modern world',[67] had devoted two articles to Walter Starkie in the monarchist daily *La Época*.[68] Both these articles[69] may be considered as contributing to the fast-growing myth of Starkie as wanderer and in

---

62 N. Starkie to E. Starkie, 13 Aug. 1931 (ES Bodl.).   **63** *Libro de Portería* [Gatehouse Book], 1927–33, p. 191 (Archivo del Monasterio de Santo Domingo de Silos, 5–a–21).   **64** The new Ambassador presented his credentials on 29 May 1931 (A. Coletes Blanco, *Gran Bretaña y los Estados Unidos en la vida de Ramón Pérez de Ayala* (Oviedo, 1984), p. 299).   **65** W. Starkie, 'Salamanca. City that became a capital in a hurry' (1938), p. 7 (see Appendix).   **66** A. de Obregón, 'La vida multiple. El Monasterio de Santo Domingo de Silos y los intelectuales', *Luz*, 27 July 1933, pp 8 and 9. My translation of the original Spanish.   **67** J. Pérez de Urbel, 'La prensa, potencia formidable del mundo moderno', *La Gaceta del Norte*, 6 May 1936, p. 16. My translation. Pérez de Urbel also became a regular contributor to the Madrid Catholic daily *El Debate* over the 1930s. (Fray Clemente de la Serna, 'Fray Justo Pérez de Urbel' in *Homenaje a Fray Justo Pérez de Urbel*, OSB, 1, *Studia Silensia* 3, p. 29.   **68** On *La Época*, see: C. Barreiro, '*La Época*, la conciencia de una monarquía liberal', *Arbil*, 74 http://www.arbil.org/(74)epoc.htm, accessed 1 Jan. 2011.   **69** Fray Justo Pérez de Urbel, 'Walter Starkie. I. El celta

pursuit of Gypsies, already projected in the late 1920s by Starkie himself, as well as by the New York impresario J.B. Pond for the former's whistlestop lecture tours in the United States. The myth would be consolidated over the 1930s through a strategic formation composed of articles and comment in the press produced by Starkie himself and others, through his travel books as well as broadcasting on the BBC.

In the first of his articles, Pérez de Urbel explains that he had read the name of Walter Starkie in the Madrid press: a Mr Starkie had given some erudite lectures on literature and been highly applauded by his audience.[70] However, he had subsequently been introduced to the Benedictine monk as a painter. The monk had then discovered he was a violinist and it was only when he had occasion to speak to him personally that he discovered that he was a director of the Abbey Theatre and a lecturer in Romance languages [sic] at the University of Dublin. Thus, Starkie's identity is initially presented in terms of hearsay, half-truths, even untruths (a painter), together with a degree of accurate data.[71] This ambiguity will become something of a trend in representations of him over the decade, that is, texts carrying some truth yet through and around which fictions abound, Starkie coming to acquire a variety of identities as he wanders through 1930s Europe. Pérez de Urbel already describes him as 'an ardent adventurer, a restless traveller, a tireless pilgrim, who goes round the world [sic] stirred by a longing to see and to know',[72] features which the Spanish friar associates with 'the Celtic soul',[73] mentioning Ossian, Brendan and Columbanus to substantiate his claim. He will also refer to a story told by Starkie himself in which he becomes something a a latter-day Kim, a fiction he had already drawn on in the lecture delivered in Montreal in September 1930, which spoke of his escaping from home at the age of twelve with a bearded old man (as in Kim's Tibetan lama) who played the violin and sang ancient Gaelic songs, a troubadour figure who taught the boy how to play the violin, how to tell the old stories and to sing the airs of his native land. The Benedictine also reports that Starkie, son of a Greek scholar, mentioned his having read the *The Odyssey* by this time, spoke of Ulysses as his favourite hero (echoing Joyce)[74] and his own will to wander as the Greek did. In the Montreal lecture, Starkie had mentioned the Pied Piper of Hamelin and Orpheus. Thus one can also perceive how he wove a web of fictional threads, created out of his childhood reading, perhaps coupled with a desire to escape from family tensions and debt in the present, as well as from an Ireland which was becoming increasingly less home to him, fictions which, moreover, came to play a part in the service of empire: Britain's, Spain's or Italy's.

vagabundo' [The vagabond Celt], *La Época*, 22 Aug. 1931, Suplemento, p. 1; 'Walter Starkie. II. Entre los gitanos' [Among gypsies], *La Época*, 29 Aug. 1931, Suplemento, p. 1.   70 Pérez de Urbel was no doubt evoking the lectures Starkie had delivered at the *Residencia de Estudiantes* in 1924 and 1928. 71 Starkie's having been identified as a painter may have resulted from confusion with his father's sister Edyth Starkie, awarded a gold medal for her painting 'The Black Veil' at the Sixth International Art Exhibition held in Barcelona in 1911 (J. Hamilton, 'Edyth Starkie', *Irish Arts Review Yearbook*, 1991/2, p. 162.   72 Fray Justo Pérez de Urbel, 'Walter Starkie. I. El celta vagabundo', *La Época*, 22 Aug. 1931, Suplemento, p. 1. My translation.   73 Ibid.   74 Joyce read Lamb's *Adventures of Ulysses* in the year that Starkie was born, 1894, and wrote on the Greek as 'My favourite hero' (J. Johnson, 'A chronology of James Joyce' in J. Joyce, *Ulysses*, p. lxiv).

The second article dedicated to Walter Starkie by Pérez de Urbel focuses on the former's Gypsy pursuits, projecting him as one of a brave and fortunate few who have managed to introduce themselves into the community, referring specifically to long periods spent by him in the Andalusian caves of Guadix, Granada and in the Madrid quarter of Tetuán de las Victorias as well as having experienced the life of nomadic tribes in Hungary and Czechoslovakia [*sic*]. The article is full of Starkie's tales: of his experiences with his violin in the company of Gypsies, stories of seduction, of cures for sickness, of garlic as an antidote for the evil eye, indeed, the stuff of his 30s travel books in embryo. Pérez de Urbel would add two other descriptions of Starkie in this second article which also contribute to the mythical identity in the making. Starkie is 'the bohemian Irishman' or 'Irish bohemian',[75] thus national and marginal identities (something of an oxymoronic mix) are reiterated, and he is also an 'improvised gypsy'.[76] The concept of improvisation evokes the *commedia dell'arte*, the theatrical form that Starkie had focussed his academic attention on in the 1920s.

According to the news relayed by sibling Nancy to Enid in Oxford, after leaving Santo Domingo de Silos Starkie was heading for 'the gypsy quarter' in Madrid and Seville. By the time the new academic year began, he was back in Dublin his hopes (and Italia's) of relocation in England dashed: W.J. Entwistle proceeded to win the Oxford Chair. Writing to Enid following a further disappointment in 1953, Starkie recalled that just as in 1928 the Ambassador Merry del Val had supported him, so in 1931 Pérez de Ayala had done likewise, but the Spanish vote was not decisive. By the time Nancy was writing to Enid at the end of October 1931, she could report that Walter was already feeling better though he had been 'very disappointed about Oxford.'[77] His eight-year-old son, Landi, had started school at Blackrock College in County Dublin and was learning Irish but before the end of the decade he, at least, had been relocated in England, boarding with the Benedictine order at Ampleforth in the north of England. His sister, Alma, would follow him, to become a boarder in the south, at Roedean.

Much change was afoot in the Free State: the Dáil was dissolved on 29 January 1932 and the elections took place on 16 February, the month in which the Army Comrades Association was founded, destined to develop into the Blueshirt movement in the following year.[78] Cumann na nGaedheal was having difficulty handling the economy in the wake of the Wall Street crash and did not possess a programme that could compete with Fianna Fáil's. The government party was being pilloried[79] and found itself reduced to employing scaremongering tactics, as in its front-page advertisement on the very day of the election in 1932: 'the gunmen and the communists are voting for Fianna Fáil today'.[80] But the support de Valera had garnered since the founding of the party in 1926, recently crowned with the launching of a daily newspaper, the *Irish*

---

75 Fray Justo Pérez de Urbel, 'Walter Starkie. II. Entre los gitanos', *La Época*, 29 August 1931, Suplemento, p. 1. My translation. The original Spanish reads: 'el bohemio irlandés' and might be translated in either of the forms indicated in the corpus of the text, above. **76** Ibid. My translation. **77** N. Cooper to E. Starkie, 30 Oct. 1931 (ES Bodl.). **78** See Chapter 8 in F. McGarry, *Eoin O'Duffy. A self-made hero* (Oxford, 2005). **79** T. Brown, *Ireland*, p. 130. **80** Cited by D. Ferriter, *The transformation* (London, 2005), p. 364.

Press (in September 1931), afforded Fianna Fáil the necessary seats, an overall majority being achieved in the General Election of January 1933. The *Irish Times* registered the radically transformative nature of the result of the February general election in the twenty-six counties following the formal transition of power in the Free State on 9 March 1932 in biblical-sounding solemnity: 'The Old Order Changeth'.[81] The change would remove the likes of Starkie from the corridors of Irish power. Thus, he looked to where the Old Order prevailed, addressing himself to the British metropolis. He had lost the opportunity of the Oxford Chair but he was already a published author in England and might well be again. It appears that he now set to finishing 'the gypsy book' he had referred to when writing to Pond on his return from Hungary and Roumania in the latter part of 1929. By August 1932, he was able to approach John Murray of Albemarle Street, who would become the publisher of the major part of his output over the next thirty years.

However, as so often throughout Starkie's life, his energies were not channelled in any single direction. He did not devote himself exclusively to writing the travel book; he also produced a translation of the novel that had afforded Ramón Pérez de Ayala the National Literary Prize (*Premio Nacional de Literatura*) in Spain in 1927, *Tigre Juan*.[82] Why Starkie should choose to translate the Spanish Ambassador's novel at this juncture (if, indeed, the choice was wholly his) is intriguing, as intriguing as his first sojourn in Santo Domingo de Silos, precisely in the wake of the declaration of the Second Spanish Republic, but perhaps intrigue is to be expected when one is dealing with an *aficionado* of the *commedia dell'arte*. However, no *zanni* could improvise a translation, and, moreover, in a matter of months as one's nation underwent a radical change of government, one was trying to complete a first travel book and answer to academic responsibilities. Italia with her native knowledge of Spanish was by the translator's side. She may have helped in the first draft, saving her husband the preliminaries, while he polished the final manuscript, introducing, for instance, Hiberno-English to render Pérez de Ayala's use of the Asturian dialect, *bable*.[83]

Another path of possibility in the British metropolis was BBC broadcasting. Thus,

---

81 'The Old Order Changeth', IT, 10 Mar. 1932, p. 7. 82 Agustín Coletes Blanco, who has documented the translations and selections from Ayala's works published in Britain and the United States, records that Methuen and Co. originally contacted Pérez de Ayala with a view to translating *Tigre Juan*. He does not explain why Jonathan Cape finally became the publisher or how Starkie came to be the translator. Neither does correspondence held in the Archivo Ramón Pérez de Ayala (henceforth ARPA) at the Biblioteca de Asturias Ramón Pérez de Ayala in Oviedo throw light on the matter. Coletes Blanco mentions a letter (though no date is supplied) from Starkie to Pérez de Ayala, in which he queried certain turns of phrase and idiomatic expressions, which was in the copy of the translation in Pérez de Ayala's home. (A. Coletes Blanco, 'Traducciones y selecciones de la obra de Pérez de Ayala publicadas en Gran Bretaña y los Estados Unidos', *Boletín del Instituto de Estudios Asturianos*, p. 48.) I have been unable to trace the letter through Coletes Blanco, the Pérez de Ayala family or the librarian Santiago Caravia Nogueras in the Oviedo library. I am grateful to A. Coletes Blanco for supplying me with material he has produced on Pérez de Ayala and enabling me to contact the Pérez de Ayala family in Madrid. I am also grateful to Santiago Caravia Nogueras for his efforts on my behalf when I consulted the Pérez de Ayala material in Oviedo and subsequently through telephone contact. 83 Note, for instance, Tiger Juan's use of 'gossoon' when addressing the character Nachín de Nacha. (R. Pérez de Ayala, *Tiger Juan* (London, 1933), p. 50.)

Gerald Christy addressed himself to J.R. Ackerley at Broadcasting House in order to promote his client:

> I would like to draw your attention to a man who I think would be a great success at broadcasting, namely Dr Walter Starkie[,] whose circular I enclose herewith. He illustrates his lecture with violin music which he plays himself – mostly unaccompanied. He is a delightful personality and a great success as a lecturer, and has done a lot of broadcasting in America for the National Broadcasting Company, and awhile [*sic*] ago gave a series of talks from Dublin and also from Belfast. He would like to call the talk 'Gypsies and their Music' and he could give it without the musical illustrations if desired.[84]

Initially, there appeared to be some interest but, come September, Christy was informed that a planned series of talks on Gypsies had fallen through. For the time being, therefore, Starkie would be off the air. In any event, there was a translation to be completed.

In an interview granted to the Editor of the Madrid monarchist daily *ABC*, held in a London hotel in the wake of the Spanish King's abdication, King Alfonso XIII was gracious in alluding to the Spanish Republic's recently appointed Ambassador in the British metropolis, claiming to have read 'a number of his books and several articles'.[85] The remark might be considered as having been aimed at disassociating Pérez de Ayala from the Republican government he was about to represent in London, a feat which the author himself would perform in 1936, finally coming to lend full support to General Franco's cause during the Civil War.[86] The decade became one of shifting identities. In Starkie's introductory essay to the translation of Pérez de Ayala's novel, the gaping admiration of Primo de Rivera reflected in the *Daily Express* piece of 1928 is now cast aside, replaced by news of the recently declared Second Republic though the allusion to the latter-day change can hardly be described as registering enthusiasm. It is a fact that the new order is repeatedly identified with a rousing vitality but the events are reported in a bald style which conveys the historical phenomenon in a mechanical manner. The 'Epilogue' (to the introductory essay) begins with a statement in which the use of 'strange' fogs the nature of the struggle that had given birth to the Republic, just as the allusion to Don Quixote in what follows confuses rather than clarifies the issue. Thus, the opening: 'The novels of Pérez de Ayala lead us into the strange universe of modern Spain with its struggle between the old and the new.'[87] The text then continues:

> Unamuno some years ago was standing like Don Quixote at the Spanish frontier crying aloud: 'How long must this endure?'[88] In Spain there was martial dicta-

---

84 G. Christy to J.R. Ackerley, 14 June 1932 (BBC Written Archives Centre, Professor Walter Starkie, RCONT 1 Talks File 1, 1932–62). 85 J.I. Luca de Tena, 'Entrevista con D. Alfonso XIII, en Londres', *ABC*, 5 May 1931, p. 24. 86 See: Chapters 7 and 8 in A. Coletes Blanco, *Gran Bretaña y los Estados Unidos en la vida de Ramón Pérez de Ayala* (Oviedo, 1984), pp 424–83 in particular. 87 W. Starkie, 'An introductory essay' in R. Pérez de Ayala, *Tiger Juan*, p. 37. 88 A brief account of

torship and it seemed as though Don Quixote would never return to ransom the country from barbers [*sic*] and canons. And yet the impossible happened. The Spanish people awoke to life and went out into the streets to vote for the Republic. Modern Spain sprang into life in April 1931 with a shout of triumph.[89]

The equivocal use of 'martial' in reference to General Primo de Rivera's military rule is striking and it might be claimed that the victorious 'shout', rather than cry, call or ring of 'Modern Spain' likens her to a delinquent. However, the text may be a case of Italia's (mis)use of English. In the light of Starkie's expression of support for the military dictatorship in the 1920s, the 'Epilogue' could be explained as exhibiting a politics of pragmatism, but why Starkie should lend himself to such pragmatism is a further intriguing question. The matter of remunerated labour cannot be ignored: family finances were an ongoing issue and the translation would bring in funds. However, Starkie's lending himself to such *volte-face* acrobatics may possess a further explanation, one which reaches beyond the maverick personality he has been attributed with and which will be further substantiated in diverse 'performances' over the decade and into the 1940s.

By mid-July 1932, the ambassador's private secretary Luis Calvo[90] was writing to the publisher of *Tiger Juan*, Jonathan Cape, to pass on the news received by Pérez de Ayala from Starkie: 'he has almost completed the translation of the second part of *Tigre Juan – El curandero de su honra* – and can send it as soon as it is required.'[91] Luis Calvo informed Starkie that the ambassador did not need to consult the translation of the sequel since Starkie's 'excellent knowledge'[92] of Castilian Spanish was sufficient guarantee. In the last fortnight of July, the publisher was anticipating that the novel would be printed 'in time for autumn publication'[93] and come September, the *Irish Times* reported that it would be published 'in a few weeks'.[94] However, by late November the novel had still not appeared and by this time Cape considered that it was 'too late in the publishing season to give the book the very best possible chance of success'.[95] Therefore, it was decided to bring the translation out in January 1933.

Surviving correspondence in the Pérez de Ayala Papers provides no indication of exactly when Starkie submitted the final part of his translation of *Tiger Juan*, but his

Unamuno's exile under the Primo de Rivera regime is provided in 'Primo and Unamuno', S. de Madariaga, *Morning*, pp 143–8. **89** W. Starkie, 'An introductory essay', p. 37. **90** The L.C. who interviewed Starkie in Madrid in 1928 for *ABC*. For further information on Calvo see his own 'Memento de RPA', *ABC*, Sábado cultural, 22 Nov. 1980, pp 41–3, and J. Burns, *Papa spy*, pp 158–61, passim. **91** Private Secretary [Luis Calvo] of the Ambassador R. Pérez de Ayala (no signature provided) to Messrs. Jonathan Cape Ltd, 14 July 1932 (Correspondencia a propósito de la traducción al inglés de *Tigre Juan* por Walter Starkie, henceforth Correspondencia, ARPA). **92** [Luis Calvo] to W. Starkie, 16 July 1932 (Correspondencia, ARPA). **93** P. Gilchrist Thompson to Private Secretary to the Spanish Ambassador, 18 July 1932 (Correspondencia, ARPA). **94** 'Spanish Minister's novel', IT, 19 Sept. 1932, p. 3. **95** Hughes Massie & Co. to Senor [*sic*] Calvo, 22 Nov. 1932 (Correspondencia, ARPA).

letter to the publisher John Murray in late August indicates that his energies had also been devoted to producing 'Off with the Raggle-Taggle Gypsies'. Starkie outlined the content of the proposed publication: 'The book describes my adventures as a vagabond fiddler wandering with Gypsies, tramps[,] through Hungary and Transylvania,' explaining that he was addressing John Murray 'because the late Mr Murray knew me and took an interest in my writing',[96] and adding that he had contributed to the *Quarterly Review*.[97] Starkie's letter soon makes clear that he is impatient to see the book on the market, particularly with a view to taking advantage of Christmas sales. With this end in view, he claims that the manuscript can be sent immediately and that he would be 'very grateful' for 'a very quick decision'. He explained that he had been lecturing on the 'adventures' contained in his book 'for the past three years all over England, Ireland, Scotland and ha[d] had three extensive American and Canadian tours'.[98] Furthermore, he claimed to be 'booked up for lectures on Gypsy adventures all over England as well as France'[99] for later in the year and would be going on an American tour in March 1933. Poet, educationist and parliamentarian Lord Gorell replied within the week on behalf of the publishing house, requesting that Starkie submit his manuscript and committing himself to ensuring that the text would be read 'at once, so that an answer [might] be given … without delay'. However, he argued against publishing before Christmas as the book would not be given 'a proper chance' since: 'it [could] not be offered round adequately by the travellers; it jeapordise[d], or limit[ed], orders from abroad, and it ha[d] a bad effect inevitably on sales in the Dominions.' Finally, Lord Gorell suggested that Starkie's proposed title might be shortened to 'Raggle-Taggle'.[1]

Starkie was most fortunate: by the end of the first week of September, Lord Gorell was writing to inform the author that he had found the manuscript 'as interesting as I had expected' and that John Murray would be 'glad' to publish it, proposing early in the new year as the date they would work towards. Thus, Lord Gorell enclosed a contract with his letter and requested that Starkie forward 'the short sections which have still to be sent and the bibliography'. He also took advantage of the opportunity the letter afforded to diplomatically comment on the length of Starkie's production: 'The book would appear to be a little long'.[2] However, he took note of Starkie's disposition to make cuts should they be thought necessary.[3] Finally, Lord Gorell recommended that a table of contents be included, 'giving a synopsis of the adventures …: brief headings, like a sort of running commentary' and requested that Starkie compose 'a descriptive paragraph of about 120 words'[4] for promotional use. Starkie

96 W. Starkie to J. Murray, 20 Aug. 1932 (JMC).   **97** W. Starkie, 'Richard Wagner and the music drama', *Quarterly Review*, 485 (July 1925), 115–29.   **98** There is some evidence of Starkie's presence in Toronto and Ottawa. A letter from Starkie to J.B. Pond, undated, was written on headed paper from The York Club, Toronto 5, and Starkie sent a cable from Ottawa to Pond on 5 March 1929 indicating that he would be arriving in New York on the following day (JBP SIUC).   **99** W. Starkie to J. Murray, 20 Aug. 1932 (JMC).   **1** G. [Lord Gorell] to W. Starkie, 26 Aug. 1932 (JMC).   **2** G. [Lord Gorell] to W. Starkie, 7 Sept. 1932 (JMC).   **3** Starkie's own declaration in this connection is not preserved in the correspondence concerning *Raggle-taggle* in the JMC. However, later correspondence relating to other publications reveals Starkie's unfailing readiness to accept cuts if required.   **4** G. [Lord Gorell] to W. Starkie, 7 Sept. 1932 (JMC).

may have been in England for lectures in early September, in any event, judging from a post scriptum added by Lord Gorell under his signature, the future Murray author visited the publishing house on the morning of Wednesday, 7 September, and may have signed the contract there and then as it is dated on the same day as Lord Gorell's letter and Starkie's visit to Albemarle Street.[5]

In response to a 'kind letter'[6] from Dora E. Yates, the Honorary Secretary of the Gypsy Lore Society and Assistant Editor of the *Gypsy Lore Society Journal*,[7] Starkie wrote that he had hoped to meet her while he was in Liverpool and regretted that he had not managed to: 'I want above all to meet you and the Editor of the Gypsy Lore Society [Journal]. I am a member and I am intensely interested in it always.'[8] The undated letter appears to indicate an early contact with the GLS and must have been written in the last quarter of 1932, possibly in early 1933, though there is another letter to Yates dated in late December 1932, which suggests that the undated one was written earlier. Starkie explained that he had finished a book on Gypsy experiences that would soon be published and expressed his intention of sending Miss Yates a copy. He also declared that 'in a week or so' he would send 'the article of personal experiences'.[9]

The final quarter of the year promised to be busy: there would be proofs from the Pérez de Ayala translation, material to be completed and submitted to the publisher for *Raggle-Taggle* as well as Starkie's lectures and other commitments within the College. Italia could help at home but now, moreover, she was brought into TCD, being appointed assistant to the Professor of Spanish.[10] In spite of his publishing commitments, before the end of the year Starkie travelled to France, to lecture 'in the south',[11] only travelling back on Christmas morning. He returned with a new violin, 'a genuine Landolphi of 1760' which, he informed Miss Yates with the passion of one seduced, he found to be 'much more beautiful' than one he had formerly contemplated in Liverpool. Moreover, as he confessed to the Honorary Secretary, he had succeeded in smuggling the prized possession through customs, dismissing judgment on his action with a Harlequinesque flourish: '– as to my honesty "dosta"!'[12]

---

5 'Agreement between John Murray, of 50 Albemarle Street, London, W.1., hereinafter called the Publisher, and Pro. Walter Starkie, Litt. D. of The Athenaeum, Pall Mall, S.W.1 hereinafter called the Author, in respect of a work entitled *Raggle-taggle*' (JMC). 6 W. Starkie to Dora E. Yates, [no date] (University of Liverpool, Library, Special Collections and Archives, Gypsy Lore Society [henceforth ULL, GLS] 7 26). 7 Dora E. Yates was 'the first Jewish woman to be awarded an M.A. by an English University', the University of Liverpool (A.J. Clinch, 'Obituary: Dora E. Yates', *Keystone Folklore. The Journal of the Pennsylvania Folklore Society*, 19:4 (Winter 1974), 225–30 at 225–6). 8 W. Starkie to D.E. Yates, [no date] (ULL, GLS 7 26). Walter Fitzwilliam Starkie, M.A. Litt.D, Trinity College, Dublin, first appears in the published 'List of members' in the journal, as member number 496, in 1931. His membership appears to have been recent: the highest number of a member recorded at the time is 505 (*JGLS*, Third Series, 10:1 (1931), p. xv). 9 Ibid. I have found no record of an 'article of personal experiences' by Starkie in the *JGLS* at this time. His first contribution to the journal appeared later, W. Starkie, 'The Gypsies as minstrels', *JGLS*, Third Series, 12:2 (1933), 65–82. 10 'Trinity College Notes', IT, 22 Oct. 1932, p. 6. 11 In a CV presented to UCLA, under 1932–33, Starkie provided the following information: 'Lecture tour in France at the Universités Populaires: Niort, Thonars, La Rochelle, St Maxent, Bordeaux and Lyon' (UCLA University Archives. Biographical Files (Walter Starkie). (University Archives Record Series 745)). 12 W. Starkie to D. E. Yates, 26 Dec. 1932 (ULL, GLS 7 27). 'Dosta' signifies 'enough' in Romani.

With reference to the life of Oswald Mosley and the pursuit of an antidote to counter the spread of communism in early 1930s England, Robert Skidelsky has observed: '[T]he challenge ... would have to come from a new movement with an alternative faith and an alternative system capable of winning mass support. Such movements had already risen on the continent.'[13] Six weeks on from the declaration of the Second Republic in Spain, 'Patria' in the *Irish Independent* explained his/her sense of menace, fearful that the 'monster' might strike Ireland, wreaking havoc in the Christian ranks:

> It is an acknowledged fact that there exists today a strong international organisation whose chief aim is the destruction of the Christian social order. This monster has gripped many nations, notably Russia, China, Mexico, Spain, and it has been and still is spreading out its tentacles in our own land. The Pope's call to all Christians to stand together and crush its head is timely.[14]

Growing fears about support for and in relation to the spread of communism led to radical political responses and crude propaganda in the 1930s in countries through which Starkie had moved in the 1920s and continued to do so. Almost ten years on from the so-called March on Rome, and following an 'invigorating' visit to the Italian capital to study fascism *in situ*, on 1 October 1932 Oswald Mosley formally launched the British Union of Fascists in London. April 1933 would find him in Rome again: 'where he made a spectacular appearance with Mussolini on the balcony of the Palazzo Venezia'.[15] In the Free State, General Eoin O'Duffy, in his capacity as Gardaí Commissioner, had also visited Italy and met Mussolini, whose 'great experiment' and 'fierce opposition to communism' impressed the Irishman. O'Duffy's dismissal by de Valera in 1933 and subsequent taking up of the leadership of the Blueshirt movement led to his being embraced by the ousted Cumann na nGaedheal party as 'its saviour'. Fearghal McGarry has drawn attention to the promotion of authoritarian ideas within the movement by 'prominent academics' James Hogan, Professor of History at University College Cork, and Michael Tierney, Professor of Classics at University College Dublin, though, he asserts, neither supported 'the principle of dictatorship.' Their proposal consisted of 'a corporate state, similar to that which existed in Italy, but influenced more by the teachings of Pius XI's recent encyclical *Quadragesimo Anno* than Mussolini's fascism'. McGarry also points out that the 'reactionary agenda' promoted by Hogan and Tierney won the support of 'a wide circle of intellectual priests' and concludes that '[r]eactionary Catholicism was a more important ideological influence than was fascism in 1930s Ireland, even if the distinction was often difficult to discern.'[16]

The promotion of Italian fascism had been a feature of Starkie's pronouncements in the press and of his political practice since 1922 and his dealings with O'Duffy would be acknowledged by the latter in the opening to his *Crusade in Spain* in 1938. He would

---

13 R. Skidelsky, *Oswald Mosley* (London, 1990), p. 289. 14 Patria [*sic*], II, 30 May 1931, p. 8. 15 R. Skidelsky, *Oswald Mosley*, pp 284, 297. 16 F. McGarry, *Eoin O'Duffy*, pp 211, 203, 205, 206.

certainly be able to sympathize with O'Duffy's Catholicism though perhaps less with the General's nostalgia for Ireland's lost golden age. None the less, he cultivated the Blueshirt leader's company, as he cultivated that of so many others. There is no evidence that Starkie was in the *Teatro de la Comedia* in Madrid on 29 October 1933 when the son of the deposed dictator, José Antonio Primo de Rivera, pronounced his maiden speech as leader of *Falange Espanola y de las Juntas de Ofensiva Nacional Sindicalista* (FE de las JONS), outlining the movement's main points, but Starkie's 1930s profile does reveal his contacts with the forces of reaction in Spain. However, before pronouncing at any length on the country over the decade, his energies were channelled towards providing an account of his 'adventures' in Hungary and Roumania.

Reviewing *Raggle-taggle. Adventures with a fiddle in Hungary and Roumania* in the *Dublin Magazine*, Æ highlighted a fundamental question in relation to all Starkie's publications over the 1930s, the first of which set him on the path of popularity as a travel writer, that is, the distinction and border-crossing between reality and fantasy: 'He tells us how he met the Pied Piper of Hamelin and got the whole story from him, and by that tale, set in his narrative with cunning art, he makes it impossible for the censorious to know exactly what tales are history and what are fantasy.'[17] In Starkie's writing the frontiers between fact and fiction become blurred and, if Æ's assessment is accepted, this has been achieved purposely so: 'with *cunning* art'. While concluding that his former fellow contributor to the *Irish Statesman* had produced 'the most engaging book of adventures', Æ's review repeatedly alerts the reader to the duplicitous quality of Starkie's text. The former editor refers to Starkie's '[spraying] a subtle *camouflage* of fantasy over his book', to his 'putting on the *disguise* of a vagabond musician' though he questions whether it wasn't 'the real man casting off a *mask*' and, finally, he will specifically refer to the notion of truth, highlighting the author's equivocal smile, evocative of Dinah the cat's in Lewis Carroll's *Alice in Wonderland*: 'He will not tell us what is the truth about it. He will smile that smile of his which *seems* so open and is really so *concealing*.'[18]

Peter Hulme and Tim Youngs have spoken of the 'close and often troubling' relationship between prose fiction and travel writing, while pointing to readers' expectations with regard to the latter: 'Many readers still hope for a literal truthfulness from travel writing that they would not expect to find in the novel'.[19] Whether readers of *Raggle-taggle* approached Starkie's text in pursuit of 'literal truthfulness' or to be seduced by stories may be difficult to gauge but motivated by truth or tale, it is a fact that Starkie's first travel book was soon successful. It appeared in the month of March and before the year was out, it had gone through three further printings: in April, May

---

17 Æ [George Russell], '*Raggle-taggle. Adventures with a fiddle in Hungary and Roumania*. By Walter Starkie. (John Murray. 10s. 6d. net)', *Dublin Magazine*, n.s., 8:3 (July-Sept. 1933), 69–71. 18 Æ [George Russell], '*Raggle-taggle*', pp 70, 71. My italics. The Pied Piper figure who is introduced into Chapter 27 of *Raggle-taggle* disappears at the end of the chapter, leaving a lingering smile behind, reminiscent of the Cheshire cat's grin in *Alice in Wonderland* (Chapter 8): 'he began to disappear slowly … and all that was left for a time was his queer, sardonic smile' (W. Starkie, *Raggle-taggle. Adventures with a fiddle in Hungary and Roumania* (repr. London, 1940) p. 262). 19 P. Hulme and T. Youngs (eds), *The Cambridge companion to travel writing* (Cambridge, 2002), p. 6.

and July.[20] In a decade of economic depression, mounting class conflict and political polarization, *Raggle-taggle* offered the reader escape into a world of adventure, of carefree fiddling and fun in what is presented as the magic domain of Gypsy folk. These elements are already anticipated through the subtitle of the text, *Adventures with a fiddle in Hungary and Roumania*, the three stanzas of the 'old English song',[21] 'I'm off with the raggle-taggle Gypsies, O!', standing as epigraph to the text, as well as through the paratextual support provided by Starkie's uncle Arthur Rackham. The illustrator signed a sketch placed opposite the frontispiece, entitled 'The Gypsy Spell', in which a male Gypsy plays the violin while another, together with three women, watch him. He also produced a miniature of a Gypsy woman in traditional dress, arms akimbo, placed at the centre of the title page.

It is worth drawing attention here, too, to the 'Old Song',[22] which begins with a question which is dismissive about property and *patria*: 'What care I for my house and land?' The text will travel through territories, Hungary and Roumania, where 'house and land' had been the subject of much division and debate both before and in the wake of the Treaty of Trianon at the end of the First World War. The 'Old Song' seems to explode the importance of such concerns. Moreover, as Æ pointed out in his review, the protagonists of Starkie's text are 'those wild folk who remain unabsorbed by civilization, who have never yielded to the enticements to be one hundred per cent American, English, German, Italian, Hungarian or Spanish, who remain each a perfect character, unique, in unlikeness to any other person'.[23] In their lack of fixed attachment to any one nation, they stand in contrast to a latter-day Europe, which, as the blurb on the front flap of the volume's dustcover announced, 'is full of the ferocious [*sic*] spirit of nationalism'.[24] Therefore, ultimately, the object of the exercise may be read as the tempering of what is conceived of as radical nationalist vindication as, moreover, and to come nearer to home, de Valera moved more closely towards fully reclaiming Cathleen Ni Houlihan's 'four beautiful green fields'.[25] The 'wandering minstrel' who narrates his journey repeatedly evokes Ireland, by intertextual allusion to a wide range of Irishmen and Irish cultural practice, for instance, the actor Joe Kerrigan, Home Rule champion Charles Stewart Parnell, Irish authors in English related to the Irish Literary Revival: Synge (most frequently), but also contemporary (Protestant) playwrights and authors O'Casey, Shaw and Lord Dunsany, keening in the west of Ireland, or to Irish airs such as 'Emer's Farewell' and the song of the Irish Wheelwright,[26] while also representing himself as 'an Irish Gypsy' as well as in his capacity as a Director of the Irish National Theatre.[27] Yet the British tie is a strong one

20 The reprints cited above are listed in the November 1940 reprint. In the meantime, there had also been a reprint in September 1934. 21 Identified as such in the 'Index and Glossary' (W. Starkie, *Raggle-taggle*, p. 397). The whole text appears as 'The wraggle-taggle Gypsies' in J.R. Murray, *Old chestnuts warmed up* (London, 1997), pp 101–2. The three stanzas reproduced as epigraph in *Raggle-taggle* are the final three. 22 Identified as such under the three stanzas (ibid., opposite p. 3). 23 Æ [George Russell], '*Raggle-taggle*', p. 70. 24 I am grateful to John R. Murray for providing me with a copy of the front flap of the dustcover of the first edition. 25 W.B. Yeats [and Lady Gregory], *Cathleen Ni Houlihan* (1902) in *The collected plays of W.B. Yeats* (London, 1953), p. 81. 26 W. Starkie, *Raggle-taggle*, pp 237, 228, 210 (Synge), 305 (Synge), 337 (Synge, O'Casey and Lord Dunsany), 338 (Shaw), 139, 18 and 189, respectively.

and is not neglected in the text, either by means of reference to particular places in the metropolitan south-east of England or through the narrator's reference to his 'Anglo-Celtic nature'.[28] He will also identify himself as both 'English' and a 'Briton' as well as assenting to the classification of an apparently innocent outsider, Nemeth Nándor, the proprietor of the Hotel of the English Queen in Debrecen: 'Mr Nemeth ... was a great admirer of England, and he explained to me that the Hungarians in Debrecen would give me unbounded hospitality because I was English. I hastened to assure him that I was not English, but Irish, but he did not understand the distinction, though he acquiesced in calling me British.'[29] Therefore, Starkie's text of travel and folklore acquires an ideological dimension in the contemporary context of redefined national boundaries and territorial claims in both Ireland and Europe.

Dora E. Yates claimed that nineteenth-century enthusiast of Gypsy life and lore George Borrow had 'deliberately misled readers by mingling fiction with fact [when] describing his own life'.[30] Arguably, the first-person narrator of *Raggle-taggle* performed a similar feat. Certainly, the author's debt to Borrow is acknowledged in the 'Short Bibliography of Initiation' appended to Starkie's first travel book, where he declares: 'At school in England Borrow educated my vagabond personality.'[31] The first-person narrator of *Raggle-taggle* appears in a number of guises, from the moment he sets out, dressed in the 'rough costume and boots' provided by a *contadino*[32] employed in the garden of the family villa in Masone, to occasions en route when he dons conventional dress in order to meet intellectuals or other figures of authority, such as the Metropolitan of Transylvania. He is a 'solitary wanderer', 'wandering minstrel', 'vagabond', 'not ... a normal man, ... a grotesque Gypsy ... like a stupid clown', a 'solitary troubadour', 'poor fiddler', 'lonely stranger', 'mad foreigner', 'the white-fleshed Irishman', another *flâneur* on calea Victoriei in Bucharest, as well as the bronchial asthma sufferer, familiar from Walter's childhood, fighting 'the battle for breath', and still the Irish Catholic, reciting his Hail Mary in a fear-stricken moment.[33] Apart from the variety of the narrator's (dis)guises, the facts of location together with reference to contemporary as well as historical figures and events of significance are interwoven with a wide range, medley, indeed, a plethora of literary fictions and styles. The product of so many ingredients is a headily hybrid text, all of which is permeated by an atmosphere of carnival. However, alongside the carnivalesque, the feasting, merry-making and physicality, a sense of lamentation and loss filters through; thus, the narrative also acquires a political hue in relation to postwar Europe.

The traveller departed '[o]ne day in July 1929' from the Ligurian village of Masone, ostensibly on a 'gypsying expedition',[34] and ends his journey in Belgrade, bringing the text to a close some seven weeks on.[35] In the meantime, he made his way into Hungary, via Genoa, Venice, Trieste, Postumia and Rakek: 'the first town on the Serbian border', where he visited the town of Siófok on Lake Balaton before moving on to Budapest

---

27 Ibid., pp 83, 337.   28 Ibid., pp 325, 72.   29 Ibid., pp 34, 327, 147.   30 D.E. Yates, *My Gypsy days* (London, 1953), p. 11.   31 W. Starkie, *Raggle-taggle*, p. 382.   32 Ibid., p. 8.   33 Ibid., pp ix, 3, 8, 94, 203, 204, 301, 365, 375, 340–1, 122, 361.   34 Ibid., p. 7.   35 The narrator mentions being away over a period of seven weeks (W. Starkie, *Raggle-taggle* p. 205), but there is no clear indication of exactly when he was in any of the places mentioned.

via the town of Lepsény, Mezőkövesd on the Hungarian Plain, nearby Miskolc, and onto the plains of the Puszta. A halt is made at the little town of Polgár before continuing on 'the weary road at [sic] haphazard'.[36] He then travels by train from Füzes-abony to Debrecen, 'city of merchants [and] bulwark of Protestantism', visiting nearby Hajduböszörmény and Hajdunánás, before joining 'the traditional herdsmen and cowboys' on the Hortobágy, an area of 'tedious, barren steppe'.[37] Finally, he takes a rest at the village of Puspökladány, en route for the frontier with Transylvania, feeling 'sad' since he is leaving 'hospitable Hungary', whose sentiment for her people will subsequently be expressed as 'deep love'.[38] The Hungarian journey constitutes Part I of *Raggle-taggle* before moving into Roumania through the city of Oradea Mare, 'or', we are informed, 'as it is called in Hungarian, Nagy-Várad',[39] to which Part II of the text is devoted. A similar number of places are then visited, 'the wanderer' first halting at Huedin, 'or, as it was called by the Magyar, Bánffy-Hunyad,' before tramping to Almás and on again towards Cluj, the Hungarian Kolozsvar, the capital city of Transylvania, where he became 'the guest of several charming families' and a member of 'the small *cénacle* of artists and intellectuals'[40] before he transferred to the so-called Street of Spoons in the gypsy quarter. The village of Orlat is briefly mentioned before the Saxon town of Sibiu or Hermannstadt, the next stop, prior to a thirty kilometre hike to the 'tiny town' of Sălişte at the foot of the Carpathian mountains, which the traveller is 'eager' to visit since, given its size, 'it had produced more great men than anywhere else in Roumania'.[41] Fagaras follows, with pauses at 'various villages such as Porumbac' for refreshment and rest before the train journey from Brasov to beautiful Bucharest, whose colours will exercise 'a siren's charm upon the foreigner.'[42] A stop at Sinaia en route affords the opportunity to highlight the country's monarchical inheritance. The narrator reflects on the village and the crown residence there metaphorically, as being maternally protected by nature: 'I thought of Sinaia bosomed in its mountains with the country palace of Roumania's King' and further renders a nostalgic echo of the institution: 'Up there [in the mountains] were cool woods and rippling streams: I saw the vision of a beautiful queen walking in the gardens with a boy king.'[43]

The narrative begins and ends in carnival mode. The Hungarian notion of *mulatni*, explained as signifying 'to enjoy oneself with Gypsies', is introduced as the Hungarian experience is embarked on and the final chapter focuses on what is presented as the Roumanian equivalent: '*a petrece*'. An 'Epilogue' follows in which the narrator travels 'on a small peasant-boat gliding up the Danube,' described in patriarchal terms as 'the great Father of rivers' and represented as accomodating 'the citizens of many countries' while drawing them together peacefully: 'Its flood harmonizes every discord and nationality and its spirit is the spirit of pan-Europe.' This 'spirit' (comparable

---

36 W. Starkie, *Raggle-taggle*, pp 9, 126 ('at [sic] haphazard' should, presumably, read: 'haphazardly' or 'in a haphazard fashion'. This may be another instance of Italia's English). **37** Ibid., pp 143, 144, 152, 153. **38** Ibid., pp 164, 215. **39** Ibid., p. 165. **40** Ibid., pp 217, 224. **41** Ibid., p. 275. **42** Ibid., pp 284, 334. The residence is Peles Castle, built in the reign of King Carol I. The allusion to the 'beautiful queen' and 'boy king' refers to Queen Marie and the future King Carol II, who was born at the castle in 1893. **43** Ibid., p. 330.

13 W.F. Starkie (centre) on the Hungarian *putzsa*, summer 1929.

with the earlier reference to 'the spirit of music') conveys what may be read as an essential message in a text that seeks to counter division, whether it be at the level of wrangling between peasants and Gypsies, a phenomenon repeatedly referred to, or what is conceived of by the narrator in his guise of 'Irish Gypsy' as the 'narrow nationalism [of] post-War Europe.'[44] The final section of the epilogue displays a further vision, perhaps marked by a reading of Æ's *The Interpreters* (1922), which also evokes elements found in the utopian and dystopian literature of the late nineteenth century, one that complements the rejection of modernity voiced earlier in the text. By means of elements that draw on science fiction ('Death Ray', 'whizzing meteoroids'), 'skyscrapers fall into heaps' and the world fragments, giving rise to an antediluvian planet of artisans, lorded over by a 'ragged Gypsy violinist' whom the traveller had met and joined forces with along the way. Perhaps the narrator no longer recalled that he had parted company with Rostás, the Hungarian Gypsy in question, having found him 'the most dictatorial Gypsy ... ever met', who treated him 'as a kind of white slave',[45] or perhaps he hadn't. Rostás had exercised a fascination over his subject, not unlike the charisma which the author appears to have succumbed to in a number of European dictators over the 1920s and 30s.

44 Ibid., pp 12, 362, 373, 83, 82.   45 Ibid., pp 379, 202.

Not inappropriately, it is in the chapter entitled 'Mulatni' that the traveller reports savouring his first dish of *gulyás*, followed by typical fritters, *csorge fank*, for desert, accompanied by the 'golden wine', Tokay. Worth highlighting here is not so much the fare, though eating and drinking are a constant feature of the text and cannot be ignored (this is the first of a number of dishes of goulash, glasses of Tokay or beer to be enjoyed *en route*), as the weaving into the narrative of reference to 'the national hero', Francis II Rákóczi, whose name will surface on six subsequent occasions. The early eighteenth-century Hungarian is the first of a number of nobles and rulers to be mentioned over the pages that follow, politicians as well as monarchs, who will contribute to creating a sense of Hungary's glorious past. There are those who, like Francis II Rákóczi, sported the title of Prince of Transylvania and are also referred to: Gabriel Bethlen and Stephen Bocskai, a number of kings: Béla IV, Ladislaus, Matthias Corvinus, Stephen I, together with the Emperor Sigismund, and political figures, from Lajos Kossuth in the nineteenth century to the ruler of Hungary in the period of the traveller's journey, Regent Horthy. The latter is introduced by reference to the procession celebrated in Budapest on St Stephen's Day (20 August), witnessed by the narrator, and in which Horthy took part. The occasion leads the spectator to express regret over the loss of past splendour: 'Before the War there was still the glamour of pageantry in Europe, but now it is all dead' and, more recently, over the territorial expropriation of Transylvania as a consequence of the Treaty of Trianon in 1920.[45a] Solidarity is expressed with Hungary's dispossession: 'The music played by the band is solemn and heartrending in its sadness: it is a Magyar folk-song, and today seems more poignant because it makes *us* all think of the provinces that disappeared from the Kingdom'.[46] Yet before this point in the text 'Magyar heroism' has been evoked and the Magyars represented as 'an unconquerable people'. The spectator's sentiments are underlined by the contribution of 'a Magyar Baron – a real baron with estates who might have strayed out of eighteenth-century romance.' He recalls 'the greater Hungary alas' of his youth, leading the traveller to lament further: 'It is sad to think that countries such as Hungary and Spain are the last bulwarks in this modern standardized world of the *Grand Seigneur*'. Finally, he returns to a comparison with Spain as he reflects on the relationship between the aristocratic family and the peasants employed on the estate, a reflection which harks of a Carlylean idealization of feudal society: 'I was irresistibly reminded of Spain, where the peasant stood in the same relation to the lord of the Manor and both possessed the characteristic of true *Nobleza*'.[47] Thus, the lamentation relates to both nation and class structure. The 'plea for the *Grand Seigneur*'[48] constitutes a defence of the feudal regime, indeed, a pining for its lost nobility.

A strong sense of the nation's past glories is resolutely expressed in relation to Hungary whereas a different procedure is generally adopted for Roumania. In the case of the latter country, the strategy consists of citing contemporary artists and intellectuals, Church representatives, politicians and government officials who are bent on

45a On the Treaty of Trianon, 'signed by a truncated Hungary on 4 June 1920', see R. Bideleux and I. Jeffries, *A history of Eastern Europe. Crisis and change* (London, 1998), p. 408.   **46** Ibid., pp 87, 85 (my italics).   **47** Ibid., pp 21, 104, 106, 104, 107.   **48** Ibid., p. xii: see the heading for Chapter 10.

14 W.F. Starkie (right) on the Hungarian *putzsa*, summer 1929.

'Roumanizing'[49] the annexed Transylvanian territory. The narrator appears to take up a position of ambivalence with regard to the annexation, stating: 'At present it is very difficult for the stranger to understand the situation clearly, for he is torn this way and that by the conflicting partisans'.[50] However, the empathy expressed in relation to Hungarian loss and, more particularly, for the lot of the Magyar aristocracy, is sustained. The traveller highlights the sorry state of its members in Cluj, where they reside 'in sad retirement ... and cry out against the sad change that has come over their lives. Before the war of 1914 they were a ruling race and their privileges were feudal. Now, after the conflict, their country has been drawn and quartered ... and their richest province, Transylvania, lies in the power of the hated enemy.'[51] Also in Cluj, the traveller meets university professors, among them the historian and parlamen-tarian Nicolae Iorga, 'a bastion of conservatism, with clear pro-monarchist views',[52] the painter Grigore Negosanu and Roumanian National Theatre actresses Athena Dimitrescu and Nunuta Hodos. Towards the end of his journey, and as a consequence of being taken in by two flighty females in Bucharest, the traveller regrets finding

49 Ibid., pp 267, 276. 50 Ibid., p. 212. 51 Ibid., p. 213. For further information regarding Roumania, see 'Making a Great Romania' in I.T. Berend, *Decades of crisis. Central and Eastern Europe before World War II* (Berkeley, 1998), pp 173–7. 52 R. Ioanid, 'Nicolae Iorga and fascism', *Journal of Contemporary History*, 27:3 (July, 1992), 467–92 at 469.

himself without funds to buy books by contemporary writers Ion Creanga and Ion Luca Caragiale. From Sibiu, and having borrowed 'a suit of clothes from a commercial traveller in the inn', the transformed vagabond called on the Metropolitan, identifying him as 'one of the great figures of Eastern Europe from a political as well as a religious point of view' while further explaining: 'I was told that he was the moving spirit in the revolutionary period after the War and that he had played a great part in securing Transylvania for the Roumanians.'⁵³ Lesser members of the clergy will also be introduced: a young Greek priest or *popa*, 'a pale, ascetic young man dressed in a black soutane buttoned up to his neck,' appointed to be the traveller's guide in Sibiu by the Metropolitan, who will escape in a fright when the traveller leads him astray, into the gypsy quarter; another *popa*, Dr Borcia in Sălişte, provides a redeeming contrast, being: 'a most wordly-looking man, with a bright sense of humour.'⁵⁴ Finally, the traveller meets a number of government civil servants: Emil Isac, the Government Inspector of Theatres and Fine Arts in Transylvania, Dr Petrescu, Director of the Museum of Popular Art in Sibiu, Liviu Rebreanu, Director of the Roumanian National Theatre in Bucharest, who, according to the traveller: 'exercises a government-imposed dictatorship [*sic*] over the playhouses and cinemas of the city',⁵⁵ Dr Breasu, Director of the Library of Folk Music in the city and one Oresanu, an Inspector of Finances in Sălişte. Apart from these prominent citizens in positions of power, a host of other characters are mentioned in episodic fashion. In the Roumanian section of the book, one who is afforded greater space than others and who stimulates 'wonder and interest' in the traveller, is Dr Constantin Popa, a lawyer of some repute in Sibiu. He is represented as frequenting 'the very select restaurant Hager', as a 'great supporter of the Liberal leader [Ion] Bratianu' and also serves to evoke the monarchy. The traveller relays information provided by friends: 'According to my friends, [Dr Popa] is one of the most famous singers in the country, and when the old King of Roumania used to come to Sibiu the first request he made was for Dr Popa to sing.'⁵⁶ In spite of being in the habit of spending hearty evenings at Hager, '[drinking] and [being] merry until the small hours of the morning' in the company of Gypsy music, the traveller detects 'a tragic air'⁵⁷ in the lawyer.

Dr Popa finds some consolation, sometimes, in the playing of a Roumanian Gypsy violinist, one Alecsandru. The latter is one of numerous Gypsies met along the road, beginning with Karoly Arpád, 'one of the well-known Gypsy violinists of Hungary' in Siófok, and the 'Gypsy Violin King', Magyari Imre, on Margaret's Island, finishing with the 'wild Romany music of Roumania' played by the celebrated Gypsy player' Grigoras Dinicu and the 'frenzied fiddling' of Catinca in the 'Bucharest of the shadows' inhabited by the traveller towards the end of his journey.⁵⁸ Apart from Gypsy musicians, he also comes into contact with diverse waifs and strays, a number of whom are women, by whom the traveller is tempted, charmed, nursed, or whose life stories he listens to, taking on an avuncular role, thus Anna, Manczi, Gilda, Juliska, Rosa, Mara, Elsa and Tintea. Diversity is further created by reference to the range of

---

53 Ibid., p. 269. **54** Ibid., pp 271, 277. **55** Ibid., p. 336. **56** Ibid., pp 272, 273. **57** Ibid., p. 273. **58** Ibid., pp 13, 57, 340, 354, 346.

citizens encountered in his path: the inn-keeper Gluck in Mezökövesd; the 'big farmer', chairman of the Electricity Board and Director of the People's Bank, Gyula Patay de Baji, in the same town; the ex-circus acrobat and fakir of Egyptian descent, Ali Hussein; an old pedlar, further identified as a Polish orthodox Jew, now resident in Hungary and heading for Nagy Várad, 'where there were many Jews'; in Debrecen: Gyula Hadfy, a sugar inspector; Nemeth Nándor, a hotel proprietor; Dr Dicsig, a well-known jurist and member of the city council; a 'dreadful little man'[59] met in Huedin who is intent on modernizing the town, much to the traveller's alarm, and so many more. The accumulation of characters is overwhelming, creating a maze of mentions, all of which lie within a web of wide-ranging literary lore and allusion. Indeed, the intertextuality becomes bewildering, moving from the frequently invoked classics and specific stories or characters from the *Arabian Nights* to the science fiction features of the epilogue, passing through fairy stories: Grimm, Perrault and Madame D'Aulnoy; nursery rhyme; Boccaccio; Dante; Cervantes' *Don Quixote* and his story 'La Gitanilla' [The Little Gypsy]; Harlequin and Brighella of the *commedia dell'arte*; Walter Scott's Meg Merrilies and Robert Burns' Cutty Sark as sources for witch-like characters, the conversation between the Master Houyhnhnm and Lemuel Gulliver and the experience of the latter in Lilliput in Swift's *Gulliver's Travels*, Coleridge's Ancient Mariner, Keats' 'Ode to a Nightingale', Byron's Don Juan, Walter Pater on Leonardo da Vinci, the dream world of Lewis Carroll's Alice and George Borrow's adventures with Gypsies. Different characters are also represented in literary terms, evoking the works of Shakespeare, Dumas and Verga: in Mezökövesd the trio of *The Tempest* appear: Gyula Patay de Baji is identified as 'the Prospero of the party' while a local landowner is Ariel and one Kovács, Caliban; prominent Cluj citizens become the three musketeers: Professor Grimm is 'the dashing d'Artagnan', lawyer Amos Francu, with his subtle wit', the Abbé Aramis, and the painter Negosanu, 'the bluff Porthos', and a girl in a wine-shop in Huedin is viewed by the traveller as 'the living embodiment of Verga's Santuzza'.[60] Finally, further allusion to other western modes of artistic expression appear: opera, particularly Wagner; classical music, through reference to Beethoven and Schubert, and the painting, drawing or engravings of Velázquez, Goya, Doré and Hogarth.

In terms of style, the text reflects the factual, documentary mode of travel narrative in the mapping out and following through of the route while also providing reference and drawing on data supplied by experts in the field of Gypsy studies over the nineteenth century: George Borrow, Charles Godfrey Leland and Henrik Wlislocki, among others. Studies devoted to particular peoples further lend authority: Charles Boner on Transylvania and Emily Gerard, Mrs Gerard as she appears in the text, whose *The land beyond the forest* is described in the annotated bibliography as 'An excellent book, full of information concerning Hungarians, Roumanians, Saxons as well as Gypsies.'[61] The English translation of *Europe* by Count Keyserling also appears in the list of texts dealing with Hungary, with particular reference to an essay devoted to the country.[62] Narrative strategies deployed by Swift and Dickens, description as

---

59 Ibid., pp 97, 126, 181.   60 Ibid., pp 97, 233, 176.   61 Ibid., p. 387.

encountered in Gothic fiction, titillating accounts of the female body or feminine dress as found in nineteenth-century *risqué* literature, or the lay-out of dialogue as represented in theatrical texts are also characteristic features of the style while the episodic structure overall evokes the Spanish picaresque, the protagonist here a latter-day Lazarillo, a rogue and a survivor. The conversation between the traveller and the old pedlar out on the *puszta* is reminiscent of the ironic dynamic employed by Swift in 'A Voyage to the Houyhnhnms', whereby the Master Houyhnhnm poses apparently innocent questions or makes seemingly ingenuous comments that prompt the traveller to supply potentially controversial or politically delicate information. The additional understatement with regard to the challenge represented by the tragic information to be provided, given the high temperature on the plain, supplies a potentially humorous vein, also found elsewhere in the text:

> The old fellow … never stopped his confounded questions. He managed to extract from me the information that I came from Ireland and he wanted to know was it not in England. 'Ah, yes, I remember once reading in the paper of a mayor who starved himself to death for the love of his country.' I had then to tell him all the story of MacSwiney, the Lord Mayor of Cork, in every detail, and explain all the vicissitudes of the Irish struggle for freedom – no easy task on a boiling day on the Puszta.[63]

In the Gypsy quarter in Bucharest, the traveller finds accomodation in a house recommended to him where 'a little man' emerges to answer his enquiry. The description of his face evokes Dickensian caricature: 'He was an old man and his face was so thickly covered with beard and furrowed with wrinkles that it resembled a waste country whose ravines are overgrown with brambles. In his wild face the silver spectacles gave the one and only touch of normality and they were like windows in a ruined mansion.' The description of the traveller's circumstance once night has fallen deploys stock elements of the Gothic: 'Night had fallen and the landscape was illuminated by a wan moon that gave every tree and shrub a ghostly appearance. In the shadows there seemed to lurk hidden beings, and I had the overpowering sensation of being followed.'[64] Elsewhere, vampires, demons and upirs appear and the text is spiced with titillating reference to women's bodies and dress in the low-life establishments in which the traveller finds accomodation. Thus, a girl's 'budding breasts above her very low-necked chemise', another's 'silk *peignoir* of very short dimensions', a 'Gypsy violinist's breasts gleam through her torn bodice' and the 'ribald laughter'[65] of a prostitute is also be heard. On two occasions, the traveller imagines conversations between himself and mythical characters, the first: 'the renowned Gypsy minstrel of sixteenth-century Hungary', Demetrius Kármán, and the second: 'a very strange fellow … with a springing step',[66] the Pied Piper of Hamelin, both of which

---

62 Like Starkie, the German author lectured at the *Residencia de Estudiantes* in the 1920s and frequented Spanish philosopher Ortega y Gasset's *tertulia* in interwar Madrid. His ideas on aristocracy were echoed by Starkie in his writings, not least in *Raggle-taggle*. **63** Ibid., p. 127. **64** Ibid., pp 350, 323. **65** Ibid., pp 333, 299, 355, 357. **66** Ibid., pp 203 258.

encounters are presented in dialogue form, as in a theatrical text, each speaker signalled in turn with the words he pronounced following on. The text also yields a biblical turn of phrase, evocative of a gambit found in the Authorized Version. The narrative of Manczi's lifestory reads: 'Thus, *it came to pass* that Manczi grew up without any discipline of any kind.'[67] Some Hiberno-English also trickles into the text, in the description of local petty squires at the inn in Mezőkövesd, pretentious 'in their knickers and green sporting-coats', who are referred to as 'squireens'.[68]

As may be appreciated from the above references, *Raggle-taggle* operates on a variety of levels. It is a travel book, documenting the journey from the Austro-Hungarian border area around Lake Balaton to the Rumanian capital, Bucharest, while the encounters along the road and the adventures experienced by the first-person narrator also provide entertainment, evoking the picaresque as well as Victorian fiction of colonial adventure. It also makes some claim to be contributing to Gypsy studies and in this connection a variety of authorities are brought to bear: Borrow and others who are representative of the scholar-Gypsy tradition, defined by A.J. Clinch as 'that curious blend of scholarship, sentimentality and individualism.'[69] At the same time, the text conveys a vindication of the Gypsy community and a defence of ethnic diversity. It functions as a vehicle for anti-Marxist discourse and last, but certainly not least, as a vindication of Hungary's right to recover territory taken from her in the wake of the First World War. These last two strands are fundamental since they may be related to the capital, the funds, which enabled the 'adventures with a fiddle in Hungary and Roumania' to take place and ultimately determined the monologic message of a text which is structured dialogically. Both the dedication of *Raggle-taggle* to the author's friends Emily [*sic*] and Cecil Harmsworth and the invocation in the text of Cecil's brother Harold, Lord Rothermere, are revealing of Starkie's ongoing connection with the Harmsworth family, further sustained at a public level in 1936 with the Dublin professor's delivery of the Lord Northcliffe Lectures at University College London, created in memory of Harold and Cecil's deceased elder brother, Alfred.

The anti-Marxist thrust is introduced in *Raggle-taggle* in the chapter devoted to the town and people of Fagăras. Before honing in on a clerk from Bucharest, the traveller conveys the idea that the Roumanian is not consistent in his criticism of the government in power, going on to express a cynical view with regard to the handling of power by the common man. Thus, he pronounces:

> In discussing the problems of his country, the Roumanian reminded me of the Spaniard; he will tell you many tales of hopeless misery and put all the blame down to the government, but when you take his opinions as your norm[,] he will turn in a sudden fit of patriotism and contradict you for generalizing about his

---

67 Ibid., p. 121. My italics. 68 Ibid., p. 96. 69 A.J. Clinch, 'Obituary: Dora E. Yates', p. 227. See also the definition of 'Gypsylorist' in M. Burke, *'Tinkers'. Synge and the cultural history of the Irish traveller* (Oxford, 2009), p. 289.

country. [...] The Government of [Iuliu] Maniu has given the peasant a taste of power, and he will soon want to play the tyrant.[70]

The depiction of the clerk somewhat echoes Dickens' union leader in *Hard times*. Like Slackbridge, the clerk is singularly unattractive, bearing no comparison with the hearty, 'agreeable'[71] farmers of the yeoman class, who invite the traveller to their table at the Mercur Hotel. However, he commands authority in the company when politics comes to the fore, depicted as the equal of a latter-day union representative in Lancashire or Wales:

> He might just as well have come from Burnley or Cardiff as Roumania; he was underfed, undersized, with an unhealthy, pimply face, and he wore ... threadbare, shiny-trousered suiting ... The little man worked himself up into a paroxysm of rage in his abuse of the Government, ... There was nobody to answer the revolutionary arguments save one very competent farmer who was a strong supporter of the present Government.[72]

But the clerk, repeatedly labelled 'the little man', forfeits his authority when he sets Lenin above Christ: 'The clerk considered [Lenin] the greatest benefactor humanity has ever known. ... the little man ... quoted Karl Marx on Christianity as the religion of the Capitalist and said that Lenin was greater than Christ. At this the whole party became very shocked and the little man saw he had gone too far.' At this point, a short paragraph or long sentence in which the traveller expresses his opinion reads like the text of a political commentator or provider of intelligence: 'The Roumanian peasant will not suffer people to interfere with his religion and Bolshevistic propaganda will not, in my opinion, make any headway, for a time at any rate, in a country so attached to the Orthodox Church.'[73]

While in Budapest, the traveller also heard his old landlady lamenting the condition of her country: 'We Hungarians ... have a maimed country',[74] though the people's determination to resist is also highlighted. The awareness of Hungary as mutilated by the Treaty of Trianon was Viscount Rothermere's conviction, leading him to produce an article in the *Daily Mail* on midsummer's day 1927 in which he declared: 'the time has come for the Allied Powers who signed that arbitrarily drafted instrument the Treaty of Trianon to reconsider the frontiers it laid down', going on to qualify the Peace Treaty as 'ruthless'[75] for Hungary. The article and campaign that followed awarded Rothermere heroic status in Hungary, documented by the Viscount himself

---

70 Ibid., p. 301. 71 Ibid., p. 302. 72 Ibid., pp 302, 303. The character of the clerk may be a caricature of the Hungarian-born communist Béla Kun, described by Rothermere as 'infamous' (Viscount Rothermere, *My campaign for Hungary* (London, 1939) p. 66). On Rothermere's 'Violent anti-Bolshevism' and acclaim for the Nazi regime in the *Daily Mail* between 1933 and 1938, see R. Griffiths, *Fellow travellers of the right*, pp 163–4. 73 Ibid., p. 303. 74 Ibid., p. 48. 75 Viscount Rothermere, "Hungary's place in the sun", *Daily Mail*, 21 June 1927, reproduced in Viscount Rothermere, *My campaign*, pp 63, 66. For further information regarding Rothermere's motivation in supporting Hungary's territorial vindications, see P. Lendvai, *The Hungarians. A thousand years of victory in defeat* (2003), trans. A.

in *My campaign for Hungary*, and the Hungarian enthusiasm for the British peer is reflected in *Raggle-taggle*, appropriately situated in the business-minded, Protestant town of Debrecen: 'The great hero of the English in that part of Hungary is Lord Rothermere and one of the streets in the city is called Rothermere *utca*. His advocacy of Hungarian interests in the *Daily Mail* has filled the people with gratitude and on all sides, even in the hovels of the Gypsies, I heard the cry "Lord Rothermere: *éljen! éljen!*"'[76]

The mention of 'Bolshevistic talk' or 'Bolshevistic propaganda'[77] and Rothermere's intervention on behalf of Hungary connect the text with developments, fears and disappointments in the wake of the Russian revolution and the First World War. There are other mentions that also evoke the more immediate political context in which *Raggle-taggle* was produced: Mussolini, projected as a friend of Hungary, whom Rothermere had visited at the Palazzo Chigi in March 1928,[78] and a representation of Jews which smacks of the late nineteenth- and early twentieth-century anti-Semitism afoot in Europe.[79] Thus, the text veers between the real and the imaginary. Apart from historical and political reference to the past as well as the present, there is much of the imaginary, the reader being met, arguably, with excess in terms of the range of literary allusion, tales within tales, such as the old man's, contained in Chapter 4, and the narrator's own flights of the imagination or dream sequences. On occasion there are also bars of music set out on the page, presumably an attempt at making the text more authentically musical as well as providing yet further variety. The overall sense of excess is further intensified by frequent references to eating, drinking and earthy allusion to women's seductive bodies and attire. Ultimately, the reader is left with a labyrinthine sense, of names, places, characters, stories, myths, music and merry-making where a border crossing between the real and the imagined is constantly at work. The headiness of it all is reflected in an uneven structure which may, in part, be explained by the charged nature of the text but may also be attributable to haste or afterthought, as in the four footnotes included in the final chapter, perhaps aimed at lending, albeit last-minute, scholarly authority. However, it could be argued that much of the material that accumulates as the text progresses constitutes so many red herrings, geared to distracting the reader who, judging from the five reprints in 1933 alone, enjoyed being thus distracted. The text's fundamental political purpose was to vindicate revision of the Treaty of Trianon in favour of Hungary and to discredit communist-inspired theory and practice; much of the rest is masquerade. With regard to disguise or masquerade, it is worth consulting the first-person narrator's statement of purpose in the preface to *Raggle-taggle*, where he declares: 'My main object in making the journey was to try to live the vagabond life of a gypsy minstrel ..., but I also wanted to investigate as an amateur, not as a scholar, the wealth of folk music and folk legend which is so essential a part of the lives of those peoples.'[80] Thus he states that he intended to attempt to live the vagabond life while safeguarding

Major (London, 2003), pp 398–405.   **76** W. Starkie, *Raggle-taggle*, pp 147–8.   **77** Ibid., pp 302, 303.
78 Rothermere published an account of his interview with Mussolini in the *Daily Mail*, 28 Mar. 1928. See also Chapter 5 in Viscount Rothermere, *My campaign*, pp 91–106.   **79** See J. Katz, *From prejudice to destruction: anti-Semitism, 1700–1933* (Cambridge, MA, 1980).   **80** W. Starkie, *Raggle-taggle*, p. ix.

himself with regard to possible criticism regarding any claim to wholly serious scholarship.[81] In the text, he is seen to be experiencing the vagabond life, though not exclusively. There is much, vague, reference to 'friends' who provide letters of recommendation or entertain him at choice restaurants such as the Hager in Sibiu, perhaps enabled through Rothermere's connections. Therefore, try as he might, the traveller's seven-week stint was not all raggle-taggle, indeed, was never intended to be so. On the study of folk music and legend, he would only interest himself as an 'amateur' since he was not motivated or required to commit himself as a rigorous researcher; the narrative was, in effect, seriously driven in another direction. As it turned out, the masquerade seduced and awarded Starkie a degree of fame as well as a new source of income.

Finally, it is worthwhile pondering the liberal use of 'queer' and, less so, 'strange', in the text whereby a sense of doubt, uncertainty, of being nonplussed, is created, of identities beyond clear definition. In this connection, it may be argued that playfulness is generated by reference to the spy and the narrator's identity. There are some four mentions of the spy or spying in Part II of the text, the most significant one staged as a conversation between Hungarians and the traveller bound for Roumania in which a statement regarding the latter is disguised by its being voiced by Hungarians:

> In Hungary people warned me against *playing the vagabond* in Roumania. 'You will be treated badly,' they said, 'and the police will *think you* are a *spy*.' It was useless for me to say that I was going to Roumania, where my only spying would be done against the Gypsies. 'Nobody will believe that you are not some *correspondent in disguise* of an English newspaper with Hungarian sympathies.'[82]

As can be readily appreciated, the diction foregrounds masquerade: playing a part, mistaken identity, sporting a mask, together with indirection through the use of irony. As earnest Æ remarked in his review of *Raggle-taggle*, perhaps frustratedly: 'He will not tell us where the truth lies'. Indeed, he would not; then the (great) game would have been up. If truth there were, it was the truth according to Rothermere (owner of an English newspaper with Hungarian sympathies), but that was hardly entertaining. Thus, 'the correspondent in disguise' rollickingly covered his tracks. The ubiquitous sense of excess is the measure of the masquerade and readers appear to have delighted in it, stimulated by the traveller's zest, his fascination with the Gypsies and the contagious pursuit of adventure. The anonymous reviewer in the *TLS* remarked on the rousing impact of the text: 'from his armchair ... the cautious Northerner ... has the itch to shed the shackles of comfort, respectability and a regular time-table' and writing in *Time and Tide*, Anne Fremantle found it: 'the perfect travel book', precisely because of its energizing potential: 'no single person, reading it, could sit a day longer in his chair at home and be content'.[83]

81 However, Starkie did receive some recognition as 'a real authority on Gypsy music' (Dr Andre Spur, 'A supplementary note on the Gypsy orchestras of Hungary', *JGLS*, Third Series, 16:1–2, 1937, 106–110 at 106.   82 *Raggle-taggle*, pp 164–5. My italics.   83 [Anonymous], 'Raggle-taggle', *TLS*, 30 Mar. 1933, p. 219. A. Fremantle, 'The Gypsy trail', *Time and Tide* 14:19, 13 May 1933, p. 578.

Overall, *Raggle-taggle* was well received in British newspapers and journals, reviewers hailing 'a most original and entertaining book', 'a book that will charm everybody', a 'very clever and amusing book', a 'fascinating volume', a 'book packed with extraordinary adventure and ... immensely readable', 'one of the most entertaining and novel of travel books', 'an extremely lively record', 'refreshing, fascinating ... adventurous' and 'full of fun'.[84] Its entertainment value was repeatedly highlighted, with only three reviewers introducing concepts related to the masking that so preoccupied Æ in his review in the *Dublin Magazine*. At the end of March, Wilson Pope observed: 'the absence from [Starkie's] narrative of any evidence of detentions or expulsions rather suggests that somewhere *concealed* in his ragged habillements he carried very useful credentials' while the anonymous reviewer in the *TLS* summed up Professor Starkie's account as signifying his being 'all things to all men for about two months', referring to his experience in the 'Hungaro-Rumanian town of Cluj' as resembling that of 'the *chameleon* that was placed on a plaid'.[85] In June, V.S. Pritchett expressed his scepticism though this was motivated by previous disappointments with regard to the genre rather than by what he found in *Raggle-taggle*:

> We have suffered so much from our professional Catholic romantics, flagon-thumpers and pot-belly boilers who have turned the wind on the heath into a monotonous literary draught, that when we find a professor setting out in heavy peasant *disguise* to fiddle his way among the gypsies of Hungary and Rumania and calling his book *Raggle-Taggle*, we approach the matter with suspicion.[86]

In Dublin, in the second week of March, Starkie may well have given publicity to his forthcoming book when he delivered a lecture on 'Life among the Gypsies'[87] in the ballroom of Lord Iveagh's residence in St Stephen's Green. Elizabeth, countess of Fingall, introduced the lecturer who spoke in aid of the Soldiers' and Sailors' Help Society (Employment Bureau). Judging from the report in the *Irish Times*, Starkie appears to have drawn on his story-telling talent while also projecting the lure of Gypsies as long-standing in his life: 'Professor Starkie told a series of short stories of his experiences among the gypsy tribes of several countries in Europe and in California. [...] Very far back in his own life, said the lecturer, he was attracted by the

---

84 E.M., 'The vagabond professor', *Everyman*, 25 Mar. 1933; [Anonymous], 'An amateur Gipsy', *John O'London's Weekly*, 22 Apr. 1933; Wilson Pope, 'A don in rags', *The Star*, 30 Mar. 1933; Ernest Newman, 'The world of music. The professor goes native', *Sunday Times*, 2 Apr. 1933; V.S. Pritchett, '*Raggle-taggle*', *Fortnightly Review*, June 1933; G.M.L., 'A book of the week. A professor among the Gypsies', *Bulletin and Scotts Pictorial*, 22 April 1933; [Anonymous], 'Adventures with a fiddle', *Books of Today*, May 1933 (ULL, GLS K10 55 (1); K10 55 (1); K10 81; Newspaper K10 P 62; K10 68 (1); K10 P 65; K10 66 (2); K10 p. 63; K10 66 (2)). My italics.   85 W. Pope, 'A don in rags', *The Star*, 30 Mar. 1933; [Anonymous], 'Raggle-taggle', *TLS*, 30 Mar. 1933.   86 V.S. Pritchett, '*Raggle-Taggle*', *The Fortnightly Review*, 133 (1 June) 1933, p. 806. My italics.   87 The title of the lecture as 'Life among the Gypsies' was reported in the *Irish Times*, 'Life among the Gypsies', 13 Mar. 1933, p. 4, while the *Sunday Independent* recorded the title as 'My Life among the Gypsies', 12 Mar. 1933, p. 9.   88 'Life among the Gypsies', IT, 13 Mar. 1933, p. 4.

gypsies and he got to know them very intimately in Italy, Hungary, Spain and other countries.'[88] However, the Gypsylorist was not going to be in Ireland or England for very much longer to aid in promoting sales of his book. In the week following his lecture, he wrote to Sir John Murray at Albemarle Street, explaining that he was off to Spain for a month,[89] but his commercial interests were not neglected. Italia took command, displaying very forthright ideas as to what needed to be done. In correspondence with the publisher at the end of March and writing in response to a letter from Sir John Murray querying whether extracts from the book might be serialized, the author's wife declared: 'I think *Raggle-taggle* needs advertising *more than anything*! I would suggest that, perhaps, a *short, brillant* [sic] extract from the book would make it better known.'[90] Italia's letter also revealed that she was watching developments with a keen eye. She expressed her awareness of the book's 'good reception'[91] in the English press and noted the absence of any comment in Irish newspapers so far. She also enquired as to how the book was selling in London and registered her surprise that a list of Murray's new publications had not appeared in the Sunday papers though she conceded that the publisher might intend to produce such a list presently. In the meantime, Mrs Starkie occupied herself with the business of promotion, explaining her strategy and achievement in a letter to the publisher a week later:

> The selling is going nicely here and in order to help [it] I have thought to print [sic] some cards of a foot square approximately … it is printed in red over white: it is very clear and convincing, I brought [sic] one copy of each in every bookseller shops in Dublin asking specially that it should be put near the book in a very prominent place on [sic] the windows. Additionally [sic] to this I have taken the arrangements to do the very same in all railway stations in Dublin and in the more important towns of the Irish Free State and if possible I will try to manage the north of Ireland too![92]

With a view to making herself clear, Italia accompanied her explanation with a drawing of the type of card she had produced. It carried the title, the name of the author, the publisher and the price of the volume, ten shillings and sixpence, followed by favourable comments from such writers as Compton Mackenzie, J.B. Priestley and *The Times* music critic Ernest Newman.

Starkie left Dublin on 17 March, passing through London to visit Sir John Murray at Albemarle Street on Saturday the 18th, in order to talk over E.B. Dutton's publishing of *Raggle-taggle* in the United States, and departing for Spain on the 19th. As he explained to Sir John, he intended 'to live for a month among Gypsies' with a view to his next project: 'I am tramping through all the Don Quixote country and playing my way down to the south[,] to Granada[,] when I hope to spend some time in the Gypsy caves. I am doing this to finish my book on wandering in Spain.'[93] How

---

89 W. Starkie to Sir John Murray, 16 Mar. 1933 (JMC). 90 I. Starkie (née Porchietti) to Sir J. Murray, 29 [March 1933] (JMC). The italics are in the original. 91 Ibid. 92 I. Starkie (née Porchietti) to J. Murray, 7 Apr. 1933 (JMC). 93 W. Starkie to Sir J. Murray, 16 Mar. 1933 (JMC).

long Starkie wandered in Spain and where exactly he went is not clear though his 1936 travel book *Don Gypsy* reflects the route outlined in his letter to Sir John Murray. In *Don Gypsy*, the traveller records that he 'passed through'[94] the village of Casas Viejas in the southern province of Cádiz, in April 1933, that is, some three months following an anarco-syndicalist uprising that led to a violent silencing of the local peasantry by the authorities.[95] Easter 1933 was in mid-April so, conceivably, he wasn't back in Dublin much before May. In June, Æ's review of *Raggle-taggle* appeared in the *Dublin Magazine* and in July an agreement was reached between John Murray and the Stockholm publishing house Holger Schildt for the translation of *Raggle-taggle* into Swedish.[96] However, Starkie may not have had much time to discuss Æ's review or concern himself with the fortunes of *Raggle-taggle* in Sweden, but not because he was leaning on his laurels in Liguria: he was bound for Bayreuth.

In 1933, the Wagner Festival at Bayreuth took place between 21 July and 19 August and was marked by Adolf Hitler's attendance as Chancellor of Germany. Twenty-two-year-old Diana James, future wife of John Grey Murray, the publisher, the John Murray, 'Jock', with whom Starkie was to forge a firm friendship over the years ahead, also attended.[97] She recalled the 'wonderful café life'[98] enjoyed there and remembered Starkie's presence as well as that of the *Sunday Times* music critic, Ernest Newman. No account of Starkie's sojourn remains[99] but some idea of the period he was there may be gleaned from a letter he wrote to Manning Robertson on his return in response to an enquiry from Robertson regarding the English soprano Dorothy Silk. He replied to Robertson from Brittas Bay in County Wicklow on 14 August, explaining that he had not written at an earlier date since he had just returned, 'a few days ago',[1] from Bayreuth. Who financed Starkie's spell in Bayreuth and why he went to the Festival in the first year of Hitler's attendance as Chancellor are further intriguing questions. In September, he was in Dublin to see the play 'Grania of the Ships' by *Irish Independent* journalist David Sears. He wrote to the author to congratulate him on the 'great success' of the play.[2] As for his own output, he now turned to producing for Spain what he had achieved for Hungary (rather than Roumania) in *Raggle-taggle*, that is, a text which would masquerade as travel literature, gypsies and jest to the fore, while providing propaganda for a particular caste and its interests.

The attraction felt by young Michael Fane towards the unkempt and free-roaming

94 W. Starkie, *Don Gypsy* (London, 1936), p. 140. **95** See J.R. Mintz, *The anarchists of Casas Viejas* (Bloomington, 2004). **96** The Memorandum of Agreement between John Murray and Holger Schildt is in the *Raggle-taggle* correspondence file (JMC). **97** Diana Murray was 'a musician by profession' [and] also wrote about music for various papers.' (Diana Murray (née James) interviewed by Sue Bradley, 15 June 2000, Book Trade Lives, The British Library (henceforth BTL, BL), C872/41, F8164–F8165). **98** Author's interview with Diana Murray, London, 17 Feb. 1995. **99** A cardboard cover is all that has been salvaged of what is announced on the cover in Starkie's handwriting as a 'Diary Bayreuth Wagner Festival July 1933' (TCD, Papers of Walter Fitzwilliam Starkie 1894–1976, Manuscript 9196: Miscellanea). Starkie told David Gordon, who met the former in his final undergraduate year at UCLA, 1969, that he had met Hitler at the Bayreuth Festival in 1933 (author's interview with D. Gordon, Los Angeles, 6 Dec. 2005 **1** W. Starkie to M. Robertson, 14 Aug. 1933 (National Library of Ireland, Manuscript 24.282 (viii)). **2** W. Starkie to D. Sears, 12 Sept. 1933 (National Library of Ireland, Manuscript 21.777).

15 W.F. Starkie (right) and Italia (centre back) with their children Landi and Alma together with friends, Brittas Bay, Co. Wicklow, 1933/4 (?).

fellow, spied beyond the window of 'the beeswaxed dining-room'[3] of his family home, in Compton Mackenzie's *Sinister Street* (1913), might be said to echo the boy Walter's own response with regard to the local lads with whom he played in Killiney and to have influenced his subsequent determination to don the trappings of vagabond. Master Michael saw 'a boy ... with tousled hair and dirty face, a glorious figure of freedom in the rain', which moves him to determination: 'He made up his mind that it was better to be a raggle-taggle wanderer than anything else.'[4] Whether or not Mackenzie's protagonist struck a chord in young Walter's consciousness and led to later resolve is debatable. Doubtless the New Order in the twenty-six countries would have been a contributing factor in the adult's decision-making process. However, it is a fact that following the publication of *Raggle-taggle* in 1933, Starkie dedicated energies to 'wandering' in Republican Spain, at intervals between 1934 and 1936. These wanderings, together with the author's earlier contact with Spain over the 1920s and into the 30s, led to the creation of two more travel books, also published by John Murray: *Spanish raggle-taggle. Adventures with a fiddle in North Spain* (1934) and *Don Gypsy. Adventures with a fiddle in Barbary, Andalusia and La Mancha* (1936).

There is no correspondence in the John Murray Collection that provides evidence of Starkie being afforded financial assistance to enable him to travel to Spain. No doubt profits from the successful *Raggle-taggle* could have helped him on his way. In any event, he had already established contacts with people powerfully placed over the

3 Ibid., p. 36. 4 C. Mackenzie, *Sinister street* (London, 1960), pp 35, 36.

Primo de Rivera years of the 1920s, not least the Duke of Alba and other members of the aristocracy, as well as writers and artists sympathetic to the regime together with others who were not, such as the poet and playwright Federico García Lorca, whom Starkie claimed to have come into contact with at the *Residencia de Estudiantes*.[5] The powerfully placed could provide hospitality and he now widened his scope, coming to frequent the *Revista de Occidente* gathering, led by philosopher José Ortega y Gasset, one of the signatories of the manifesto in favour of establishing a second Spanish republic.[6] Ortega had founded the Madrid-based journal, the *Revista de Occidente*, in 1923, following the founding of *The Criterion* by T.S. Eliot in London in 1922, the latter financed by Lady Rothermere, wife of Harold Harmsworth. The two journals shared an interest in cultivating an educated readership in their respective countries, in developing a European consciousness, while providing information regarding developments in the arts and publishing contemporary writing. Thus, ideas and materials were exchanged. In the final chapter of *Spanish taggle-taggle*, the narrator claims to have already been made 'a member of several *tertulias* of men of letters' when he was in Madrid in 1924 and goes on to refer to the *tertulia* of Ortega, comparing the latter's efforts to those of the editor of the *Irish Statesman* in 1920s Dublin: 'I was intensely interested in the *tertulia* of this Spanish Socrates because he has succeeded in doing for modern Spain what George Russell (Æ) valiantly tried to do for modern Ireland with the *Irish Statesman*. Ortega y Gasset like the bearded philosopher Æ has the great range of mind and the wide sympathy that attracts the young idealists as well as the old.'[7] Starkie's contact with the *Revista de Occidente* circle over the Republican years is reflected in two pieces by the Galician-born writer and critic Lino Novás Calvo[8] in which he refers to *Spanish raggle-taggle* and *Raggle-taggle*, respectively. Having read the former, Novás Calvo highlights the author's remarkable degree of malleability and finally refers to the immense variety in the text, all of which he sees as being drawn together by 'this string of wax',[9] Walter Starkie. Novas Calvo's metaphor aptly conveys the shape-shifting nature of an identity that melts into myriad others, a number of which would be adopted by the narrator in the first travel book relating to Spain, *Spanish raggle-taggle*, to be followed by a no less performative production, *Don Gypsy*.

In the 'Wanderer's Library', a 'short bibliography'[10] appended to *Spanish raggle-taggle*, foremost mention is made of Borrow's 1843 text: '*The Bible in Spain* still makes the greatest appeal to the true wanderer, who longs for hardship, provided that he can meet with an adventure at every turn of the road.'[11] Two other influential nineteenth century travel narratives on Spain: Richard Ford's *Gatherings from Spain* (1846) and

5 In the interview with Bernard Galm, Starkie states that he first met Lorca in 1922 at the *Cante Jondo* festival in Granada (B. Galm interview with W. Starkie, OHP, UCLA, 1970–1). 6 The manifesto was also signed by the Republican Government's future Ambassador to Great Britain, Ramón Pérez de Ayala, and by the doctor and writer Gregorio Marañon. 7 W. Starkie, *Spanish*, pp 442, 445. 8 L. Novás Calvo, 'El profesor excéntrico', *Revista de Occidente*, Año 12:136 (Oct. 1934), 97–101; 'Carta crítica al profesor andante', *Revista de Occidente*, Año 13:139 (Jan. 1935), 118–21. 9 L. Novás Calvo, 'El profesor excéntrico', p. 101. My translation. The original reads: 'ese hilo de cera', literally, 'that thread of wax'. 10 W. Starkie, *Spanish*, p. 466. 11 Ibid., pp 466, 469.

Théophile Gautier's *Voyage en Espagne* (1843) are accompanied by the compiler's assertion: 'Those three books do not grow old, … age mellows them.'[12] Starkie's text alludes to all three of these authors, with both the picaresque and Romantic heritage being reflected in *Spanish raggle-taggle* through the Gypsy focus and pattern of life on the road, features already contained in his *Raggle-taggle* of the previous year. If a longing for hardship defines 'the true wanderer', Starkie might fall short of the title since his tales of wandering are not hardy accounts of difficulties endured but they do display a desire for adventure and, in this sense, they are also reminiscent of British nineteenth-century popular fiction for boys. Thus, in *Spanish raggle-taggle*, the traveller's reports his restlessness after some days spent in the Monastery of Santo Domingo de Silos while indicating his eagerness to be off in pursuit of new adventure:

> My hours pass slowly in this monastery, for I have no task to absorb my restless mind. Every day there are the same silent meals in the refectory, the regular church services, but between those routine duties, time hangs heavy on my hands. […] I began to feel the virus of Gypsy wandering again in my bones and a tingling desire to dash away out of the cloister into the open world once more.[13]

The sense of adventure is already captured at the beginning of the two first chapters of the travelogue. They present the narrator expressing a sense of release on 'the first day of the vacation', which leaves him 'free to wander away from the tedious daily round of duty' and registering a schoolboy's excitement before what lies ahead: 'We are off to Spain! Tomorrow morning will find me tramping along the road from Hendaye to San Sebastian.' In the opening chapter, the narrator refers to what he represents as his two selves: a 'conventional self' and 'vagabond second self', the latter being the adventurous fellow, but as the text progresses a wider range of identities will be exhibited, the narrator coming to perform a variety of roles as he travels into the Spanish state through the Basque Country, into the territory of Old Castile and on to Madrid. In the 'Preface' to the text proper, the traveller explains that he has 'endeavoured to describe a summer journey [he] made alone on foot in Spain, earning [his] living as a wandering minstrel'. This is the guise he will adopt predominantly, his minstrel status rooted in his accompanying fiddle, which he is ever ready to play, and resolutely not hampered by a 'squat, uncourtly figure', … portly form, … puffiness and …short legs', but rather viewing himself as upholding a tolerant tradition, as he declares: 'the best minstrels and storytellers were gifted with a pleasant rotundity of mind and body'.[14] There are variations on the guise of wandering minstrel. The Spanish form *juglar* is drawn upon, and, in this connection, the linguist and cultural historian Ramón Menéndez Pidal's 1920s publication is acknowledged as having been inspirational,[15] while the traveller also projects himself as being 'like a hardened old

12 Ibid., p. 469. The statement carries an echo of Laurence Binyon's First World War poem 'For the Fallen'. 13 Ibid., pp 321, 322. 14 Ibid., pp 3, 7, 3, ix, 5, 284. 15 R. Menéndez Pidal, *Poesía Juglaresca y Juglares: aspectos de la historia cultural de España* (Madrid, 1924). For Starkie's acknowledgment, see the final paragraph of the 'Preface' to *Spanish raggle-taggle*, where Menéndez Pidal is identified as the author's 'friend'. References to the scholar may also be found in Chapter 29 of Starkie's

Irish minstrel of the fourteenth century, setting out on the boat for Spain to wander along the way of St James to far-off Compostela, ready to play and sing his way'.[16] The traveller/narrator's additional identity reflected here, as Irish, is flaunted throughout the text though its meaning is not related to de Valera's latter-day nationalist project but, as is manifest in the text just quoted, the connotation is consciously Catholic.

Therefore, the foremost identity adopted by the traveller is rooted in a popular figure of fourteenth-century western culture. The Middle Ages as a cultural referent are important in the text, as may be appreciated in the mentions of the medieval Spanish monk, the Arcipreste de Hita and his earthy text *El libro de buen amor* [The book of good love], the 'bibulous minstrel [Alfonso Álvarez de] Villasandino', as well as of the ballad form and, in particular, the famous narrative of the 'Siete Infantes de Salas' [The seven princes of Salas]. However, Spanish picaresque prose fiction of the sixteenth and seventeenth century also looms large in the construction of the travelling 'I'. Thus, the anonymously authored *Lazarillo de Tormes* is reflected in the traveller's 'henchman',[17] who joins him in his performances in the town of Salas de los Infantes and to whom he gives the name of Lazarillo; the 'W.S.' who signs the preface to *Spanish raggle-taggle* compares himself to the 'arch-mentor of rogues', the protagonist of Mateo Alemán's *Guzmán de Alfarache*: 'I shall leave my home like the picaresque knave Guzmán de Alfarache "to see the world and travel from place to place, commending myself to God and well-disposed persons",' and on being queried about his adventures by Fray Justo Pérez de Urbel at the Monastery of Santo Domingo de Silos, the first-person narrator of *Spanish raggle-taggle* confesses to feeling like the protagonist of Jerónimo de Alcalá's *Alonso mozo de muchos amos* [Alonso, servant of many masters]: 'when he gratifies the curiosity of the Vicar of the convent.'[18] While at Silos, too, he will have occasion to quote 'the picaresque knave', the protagonist of Vicente Espinel's *Relaciones de la vida del escudero Marcos de Obregón* [An account of the life of Squire Marcos de Obregón] and to recall Estebanillo González, 'the good-humoured rogue',[19] protagonist and apparent author of *La vida y hechos de Estebanillo González, hombre de buen humor, compuesta por él mismo* [The life and deeds of Estebanillo González, a merry man, according to his own account]. Cervantes' *El Ingenioso Hidalgo Don Quijote de la Mancha* [The ingenious nobleman Don Quixote of La Mancha] is also drawn upon. The narrator 'proudly assume[s] the title of Knight-errant of Fiddlers', projecting his 'fiddle' as his 'Rozinante [sic]' and also compares himself in another instance to Monipodio, chief of the underworld in Seville in the story of the Golden Age author 'Rinconete y Cortadillo'.[20]

Diverse as these identities are, the narrator fashions himself in many more, ranging from the mischievous character in Shakespeare's *A midsummer night's dream* to the lampooned form of his forename employed in the *Catholic Bulletin*. Thus, he is 'a

text (W. Starkie, *Spanish*, pp 359, 373, 375).   **16** W. Starkie, *Spanish*, p. 6.   **17** W. Starkie, *Spanish*, pp 6, 355.   **18** Ibid., pp 400, x, 314. Tribute is paid to the dialogue form adopted in Alcalá's text by the traveller's conversation with Fray Justo being reproduced under 'Myself' or 'Fr Justo' (W. Starkie, *Spanish*, p. 314).   **19** Ibid., pp 322, 400.   **20** Ibid., pp 9, 285. The name of Don Quixote's horse in the original Spanish of Cervantes' novel is Rocinante. 'Rinconete y Cortadillo' is one of the stories contained in Cervantes' *Novelas Ejemplares* [Exemplary novels].

Merry-Walter', 'a Robin Goodfellow', 'the poor vagabond', 'Don Gualtero', 'Don Gualtero (or, simply, Gualtero) de muchos caminos [Walter of many highways and byways], 'a free untrammelled vagabond', a 'frugal tramp', 'the sympathetic listener', 'a humble vagabond', becoming 'the limping minstrel', when suffering from a sore foot, even 'an interloper', and his urge to roam is also explained as a consequence of 'a tinker's curse'.[21] When feeling 'the restless desire to escape over the monastery wall' at Silos, the would-be-traveller-again draws on Thomas Dekker's fifteenth-century account of the Gypsies, contained in the *English villanies*. Dekker explains that the Gypsies are known as 'moonmen', elaborating further:

> Their name they borrow from the moon, because the moon is never in one shape two nights together, but wanders up and down heaven like an antic, so these changeable stuff companions never tarry one day in a place but are the only base runagates on earth. [...] They are a people more scattered than Jews, and more hated, beggarly in apparel, barbarous in condition, and beastly in behaviour, ...[22]

Thus, the unquiet guest at the monastery, frequenter of Gypsies, declares: 'I am becoming a Moonman again'.[23] This account of metamorphosis and of the narrator/traveller's constant shape-shifting in the text, is reinforced by his reference to Starkie's contemporary, the American one-woman theatre artist, Ruth Draper, famous for a unique ability to transform herself into a vast array of characters. When attempting to play a number of parts in a monodrama, produced by the traveller following a tale told him by a monk at Silos of one Fernando, the American's talent longingly comes to mind: 'As I improvised the monodrama, I thought of Ruth Draper and wished devoutly I had a spark of her genius'.[24] Further, in this connection, it is worth recalling that before crossing the border into Spain at the beginning of his journey, the traveller registers the response of guests at his hotel who cannot determine his identity, assessing him in a variety of ways: 'a queer suspicious fellow ... perhaps a refugee from Spain in disguise ... Perhaps a Russian [and] "drôle de type".' The traveller admits to drawing enjoyment from their perplexity, deliberately adding to the confusion by creating further fantasy, initially for the benefit of the hall-porter:

> I started my campaign by telling the hall-porter my fake story – a rigmarole romance of wandering into Spain to gather news for a Royalist paper. 'Je vous dirai un secret: je suis lié avec l'aristocratie espagnole,' said I, blushing slightly from the emotion of weaving my tale. [...] The French porter was incredulous, but polite. Anyhow, thought I, he will tell my story to the rest, and embroider it in his own colours.[25]

---

21 Ibid., pp 8, 14, 57, 335, 441, 79, 256, 311, 386, 400, 312.   22 T. Dekker, 'Of moone-men', Chapter 7 in *English villanies eight severall times prest to death by the printers, but are now the ninth time (as at first) discovered by lanthorne and candle-light, and by the helpe of a new cryer (1648)* (London, 1648), page not numbered.   23 W. Starkie, *Spanish*, p. 322.   24 Ibid., p. 354.   25 Ibid., p. 18.

Other characters add yet further to the variety already highlighted. The narrator suspects that Fray Antonio in Silos has detected 'the professor on holiday', in spite of his 'dishevelled appearance', and communist Mariano in Sepúlveda is not convinced by the traveller's claim that he is 'only a poor wandering minstrel', declaring: 'You are not the type of the *vagamundo* [*sic*] [vagabond], ... your disguise is too thin: I can see by your face that you are a communist agent. Believe me, the disguise of a fiddler is as good as any other for spreading the doctrines of communism in the villages.' Mariano's use of the notion of disguise (already introduced in one of the supposed attempts by the hotel guests in Biarritz to determine the traveller's origin) is also used by Paquita, one of 'three exotic girls' met in the Basque fishing village of Motrico. The traveller insists on his vagabond, elusive identity: 'I'm only a *vagamundo*, here today, gone tomorrow' while she contests the veracity of his claim, having obtained information from another source, deemed more reliable: 'I don't believe you, Señor. The old man said you were really a foreign gentleman with money too, but disguised.'[26]

Together with the above (dis)guises, the narrator identifies himself in other ways which acquire further significance in relation to contemporary developments in Ireland and Europe. Firstly, in the con-text[27] of a shifting Irish identity as, following the 1932 general elections, de Valera began to steer the twenty-six counties away from dominion status towards an independent Constitution and, second, in the con-text of threatened ethnicities in Europe following Hitler's accession to the chancellorship of Germany in 1933. Early on in the narrative, the traveller refers to himself as 'a lonely man who is out of tune with the world'.[28] The description most immediately corresponds to a given circumstance, the traveller's solitary contemplation of bathers in Biarritz, but when coupled with the not infrequent references to himself as 'the stranger', 'a strange creature' and with the look of a heretic ('*cara de hereje*')[29] who, moreover, is treated with suspicion and even slapped in the face, albeit by a relatively harmless adolescent girl, the traveller/narrator's projection as (persecuted) Other begins to take shape. In this connection, therefore, it may not be surprising to also find references to 'the Wandering Jew', first alluded to when the traveller refers to keeping half of his winnings from the gambling table at the casino in Biarritz in the bottom of his rucksack as a reserve fund: 'It will be like the nest-egg of the Gypsy nomad or the silver coins which God ordained that the wandering Jew should always find in the bottom of his wallet at the hour of need.'[30] As regards Irishness, the Ireland Starkie had comfortably grown up in was rapidly changing. Thus, the narrator becomes a lonely man, estranged from his point of origin, his established sense of selfhood, and the text records the traveller's feeling of isolation on a number of occasions. In the wider European con-text, the discrimination against difference also evokes the scapegoating of Jews and Gypsies in contemporary Germany. In this connection, it is revealing to find that *Spanish raggle-taggle* carries none of the trite anti-Semitic remarks registered in the travel book published a year and eight months earlier, *Raggle-*

26 Ibid., pp 311, 392, 172.   27 I use 'con-text' following F. Barker & P. Hulme, 'Nymphs and reapers heavily vanish: the discursive con-texts of *The Tempest*' in J. Drakakis (ed.), *Alternative Shakespeares* (London, 1985), p. 236, n. 7.   28 W. Starkie, *Spanish*, p. 21.   29 Ibid., pp 224, 110, 111.   30 Ibid., pp 16–17. Later references to the Wandering Jew appear on pp 74 and 412.

taggle, dictated by other interests and concerns. Finally, the narrator will refer to himself as 'a gross Silenus', drawing on the figure of Greek legend.[31] Silenus possessed a deceptive appearance, appearing to be a foolish fellow while conveying pertinent truths. Herein may lie a key for interpreting the further significance of the carefree minstrel, the wanderer, the roguish character. Donning these (dis)guises makes for movement and variety as well as enabling the traveller to penetrate places he would probably not have gained access to in conventional guise: gypsy camps, caves and their company but, paradoxically, the particular truths he conveys tend towards the containment of change and diversity. A.J. Clinch's observation with regard to Gypsylorism as a 'politically inert'[32] practice might be cited in this connection.

Chapter 3 of *Spanish raggle-taggle* highlights (characteristically, through apparently casual conversation) the plight of members of the nobility in the wake of the founding of the Republic in 1931: 'a chatty Parisian … insisted that Spain since the Revolution [*sic*] began at Biarritz, not at Irún. "There are nearly as many Spaniards as French on the Côte d'Argent – why, the entire *noblesse espagnole* sits along the coast and looks with melancholy longing across the bay at Fuenterrabía".'[33] The following chapter hones in on the sorry lot of an 'old friend' of the traveller's, one Don Gonzalo,[34] who 'had striven all his life to be a worthy henchman of the monarchy' and followed the King into exile. The Marquis tells of 'the burning of convents and churches by bands of wild revolutionaries, led by "irresponsible intellectual theorists"', though he assuredly asserts: 'Spain has witnessed those scenes of destruction before, and such revolutions are but faint ripples on the surface of Spanish History [*sic*].'[35] This initial focus on the lot of an (exiled) élite and its views (with whom Starkie might well empathize given his class's sense of loss of privilege in the twenty-six counties) and the apocalyptic vision of contemporary Spain conveyed by Don Gonzalo sets the tone for much of what follows in Starkie's first Spanish travel book.

As is indicated in the map at the end of the text tracing the 'Route of Dr Starkie's Travels', the traveller/narrator crosses into Spain from Hendaye, to the town of Fuenterrrabía, from where he journeys on through the Basque Country into Old Castile and on to the Spanish capital. The text is entitled *Spanish raggle-taggle* but the Spain which is represented possesses a strong ideological thrust, seeking to contest the (in the dismissive words of Don Gonzalo) 'faint ripples', lest they become deep roars, destructive of 'Spanish History', envisaged as a fixed flow along feudal lines. Paradoxically, therefore, in a text in which polyphony seems paramount, which is constructed on encounters with human variety, ranging over class and condition, and which carries the intertextual irreverence of Rabelais, Sterne and Fielding's *Tom Jones*, the fantasy of fairy story, of dream and nightmare, together with a

31 Silenus was instrumental in the construction of the figure of Folly in Erasmus's *Praise of Folly* and for the character of Raphael Nonsenso in Thomas More's *Utopia*. I am using the rendering of the protagonist's surname in the latter text as it appears in the translation by Paul Turner (T. More, *Utopia*, trans. P. Turner (London, 1976)). 32 A.J. Clinch, 'Obituary: Dora E. Yates', p. 227. 33 W. Starkie, *Spanish*, p. 13. 34 In the interview with B. Galm, Starkie states that Don Gonzalo was a rendering of Alfonso Merry del Val, Spain's Ambassador in London, 1913–31 (B. Galm interview with W. Starkie, OHP, UCLA, 1970–71). 35 W. Starkie, *Spanish*, pp 27, 28.

consciousness of the (persecuted) Other, a monologic discourse holds forth: Spanish History, which means, as is amply illustrated, traditional Catholic and heroic Castile. The monologism will be further substantiated in *Don Gypsy* (1936), dated in 1935 and also accompanied by a map indicating the 'Route of Dr Starkie's Travels', which carries an itinerary stretching from Spanish Morocco to Argamasilla de Alba in La Mancha, via what was Moorish Spain, riven with the rhythm of flamenco's *cante hondo* [deep song] and coming to a climax in Seville's Holy Week. Thus, the two texts together convey a Spain vertebrated by the North African territory she had colonized together with territory within the Peninsula's borders that exemplify her own successful resistence to colonization and change by Arab settlement. In this latter connection, it is pertinent to signal the exclusion from 'Dr Starkie's Travels' of the industrialized and commercialized western or eastern seabords of the Peninsula and those in which home rule had become an issue, if not a reality, with the exception of the Basque Country, which is portrayed in *Spanish raggle-taggle*. None the less, the point of view is that of canonical 'Spanish History'. Bilbao is mentioned, but is only identified as a place with a bar, serving as a meeting place and as a point of railway departure, and Catalonia, which had obtained a Home Rule Statute in 1932, is not included in either of the travel books. There is an allusion to Catalan autonomy through a comment made by the Galician friend of the Gypsy Lucas, with whom the narrator travels to Bilbao from Guernika, one Tío Anselmo [Uncle Anselmo]. Tío Anselmo is presented as 'a fierce partisan of the Galician separatist movement' and he insists: 'It is time for us to copy the Catalans and cry out for independence.' However, no semblance of discussion follows, nor is further information provided as to Galician separatism or the Catalan *Estatut d'Autonomia* [Home Rule Statute]. These Brother Celts, Irishman and Galician, move on to making music and drinking wine: carnival rules, with Anselmo playing his concertina and the traveller his fiddle, the Galician providing further folkloric fancy through story-telling and the reciting of folk poems. The encounter is brought to a close with the traveller rejecting the label of Celt and, not very convincingly, claiming that Irishmen are only Celts 'when they live in exile in the United States'.[36]

The only sympathetic comment to be found in favour of Republican reform is expressed in the last of three chapters devoted to Madrid at the end of *Spanish raggle-taggle*. The task being carried forth in the field of tertiary education by Alberto Jiménez Fraud through the *Residencia de Estudiantes*, by Ramón Menéndez Pidal in the *Centro de Estudios Históricos* [Centre for the Study of History] and by José Castillejo's work in schools is duly awarded recognition at the close of a text the main thrust of which has undermined the Republican enterprise. With comments on the age that range from 'these troubled times', 'the turmoil of today', to 'the evil that is in the world', with contemporary Spain seen as possessing 'many ragged villages where in former days proud heroes dwelt' and being 'topsy-turvy after the Revolution',[37] the depiction of the country under the Republic in *Spanish raggle-taggle* is well-nigh ubiquitously negative. Raymond Carr has observed that the attack

36 Ibid., p. 194.   37 Ibid., pp 313, 212, 248, 247, 269.

suffered by the Catholic Church on its 'privileged position' in the wake of 1931 constituted 'a godsend to conservatives searching for a decent stick with which to beat the Republic'.[38] *Spanish raggle-taggle* bears no beating but does drum up sympathy for members of the clergy who are represented as hounded. The traveller is romantically rowed into the country from Hendaye to Fuenterrabía by an old Basque fisherman who tells 'lurid tales of refugees escaping from Spain to France at dead of night', many of whom are 'priests carrying, hidden beneath their soutanes, church ornaments, which they hoped to deposit in some place of safety abroad.'[39] Fuenterrabía itself is represented as lacking its former glory: 'In the Middle Ages [the town] must have been a stronghold for the King of Navarre, with its stout wall and castle, but to-day it is sadly tottering.'[40] The encounter with the fisherman also serves to promote antinationalist sentiment with regard to minority cultures, Spanish and English being presented as 'international',[41] as opposed to Basque and Gaelic. The universal validity of Spanish is further illustrated when the traveller visits the Basque painter Ignacio Zuloaga at his home in Zumaia.[42]

The first eighteen chapters of *Spanish raggle-taggle* constitute Part I of the text and are devoted to the the traveller's approach to Spain through Biarritz, Hendaye and into the Basque Country. The carnivalesque: Gypsies and jollity, wine, food, sensual women and minstrelsy are not found wanting but once in the Peninsula, a substantial amount of text is devoted to upholding a Catholic Spain unified under Castile, reflected in Zuloaga's pronouncements, in the homage paid at the shrine of St Ignatius of Loiola, founder of the Society of Jesus, and the chapters devoted to 'The visions at Ezquioga', where views that express opposition to the Republican government's policies and practice are rife. The traveller explains that he was sent to Zuloaga by the author of *Tigre Juan*, Ramón Pérez de Ayala, the Spanish Republic's Ambassador in London. The name of Zuloaga's home on the coast of the Bay of Biscay, Santiago Etxea [The house of St James], acknowledged the ancient chapel on the site where pilgrims might halt en route for Santiago de Compostela. As the traveller waits to be admitted to the estate, he notices 'a little statue of Our Lady in a niche in the wall', leading him to '[mumble] a prayer',[43] one of a number of instances in the text that provide evidence of the narrator's Catholicism and, here too, that of his host. Zuloaga identifies himself as Basque though strongly in favour of, and prescriptive, with regard to the citizen's commitment to imperial Castile: 'I am born a Basque from Eïbar yet I refuse to sacrifice my universal heritage for any regionalism. It was Castile made Spain and every one of us whether we are Basques, Galicians or Andalusians must go forth from *our narrow regions* and become Castilian, for it was Castile that made the Spanish world.'[44] Zuloaga's pronouncement is further supported by later reference to three

---

38 R. Carr, *Modern Spain, 1875–1980* (Oxford, 2001), p. 123. 39 W. Starkie, *Spanish*, p. 33. The fisherman's 'lurid tales' are perhaps an echo of fears following the church burning that occurred in May 1931 in Madrid, assessed as 'Mediterranean fetishism' by Ortega y Gasset, which the provisional government of the Republic took no measures to stop (R. Carr, *Modern Spain*, p. 123). 40 Ibid., p. 37. 41 W. Starkie, *Spanish*, pp 37, 36. 42 The Spanish spelling of the Basque place name is supplied in Starkie's text: Zumaya, as is also the case with the name of Zuloaga's home, 'Santiago Echea' [from the Basque 'Etxea', meaning 'home']. 43 W. Starkie, *Spanish*, p. 89. 44 W. Starkie, *Spanish*, p. 97. My

other contemporary Basques: two writers, Miguel de Unamuno (whom Starkie had met in 1921) and Pío Baroja (who was to become something of a fixture at British Institute gatherings in post-Civil War Madrid)[45] together with the Spanish nationalist politician Ramiro de Maeztu. The latter's *Defensa de la Hispanidad* [A defence of the Hispanic world] was also published in 1934 and included in the 'Wanderer's Library' attached to *Don Gypsy*, where Maeztu is described as 'a valiant conservative who laments the passing of old values'.[46] The three intellectuals are represented as 'Basque by race but Castilian by tradition' with the rider: 'for Castile is universal Spain – the Spain that exists not only in the Iberian Peninsula but over the sea in the new world.'[47] Given this ethnocentrism, it is not surprising to find the Basque language described as possessing 'a harsh, barbaric sound' and the Tree of Gernika, symbolic of the Basque race, dismissed as 'a pathetic relic of the past' and 'this melancholy tree', situated in a 'scrubby, imitation Greek temple'.[48] The chapter in which these references are found is entitled 'The tree of Guernica'[49] and opens with a bar of music from the Basque anthem of the same name, accompanied by the opening words of the anthem: 'Guernikako arbola da bedein catuba [sic]'[50] [Blessed is the Tree of Gernika], all of which announces what might be expected to be a more deferential treatment towards Basque national identity than that which is subsequently represented. In effect, the strategy might be seen as characteristic of the tendency towards camouflage in the text.

The chapters devoted to what the traveller is informed has become 'the talk of all Spain'[51] focus on what were claimed to be apparitions of the Virgin Mary in the Basque village of Ezkioga in 1931. William A. Christian has shown the extent to which the phenomenon was given widespread coverage in the Catholic and right-wing press of the time while claiming that '[e]ven leftist newspapers depended on these sources.'[52] It is here that the traveller frequents the company of the forbidding 'Doña Carmen de Medina, sprung from one of the old noble families of Spanish aristocracy and a sister of the Duquesa de Tarifa' and admits to feeling 'touched' by her piety.[53] The traveller claims that she first addressed him in the knowledge that he was 'an Irish Catholic' and came to question his wisdom in leaving Ireland for Republican Spain: 'Why have you come from your beautiful island of Faith to this land of Sin [sic] and blasphemy against God?' She also expresses her conviction as to what is needed to remedy the situation: 'soldiers with stout hearts to fight the battle of the Church

italics. Madariaga speaks of Zuloaga as being like Unamuno: 'un vasco … conquistado por el espíritu castellano' [a Basque … conquered by the Castilian spirit] (S. de Madariaga, 'Ignacio Zuloaga' in *Españoles*, p. 122). **45** See J.-C. Mainer, *Pío Baroja* (Madrid, 2012), pp 348, 424–5, n. 27. **46** W. Starkie, *Don Gypsy* (London, 1936), p. 509. Maetzu was assassinated during the Civil War, already in 1936. (P.C. González Cuevas, *Maeztu. Biografía de un nacionalista español* (Madrid, 2003), pp 358–9.) See also: R. de Maeztu, *Defensa de la hispanidad* (Madrid, 1941). **47** W. Starkie, *Spanish*, p. 186. **48** Ibid., pp 132, 182. **49** The Spanish spelling, 'Guernica' is given preference over the Basque 'Gernika'. **50** W. Starkie, *Spanish*, p. 182. 'bedein catuba [sic]' should read 'bedeinkatua' in present-day Basque. I am grateful to Maria Colera for assistance with the language. **51** Ibid., p. 111. **52** W.A. Christian, *Visionaries. The Spanish Republic and the reign of Christ* (Berkeley, 1996), pp 25; 25–6. **53** For further information on Carmen de Medina Garvey, see W.A. Christian (1996), pp 53–6, passim. **54** W. Starkie, *Spanish*, pp 121, 122. **55** W.A. Christian, *Visionaries*, p. 60.

against the forces of Satan.'⁵⁴ Doña Carmen also raises the spectre of civil war, her assertion being reinforced by one Francisco Goicoechea, the so-called 'Chico de Ataún' [The lad from Ataun],⁵⁵ who tells of his vision of the Virgin who, he claims, told him: 'there would be Civil War in the Basque Country between the Catholics and the non-Catholics. At first the Catholics would suffer severely and lose many men, but ultimately they would triumph with the help of twenty-five angels of Our Lady.'⁵⁶ The militant Catholic group 'Acción Católica' [Catholic Action] is also represented in the Ezkioga episode, revealing a connection with the influential former editor of the Catholic daily *El Debate*, Ángel Herrera Oria, who had become mentor to the group of political Catholics who brought about the right-wing party commonly known as the CEDA (*Confederación Española de Derechas Autónomas*). As Carr has signalled, the party's 'immediate aim ... was the defence of the persecuted Church against the onslaught of the secularising left.'⁵⁷ Doña Carmen introduces the traveller to a youth described as 'a charming young man called Llorente from Pamplona – a strong member of the "Acción Católica"', who, charming as he is reported to be by the traveller, is none the less forthright in voicing a threat to the Republican order: '[He] informed me that I might expect any day a rising of the Basque province and Navarre against the Republic in defence of their religion.' 'Acción Católica' is further represented in Ezkioga in the shape of 'four austere-looking young men dressed in black – fervent members'⁵⁸ of the association, who constitute a bodyguard for Francisco Goicoechea. Finally, the traveller also refers to 'a pale-faced priest' sitting near him at table, 'a member of an order which devotes itself to the teaching of the poor.' The priest's fallow state is illustrative of the consequences of 'Article 26 of the new constitution and the subsequent legislation [which] separated Church and State, expelled the Jesuits, and clipped the Regular Orders' control over education.'⁵⁹ The unemployed priest has reproduced the whole of St John's Gospel in minute writing on a postcard and wryly comments: 'I might just as well spend my time thus, as in any other way nowadays: I am not allowed to have my school: Spain does not want me.'⁶⁰

The traveller's other major port of call in the Basque Country is the sanctuary of Loiola where he converses with a young Jesuit, seen 'praying devoutly' in the Oratory. The Jesuit's views will echo Don Gonzalo's assurance that present misfortune, those 'faint ripples', will pass and they also connect with Doña Carmen's conviction that there must be a fighting response to the Republic. His account also highlights the current plight of members of the Jesuit community whose services, like those of the pale-faced priest referred to above, were dispensed with as a consequence of Article 26 of the new Spanish constitution:

> Loyola is crowded with members of our order who have had to flee from the incendiarists in the cities. We are ready to leave at any moment [...] But ... we shall return to this *Casa Santa* [Holy House] of our founder one day soon, even

56 W. Starkie, *Spanish*, p. 135. For Doña Carmen's words, see p. 125.   57 R. Carr, *Modern Spain*, p. 127.   58 W. Starkie, *Spanish*, pp 137, 136.   59 R. Carr, *Modern Spain*, p. 123.   60 W. Starkie, *Spanish*, p. 138.

if they scatter us to the ends of the earth. [...] in this hour of peril for Spain, the Church looks to the Basques to fight for their faith. [...] we are soldiers of Christ, and soldiers do not speak, they act.

The Jesuits' educational service in the production of an élite is vindicated by the young priest who recalls the adoption of a knightly guise by their founder, conscious of the need for dedication to a chivalrous ideal. His reference to Cervantes' protagonist and antagonist evokes the rejection of the '*hombre masa*' [mass man, the barbarian mass] in Ortega y Gasset's *La rebelión de las masas* [The Revolt of the Masses] (1930), whose rise, in Ortega's view, threatened '*el hombre selecto*' [the select man, the élite]:

> The Socialists speak truly when they say that we educate a caste of nobles. Yes, we still believe in the age of chivalry. ... St Ignatius ... set out as a knight-errant. [...] Today we need a noble caste to carry on such chivalry. Alas, ... Don Quixote, the ideal Knight of Spain, was chaste and left no descendants, whereas Sancho Panza has begotten children in every corner of our country.[61]

In contrast to Zuloaga, Doña Carmen, the Jesuits and the Catholic Action contingent, the traveller comes across working men of the left, the description of whom is far from summoning respect or sympathy, indeed, it is crudely propagandistic. Juan José, a comb-maker, who claims to be 'a Spanish republican', expresses his anti-clericalism in an uncouth manner: 'To hell with the Church, the clerics and all their machinations.' His 'coarse blue jacket [and] big tie of violent red' together with ill-fitting trousers connote vulgarity while he is reported as having become 'more and more blasphemous' as the traveller and himself approached Ezkioga, suggested as attributable to indulgence in alcohol en route. In Part II, Mariano is identified as 'the communist of Sepúlveda', who expresses the belief that 'the true Revolution has yet to come to Spain.' He possesses a classier wardrobe than Juan José though he also sports a red tie, in this instance described as 'flaming'. His anti-clericalism is vehement and the reader is tendentiously informed that 'like most revolutionaries, [he] was a suspicious fellow'. Furthermore, Mariano and his fiancée are used to illustrate what is presented as the misconception that gender relations can be transformed, in contrast to progressive thinking in the Republican period. Thus, Mariano is shown to be as jealous as a traditional Spaniard when the traveller dances with his fiancée and she declines to take an active part in demanding her rights or participating in political meetings, apparently content to conform to woman's domestic lot: 'I am in love with Mariano. That is enough for me. I leave all these theories and ideas to him and I say every day: "You, Mariano, must have eyes, brain and speech for both of us: my part is to mind the home".'[62]

The second group of eighteen chapters, Part II of *Spanish raggle-taggle*, takes us into Old Castile. A 'mighty scene' meets the traveller, awarded a Wagnerian majesty through the description in the opening paragraph of Chapter 19: 'When the gods

---

61 Ibid., pp 106, 107.   62 Ibid., pp 113, 115, 392, 394, 396.

created the kingdom of Castile, they ordered the race of giants to build a gateway of bolders wrenched from mountainous peaks. "It is like Wotan's Walhalla raised by Fafner and Fasolt," said I to myself as I approached the Pass of Pancorbo.' The traveller climbs the Pancorbo Sierra where he spends the night in a cave. Vultures have nests in the rocks above and reinforce the Wagnerian vein, being described as 'sinister watchers like the ravens of Wotan'. Having spent a sleepless night, the traveller claims to have felt 'like a mediaeval noble of Castile watching over his armour on the night before he was dubbed a *caballero* [knight].' The comparison complements the content of this second part of the text, which highlights Castile's medieval heroes (the Cid, Fernán González, Muño Sánchez de Hinojosa) while also underlining the religious message of Part I. The traveller's itinerary takes in a number of monasteries and holy places: the Monastery of Santo Domingo de la Calzada, the shrine of San Juan de Ortega, the Charterhouse of Miraflores, the Monastery of San Pedro de Cardeña and that of Santo Domingo de Silos, where Starkie had met Fray Justo Pérez de Urbel in the early 1930s and who is introduced here as the traveller's 'closest friend and mentor'. Thus, at the end of the opening chapter of Part II, the plain of Castile is spread before the reader in all its heroic and Catholic glory as the traveller eagerly sets out following his night in the cave:

> There before me lay Castile of the Cid Campeador, national hero of Spain. [...] The slender ribbon I see winding over the brown expanse is the famous way of Saint James. Along that road thousands of pilgrims through all the ages journeyed towards the distant western shrine of the Apostle. [...] Who could travel today over that plain and not feel that from its brown earth sprang all that was noblest in the Spanish race?[63]

Over this second block of chapters, three characters are introduced who further illustrate resistence to change or express disillusionment with the Republican present: Gabriel Ureña, a commercial traveller, born in Chile, Doña Leocadia, the traveller's landlady in Burgos, and Moreno, a peasant from Covarrubias. There are also significant, albeit briefer, contributions in this connection from Juanito, a *pica*[64] from Valdepeñas, and Pablo, a waiter in Burgos.

Both Ureña and Doña Leocadia signal devotion to Catholicism and support for the monarchy; the former also illustrates the respect of the colonized culture for the colonizing nation. In spite of his Chilean birth, Ureña is 'Castilian to his fingertips', living in Burgos and '[loving] all the churches and castles of Old Castile because they [remind] him of the glorious past of Spain'. Moreover, he is depicted as 'a loyal monarchist and a fervent Catholic'. Doña Leocadia is also resident in Burgos and is presented as the landlady of the lodgings where the traveller had stayed with his wife a decade earlier. He 'often' goes to morning mass with her and her neighbours and will also find her meditating in the cathedral at dusk. This devout member of the

---

63 Ibid., pp 209, 314, 216. 64 In the bull-fight, the *picador* is responsible for introducing arrows into the animal with a view to weakening it before the *matador* [bullfighter] takes it on.

community is displeased on hearing her guest playing 'La Marseillaise'. She hands him a peseta, making it clear that it is a reward for the Spanish songs he has gone on to play since he noticed 'some scowling faces' in the street audience. The traveller reports that on handing over the piece of money, his landlady declared '[w]ith bitter sarcasm ... "[H]ere is the image of my King."' Like Doña Leocadia, the traveller had met the waiter Pablo on his earlier visit to Burgos, when he was employed at the local casino. He now surfaces in one of Burgos's cafés and the traveller notes that he is no more content with either Alcalá Zamora or Azaña, both presidents of the Republic, than he had been with the monarchy in 1921. Moreover, Pablo is pessimistic about what amounts to the country's loss of stature, boding disintegration: 'Spain will soon be just an island of memory'. The traveller seeks to rouse his 'old friend' from the doldrums with the help of wine while proposing a challenging toast: 'Bring two glasses of *manzanilla* and let us drink to the newly awakened Spain; may she never prove unworthy of her ancient glories.' In contrast to Pablo, *picador* Juanito considers himself to be worse off than under the monarchy and dictatorship of General Primo de Rivera: 'What good has the Revolution done me? When the King disappeared I said to myself – "Aha, ... your time is coming." [...] But ... it is worse under the Republic than before. I am leaner than I was in the days of Miguelito Primo de Rivera.' His use of the diminutive in the dictator's forename (Miguelito for Miguel) conveys a degree of affection for the former ruler and he remembers a time when he possessed 'hopes for the future'[65] whereas his present is one of disenchantment.

The most sustained example of resistance to change and a defence of tradition is expressed through the contribution of Moreno, a rural worker, who is averse to modernization of the land and registers a sceptical attitude with regard to freedom as currently preached from the capital by urban intellectuals and politicians. The traveller's role in the conversation here, as on other occasions in the text, becomes that of devil's advocate:

> The revolution has been all words and foam. [...] The *Señoritos* [rich young men] from Madrid tell us there has been a revolution and that we are as free as the birds in the air. But I ask you ... , is anybody in this world free? Must we not lead our sheep and goats to pasture and till our piece of land and sweat like the Devil himself until we give up the ghost? What's all that revolution but words, and words won't till the land or rear my goats and sheep here in Castilla la Vieja [Old Castile].
>
> Come now, Moreno, what about the agrarian reform?
>
> Who cares a curse about the agrarian reform except the politicians? Why, here in Castile we all have our piece of land and what we want is to be left alone to work it. [...] My father, my grandfather and my great grandfather reaped and threshed in [the] old traditional way and they were able to live *una vida honrada* [an honourable life]. Why should I worry my head over those newfangled notions?

---

65 Ibid., pp 229, 230, 256, 267, 266, 163.

The narrator's observation might suggest that he finds Moreno's response wrong-headed, that he is on the side of change, but the description which follows of the workers in the fields aligns him with the traditionalist:

> It was useless to urge Moreno to consider the benefits of modern methods, new inventions and mechanical contrivances that would increase his output. [...] we walked along through the golden afternoon ... All around us in the fields men and women were gathering in the harvest in the primeval way. The method of threshing had not changed in the slightest since the days of Fernán González and the Cid. [...] The sight of those innumerable workers in the golden fields was a majestic one.[66]

As can be appreciated from the references to the range of characters above, the majority speak out against the Republic and those who do not are represented as unattractive, the case of Juan José, or motivated by personal gain, as is illustrated by an inn-keeper, Old Simón, and his son, Florencio, in Ezkioga. The traveller recalls that in the Middle Ages, 'the minstrel was looked upon as a collaborator of the nation's history'.[67] It may be said that in *Spanish raggle-taggle*, dedicated 'To his Grace the Duke of Berwick and Alba' (Starkie's host at the *Residencia de Estudiantes* in Madrid in 1924), the author was collaborating with the historical discourse of the Spanish nation as propounded in the text by Don Gonzalo, another aristocrat, one which was rooted in the Catholic Church of the *ancien regime* and in feudal Castile, whose exponents were defiant in the face of change. Moreover, they found they were able to continue counting on the collaboration of the latter-day Irish minstrel. He went on to produce a further prolix account of rambling in Spain, *Don Gypsy*, published a month before the coup led by General Francisco Franco, which was to lead to civil war.

In Starkie's second travel book on Spain, a Greek Gypsy coppersmith, one Pavo from Corfu, whom the traveller comes across in Tetuan poses the question: '[W]hat's an island ... to all of us who wander over the face of the earth?' The rhetorical formulation communicates (Starkie's?) bravado, expressing something of a dismissive attitude as well as one of triumph: an island lost but a world gained. In contrast, the traveller and first-person narrator (initially more readily identifiable with the author) does register the loss of and longing for his island when exposed to the fierce light and piercing contours of the south: 'Andalusia is so drenched with sunlight and so sharply outlined in the clear air that at times I long for the misty, melancholy line of Irish hills and the grey sea edged with foam, which would soothe a dreamy temperament.'[68]

The blurring of boundaries between fact and fiction is captured in a passing comment on the part of the narrator in *Don Gypsy*. He declares: 'This Gypsy adventure of mine among the nomads was certainly creating as many coincidences as a novel.'[69] Certainly, the merging of the real and the fantastic is no less a feature of this second travel book on Spain than in the former, and, as in *Spanish raggle-taggle*, the

66 Ibid., pp 301–2.   67 Ibid., p. 359.   68 W. Starkie, *Don Gypsy*, pp 88, 169.   69 Ibid., p. 127.

identities adopted by the traveller are legion. In the 'Prologue', he immediately
projects himself as 'a musical picaroon', who will become a 'Pilgrim' along the route
of Don Quixote, in pursuit of the latter's windmills in La Mancha. However, very
soon, in the opening chapter, he will assert his identity as 'Pied Piper', following up
with others, some of which are already familiar to readers of *Spanish raggle-taggle*: 'the
Wandering Jew', a *'juglar'*, 'wandering minstrel', 'a poor wandering minstrel', 'the
picaresque wanderer', 'a vagabond', 'the fleeting vagabond', 'a stranger'[70] and there is
reference to disguise and being judged to be a spy.[71] Identities also multiply by means
of the traveller comparing himself to characters in fiction or myth. Thus, in Tetuan's
labyrinth of streets, he compares himself to 'Theseus without Ariadne's skein of
thread'; as he wonders what goes on behind the closed, even 'heavily barred' doors, he
declares that he is 'becoming as inquisitive as Agib the Third Kalandar, struggling
against the temptation to open the forbidden golden door'; walking down the Street of
the Seven Turnings in Málaga, he confesses to feeling 'like Emperor Jones in the
forest: the further I penetrated into the maze[,] the more vestments of civilization I
cast off'; while tramping around the streets of Seville during the Holy Week celebrations, he feels like 'the student Cleophas accompanied by the little lame devil'; the
'diaphanous' atmosphere of La Mancha leads the traveller to feel that he is 'travelling
in seven-leagued boots' and by the time he arrives at his final destination, Argamasilla
de Alba, identified as Don Quixote's home town, he claims the title of 'Knight of the
Fiddle', arguing that his violin has supported him like the Manchegan knight's horse
his master while admitting to being 'as proud of my prowess as Amadis of Gaul
himself'.[72] Further to the variety of identity, the traveller also appears in different
professional guises: as linguist or ethnologist, eagerly jotting down the 'vitriolic words'
expressed by a Gypsy mother in Puerto de Santa María in both *Caló* (the language of
Spanish Gypsies) and Spanish; he speaks of himself at different junctures as 'playing
the historian or archaeologist' and having gone to Puerto de Santa María 'to play the
minstrel', but finding that he shall 'soon be playing the fisherman'.[73] These multiple
identities are reinforced by characters met by the traveller, who also take on likenesses
that draw on story, nursery rhyme or myth. The picaroon Jules Rangoni whom the
traveller meets in Tangier is described as being 'like the dragon in the myth; as soon
as you have slain one head, another arises to take its place'; also in Tangier, he labels
the Gypsy Blas Núñez Malolo 'the Tom Thumb Gypsy' because of his size;
Bardomero Núñez, one of 'two very fat men' met in the Café Resbaladero in Puerto
de Santa María, is listened to by the traveller 'as if he had been the Barber's Sixth
Brother'; Manuel Collantes Lara, the traveller's confederate in his street-playing antics
in Cádiz, is compared to 'the Carpenter in *Alice through the Looking-Glass*, he knows
when the butter is spread too thick'; the behaviour of the legendary Don Juan is
compared to 'the wicked goblin in the fairy stories'; a miller in a windmill in La
Mancha is 'all white with flour like the nursery rhyme miller' and when the traveller

70 Ibid., pp ix, 4, 20, 63, 92, 108, 397, 238, 369, 370.   **71** See the conversation between the traveller
and a representative of the *'guardia civil'* in Chapter 12 (W. Starkie, *Don Gypsy*, p. 166).   **72** W. Starkie,
Don Gypsy, pp 41, 42, 398, 450, 495, 477.   **73** Ibid., pp 418, 391, 415.

attends the funeral in Criptana of one Blas Moreno, nicknamed Sancho, it seems to him that he is taking part 'in the memorial service to Sancho Panza'.[74] The representation of national identity is also present, the traveller referring to his 'Anglo-Celtic nature' and identifying himself as 'Irish' to a Galician though also alluding to 'we in England' while being introduced as '"Un Irlandés"[75] [an Irishman] who calls himself Don Gualtero', 'Un Inglés que chamuya el *Caló* [an Englishman who speaks *Caló*].' There is a fluctuation between Irish and English identities, as in the earlier travel books of the decade. However, the traveller's identification of his passport as 'British', not 'English',[76] as interpreted by the Gypsy Lalin, also becomes an occasion to demonstrate an ongoing assertion of imperial identity.

In *The dialogic imagination*, Mikhail Bakhtin speaks of the rogue, together with the clown and the fool, as 'three prominent types' who were already familiar figures in classical antiquity and the ancient Orient, subsequently appearing in the 'literature of the dregs of society'[77] in the Middle Ages. The Russian critic further asserts: 'Their very appearance, everything they do and say, … must be grasped metaphorically … one cannot take them literally because they are not what they seem … They are life's maskers.'[78] In *Don Gypsy*, the traveller will be awarded the three identities of these 'maskers'. The epigraph to Starkie's third travel book represents a piece of dialogue from Shakespeare's *As you like it*, a play that *Don Gypsy* speaks to in a number of ways, from the theme of exile to Jaques' 'All the world's a stage' speech. The epigraph carries part of the dialogue between Jaques and Rosalind in Act IV, scene 1 of the play in which the former, in characteristic melancholic mode, asserts that he has gained experience through his travels. Rosalind challenges Jaques by declaring: 'I had rather have a fool to make me merry than experience to make me sad; and to travel for it too!' The play speaks much of the fool and the figure is highlighted again in the opening chapter as the traveller contemplates his Tarot pack, carried in his knapsack 'as a talisman'. The first card he sees is '"Le Mat", the fool dressed in his clown's costume.' Later in the text, it may be said that the traveller plays the fool in so far as he feigns particular guises as a strategy ('a Machiavellian one', as the traveller himself admits on one occasion) for obtaining information. He confesses that in Granada:

> I spent more time eavesdropping in bars and taverns, skinning my ears to hear conversations, than I did in playing. A stranger has a great opportunity of picking up stray scraps of information if he sits in a corner with a far-off, abstracted look on his face, for the rest of the company pay no more attention to him than if he was as deaf as a doorpost.

---

74 W. Starkie, *Don Gypsy*, pp 19, 23, 424, 429, 454, 488, 490.   75 The inverted commas appear to indicate an acquired or stage identity, as in the case of 'Er Niño de Graná' [The Boy from Granada], the flamenco performer mentioned immediately beforehand. The capital letter is used in 'Irlandés' as in the following quote, 'Inglés', though they are not required in these instances in Spanish.   76 W. Starkie, *Don Gypsy*, pp 223, 485, 443, 286, 319, 126.   77 M.M. Bakhtin, *The dialogic imagination*, p. 158. 78 Ibid., p. 159.

In another instance, he speaks of having made efforts to adopt 'a look of lonely, forlorn honesty'.[79]

Apart from the mention of the clown in relation to the Tarot card, the traveller encounters a circus troupe on the outskirts of the town of Huétor-Tájar in the province of Granada, as he makes his way towards the city. Thrust into the arena of greasepaint, midst 'the beating of the drums and the discordant [*sic*][80] din of trumpet and saxophone', he finds himself transformed into a clown by the circus master Don Ricardo: 'I felt like a lump of plaster in his hands. I was plastered, powdered, rouged and blackened.' On looking at himself in 'a piece of cracked mirror' provided by the circus master, he supplies an account of his appearance and transformed identity: 'a bloated white mask with red-tipped nose, gaping red wound for a mouth and long black eyebrows slanting upwards. I was no longer Don Gualtero the lonely minstrel or village Paganini, but Canio the clown dressed up for his song "On with the motley".'[81] The reference to the traveller as Don Gualtero or a village Paganini were already masks and now an operatic one is adopted, inspired in Ruggero Leoncavallo's *Pagliacci* [Players or Clowns]. Canio's poignant 'Vesti la Giubba' [On with the motley] is sung in the wake of the clown's discovery that he has been deceived by his wife. Thus, the theme of betrayal comes into play and a further significance in this connection is perhaps wrought in *Don Gypsy* through reference to the traveller looking at himself in 'a piece of cracked mirror.' In the opening episode of Joyce's *Ulysses*, Stephen looks at himself in a mirror 'cleft by a crooked crack', subsequently declaring bitterly: 'It is a symbol of Irish art. The cracked looking glass of a servant.'[82] As Jeri Johnson has pointed out, the servant is a metaphor for Ireland[83] and Starkie's text may consciously be echoing the incident in *Ulysses*. In any event, it is striking that the circus mirror is cracked and the reflection perceived undoubtedly constitutes a grotesque image: 'bloated', 'gaping', '[slanted] upwards.'

Further to Canio's song, which alludes to Harlequin, the narrator also mentions the *commedia dell'arte* character. Indeed, in the antics forged in the circus arena, he becomes 'Harlequin, the stupid clown'.[84] Harlequin's 'uncertain nationality' and 'chameleon-like nature'[85] connect with the description of '[t]he picaroon of today' described by the traveller in *Don Gypsy*. Most immediately in the text, the profile is related to Jules Rangoni, met in Tangier, but in the prologue the narrator already identifies himself as a picaroon and particular traits of the description of the latter-day rogue may undoubtedly be related to a position fashioned by Starkie in the 1930s as a strategy for survival: 'The picaroon of today has no country ... his personality is like a patch quilt made up of the different coloured rags of each nationality. He believes in none of them and he will tune his discourse to suit his company and vary his hue like the sympathetic chameleon.'[86] The figure of the picaroon constitutes one of the many masks adopted by the traveller so perhaps the author of *Don Gypsy* should not readily

79 W. Starkie, *Don Gypsy*, pp 5, 6, 149, 251, 168.   80 The 'discordant' is redundant given the use of 'din', which follows.   81 W. Starkie, *Don Gypsy*, pp 219, 220.   82 J. Joyce, *Ulysses*, pp 6, 7.   83 J. Johnson, 'Explanatory notes' in J. Joyce, *Ulysses*, p. 770, note 7.2.   84 W. Starkie, *Don Gypsy*, p. 223. 85 J.A. Stevens, *The Irish scene* p. 153, drawing on E. Welsford, *The fool: his social and literary history* (London, 1935), a text that Starkie may have been familiar with.   86 W. Starkie, *Don Gypsy*, p. 17.

be associated with the rejection of belief in any nation that is expressed in the above passage. Given contemporary evidence, the extent to which Starkie might have believed in no nation by 1936 is debatable. Before the publication of the so-called Italian autobiography of 1938, *The waveless plain*, which speaks out in defence of the Italian nation under Mussolini, he had signed articles in the Irish press supporting the Italian colonization of Abyssinia and in *Grand inquisitor* (1940), he also speaks out in defence of the Spanish nation led by General Franco, having produced articles for the Irish press supporting the General's cause during the civil war.[87] On the other hand, perhaps his service to the particular visions of Italy and Spain as represented by the dictators did not entail belief in them. As to Great Britain, the allegiance of Mrs W.J.M. Starkie to the Empire never flagged and her son firmly expressed his own having been appointed the British Council's representative in Spain in 1940. Writing to the Archbishop of Westminster to acknowledge the latter's support of his candidature for the post in Madrid, he declared: 'I am sure that the Spaniards will welcome British Catholics, and as a Catholic from Ireland who is a loyal member of the British Commonwealth of Nations[,] I am eager to work for our cause in Spain.'[88]

In *Don Gypsy*, the traveller comes to lament his lot as minstrel, now exploiting the figure to vindicate the outsider: 'Alas! What a sad profession is a minstrel's. He is also fated to be a pariah and an outcast ... hurrah! hurrah for the pariahs!' An oft-repeated experience of the traveller over *Don Gypsy*, alongside the picaresque playfulness and carnivalesque creation, is lack of funds while loneliness and his rejection by communities or individuals along the way, given his distinct appearance, are also significant features. All these elements may be related to Starkie's own circumstances: the family's clipped finances, together with a sense of uprootedness and a loss of belonging in an Irish nation now undertaking a major process of transformation, on the verge of acquiring a new constitutional identity. The repeated highlighting of the traveller's rejection in *Don Gypsy* because of his difference might be interpreted as a metaphor for Starkie's personal sense of rejection in his community of origin. When in Puerto de Santa María, the traveller's response is reminiscent of Lemuel Gulliver's towards the Yahoos on his arrival in Hoyhnhnmland. The latter-day traveller encounters a wide variety of physical type: 'bull-necked, dark, fat, wizened, wrinkled, baby-faced, dwarfed, spindle-shanked', whom he classifies as 'queer' and 'grotesque', in contrast to what he regards as his own 'normal appearance'. However, in turn, he will himself be perceived as beyond the norm, reactions varying from staring to ridicule: 'When I played [the violin] in the streets[,] the girls would stand and laugh at me. When I walked into the *Iglesia mayor*...I aroused curiosity, for many of the congregation turned round to look at me.' Yet he will go on to reveal his own inability to appreciate the narrowness of his ethnocentric perception: 'I cannot imagine what they consider unusual about me.' A loaded question follows: 'Why is a stranger always mocked and made the cynosure of neighbouring eyes?' The response reveals intolerance. And the

---

87 For further information on the articles published in the *Irish Independent* from Abyssinia (1936) and Spain (1938), see below. A full listing of the articles in question is also supplied in the Appendix. 88 W. Starkie to Cardinal A. Hinsley, 11 June 1940 (Westminster Diocesan Archives, AAW, Hi2/217).

traveller will be subjected to more. Having left Argamasilla early in the morning: 'to avoid the attentions of the urchins who turn mockery to bitter account by pelting the lonely wanderer with stones', the 'stranger' will be persecuted by the local children in Herencia and have to take sanctuary in the church. Finally, it is only the passing of time which ensures refuge:

> A crowd of children of both sexes followed me making rude remarks about my person and jeering at my fiddle. I tried to keep my dignity … But the children … continued their teasing. Some of them threw pieces of earth and pebbles, others ran along and pulled at my coat-tails…I halted at various shops in an effort to lose them, but when I came out[,] I found them all ready to form up in a mocking procession behind me … Fortunately … the shades of evening were falling, and the children soon became wearied of their game of baiting the Pied Piper.

Following the children's disappearance, the traveller is approached by 'a very good-looking little boy' who constitutes an exception to the barbarous breed who have humiliated him. The boy apologizes for the behaviour of his companions and explains that the outsider was persecuted simply because he was 'a stranger' and because the children found it amusing to contemplate him going into church given his rotund physique 'and all'. The episode is brought to a close with a reflection on prejudice, ultimately the purpose of these episodes: 'My experience with the urchins of Herencia proved to me how difficult it is for a man to be a follower of Don Quixote when the world insists upon considering him a Sancho Panza.'[89]

Such scenes of persecution as described above, albeit by 'urchins', are striking in the context of 1930s Europe and in a text which foregrounds 'Gypsy' in the title. Furthermore, Starkie's third travel book was dedicated to the Barcelona-born mezzo-soprano Conchita Supervía. The dedication of a book on Spain to a Spanish singer might be considered a fitting tribute and especially appropriate given her untimely death a few months earlier in the capital city where the text was published. On the other hand, Supervía might evoke Mussolini's Italy since she perfomed at La Scala in Milan over the 1920s. However, more recently, the singer had also married the London businessman of Jewish descent Ben Rubenstein, in 1931, and would be buried in Willesden United Synagogue Cemetery following her passing five years later. Thus, she also comes to signify Jewishness. Indeed, it might be said that the 1936 text wavers between different signifiers, two of which, Jew and Gypsy, came to acquire haunting signifieds in a Europe where 'violence, persecution, and discrimination'[90] had been threatening the survival of the Other in the Third Reich since 1933.[91] The most striking instance of the text's awareness, if not preoccupation, with contemporary racial prejudice and genocide in Nazi Germany is the claim expressed in an imaginary conversation between the traveller and the ghost of the Spanish nineteenth-century

89 Ibid., pp 47, 100, 421, 422, 480, 482, 483, 484. 90 I. Kershaw, *Hitler* (London, 2008), p. 518.
91 For fuller reference in this connection, see: V. Klemperer, *The language of the Third Reich*, trans. M. Brady (London, 2010); I. Kershaw, *Hitler*; *http://www.yadvashem.org.il*, accessed 23 Mar. 2012.

author Ángel Ganivet. Speaking of literary characters who come to function symbol-
ically within their cultures, the ghost of Ganivet voices racial reconciliation: 'Ulysses
is the symbol of ancient Greece: he possesses all the Aryan virtues – prudence,
constancy, strength, restraint and, in addition, the astuteness and resourcefulness of
the Semitic race.'[92]

Don Gypsy is subtitled *Adventures with a fiddle in Barbary, Andalusia and La
Mancha*. The traveller approaches Spain by way of North Africa, represented in the
subtitle from a Eurocentric perspective, as a land of barbarians. The ethnocentrism
recalls Mr Rochester's reaction to the Caribbean in Charlotte Brontë's *Jane Eyre*. The
Victorian English gentleman is overwhelmed by what he perceives as excess in the
West Indies[93] and the Irish/English/British traveller in 'Barbary' in 1935 longs for a
relief similar to that which was afforded Rochester in the shape of '[a] wind fresh from
Europe',[94] enabling him to reach resolution. The traveller posits the colonialist binary
opposition:

> In the streets and *zocos* of Tangier, Tetuan and Xauen I had become dulled in ear
> and eye by too many chaotic sounds and colours. So many picturesque sights
> passed before my eye, so many unwanted sounds were dinned into my ears, that
> I lost all power to distinguish between them. I was so sated with picturesqueness
> that I should have felt a sense of relief if a genii had suddenly dumped me down
> in the middle of the Castilian plateau.[95]

In the early pages of the text, there will be reference to Jews resident in Tangier and
the description smacks of the anti-Semitic comment already referred to in *Raggle-
taggle*. Such comment corresponds to the merchant class who are represented as
undermining established trade. Thus, finding himself in a *fonduk* in Tangier, in the
company of a Gypsy, one Blas Núñez Malolo, the traveller notes that among 'the
Arabs, and Berbers in turban, fez and Phrygian cap[,] there were many bearded Jews
in greasy dark gabardines' and as he leaves the *fonduk* at midnight, the 'only signs of
activity' he registers are those of 'a group of Jews…haggling over goods in a corner.'
The traveller's Gypsy companion finds the merchant Jews anathema: 'As soon as he
saw the Jews Don Blas mumbled a curse and said: 'There is the plague of my life.
Twenty years ago I used to be as solitary as a king in the Zoco Grande and I had no
rivals. To-day there are so many of these *judíos* [Jews] selling cloth – aye and under-
selling me, that I can hardly earn my expenses.' However, in contrast to this negative
profile, the traveller introduces his 'friend', Cansinos, a descendant of Sephardic Jews
and bookseller in the Jewish quarter of Tetuan, who provides the traveller with 'intel-

---

92 W. Starkie, *Don Gypsy*, p. 245. See also W.F. Starkie, 'A few glosses on *Don Quixote* and La Mancha'
in H.D. Crotty, *Glimpses of Don Quixote and La Mancha* (Los Angeles, 1963), where Ulysses is represented as possessing 'all the virtues of the Aryan – prudence, constancy, effort, self-control with Semitic
astuteness and fertility of resource.' (p. ix) The reference is footnoted as coming from J.A. Carey's translation of A. Ganivet, *Idearium Español* (A. Ganivet, *Spain: an interpretation*, trans. J.A. Carey (London,
1946), pp 134–5). **93** C. Brontë, *Jane Eyre* (London, 1985), p. 335. **94** Ibid. **95** W. Starkie, *Don
Gypsy*, p. 136.

lectual companionship' during his stay in the city. As Cansinos recites traditional ballads, shepherd songs, marriage airs or songs of pilgrims en route for Jerusalem, the traveller sympathetically, perhaps to some degree empathetically, perceives in him the history of a people and a will to survive: 'It was a face Ribera would have painted, a solemn patriarchal face, armed with centuries of determination – the face of one who had wandered from one country to another, carrying with him his perpetual sorrow for the beloved country lost to his race, and the consciousness of his Jewish destiny in the world.'[96]

The other ethnic group who are presented as suffering the consequences of intolerance are Gypsies. While still in Tetuan, the traveller will be exposed to prejudice on the part of a local Arab towards Greek nomad coppersmiths, making him realize that the Gypsy is 'as much of a pariah to Moor as to Christian', harassed by both cultures: ' "Ah!" said the Moor, "so you are looking for the Greeks. You will find them down at the bottom of that slope over there. Follow the ditch and you'll soon see wooden hovels and tents, where they live like dogs." As he said this[,] he looked at me scornfully.' By means of reference to pertinent bibliography, F.H. Groome's *Introduction to Gypsy Folk Tales*, Andreas's *With Gypsies in Bulgaria* and a text by G. Georgeakis together with L. Pineau, *Le Folklore de Lesbos*, the traveller shows how 'prejudice against the Gypsy smiths is a deep-seated one in Europe.' Furthermore, once in Spain, in Granada, and on the subject of *cante hondo*, the traveller speaks of *martinetes*, assessing them as 'survivals of days long ago when the Gypsy race was hounded from one place to another by society [*sic*].'[97]

The traveller's favourable impression of the unity found in Arab culture, registered in *Don Gypsy*, recalls Starkie's reviews in the *Irish Statesman* which sought to promote unity in 1920s Ireland: 'In Tetuan and Xauen one has the certainty that Arab life is a hardy organism, enduring for ever unchanged through its tremendous unity - the song of Islam.' This ideal cohesion is contrasted to 'the chaotic individualism of the European' and, with particular reference to Spain: 'the fierce individualism of the Spaniard.' The antidote to disintegration in the Spanish context is presented in *Don Gypsy* by means of the recognition awarded the Catholic Sovereigns, Ferdinand and Isabella, who unified Spain in the wake of their victory over the Arabs following eight centuries of occupation by the latter. Indeed, resistance to foreign invasion is touched upon elsewhere in the text: out on the old walls and fortifications of Cádiz, for instance, the traveller will recall 'the heroic stand made by the city against the French in 1812.' However, the Catholic Sovereigns will particularly be focussed on, the traveller's contemplation of their tombs leading him to reflect on their reign and the policy of unification which brooked no opposition: 'It was owing to their belief in the absolute necessity of having one crown, one country, one faith that they subsequently cast all thoughts of tolerance to the winds and swept down with avenging fury upon the vanquished.'[98] Attention to the figure of King Ferdinand is filtered through selected allusions to the Spanish monarch in Machiavelli's *The Prince*. Quoting from Chapter 18, 'How princes should honour their word', and Chapter 21, 'How a prince

96 Ibid., pp 28, 30, 78.   97 Ibid., pp 93, 121, 293.   98 Ibid., pp 136, 137, 437, 233–4.

must act to win honour', the traveller first quotes the whole of the opening paragraph of the latter chapter in which the reader is invited to consider Ferdinand's deeds, all of which are qualified as 'great and some of them extraordinary', and the King's strategy for success is traced, from his attack on Granada at the beginning of his reign, the use he made of religion in order to advance greater ambitions, and the speed with which he worked so that potential enemies had no time to organize any opposition to him. The traveller then turns to the opening passage of Machiavelli's Chapter 18 which baldly, and boldly, undermines what might be expected from the title: 'Those princes who have done great things have held good faith of little account and have known how to circumvent the intellect of men by craft, and in the end have overcome those who have relied upon their word.'[99] In the paragraph that follows, Machiavelli outlines how fighting might proceed and these are reproduced in *Don Gypsy*: 'there are two ways of carrying on a contest, the one by law, the other by force. The first way befits men, the second befits brutes. But as the first is often unsuccessful, it is necessary to have recourse to the second.'[1]

In an isolated sentence that follows the paragraph translated from Chapter 21 of *The Prince*, in which Ferdinand's success is highlighted, the traveller exclaims: 'How many times in the subsequent history of the world have those words echoed through the minds of dictators!' Subsequently, the King's reply to the Italian ambassador's query regarding Spain's having been conquered by 'Gauls, Romans, Carthaginians, Vandals and Moors' is delivered in indirect speech: 'The King had answered saying that the Spanish people were good enough as fighters but undisciplined. Only great things could be accomplished by them when they were led by one who knew how to unite them and keep them in order.'[2] The allusion to 'dictators' in the traveller's exclamation and the King's conviction that the state's success depends on a strong leader ('one who [knows] how to unite [the people] and keep them in order') cannot but bring contemporary Europe to mind and, more particularly, Spain. The coup led by General Franco took place in the month following the publication of *Don Gypsy* and the text seems, on occasion, to be anticipating it. While in Granada, the traveller meets up with the Granada banker and painter José María Rodríguez-Acosta[3] (a friend of Pérez de Ayala and Zuloaga, among others, including the traveller), who will deliver a diatribe on the current (dis)order:

> The Republic has misled people sadly and the people have been the prey for unscrupulous propagandists, who announced that as soon as the Revolution broke out[,] the Millenium would come with Socialism. I remember when the King left Spain in 1931[,] the ignorant workers in the towns sat in the cafés

---

99 Starkie does not acknowledge the translator of the extract from Machiavelli's text; it may have been himself. George Bull's 1961 translation of the part of the opening sentence/paragraph cited by Starkie reads: 'princes who have achieved great things have been those who have given their word lightly, who have known how to trick men with their cunning, and who, in the end, have overcome those abiding by honest principles' (N. Machiavelli, *The prince*, trans. G. Bull (London, 1975), p. 99). **1** W. Starkie, *Don Gypsy*, pp 231, 232. **2** Ibid., pp 232, 233. **3** For further information on José María Rodríguez-Acosta, see *www.fundacionrodriguezacosta.com*, accessed 28 March 2012.

drinking and called out to the bourgeois –'Now it is your turn to work: we're going to do as you did in the past – sit in cafés and watch the crowd go by.' And so the [*sic*] Spaniards do not work, production declines, wages increase and the result is chaos. And the demagogues who shout still have their way, but it will not be for long, for the people are disillusioned and there is hunger everywhere.

The traveller does not dispute the banker's account. He confirms the picture of ubiquitous hunger in the area while spelling out the conservative solution and presuming that a military dictatorship would find support in the population on the grounds of their familiarity with the model of government, having experienced it over the Primo de Rivera years:

> I could certainly agree with Don José that there was plenty of hunger in Andalusia, for I had been living among pinched faces ever since I had come to Granada. The remedy which most of the Conservatives suggest for present ills in Spain is to go back to strong government by the army until order is restored. How often in Spanish history has that remedy been applied! The mass of the people are familiar with it and they would, presumably, welcome it on the principle that the Devil you know is better than the Devil you do not know.[4]

In the chapter in *Don Gypsy* which evokes the Spain of the Catholic Sovereigns, a downward path is traced from the time of their achievements, together with those of Charles V and the first twenty years of Philip II's reign. From the late sixteenth century on, Spain's disintegration is registered, marked by the gradual loss of her colonies. The account reaches a climax recording fragmentation within the state as a further illustration of decline: 'And then after 1900 when Spain was reduced to its peninsula[,] the cry of regionalism, separatism rose from within the country.' The Republic is presented as further responsible for accelerating the decay into which Spain has fallen, a state riddled with division. Thus the traveller's voice lends itself to registering deep nostalgia for a time now forfeited, related to the feudal order which patronized popular culture: '*Ou sont les neiges d'antan?* Said I to myself as I wondered disconsolately past the shuttered windows of a palace where I had heard many *soleares* and *bulerías*.' In the divided present, he comes across political tension in towns from inland Guadix, in the province of Granada, where 'two irreconcilable camps…the Conservatives, Diehards, clerical sympathisers, on the one side, and the Republicans, Socialists of the red to deep pink variety on the other' gather on opposite sides of the room in the Café Pasajes, to coastal Torremolinos, in the province of Málaga, 'divided into two camps – communist and clerical.'[5]

Rodríguez-Acosta is not the only Spaniard who expresses disagreement with or opposition to the Republican regime. As in *Spanish raggle-taggle*, the discontents cover

4 W. Starkie, *Don Gypsy*, pp 233, 285, 286. Note the exclamation in the final quote cited here (from p. 286 of *Don Gypsy*) which is evocative of the earlier exclamation cited at the beginning of my paragraph (from p. 232 of *Don Gypsy*). The two together seem to be suggesting the inevitability of a coup.
5 Ibid., pp 237, 409, 369–70, 402.

all classes: from banker to goatherd, passing through an old lottery-seller, one Juan José; Pedro el indio, a bootblack, together with the *saeta* singer and renegade socialist and defender of votes for women, Francisco Borrachera. There is also reference back to the incident in Casas Viejas in 1933 which was damaging for the embryonic Republican order, referred to as 'the abominable massacre' of 'nineteen starving peasants.' The lottery-seller, Juan José, vehemently declares: 'The blood of the poor victims who were butchered in that hut at Casas Viejas has stained the purple of the Republican standard red.[6] Yes ... that flag will turn to *sangre y oro* (blood and gold) again',[7] the determination ominously expressed in his final statement clearly prophesying a return to the old order.[8]

Undoubtedly, a strong sense of nostalgia permeates the text and is repeatedly expressed by the traveller. He muses on happier days in the 'aristocratic' and 'firmly monarchical' Jerez de la Frontera of 1928 when he was the guest of the Marquis of Almocaden: 'the head of the house of Domecq.' The Marquis had died in 1933 but other 'good friends' of the late 1920s, 'such as the Conde de los Andes who had entertained [the traveller] with wine and *zambras* [Andalusian Gypsy dancing]' were now in the company of those other members of the aristocracy portrayed in *Spanish raggle-taggle*, residing in exile, like the king himself. There are a number of sympathetic allusions to the Spanish monarchy over the text, whether it be indirectly, as in the reference to the Málaga *merendero* (bar-restaurant) of Antón Martín, who had served King Alfonso XIII and Queen Victoria Eugenia in 1926,[9] or directly, as when the traveller is enjoying a sampling of wines in the González Byass *bodegas*: 'I went on drinking the priceless wine from the "Queen Mercedes" cask, which had been made for the first wife of Alfonso XII.' Two casks seen in the Domecq bodega in 1928 which carried the signatures of the now exiled monarch, Alfonso XIII, and his spouse are highlighted too. Sympathy is also expressed for the former dictator under Alfonso XIII's reign, Primo de Rivera, projected as an efficient man of action in both home and foreign affairs. Admiration for the General is voiced by 'an Andalusian of the old school' and ex-soldier 'who had served the King in Morocco', now landlord of an inn, The traveller qualifies Don Miguel's words a 'harangue', but they are delivered none the less, mediated through a free indirect style:

> He admired Primo de Rivera more than any Spaniard of recent times. 'Primo de Rivera ... was the best man Spain has had for a hundred years. Why? Because he didn't talk, he acted. And when he acted[,] he did so after taking the best advice. He it was who gave us the roads and the *Chorro* at Málaga for irrigating the countryside. And when matters were dragging on in the Riff[,] he slipped over to Africa between one meeting of the *Cortes* [Parliament] and another and in the twinkling of an eye the war was finished.'[10]

6 The Spanish flag during the Second Spanish Republic was a tricolour of red, yellow and murrey. 7 W. Starkie, *Don Gypsy*, p. 140. 8 Juan José will also be used to convey an, at best, naïve, in effect, negatively charged representation of Libertarian Communism: 'it means that everyone may do exactly what he pleases' (W. Starkie, *Don Gypsy*, p. 140). 9 'Merendero Antonio Martín', *http://sinalefa5. wordpress.com/2011/07/31/merendero-antonio-martn/*, accessed 25 May 2012. 10 W. Starkie, *Don*

On the road from Granada to Guadix, Primo de Rivera also comes into the conversation the traveller holds with a goatherd, who, we are pointedly told: 'was not a socialist' and who considers that the country requires some fierce shepherding. The words of this man of the people are reproduced in direct speech: '[T]he people are like mountain goats … they need a shepherd with a crook to count them and drive them home. That's what we need in Spain … a real shepherd with a shout out of him that could be heard a mile off and a stick, too, which would prevent us from straggling like stray goats.'[11]

Apart from the monarchy and/or military dictatorship, the traditions which are celebrated in *Don Gypsy* are rural life; the music, song and dance of the folk; Catholicism and colonization, all of which may be related to the ubiquitous strain of anti-modernity in the text. Life in villages or the countryside is sometimes combined with music and song, creating a sense of pastoral Arcadia. Finding himself in Cadiar, 'a small town bosomed up high in the Alpujarras', the traveller finds 'a town of [male] fiddlers' and girls who sang the local folk-songs. He also mentions men in the casino, as well as the girls, giving voice to love-songs and he describes their singing in contrast to the *Cante Jondo* or *Flamenco* heard in Granada as 'tender and elegiac', interpreting it as an expression of their collective experience: 'The people sang together in a serene, spontaneous way, as though to express their life as a community. For them singing as well as dancing was an expression of collective solidarity. They sang together as they worked in the mill or as they sat sewing on the terrace of the house.' Later, sallying forth from Jerez de la Frontera into the 'peaceful' countryside by the banks of the river Guadalete, the traveller hears a glory of voices, evocative of the peasants in the fields of Castile depicted in *Spanish raggle-taggle,* far removed from the cries of workers in the city vindicating rights and revolution: 'singing on all sides: the fishermen standing on the banks sang, the men working in the fields sang, and along the roads I heard a band of muleteers singing a slow, rambling song in unison as they advanced in long line towards the city.' These men, like the inhabitants of Cadiar, are not the stuff of revolutionaries; they preserve the established peace. Gypsy music, song and dancing also exemplify tradition with such instances as Fernando de Triana, visited by the traveller in Camas. Triana is portrayed as representing 'the survival of the golden age of Gypsy song', upholding a tradition which he speaks of as currently in a state of decay. Thus, he laments: 'When [La] Niña de los Peines[12] and a few others have gone[,] there will be nothing to remind us of the proud, metallic harshness of the Gypsy voice.' He also finds Gypsy dancing ailing from 'corruption': 'No genuine Gypsy dancer in a *cuadro flamenco* [flamenco troupe] would ever have used the castanets…she would dance to the rhythm of handclapping with guitar and singing.'[13]

In *Don Gypsy*, the traveller identifies himself as a Catholic, through allusion to his guardian angel, for instance, or there is reference to Catholic culture, such as the

Gypsy, pp 409, 406, 409, 443, 396.   11 Ibid., pp 406, 409, 443, 396, 355.   12 Pastora Pavón Cruz (1890–1969) was known as 'The Girl with the Combs' (with reference to the tall Spanish combs worn by women as part of traditional head dress on festive or ceremonious occasions, over which the mantilla is draped). She was considered to be the most distinguished female flamenco singer of the twentieth century.   13 W. Starkie, *Don Gypsy*, pp 386, 387, 389, 390, 411, 464, 467.

Spanish meat dispensation on Fridays. Catholicism is very much present in *Don Gypsy*, as it was in *Spanish raggle-taggle*: here, from the traveller's departure 'On the morning after St Patrick's Day, 1935,' to the climactic final chapter in the Seville of Holy Week. Apart from informing on the atmosphere in the city and the spectacular *pasos* [floats] bearing the statues of Our Lady of Macarena, the Christ of Great Power and the Christ of the Gypsies, the traveller will go back to 'the famous bar of "Tío Cornelio"', apparently with a view to illustrating Catholicism's current pre-eminence over communism. As he explains: 'It was here that in 1931 a regular battle took place between revolutionaries and the government, and the original bar was bombed to bits. Tonight there was no talk of communism, but a great deal about the religious significance of Our Lady of Macarena.' Alongside Seville, Jerez de la Frontera is described as 'a profoundly religious city' and in the countryside, the traveller will visit the 'pathetic relic' of the Carthusian monastery founded in the late fifteenth century, from which the monks were ousted in 1835. The traveller's contemplation of the ruin will lead him to express solidarity with the ousted brethren who, furthermore, become another representation in the text of the persecuted other:

> I wondered how the people of Jerez ever had the heart to allow those Carthusian monks to depart for ever from the monastery which had been such a beneficial institution to the whole countryside … The monks of Jerez deserved well of their country as well as of their city … What a tragic day it was in 1835 when the community … were cast out into the turmoil of the world to become beggars wandering over the roads of Spain, unable to adapt themselves to the lives of other men.[14]

Finally, the question of colonialism is broached in the opening chapter of the text through the mention of 'a fierce argument' between an Englishman and a Spaniard on the subject of Gibraltar. The argument is prevented from becoming either further heated, or more substantial, by means of a playful literary device found in Thomas More's *Utopia* whereby information is forfeited at a crucial moment as a consequence of an unexpected occurrence. In *Don Gypsy*, 'a sudden heaving movement of the ship'[15] leads the Spaniard to hasten towards the taffrail and lean over the side, bringing the episode to an end. However, it is the references to Spain's colonialist[16] activity in North Africa, represented as a civilizing mission by the traveller himself at a number of points, which might be conceived as connecting with other instances of tradition given the evocation in the text of the authorization awarded Columbus by the Catholic Sovereigns, which enabled him to sail for 'the New World' in 1492. Thus, Spain's current colonialist activity may be perceived as echoing the exploits of the former glorious reign. In conversation with the Jewish bookseller in Tetuan, Spain's colonization is praised by both the traveller and Cansinos, respectively:

---

14 W. Starkie, *Don Gypsy*, pp 3, 470, 406, 412. 15 Ibid., pp 4, 5. 16 I use 'colonialist' here as defined by Elleke Boehmer when referring to colonialist literature, i.e., 'specifically concerned with colonial expansion.' (E. Boehmer, *Colonial and postcolonial literature* (Oxford, 1995), p. 3.)

The Spaniards have brought a civilizing influence to this part of the world. I have been greatly struck by the pleasant spirit of companionship and tolerance between the Moors and the Spanish soldiers [...]

... today there has been a wonderful change owing to the wise measures taken by Spain in her relations with the Protectorate. Her influence has been truly beneficial in education. Little by little the spirit of Spain will, as you say, *Señor*, civilize those Moors ...

In Algeciras, in conversation with the old lottery-seller Juan José, the traveller declares that life is better in Morocco 'since the Protectorate was established' and in the exchange staged between 'the ghost of Ganivet' and himself, the traveller again pronounces in favour of Spain's beneficial impact in the region while also recognizing that of France: 'Spain in recent years has established peaceful government in Africa and brought civilization to the Riff. She has followed the example of France.'[17]

* * *

The change of government in Ireland following the victory in the general elections held in the Free State in 1932 prompted a partial refashioning of Starkie's career, beginning with the letter he addressed to John Murray that same year regarding the manuscript of what became *Raggle-taggle*. The two other 'travel books', *Spanish raggle-taggle* and *Don Gypsy*, followed within the next three years: the former just twenty months after the author's initial success with *Raggle-taggle* and with a span of only eighteen months between the first travel book on Spain in 1934 and the second in 1936. The response to *Raggle-taggle* had been widely enthusiastic but it became less so in the case of the later publications[18] in spite of, for instance, favourable criticism in Ireland from writer Kate O'Brien in relation to *Spanish raggle-taggle*[19] and approval from novelist Francis MacManus for *Don Gypsy*.[20] The author himself appears to have possessed high ambitions and, therefore, came to experience disappointment with the response of reviewers. Indeed, over the 30s, his dismay in this instance becomes something of a *leitmotif*, reflected in correspondence both with his sister Enid and his publisher John (Jock) Murray at Albemarle Street. Writing to Enid in the wake of the publication of *Don Gypsy*, he confessed his lofty aspiration: 'I always long to try [sic] to express myself in a work of art' and also lamented: 'I despair of reviewers: they always succeed in diminishing and cheapening one's work. They try to make out that one was just pegging one's way at some wretched little point of folklore or music or else they class one with the vulgar travelogue!'[21] Almost two years on, he considered

17 W. Starkie, *Don Gypsy*, pp 80, 138, 242.   18 See, for instance, the review 'Spanish raggle-taggle' in *The Spectator*, 8 Nov. 1934, p. 771, and of *Don Gypsy*, 'A scholar Gypsy', in *The Times*, 12 June 1936, p. 10. Starkie found the latter 'the limit of foolishness and so flippant as to be insulting'. (W. Starkie to J. Murray, 13 June 1936, JMC). See also Starkie's own reference to the 'snippets' produced by Waugh and Nicolson, cited in the corpus of the text above.   19 K[ate]. O' B[rien]., 'A fiddle in Spain. Dr Starkie's latest book of adventures', II, 6 Nov. 1934, p. 3.   20 F[rancis]. MacM[anus]., 'Knight of the Fiddle', IP, 16 June 1936, p. 6.   21 W. Starkie to E. Starkie, 9 July 1936 (ES Bodl.).

Enid to have been fortunate in being awarded space in the *TLS* following the publication of her *Arthur Rimbaud* in contrast to the treatment given his own efforts. He tartly observed: 'I never expect more than a column of frigid futility and miscomprehension.'[22] And in the wake of publication of *The waveless plain*, his plaint carried no less indignation:

> I got snippets from people like Evelyn Waugh and Harold Nicholson [*sic*] –
> showing that they had not even read the blurb of my book. It is terrible to see how
> low book-reviewing has sunk in England. Some cold-shoulder my book simply
> because it is on Italy. Others who are in the political-writing 'racket' don't even
> bother to mention my close study of the origins of Fascism.[23]

He also had occasion to protest before his publisher, who chided him for not writing as 'a Professor should'[24] while Starkie was embarked on the narrative of *Don Gypsy*. Initially, the Professor was challenging in his response: 'I hope I never do [write as 'a Professor should'] ... I'm afraid I cannot say an act of contrition for my sins as a vagabond – "*j'écris comme je suis*"[,] that is all.' However, the defiance was not sustained. In the following sentence, he deferred to Murray's criterion, claiming that he was 'eager' to see the corrections produced by the publisher since the latter would have diagnosed what was wrong with one of the chapters in *Don Gypsy* which had given Starkie more trouble than most. He then went on to recognize that his text 'need[ed] to be manicured somehow,' finally expressing how 'deeply grateful' he felt towards Murray for his 'kindness in advising [him].'[25]

In spite of having made his mark within the travel writing genre and acquired popularity in Britain through lecturing,[26] by 1938 Starkie was expressing a sense of insecurity and vulnerability. His anxiety is reflected in a letter to his sister Enid: 'I always feel on the edge of a precipice [,] waiting to be blown over the edge but praying for divine aid from Mercury, god of luck – i.e. the sweep or the more unlikely break of luck from a book.'[27] None the less, university life ticked over at Trinity and beyond the gates of the institution he was busy throughout the 30s with a host of activities in the city, from the Bicentenary celebrations of the RDS, to commitments related to the Abbey, passing through the Irish Academy of Letters, as well as having access to escape from daily routine through travel abroad, yet all was far from well. The decade was plagued with a series of domestic tensions regarding family finances and his marriage while being further aggravated by his son's adolescent antics. And further afield, as the decade advanced, the situation in Europe was acquiring more menacing proportions.

By 1934, Walter's mother had moved from 129 Anglesea Road to a flat at 84 Northumberland Road, still within the Dublin suburb of Ballsbridge, though closer to

---

22 W. Starkie to E. Starkie, 20 May 1938 (ES Bodl.). 23 W. Starkie to E. Starkie, 18 June 1938 (ES Bodl.). 24 W. Starkie to J. Murray, 21 Sept. 1935 (JMC). Starkie quotes John Murray's words in this reply to a letter from the publisher addressed to the author. 25 Ibid. 26 The lecturing appears, for the most part, to have been related to his Gypsy ventures and, therefore, became a means of advertising his writing. 27 W. Starkie to E. Starkie, 18 June 1938 (ES Bodl.).

the centre of the city and within easier reach of son and daughter-in-law at Botanic House. Muriel and Chou-Chou no longer lived with their mother, having married, and by early 1935, Nancy was working in London so a smaller property was certainly in order. However, in April 1936, Nancy would be writing to Enid of their mother's plans to move come October, when the lease of the flat ran out, since she felt unable to afford the annual rent of £91, a move that Walter appears not to have been in favour of: 'Any time mother mentions leaving to Walter, he says he thinks it a mistake, that she won't get anywhere cheaper,' yet, according to Nancy, he had done nothing to enable his mother to keep the flat on. She blamed her brother for not providing the $1 per week he had promised the widowed Mrs Starkie in order to enable her to meet her expenses while also pointing out that 'Walter's family' (presumably his two children since Italia was giving her mother-in-law short shrift by this time) were 'continuously feeding' at Northumberland Road. Twenty-seven-year-old Nancy held her senior sister-in-law responsible for squandering her husband's income, labelling her 'a bad manager' and 'extravagant'.[28] In the same letter, Nancy also insisted that in her view the financial priority should have been paying off the 'overdraft'.[29] In 1930, Nancy was already speaking to Enid of an overdraft of 'very nearly £1,400'[30] and, come 1936, the youngest sister believed Walter to be 'about £800 overdrawn.' The former overdraft may have been generated by May Caroline's spending over the decade of the 20s while her son's may have been a consequence of Italia's poor household management.[31] Nancy certainly thought so, though she also awarded Walter some responsibility in the matter: 'They have not any real idea how to run a house. Italia is extravagant in such a foolish way.'[32] In the same letter to Enid she also spoke of her brother's having to seek for signatures to support his solvency in 1935,[33] a year, moreover, in which he had pawned his father's gold medals in London for some £20. The amount in question was destined for his mother, though it appears to have fallen to her to pay the £2 quarterly interest.[34] By 1938, the widowed Mrs Starkie's financial distress had come to a head. Writing to Enid from a hotel in Kilmarnock in July, following a stay with Walter and Italia (over which Nancy had found her brother and his wife 'very decent' and Italia 'very kind, so spontaneously so'), May Caroline's youngest child was now censorious of her mother. She also recognized that Walter, and especially Enid, had been 'wonderful children' to their mother:

> I think the position [mother] has got herself into is lamentable. But there is no use saying anything now. The whole thing was so grossly mismanaged in 1920. And Mother right through, being so proud, has acted in such a stupid way, never foreseeing what was bound to happen in the end. It is hard to imagine someone

28 N. Starkie to E. Starkie, 28 Apr. 1936 (ES Bodl.).   29 Ibid. Nancy's conviction is demonstrated by her underlining the sentence in question.   30 N. Starkie to E. Starkie, 3 May 1930 (ES Bodl.).   31 Starkie's debts may not have been a consequence of poor household management on the part of his wife. He explained to Enid at this time that he had taken on responsibility for loans requested by his mother (W. Starkie to E. Starkie, 18 June 1938, ES Bodl.).   32 N. Starkie to E. Starkie, 14 May 1936 (ES Bodl.).   33 Nancy mentions three names in this connection, one of which is 'Harmsworth', presumably Cecil.   34 N. Starkie to E. Starkie, 28 Apr. 1936 (ES Bodl.).

with intelligence behaving as she did. It is too hard on you and Walter, and also[,] I think[,] hard on Walter's wife.[35]

Thus, Walter was condemned to dedicating his energies to earning money, as much as possible. Apart from his salary at TCD, his public lectures were a further source of income as well as his books, but there never seemed to be enough. After *Don Gypsy* in 1936, he published one further book in the 1930s with John Murray, *The waveless plain*, and as the decade drew to a close, he was struggling to finish both his biography of the Spanish inquisitor Cardinal Cisneros, to be published by Hodder and Stoughton in 1940, together with the translation of the Second Part of *Don Quixote* for Macmillan. In a letter to Enid in September 1939, Italia was looking forward to her husband's being paid for his efforts: 'I hope [Walter] will be able to get his 450 pounds when the publishers get the manuscripts: two more payments ... , one now and one for [*sic*] the beginning of December[,] would come to a total of nearly 900 pound [*sic*] before Xmas.'[36] Italia may have been planning for Christmas though it is more likely that by then she was concerned with calculations regarding the funds that would be needed to satisfy public school fees in England: Landi's at Ampleforth and Alma's at Roedean, together with other items.[37] Her preoccupation with making funds stretch, as well as the energies she devoted to contemplating how the family's finances might be improved by way of an active contribution from herself, through her teaching at Alexandra College and TCD, are reflected in correspondence with her sister-in-law. Early in 1938, she communicated her calculations and determination to Enid:

> 40 pounds and travelling expenses and clothes will probably come to 75 or 80 pounds a year and the vacations time at home. We must face all this and we shall. When both the children will be [*sic*] away[,] the expenses of our living at home will be reduced to nothing, at least for the 36 weeks the children are away [...] I shall do as many lessons as I can find and perhaps I could take in for the term's weeks some good post-graduate student or lecturer ... we shall see [...] I hope next year to have more work at the [*sic*] Alexandra, and I shall ask a little more money for my work in Trinity.[38]

Another likely source of anxiety for Starkie over the decade was the deterioration in Italia's relationship with her mother-in-law and at least two of his siblings, Chou-Chou and Nancy, which led to tensions within the couple's married life. As Italia's second decade in Ireland began, she was hoping that her husband would win the Chair

---

35 N. Cooper (née Starkie) to E. Starkie, 12 July 1938 (ES Bodl.). 36 I. Starkie (née Porchietti) to E. Starkie, 19 Sept. 1939 (ES Bodl.). 37 Alma started school at Roedean in September 1938, where she benefitted from a scholarship (W. Starkie to E. Starkie, 20 May 1938; 31 May 1938, ES, Bodl.). 38 I. Starkie (née Porchietti] to E. Starkie, dated 31st only (ES, Bodl.). From other information in the letter, the year may be calculated to have been 1938. At the end of the letter, Italia expresses her good wishes for Easter. Easter Day 1938 was on 17 April. Therefore, the date on which the letter was written may be calculated to have been 31 March 1938.

of Spanish at Oxford and, thus, provide a way of escape. When Nancy wrote to Enid in July 1931, a fortnight on from Italia and Walter's son Landi's first communion, she informed her sister that Italia had written to Nancy 'to say that if Walter gains [*sic*] Oxford, it will be possible for them to go on living together, but if he continues in TCD[,] she will probably go and live in Italy'.[39] W.J. Entwistle won the Chair, and Italia stewed for the decade in Dublin.

In May 1934, as Nancy busily typed the manuscript of *Spanish raggle-taggle* so that her brother could send the first part to his London publisher, Italia visited Mrs O'Reilly, the mother of Chou-Chou's Garda husband, Superintendent Michael O'Reilly. Writing to Enid, Nancy relayed nine points, her listing of information provided by brother-in-law, Michael, who had heard 'all Italia said' from his indignant mother the following day. According to Mrs O'Reilly, via Michael, Italia had criticized Nancy, Chou-Chou and her mother-in-law, with an indictment of Mrs Starkie which Mrs O'Reilly had felt obliged to censor: 'Dreadful things about Mother, which Mrs O'Reilly would not tell'. The straw which broke the camel's back was 'How much she, Italia, had suffered at the hands of the Starkie's [*sic*].' The consequence of the day's gossip was that Mrs O'Reilly 'would never have [Italia] in her house again,' Chou-Chou and Michael '[would] not have anything to do' with their sister-in-law for the time being, and Italia herself hadn't been seen since, though Nancy was able to provide Enid with an account of Italia's current state of mind and intentions: '[S]he seems to be in a very bad humour. She is on the warpath again, about taking Landi and Alma to live in London, for their education, and Walter to live in Trinity, except for the holidays.'[40] Just over a year later, Nancy was working in London and had no news to deliver to Enid regarding Italia and the children: 'except that [Italia] was in rather bad form,'[41] an impression presumably relayed from a member of the family in Ireland. However, in May, the Danish writer resident in Dublin, Signe Toksvig, had met Italia at Bray motor races and found her 'quite lovely and quite intelligent' though she also observed 'something schoolmistressed [*sic*] about her,' further noting that Italia had much to say about the separation of the Swedish consul in Dublin, Harry Eriksson. Her being '[f]ull of it',[42] as Toksvig remarked, was perhaps indicative of a circumstance which Italia was personally mulling over. Nancy also disclosed in her letter from London that Italia would be taking the children to Belgium in August to spend the month there.[43] Meanwhile, her husband was occupied in Cambridge, delivering a course of five lectures on D'Annunzio, Pirandello and modern Italian drama.[44] In contrast, in 1936, there were plans for the whole family to spend July and August in Mallorca. Lady Sheppard, who had attended Starkie's lectures at TCD in 1935, had

---

39 N. Starkie to E. Starkie, 13 July 1931 (ES Bodl.). Landi made his first communion on 30 June 1931 at the convent of St Mary Magdalen, Donnybrook, Co. Dublin.   40 N. Starkie to E. Starkie, 10 May 1934 (ES Bodl.).   41 N. Starkie to E. Starkie, 1 June 1935 (ES Bodl.).   42 L. Pihl (ed.), *Signe Toksvig*, p. 317.   43 There is no indication in the correspondence regarding where Italia and her offspring were going to in Belgium or whom they stayed with. However, Walter and Italia moved in diplomatic circles in Dublin and they had struck up a friendship with the Belgian consul, Louis de Goor and his wife, therefore, it is possible that an invitation to Belgium had come from them (author's interview with T. de Vere White, London, 7 Dec. 1989).   44 W. Starkie to J.G. Murray, 2 Aug. 1935 (JMC).

placed her property (originally a monastery) at the disposal of the Starkies, complete with servants, and Enid was invited to join them. In the event, Italia travelled to the Balearic island with her children but without her spouse or sister-in-law. On 30 July, a cold and rainy day, together with Lady Sheppard, Mrs Starkie called on Robert Graves at his home in Dènia. In the course of the visit, Lady Sheppard appears to have voiced her support of General Franco, whose *coup* had been carried out twelve days earlier. Graves noted the call and political pronouncement in his diary: 'Visit from Lady Shepherd [*sic*] and Mrs Starkie and her children from Fornalutx. "We are very Right in our village" and talked of chances of bringing down an aeroplane.' Her Ladyship's remarks caused offence to Laura Riding, though she remained courteous, as Graves noted: 'Offensive to Laura, who replied warmly.' Lady Sheppard's allegiance had not wavered the following week, Graves further noting that Lady Sheppard and Mrs Starkie were then 'queening it'.⁴⁵ Starkie appears not to have reached Mallorca either before or following the outbreak of the Spanish Civil War. On 11 August he was in Genoa where he helped with the influx of 'Spanish refugees … arriving in thousands every day,'⁴⁶ having lectured in Budapest in July,⁴⁷ been in France,⁴⁸ and by the 24th, when he was writing to John Murray, he had been 'mainly tramping' in Sardinia. In spite of the heat and the struggle to fight off malaria 'by doses of 5 tablets of quinine per day', the postcard to his publisher reads as though he had been on holiday: 'Sardinia is a wonderful place – very desolate, parched, full of folklore and colour – wonderful costumes, wild characters and as for the wines[,] they are unique – more fragrant than any in Italy'.⁴⁹ Apart from for the joy of tramping, Starkie's task with the Spanish refugees is not mentioned to Murray, neither is a reason for his visit to France or information regarding exactly where he went provided in a letter addressed to Commendatore Guido Crolla, *Chargé d'Affaires* at the Italian Embassy in London.⁵⁰ The military coup in Spain thwarted the Starkies' summer plans though Italia and children were able to enjoy a degree of Balearic beauty before being rescued from the war zone, taxied home on a British warship.⁵¹

In the autumn of 1938, Italia was still expressing discontent with her lot in Ireland, pondering ways of escape, wondering what path might be taken. Writing to Enid in September 1938 from the Hyde Park Gardens residence of Cecil and Emilie Harmsworth, Italia confessed that when she was in London, she experienced 'the sad

45 Entries for Thursday, 30 July 1936 and Monday, 3 August 1936, Diary of Robert Graves 1935–9, St John's College, Oxford.   **46** W. Starkie to Commendatore Lodi Fé, Italian Consul in Dublin, 29 Sept. 1936 (Archivio Centrale dello Stato (henceforth ACS), Fondo/Serie Ministero della Cultura Popolare (henceforth MCP), Busta 364 (currently being recatalogued). Henceforth Busta 364).   **47** W. Starkie to E. Starkie, 9 July 1936, where he speaks of '[having] to go to Budapest for a lecture' before going on to Italy. He also explains that he will be in Mallorca on 1 August (ES Bodl.).   **48** W. Starkie to Commendatore Guido Crolla, 11 Aug. 1936 (ACS, MCP, Busta 364).   **49** W. Starkie to J.G. Murray, 24 Aug. 1936 (JMC).   **50** Writing to Lodi Fé in late September, Starkie explained that he had been in Caprera as the guest of his brother-in-law, Mario Bonetti, Commander of the Montecuccoli ('the finest cruiser in the Italian fleet'), and had spent a day with Garibaldi's daughter, Donna Clelia, at La Maddalena (W. Starkie to Commendatore Lodi Fé, 29 Sept. 1936, ACS, MCP, Busta 364). The visit to La Maddalena is incorporated into Chapter 28 of *The waveless plain*.   **51** W. Starkie to Commendatore G. Crolla, 11 Aug. 1936 (ACS, MCP, Busta 364).

16 W.F. Starkie with musicians in Budapest, July 1936.

sensation to have [sic] lost seventeen years of [her] life in Dublin'⁵² and over the same period, in correspondence with her husband's publisher, John G. Murray, the forty-eight-year-old discontent expressed her desire to flee in a wholly Romantic strain: 'If duties and responsabilities [*sic*] were less heavy on us, I would make Walter break with Ireland and would go with him to Paris to live and suffer among the people: we cannot do it now and later will be too late: What to do then? What directive [*sic*] to take?'⁵³

Italia's state of mind at this time was also affected by her son Landi's conduct. The boy's progress had been a source of anxiety for some time. Before the children went back to school in January 1936, a tutor was going to Botanic House daily 'to make Landi work and leaving him work to do'.⁵⁴ The thirteen-year-old was sent to Ampleforth in January 1937 and in 1938, while his father was involved in vivas in England in the month of September, he received a telegram informing him that Landi had 'done a bunk'⁵⁵ to York. Starkie immediately travelled to Yorkshire to speak to the Headmaster, Fr Paul Nevill, and to be given an account of his elder child's wayward

52 I. Starkie (née Porchietti) to E. Starkie, 2 Oct. [1938] (ES Bodl.).   53 I. Starkie (née Porchietti) to John G. Murray, 15 Sept. [1938] (JMC). Italia's forceful character is reflected here as she expresses with conviction what she would 'make' her husband do, were they freer to move.   54 I. Starkie (née Porchietti) to E. Starkie, 7 [Jan. 1936] (ES Bodl.).   55 W. Starkie to E. Starkie, 6 Sept. 1938 (ES Bodl.). Starkie pointed out to his sister that the expression with reference to his son's playing truant was Landi's.

behaviour. He subsequently concluded that the Irish, Landi, and English, Fr Sebastian Lambert OSB, the boy's housemaster, had clashed on ethnic grounds: '[Landi] has the misfortune to have a housemaster who is English of the English and gets frantically worried by Landi's Irish brand of wildness.' However, the school recommended that Landi be seen by a Harley Street psychoanalyst, a Dr Strauss, 'a Catholic doctor,' who diagnosed Landi as 'an anti-social type', an assessment interpreted as 'natural' by his father, given his own 'nomadic tendency' together with 'his grandfather on [his] mother's side [having run] away to sea at fourteen'. Starkie accompanied his son on the first visit to the London practitioner; it then fell to Italia to accompany Landi on subsequent ones since Walter, intent on focussing on his Ximénez book, was due to leave for Spain on 7 September, though 'only'[56] for three weeks, as he assured his sister. There was some consolation for Italia: she could be in London rather than Dublin,[57] where, moreover, she made efforts to show her son and his sister (en route for Roedean) the 'tresors'[58] [*sic*] of the metropolis while they were guests of the Harmsworths. Some eight months on, the school was reporting that Landi was 'much better' and 'working hard'[59] though Italia feared he would not pass his School Certificate. She seems to have felt utterly hopeless by this time, confessing an absolute sense of disappointment and despair to her trusted sister-in-law regarding her son's lack of achievement: 'Poor Landi: what a pity he has turned out like that! We must resigne [*sic*] ourselves: no success from him would ever console me from such a defeat concerning my son.'[60] In the wake of the news of Landi's having bunked in September 1938, Walter had written to Enid of 'how worried and wrung [?]' Italia had been, going on to exclaim: 'our house on some occasions has been a storm!'[61] Thus, the Benedictine monastery of Santo Domingo de Silos in north-west Spain would offer the harassed parent a welcome refuge from the trials and tribulations of family life.

Beyond domestic conflict and troublesome offspring, the 1930s became an increasingly tempestuous decade in Europe. On the political front, the Starkies appear to have remained firmly pro-Mussolini, at least until into 1938. Starkie's contact with the Italian Fascist Luigi Villari[62] was maintained over the 1930s through the All Peoples' Association,[63] founded in 1929 by Ulsterman Sir Evelyn Wrench, of which Villari became Italian representative on the International Governing Council and Starkie the Chairman of the Dublin Branch in the Irish Free State.[64] According to Wrench,

---

56 W. Starkie to E. Starkie, 6 Sept. 1938 (ES Bodl.). **57** Writing to Desmond Harmsworth, Cecil and Emilie Harmsworth's son, and his family while staying with the Harmsworths at Hyde Park Gardens in July 1938, Italia referred to enjoying his parents' hospitality and 'adoring London once more.' (I. Starkie (née Porchietti) to Desmond, Dorothy and Margaret Harmsworth, 10 July [1938] (Daniel Harmsworth)). **58** I. Starkie (née Porchietti) to E. Starkie, 2 Oct. [1938] (ES Bodl.). **59** I. Starkie (née Porchietti) to E. Starkie, 18 May 1939 (ES Bodl.). **60** Ibid. **61** W. Starkie to E. Starkie, 6 Sept. 1938 (ES Bodl.). **62** For further information on Villari's propaganda activity in London between the 20s and 30s, see C. Baldoli, *Exporting fascism*, pp 8–10, passim. Villari was programmed to deliver the first address at the Second Summer Conference of the All Peoples' Association, held at Digswell Park between Friday, 24 Aug. and Tuesday, 28 Aug. 1934, on 'The *Dopolavoro* Movement in Italy'. In his absence, the paper was read by Harold Gould, Head of the British Institute in Florence. **63** Henceforth APA. **64** In the first *News Bulletin* of the Association the Right Honourable Lloyd

sometime-associate of Lord Northcliffe,[65] APA's vision signified: 'a group of friends in all countries who are determined that there shall be no more war, that the nations of the world shall get to know one another better, that no member of our society shall ever feel a stranger again',[66] in effect, as the 30s advanced, the stuff of appeasement.[67] The Starkies took an active part in the gatherings of the Dublin Branch as is documented in a report on activities in 1934. The Branch organized 'Language Evenings' twice a month when tables were set up 'for the practice of seven languages'. Italia's command of Spanish appears to have been inspirational: 'Madame Starkie, the wife of our popular Chairman, Professor Walter Starkie, is chiefly responsible for the extraordinary success of the Spanish Tables. She is a native Spanish speaker, and has imbued our members with a keen desire to become proficient in the language.' The report also noted that the group was promised a taste of the Professor's popular fare: 'We are looking forward to one of Dr Starkie's well-known Lectures on Recent Adventures of a Collector of Gypsy Folk-lore and Language, with Violin illustrations.'[68] As in the summer of 1933, in 1934 the Starkies rented a bungalow in County Wicklow, not far from Dublin, by the sea at Brittas Bay. On a July day graced by sunshine, members of APA travelled out to 'Halcyon', where they were hosted by the couple:

> Thanks to the hospitality of Professor and Madame Starkie it was possible for us to organize a most enjoyable bathing outing to Brittas Bay … , where Professor Starkie was spending the summer in a bungalow situated at the edge of the sand dunes, which stretch for miles along a silver strand. A drive of thirty miles, a bathe, tea alfresco [*sic*] and a glorious sun.[69]

George, O.M., M.P., and the Right Honourable Viscount Cecil of Chelwood, Under-Secretary of State for Foreign Affairs during the First World War, figure as Honorary Presidents. Another Ulsterman, the Marquess of Londonderry together with Starkie's initial contact at John Murray when he first approached the publishing house in 1932: Lord Gorell, and one whom Starkie was to find himself subject to in post-Civil War Spain, the Right Honourable Sir Samuel Hoare, were three of twenty-four Vice-Presidents, eighteen of whom possessed titles of civil distinction (*News Bulletin of the All Peoples' Association*, Number 1, Apr. 1930).　**65** '[Evelyn Wrench] began the manufacture of picture cards within a few months of leaving school. After four years of it, Lord Northcliffe (still Harmsworth then) offered to take the business over and to make its young founder a journalist' (H.F., 'Sir Evelyn Wrench and his work by a friend of thirty years' (*APA News Bulletin*, Jan. 1932, p. 17). Wrench would become Editor of *The Spectator*.　**66** E[velyn]. W[rench]., 'About Ourselves. Why APA was started. By the Editor'. *APA News Bulletin*, April 1930, 3–13, at 13.　**67** Issue number 12 of the *APA News Bulletin* reported that Sir Evelyn Wrench had been received by Mussolini in October 1933 and made reference to a visit to Rugby on 2 June 1933 when Wrench addressed 'a large meeting in the Temple Speech Room on the subject of "Germany and World Peace".' The report stated: 'Sir Evelyn Wrench gave a lucid account of Germany under Herr Hitler, which in its significance and interest was widely appreciated by the audience' ('Italy. APA in Rome', *APA News Bulletin*, 12, p. 60; 'APA in Rugby', *APA News Bulletin*, 12, p. 55).　**68** 'Irish Free State. APA in Dublin (communicated by Mrs. Powell Anderson)', *APA Magazine*, 15 (1934), p. 70. Starkie's lecture 'New adventures of a collector of Gypsy foklore and language' was delivered in May (II, 24 May 1934, p. 12).　**69** 'Irish Free State, APA in Dublin (communicated by Mrs Powell-Anderson)', *APA Magazine*, 16 (1934), p. 55.

As has been seen, Starkie's alignment with the forces of reaction in Spain were made manifest in *Spanish raggle-taggle* and *Don Gypsy*. His last publication with John Murray in the decade of the 30s, *The waveless plain*, reiterated his continuing support for Mussolini's regime, but for some time before the publication Starkie had been liaising with representatives of the regime in both Dublin and London as well as with General Franco's forces in Spain. The most immediate results were a number of newspaper articles in support of Mussolini and Franco's imperial 'adventures'. The material for the articles was derived from first-hand experience of territory colonized by the Italians in East Africa and General Franco's advancing troops in war-torn Spain.

In between *Spanish raggle-taggle* and *Don Gypsy*, some five months before the publication of the latter, Starkie travelled to Abyssinia under the auspices of the Italian government, by then engaged in a warring offensive in the country. On 4 March 1936 a series of propaganda articles began publication in the *Irish Independent*, all of which, with the exception of the first, were headed 'With Dr Starkie in Abyssinia.' The final article would appear on 17 March, St Patrick's Day.[70] In description evocative of peasants in Castile or local people in the Andalusian village of Cadiar, as represented in the travel books on Spain, Dr Starkie depicts the Italian soldiers on board the troop ship 'Sardegna' as '[singing] their way to battle'. Just as the travelling narrator was depicted in the earlier 30s publications, the reporter is again the Pied Piper of Hamelin, his musical talent now lent to playing Italian airs of the 'Great War': 'The Song of the Alpino' and 'The Bridge of Bassano'. But juxtaposed to the relaxed rhythm, reminiscent of the cruise liner,[71] is the exaltation of war pronounced by 'a colonel from Libya,' whom Starkie qualifies as a friend and, further, a poet and friend of Gabriele D'Annunzio:

> War … is the reason for life. It is war that brings man to his full stature. It is in war that all egoism and meanness disappears [*sic*]. It is in war that we meet with the virtues of sacrifice to an ideal. People become sluggish without the spirit of war to quicken their blood […] nothing is finer than those big, modern ships vomiting soldiers on to this African land.

---

70 For full details of each of the articles, see Appendix. According to the author, the articles were republished in the British and American press (W. Starkie to Commendatore G. Crolla, 11 August 1936 (ACS, MCP, Busta 364). Further to Starkie's time in Abyssinia, see Chapter 33 of *The waveless plain*, where material from the *Irish Independent* articles is incorporated.   71 The carefree, carnivalesque atmosphere is further made manifest in a letter to John G. Murray to whom Starkie forwarded from Asmara 'the manuscript of the chapter on Seville' for *Don Gypsy*, claiming to have managed to finish the text over the seven-day sea voyage. (In effect, the material draws on three articles he published in the *Irish Independent* in 1928 on Holy Week in Seville: see 'Holy Week in Seville', 1, 2 and 3, II, 12, 13 and 14 April 1928, p. 6.) Having referred to the '3,500 troops of many kinds from all over Italy [who] spend nearly all their day singing together,' he nonchalantly declares: 'We are like a carnival ship gliding through the Red Sea to the sound of innumerable Italian folk songs. […] The officers are charming and we have the most amusing time' (W. Starkie to J.G. Murray, 27 Jan. 1936 (JMC)).

The reporter will distance himself from the warmongering rhetoric of the colonel but not without some recognition of the latter's distinction: 'My friend the colonel was certainly a personality – a disturbing one to an unwarlike vagabond like myself!'[72]

Starkie's articles are accompanied by photographs. His first carries, among others, one of himself surrounded by soldiers with the caption: 'Dr Starkie with Blackshirt troops at Maidolo, on the Northern Front of Abyssinia.'[73] His fourth also carries photographs of Dr Starkie-the-reporter, textually playing out colonialist travel accounts, as found in Defoe's *Robinson Crusoe* or R.M. Ballantyne's *Coral Island*, where foreign lands are visited by white westerners ready to purchase and/or prose-lytize, the white man being projected as the master race.[74] Thus, Starkie tells of bargaining and eventually paying two thalers for a scimitar, while the spear he is photographed with is a gift from one who seeks surrender, as he explains:

> One of the Gallas attached himself to me. He was a man of about 40, very black-skinned, with hair just beginning to turn grey. A fine, noble figure of a man, with something wistful about his expression. [...] He just stood by me and *gazed* at me. Then he handed me his long, heavy spear, saying 'Zubu,' which means 'Good.'
>
> 'What does he want me to do with the spear?' said I to [our Ascari boy-servant] Tessayam.
>
> 'He wants to give it to you as a gift,' was the reply.
>
> I took the spear and I offered him two thalers in return, but he shook his head.
>
> 'He won't take money from you because he wants you to be his "Guetana".' (a master).
>
> The Galla then came up and spoke excitedly to Tessayam, who said:
>
> 'The Galla wants to become your son.'
>
> 'My son?' said I incredulously.
>
> 'Yes: he says he wants to become your son and go far away with you forever.'
>
> 'But why should he want to go away with me?'
>
> 'Because you are white and have blue eyes. The white man has all the graces of God.'
>
> The Galla then looked at me imploringly in the hope that I would take him under my wing. He pointed to the motor-car lamps which had been turned on saying (as Tessayam told me) that the light was the eye of God.
>
> When he saw me depart, he bowed his head and sat apart from the rest, the picture of unrelieved sorrow.[75]

Prior to publication of the *Irish Independent* articles, Dr Starkie's voice had also been heard over the air in support of the Italian occupation. Having returned from a tour

---

72 W. Starkie, 'An Irishman visits the warfront', II, 4 March 1936, p. 11 (see Appendix).　73 Ibid.　74 On such fictions, see P. Hulme, *Colonial encounters: Europe and the native Caribbean, 1492–1797* (London, 1986), J. Bristow, *Empire boys: adventures in a man's world* (London, 1991) and R. Phillips, *Mapping men and empire. A geography of adventure* (London, 1997).　75 W. Starkie, 'Native Allies of Italy', II, 11 March, p. 11 (see Appendix). The italicization of 'gazed' is mine. The reader will recall Starkie's use of 'gaze' in the report of his interview with Mussolini in 1927.

of the northern front in early February 1936, he broadcast his impressions to Ireland while praising 'the great colonizing work which Italy is doing in this far-off land.'[76] On the journey to the Italian colony, the reporter had travelled in first-class accommodation[77] and on the return journey to Italy, he also voyaged in style, on 'an Italian luxury liner [en route] from Shanghai',[78] the *Victoria*. Back in Dublin in the month of May, Dr Starkie and his wife were fêted by the Italian colony at the lunch held at the Broadway Soda Fountain to celebrate 'Italy's victory in Abyssinia' and at which Dr Walter Starkie made a speech. Both the Italian national anthem and Fascist anthem were played and Romano Lodi Fé, the Italian consul in Dublin, 'paid homage to an Irish author – Dr Walter Starkie', who, the consul claimed, 'ha[d] been the only one to narrate with serenity and objective spirit what he witnessed in East Africa.'[79] Four months on from the publication of the last of Dr Starkie's articles on Italian East Africa in the *Irish Independent*, and in the month following the appearance of *Don Gypsy*, the rising in Spain led by General Francisco Franco took place.

Helen Graham has observed that the military coup of 17–18 July 1936 'aimed to halt the mass political democracy set in train by the effects of the First World War and the Russian Revolution, and accelerated by the ensuing social, economic and cultural changes of the 1920s and 1930s.'[80] With little exception, Starkie's two travel books on Spain of 1934 and 1936 may be assessed as lending support to the halting of 'the mass political democracy' which the Second Spanish Republic had set about achieving from 1931.[81] Undoubtedly, both texts reveal an overall sympathy for the pre-Republican era and it is not surprising, therefore, to find Starkie already expressing support for the rebel general's coup in 1936[82] and coming to pronounce favourably in the press as Franco and his forces gained ground.[83] In the second year of the war, 'Dr Walter Starkie' produced a series of articles for the *Irish Independent*, which appeared over a three-week period between January and February 1938. On occasion, the articles have an air of the travel guide, providing history in a nutshell or informing as to the best local bar or restaurant, thus 'Chicote' in San Sebastián, or 'Paredes' in Oviedo, to name but two of a number (food and drink certainly claim a presence in the articles, as in the

76 'Radiotransmissione all' Irlanda del Prof. Walter Starkie dell' Università di Dublino', dated in Asmara, 9 Feb. 1936 (ACS, MCP, Busta 364).   **77** Ministero della Guerra Comando del Corpo di Stato Maggiore, Ufficio Trasporti, Giulio Perugi, Il Colonello di S.M., Capo Officio to the Ministero della Stampa e della Propaganda, Roma, 13 Jan. 1936 (ACS, Fondo/Serie MCP, Busta 364).   **78** MS of *The waveless plain*, typed pages clipped together, numbered 52 to 59, p. 54 (JMC).   **79** 'Italy's Victory in Abyssinia', EH, 2 May 1936, p. 2.   **80** H. Graham, *The Spanish Civil War. A very short introduction* (Oxford, 2005), p. 1. See also Graham's Chapter 1, 'The challenge of mass political mobilisation (1931– 1936)' in H. Graham, *The Spanish Republic at war* (Cambridge, 2002).   **81** Statements such as the one in the final chapter of *Spanish raggle-taggle* awarding '[c]redit' to the government of the Republic for the 'attempts' being made 'to cope with the problem of education in the backward rural parts of the country' do not invalidate the claim (W. Starkie, *Spanish*, p. 451).   **82** 'The situation in Spain. Dr Starkie on Franco's aim', IT, 23 Oct. 1936, p. 8. See also W. Starkie, 'Spanish Kaleidoscope: a background', *The Fortnightly*, Dec. 1936, 682–8.   **83** 'People 85 P.C. with Franco. Re-visit to Spain,' II, 4 Jan. 1939, p. 10. In the meantime Starkie would also pronounce on latter-day Ireland, seen as a lesser entity than that of the Free State (W. Starkie, 'Ireland today', *Quarterly Review*, 538 (October, 1938), 343–60).

travel writing). Fundamentally, however, they constitute propaganda pieces, speaking out crudely against 'the Reds' and in support of the rebellion.[84]

Starkie travelled into Spain from Lisbon,[85] to the territory occupied by General Franco and his troops in the north-west of the country, spending, according to his account, Christmas 1937 and New Year 1938 on the Madrid front. His return was announced in the *Irish Independent* in an advertisement which explained that 'the brilliant writer and famous traveller', Dr Walter Starkie, would be telling readers of the newspaper about his 'unique experiences' (a variant on adventures) in both Portugal and Spain from the coming week on in a series of '*exclusive* special articles'.[86] Starkie produced sixteen articles on Spain, which were immediately followed by eight on Portugal. The first appeared on 24 January, on page 5. Should the reader of the *Irish Independent* have overlooked it, page 9 carried a reminder, where the author was projected as scholar, fiddler and wanderer ('he wanders over Europe', readers are informed, the reminder reaching a climax by bestowing the title of 'world-wanderer' on Starkie as the column draws to a close), boldly (that is, in bold print) promoting him in discourse that smacks of consumer-culture salesmanship: 'He talks well, he walks better and he writes best of all'.[87]

There is an echo of 'the wanderer' in the opening article but Dr Starkie maintains a more professionally defined identity here, becoming 'the visiting Hispanist', 'an observer' though also, less objectively: 'a fervent devotee of Castile'. Moreover, his fiddle will continue to accompany him, Dr Starkie recalling that the Duke of Alba declared he should become 'a foreign minstrel [*sic*] of General Franco.'[88] The articles are built on a binary opposition of heroes and villains, as is reflected in the first article. General Franco and his men are portrayed as fighting for Old Spain: the 'true Spain,' 'eternal Spain,' 'the bulwark of Christianity,' 'preserver of Western civilization' against 'the Other [new] Spain,' associated with 'outlandish modern theories' and even awarded the status of 'a plague'. Destructive ideas have been imported from abroad, that is, post-revolutionary Russia. Thus, the occasional use of bold print in the article highlights references to the Bolshevization of Spain:

> As far back as 1920 the Russian leaders considered that Spain could be Bolshevised with the same facility as Russia [...] The grand rehearsal of the civil war was the miners' rebellion in the Asturias in 1934. By that time Bolshevik

---

84 In this sense they bear similarities to the writings of other pro-Franco partisans. See J. Keene, *Fighting for Franco. International volunteers in nationalist Spain during the Spanish Civil War, 1936–39* (London, 2001), Chapter 2.   85 Starkie travelled to Lisbon as TCD's representative for the celebration of the fourth centenary of the University of Coimbra in December 1937. Articles on the Portuguese dictator Salazar followed his articles on Spain in the *Irish Independent* (see above, following reference to the articles on Spain).   86 'Just back from Spain', II, 18 Jan. 1938, p. 10 (see Appendix). The italics in the final quote are in the original.   87 'Behind the scenes in war-torn Spain. The old Spain and the new', II, 24 Jan. 1938, p. 9 (see Appendix). Ian Kenneally has referred to the *Irish Independent*'s reputation by 1919 as being 'the most receptive to the desires of the mass market' (I. Kenneally, *The paper wall. Newspapers and propaganda in Ireland, 1919–1921* (Cork, 2008), p. 102).   88 II, 3 Feb. 1938, p. 6; 11 Feb. 1938, p. 6; 31 Jan. 1938, p. 7; 25 Jan. 1938, p. 7; 26 Jan. 1938, p. 6 (see Appendix).

influence was rampant. Even in the years before I had seen communist marriages with hammer and sickle in tiny, primitive towns of Castile.

And the text questions whether 'true Spaniards', that is, the ruling class, could have tolerated such an affront: 'Were the true Spaniards, the inheritors of the Cid, Pizarro and Cortes, to fold their arms and wait timidly for their own annihilation? Were they to give up not only themselves, their families, their ideals, but their country without a struggle? Were they to suffer the same fate as the White Russians in 1918?'[89]

The first article also promotes an idea that echoes what became an outstanding feature of the *Irish Statesman* reviews in the later 1920s in relation to Ireland: the question of unity. It is now reiterated over these *Irish Independent* articles in relation to Spain, a country to be united under Castile. Thus, he/she who hails from the Basque Country, Galicia, Catalonia or Andalusia must be born again in loyalty to the state: 'whether the Spaniard is Basque, Galician, Catalonian [*sic*], or Andalusian, if he is to be true to Spain, he must be born again into the living spirit of Castile.'[90] The eighth article signed by Starkie will assert that the 'desire for unity' is 'a fundamental creed of those with fascist ideas.'[91] The presence of Catholicism is a constant point of reference in the articles, introduced by Dr Starkie himself, who '[insists] on halting'[92] in Avila to invoke the spirits of St Teresa and St John of the Cross, and it is also represented as a unifying component in Spanish culture. Thus, the reference to blessed virgins identified with different parts of the country: Our Lady of Pilar in Saragossa, of Covadonga in the highlands of Asturias and of Andujar in Andalusia; to St James the Apostle, Santiago, in Galicia, and to the Irish College in Salamanca. Neither will the reader of the *Irish Independent* be spared images of the destruction wreaked 'by the Reds'[93] on a religious painting and statue.

The articles are also used as a vehicle for clarifying particular aspects and ideas with regard to General Franco and those who are fighting with him. The difference between the Carlist 'Requetés' and fascistic 'Phalangists'[94] are minimized, coupled with the assurance that the General has been capable of harmonizing the discordant elements. Fascism is explained as a fundamentally Italian movement and there is an insistence on Spain finding her own way, based on her traditions, not merely reproducing Italian fascism. Regarding the destruction of Guernica [*sic*], the bombing is justified 'because it was a nodal point in the Red defence.' Furthermore, the article in which Gernika is referred to, the sixteenth, is accompanied by a 'Plan prepared on the instruction of General Franco for the building of the new Guernica'.[95] An article is also devoted to the 'Moors' who were fighting alongside General Franco and his troops. Apart from highlighting questions of cultural difference in their diet, the article underlines the satisfactory colonial relationship established between the General and his officers in relation to the Moroccan mercenaries. Dr Starkie explains:

---

89 II, 24 Jan. 1938, p. 5 (see Appendix). 90 Ibid. See Zuloaga's similar comment in W. Starkie, *Spanish*, p. 97. 91 II, 1 Feb. 1938, p. 12 (see Appendix). 92 II, 25 Jan. 1938, p. 7 (see Appendix). 93 II, 29 Jan. 1938, p. 7 (see Appendix). 94 II, 31 Jan. 1938, p. 7 (see Appendix). 95 II, 12 Feb. 1938, p. 7 (see Appendix).

Some of the older, bearded Moors in their hooded cloaks resembled Abraham in Majesty. Their loyalty to their Spanish officers is a thing of wonder. Some of the latter told me that the Moors shield their officers with their bodies, and throw themselves in the way of bullets and bayonets to save them. They have an extraordinary devotion to General Franco. He is for them the Great White Chief.[96]

Finally, the tenth and eleventh articles are devoted to General Franco and his cause. Dr Starkie claims that his heart 'warms' towards General Franco 'because he is a *Gallego* [Galician] from the north-west corner of Spain where the inhabitants … call us Irishmen Hermanos Celtas (Brother Celts)'. The articles provide a history of the General's career, projecting him as a 'leader of men,' the incarnation of 'aspirations of a whole nation struggling to raise itself up', a man with 'a cold, methodic forcefulness of character' with 'no traces … of the impetuousness we note in some other dictators' and of 'exceptional courage'.[98] His ideal is 'Christian family life'.[99]

Before turning to the eight articles on Portugal, it is worth paying attention to a photograph that appeared in the *Irish Independent* early on in January 1938, before any of the Spanish articles appeared, with the caption 'Journalists in the Danger Zone'. Dr Starkie is the 'journalist' on the right of the photograph, complete with trilby to protect the chronic asthma sufferer against the minus 18 temperature. Those posing next to him are identified in their capacity as War Correspondents for the *Daily Telegraph* and *Morning Post*, Karl Robson, on the left, and for *The Times*, H.A.R. [Kim] Philby, in the centre, bandaged following an accident in which three other journalists were killed.[1] Philby, recruited by the Russians in the 1930s, 'toadying to the fascists'[2] in Civil War Spain, would eventually defect, fleeing to Moscow some twenty-five years on, in January 1963.[3] The question of exactly what role, or roles, 'Dr Walter Starkie, Dublin' (not identified as a war correspondent like his companions in the photograph) was playing at this juncture is, again, intriguing.[4]

---

96 II, 26 Jan. 1938, p. 6 (see Appendix).   98 II, 3 Feb. 1938, p. 6 (see Appendix). I understand the allusion to impetuousness in certain other dictators to allude to Hitler.   99 II, 4 Feb. 1938, p. 6 (see Appendix).   1 The photograph also appears in Starkie's fourth article (II, 27 Jan. 1938, p. 6 (see Appendix) and he will mention Philby's recommending a restaurant in Salamanca ('El Gorujo') in the eighth article (II, 1 Feb. 1938, p. 12 (see Appendix). For reference to the journalists who lost their lives, Edward Neil, Richard Sheepshanks and Bradish Johnson, see K. Robson, 'With Franco in Spain' in W. Hindle (ed.), *Foreign correspondent. Personal adventures abroad in search of the news* (London, 1939), pp 253–69).   2 N. Rankin, *Telegram from Guernica* (London, 2003), p. 147.   3 P. Seale and M. McConville, *Philby. The long road to Moscow* (London, 1978).   4 Jimmy Burns, son of Tom Burns, Press Attaché during the Second World War at the British Embassy in Madrid, has no doubt, at least in relation to the period of the Second World War: 'Starkie was a British agent, his *eccentric public persona* belying a background of discreet service to His Majesty's Government as an Anglo-Irishman who strongly identified with the Allied cause and equally strongly opposed his native Ireland's neutrality in the war on the grounds that he considered it part of the British Empire' (J. Burns, *Papa spy*, p. 252. My italics). See also P. Day, *Franco's friends. How British intelligence helped bring Franco to power in Spain* (London, 2011), pp 174–5. Apart from touring the war zone with a view to producing pro-Franco articles in the press, Starkie may have been sent to observe Philby, who continued to work for British Intelligence following Starkie's taking up his post in Madrid as British Council Representative (P. Preston, *Franco. A biography* (London, 1991), p. 461).

17 W.F. Starkie
(right) with Karl
Robson (left) and
Kim Philby (centre),
on the Ebro front,
Spain, 31 Dec. 1937.

In the articles on Portugal, the importance awarded Christian civilization by Francisco Franco is seen to be shared by Antonio de Oliveiro Salazar, the Portuguese President, who also held a conviction with regard to the need for a dictatorial regime as a means of generating national order. Dr Starkie explains that he is back in Portugal after a period of twelve years,[5] having previously visited the country as 'a student of antiquity' or as 'a vagabond in search of the folk'. Now he styles himself 'the traveller' and reports that he arrived 'early one December morning at the mouth of the Tagus', though he does declare possessing a particular focus on the *Estado Novo*: 'On this occasion my thoughts concentrated on the New Portugal which has arisen, full of hope, under the guidance of Europe's most modest dictator.'[6] His concentrated thoughts lead to his remarking that he has been 'greatly struck' by 'the amount of foreign propaganda in Portugal,' arguing that now that the country 'has raised herself up, [she] is being courted by different nations'.[7] Herein may lie an explanation for Dr Starkie's presence in Portugal: to obtain information on the 'courting' of the country, by whom [for whom?], how it was proceeding and to what end.

In Lisbon, Dr Starkie focuses on predictable aspects of Portugal and her culture: the climate, the melancholy expressed through *saudade*, her lyric poetry and the *fado*, but also turns his attention to 'the stately Avenida and streets constructed under the new progressive regime',[8] dwelling on the cosmopolitan atmosphere in the city's cafés and theatres. One reason for being in Portugal at the time becomes clear in the second article, that is, the celebration in Coimbra of the university's fourth centenary.[9] Starkie was a delegate at the celebration, which afforded him the opportunity of paying his respects to Archbishop and Cardinal Dr Cerejeira and of sharing banter with the

---

5 I have found no record of time spent by Starkie in Portugal in 1926. 6 II, 16 Feb. 1938, p. 7 (see Appendix). 7 II, 17 Feb. 1938, p. 5 (see Appendix). 8 II, 16 Feb. 1938, p. 7 (see Appendix). 9 See: 'Famous Portuguese University Celebration of Fourth Centenary' (GH, 7 Dec. 1937, p. 11). The article mentions that there were delegates from fourteen countries present.

fascist historian Volpe, though also the occasion to ponder Italy's current relationship with Portugal:

> My neighbour at table was the famous Gioacchino Volpe, the Italian historian. We had an animated conversation on European affairs. He tried to pull my leg about Ireland and England, while I tried to pull his about the Mediterranean. Conversation with him, however, was a reminder that Italy today feels herself closely linked to countries such as Portugal, which have followed with their own individual variations her great idea of the Corporative State.

In a manner familiar from the travel books, another of Dr Starkie's 'interlocutors' (unnamed) is quoted, expressing the hope that General Franco will win the war being waged in neighbouring Spain for the sake of Christianity and empire: '[W]e hope and pray that Franco will win this war, for if he does, we shall save Christian civilization, not only in the Iberian peninsula , but also through the great Iberian world – that is to say, Brazil and the South American States'.[10]

The five articles which follow are devoted to the figure of Salazar, styled a 'dictator in spite of himself',[11] to explaining the principles of the Corporative State,[12] to rejecting communism on the grounds that it is incompatible with freedom[13] and to reflecting on the relevance of fascism to Salazar's regime.[14] The 'wanderer' returns in the final article to take us 'From the Tagus to the Douro',[15] an article that reads like the narrative of a tourist brochure, with a final focus on the port wine trade, the visitor being treated to lunch and dinner at the Factory House of Guimaraens, Fonseca and Monteiro.

It is worth observing that in the articles devoted to Spain as well as in those dealing with Portugal, the texts also carry elements of relevance to the question of latter-day Irish identity. Thus, among the articles on Spain, there are stories involving two Irish citizens in the Basque Country. One tells of a Miss Boland, attempting to protect a Spanish aristocrat and his two sons by hiding them in her flat. Dr Starkie nostalgically tells *Irish Independent* readers: 'She felt quite safe because she had an Irish Free State passport'. Predictably, Miss Boland is no Fianna Fáil supporter. The following sentence declares: 'In addition, she hoisted the Union Jack'. However, neither passport nor flag were able to save her from being shot by 'a Red militia man'. In the same article, Dr Starkie refers to 'an Irish friend [again, unnamed] … who had lived through the whole period of the war' and been resident in Bilbao for twenty-nine years. He speaks out in favour of a centralized Spain, a claim that could be extrapolated to the unity of the British Empire: 'as a good Irishman he agreed with encouraging [the

---

10 II, 17 Feb. 1938, p. 5 (see Appendix).   11 II, 19 Feb. 1938, p. 7 (see Appendix). The article carries the heading 'A dictator in spite of himself', a claim which is included in the article in the following sentence: 'He is dictator in spite of himself – that is to say, dictator owing to his deep sense of national duty' – where the indefinite article does not appear. The error may simply have been a misprint but in a number of the later articles (numbers 5, 7 and 8), the use of English in terms of expression and/or syntax is incorrect. Italia may have had a hand here too.   12 II, 22 Feb. 1938, p. 8 (see Appendix).   13 II, 23 Feb. 1938, p. 6 (see Appendix).   14 II, 24 Feb. 1938, p. 9 (see Appendix).   15 II, 25 Feb 1938,

Basques'] local customs. "But," he added, "encourage their local autonomy; give them back their "Fueros" or charters, but do not let them sacrifice the unity of Spain'",[16] a plea which is immediately followed up in the article by reference to the Basque writers Unamuno, Baroja and the painter Zuloaga who, we are told in an echo of *Spanish raggle-taggle*,[17] think and write in Spanish. Within the articles devoted to Portugal, there are a number of references to England's relationship with Portugal, her oldest ally. The point being conveyed is how fruitful long-standing relationships with England may be, the inference being that Ireland might take note; as she also might in the article devoted to the University of Coimbra's fourth centenary celebrations where, Dr Starkie observes, he was the only Irish delegate.

The articles I have been referring to were published early on in 1938. Towards the end of the year, following the Munich Pact of September, citizen of the commonwealth Walter Starkie wrote to the Editor of the *Times*. The correspondent hailed the British Prime Minister Neville Chamberlain as 'Paladin of Peace',[18] further substantiating Starkie's alignment with the appeasers. His wife shared his enthusiasm and support for Chamberlain's action. In a letter to John G. Murray, written on the day the sixty-nine-year-old statesman left London to see Hitler at Berchtesgaden,[19] Italia qualified the visit as 'a beautiful gesture'[20] on the part of the PM and conveyed to her sister-in-law what she interpreted as inspiration for her son, found in the reference to his childhood: 'those beautiful words of Chamberlain: "When I was a small boy of twelve[,] I used to repeat to myself when in difficulty[,] I must try, and try and try again".' She further expressed admiration for such determination, qualifying it as heroic, and expressing her satisfaction that Landi shared Chamberlain's nationality: 'I think those words tell us all the greatness and simplicity of an hero. I felt so happy that my son is[,] like him[,] a British subject.'[21] Italia might also have felt happy that Landi was not an Italian subject and, therefore, at least for the time being, she was spared her sister's anxiety. She saw Eva briefly in Ventimille in late September, before returning to Dublin from London, describing her to Enid as 'very afflicted at the thought of her elder son being called up at any moment by Mussolini.'[22] Yet, and paradoxically, in the year that her husband finally published *The waveless plain* and she was able to register relief in July over 'the very good reviews ... just lately',[23] Italia might also have been drawing away from the Italian regime given the anti-Semitic turn that had been taken. She certainly didn't mince her words in this connection when writing to Enid early in 1938: 'The Anti-Jews policy followed in Italy now is desgusting [*sic*] and I gather Toscanini will eventually refuse to conduct in Italy.'[24] However, in November 1939, in correspondence with Enid, Nancy spoke of her brother and sister-in-law's German sympathies, though she did qualify her statement: 'Walter and Italia are *of course* very

p. 13 (see Appendix). **16** II, 10 Feb. 1938, p. 6 (see Appendix). **17** W. Starkie, *Spanish*, pp 97, 184–6. **18** W. Starkie to the Editor of *The Times*, 3 Dec. 1938, p. 13. **19** I. Kershaw, *Hitler*, p. 434. **20** I. Starkie (née Porchietti) to J.G. Murray, 15 Sept. 1938 (JMC). **21** I. Starkie (née Porchietti) to E. Starkie, 2 Oct. [1938] (ES Bodl.). **22** Ibid. Eva's son, Orazio Bonetti, was killed on 7 August 1943. **23** I. Starkie (née Porchietti) to E. Starkie, 7 July 1938 (ES Bodl.). For an instance of 'the very good reviews', see 'Dr Walter Starkie on Italy and its people. A brilliant autobiography', II, 28 June 1938, p. 4. **24** I. Starkie (née Porchietti) to E. Starkie, 31 [Mar. 1938] (ES Bodl.).

pro–German – perhaps I am wrong in saying that – but anyway they are anti-English.'[25] Over a month earlier, she had reported that her brother looked 'blooming', adding: '*Of course* he really has great belief in Hitler and Mussolini, and none in the others' while she also expressed the opinion that Italia was 'rather anti-British … though, *of course*[,] she rigorously denies it[.] Even so one can *easily* see her feelings.'[26] In the light of her brother's inclination towards masquerade, it might be argued that Nancy was perhaps being presumptuous. With regard to Italia, following the anti-Semitic legislation passed in Italy on 14 July 1938,[27] and given the disgust she had plainly expressed to Enid in relation to such discrimination earlier in the same year, her allegiance to the Italian Fascist regime may well have shifted so that when she 'rigorously denie[d]' being anti-British in 1939, her disavowal was sincere.[28] On the other hand, Italia was not, or had not been, the only Mussolini supporter among the women in the Starkie family: Walter's mother appears to have been so too. When Nancy wrote to Enid in November 1939 to impress upon her sister that she should stay with her over Christmas and not with Italia where, according to Nancy, Enid 'would be too martialled',[29] she spoke of her own agreement with her mother's sister, Aunt Ida, that Mussolini had been the first to introduce force into Europe since 1919, explaining her mother's annoyance at such an interpretation as a consequence of being 'educated in the "Totalitarian Starkie [S]chool"',[30] undoubtedly an allusion to WJM's despotic rigour.

Walter Starkie addressed John G. Murray from Salamanca in December 1937 on his intentions regarding *The waveless plain*, projecting himself as embarked on an impassioned 'crusade' to reconcile two countries: 'My whole idea is to try and bring England and Italy together and to show that my life in Italy and love for Italy is linked up with the fundamental traditions of the country. I believe passionately in the crusade for bringing England and Italy together in friendship and harmony'.[31] Starkie's sub-titled *Italian autobiography* was a text with a history going back to at least 1935. Writing to his publisher in October of that year, he referred to 'the letters' he had previously sent to Murray together with some 'Italian letters', that Starkie requested should be treated as 'confidential'. The letters may have carried information regarding opportunities afforded journalists by the Italians, as commented on by R.J.B. Bosworth: 'In general, the approach of the Ethiopian war and its prosecution ended the love affair between foreign journalists and Mussolini […] To improve their deteriorating image, the Italians

---

25 N. Cooper (née Starkie) to E. Starkie, 27 Nov. 1939 (ES Bodl.). My italics.   **26** N. Cooper (née Starkie) to E. Starkie, 7 Oct. 1939 (ES Bodl.). My italics.   **27** R. Lamb, *Mussolini and the British* (London, 1997), p. 218.   **28** As the Second World War progressed, she may well have become more pro-British: 'in the years 1941 and 1942, when the annihilation of the Jews was no longer terrible rhetoric [on the part of Hitler], but terrible reality' (I. Kershaw, *Hitler*, p. 469).   **29** Nancy's insistence suggests that she too could martial. Following her sister Enid's death in 1970, her brother Walter was impressed by the 'commanding personality' she brought to bear in organizing the funeral arrangements, leading him to a comparison with the siblings' father (W. Starkie to J.G. Murray, 4 Jan. 1971, JMC).   **30** N. Cooper (née Starkie) to E. Starkie, 27 Nov. 1939 (ES Bodl.).   **31** W. Starkie to J.G. Murray, 20 Dec. 1937 (JMC). Further to Starkie's 'crusade', see his address to the Newman Society: 'Italian memories' (CH, 'Italy's part. An address to the Newman Society', 22 Oct. 1937, p. 14).

funded friendly journalists. In London, [Count Dino] Grandi had *carte blanche* to pay for sympathetic explanations of Italy's imperial thrust into Ethiopia'.[32] In his letter to Murray, Starkie went on to refer to correspondence he had addressed 'to Rome' while insisting on his desire, and right, to remain an independent commentator:

> I am determined to renounce the Italian offer of support so that I may be absolutely free. I stated in my letter to Rome that I was not Fascist and that I wanted to write only what I actually saw. In any case[,] I should have published the book whatever the Italian government said. Surely as a wanderer I am allowed to treat the subject as I did Spain and Hungary. I really want to do a book on Italy and I think now is the time for many reasons.[33]

Starkie's claim that as 'a wanderer' he should be able to deal with Italy as he had in the case of his raggle-taggle books and *Don Gypsy* is striking in its naïvety in the light of those earlier texts in which 'the wanderer' was not above pointed political comment. Or did he make such a point because the pointed political comment was not the wanderer's own conviction, he saw himself to be merely the messenger?

Once in Genoa, following his tramp in Sardinia in the summer of 1936, Starkie replied to a letter from Commendatore Guido Crolla at the Italian Embassy in London, which had been waiting for him, Starkie asserted, on his return from France. First of all, the correspondent expressed his surprise that he had received no acknowledgment of the articles on Abyssinia he had published in the *Irish Independent* and which, he informed Crolla, 'External [*sic*] Affairs in the Irish Free State' had assured him 'were responsible for changing the attitude of the Irish people towards the conflict and for disposing them towards Italy.' He then explained to Crolla what, he declared, he had already told the Italian Consul General in Dublin, that is, that he would need to modify 'the plan of the book' as a result of 'the amazing Italian victory and the early termination of the campaign'. He subsequently turned to arguing his case, initially bringing to bear the impact of events in Abyssinia:

> I want my book to include the whole development of the New Italy[,] from the War to the Empire. It is impossible for me to produce a book of such weight in a few months. It was understood originally that I should give the manuscript to you at the end of April for perusal, but this was impossible owing to the precipitation of events culminating in the Italian victory.

His next tactic was to substantiate his argument for delaying the book by bringing in the House of Murray: 'As a matter of fact I have already done most of the part of the book which deals with Abyssinia but my publishers think I should widen the scope … so as to bring in the countless other events which have gone to create [*sic*] the New Fascist Italy',[34] adding that he had told his publishers to write to Crolla. Marginal

---

32 R.J.B. Bosworth, *Mussolini* (London, 2002), pp 303, 304. Grandi was Italian Ambassador in London from 1932 until 1939. 33 W. Starkie to J. Murray, 18 Oct. 1935 (JMC). 34 W. Starkie to

handwritten comment on Starkie's letter in the Italian State Archive expresses impatience and scepticism in relation to the correspondent and his argument with reference to his publishers: Crolla, or someone else, wrote in the left-hand margin of the sheet where the publishers are mentioned: 'Cretino! Va a dire all'editore che il nostro Ministero se interessa al suo libro'.[35] Later in his letter to Crolla, Starkie had returned to his astonishment at not having received any acknowledgment from the Italian Ministry regarding his articles in the Irish press, claiming that the position he had placed himself in was far from easy: 'As a matter of fact I had to submit to a great deal of abuse and criticism from the sanctionists and on several occasions I even received threatening letters because I had stood out for Italy.' Italian marginal comment at this juncture was cynically dismissive: 'Tutti eroi; e vogliono premi e riconoscimento!'[36]

The purpose of Starkie's letter was delay tactics. With Anthony Eden occupying the post of British Minister for Foreign Affairs and given his hostile attitude towards Mussolini,[37] the time was far from right for Starkie to publish his book. Thus, John G. Murray followed Starkie's letter up with one from himself, representing 'the publishers'[38] and addressed to the Commendatore, in which he further substantiated the delay tactics. He referred to the recent publication of *Don Gypsy*, arguing that for the sake of Starkie's literary reputation his books should not be published 'at too short intervals'. He also claimed that it was 'unwise to hurry [Dr Starkie] over his books' since they were 'always the outcome of wide experience and much knowledge.'[39] Murray added that the publishers were hoping to have the text out for January or February 1937. However, with the same Minister for Foreign Affairs occupying the post, the time remained unripe. It was not until Viscount Halifax took over, following Eden's resignation on 20 February 1938[40] that publication became a possibility. In the meantime, Murray brought out a conciliatory edition of Starkie's 1920s publication on Pirandello.[41] *The waveless plain* finally appeared on 1 June, subsequently celebrated with a party at Albemarle Street on Bloomsday. Thus, advantage of improved relations was briskly taken, in the wake of the Easter Agreement between Italy and Great Britain, signed in Rome on 14 April 1938.[42]

In July 1938, Walter and Italia Starkie were staying with the Harmsworths, enjoying London prior to a busy month in Dublin. Italia described her husband as allowing himself some respite from what she summed up as 'his monotonous and laborious

Commendatore G. Crolla, 11 Aug. 1936 (ACS, MCP, Busta 364). **35** 'Cretin! So he's going to tell his publishers that our Ministry is interested in his book.' My translation. **36** W. Starkie to Commendatore G. Crolla, 11 Aug. 1936 (ACS, MCP Busta 364). 'They all think themselves heroes; and they want prizes and recognition.' My translation. **37** According to Bosworth, Eden regarded Mussolini as 'a complete gangster' and 'the Anti-Christ' (R.J.B. Bosworth, *Mussolini*, p. 303). **38** J.G. Murray wrote on John Murray headed paper, which carried the names of 'the publishers': Sir John Murray, K.C.V.O, D.S.O.; Lord Gorell, C.B.E., M.C.; T.R. Grey and himself, John Grey Murray. **39** J.G. Murray to Commendatore G. Crolla, 11 Aug. 1936 (ACS, MCP, Busta 364). **40** R. Lamb, *Mussolini*, p. 203. **41** A sheet headed 'Professor Starkie's rights', handwritten and dated 30 September 1954, indicates that the terms for *Pirandello* (1937) were 'exceptional'. (JMC) **42** R. Lamb, *Mussolini*, pp 209–10.

life'. The assessment may suggest something of the quality of her own, as companion to monotony and intense labour. Were this the case, it would certainly fall short of satisfying. Following the break in London enjoying the Harmsworths' 'charming hospitality',[43] Starkie was involved with the Abbey Theatre Festival in August. He delivered a paper on Sean O'Casey[44] and took some responsibility for delegates, accompanying them on a visit to the Book of Kells during their stay.[45] In September he was off to Santo Domingo de Silos to work on his next publication, the Cisneros biography, and he would move between Dublin and London over November and December, lecturing at the Book Fair in London on 15 November and travelling back again in December to deliver a number of lectures.[46] He had broadcast on RÉ with a distinct religious emphasis in the month of August: on 'The Assumption in Art and Music' and he would again in December: on 'Christmas and the Arts'.[47] His voice was also heard over the BBC: on 1 April he broadcast to schools on 'Gypsying in Barbary', on 28 June his engagement was entitled 'Raggle-taggle' and towards the end of the year a discussion between Starkie and Alan MacKinnon was heard over the regional service.[48]

The tempo was intense. Starkie's course over the 1920s had hardly been quiet but the following decade was extraordinarily charged given the ever-increasing pace of publication, lecturing, some broadcasting and much travel. Apart from the crossings to England and the sojourns in Italy and Spain, in 1935 he was planning to travel to Tunis and Tripoli as well as Italy, where he would be lecturing in Rome, with further sessions programmed for Belgrade, Zagreb, Mostar and Sarajevo.[49] In 1936, between November and December, he delivered the Lord Northcliffe Lectures in Literature at University College London. The lectures touched on what, by this time, were predictable Starkie subjects: wandering, the minstrel, actor, picaroon, adventures and gypsies.[50] By this stage in the year, he had spent time in Abyssinia and Italy, been back in Budapest and visited the Greek island of Rhodes.[51] In March 1937, he was in

43 I. Starkie (née Porchietti) to D. Harmsworth and family, 10 July [1938] (Daniel Harmsworth). **44** The Festival took place over the fortnight of the 6 to 20 August 1938. Starkie's paper was published together with other contributions in L. Robinson (ed.), *The Irish theatre. Lectures delivered during the Abbey Theatre festival held in Dublin in August 1938* (London, 1939), pp 149–76. **45** 'Great honour for visitors. The Book of Kells', II, 11 August 1938, p. 11. **46** W. Starkie to J.G. Murray, 22 Nov. 1938 (JMC). **47** 'Talk by Dr Starkie', II, 17 Aug. 1938, p. 3; 'Church festivals and the Arts. Dr Starkie's views', II, 24 Dec. 1938, p. 8. **48** W. Starkie to E. Starkie, 18 June 1938 (ES Bodl.); W. Starkie to J. Murray, 23 June 1938 (JMC). Director of Schools Broadcasts to W. Starkie, 25 Oct. 1937 and F.N. Lloyd Williams to W. Starkie, 13 Apr. 1938; BBC International Circulating Memo. From F + D Ex. to Talks Booking, Subject: 'Raggle-taggle': Tuesday, 28 June 1938, 8:00 – 8:30p.m. Reg. Dated: 2 June 1938; W. Starkie to The Editor, *The Listener*, 9 Dec. 1938 (BBC Written Archives Centre. Professor W. Starkie, RCONT 1 Talks File 1, 1932–62). An account of the discussion between Starkie and MacKinnon, 'Do we get too much fresh air?' was published in *The Listener*, 15 Dec. 1938, pp 1299–300. **49** W. Starkie to J.G. Murray, 18 Oct. 1935 (JMC). One other destination is mentioned following Sarajevo but is illegible. **50** Like others who delivered the Northcliffe lectures, Starkie delivered six in all, which were open to the public: (1) 9 Nov. – Wandering minstrel; (2) 16 Nov. – Wandering actor; (3) 23 Nov. – The novel of the picaroon; (4) 1 Dec. – Cervantes, ex-serviceman, and Don Quixote, the wandering knight; (5) 7 Dec. – Adventures of the eighteenth century; (6) 14 Dec. – Gypsies in literature and music. The Chair at the first lecture was taken by Cecil Harmsworth. **51** An account of a visit by Starkie to Rhodes in 1936 is recorded in manuscript of what became *The waveless plain* (JMC). The account, which

Northern Ireland, addressing the Belfast Natural History and Philosophical Society,[52] in Rome in September,[53] Portugal and Spain in December. In 1938 and 1939 around Eastertime, he travelled on cruises: to mainland Greece and the island of Crete in 38; to Greece and Turkey in 39, passing through France on both occasions.[54] As the decade drew to a close, no let-up in his labours was in view: the Cisneros biography and *Don Quixote* translation were pending and the travel writer had plans for a further Gypsy book,[55] following a stint in Provence in late May at the Gypsy gathering of Saintes-Maries-de-la-Mer.[56] Come November 1939, he was able to tell John G. Murray that he had completed his book on Cisneros for Hodder and Stoughton[57] and Italia wrote in December, explaining that her husband was finishing his translation of *Don Quixote* for Macmillan.[58] The Gypsy book was postponed. Since the conversation with Murray in November 1938 and the drawing up of a contract in 1939,[59] Europe had become engaged in another major conflict.

January 1939 was marked by the death of Yeats. Starkie produced an obituary article for the *Irish Independent*[60] but his energies were to be less taken up by the press over the year ahead. Writing to Enid in March, he explained that it had been 'a terrible term for work'.[61] Apart from his task at Trinity, he had been lecturing in England, from Cheltenham to Harrogate, but on 17 March he left for Greece, returning to England via Paris. On 1 April 1939, General Franco's troops made their triumphant entry into Madrid but any satisfaction Starkie might have felt appears to have dissolved by early August when he wrote to Murray in a 'very depressed' state, attributed by him to 'IRA bombs, Hitler, Ciano, [Serrano] Suñer, *et compagnie*'.[62] Nonetheless, a month after war had been declared, Nancy saw him to be 'blooming'.[63] Certainly, when he wrote to

was discarded (a note in the margin indicates 'Not used'), appeared towards the end of what was published as Chapter 33, the final chapter in *The waveless plain*, following the penultimate paragraph of the published text. The text was devoted to promoting Italian achievement on the island since 1925. **52** 'The tragic war in Spain. Dr Starkie's views', II, 10 Mar. 1937, p. 6. **53** 'Epilogue' (W. Starkie, *Waveless*, p. 498). **54** W. Starkie to E. Starkie, 5 May 1938; W. Starkie to E. Starkie, 10 Mar. 1939 (ES Bodl.). David Gordon recalls Starkie telling him that he had '[run] into Dr Goebbels in March 1939 on the isle of Rhodes.' (D. Gordon, 'Walter Starkie and the greatest novel of all', *First Principles* (4 Oct. 2008). http://www.firstprinciplesjournal.com/print.aspx?article–579&loc–b&type–cbtp, accessed 26 May 2012. In interview, Gordon recalled Starkie claiming to have met Goebbels on Rhodes in 1938 (author's interview with D. Gordon, Los Angeles, 6 Dec. 2005). However, in e-mail correspondence in 2005, Gordon mentioned 1939, as in the piece published in *First Principles*. **55** Starkie had talked to John G. Murray about the future book in November, when he was over in London for the Book Fair (W. Starkie to J.G. Murray, 22 Nov. 1938 (JMC)). *In Sara's tents* was eventually published in 1953, as his post with the British Council in Spain was drawing to a close. **56** Starkie had been commissioned by the National Broadcasting Corporation of America to cover the event in 1938 (W. Starkie to E. Starkie, 20 May 1938 (ES Bodl.). **57** W. Starkie to J.G. Murray, 10 Nov. 1939 (JMC). **58** I. Starkie (née Porchietti) to J.G. Murray, 11 Dec. 1939 (JMC). Macmillan didn't bring out *Don Quixote of La Mancha* until 1954: 'Dr Starkie's New Version of a Classic', II, 8 May 1954, p. 8. **59** '1953 – *In Sara's Tents* – contract … made in 1939' (Sheet headed 'Professor Starkie's rights', handwritten and dated 30 Sept. 1939, JMC). **60** W. Starkie, 'An Appreciation', II, 30 Jan. 1939, p. 9. **61** W. Starkie to E. Starkie, 10 Mar. 1939 (ES Bodl.). **62** W. Starkie to J. Murray, 11 Aug. 1939 (JMC). It will be noticed that neither Mussolini nor Franco are mentioned following Hitler but their foreign ministers, both of whom were rabidly pro-German. However, Starkie's addition of '*et compagnie*' might be understood to include them. **63** N. Cooper (née Starkie) to E. Starkie, 7 Oct. 1939 (ES Bodl.).

18 W.F. Starkie (forefront, seated) with Diana Murray (née James)
(on his left), on land during a cruise in the Aegean, April 1938.

John Murray in September, telling him that he would be crossing the Irish Sea on the
20th with his daughter Alma (en route for Roedean) and intended to call into 50
Albemarle Street on the following day, his tone was light-hearted, in spite of the state
of war: 'I have not yet got a gas mask, and I know nothing about decontamination! Will
you please help me Sir Air Warden? Let me at any rate take refuge in your anti-gas
cellar – that is to say if you don't suspect me as a neutral.'[64] In spite of the manifest
playfulness of the text, it might be argued that it conveys a loss of bearings. Whether
or not this was the case, Starkie's activities over the last quarter of the year certainly
reveal distinct directions, his allegiance apparently not being fixed as the war began
with regard to the contending parties.

Between November and December 1939, following a speech delivered by Starkie on
Armistice night at the Dublin Technical Schools, there was an exchange of letters with
the Irish correspondent of the *Sunday Times*, Frank MacDermot. Starkie spoke in the
context of 'a public discussion … on the subject of the organization of Europe after
the war', MacDermot having put forward a motion on 'The United States of Europe',
which the former had seconded. In his Irish Letter, the anti-neutrality correspondent
cited Starkie as an instance of the existence in Éire even in pro-British circles, of a
good deal of the 'muddle-headed type of pacifism which has had such a vogue of
recent years in democratic countries.' MacDermot then went on to explain that with

64 W. Starkie to J. Murray, 11 Sept. 1939 (JMC).

reference to the First World War, the Professor had been critical of British and French (Foreign) Ministers, labelling them as 'bellicose old men heartlessly despatching youngsters to their doom' while also '[deploring] the behaviour of the American Government and Congress in lifting the embargo on the export of war materials'. MacDermott observed that Starkie's speech had been the 'most applauded ... of the evening' though he indicated that the audience were not discerning, having failed to perceive a lack of consistency between the 'sentiments' expressed by the speaker and his 'laudation of Italy and Fascism', identified by the correspondent as an 'essentially militarist philosophy and educational practice'.[65] According to Nancy, her brother responded to MacDermot's account of his speech by falling into a rage and taking a taxi to MacDermot's home, 'where he told the correspondent he was dishonest and dishonourable'.[66] MacDermott responded in writing to Starkie, objecting to the terms in which he had been assessed and pointing out that 'if [Starkie] made political speeches, he must not be so thin-skinned'.[67] Starkie then proceeded to write a letter of protest to the *Sunday Times* (vetted by a solicitor on Nancy's insistence, it having fallen to her to type the letter out), in which he argued misrepresentation of his speech while pointing out that he had been critical of 'the statesmen of all countries without distinction.' He also denied expressing regret over the American Government's lifting the embargo on the export of war materials, providing an account of his words in indirect speech. Finally, he rejected the praise of fascism in the terms referred to by MacDermot, claiming that he had 'paid tribute to the Italian Government's persistent attempts to save the peace of Europe' over 1938 as well as on the eve of the war. Starkie ended his letter by quoting from himself in the 'Epilogue' to *The waveless plain* where, he stated, he had expressed his own attitude towards Europe,[68] a text which preached reconciliation, is replete with idealism and, it might be said, not without a degree of muddle-headedness (as well as dead metaphor and triteness):

> The Romans of today must weave their great and ancient civilization into the general European pattern. They must bestow their qualities on the neighbouring

---

65 Our Irish Correspondent [Frank MacDermot], 'Irish pacifists', ST, 19 Nov. 1939, p. 8.   66 N. Cooper (née Starkie) to E. Starkie, 27 Nov. 1939 (ES Bodl.).   67 Ibid. Starkie provides his own account in a letter to his publisher: 'As soon as I saw the paper [ST, 19 Nov. 1939] I took a taxi to [Frank MacDermot's] house and demanded to see him. I asked him whether he was the Irish correspondent. When he answered in the affirmative, I said to him: "You are better dishonest and dishonourable. You have knifed me in the back." With that I walked out, wishing in my heart that we were back in the good old 18 [*sic*] century when such affairs are [*sic*] settled with revolver or Toledo rapier' (W. Starkie to J.G. Murray, 28 Nov. 1939 (JMC)).   68 With, perhaps, some input from his wife. In correspondence with Enid in early 1939, Italia prescribed, putting forward ideas with a view to solving the ills which beset Europe: 'to understand those that are different from us ... is conquest or failure in life ... and on [*sic*] a wider sense, to make friend [*sic*] with the unfriendly and furthermore, to make a friend of your enemy is the achievement of few and should be the object of educated men. How fruitful life should be and how less anxious today we should be if this fact could come to realisation. I don't see a solution for the [*sic*] tortured Europe unless the big nations change parteners [*sic*]: England should make of Germany her best friend and so Italy of France ...The situation is everyday more serious' (I. Starkie (née Porchietti) to E. Starkie, 25 Mar. 1939, ES Bodl.).

nations, and receive from the latter their gifts in return. From France, the natural ally and partner in the Mediterranean, they may draw inspiration, for France, since the eighteenth century, has been the fairest garden of culture in the world; from Germany, with its North and South Teutonic tensions, they will draw the Germanic ideals of a natural hierarchy of nations; and, above all, from friendly relations with England and the British Commonwealth of Nations[,] they may derive that spirit of human toleration and frank individualism which may be summed up in the two phrases: 'Live and let live' and 'The Englishman's home is his castle.' From England's island empire they may learn that instinctive spiritual quality of happiness which causes the idea of imperial unity to bloom into the Commonwealth of free nations combining as members of the same family in the defence of their common heritage.[69]

Starkie used the final paragraph of his reply to MacDermot to align his position with that of the British Minister for Foreign Affairs, a spokesman for appeasement: 'Lord Halifax, in a recent broadcast, appealed to his listeners to give deep thought as to the possibilities of establishing a just and lasting European peace'.[70] Starkie declared that it was on this understanding that he had agreed to speak at the event, though by the time of his speech nations in Europe were already at war.

In his reply to Starkie's response, MacDermot argued that the former couldn't possibly claim to have stated what he presented in his letter since he had not read from a manuscript, going on to provide further illustration of Starkie's criticism of French, American and British politicians. He also insisted on Starkie's expression of opposition to the lifting of the American embargo and ironically commented on the speaker's selective assessment in relation to the Italian dictator and his regime:

> [Professor Starkie's] allusion to the 'old men' immolating the youngsters was even followed by the dramatic question (thunderously cheered), 'Why don't they go and fight themselves?' while Clemenceau, Wilson and Lloyd George were referred to as 'buffoons'. The removal of the American embargo on the export of munitions was, in fact, deplored. In spite of the apparent inconsistency, Italy and Fascism were praised, although, I quite agree, Professor Starkie did not describe them as militarist, nor did he enquire why Signor Mussolini did not himself fight in Abyssinia or Spain instead of sending young men to perish there.

In his final paragraph, MacDermot added: 'a more unfriendly critic might have put a more sinister construction on the speech than that adopted and adhered to by Your

---

69 The much-revised manuscript of *The waveless plain* reveals that Starkie continued the sentence in which he referred to 'the Germanic ideas of a natural hierarchy of nations', quoted above. His text had read: 'for, as Count Keyserling said in his book on Europe: "Only Weimar, Potsdam and Vienna taken together delimit with some exactness the full richness of the German substance as it presents itself today"' (MS of *The waveless plain*, JMC).   70 W. Starkie to the Editor of the *Sunday Times*, 26 Nov. 1939, p. 8. See also W. Starkie, *Waveless*, p. 504. The only difference in the text is the use of the past tense: 'caused', where the present was used in the letter.

Irish Correspondent',[71] thereby suggesting that Starkie's position might have been interpreted as pro-Axis.[72] The gloss would certainly complement Nancy's claim in her letters to Enid in October and November 1939 that her brother possessed 'great belief in Hitler and Mussolini, and none in the others', that her sister-in-law was 'rather anti-British'[73] and, again, that husband and wife were 'anti-English' and, possibly 'very pro-German.'[74] Certainly, Starkie was not above identifying himself with a hatred of 'the [colonizing] English' felt by 'the [colonized] Irish'. Responding to a letter from Enid in 1937 in which Starkie's eldest sister had been describing the English in Rome, her brother expressed his amusement at her account as well as agreeing with her assessment:

> I never read a better description of the pathetically absurd English in Rome than yours: I laughed and in all laughed most heartily at it. It is quite true: the English think they own Rome and they won't look at the natives. It is that curious lofty superiority that makes every country in the world – including ourselves the Irish – hate the English. *Qu'allais tu faire dans cette galère.* [75]

This sentiment, together with a grooming in the 'Totalitarian Starkie School', which had promoted a belief in Carlylean heroics and 'personality'[76] of the *Übermensch* variety, further substantiated by Italia's loyalty to her *patria*, would have inclined Starkie towards Mussolini, if not also, as Nancy suspected, Hitler, though her brother had cited the Führer as one of the causes of his state of extreme depression in August 1939.[77] It is also relevant to highlight that apart from such considerations and any conviction Starkie may have held about the importance of avoiding war at all costs, of striving for peace given the experience of much painful loss in the context of the First World War,[78] another more immediate personal concern was his son of sixteen. Landi,

---

71 F. MacDermot to the Editor of the *Sunday Times*, 3 Dec. 1939, p. 8.   72 Writing to Enid, her brother explained: '[Frank MacDermot] ... completely misinterpreted me: I attacked the Versailles Treaty[,] not Daladier and Chamberlain' (W. Starkie to E. Starkie, 18 Dec. 1939, ES Bodl.).   73 N. Cooper (née Starkie) to E. Starkie, 7 Oct. 1939 (ES Bodl.).   74 N. Cooper (née Starkie) to E. Starkie, 27 Nov. 1939 (ES Bodl.). The Starkie couple's support for Hitler could have been rooted in the dictator having been fashioned as, in the words of Hermann Esser, 'Germany's Mussolini'. In this connection, Kershaw quotes from an interview with Hitler in the Harmsworth *Daily Mail* in the early 1920s in which the future *Führer* revealed his consciousness of the adoration afforded the *Duce* and what a German version might expect: 'If a German Mussolini is given to Germany ... people would fall down on their knees and worship him more than Mussolini has ever been worshipped' (I. Kershaw, *Hitler*, pp 110, 112).   75 W. Starkie to E. Starkie, 2 Nov. 1937 (ES Bodl.). Referring to reviews following the publication of Enid's *Rimbaud*, her brother returned to his plaint about reviewers interpreting a particular assessment as smacking of racial condescension: 'some of [the reviews][,] like Herbert Wolfe's[,] are so patronising, so righteously and Britishly conceited and superior' (W. Starkie to E. Starkie, 18 June 1938 (ES Bodl.).   76 I. Kershaw, *Hitler*, pp 110–13; 119–20. Evelyn Waugh provides an instance of Mussolini's 'rhetorical and uncompromising' public utterances which could have reminded Starkie of the imposing personality of Pater (E. Waugh, *Waugh in Abyssinia* (London, 1985), p. 27).   77 W. Starkie to J.G. Murray, 11 Aug. 1939 (JMC). Rather than pro-Nazi, Starkie might be more convincingly numbered among the British Italophiles who were anti-German (C. Baldoli, *Exporting fascism*, p. 105, passim).   78 That Starkie felt strongly about the sacrifice of young life in the

would be called up, to fight against the nation of his mother's origins if the war were to last as long as the former one and, initially, it was in the unarmed British interest to stretch matters out with a view to gaining time for building up necessary supplies.[79]

A little over a fortnight before Starkie's Armistice Night speech in November, he had lectured to the Dublin French Society on 'Chopin's Work for Poland', a lecture that served to give voice to 'the heroism, the dignity, the passionate lyricism of the Polish genius' in the wake of recent German aggression.[80] According to the *Irish Independent* account, Starkie's lecture was illustrated by gramophone recordings, one of the pieces played having been produced following an earlier instance of invasion: 'the revolutionary study in C Minor … written in a burst of agony and fury when news came in 1831 of the taking of Warsaw by the Russians'. While there was this allusion to past abuse by the Russians, the lecturer appears to have made no reference to the current invasion and annexation. However, the description of Chopin as 'the ideal national composer'[81] may certainly be interpreted as expressing support for Poland's identity as a nation and, therefore, aligning Starkie with those who opposed Nazi aggression. Furthermore, it would not be surprising to find Starkie supporting the Allies given the Starkie family's Unionist allegiance, friendships and contacts in both England and other parts of the British Isles, as well as his knowledge of the French language and familiarity with the achievements of the nation and culture of his formidable governess, Léonie Cora. Writing to his son Desmond in the United States from Hyde Park Gardens at the end of 1938 while Starkie was a house guest, Cecil Harmsworth observed: 'Feeling here against the Nazis runs high after the Jewish pogroms and it is national passions I have been most afraid of all along. The suspicion grows in my mind that Hitler and Musso[lini] are deliberately seeking a quarrel. If it's not one claim[,] it's another … A pretty bad outlook generally I would say.' In the same letter, he alluded to Ireland seeming something of a 'Sleepy Hollow'[82] by contrast. Certainly, part of the Starkie family were absorbed in peaceful pursuits there by springtime 1939.

In a letter to Enid in May, Italia explained that the family had acquired 'something on four wills [*sic*] [,] said to be a car.'[83] Italia applied herself to learning to drive so that by the summer she and Landi were able to take a motoring holiday. Come September, Italia informed Enid that mother and son had enjoyed 'a lovely holiday around Ireland: from Dublin to Achill; from Achill to Clifton and Galway, then to Wexford, Waterford and back home', with her son mostly at the wheel: 'Landi had the most long-wished

---

war was also illustrated in an argument he engaged in with his mother's sister, Aunt Ida, in which he labelled her ' "an armchair critic, sending young men to their death while sitting comfortably at home".' (N. Cooper (née Starkie) to E. Starkie, 7 Oct. 1939 (ES Bodl.).) The double inverted commas in the quote indicate Nancy's quoting of her brother's words. In remembering the years of the First World War, Enid recalled: 'We were … surrounded by sadness. Many of Walter's closest friends were killed at Suvla Bay in 1915, when there was scarcely a family around us who had not lost someone' (E. Starkie, *Lady's child*, p. 201).   **79** See the entries on air power and artillery in I.C.B. Dear and M.R.D. Foot (eds), *The Oxford companion to the Second World War* (Oxford, 1995), pp 14, 57.   **80** I. Kershaw, *Hitler*, pp 514–27; R. Overy, *1939. Countdown to war* (London, 2010).   **81** 'Chopin's Work for Poland. Lecture in Dublin', II, 26 Oct. 1939, p. 9.   **82** C. Harmsworth to D. Harmsworth, 11 Dec. 1938 (Daniel Harmsworth).   **83** I. Starkie (née Porchietti) to E. Starkie, 18 May 1939 (ES Bodl.).

for [*sic*] experience of driving practically all the time.' His mother judged him to have driven 'quite well' and was already prescribing Landi's next step: 'he should now learn what an engine is and become useful to himself and his people.'[84] In the meantime, a 'worn-out' husband and father remained in Dublin, 'trying to finish off the Ximenez [*sic*] book and [the translation of] *Don Quixote*', which had been 'hanging round [his] neck like a millstone'. On 11 August he responded to a letter from his Albemarle Street publisher who had written to request the delivery of the manuscript 'within a fortnight' of what became *In Sara's tents*. In spite of claiming that he was 'terribly busy' working on his books and 'especially' the latter, Starkie stated that it would be impossible for him to deliver the Gypsy book in the time required, claiming that Murray's letter had given him 'a shock' and comparing his demand to 'an ultimatum from Adolf!'[85] He would complete the biography of Cardinal Cisneros but both *In Sara's tents* and the *Don Quixote* translation would be shelved until his post in Madrid with the British Council was drawing to a close.

---

84 I. Starkie (née Porchietti) to E. Starkie, 17 Sept. 1939 (ES Bodl.).   85 W. Starkie to J.G. Murray, 11 Aug. 1939 (JMC).

7

From Rags to Representative: in Majesty's Service Once Again

[A] Council representative in Spain should be like that famous Italian illusionist, Fregoli, who had to perform a whole opera himself with all the voices, male and female, by going behind a curtain every second and emerging dressed in a different garb![1]

In the wake of the declaration of war on Germany by France and Britain on 3 September 1939, Italia expressed a sense of bewilderment to her sister-in-law Enid: 'In the last two weeks the face of the world has changed and we don't know where we are.'[2] Almost two months on, her husband was still expressing the likelihood of Italy's joining forces with the Allies by spring 1940[3] and this may have been what Italia also hoped. However, come April 1940, the energy, sentiment and enthusiasm Starkie had exhibited and channelled into the Italian regime since the 1920s had been transferred to the Allied cause.

In the first springtime of the war, Starkie was in Paris. He addressed a postcard to The Lady Harmsworth,[4] asking if he might stay with his old friends, Cecil and Emilie, over the week-end following his flight back to London on Saturday, 20 April. Why Starkie should have been in Paris in April 1940 is not commented on in the brief missive but he reported having spent 'a most exciting and interesting time' and being off to the front that day: 'so delighted to see the Tommy and the *Poilu*'. He also assured his Irish friends: 'Here there is marvellous confidence in our [*sic*] eventual victory. [...] I have never seen France so serene, so united, so resolute in victory. It has been a great experience for me to see this great country rise in defence of civilisation.'[5] Back in Dublin at the end of the month, he wrote to Enid, providing a fuller report, though where the obligation ('had to') to fly to Paris originated is not explained, perhaps because Enid knew. In any event, the 'traveller' obtained access to the French Ministry of Information, recording the fact of being detained there as if it were to be expected ('of course'), even familiar, and from there he obtained permission to visit the front. The account of the visit and his observations convey a similar tone to that registered on the postcard to the Harmsworths, one which is rousing, resolute, as well as informative and anecdotal, coming to a climax in this instance with a rejection of the nation which had now become the enemy:

> I only passed through London in a dreadful hurry. I *had to* fly over to Paris and *of course*, when I got there[,] I found myself bogged in the ante-rooms of the

1 W. Starkie to A.J.S. White, 15 June 1944 (The National Archives of the UK (henceforth TNA), British Council (henceforth BC), BW56/7). 2 I. Starkie (née Porchietti) to E. Starkie, 19 Sept. 1939

Ministère d'Information at the Hotel Continental. [...] I got a special permit for the front and I had an amazing time. I visited all the Maginot line from Strasbourg up to near Luxembourg. I also visited all the defences down at the back of Switzerland. Most of my time was in Alsace[,] which was very interesting as I was able to study the French method of dealing with their minorities – such a glowing contrast to the foul cruelty and tyranny of the Nazis and Communists. I am thrilled by my visit to France: I could never have imagined that 2 [4?] years could have worked such a miracle in the French people. When I remember the lassitude of the people at the time of Munich and the dangerous disintegration and communistic tendencies of 1936[,] I am amazed at their wonderful unity today [...] Their security [sincerity?], their discipline, and sacrifice is a lesson to all other peoples [...] They are full of the idea of creating a new Western Europe of cooperation [...] Their patriotism is warm-hearted, generous, expansive, not restricted like the German[,] who always seem to me to narrow their conceptions down until all the rest of the world becomes in their eyes one vast grovelling mass of parias [*sic*]![6]

At the end of March, before leaving Dublin, Starkie had written to Jock Murray, informing his publisher that he would be seeing him in London before crossing the Channel. His use of the passive voice when going on to provide further information about the trip suggests that he was acting under orders (as well as enabling anonymity as to who gave the order): 'I am coming over Thursday night to London and shall see you Friday. I am en route for France: I *have been told* that I am getting permits to visit France from the authorities and hope to fly to Paris next Saturday morning.'[7]

It is also worth recalling here that following the party that Murray threw on Bloomsday 1938 to celebrate the publication of *The waveless plain*, Starkie remarked to his sister that he had noticed her speaking to a person whose identity he queried, wondering whether it might have been Sir Leonard Woolley and going on to ask: 'When shall we meet[?] – I suppose in Oxford.'[8] As has been documented,[9] apart from being a leading archaeologist,[10] Sir Leonard worked for the Intelligence Service[11] and it is conceivable that Starkie's visit to France in the spring of 1940 was an intelligence mission. Apart from the travel books of the 30s, which already provide some inkling

(ES Bodl.). 3 'Italy will probably be in with us next spring' (W. Starkie to J.G. Murray, 10 Nov. 1939, JMC). Starkie's ongoing belief would align him with Lord Halifax's tolerant attitude towards Mussolini (R. Lamb, *Mussolini*, p. 285). See also C. Baldoli, *Exporting fascism*, p. 4. 4 Cecil Harmsworth was distinguished with a peerage in the New Year's Honours of 1939, taking on the title of Baron Harmsworth of Egham, C. Kidd and D. Williamson (eds), *Debrett's peerage and baronetage* (London, 1990), p. 578. 5 W. Starkie to The Lady Harmsworth [Emilie Harmsworth, née Maffett], 13 Apr. 1940 (Daniel Harmsworth). 6 W. Starkie to E. Starkie, 30 Apr. 1940 (ES Bodl.). My italics. 7 W. Starkie to J.G. Murray, 31 Mar. 1940 (JMC). My italics. 8 W. Starkie to E. Starkie, 18 June 1938 (ES Bodl.). 9 H.V.F. Winstone, *Woolley of Ur. The life of Sir Leonard Woolley* (London, 1990). 10 In archaeologist guise, Woolley had delivered a lecture in Madrid under the auspices of the *Comité Hispano-Inglés-/Hispano-British Committee* on 19 June 1929, entitled 'La vieja ciudad de Ur y el descubrimiento de las tumbas reales' [The ancient city of Ur and the discovery of the royal tombs] (ADDA, FDJ). 11 H.V.F. Winstone, *Woolley*, Chapter 4.

of intelligence (the, albeit playful, reference to spies, to disguise, the traveller adopting a discreet profile on occasions, positioning himself so as to overhear particular conversations), further evidence might also be gleaned from the letter addressed to his publisher in 1935 in which he spoke of delivering lectures in a number of places in the Balkans, subsequently declaring: 'I shall have a good opportunity of observing affairs in those countries.'[12] Therefore, when the Chairman of the British Council, Lord Lloyd of Dolobran,[13] interviewed Starkie for the post of British Council Representative in Spain on 6 May 1940,[14] apart from the candidate's knowledge of Spanish and well-nigh twenty years of contact with the country, the forty-five-year-old could offer a substantial range of experience in teaching, organizing activities and developing contacts both at home and abroad, dating back to his task with the YMCA and War Office in Italy at the end of the First World War, his frequent visits to Spain under the Primo de Rivera regime and during the years of the Second Republic, passing through his proximity to the corridors of power during the Free State years in Ireland. Moreover, Starkie had acquired contacts with associations or individuals in England and Spain who were to occupy posts of importance in the cultural and political landscape of the 1940s in both countries, thus, Lieutenant-Colonel Charles Bridge, Secretary-General of the All Peoples' Association (of which Starkie was the Irish Representative), described as Evelyn Wrench's 'right hand man',[15] and subsequently first Secretary-General of the British Council,[16] together with the Duke of Alba, Spanish Ambassador to Britain during the Second World War, whom Starkie had first met in Madrid in 1924 when he lectured under the auspices of the *Comité Hispano-Inglés* [Hispano-English Committee] at the *Residencia de Estudiantes*. Bridge had addressed the secretary of the Hispano-English Committee, the Marquis de Silvela, in 1935, in the wake of the founding of the British Council, following the desire of the Council, 'to take an active interest in your work'. Consequently, Bridge explained: 'I have ... been instructed to place myself unreservedly at your disposal for any assistance that I may be able to give you'.[17] It was a time when the Chairman of the Committee, the Duke of Alba, had little good to express in relation to Spain,[18] but

12 W. Starkie to J.G. Murray, 18 Oct. 1935 (JMC). 13 The Right Honourable Lord Lloyd of Dolobran, GCSI, GCIE, DSO was appointed Chairman of the British Council in 1937 and held the post up until the time of his death in February 1941. In 1940, he took on the post of Secretary of State for the Colonies in the Churchill government 'but ... insisted on continuing as Chairman of the British Council' (F. Donaldson *The British Council. The first fifty years* (London, 1984), p. 76). His 'colossal achievements' (F. Donaldson, *The British Council*, p. 50) as Governor of Bombay have been recognized though his contribution as High Commissioner in Egypt has been assessed as 'controversial' (M.E. Yapp (ed.), *Politics and diplomacy in Egypt. The diaries of Sir Miles Lampson, 1935–1937* (Oxford, 1997), p. 13). 14 There appears to be no record of the interview or of a contract made out for Starkie in British Council files or in Lord Lloyd's Papers at Churchill College Cambridge. The date of the interview is mentioned by Starkie in correspondence with his sister Enid and the Duke of Alba (W. Starkie to E. Starkie, 30 Apr. 1940 (ES Bodl.); W. Starkie to the Duke of Alba, 2 May 1940 (ADDA, FDJ). 15 The description was C.M. Pickthall's, employed in the Department of Overseas Trade and a member of the Committee of International Understanding and Cooperation, 'a forerunner of the British Council' (F. Donaldson, *The British Council*, p. 26). 16 Ibid., p. 27. 17 C. Bridge to the Marquis de Silvela, 17 Apr. 1935 (ADDA, FDJ). 18 'You are welcome at [the Palace of] Liria. People here are all agog to hear you. [...] I hope you will be staying a few days, though I cannot say that Spain is very pleasant under this damned Republic' (The Duke of Alba to Sir Edwin L. Lutyens, 10 May 1934;

following General Franco's victory and Lord Lloyd's interview with the Spanish *Caudillo* in October 1939, collaboration would prosper.

The offer in April 1940 to found the British Council Institute in Madrid might have been interpreted by Starkie as a stroke of the good fortune he was always hoping for. Italia had written to her sister-in-law in January, referring to amounts to be paid to her mother-in-law and, visibly, in a state of anxiety over the family's stretched finances, with the prospect of even leaner days ahead:

> the times are difficult and they promise to get harder and harder: I imagine we shall have soon[,] from the very next year, to live on the only income from Trinity[,] which is not a penny more than 800 + 50 (that is all) for my work in Trinity. The lectures in England are not existing [*sic*] at present; in Ireland he [her husband] makes [*sic*] this year 1940 about 100 pound [*sic*] between broadcasts and RDS lectures.

Italia then went on to chalk up the amounts which would be required for the house and coal, Walter's mother, income tax, life insurance policies, clubs, clothing for the family, the children's schooling as well as what would be needed for Landi were he to go up to TCD at the beginning of the 1940–1 academic year. The total calculated by Italia, without taking into consideration a series of other expenses, among which she cited food, maid, garden, electricity, telephone, gas, laundry, vacations, occasional trips and doctors, was £575. She also mentioned another source of funds, '[m]y income from America', perhaps obtained from family interests in the *Colegio Internacional* in Buenos Aires or other business interests derived from investments in Argentina, but insisted that this was not a steady source. Thus, she concluded: 'You see the [ac]counts are rather stiff. From 1941 we shall have [a] very difficult time.'[19] Starkie's biography of the Spanish Renaissance Cardinal Ximénez de Cisneros, entitled *Grand Inquisitor* and dedicated to the Duke of Alba, was published on 20 May and sales could have signified additional funds. However, as Representative of the British Council in Madrid, Starkie's salary would be at least £1,000,[20] plus a 'suitable'[21] entertainment allowance, a notable improvement on his current earnings and, therefore, some financial peace of mind for Italia. Starkie expressed the feeling to his sister that he could not turn the job down, the question of finance also being commented on by him. Writing to the Duke of Alba just before the interview with Lord Lloyd, he declared that he had replied to the Chairman's invitation to take up the post in Madrid, indicating his willingness 'to accept the offer on patriotic grounds for', he claimed: 'nothing would give me greater satisfaction than to be able to establish closer relations between Spain and Great Britain and draw the true Spain nearer to the true England,'[22] the 'true' nations understood to be monarchies. Indeed, Starkie explained

'the post in Spain is nowadays[,] as [*sic*] everything else[,] infernally bad.' (The Duke of Alba to Arnold Lunn, 2 May 1936 (ADDA, FDJ)). **19** I. Starkie (née Porchietti) to E. Starkie, 27 Jan. 1940 (ES Bodl.). **20** W. Starkie to E. Starkie, 30 Apr. 1940 (ES Bodl.). The amount cited by Starkie in his handwritten letter to Enid may have been £1,100. The first zero could be a number 1. **21** Ibid. **22** W. Starkie to the Duke of Alba, 2 May 1940 (ADDA, FDJ).

his purpose to the Duke in producing *Grand Inquisitor*: 'my object in writing the book was to bear tribute in a subtle way to the renovated [*sic*] spirit of Franco[23] and to express the hope that "El Mejor Alcalde el Rey" [The Best Legislator, the King] will return.'[24] The biographer claimed that he accepted the post of Representative in Spain on patriotic grounds but the letter received from the Council had also appealed to the candidate's sense of personal pride. Starkie quoted from the letter for his sister's benefit: '[T]hey say that "whoever accepts [the post] can rest assured that he is undertaking a task of real national importance".'[25] Undoubtedly, Walter, and his mother aspired to the achievement of 'real national importance', something akin to that commanded by the last Resident Commisioner of Education under the Union. Here was Walter's opportunity to emulate his father, to obtain the recognition denied him so often by reviewers (according to his own plaint) or as government-appointed Director of the Abbey Theatre[26] as well as to reiterate the Starkie family's ongoing service to the British crown.

In the meantime, Italia seemed to be souring. There was the matter of where Landi would live when, and if, he went to TCD later in the year. His mother pointed out to Enid that his grandmother had 'unwisely'[27] suggested he live in college whereas she wished him to live at home. By April, Nancy was reporting to Enid that Italia was estranged from Walter's mother and had become 'so bitter looking'[28] while matters did not improve following the departure of her husband for Spain. Some three months on, Nancy perceived that her sister-in-law was missing her husband though she 'never' went to see his mother and she now described Italia as 'dreadfully bitter and bad-tempered looking'. Moreover, with Landi about to return to Ireland from Ampleforth, Nancy forecast that Italia would become 'worse-tempered'.[29] Walter was over a thousand miles away so not in a position to seek reconciliation between his mother and her daughter-in-law *in situ* or to take his rebellious son in hand. In any event, the job in Madrid was all absorbing, presenting him with a number of challenges; he had little time to address domestic distress at home. Thus Italia was condemned to persevering under the Irish Emergency, though not for long. With her daughter safely boarding at Roedean and Landi set to join the forces, she would be able to leave the country she had persevered in for twenty years, her departure enabled by an imperial nation at war with her own. Presumably she had no regrets with regard to leaving Ireland but the bitter look would linger.

Starkie was no stranger to Spain when he flew into Madrid in July 1940 to take up the post of first Representative of the British Council. Close to retirement in the early 1950s, he recalled promising the Chairman, Lord Lloyd of Dolobran, at his interview

---

23 See in this connection the 'Epilogue' to W. Starkie, *Grand inquisitor* (London, 1940), pp 451–64. 24 W. Starkie to the Duke of Alba, 24 May 1940 (ADDA, FDJ). 'El mejor alcalde el rey' evokes the title of Spanish dramatist Calderón de la Barca's play, written between 1621 and 1623 and published in 1636. 25 Cited in W. Starkie to E. Starkie, 30 Apr. 1940 (ES, Bodl.). 26 'Poor Walter does so feel that he is a cardboard and cotton wool director and does so like to be consulted!' (G. Yeats to W.B. Yeats, 1 Feb. [1932]. Cited in A. Saddlemyer (ed.), *W.B. Yeats and George Yeats. The letters*, p. 292). 27 I. Starkie (née Porchietti) to E. Starkie, 27 Jan. 1940 (ES Bodl.). 28 N. Cooper (née Starkie) to E. Starkie, 22 Apr. 1940 (ES Bodl.). 29 N. Cooper (née Starkie) to E. Starkie, 24 July 1940 (ES Bodl.).

that he would impose 'a self-denying ordinance' whereby he swore 'to put the Raggle-Taggle Gypsies to sleep for the duration'.[30] Once his contract with the Council drew to a close, he picked up the genre again with the publication of the manuscript he had abandoned as war broke out, *In Sara's tents*, and went on to author *The road to Santiago* later in the decade. From the time of his arrival in Madrid, however, his energies were focussed on making his contribution to the war effort by seeking to build cultural bridges between Spain and Britain, initially through activities at the Institute in Madrid and, as the decade progressed, on working to maintain what had been achieved as well as developing the Council's work both in the capital and around the country.

A bare six months after General Franco's victorious entry into Madrid on 1 April 1939, Lord Lloyd travelled to the Spanish capital in pursuit of the *Caudillo*'s approval for the setting up of a Council institute. The Chairman of the British Council was received by General Franco at the *Palacio de Oriente* on Monday, 23 October. A meeting of 'about an hour' took place, which Lloyd summed up as 'friendly'.[31] In his 'Spanish Diary', he recorded having identifed himself before the General as a supporter of his 'crusade' in defence of Christianity and against the spread of Communism:

> I was one of those who throughout the recent struggle in Spain had believed in the sincerity of the cause which he, General Franco, had so brilliantly led, and I had never doubted that the whole of their sacrifices had been made in order to rid Spain of the curse of Bolshevism and to rescue the Church and religion from the Atheist propaganda which under the Red government was corrupting Spanish youth.[32]

In turn, Franco is reported by Lloyd as declaring respect and admiration for 'the British cultural standards more than those of any other country', and enunciating the consent which Lloyd had travelled to Madrid to obtain: '[he] would unreservedly welcome the establishment of British Council activities in Spain in as full a measure as we cared to develop them'.[33] Subsequently, a series of conditions were imposed by the Spanish government,[34] not least the fact that the Director of the Institute and all members of staff should be Roman Catholics, a requirement which constituted something of a challenge for a predominantly Protestant Great Britain and, moreover, in wartime.

The day following his interview with Franco, Lloyd travelled to Toledo, sent by Cardinal Hinsley to see Cardinal Gomá, the Cardinal Primate of Spain.[35] In coming to

---

30 W. Starkie, *In Sara's tents* (London, 1953), p. 9. 31 Lord Lloyd's 'Spanish Diary' (henceforth LLSD), TNA, BC, BW 82/13, 23 Oct. 1939, p.11. 32 LLSD, TNA, BC BW 82/13, 23 Oct. 1939, pp 10–1. 33 LLSD, TNA, BC BW 82/13, 23 Oct. 1939, p. 7. 34 Listed in J. Hurtley, *José Janés: editor de literatura inglesa* (Barcelona, 1992), pp 308–9. 35 LLSD, TNA, BC, BW 82/13, 23 Oct. 1939, p. 12. 36 See, for instance, A. Beevor, *The battle for Spain. The Spanish Civil War, 1936–1939* (London, 2007), pp 88–9, 222–4, 247. On Mussolini and the period of Spain's Second Republic, see I. Saz Campos, *Mussolini contra la II República. Hostilidad, conspiraciones, intervención (1931–1936)* (Valencia, 1986).

a decision as to a candidate to head the Council venture in Madrid, no doubt Lloyd would again refer himself to Cardinal Hinsley, who supported Starkie. However, apart from being a Roman Catholic, Starkie possessed a number of other qualities which undoubtedly made of him a promising candidate for the post. As has been documented, Franco received support from Mussolini's Italy during the Spanish Civil War[36] and Starkie had established significant Italian connections over the 1920s. Furthermore, he had occupied the Chair of Spanish at TCD for some fourteen years and had been lecturing and travelling in Spain since the early 1920s. Finally, his experience with the YMCA in conjunction with the War Office in Italy at the end of the First World War had provided him with a wealth of experience, which he could now draw on in the setting up of the first British Council Institute in Spain. And, to boot, the newly-appointed Representative played the violin and possessed a talent for telling a tale. Indeed, in 1938 he had himself declared: 'A man with a fiddle in his hands and a host of anecdotes on the tip of his tongue could win his way into the hearts of all the soldiers in the world.'[37] He was now being called on to exercise his charm on the victorious Spanish general and his cohorts.

In the search for a suitable candidate for the Madrid post, a number of names were mooted: Professor Antonio Pastor, Reader in Spanish at King's College London; the historian and Italophile Sir Charles Petrie;[38] the diplomat and British Government agent in Burgos during the Spanish Civil War, Sir Robert Hodgson,[39] and Professor Thomas Bodkin,[40] Director of the Barber Institute of Fine Arts at the University of Birmingham, before the latter's friend, Professor Walter Starkie, was approached.[41] In a letter to the British Ambassador in Madrid, Sir Maurice Peterson, in April 1940, the Secretary-General of the British Council, A.J.S. White, explained that Spain's Ambassador to Britain, the Duke of Alba, had recommended that the Council comply with the first of the nine conditions laid down by the Spanish Government for the setting up of a Council Institute in Madrid,[42] that is, that the Director should be a Roman Catholic. White went on to affirm that the Council intended to do so and hoped to find 'the right man in the very near future'.[43] By the end of May Starkie had indicated that he would accept the appointment. A.J.S. White wrote to inform Ambassador Peterson in Madrid and to elicit his approval: 'Walter Starkie of Dublin

---

37 W. Starkie, *Waveless*, p.31; W. Starkie, *Scholars*, p. 202. **38** Petrie was a 'close [friend]' of Luigi Villari (C. Baldoli, *Exporting fascism*, p. 102). **39** See R. Hodgson, *Spain resurgent* (London, 1953). **40** In a report which Bodkin produced following a Council lecture tour, he made the point that he had himself been 'pressed' by Lord Lloyd to take up the post in Madrid ('Extracts from a report dated August 6th by Professor Bodkin on his Lecture Tour in Spain and Portugal, 1942', TNA, BC BW56/4). **41** In the 'Prelude' to *In Sara's tents*, Starkie recalls receiving a letter from Lord Lloyd a fortnight after 10 May in which the Chairman of the British Council invited him to proceed to Madrid in order to found a British Institute and he further notes that he signed his contract with the Council on 18 June 1940. I have found no record of the letter from Lord Lloyd in either Lord Lloyd's Papers at Churchill College Cambridge nor do the British Council files carry a copy. No copy of Starkie's contract remains in the Council files either (e-mail communication with Peter Bloor, British Council Records Management Officer, 3 Aug. 2009). **42** See 'Translation of Note Verbale No. 27 addressed to His Majesty's Embassy by the Ministry of Foreign Affairs, dated: 16 Feb. 1940' (TNA, BC, BW 56/2). **43** A.J.S. White to Sir Maurice Peterson, 8 Apr. 1940 (TNA, BC, BW 56/2).

would accept Directorship of Institute. He is highly recommended by various authorities here and [the Duke of] Alba cordially approves. We do not think we can get a more
suitable candidate. Please confirm urgently that he would be acceptable.'[44] Spanish
confirmation tarried but the newly appointed Representative was able to set out for
Madrid in late June 1940.

While Starkie was found by the Council to be 'the right man' and expected to be 'a
most useful person',[45] in Spain his author profile was not rated highly by certain representatives of the regime. Not long after the end of the Civil War when authorization
for all publications was required,[46] an application was made for permission to publish
Spanish raggle-taggle, a text which had already been published in Spanish translation
as *Aventuras de un irlandés en España* [Adventures of an Irishman in Spain] during the
course of the Civil War.[47] Enrique Conde Gargallo, employed as a censor/reader
within the new censorship apparatus, reporting in late May 1939, considered that
Starkie's travel book carried chapters which expressed 'a distorted and whimsical sense
of regional reality' and it was because of the chapters in question, together with what
he diagnosed as a 'Republican tone',[48] that he deemed the text inappropriate for publication.[49] This judgment was exercised prior to Lord Lloyd's visit to Spain in the
month of October and a little more than a year before Starkie's arrival in the country
as Representative. However, once the author himself had landed, there appears to have
been no looking back to such reservations: a number of his books would be published
in Spanish translation and he increasingly garnered support for the Council's initiatives and the Allied war effort.

In a letter to the British Council in London during his first autumn in Madrid,[50]
Starkie quoted the strategic advice 'patience and shuffle the cards'[51] issued from the

44 Quoted in the Secretary-General, A.J.S. White, to the Chairman, Lord Lloyd, 31 May 1940 (TNA,
BC, BW 56/2). **45** F.R. Cowell of the British Council to G.P. Young at the British Embassy in
Madrid, 13 June 1940 (TNA, BC, BW 56/2). **46** For further information on censorship under the
Franco regime, see M.L. Abellán, *Censura y creación literaria en España* (Barcelona, 1980) and, more
recently, in relation to the censorship of English literature, J.A. Hurtley, 'Tailoring the tale. Inquisitorial
discourses, and resistance, in the early Franco period (1940–1959)' in F. Billiani (ed.), *Modes of censorship
and translation. National contexts and diverse media* (Manchester, 2007), pp 61–92. **47** The text is listed
in the database of the Archivo General de la Administración (henceforth AGA) in Alcalá de Henares
(Madrid) as 'Narrativa y pintoresca de un viaje por España [Narrative and the picturesque on a journey
around Spain].' The file does not contain the customary application presented by the publishing house,
only the censor/reader's report (AGA, Caja 21/06393, Expediente CIR 1072). See the Bibliography for
full reference to editions of Starkie's *Aventuras de un irlandés en España* (1937; 2007). **48** The original
Spanish of the two quoted pieces from the report is: 'un sentido deformado y caprichoso de la realidad
regional' and 'tono republicano'(AGA, Caja 21/06393, Expediente CIR 1072). My translation. The
Republican tone would be detected in the chapter entitled 'Madrid', where Starkie spoke of Ortega y
Gasset and the *Revista de Occidente* gathering (*tertulia*), of Alberto Jiménez Fraud and the enlightened
significance of the *Residencia de Estudiantes* as well as recognizing the Republican government's efforts
in favour of educational reform, as commented on earlier. **49** AGA, Caja 21/06393, Expediente CIR
1072. **50** W. Starkie to Mrs. C. Wiggin, with whom Starkie liased in London until she was transferred
to the Madrid Institute in 1942, 26 Oct. 1940 (TNA, BC, BW 56/2). **51** The original is 'paciencia y
barajar' (M. de Cervantes, *Don Quixote*, Part II, Chapter 23). The English rendering in the corpus of
the text above is taken from Starkie's own translation of Cervantes' novel (W. Starkie, *Don Quixote* (New
York, 2001), p. 690).

mouth of Durandarte in Cervantes' *Don Quixote*. Thus he envisaged the challenge represented by a capital city enveloped in Axis propaganda as requiring the forbearance and determination exercised by the valiant knight subject to enchantment in Cervantes' novel and braced himself accordingly. The Representative's arrival was preceded by that of the new institute's Secretary-Registrar George Reavey. A report he submitted from Madrid early in 1940 speaks of German influence being 'very apparent'[52] and another, a month later, delivered news of the Italian presence acquiring further visibility through the founding of an institute.[53] Thus, given the disadvantage under which the Allies and, more particularly, a poorly armed Britain laboured in 1940, together with the ubiquitous penetration of Axis propaganda in the Spanish media, Starkie was certainly setting to work against heavy odds.

The search for suitable premises was an early challenge and a number of properties were considered before the lease of a building situated in Méndez Núñez, a street at only a short distance from the Retiro Park and the Prado Museum, was agreed upon.[54] Moreover, the house contained a space resembling 'an English baronial hall',[55] which might further recommend it when considering receptions, concerts and public lectures. In spite of difficulties ranging from shortages of food and furniture in a devastated Madrid,[56] to the insecurity created by 'spies and counterspies', the Director of the new British Institute succeeded in laying on a housewarming in late August 1940 to which over seventy distinguished guests, British, Spanish and American, were invited and at which Starkie delivered 'a short speech of welcome defining the objects of the British Institute and ... made a special point of linking the names of Shakespeare and Cervantes as symbols of the two countries.' He also explained to the select gathering the attitude of the British Council towards cultural relations – the practical policy and the general humanistic outlook. At this early stage, Starkie already had plans for giving 'a short intensive course of English to young ex-servicemen who wish to present themselves ... for the Diplomatic Service examinations', appreciating that the situation of ex-servicemen returning to civilian life was not unlike that experienced by their British counterparts in the wake of the Armistice in 1918. His report reveals that he had listened to potential students expressing their needs: 'They wish to receive not only instruction in English language and literature but classes and lectures in economic and general political affairs from an English point of view.'[57] Another early project was the setting up of an infant school, where classes began in the month of September 1940.

There were numerous needs as the Institute set itself in motion in 1940, from typewriters to paper, tables and chairs, books and bricks for the infant classes, pictures,

---

52 A report from G. Reavey, 2 Feb. 1940 (TNA, BC, BW 56/2). 53 A report from G. Reavey, 1 Mar. 1940 (TNA, BC, BW 56/2). 54 See: 'British culture in Spain', TT, 4 Dec. 1940, p. 3. 55 W. Starkie, 'Report of a pianoforte recital given by the celebrated pianist Rudolph [*sic*] Firkusny [*sic*] at the British Institute on the 13th of October [1940]' (TNA, BC, BW 56/2). 56 P. Montoliú, *Madrid en la posguerra, 1939–1946* (Madrid, 2005). Carlton J.H. Hayes recorded feeling 'dejection at seeing so many signs of poverty and malnutrition' as he was driven into Madrid from Barajas airport to take up his post as United States ambassador to Spain on 16 May 1942 C.J.H. Hayes, *Wartime mission in Spain, 1942–1945* (New York, 1945), p. 22. 57 W. Starkie to A.J.S. White, 27 Aug. 1940 (TNA, BC BW 56/2).

other classroom materials, a film projector and, not least, teaching staff. Christopher Howard, future Director of the Institute in Barcelona, did not arrive until December and two other male teachers, A.R. Milburn and R.C. Taylor, only followed in 1941 so classes in the Institute were at a minimum until after the Christmas break. However, the Director was far from idle. Activities were not to be limited to delivering classes; cultural events such as concerts, lectures, film shows and exhibitions were also contemplated. Thus, Starkie took advantage of the Czech pianist Rudolf Firkušný's passing through Madrid in October 1940, en route for the United States, to have him give a recital. The Director's report on the setting up of the concert provides some idea of the difficulties he faced. On this initial occasion there was the challenge of finding a grand piano, no mean task in postwar Madrid. However, he managed to find: 'a brand new Steinway grand piano ... in a small French shop.' He then had to organize the recital and send out invitations all within twenty-four hours as the pianist was in transit to Portugal and could only stay in Madrid for two days. The invitations were made over the telephone as well as via messenger boy so that in spite of such short notice, Starkie managed to assemble 'the most influential people': the Madrid aristocracy, the world of music, politics and diplomacy. He reported back to London:

> I am glad to say that the whole musical [*sic*] public turned up, including the principal composers, conductors, pianists, string instrumentalists, and the musical [*sic*] critics of all the papers. The hall of the Institute where the recital was held was thronged and we also filled the gallery above. There were over 220 people present. [...] Among the musicians who came were Turina, the well-known composer, Guridi, the brilliant new Basque composer, Conrado del Campo, José María Franco, the conductor, Luis Galve and [Enrique] Aroca, Spanish pianists. Of the nobility many came including the Duquesa de Tetuán, the Marquis and Marchioness of Casa Valdés, the Duchess of Lécera, la Princesse d'Orléans, el Duque de Montellano, Conde de Gamazo, etc. Lady Maud Hoare [the wife of the British Ambassador to Spain Samuel Hoare] took the seat of honour. All the other political groups were very well represented, for I asked many of the heads of the Falange party. The Director of the French Institute came and brought a party of twelve French men and women [...] The son and daughter of the French Ambassador also came.

There was also diplomatic representation from the American Embassy and a number of Ministers, Dutch, Polish, Egyptian, Turkish and Czech, were present. The political moment for the delivery of a Czech soirée was a potentially delicate one, given that the Germans appeared to have 'issued all kinds of orders against Czech and Polish artists'. Thus, Starkie transformed the recital into a tribute to the recently deceased Enrique Fernández Arbós, sometime principal violin professor at the Royal College of Music in London, subsequently conductor of the Madrid Symphony Orchestra and, later, a guest conductor in America, whose name, therefore, as Starkie argued in his report, constituted a link between England, Spain and America. The autumn evening glowed as logs burnt in 'the huge fireplace' situated in the hall and 'all the ladies'[58] graced the event by donning evening-dress. Later there were refreshments and a cold buffet for about fifty of the principal guests, the evening ending with Firkušný and Starkie playing the César Franck and Lekeu violin and piano sonatas. The Czech pianist also accompanied Starkie's rendering of Hungarian, Roumanian and Greek Gypsy tunes. The occasion echoes a model familiar to Starkie from his mother's music parties[59] as well as from social events over the Free State years in Dublin: guests were introduced to one another, agreeable conversation was generated, food was provided, drinks were served and entertainment was supplied. The new Representative was already a past master at such events. As long as 'suitable' funds were made available, much might be achieved.[60]

By December 1940, the relatively mundane task of designing membership forms had been completed[61] and norms had been established. Students of the Institute would be admitted from the age of seventeen onwards and classes would take place from 5 until 9 in the evening. Ten pesetas was charged for registration while fees for classes varied, depending on the number attended, either three or six per week.[62] The Institute also offered membership to those who were not students by means of which access to the library was allowed as well as to the variety of activities provided, such as lectures, concerts, teas and art exhibitions.[63] In a letter just before Christmas, Starkie reported that the Institute was being 'besieged by people who are interested in our work'. There also seems to have been a growing show of sympathy and solidarity since 'small donations' were also accompanying the subscriptions for membership. As the year 1940 drew to a close, Starkie arranged for Midnight Mass to be celebrated in an oratory set up at the Institute, calculating that 'at least 150 people'[64] would be present.

With almost five hundred students enrolled by early December 1941, the premises

---

58 W. Starkie, 'Report of a pianoforte recital' (TNA, BC BW 56/2).   59 Reviewing Enid Starkie's *A lady's child*, Stephen Gwynn recalled the Starkie sisters, Enid, Muriel and Chou-Chou, together with their brother, giving 'concerts' at their mother's 'parties' and their becoming 'head and front of Dublin's musical world' (S. Gwynn, 'A Dublin conversation piece', *Time and Tide*, 23:2, 10 Jan. 1942, p. 32).   60 On Starkie and music at the Institute in Madrid, see S. Llano, 'Walter Starkie y el British Council en España: música, cultura y propaganda' in J. Suárez Pajares (ed.), *Música española entre dos guerras: 1914–1945* (Granada, 2002), pp 187–217. Further to the subject of cultural propaganda, see J.F. Berdah, 'La "propaganda" cultural británica en España durante la Segunda Guerra Mundial a través de la acción del "British Council": un aspecto de las relaciones hispano-británicas (1939–1946)' in J. Tusell, et al. (eds), *El regimen de Franco. Política y relaciones exteriores* (Madrid, 1993), pp 273–86.   61 G. Reavey to Mrs C. Wiggin, 10 Dec. 1940 (TNA, BC, BW 56/2).   62 'The fees for the classes are as follows: for three classes a week, 20 pts. [pesetas], six classes a week, 30 pts. Three classes a week for a term of three months, 45 pts., six classes a week for the same term, 60 pts. Three classes a week for the scholastic year, 100 pts., six classes a week for the same time, 150 pts.' (W. Starkie, 'A minute for Mr Tunnard-Moore', TNA, BC, BW 56/2).   63 '[M]embership of the Institute ... is open to Spanish and British subjects, citizens of the USA and South-American Republics may be admitted to Associate membership. Prospective members must be recommended by persons known to the British Institute. Individual members pay Pts. 50, i.e. 25/-, teachers of English pay Pts. 25, i.e. 12/6, student members pay Pts. 25, associate members pay Pts. 100, i.e. 2 pounds sterling and 10 shillings.' (W. Starkie, 'A Minute for Mr. Tunnard-Moore', TNA, BC, BW 56/2).   64 W. Starkie to Mrs C. Wiggin, 18 Dec. 1940 (TNA, BC BW 56/2).

in Méndez Núñez were already becoming cramped. Writing to London in October when the Director had taken to his bed, 'very tired and run down', Christopher Howard reported on the 'great'[65] increase in the number of pupils. Italia had joined her husband in Madrid in January[66] and by the time Howard was writing his report, part of the accommodation allotted to the Representative and his wife had been sacrificed to provide classroom space. Some three weeks later, with 460 students attending classes, Starkie himself described the building as 'a hive of industry from 8:45 in the morning until 9p.m.'[67] so that when student numbers reached the 500 mark as the calendar year drew to a close, the comparison to 'a London railway station in rush hour'[68] might well have seemed no exaggeration. But Starkie seemed energized by the challenges around him, recognizing that he held 'a tough[,] fighting job' and asserting that Madrid was 'not the place for drones'.[69]

When the Representative came to assess the period towards the end of the year, he spoke of 'having such a boom',[70] and of 'our great success', even 'triumph',[71] in spite of the 'ceaseless spying and Gestapo work going on all around us'.[72] His efforts were also publicly recognized by the Council: 'Professor Walter Starkie, the Director, ha[s] performed the task set him with originality and discretion. His work in Madrid is of great interest.'[73] The accomplishment might be measured on the basis of the increasing enrolment of both students and members at the Institute but a whole programme of events over 1941 also contributed to the growing success story. Thus, lectures were delivered by the neurologist Sir James Purves-Stewart, the British and American ambassadors, Sir Samuel Hoare and Alexander Weddell, while Spanish members of the Jesuit and Agustinian orders were also invited to deliver talks. Starkie qualified Purves-Stewart's two lectures as 'a great success'[74] while remarking on Sir James's ability to win over the sympathy of the Spanish doctors in the audience. The Director also noted that the lectures had also broken ground in that they achieved greater press coverage for the Council: 'for the first time we were given generous prominence in some of the papers.'[75] He contributed to the series of lectures too, drawing on his 30s lore with the subject 'Music, magic and minstrelsy – some experiences of a folklorist', illustrated by his playing of some of the tunes he had collected from Spain, Hungary, Roumania and Greece. Starkie argued that Father Heras's lecture achieved 'a great deal of popularity among Spaniards'[76] and both Sir Samuel's lecture and his own appear to have drawn the crowds: an audience of 350 listened to the Ambassador while 300 attended the Director's performance. Before the year was out, Arnold Lunn, Catholic convert and 'publicist for right-wing Catholicism',[77]

65 C. Howard to Mrs C. Wiggin, 31 Oct. 1941 (TNA, BC BW 56/3).   66 *Report of the British Council, 1940–1941* (1941), p. 63.   67 W. Starkie to A.J.S. White, 21 Nov. 1941 (TNA, BC BW 56/3).   68 W. Starkie to A.J.S. White, 2 Dec. 1941 (TNA, BC BW 56/3).   69 Ibid.   70 W. Starkie to A.J.S. White, 21 Nov. 1941 (TNA, BC BW 56/3).   71 W. Starkie to A.J.S. White, 2 Dec. 1941 (TNA, BC BW 56/3).   72 W. Starkie to A.J.S. White, 21 Nov. 1941 (TNA, BC BW 56/3).   73 *Report of the British Council 1941–1942* (1942), p. 28.   74 W. Starkie to Lord Lloyd, 15 Jan. 1941 (TNA, BC BW 56/3).   75 W. Starkie to Mrs C. Wiggin, 29 Jan. 1941 (TNA, BC BW 56/3).   76 W. Starkie to A.J.S. White, 14 Mar. 1941 (TNA, BC BW 56/3).   77 J. Keene, *Fighting for Franco*, p. 61. On Lunn's connection to Douglas Jerrold's *English Review* see R. Griffiths, *Fellow travellers of the right*, p. 22.

speaking 'as a 100% Briton', according to Starkie, 'won the hearts of all with a magnificent lecture on mountaineering and ski-ing'.[78]

Apart from lectures, there were musical events, film shows, which drew large audiences, and social gatherings. In January 1941, a string quartet concert was organized, composed of the British Vice-Consul John Milanés and the Spanish musicians Meroño, Casaux and Conrado del Campo. On the following day, the concert was awarded a favourable review in the Falange daily *El Alcázar*.[79] However, the musical event of the calendar year was the three vocal recitals given by the British contralto Astra Desmond in the month of November. Starkie reported that Desmond performed as 'a veritable ambassadress of British song' and claimed that her recitals had 'stirred the imagination of the Madrid educated public as nothing else we have ever had before'.[80] In May a student dance was organized which drew 120 students, for whom a jazz band was provided. By June the Institute had 'a fine roof garden' which would be used over the summer for parties, teas and dances and in July a flamenco party took place: some hundred guests attended and the hall of the Institute premises, complete with log fire at Christmastime, took on the air of an Andalusian patio, complete with canaries and plants. According to Starkie, the party was 'a decided success'. But not all was *fiesta*. Fifty students attended a summer course which three members of staff took responsibility for: Christopher Howard, Derek Traversi, the future Shakespeare critic and Director of the British Institute in Barcelona in the wake of Howard, and a Miss Jackson, who would go on to teach at the school. The students were mostly employees in government offices and shops; Starkie qualified them as 'hard workers', finding them 'very keen to learn English'.[81] A 'film apparatus'[82] had arrived by early July and there were plans to show weekly films in the summer courses.

Another activity developed over 1941 under the auspices of the Institute was the charitable work carried out by Starkie's wife (whose second forename, Augusta, now came to be used more widely) together with a number of other well-intentioned wives. The American Red Cross provided flour and milk and this was distributed among 400 families of poor children. Every Tuesday between forty and fifty Spanish and British women would go to the Institute to make garments out of the sacks in which the food relief was transported, thus enabling destitute children to be clothed. Writing to the secretary-general of the Council in November 1941, Starkie explained that in the previous week a reception had been given in honour of Mrs Weddell, the wife of the

---

78 W. Starkie to A.J.S. White, 21 Nov. 1941 (TNA, BC BW 56/3). A lecture by Lunn had been planned for spring 1936, to be delivered in Madrid under the auspices of the *Comité Hispano-Inglés*, but the Duke of Alba, co-founder of the *Comité* in 1923 with the then British Ambassador to Spain, Sir Esmé Howard, wrote to Lunn cancelling the lecture: 'Unfortunately, the situation in Spain is so chaotic that after due consideration and after having consulted the Ambassador we thought it was best to have no lecture this spring' (The Duke of Alba to A. Lunn, 2 May 1936 (ADDA, FDJ)). 79 EMA [*sic*], 'Una interesante sesión de cámara', *El Alcázar*, 25 Jan. 1941, p. 2. David Wingeate Pike identifies *El Alcázar* as leader of 'the military press' (D.W. Pike, *Franco and the axis stigma* (Basingstoke, 2008), p. xiv). 80 W. Starkie to A.J.S. White, 21 Nov. 1941 (TNA, BC BW 56/3). 81 W. Starkie to Mrs C. Wiggin, 26 July 1941 (TNA, BC BW 56/3). 82 W. Starkie to Sir M. Robertson, 2 July 1941 (TNA, BC BW 56/3).

American ambassador, in order 'to show her the distribution of the loaves and the milk to the families'.[83] When giving an account of the Council's work in Madrid to the new chairman Sir Malcolm Robertson, in the wake of Lord Lloyd's 'short illness'[84] and death, Starkie outlined the distinct cultural areas he had exploited so far: scientific, literary, musical and artistic. These areas were further developed over the forthcoming year. A *tertulia* of writers and artists, among them the novelist Pío Baroja and painter Ignacio Zuloaga (both of whom Starkie had written about in the travel books on Spain in the 30s), became a particularly successful initiative.[85]

In the wake of a visit to the Madrid Institute in January 1942 by the Council's Educational Director, Professor Ifor Evans, it was decided that the Starkies should no longer live on the Institute premises. In spite of the the couple having given up part of their living quarters in the Institute, space had remained an issue as numbers of students and members continued to grow as well as children attending school on the same premises. After passing through hotel accommodation, the Starkies took up residence at a 'large flat' on calle del Prado in Madrid, 'to be used by the [British] embassy as a safe house for escaping prisoners of war and Jewish refugees.'[86] On 12 March, there were 700 students and 340 members,[87] the number of members rising by ten over the following week,[88] and as July drew to a close, Starkie reported a further 762 students while members numbered 408.[89] With 94 children to accommodate as well, reorganization of the premises was undertaken.[90] Furthermore, with a view to improving organization, Carmen Wiggin transferred to Madrid as secretary-organizer and a confidential secretary was appointed to the Director. Starkie appears to have appreciated the increase in staff in an administrative capacity, expressing satisfaction with regard to Mrs Wiggin's imminent arrival[91] at a time, moreover: 'when dangers [were] certainly not decreasing'.[92] Indeed, it is worth remembering that by the end of 1942, Spain, Portugal and Sweden were the only accessible parts of Europe for the Allies.[93]

The year 1942 marked the fourth centenary of the birth of Spain's Renaissance mystic Saint John of the Cross as well as the centenary of the death of the Romantic poet José de Espronceda. Starkie took advantage of both these events to forge further links with the Church authorities and to reinforce cultural connections between Spain and Great Britain, respectively. In the month of March one of the two Vicars-General of the Madrid Diocese, Manuel Rubio Cercas, delivered a lecture on the Carmelite poet and in May Starkie himself lectured to a 'crowded' audience on 'Byron and Espronceda'.[94] The Institute Director also lectured on 'The Gypsy scholar in English

83 W. Starkie to A.J.S. White, 21 Nov. 1941 (TNA, BC BW 56/3). 84 'Foreword' in *Report of the British Council, 1940–1941*, p. 5. Lloyd died on 5 Feb. 1941. 85 W. Starkie to Sir M. Robertson, 2 July 1941 (TNA, BC BW 56/3). 86 J. Burns, *Papa spy*, p. 253. See also J.A. Michener, *Iberia. Spanish travels and reflections* (New York, 1968), p. 794. 87 W. Starkie to Mr Seymour, 12 Mar. 1942 (TNA, BC BW 56/4). 88 W. Starkie to A.J.S. White, 20 Mar. 1942 (TNA, BC BW 56/4). 89 W. Starkie to R. Braden, 29 July 1942 (TNA, BC BW 56/4). 90 Ibid. 91 W. Starkie to A.J.S. White, 20 Mar. 1942 (TNA, BC BW 56/4). 92 W. Starkie to A.J.S. White, 31 Mar. 1942 (TNA, BC BW 56/4). 93 A.J.S. White, *The British Council. The first twenty-five years, 1934–1959* (London, 1965), p. 36. 94 W. Starkie to M. Blake, 12 May 1942 (TNA, BC BW 56/4).

literature' and delivered a series of six lectures on 'England in song and symphony', illustrated by violin and gramophone records.[95] Other members of staff at the Institute, Christopher Howard and Derek Traversi, contributed to the programme of lectures over the year and also lent their talents to play-directing for the student play-reading circle.

Early in 1942 the first art exhibition, comprising 160 pictures, was set up at the Institute which, Starkie argued: 'brought a great many new members …, not only the artists and art students but also rich people and members of the nobility who up to this time were inclined to patronize Axis institutions.'[96] The exhibition also enabled the Institute to connect with the university sector. The Chief Librarian of Madrid's Complutense University, Javier Lasso de la Vega, took along a group of Library Studies students and lectured to them against the backdrop of the pictures. The exhibition also signified something of a financial success with almost half the pictures being sold and 30 orders for reproduction being requested. The exhibition was further bolstered by an art expert brought over from England: Professor Thomas Bodkin, former Director of the National Gallery of Ireland in Dublin between 1927 and 1935 and an old friend of Starkie's. Bodkin lectured in April and later in the year, the National Gallery expert John Steegman organized a historical print exhibition which led to the Institute being 'thronged every day'.[97] Recognizing that the Spanish capital was 'a great centre for stamp collecting', where philatelists were 'legion',[98] a stamp exhibition was set up, proving a great success. A further distinguished visitor from England completed the lecture programme in the arts field, the ex-Governor of Jerusalem and Cyprus, Sir Ronald Storrs. Efforts were also made to be of service to the medical profession. Already in March, Starkie reported that '[a] close relationship' was being forged with the profession, some of whom were becoming members of the Institute in order to read the 'Monthly Medical Bulletin' sent to the Institute from England.[99] In June, the brain specialist Dr H.W.B. Cairns read a lecture in Spanish on 'Brain abscesses' to 'a packed hall of Spanish medical men'[1] and in December a British film on 'Blood transfusion' was shown to 'a select audience of 75 doctors and medical students.'[2] Popular entertainment was also provided over the year through cinema evenings.

No summer courses were run in the Axis institutes in Madrid in 1942, but Starkie persevered, in spite of the absence of competition, convinced that 'the holiday course is necessary in time of war to counteract enemy propaganda and to prepare the way for the autumn'.[3] The classes were kept: 'at a cheap rate so as to attract the poorer employees', a strategy which the Institute Director judged to be 'excellent propa-

---

95 See a report headed 'British Institute Activities. 3rd Term: April 13th – June 28th', dated 29 July 1942, attached to a letter from W. Starkie to R. Braden, 29 July 1942 (TNA, BC BW 56/4). 96 W. Starkie to A.J.S. White, 20 Mar. 1942 (TNA, BC BW 56/4). 97 W. Starkie to Mr Braden, a report headed 'The Term's Activities', no date (TNA, BC BW 56/4). 98 Ibid. 99 W. Starkie to A.J.S. White, 20 Mar. 1942 (TNA, BC BW 56/4). 1 A report headed 'British Institute Activities. 3rd Term: April 13 – June 28', dated 29 July 1942, attached to a letter from W. Starkie to R. Braden, 29 July 1942 (TNA, BC BW 56/4). 2 W. Starkie to Mr. Braden, a report headed 'The Term's Activities', no date (TNA, BC BW 56/4). 3 W. Starkie to A.J.S. White, 30 June 1942 (TNA, BC BW 56/4).

ganda'. The course was 'in full swing' by mid-August with well over a hundred students attending 'mostly from Government and private offices, eager to study English.' Ambassador Hoare proposed that a course should be set up in the Basque town of Zarautz, where members of the Spanish aristocracy took up residence over the summer months, at a cool remove from the scorching heat of Madrid. Starkie went up to Zarautz to supervise the setting up of the classes, finding himself at the Grand Hotel in San Sebastian: 'cheek by jowl with German officials who were sprinkled about in great profusion among the various dukes and duchesses'.[4] Developments in the world war led to a fall in the number of students expected on the course but Starkie insisted on carrying it through, and remained optimistic.

In spite of periodic setbacks as a consequence of developments in the war and Axis manoeuvring in Madrid, the Institute's increasing success overall enabled Starkie to sally forth to establish or reinforce connections with individuals and institutions outside the Institute's walls. Hence, links with the influential Church authorities were intensified. Attending the weekly meetings of the Royal Spanish Academy [Real Academic Española], the Representative met up with the Bishop of Madrid-Alcalá, Leopoldo Eijo y Garay. The Bishop took a keen interest in the school and had confirmed the children there in 1941. Starkie claimed, moreover, that the Bishop felt 'a sense of gratitude towards the British Council because we have been able to create a lectureship in English in the seminaries of the diocese'.[5] Another member of the clergy, the prominent Basque Jesuit, Father Nemesio Otaño, Director of the *Real Conservatorio de Música y Declamación* [Royal Conservatory of Music and Recitation] and 'a close personal friend of General Franco', was afforded 'a big gift of music and books'.[6] The Church wielded much authority in the educational field[7] but Starkie did not limit his contacts to the clergy. The Minister of Education, José Ibáñez Martín, was also grateful for the collaboration of the British Council in providing books and the Representative was able to report that in spite of the Minister's being 'a strong Falange Party man,' he had expressed 'very friendly feelings'[8] towards him. Another educational contact which was qualified as 'of decided importance ... from an educational point of view, as well as excellent propaganda for the Council'[9] was the collaboration wrought with the *Instituto de Selección Escolar* [The Schools Selection Institute], founded in 1931 with the purpose of making secondary and university education available to children who showed promise but whose families were without means. Finally, before the year was out, a further foray was achieved in the theatre world. The translation of J.B. Priestley's *Time and the Conways* [La herida del tiempo] was staged at the María Guerrero Theatre in Madrid, translated by Luis Escobar and directed by him. The play drew full houses and Starkie hosted a reception on the stage for director and company.[10]

4 W. Starkie to A.J.S. White, 14 Aug. 1942 (TNA, BC BW 56/4).   5 W. Starkie to T.F. Lindsay, 9 July 1942 (TNA, BC BW 56/4).   6 Ibid.   7 With reference to the Church's power at this time, Helen Graham has noted: 'Catholic organisation and discourse provided the mediating device whereby the regime integrated and nationalised the bulk of the Spanish population' (H. Graham, *The Spanish Republic at war, 1936–1939* (Cambridge, 2002), p. 124, n.178.   8 W. Starkie to I. Evans, 17 Feb. 1942 (TNA, BC BW 56/4).   9 W. Starkie to A.J.S. White, 7 Dec. 1942 (TNA, BC BW 56/4).   10 *Report*

All told, the year ended with a sense of significant progress on a number of fronts in spite of Madrid being 'officially ... an entirely Axis city and[,] ... therefore, the atmosphere [being] one of extreme delicacy'.[11] The Representative repeatedly noted the difficulty of advertising events at the Institute given the German monopoly of the press. Thus, the success of the art exhibition early in the year was developed as 'the result of personal contacts and by word of mouth, since the press gave no publicity at all, owing to German pressure'[12] and on the occasion of Starkie's lecture on Byron and Espronceda, journalists attended but were prevented from reporting: 'The newspaper reporters came and wished to publish an account of the lecture ... but the German-controlled censorship would not allow it ... [as] I was told afterwards.'[13] However, in spite of plentiful difficulties, the success of the Representative, supported by his wife, who carried on with her '*Ropero*' or 'Sewing Society' and supervised the catering at receptions, was unanimously praised by the lecturers sent from England. Bodkin, Steegman and Storrs agreed in their recognition of the achievements of both the Representative and his wife.[14]

Following the celebration in December of a musical Nativity Play and choir-singing by the children, together with the distribution of prizes, all set against a Christmas tree and crib, 'symbolizing the British and Spanish Christmas',[15] the Madrid Representative went into the new year with flying colours. Perhaps he didn't need a film celebrity by his side to boost his popularity but such seduction was what the Council would provide: actor and director Leslie Howard, not long home from Hollywood was to take a final bow at the British Institute in Madrid. When the Barcelona journalist Ángel Zúñiga interviewed the Madrid Institute's star turn in May 1943, he recognized '[t]he same carefree elegance and the same delightful sense of humour'[16] which were familiar to him from the screen. The actor's fame preceded him and though his 1941 propaganda film 'Pimpernel Smith' had not been seen in Spain, the translation of Margaret Mitchell's *Gone with the wind* (*Lo que el viento se llevó*) was currently the rage[17] and Ashley Wilkes's appeal proved wellnigh irresistible.[18] By the

of the British Council, 1942–1943 (1943), p. 25. For further information on the translation and production, see J. London, *Reception and renewal in modern Spanish theatre: 1939–1963* (London, 1997), pp 63–5.   11 John Steegman to M. Blake, 12 Dec. 1942 (TNA, BC BW 56/4).   12 W. Starkie to A.J.S. White, 20 Mar. 1942 (TNA, BC BW 56/4).   13 W. Starkie to M. Blake, 12 May 1942 (TNA, BC BW 56/4).   14 J. Steegman to M. Blake, 12 Dec. 1942; R. Storrs to A.J.S. White, 22 Dec. 1942; 'Extracts from a report dated Aug. 6 by Professor Bodkin on his Lecture Tour in Spain and Portugal, 1942' (TNA, BC BW 56/4).   15 A report headed 'The Term's Activities', signed by W. Starkie but with no date (TNA, BC BW 56/4).   16 The original Spanish reads: 'La misma descuidada elegancia y el mismo delicioso sentido de humor' (A. Zúñiga, 'Pimpinel Smith me hace confidencias' [Pimpernel Smith confides in me], *Destino*, 29 May 1943, page not numbered).   17 The novel was published for the first time in Spanish in 1943: *Lo que el viento se llevó* (Barcelona: Aymá. Translated by Juan G[onzález-Blanco]. de Luaces and Julio Gómez de la Serna). The 1939 film produced by Victor Fleming and David O. Selznick was not shown publicly in Spain until 1950 (A. Gil, *La censura cinematográfica en España* (Barcelona, 2009), pp 18–19).   18 Howard had expressed his political misgivings about visiting Spain at the time in a letter to Foreign Secretary Anthony Eden on 12 April 1943. In his reply, Eden responded to Howard's 'scruples about hobnobbing with any Falangist leaders', arguing that the Falangists 'although tiresome and influential are only a minority in Spain' and insisting on the support which Howard's visit would signify: '[I]t is very important just now to fly the British flag

19 W.F. Starkie (at the foot of the staircase, with Italia (on his right) at the
flamenco party, British Institute, Madrid, Spain, May 1943.

time Leslie Howard arrived in Madrid, the Institute had 1,500 students, a number
which would lead Martin Blake of the Council to express the opinion that 'the time
ha[d] come to set up a waiting list.' He also pondered whether the fees might not be
increased slightly, especially the registration fee, which stood at ten pesetas, and argued
that allied nationals should no longer be accepted as students. He insisted further that
Institute classes were to be geared towards Spaniards and given that the continuing rise
in the number of students as well as members had aggravated the problem of space,
he argued that new premises were 'essential'.[19]

When writing to A.J.S. White in October 1943, Starkie listed among the Institute's
activities the fortnightly *tertulia*, chamber music concerts, gramophone recitals,
lectures illustrated with music at regular intervals, book and art exhibitions as well as
dinner parties, the latter aimed at bringing together 'leading personalities who want to
be in touch with the Embassy'.[20] However, contact was not limited to bringing people
into the Institute, Starkie also went on developing links with a range of institutions,
from the *Consejo Superior de Investigaciones Científicas* [The Higher Council for
Scientific Research][21] in Madrid to the Benedictine monastery of Montserrat in the
mountains of Catalonia and before the year was out, an Institute would be opened in
the city of Barcelona.[22] Another important development over 1943 was the promotion

in Spain and to give encouragement to our many friends there, who are to be found in all classes' (Sir A.
Eden to L. Howard, 20 April 1943, TNA, FO 954/27C Spain). See J. Burns, *Papa spy*, pp 251–60, and
J. Rey-Ximena, *El vuelo del Ibis* (Madrid, 2008), pp 124–31, for accounts of Howard's sojourn in
Madrid. **19** 'Mr Martin Blake's visit to Portugal and Spain', May 1943 (TNA, BC BW 56/7). Blake's
visit took place between 14 and 20 May 1943, thus coinciding with Leslie Howard's. **20** W. Starkie to
A.J.S. White, 30 Oct. 1943 (TNA, BC BW 56/7). **21** Henceforth CSIC. **22** For information on the

of British books. In February and March an exhibition was held on the Institute premises in Madrid, opened by the Duke of Alba on 4 February, and complemented by '[a] special series of half-hour talks during the course of the ... Exhibition on Tuesdays and Thursdays at 8p.m.'[23] In his correspondence with the Council, Starkie underlined the importance of the book enterprise, one which would come to be run most efficiently by Mrs Simpson, then working at the British Embassy in Madrid, but who was ready to transfer to the Institute having worked for the Council in Yugoslavia. In his memoirs, the publisher José Ruiz-Castillo Basala would remember her 'affectionate welcome'[24] for all the publishers who frequented the Institute as well as the cup of tea he would be served by her mid-morning when attending meetings at the Institute.

The year 1943 began with lectures from the Jesuit Father Martin D'Arcy. In his report to the Council on his return, D'Arcy summed up Starkie's post as 'a very difficult job', going on to express his support for the Representative's efforts, which echoed those of Bodkin, Steegman and Storrs:

> Professor Starkie ... does exceptionally good work, indeed invaluable work, in dissipating prejudices and misunderstandings among the Spanish about English ideals and traditions. With his knowledge of Spain and versatility he is able to use all the arts and the various customs of both countries to foster good will, and he is a persona grata with Bishops and clergy and the multitudes who believe in the European Christian tradition, whether they put their beliefs into practice or not.[25]

All told, 1943 might be regarded as one of further progress, boosted by the popular appeal of Leslie Howard. In June, Starkie himself wrote with confidence as regards the success of the Council's labours: 'We have built up a special place in the affections of the Spanish people generally, and we have made the Institute a centre of cultural life in the broader sense.'[26] The school was no less successful: in May, Blake reported that there was 'a long waiting list'[27] and by the end of October, Starkie affirmed: 'the Institute has become firmly established and is looked upon with sympathy by the people of Madrid.'[28]

On 1 May 1944 Starkie wrote excitedly to London with the news that he had been

British Council's donation of books to the monastery of Montserrat on 10 August 1943, see W. Starkie to A.J.S. White, 20 Aug. 1943 (TNA, BC BW 56/7). The Institute in Barcelona was opened on 25 October 1943 and visited by the British Ambassador to Spain, Sir Samuel Hoare, three days later. **23** From a leaflet headed 'Exhibition of English Books' (British Council Madrid Ephemera, henceforth BCME). Seven 'talks' were delivered, two by Starkie: 'Hispanists of modern England' and 'Music and drama in England today.' **24** The original Spanish reads: 'afectuosa acogida'. My translation (J. Ruiz-Castillo Basala, *El apasionante mundo del libro. Memorias de un editor* (Madrid, 1972), p. 225). **25** 'Impressions from the Reverend M.C. D'Arcy, Campion Hall, Oxford, on his visit to Portugal and Spain in December 1942 and January 1943 (extract)' (TNA, BC BW 56/7). **26** W. Starkie to Sir M. Robertson, 30 June 1943 (TNA, BC BW 56/7). **27** 'Mr Martin Blake's visit to Portugal and Spain', May 1943 (TNA, BC BW 56/7). **28** W. Starkie to A.J.S. White, 30 Oct. 1943 (TNA, BC BW 56/7).

20 W.F. Starkie in conversation with Leslie Howard at the flamenco party,
British Institute, Madrid, Spain, May 1943.

to Valencia to lecture at the invitation of the university, a significant achievement given that '[i]t was a set policy of the [Spanish] Government not to invite the British Institute to give lectures in Universities'. He lectured on 'The Hispanists of Great Britain' and reported 'a huge success' given that the Aula Magna with a seating capacity of 800 'was crowded and even all the standing room was taken.' He found the Valencia university authorities 'extremely complimentary in their references to us' and their receptiveness led him to select Luis Vives as a means of underlining Anglo-Spanish relations as well as with a view to erasing any remaining ill feeling as a consequence of the University of Oxford's rejection of a gift of books from the CSIC. As he explained to the Secretary General of the Council: 'I realised that Luis Vives, the Renaissance Liberal philosopher, was a very good card to play, so I linked up Oxford University with Valencia and in this way[,] I think I managed to dispel most of the clouds that have settled on us here owing to the Oxford action in the question of the books.' In his report to the Council, Starkie also admitted to having been surprised by the enthusiastic response at the end of his lecture, declaring: 'I can only explain this by the fact that events are moving rapidly in Spain as elsewhere.'[29] Undoubtedly, achievements for the Council in Spain over 1944 were not only a consequence of the impact of the effective programming of lectures, an attractive variety of activities and teaching success at the British Institutes in Madrid and Barcelona but also of the progress of the Allies in the war zone. Thus, on 9 June, Starkie delivered the same lecture he had given in Valencia at the headquarters of the CSIC in Madrid, stating in

29 W. Starkie to A.J.S. White, 1 May 1944 (TNA, BC BW 56/7).

his report of the event that it was 'perhaps the most conspicuous success I have had
... here for the Council.'[30] He noted the presence of the Marqués de Palomares in the
audience together with 'many other members of the former Anglo-Spanish
Committee [*sic*],'[31] the *Comité Hispano-Inglés*.

From June on, events gathered speed. In early July 1944, Starkie was summoned by
the Minister of Educación, José Ibáñez Martín, with whom he discussed 'the whole
question of English in the *Bachillerato*.'[32] English was discriminated against within the
law then in force but during the interview of an hour, the Minister invited the Council
Representative to place his request for reform of the law in writing. Starkie reported
that he was doing so and signalled what the change would mean: 'I consider that if the
Minister keeps his promise (it was a definite promise)[,] I have gained a great victory
for English in Spain and have destroyed one of the main advantages of the Germans
here.'[33] In late November, Starkie held a dinner for eleven members of the CSIC
together with the Minister himself. It was the latter's first visit to the Institute, now
installed at number 5 on calle Almagro, and he expressed the view that 'the moment
had come to push on energetically the study of English'.[34] A further move towards
closer collaboration was also made with the Minister offering the Council the summer
university of Menéndez y Pelayo in Santander for the teachers' course in the summer
of 1945.

There was also some satisfaction in 1944 for Starkie, the 1930s travel writer, with
the publication in Spanish translation of *Raggle-taggle* and *Don Gypsy*.[35] He reported
back to London that the translation of *Raggle-taggle* had been published in time for
the *Feria del Libro* (Book Fair) in Madrid and was being well received: 'The book ...
has been selling very widely ... and looks like being a bestseller this year'.[36] In a
prologue to Starkie's text, Julio Gómez de la Serna provided words of praise for
Starkie's labours at such a delicate and difficult moment.[37] By early March, the
Representative was feeling the effect of having lost both teaching and administrative
staff: Christopher Howard had gone to Barcelona and Carmen Wiggin was back in
London. Nonetheless, on the teaching front he was able to count on, among others,
the talents of Charles David Ley, who had transferred from the Lisbon Institute to
Madrid in 1943.[38] Starkie also found that his task had multiplied with the opening of
the Barcelona Institute. He travelled to the Catalan capital in February with a view to
inspecting the progress of the Institute there and gave two lectures, which appear to
have roused interest, as Starkie reported: 'Both lectures were extremely well attended,
the second had a really big audience of the most prominent Barcelona people,

30 W. Starkie to A.J.S. White, 15 June 1944 (TNA, BC BW 56/7). **31** Ibid. **32** W. Starkie to A.J.S.
White, 15 July 1944 (TNA, BC BW 56/7). **33** Ibid. **34** J. Bowker, British Embassy, Madrid, to the
Right Honourable Anthony Eden, 20 Dec. 1944 (TNA, BC BW 56/7). **35** W. Starkie, *Trotamundos y
gitanos (Aventuras de un juglar en Hungría y Rumanía)*, trans. M. Alfaro (Madrid, [1944]); *Don Gitano.
Aventuras de un irlandés con su violín en Marruecos, Andalucía y en la Mancha*, trans. A. Espina
(Barcelona, 1944). **36** W. Starkie to A.J.S. White, 15 June 1944 (TNA, BC BW 56/7). **37** J. Gómez
de la Serna '"Trailer" biográfico del profesor Walter Starkie' in W. Starkie, *Trotamundos*, p. xv.
38 For Ley's own account of his time in Madrid in the 1940s, see C.D. Ley, *La costanilla de los diablos.
(Memorias literarias 1943–1952)* (Madrid, 1981).

including such famous personalities as the veteran [architect] Puig y Cadafalch, and members of the City Council of Barcelona.'³⁹ Furthermore, a ten-minute summary of his lecture in Spanish was broadcast on *Radio Barcelona*: 'the first time that we have got on the air in Spain',⁴⁰ as Howard reported. In May Starkie was back in Barcelona in connection with a book exhibition, opened by the Consul-General Harold Farquhar on 10 May. On this occasion, Starkie also took the opportunity to visit the Bishop of Barcelona: 'a very strong influence in the city and one most necessary to us in our work.' He also entertained the bourgeoisie in style: 'I gave one big *tertulia* at the Ritz to over 90 writers, publishers, scientists, professors, etc., and this was a great success, for it enabled me to gather together an immense amount [*sic*] of pro-British Catalans, who long to get into touch with our work. I gave also a dinner for some of the wealthier publishers and writers who have helped us.'⁴¹ In the meantime, the Madrid Institute had its share of activity: 'Courses of English civilisation and letters', open to students and members of the Institute, were run from January to March. On 24 November Starkie staged a tribute to Ramón Menéndez Pidal, projected as 'Counsellor of the Hispanic world'.⁴² By the end of 1944, the Council had managed to expand its influence beyond Madrid and Barcelona, travelling north-west to establish an Institute in Bilbao, and the sphere of influence would continue to grow, with two more centres projected for Valencia and Seville between 1945 and 1946.

As the year of the Allied victory began, British Embassy official James Bowker observed that the Institute was 'on the crest of a wave' and given the favourable turn in the war was optimistic that 'our cultural relations ... offer almost unlimited possibilities.'⁴³ However, the declarations of the ex-Ambassador Samuel Hoare, now Lord Templewood, in his maiden speech in the House of Lords ruffled feathers in Madrid. Starkie reported to London that 'the severest attack of all' in response to Templewood's words had appeared in the monarchist daily *ABC* under the title 'An unfortunate speech'.⁴⁴ The rumpus led the Representative to argue that the official openings of the new building in Madrid and the latest Institute in Bilbao should be delayed and he continued in a similar vein until into the month of April, with a further institute in Valencia now contemplated: 'I think it would be best ... to go on with our solid work as before, [as] silently and efficiently as possible'.⁴⁵ He had his reasons for being wary. His 'special relationship' with the Minister of Education Ibáñez Martín had reaped benefits: the change in the status of English in secondary education and, as he reported in 1945, the change in the law with regard to the Intellectual Property Act.⁴⁶ Therefore, he considered it necessary 'to play a very cautious game'.⁴⁷ In the

39 W. Starkie to M. Blake, 7 Mar. 1944 (TNA, BC BW 56/6). Starkie does not specify in his letter what was the subject of the second lecture that he delivered in Spanish at the *Casa del Médico*. The first lecture was delivered in English at the Institute and dealt with Bernard Shaw.   40 C. Howard to D. Shillan, 1 Mar. 1944 (TNA, BC BW 56/6).   41 W. Starkie to M. Blake, 25 May 1944 (TNA, BC BW 56/7).   42 The original Spanish on the invitation card sent out by the Institute reads 'Consejero de la Hispanidad'. My translation (BCME).   43 J. Bowker to M. Blake, 11 Jan. 1945 (TNA, BC, BW 56/7). 44 W. Starkie to M. Blake, 5 Jan. 1945 (TNA, BC BW 56/7). The *ABC* article was entitled 'Un discurso desafortunado', 31 Dec. 1944, p. 43.   45 W. Starkie to A.J.S. White, 3 Apr. 1945 (TNA, BC BW 56/7). 46 W. Starkie to A.J.S. White, 2 May 1945 (TNA, BC BW 56/7).   47 W. Starkie to A.J.S. White, 3 Apr. 1945 (TNA, BC BW 56/7).

21 W.F. Starkie entertaining guests at dinner in the Japanese
Room at Madrid's Lhardy restaurant, October 1945.

meantime, Starkie embarked on a lecture tour around Spain (in early January he was already mentioning Saragossa, Valencia, Santiago de Compostela and Barcelona), organized by the Minister of Education. By the summer of 1945, he planned to have lectured at every university in the country and at Eastertime delivered an account of 'The Experiences of a British Folklorist in Europe' at the Real Academia de Alfonso el Sabio [Royal Academy of Alfonso the Wise] in Murcia.[48] In the Director's absence, a programme of lectures continued in Madrid, ranging from Frank Wallace on sport and game preservation to Douglas Woodruff, editor of the Catholic newspaper *The Tablet*, on Cardinal Newman and G.K. Chesterton, a complement to an exhibition of Catholic books in English. Connections with Spanish music and literature were also further forged. A tribute was held for the composer and National Commissioner of Music Joaquín Turina and Oxford Professor of Spanish W.J. Entwistle lectured on the Golden Age dramatist Calderón de la Barca as well as on Cervantes.

In this final year of the war, 'the question of Starkie remaining'[49] was broached. Bowker at the Embassy in Madrid felt that it would depend upon whether 'a really good man'[50] could be found to occupy the post. Remaining Council documents for 1945 certainly attest to recognition of Starkie's labours as Representative in Spain. The year began with congratulations from the Chairman following the news of the dinner held at the Madrid Institute for the Minister of Education and members of the

48 The lecture was delivered in Spanish: 'Experiencias de un folklorista británico en Europa' (W. Starkie to A.J.S. White, 10 Apr. 1945 (TNA, BC BW 56/7)). 49 J. Bowker to M. Blake, 11 Jan. 1945 (TNA, BC BW 56/7). 50 Ibid.

CSIC in late 1944 and the tribute to Menéndez Pidal, which Malcolm Robertson qualified as 'an excellent and well timed gesture'.[51] Martin Blake in London and James Bowker at the Embassy in Madrid both agreed that Starkie had carried out 'excellent work'[52] and following his lectures in April, W.J. Entwistle hailed Starkie's success, recognizing the effectiveness of his talents in what the Oxford professor deemed a fundamentally lawless country: 'In Spain all depends on personality, Professor Starkie's. He is *persona gratissima* in all circles in Spain, and with connexions and initiative to take a high line. That is necessary in a land of no law, and where diplomatic channels are choked. He … should have a brilliant year of propaganda.'[53]

In 1946 Starkie's contract with the Council came to an end. He left Madrid on 12 October after an eventful year in which he had been summoned before Franco,[54] travelled to Barcelona for a one-night performance of *Hamlet*,[55] as well as on two further occasions on which he delivered lectures and visited a book exhibition at the institute there,[56] was in Valencia for the celebration of the traditional fireworks festival, Les Falles, and for a performance of T.S. Eliot's *Murder in the cathedral*. He also entertained Sir William Beveridge, who paid a visit to Spain as the guest of the University of Madrid[57] and, finally, he lectured in Seville, Bilbao and in the Canary Islands. In November he was back in Dublin, 'anxiously'[58] awaiting news of his future. In January he had told the Spanish Minister of Education Ibáñez Martín that he had 'only been lent'[59] to the Council by TCD and should have already returned. In providing an account of the conversation between the Minister and Starkie, the latter claimed that Ibáñez Martín expressed 'deep anxiety'[60] at the Representative's departure. Certainly an article devoted to Starkie and published in 1946 in the regime's *Revista Nacional de Educación* [National Review of Education], expressed a high opinion of the Representative's labours at the head of the Institute and stated that moves had been made with a view to ensuring that Starkie might stay on.[61] He did, much to the chagrin of many of those who had been colleagues at TCD for a number of years. Addressing Cecil Harmsworth, Robert Tate expressed 'much [concern]'[62] on hearing the news from Starkie's mother that her son intended to return to the university for only two terms and was planning to resign his fellowship. Starkie made his last appearance in

---

51 M. Robertson to W. Starkie, 1 Jan. 1945 (TNA, BC BW 56/7). 52 J. Bowker to M. Blake, 15 June 1945 (TNA, BC BW 56/7). 53 A report by Prof. W.J. Entwistle on a tour in Spain and Portugal, enclosed with a letter dated 28 Apr. 1945 (TNA, BC BW 56/7). 54 For an account of the interview, see W. Starkie to Sir V. Mallet, 1 Jan. 1946 (TNA, BC BW 56/7). 55 Starkie delivered a lecture before the performance, see W. Starkie, 'Cervantes y Shakespeare' in *Semblanza de Cervantes y Shakespeare. Conferencia pronunciada en el Teatro Calderón de Barcelona la noche del 23 de enero de 1946, con motivo de la extraordinaria representación de Hamlet en homenaje a la literatura inglesa* (Barcelona (no date) [1946/7?], pp 3–16). 56 *La Vanguardia*, 15 May 1946, p. 11; *Diario de Barcelona*, 16 May 1946, p. 2. 57 On Beveridge's visit to Spain see: 'Sir William Beveridge in Madrid', *Informaciones*, 26 Mar. 1946, p. 1; Ambassador V.A.L. Mallet to the Right Honourable Ernest Bevin, 5 Apr. 1946 (TNA, BC BW 56/7) and A. Álvarez Rosete, '"¡Bienvenido Mr Beveridge!" El viaje de William Beveridge a España y la prevision social franquista', *International Journal of Iberian Studies*, 17:2 (2004), 105–16. 58 W. Starkie to A.J.S. White, 1 Nov. 1946 (TNA, BC BW 56/7). 59 W. Starkie to A.J.S. White, 31 Jan. 1946 (TNA, BC BW 56/7). 60 Ibid. 61 'Figuras del hispanismo: Walter Starkie', *Revista Nacional de Educación*, 64 (1946), 67–69. 62 R.W. Tate to C. Harmsworth, 9 Oct. 1946 (Daniel Harmsworth).

College as a Fellow on 13 March 1947. Writing from the Registrar's Office at TCD, K.C. Bailey expressed how 'sad' everyone was at Starkie's departure while recognizing that the former Fellow was 'the best judge of the way in which his talents can be used to the greatest advantage'.[63] Tate affirmed: 'We shall miss him very much', concluding that Starkie preferred 'what Horace calls "mersari civilibus undis" to the University life.'[64] Tate had no doubt that his former protégé inclined towards matters of state rather than of the Academy but Starkie did have his regrets about resigning his fellowship.[65] However, Italia's reluctance, or refusal, to return to Ireland may well have weighed the scales in favour of Starkie's decision to stay on in Spain.

Starkie returned to Madrid in December.[66] As he again took up residence in the Spanish capital, a new bout of darkness seemed to be threatening. In the wake of the closing of the frontiers between France and Spain in the month of February and the April declaration by France, Great Britain and the United States rejecting the regime, the year ended with the United Nations recommendation that member nations withdraw their representatives.[67] Thus, the period became one of increasing isolation for Spain, but Starkie was not one to be daunted by dictatorship. Moreover, he could draw much encouragement from the vindication of his labours in an article by Douglas Brown. The Reuter's correspondent wrote in the wake of the publication of Lord Templewood's *Ambassador on Special Mission* (1946), which made no mention of 'the vital work of the British Institute in Madrid' over the period that Samuel Hoare was Britain's Ambassador to Spain. Brown was trenchant in his defence of Starkie's efforts:

> Throughout the war, the underlying sympathies between Spaniards and Englishmen of all degrees were kept alive … in the genial atmosphere of the British Institute. If ever anyone had a 'special mission' in Spain it was that scholar-gypsy Professor Walter Starkie … who forged a thousand permanent Anglo-Spanish links even in the darkest days of the war.[68]

In spite of Starkie's prolonged absence in the autumn of 1946, the Madrid Institute 'Programme for the Easter Term, 1947' lists a charged series of events. Professor W.F. Starkie was scheduled to deliver the concluding lecture, which figures simply as 'Music',[70] presumably awaiting further definition on the Representative's return. The

---

63 K.C. Bailey to C. Harmsworth, 14 Mar. 1947 (Daniel Harmsworth). 64 R.W. Tate to C. Harmsworth, 9 Oct. 1946 (Daniel Harmsworth). 65 In one of the scrapbooks preserved at TCD, next to the news of his departure from the college reported in the *Irish Times*, Starkie wrote in the margin: 'The sad decision'. (TCD, W.F. Starkie Papers, MS 9202, 3 (1946: Oct.-Dec.)). See also, 'Dr Starkie to leave Dublin University', IT, 16 Oct. 1946, p. 3. 66 'Charles Morgan y Kenneth [*sic*] [Kenneth Clarke] hablarán en España. Bienvenida al Profesor Starkie'. *El Alcázar*, 11 Dec. 1946, p. 1. 67 See: R. Pardo Sanz, 'La política exterior del Franquismo: aislamiento y alineación internacional' in R. Moreno Fonseret & F. Sevillano Calero (eds), *El Franquismo: visiones y balances* (Alicante, 1999), pp 93–117; F. Portero, 'Spain, Britain and the Cold War' in S. Balfour & P. Preston (eds), *Spain and the Great Powers in the twentieth century* (London, 1999), pp 210–28. 68 D. Brown, 'Should an Ambassador tell?' (Reuter-Feature No. 3835/D. TNA, BC BW 56/7). The article was sent by W. Starkie together with a letter to A.J.S. White, dated 1 Nov. 1946 (TNA, BC BW 56/7). 70 British Council Madrid Ephemera,

variety of activities was complemented by Thursday evening film sessions, held at 8:15p.m., generally commented on by members of staff at the Institute. Following the Easter break, a highlight in the summer term was the lecture and reading of P.B. Shelley's *Adonais* by the Spanish poet Vicente Gaos, himself published in the Adonais poetry series launched in 1943 and in which his Shelley translation would appear later in the year.[71] In his preamble, Starkie claimed to be one of the first subscribers[72] and, in honour of the occasion, projected himself as Gaos's page, arguing that history provided other instances of 'an English-Irish page in the service of a Spanish nobleman'.[73] However, having cast himself in the role of servant, he went on to fulfil his task as Representative, presenting Shelley and Keats, as part of a '*cortège*' which expressed 'the spirit of England'.[74] It might be added that the Anglo–Spanish event, celebrating the translation into Spanish of an English Romantic poet by a Spanish contemporary poet, provided the opportunity for the Council to connect with a group whose star was on the rise. As José-Carlos Mainer has pointed out, the publishing house Rialp had purchased the Adonais series in 1946: 'the group piloted by Florentino Pérez Embid and conceived by the Opus Dei as an emblem of its presence in Spanish intellectual life.'[75] Before the summer, the writer and *Daily Mail* journalist, J.M.N. Jeffries and the playwright, critic and theatre manager Ashley Dukes delivered lectures while a book exhibition produced praise for both the Representative and Mrs Simpson.[76] In August, as Starkie was making plans for his departure to London later in the month,[77] the prominent Madrid daily *Arriba* assessed Spain's exclusion from the Paris conference as 'an error and perhaps a danger for the future'.[78] However, the Representative pressed on. Before leaving the country, he reaped a further success for the Council with a summer course, organized in the Catalan town of Puigcerdà in the Pyrenees. In an article in the Barcelona daily *El Correo Catalan*, the Spanish Professor José María Castro y Calvo stated: 'Professor Walter Starkie has achieved one of his greatest successes in Puigcerdá [*sic*].' He also registered how struck he was by Starkie's ability to retain his audience's attention for more than half an hour, in spite of his Spanish still being 'a little foreign'. The Representative's 'magic violin'[79] appears to have enchanted the gathering, as it did on so many occasions over his years of service.

The new Institute year 1947–8 began in Madrid on 13 October with an even greater programme of events than at the beginning of the calendar year and Starkie's input as lecturer was intense. He delivered a single lecture on 'Cultural relations between Spain and England in the 16th century' as well as a series on 'Music and literature' in which

henceforth BCME. **71** Gaos's *Arcángel de mi noche* was volume number 9. For further information on the series, see J.A. Llera & P. Canelo, *60 años de Adonais: una colección de poesía en España (1943–2003)* (Madrid, 2003). **72** Percy B. Shelley, *Adonais*, trans. V. Gaos (Madrid, 1947), p. 11. See further comment in Starkie's prologue on himself as Gaos's page on pages 9 and 15 of the text. **73** The original Spanish reads: 'un escudero inglés-irlandés al servicio de un hidalgo español' (W. Starkie, 'Prólogo' in P.B. Shelley, *Adonais*, p. 10). **74** The original Spanish reads: 'cortejo' and 'el espíritu de Inglaterra' (P.B. Shelley, *Adonais*, p. 10). **75** J.C. Mainer, 'Al final del verano de 1943 …' in J.A. Llera & P. Canelo, *60 años*, p. 17. My translation. **76** 'Exposición de ediciones del British Council.' *Misión*, 5 July 1947, p. 5. **77** 'Ha salido para Londres Mr. Starkie.' *La Vanguardia*, 29 Aug. 1947, p. 2. **78** 'La exclusión de España de la conferencia de Paris es un error y puede que un peligro para el futuro.' *Arriba*, 12 Aug. 1947, p. 6. **79** J.M. Castro y Calvo, 'Curso de verano', *El Correo Catalán*, 3 Sept. 1947, p. 1.

he dealt with 'Shakespeare and the Madrigalists', 'Dryden and Purcell' and 'Handel in England'. However, these commitments at the Madrid Institute did not prevent him from travelling around the country. On 14 October, he was already in Seville, lecturing on contemporary theatre[80] and a week later, in Quixote territory (Campo de Criptana in the province of Ciudad Real), he was pronouncing on Cervantes and Shakespeare in connection with celebrations for the Cervantes fourth centenary.[81] A week on, a journalist of the Alicante newspaper *Información* was interviewing Starkie about Cervantes and his impact on the English novel[82] while the Representative took advantage of his sojourn in Valencia to deliver two lectures at the Institute there. The first dealt with O'Higgins and Cochrane in the history of Chile and Peru (a lecture he would repeat at the Bilbao Institute in late November),[83] while the second focussed on 'The modern English theatre'.[84] His stay in Valencia also enabled him to deliver a further lecture, on Cervantes and the English novel.[85] Prior to leaving Valencia at the beginning of November, Starkie would pay a visit to the choral society, the 'Polifónica Valentina'.[86] Before the end of the month, he lectured in the Law Faculty at the University of Madrid on the meaning of Cardinal Cisneros for today.[87] In December, Starkie delivered on 'Dryden and Purcell'[88] before leaving for Catalonia to host a reception, together with the Director of the Barcelona Institute Derek Traversi, in honour of the British Council delegate Kenneth Johnstone and Dr Charles Burns. The Representative's presence in Barcelona afforded him the opportunity to lecture at the *Institut del Teatre* [Theatre Institute], where he spoke of W.B. Yeats and the Irish theatre.[89] Less than a week on, Starkie was back in Madrid lecturing at the Institute on Handel in England,[90] the last in the series on music and literature.

In December, *The Times* carried the news that Starkie had been appointed Professor of English Literature at the University of Madrid[91] and before the year was out, it was rumoured that he was to occupy the post of Literary Director at the María Guerrero Theatre in the Spanish capital.[92] Jose-Carlos Mainer has described Starkie at this time as being 'ubiquitous'.[93] As the above references to his activity over the years of the Second World War and into the postwar period show, he certainly seemed to be so although Starkie's omnipresence was not exclusive to his post in Madrid. Consideration of his industry over the previous two decades in Ireland and Europe

---

My translation.　**80** 'El profesor Walter Starkie habló anoche en el Instituto Británico sobre el teatro contemporáneo.' *El Correo de Andalucía*, 15 Oct. 1947, p. 2.　**81** 'El IV Centenario de Miguel de Cervantes … Conferencia del Profesor Starkie en Campo de Criptana', *ABC*, 21 Oct. 1947, p. 17.　**82** 'Influencia de Cervantes en la novelística inglesa. Hay que conocer el Levante a través de Gabriel Miró. Charla con el profesor Starkie', *Información*, 28 Oct. 1947, p. 3.　**83** 'Conferencia del profesor Walter Starkie en el Instituto Británico', *El Correo Español – El Pueblo Vasco*, 23 Nov. 1947, p. 3.　**84** *Levante*, 28 Oct. 1947, p. 6; *Levante*, 30 Oct. 1947, p. 2.　**85** *Las Provincias*, 31 Oct. 1947, p. 8.　**86** 'Música. Coral Polifónica Valentina', *Levante*, 2 Nov. 1947, p. 3.　**87** 'Reuniones, Lecturas y Conferencias. Convocatorias para Hoy'. *ABC*, 28 Nov. 1947, p. 15.　**88** 'Índice del Día', *Arriba*, 3 Dec. 1947, p. 2.　**89** *Diario de Barcelona*, 7 Dec. 1947, p. 20.　**90** *Madrid*, 12 Dec. 1947, p. 2.　**91** *The Times*, 11 Dec. 1947, p. 3. See also *Report of the British Council, 1947–1948* (1948), p. 61. Starkie's obituary in *The Times* states that he was 'Special Lecturer in English Literature' from 1948 until 1956 at Madrid University (8 Nov. 1976, p. 15).　**92** 'Cartel de amenidades', *España*, 27 Dec. 1947, p. 1.　**93** J.C. Mainer, 'Al final', p. 17. My translation.

reveals a pronounced proclivity for presence over a wide range of activity and territory. In 1948, the nation he had served in Spain since 1940 recognized the Representative's dedication, rewarding him with a CBE, and on he marched. Starkie's achievement was also fêted in Spain with the publication of a volume of tribute, *Ensayos Hispano-Ingleses. Homenaje a Walter Starkie.*[94] The Duke of Alba headed the tribute, hailing Starkie's creation of Spain's five flourishing Institutes.[95] The volume comprised contributions from a wide range of writers, from the Madrid poet Dámaso Alonso to the Galician writer Ramón Otero Pedrayo, both translators of James Joyce, the latter into Galician, and included pieces from a number of others whose work continues to be read, thus, Azorín, Baroja, Benavente, Gerardo Diego and, not least, the future Nobel prizewinner Camilo José Cela. A host of other artists and intellectuals also participated: significant Catalan figures, such as the composer Mompou, who dedicated some bars of music to his 'friend';[96] the architect Puig i Cadafalch and the eminent librarian as well as historian of Catalan literature Jordi Rubió i Balaguer, together with the Seville-born Professor of Spanish Language and Literature Francisco Sánchez-Castañer; the writer and member of the Spanish Academy of the Language José María de Cossío; one of the signatories of the manifesto in favour of the Republic in 1931, the Madrid doctor and writer Gregorio Marañon and the Granada-born Professor of Civil Law and Falangist intellectual Alfonso García Valdecasas. Finally, Antonio Espina might also be mentioned, the Madrid writer and contributor to the leading journal founded by José Ortega y Gasset in 1923, the *Revista de Occidente*, who had translated Starkie's *Spanish raggle-taggle* and *Don Gypsy* into Spanish. The *festschrift* was brought to a close by Juan Ventosa, Chancellor of the Exechequer in the last government prior to the abolition of the Spanish monarchy in 1931.[97] Thus, while the volume included a collection of essays and pieces produced in honour of Walter Starkie, as the subtitle makes clear, it also carried further significance. The main title echoes that of the *Comité Hispano-Inglés*, the Anglo-Spanish cultural entity founded in 1923 by the Duke of Alba and Sir Esmé Howard, as if laying bare the will to connect back in time, with a period before the Republic, Civil War and Franco regime. The volume brought together thirty-seven contributions from far and wide in the Spanish state from men (almost exclusively) of varying ideological persuasions but it might further be seen as expressing a desire for the restoration of the monarchy, ideally one which would tolerate Spain's cultural diversity. The translations

94 The text was published by the Barcelona publisher José Janés. The colophon indicates that the volume came off the press in late January 1948. 95 Duque de Alba, 'Walter Starkie' in [No editor], *Ensayos hispano-ingleses. Homenaje a Walter Starkie* (Barcelona, 1948), p. 6. The institutes which had been founded by this time were in Madrid, Barcelona, Bilbao, Valencia and Seville. 96 F. Mompou, 'A Walter Starkie' in *Ensayos*, p. 223. A tribute to the Catalan composer was held at the Institute in Madrid on 3 June 1946. 97 Ventosa recognized 'The extraordinary success of the task carried out in Spain by the British Institute, led by [Professor] Walter Starkie'. My translation (J. Ventosa, 'Una gran obra común' [A great task in common] in *Ensayos*, p. 356).

22 W.F. Starkie with Italia, Madrid, 1946[?].

of poems by Dylan Thomas and Rupert Brooke into Catalan by the poets Marià Manent and Josep Janés i Olivé bear witness to the ideal.

Further recognition was awarded the Representative towards the end of the decade with portraits being produced by two Spanish painters: Chicharro Hijo (Eduardo Chicharro Briones), and Daniel Vázquez Díaz.[98] However, sittings did not interrupt what became yet another year of feverish activity for Starkie. In January he lectured at the Madrid Institute on 'The formation of a library' and before the Easter break he spoke of the British composers Vaughan Williams, William Walton and Benjamin Britten in three sessions given the general title of 'The renaissance of music in England'.[99]

In April, Starkie gave the first lecture in a series over the summer term on 'The significance of Edmund Burke, statesman and writer (1729–1797)' as well as delivering four sessions between April and June in the 'Music and Literature' series on 'The sonata', 'The concerto', 'The symphony' and 'The tone poem'.[1] In May he was also a

98 'El arte para el pueblo en *Pueblo*. La exposición nacional de Bellas Artes' (*Pueblo*, 29 Apr. 1948, pp 1, 5). The portrait by Chicharro Hijo is currently exhibited in the Torreón de Lozoya in Segovia. The Vázquez Díaz portrait is the property of the *Bilboko Arte Eder Museoa / Museo de Bellas Artes de Bilbao* but is not currently exhibited. I am grateful to Mariano Gómez de Caso Estrada in Segovia and Ana Galilea in Bilbao for enabling me to view the portraits.   99 The lectures took place on Wednesdays at 8p.m. ('Programme. Lent term 1948', BCME).   1 The Burke lecture took place on 6 April at 8p.m. and

member of the jury of the 'Premio Internacional de Primera Novela' [International Prize for a First Novel], founded by the Catalan publisher Janés, with the Spanish Academy representatives Eugenio D'Ors and José María de Cossío, the poet and translator Fernando Gutiérrez and the British writer Somerset Maugham.² At the same time, Starkie was moving around the country: in May he opened a book exhibition at the Institute in Bilbao and lectured there on books and libraries;³ in June he was down in Granada, visiting a charitable institution⁴ and, again, lecturing, but on a less sober theme than in Bilbao: the Gypsies and their music.⁵ A 'Summer course for teachers of English and advanced students' was organized in Madrid over the month of September, Starkie delivering the inaugural lecture on 'The approach to Shakespeare'. On 13 October, a few days before his son's marriage,⁶ he delivered the opening lecture of the new Institute year on 'The Fantasticks' – Baroque poets of the 17th century' and later in the month would speak on 'The madrigalists', 'The seventeenth century' and 'The eighteenth century' in a series devoted to 'Music and poetry'. The closing lecture of the term was given by Starkie on 21 December when he focussed on 'The picaresque novel in the eighteenth century'.⁷ A number of the lectures delivered at the Madrid Institute over 1948 by outside specialists were by Spaniards, possibly reflecting the '[f]inancial stringency'⁸ experienced by the Council in the later 1940s. The tendency is perhaps reflected at the level of artistic exhibition too, Gregorio Prieto's drawings being shown at the Madrid Institute over the month of February.⁹ However, a British name whose visit was not curtailed and which would have a wide appeal was that of the founder of penicillin, Sir Alexander Fleming, who lectured in both Barcelona and Madrid between late May and early June.¹⁰ Other distinguished British speakers delivered lectures towards the end of the decade, and into the 1950s, a number of whom were returning, thus Ashley Dukes, Arnold Lunn, Sir Charles Petrie and Fr Martin D'Arcy, the latter three old friends of Starkie.

The 'daunting economic situation'¹¹ that met the Conservative party on their victory in 1951, in the wake of Labour's 'Age of Austerity',¹² did not bode well for

the 'Music and Literature' series on Wednesdays at 8p.m.: 28 April, 12 May, 26 May and 9 June ('Programme. Summer Term, 1948', BCME). 2 'Premio Internacional de Primera Novela', *La Vanguardia*, 7 May 1948, p. 3. 3 'Exposición de Libros y conferencia de Starkie y Zuazagoitia', *El Correo Español – El Pueblo Vasco*, 14 May 1948, p. 4. 4 'En el Hogar José Antonio de Auxilio Social', *Ideal*, 4 June 1948, p. 1. 5 'Sobre "Los gitanos y su música" habló Mr [*sic*] Walter Starkie en el Corral del Carbón', *Patria*, 4 June 1948, pp 8, 7. 6 Landi Starkie married Philippa Gilliland on 18 October 1948. The ceremony took place in the British Institute chapel in Madrid (*Ya*, 4 Nov., 1948, p. 4). 7 'Programme of activities. Autumn term 1948. Second half' (BCME). 8 On the question of austerity and retrenchment in relation to the British Council from 1945 until into the 1950s, see Chapter 11 ('Financial Stringency') in F. Donaldson, *The British Council*. 9 'Dibujos por Gregorio Prieto. Interpretación de los Sonetos de Shakespeare y del *Paraíso perdido* de Milton. Impresiones de Oxford y Cambridge. Paisajes de la Gran Bretaña. Retratos [Drawings by Gregorio Prieto. Interpretation of Shakespeare's *Sonnets* and Milton's *Paradise lost*. Impressions of Oxford and Cambridge. Landscapes of Great Britain. Portraits]. 7–27 febrero [1948]' (BCME). 10 'Hoy llegará a nuestra cindad – Sir Alexander Fleming', *La Vanguardia*, 26 May 1948, p. 7; 'La Vanguardia en Madrid. Homenaje popular al Dr Fleming', *La Vanguardia*, 13 June 1948, p. 1. 11 C.J. Bartlett, *A history of postwar Britain, 1945– 1974* (London, 1978), p. 94. 12 M. Sissons & P. French, 'Introduction' in M. Sissons and P. French (eds), *Age of austerity* (Oxford, 1986), p. xvii.

British Council finances or Starkie's future over the forthcoming decade. Whereas he had overseen expansion of the Council's Spanish institutes in the 1940s, by 1952 he had been obliged to implement the closure of Bilbao and Valencia as a consequence of 'terrible cuts'[13] and a year on he was going through 'a very worrying time', not least because of 'Treasury restrictions'.[14] However, come December 1953, he was commenting on the possibility of staying on at the head of the Council in Madrid beyond his sixtieth birthday, given British support for him in Spain: 'The Embassy are unanimous with the Ambassador in pressing London through the Foreign Office for me to stay on with an extension. Also Bishop Mathew is … making representations. I do not know what will happen.'[15] Apart from this eleventh-hour appeal, Starkie had been considering his approaching retirement from the Council for some time and planning for it to some degree. Moreover, by 1952, he was so caught up in cuts and bureaucracy that he declared himself to be 'nearly at the end of my British Council tether'[16] so, presumably, ready to take his leave, but a sense of looming financial insecurity nagged, becoming a recurring feature in letters to friends and family. In 1956, the year of his departure for the United States and with no sure knowledge of how he might prosper there, he was still to express regret at the absence of any 'influence in England' in order to obtain the security which eluded him, in the shape of 'a librarianship at the Foreign Office or some safe sinecure like that'.[17]

In the meantime, following the death of W.J. Entwistle in 1952, the Alfonso XIII Chair at the University of Oxford again became vacant. In spite of serious misgivings, not least given his age and having been twice rejected as a younger candidate, Starkie decided to put himself forward with the support from Spain of two of those who had already lent him their approval in the 1920s: the Duke of Alba and Ramón Menéndez-Pidal, now accompanied by the poet Dámaso Alonso. He wrote to Enid with enthusiasm as he contemplated the possibility:

> As you know, there is nothing I have longed for more in my life than to have [?] the Chair of Spanish at Oxford. [...] The ideal would be for me to end my days in Oxford. Nothing would give me greater peace of mind: I love lecturing and academic work when it is not tainted by bureaucracy and red tape worm! I should be near you … The Chair would suit me admirably.[18]

In the event, the post went to a candidate seventeen years younger than himself, Peter Russell. Later in the year, Vice-Chancellor Steele at the University of Wales Cardiff wrote to see if Starkie would be interested in a Chair of Spanish to be set up in Cardiff. He had been ready to forfeit Madrid for Oxford but the prospect of Cardiff was less appealing. He confessed to Enid: 'I am so depressed after the Oxford fiasco and so cast down after the way I have been treated that I could accept anything. At the same time

13 W. Starkie to E. Starkie, 13 Mar. 1953 (ES Bodl.). See also the Council's 1951 *Report*, which states that the European budget for 1950–1 was 'almost £100,000 less than its budget for the previous financial year' (*Report on the work of the British Council for the year ended 31 March 1951* (1951), p. 14).   14 W. Starkie to E. Starkie, 8 Mar. 1953 (ES Bodl.).   15 W. Starkie to E. Starkie, 17 Dec. 1953 (ES Bodl.). 16 W. Starkie to E. Starkie, 1 July 1952 (ES Bodl.).   17 W. Starkie to E. Starkie, 25 Feb. 1956 (ES Bodl.).   18 W. Starkie to E. Starkie, 1 July 1952 (ES Bodl.).

23 W.F. Starkie (seated, centre) at a Gypsy *zambra*, Verdú, Catalonia, Spain.

I hate the idea of leaving Spain[,] where I am very happy.'[19] Therefore, in the short term, while still resident in Spain, he opted for writing and translating. Indeed, his energies had been focussed on both these activities as he contemplated retirement at the turn of the decade and continued to be so in the wake of disappointment over the Oxford Chair.

1950 was a particularly busy year as it included a tour under the auspices of the British Council in South and Central America.[20] However, in February Starkie was reporting to John Murray that he was working 'very hard at "Sara"' and was hoping to send 'the final proof [*sic*] soon'.[21] Come September, he spent time with J.G. Murray at Albemarle Street though didn't arrive with a text. In a memo to himself following the visit, Murray noted that plans for four books had been established: 'Sara', which Starkie 'promised that he would complete ... by Christmas', to be followed by 'a provisional sequence of foreign books': "The Three Pedros", "Irish Memoirs" and "Spanish Memoirs".'[22] The second and fourth would not materialize but the the first and third did, Starkie relaunching his career as an author with *In Sara's tents* in October 1953, originally planned for publication in 1940.[23] The book

19 W. Starkie to E. Starkie, 30 May 1953 (ES Bodl.). **20** Starkie lectured on 'Literary subjects' in Mexico, Columbia, Peru, Chile, Argentina and Uruguay (*Report on the work of the British Council for the year ended 31 March 1951*, Appendix 11, p. 95). **21** W. Starkie to J.G. Murray, 4 Feb. 1950 (JMC). **22** Memo initialled J.G.M., 7 Sept. 1950 (JMC). **23** See: *John Murray's autumn list 1939*, where *In Sara's tents* is announced as 'Forthcoming' (p. 3) and *John Murray's spring list 1940*, where the text is announced under 'Forthcoming books' (p. 4). In the copy of the 1940 *Spring List* held in the JMC

was centred on the May gathering of gypsies in Saintes-Maries-de-la-Mer in Provence and Starkie was back there in the month of May 1951, not having witnessed the festivities since 1938. However, judging from the description supplied in Murray's catalogues, and as was the case with the 30s texts which drew on the genres of autobiography and travel, *In Sara's tents* had possessed other ambitions, in the context of a Europe on the verge of and very soon to be plunged into war. *John Murray's autumn list 1939* announced: 'This book is more than a travel book and more than an autobiography ... particularly is the book important in showing the position of a free and wandering people in a world of increasing Nationalism [*sic*].' This final announcement of the advertisement would be adjusted to the circumstance of wartime in 1940: 'And particularly is the book important in showing the position of a free and wandering people in a world of war and nationalism.'[24] Publication was eventually scheduled for autumn but by that date Starkie had taken up the British Council post in Madrid.

July and August 1951 were spent in the relative cool of the Spanish province of Asturias, in 'half a house in a village [Cudillero] just above the sea ... founded by the Normans in the twelfth century'. Starkie claimed he had 'worked very hard at "Sara's Tents".'[26] In the first week of January 1952 he further reported to his publisher that he had just returned from the monastery of Santa María de El Paular near Madrid, where he had been working twelve hours a day. However, in spite of the strenuous efforts made by Starkie, Murray's reader (who found 'the making of a most fascinating book' in the material he had been given to read) judged the manuscript to be 'too formless and without a plan – at least a plan that works out well in practice' while he also detected 'a lot of needless repetition ... scattered about.'[27] A contemporary common reader of Starkie's 1930s published texts might have diagnosed a degree of discursiveness but some twenty years on, around the time of his approaching retirement and exit from the British Council, Starkie was juggling with several commitments. A number of these were related to his post[28] but he was also writing, translating[29] and fitting in field work, as with his revisiting Saintes-Maries-de-la-Mer

'Autu[mn]' has been added in pencil.   **24** *John Murray's autumn list 1939*, p. 3; *John Murray's spring list 1940*, p. 4.   **26** W. Starkie to J.G. Murray, 7 Sept. 1951 (JMC).   **27** W. Mattingley to J.G. Murray, 3 June 1952 (JMC).   **28** For instance, a reception at the Madrid Institute for Britain's new Ambassador to Spain, Sir John Balfour, in October 1951; flying to Strasbourg in May 1952 to lecture on 'Le Ritual du Théâtre' (The ritual of Theatre) at the Council of Europe Committee in the University of Strasbourg; flying to Barcelona in the same month on the occasion of the celebration of the Eucharistic Congress to open the English Catholic books exhibition while also announcing the result of the international poetry competition, for which Starkie had been required to read 550 poems on the Eucharist; lecturing in Barcelona and around Catalonia in April 1953, and attending the music festival in Granada in July.   **29** Hollis and Carter published Starkie's translation of Ramón Menéndez Pidal's *Los españoles en su historia* [*The Spaniards in their history*] in 1950, which carried a prefatory essay by the translator on the author's work. In 1954 Jonathan Cape brought out Starkie's translation of *Turris Eburnea* [*Tower of ivory*] by the Uruguayan Rodolfo L. Fonseca. Fonseca's novel had won the first-novel prize (Premio Internacional de Primera Novela) in 1947 when Starkie was one of the members of the jury. The novel had been published in Spanish by Janés in 1948. In the summer of 1953, he told Enid that he had been working in Madrid 'sixteen hours a day' on the translation, only leaving the flat once a week (W. Starkie

and travelling on the Spanish pilgrim road once again, at Eastertime 1954, in connection with what became *The road to Santiago*.[30] Thus, the manuscripts Starkie handed to J.G. Murray certainly provided the latter with much labour, duly recognized by the author, who pined for guidance when he found it wanting while repeatedly revealing a readiness to bow to the criterion of Albemarle Street. In May 1954, just over six months on from the publication of *In Sara's tents*, he wrote to his publisher, declaring: 'You must take me in hand. I miss your mentorship'[31] and in correspondence related to *The road to Santiago* he comes to display a total dependence on Murray's editing, for which he expressed much gratitude. His reliance may have been motivated, as Starkie himself claims, by an impatience to see the book in print as well as by his bowing to Murray's understanding of the world of publishing. Nevertheless, a forfeiting of authorial propriety may also be detected:

> I am sure you have improved the manuscript by the titivation. [...] Do not be afraid of wielding the bisturi of the surgeon or the pruning knife or the shears of a mule clipper. I am now so fatalistic and pessimistic that I could accept anything in order to get on quicker [*sic*] with the job which seems so long drawn out for one who is impatiently waiting for galleys. [...] You have no idea how grateful I am to you for all your painstaking guidance. [...] I hope you have cut remorselessly in the rest of the book because I feel there is so much variety and incident ... that it can stand a good deal of 'montage': I have selfishly left that burden on your shoulders because you, like the Ajax of Sophocles[,] know when you have to produce the shears ... and you know what the critics, reviewers and the public want. [...] I enclose today the final chapter ... which has given me a great deal of labour. By all means cut portions if you do not think it reads well. [...] I am impatient to see how the book looks when cut. It should be possible to make it dramatic and suggestive by pruning.[32]

Starkie subsequently expressed both his own and Italia's joy on contemplation of the final product and was effusive in his praise of Murray's efforts: 'You have done a wonder! I have just received the finished book: we are both delighted with it. [...] my gratitude to you for your angelic patience and understanding.'[33] The problem of prolixity was to plague the writer's pen in the production of what he expected to be

---

to E. Starkie, 30 Aug. 1953, ES Bodl.). Starkie's translation of Ignacio Olagüe's *This is Spain*, with a ten-page introductory essay by the translator was also published in 1953. For further information on Olagüe, see D.W. Pike, *Franco and the axis stigma*, p. 83. Prior to this 'incarceration', he had spent a more entertaining time in France, at the Rabelais celebrations, followed by a week in the Basque coastal town of Fuenterrabía (W. Starkie to E. Starkie, 8 Aug. 1953, ES Bodl.). **30** I. Starkie (née Porchietti) to J.G. and Diana Murray, 11 Apr. 1954; W. Starkie to J.G. Murray, 3 May 1954 (JMC). **31** W. Starkie to J.G. Murray, 3 May 1954 (JMC). **32** W. Starkie to J.G. Murray, 27 Apr. 1956; 14 May 1956; 16 May 1956 (JMC). In a memo to himself when awaiting seventy more pages of what would become *The road to Santiago*, Murray noted: 'Starkie said that he would be very glad to have suggested prunings, and he seemed very happy about cutting to fit' (Memo initialled JGM, 19 Oct. 1955, JMC). **33** W. Starkie to J.G. Murray, 4 Apr. 1957; 1 May 1957 (JMC).

only the first volume of his autobiography: *Scholars and Gypsies*, which Murray was still on hand to mentor. This would not be the case with another ambitious project devoted to the Duke and House of Alba that crossed the Atlantic travelled with him in 1956.

Epilogue

American Bounty

> I shall find myself at 60 out in the street. [...] ... one must grasp at any straw or
> weed when one has been precipitated into the abyss of retirement[1]

The prospect of retirement from the British Council was not a happy one for Starkie,
marred as it was by concerns as to his financial survival. Writing to J.G. Murray in 1954,
he spoke of his need to earn his living through writing[2] since the British Council post
carried no pension. Some two years on, he qualified a lump sum received from the
Council as 'a paltry gratuity' and, moreover, soon to be 'exhausted', further explaining:
'For this reason it was vital for me to rely on my writing to pay for my life and that of my
wife'.[3] There were other worries and financial burdens too: his mother's illness and his
son's divorce. However, there were also sources of satisfaction: his services in Spain
were recognized by the British crown with his investiture as a Commander of the Order
of St Michael and St George on 2 November 1954[4] and he received what he deemed 'a
charming letter' from the Provost of TCD, informing him that the Board had resolved
to confer an Honorary Fellowship upon him. Writing to Enid, he expressed much joy
on being reunited with his *alma mater*: 'I am very glad to have the Fellowship as it means
linking me up again with TCD'.[5] In December, he informed J.G. Murray that he had
made no decisions as to his future except that he expected to stay in Madrid until the
autumn of 1955 as he had 'more than enough'[6] to occupy him. He was to remain at home
in the Spanish capital until October 1956 when he and Italia embarked for New York,
initially for an academic year. The period became well nigh twenty.

    In spite of Starkie's misgivings, the future yielded much more than straw and weeds.
Already in December 1954 he was in Paris 'in consultation with HMV and Columbia
Gramophone',[7] who were interested in producing records of Gypsy, Spanish and
Hungarian music in collaboration with Starkie as well as commentaries by him on
Abbey Theatre plays. In January 1955 Starkie's mother stayed on in Madrid, having
spent Christmas with the family, while her retired son remained busy 'working at [his]
books' and delivering 'quite a number of lectures at the university'.[8] The Columbia
project was also taking up precious time but Albemarle Street was again assured that it
would benefit his Murray publications.[9] He also mentioned to Murray that he had
produced 'several articles and reviews' for the *TLS*. In May he reported 'working like a

1 W. Starkie to E. Starkie, 2 June 1952 (ES Bodl.); W. Starkie to J.G. Murray, 15 Dec. 1954 (JMC).
2 W. Starkie to J.G. Murray, 21 Apr. 1954 (JMC).   3 W. Starkie to J.G. Murray, 28 July 1956 (JMC).
4 'Honour for Professor Walter Starkie', IT, 3 Nov. 1954, p. 5.   5 W. Starkie to E. Starkie, 12/17[?]
May 1954 (ES Bodl.).   6 W. Starkie to J.G. Murray, 15 Dec. 1954 (JMC).   7 W. Starkie to J.G.
Murray, 28 Dec. 1954 (JMC).   8 W. Starkie to E. Starkie, 12 Jan. 1955 (ES Bodl.).   9 W. Starkie to
J.G. Murray, 14 Feb. 1955 (JMC).

nigger at *The road of St James*'[10] (what became *The road to Santiago. Pilgrims of St James*) but in the intervening months, there had been some respite: a visit to Lisbon to lecture at the British Institute, an occasion he had taken advantage of to spend a day in Fatima and visit a fair at Leiria, which was followed by a trip to the south of Spain, to Córdoba and thereabouts for Holy Week.[11] In September he visited his mother in Dublin and took part on an examining board at TCD to establish a new Fellow in Italian.[12] By late February 1956, he succeeded in sending the 'Epilogue' of *The road to Santiago* to Murray, not long before he left for Seville to work on recordings on the Friday and Saturday of Easter Week.[13] Come June, Italia had subjected him to 'a slimming cure', in preparation for their transfer to the United States but her husband had little time to ponder his diet as he struggled 'desperately to finish the third book'[14] before departure. Indeed, the schedule was exacting: the publication on the pilgrim route to Santiago de Compostela for Murray, the Alba manuscript for Weidenfeld and Nicolson in conjunction with Harpers and a multilingual book on ' "a Spanish musical journey" (illustrated with records)', to be published by Starkie's 'friend',[15] René Kister in Geneva. Following completion of the Murray text and the Swiss commitment, Starkie was anxious to finish the Alba manuscript in order to be able to hand it over to the publisher on his arrival in New York while also concerned to obtain 'the combined publicity of the three books for my American tour'.[16]

Starkie's second American sojourn, a quarter of a century on from his last J.B. Pond lecture tour in 1931, was initially engineered through an institution he had become familiar with on his earlier visit, the Institute of International Education in New York, which produced a promotion leaflet for the lecturer on this occasion. The Starkies embarked on the transatlantic crossing at Algeciras on 19 October and on the 29th both Starkie and his wife visited Cass Canfield at Harpers in New York to hand over the Alba manuscript.[17] On the same day, Starkie delivered his first programmed lecture at Columbia University.[18] The intensity of the 29 October anticipated the rhythm of the immediate months ahead of late 1956 and into 1957. Writing to Murray before his departure, Starkie had mentioned his 'extended lecture tour all over North America from October 30 [1956] to June 1957'[19] and on a postcard sent from Austin, Texas, once he had settled in for the second semester as Visiting Professor of Romance Languages, he declared that he had delivered '53 lectures in 45 universities, colleges, museums in 23 different states in USA since October 29', no small achievement for a still somewhat overweight sixty-two-year-old. Given the number of lectures in so

10 W. Starkie to J.G. Murray, 27 May 1956 (JMC). 11 W. Starkie to S. Lowndes Marques, 5 Apr. 1955 (Harry Ransom Center, University of Texas at Austin [henceforth HRC, UTA]). 12 W. Starkie to E. Starkie, 29 Sept. 1955 (ES Bodl.). 13 I. Starkie (née Porchietti) to J.G. Murray, 7 Mar. [1956] (JMC). 14 W. Starkie to E. Starkie, 24 Aug. 1956 (ES Bodl.). 15 The book was published in English, French, German and Spanish, the title in English being *Spain. A musician's journey through time and space*. In late July 1956, Starkie explained to Murray that the manuscript of the book had been sent to EMI in Paris a month earlier and he had now 'mostly finished' the records (W. Starkie to J.G. Murray, 28 July 1956, JMC). 16 Ibid. 17 C. Canfield to W. Starkie, 30 Oct. 1956 (HRC, UTA, Harpers Papers and Correspondence). 18 J.G. Murray to Elliott B. Macrae (of E.P. Dutton, American publisher of *The road to Santiago*), 15 Oct. 1956 (JMC). 19 W. Starkie to J.G. Murray, 14 June 1956 (JMC).

many different locations in a relatively short space of time, it is hardly surprising to find that he was 'beginning to feel like an automaton'.[20]

The visiting professorship at Austin in 1957 was the first of a number, held at Austin again (February–June 1958); NYU (January–June 1959); University of Kansas Lawrence (1959–60); University of Colorado Boulder (1960–1) and at UCLA, where Starkie first taught over the 1961–2 academic year, staying on in Los Angeles until he left America to return to Madrid in the 1970s. When the Starkies first flew back to Europe in July 1957, he was able to bask in a considerable degree of financial, academic and cultural success. In spite of having felt 'very far away over in the States',[22] America provided, and could not be ignored. As May 1957 began, he wrote to J.G. Murray: 'I have done far better than I could ever have hoped in USA'[23] and was 'very pleased' a month on when he received an invitation from The Dean of Arts and Sciences, Professor Harry Ransom, to return to Austin in 1958 'as it resolve[d] ... financial problems for the moment'.[24] There were fond philanthropists in Texas too, not least Jane Blaffer Owen, who would place The Poet's House at New Harmony at the Starkies' disposal in the summer of 1958.[25] At the close of his first visiting professorship at Austin, Starkie reported that he and Italia were 'longing to be back in Europe' but recognized that they had enjoyed the USA 'enormously' and found 'everyone ... wonderfully kind'.[26] Therefore, it may be argued that on the grounds of agreeable community, the country was undoubtedly inviting but what came to make it inevitable as a place of residence was the more prosperous environment than contemporary Spain was able to furnish in the latter 1950s and a degree, at least in the foreseeable future, of financial security. Starkie soon saw 'great possibilities' so that the country also signified promise, though he expressed his need for 'guidance'[27] there too. And America delivered as the proverbial land of opportunity, early affording him splendid opportunities for lecturing on the Irish Revival, the theatre and Spanish material with which he had familiarized himself over years, not least through personal experience;[28] for radio and television

---

20 W. Starkie to J.G. Murray, [no date], also informing his publisher that he had arrived in Austin and was installed in 'a small apartment in ... Normandie House [lying] equidistant between the Michaelangelesque Capitol (floodlit at night) and the Bolognesque town of the University of Texas' (JMC).   22 W. Starkie to J.G. Murray, [no date] (JMC).   23 W. Starkie to J.G. Murray, 1 May 1957 (JMC).   24 W. Starkie to J.G. Murray, 8 June 1957 (JMC). Starkie enclosed a copy of Ransom's letter in his own to Murray.   25 W. Starkie to J.G. Murray, 13 Aug. 1958 (JMC). Jane Blaffer Owen (1915–2010) was the daughter of Robert Lee Blaffer, a founder of the Humble Oil Company, and granddaughter of William T. Campbell, a founder of Texaco. She married Robert Dale Owen, a descendant of the Robert Owen of the factory cooperative of New Lanark in Scotland, who founded the utopian community at New Harmony in the 1820s. Blaffer Owen met Starkie through the Texas oil magnate J.S. Cullinan (author's interview with J. Blaffer Owen, Houston, 31 Dec. 1998). I am grateful to Jane Blaffer Owen for hospitality in New Harmony.   26 W. Starkie to J.G. Murray, 8 June 1957 (JMC).   27 W. Starkie to J.G. Murray, 24 Apr. 1957 (JMC). The Starkies stayed with Æ's son Diarmuid Russell and his wife on arrival in New York in 1956. In 1957, Starkie was hoping that Russell, of Russell and Volkening, 522 Fifth Avenue, might become his agent in the United States though no arrangement materialized.   28 In April 1957, he outlined his schedule to Murray: 'I have 11 important public lectures in April. The University of Emory at Atlanta have invited me to give the Bernard Stipes Foundation Lectures ... on April 16 – 18 on occasion of the Pan-American Campus. This means that Atlanta will be the centre of South American states as well as visitors from the North American states.

employment;[29] travel to South America[30] and further possibilities of exploiting his work in translation from Spanish and his knowledge of Irish literature in English. In this connection, his friendship from 'the old days'[31] of 1929 with the successful publisher of the New American Library, Victor Weybright, proved particularly fruitful.

Starkie's TCD colleague Professor of Romance Languages Thomas Rudmose-Brown had dismissively remarked on Starkie's bent for the limelight in the 1930s.[32] Now, some quarter of a century on and much to Starkie's satisfaction, it shone particularly brightly on him over the 'very hectic time' he and Italia spent in New York in June 1957 before their TWA flight back to Europe. Weybright had joined forces with the American publisher of *The road to Santiago*, E.P. Dutton, setting up 'a whirlwind programme.'[33] Thanks to his fellow Gypsy Lore enthusiast, he was introduced to Dr Luce Klein, the Director of Spoken Arts, which led to recordings; lunches were given for Starkie to meet critics of the *New York Times*, the *Herald Tribune* and *Chicago Tribune*, which soon led to 'four articles on the Santiago book' in the New York paper as well as a special radio interview, and still more critics were present at the 'big cocktail party'[34] Weybright threw for his old friend on 25 June. America fêted him on the media front and seemed ubiquitously susceptible to the Irishman's charm, even over the telephone. In February Warren O'Reilly at Harpers reported that he had enjoyed 'a very pleasant chat' with the Visiting Professor at Texas, Austin, finding him 'certainly a delightful character'.[35]

The Starkies were back in Madrid for the weekend of 5 July, where further intense activity awaited. In less than a week, Starkie was off to Paris and Geneva to correct the proofs of the Swiss music book[36] and before the end of the month was participating on the jury of the International Film Festival at San Sebastián. There was also success to be recorded in Europe where a German edition of *In Sara's tents* 'ha[d] gone very well'.[37] Indeed, Starkie returned triumphant. However, it seems that not all in England

One of my lectures has to be given in English and the other in Spanish. The first subtitled "Symposium in Elysium" is an account of my memories of the 4 Nobel prizewinners; G[eorge] B[ernard] S[haw], Pirandello, Benavente and Eugene O'Neill ... The second lecture will be on Andalusia in poetry and music [and] is an account of García Lorca, Falla, Turina, Machado and will be based on my music book. I have also been invited by the University of Kansas to be the guest lecturer on April 26[,] on the Day of Cervantes[,] at which all the teachers of Spanish and Portuguese gather' (W. Starkie to J.G. Murray, 22 Feb. 1957, JMC). **29** Murray was also supplied with details regarding the media activity: 'I am doing a series of lectures on broadcasting and TV based on *The road to Santiago* and "The Spanish Musical Journey" [*Spain: a musician's journey through time and space*] entitled 'Minstrel of a Thousand Years'. These will be relayed all over USA by the Washington Board of Education' (ibid.). **30** Starkie spent 'four hectic days in Mexico City' in 1957 on which occasion he was 'entertained, wined and dined and met many writers and university professors' (W. Starkie to J.G. Murray [no date], JMC). In May 1958, he travelled to Venezuela, invited by the University of Caracas and Fundación Mendoza (W. Starkie to E. Starkie, 17 May 1958, ES Bodl.). Both these trips may have materialized from contacts made at Emory in April 1957. **31** W. Starkie to J.G. Murray, 6 July 1957 (JMC). **32** T.B. Rudmose-Brown to W.B. Yeats, 19 Sept. 1932; 24 Sept. 1932. I am grateful to John Kelly for allowing me access to the cited correspondence, to be published under his editorship by Oxford University Press. **33** W. Starkie to J.G. Murray, 8 June 1957 (JMC). **34** W. Starkie to J.G. Murray, 6 July 1957 (JMC). **35** Memo from T. [F. ?] Warren O'Reilly to C. Canfield, 4 Feb. 1957 (HRC, UTA, Harpers Papers and Correspondence). **36** W. Starkie to J. Boulenger, 10 July 1957 (JMC). **37** W. Starkie to J.G. Murray,

were eager to obtain his cooperation or impressed by his most recent publication. Before leaving Madrid the author had already expressed concern about the geographical distance between himself and publishers, which prevented him from pressing claims regarding his books, but it was the BBC which became the particular bane, Starkie considering that the corporation had been ignoring him since the end of the war. In July 1956, he assured his London publisher: 'For the past ten years I have been consistently boycotted by the BBC, though they have known me and given me many engagements in the past'[38] and he continued to express his gripe from America, with, perhaps, a thrust of aggression (certainly a solid self-assuredness) following six months of transatlantic success. Murray had attempted to mollify matters in late September 1956, organizing an interview with Stephen Wade of ITV, and later expressing his intention to pursue the matter with the BBC, the effort drew approval from his fractious author: 'I am so glad to think that you are approaching the BBC. I always feel that I have been neglected by them for the past ten years. I think it is time for them to make me some amends.'[39] Starkie also felt the right to reparation from the *TLS* for the poor assessment awarded *The road to Santiago* by a reviewer whom Starkie branded 'an ignoramus and a pedant'.[40] However, the pilgrim publication did obtain some positive response too: from Harold Nicolson in *The Observer* and in the Catholic *Tablet*.[41]

In early September Weybright wasted no time in launching an abridged paperback *Don Quixote* into the American market: 'designed to relate without digressions the principal adventures of the Knight and his Squire'.[42] For $5.95 a Mentor Record Companion, a 12-inch long-playing record, could also be purchased, which carried selections from the text 'read aloud by the translator'.[43] At the end of the month, Starkie snatched four days in London, lodging at the Athenaeum. On the 30th, he was with the Murrays at their home in Hampstead, where he dedicated a copy of *The road to Santiago* to them.[44] He then travelled over to Dublin, finding his mother 'in very good spirits',[45] ready to go out and about with him. By late 1957, J.G. Murray reported that Starkie was 'on the move from Madrid to America'[46] where his new contract at

6 July 1957 (JMC).   **38** W. Starkie to J.G. Murray, 28 July 1956 (JMC). Starkie had certainly broadcast over the BBC, both in the 30s and into the 40s though rather fewer than the 'many' engagements he claimed in his letter to Murray. During the war doubts were expressed within the corporation as to his political views but correspondence from 1954 reflects a readiness to take him on board (E. Molony to B. Tesler, 8 Nov. 1954; B. Tesler to E. Molony, 11 Nov. 1954, BBC Written Archives, Professor Walter Starkie, RCONT 1 Talks File 1, 1932–62).   **39** W. Starkie to J.G. Murray, 20 Apr. 1957 (JMC). Back in Madrid, Starkie insisted to Murray: 'Would it be possible to get the BBC to give me some talks in September-October-November[?] I have not been invited to speak for years.' (W. Starkie to J.G. Murray, 6 July 1957, JMC).   **40** W. Starkie to E. Starkie 10 July 1957 (ES Bodl.). The critic found Starkie's text neglectful of German sources yet 'over-long and discursive' (*TLS*, 17 May 1957, p. 307).   **41** For a consideration of *The road to Santiago* in the context of the Cold War, see J.A. Hurtley, 'Re-writing the road: Walter Starkie on St James's Way' in A. Camps, J.A. Hurtley, A. Moya (eds), *Traducción, (sub)versión, transcreación* (Barcelona, 2005), pp 155–63.   **42** M. de Cervantes Saavedra, *Don Quixote of La Mancha*, trans. W. Starkie (New York, 1957), title page.   **43** See the announcement opposite the title page of the 1957 publication.   **44** The dedicated copy is preserved in the JMC.   **45** W. Starkie to E. Starkie, 21 Oct. 1957 (ES Bodl.).   **46** J.G. Murray to C. Brooks of Messrs. A.M. Heath and Co. Ltd, 18 Dec. 1957 (JMC).

Austin would begin in January. By May the Visiting Professor was feeling 'up to [his] ears in work', created by 'a great number of postgraduates writing theses', which he was required 'to read and criticize',[47] as well as by the prospect of a lecture tour in Venezuela and a talk to be delivered at the Irish Historical Society in New York before the end of the month. June brought the balm of New Harmony before the couple travelled to New York to embark for Barcelona on the Italian liner *Augustus*. They arrived on 1 August, not long before the marriage of their daughter.[48] Before the ceremony Starkie described himself as 'desperately busy [and] working all day solidly' as he struggled to catch up on 'arrears' while feeling additionally anxious about showing 'a great part'[49] of his first volume of autobiography to J.G. Murray in the month of September. Mid-month, he left Italia typing his memoir and travelled to Dublin to stay with his mother for a week before going on to London, where he was able to speak to his publisher about the forthcoming volume before going down to Southampton to sail for New York on the Queen Elizabeth. He had been contracted for a lecture tour in the southern United States by the Harry Byrd Kline Celebrity Service of Dallas. The employment would tide Starkie over the final months of 1958 before he took up a visiting professorship at NYU. He spoke of it as 'my desperate attempt to make money enough to see me through this year and the next[,] up to the time when I go to Kansas'. The Kline Service certainly delivered on the financial front,[50] but by December his room in Dallas felt 'very lonely' and his wife was not in a position to offer much consolation. Italia was in Toronto with Landi or, rather, without him as he was having to travel in connection with his job and, according to her husband, she was feeling 'very depressed' on account of the Canadian cold. There were other 'depressing facts'[51] about Landi too though Walter chose not to disclose them when writing to his sister Enid in December.

In Spain, Starkie continued to command an authorial presence with the translation of *The road to Santiago* into Spanish but the year ended on a worrying note. When writing to Enid in December, he was in receipt of a letter from his sister Chou-Chou reporting their mother's being 'very ill'[52] of late. He felt frustrated, indeed overwhelmed, by the distance between Ireland and the United States and by his unsettled status and dependence on the Kline contract. He had already explained to Enid in August that travel between Spain and the US: 'five journeys for myself and Ita[lia], i.e. 10 passages',[53] had meant a considerable drain on his earnings and, therefore, he was not in a position to increase the allowance he gave to his mother. In January his Visiting Professorship at NYU positioned him within easier reach of Ireland though still an ocean away. Through a friend of Oliver St John Gogarty's, Starkie took on an apartment at the bohemian Hotel Chelsea in New York for $165 per

47 W. Starkie to E. Starkie, 17 May 1958 (ES Bodl.). **48** The marriage took place on 27 Aug. 1958 in the British Institute chapel. **49** W. Starkie to E. Starkie, 21 Sept. 1958 (ES Bodl.). **50** According to Starkie's 'Field Representative' for the late 1958 lecture tour, H.M. McFadden, Starkie's 'normal en route honorarium' was $500 (H.M. McFadden to Dr R. Vosper, 19 May 1958. Spencer Research Library, University of Kansas, Robert Vosper Correspondence (henceforth SRL, UKAN, RVC), Starkie, Walter, RG 32/1/4. **51** W. Starkie to E. Starkie, 8 Dec. 1958 (ES Bodl.). **52** Ibid. **53** W. Starkie to E. Starkie, 21 Aug. 1958 (ES Bodl.).

month. The task at NYU as 'Distinguished Visiting Professor' appears not to have taxed his energies in excess, being 'mostly public lectures and special courses on (1) Music, Magic, Minstrelsy; (2) Five Master Dramatists (Shaw, Pirandello, Benavente, Yeats, O'Neill); (3) The Irish Renaissance',[54] that is, constituted by material more than familiar to him. However, by May he was was feeling 'very lonely and neglected',[55] a state of mind exacerbated by a lack of communication with J.G. Murray (according to his own assessment) but, arguably, also influenced by Italia being away from him in Toronto and his mother's having been in a nursing home for over six months. His plaint over the BBC also persisted.[56] There was some respite from solitude in June with a flight to Toronto to preside at a TCD banquet and to take part in some TV performances, from where he flew to Dublin. He stayed at 4 Landsdowne Road, where the dismantling of his mother's home was afoot. The Dublin bookseller Hodges and Figgis was dealing with 'the Georgian books'; there was discussion as to whether Pater's Italian tables should go into auction; Larky Waldron's tea-set was destined for Enid and her brother claimed possession over 'the commemorative medal of San Lazzaro degli Armeni of Venice' and 'the gilt box from Florence'. He also preserved in a trunk 'the green Wedgewood set of plates'[57] his father's sister Edyth had left him in her will and staked a claim on some of the Rackham-illustrated books, significantly those which connected with Wagner, Shakespeare and fairy tale.[58] By mid-August he was in Madrid writing his memoir while Italia 'loyally'[59] typed and both were able to enjoy their first granddaughter. Financially, the panorama was promising. By May Starkie was aware that the Kister music book was 'doing excellently in France.'[60] In spite of the price having rendered it out of the reach of many, the first edition had sold out and a reprint of 6,000 copies had been produced. Together with this publishing success, his next visiting professorship was for the whole academic year (from 15 September until June 1960) and carried a salary of $10,000.[61] From now on he would not be obliged to cobble together his earnings since the decade brought him contracts for full academic years. While at Austin, he had spoken of Harry Ransom as 'the real live wire in Texas'.[62] Now he was to meet one of a similar ilk at Lawrence, Kansas, the Republican Chancellor Franklin D. Murphy, great grandson of a Roman Catholic Irishman, Patrick Murphy, and a Protestant Irishwoman, Martha Flanagin,[63] a medical doctor by profession, a man of 'wit', who 'interacted freely with people in high

54 W. Starkie to J.G. Murray [no date – May [?] 1959] (JMC).   55 Ibid.   56 W. Starkie to J.G. Murray, 20 May 1959 (JMC).   57 W. Starkie to E. Starkie, 15 July 1959 (ES Bodl.).   58 Starkie 'want[ed] particularly the Rheingold and Siegfried volumes, *Midsummer night's dream* and the Grimm.' (W. Starkie to E. Starkie, 15 July 1959, ES Bodl.).   59 W. Starkie to J.G. Murray, 15 Aug. 1959 (JMC).   60 W. Starkie to J.G. Murray, 20 May 1959 (JMC).   61 Card on Walter Starkie: rank of Visiting Professor in the Department of Romance Languages, 1959–60. (W.F. Starkie Individual Service Record, University of Kansas Academic Affairs Records 1953–2010, RG10, University Archives, SRL UKAN). Starkie had corresponded with University of Kansas librarian Robert Vosper in connection with the Cervantes Day celebration of 1958 and broached the subject of a visiting professorship at Kansas in letters addressed to him. It was Vosper who first introduced Starkie to the Chancellor at Kansas, Franklin D. Murphy (SRL, UKAN, RVC, Starkie, Walter. RG 32/1/4).   62 W. Starkie to J.G. Murray, 8 June 1957 (JMC).   63 M.L. Davis, *The culture broker. Franklin D. Murphy and the transformation of Los Angeles* (Berkeley, 2007), p. 396, n. 1.

places, ... loved opera and read dictionaries for fun' and who 'had made tremendous strides in bringing recognition to the [U]niversity [of Kansas]' over the 1950s. The Lawrence appointment determined Starkie's future years in America. When 'the Boy Wonder'[64] went west, Starkie was not long in following.

Murphy had been Chancellor at Kansas since 1951 and had achieved much over the decade but following Starkie's arrival, he was not to tarry in resigning the chancellorship as a consequence of on-going disagreements with the Democratic Governor of Texas George Docking.[65] Specialist in medieval Spanish sculpture, Marilyn Stokstad, was an undergraduate at the University of Kansas over the year Starkie spent there. She recalls not being impressed by the professor's 'anecdotal approach and playing of the violin, rather badly' in his classes and wonders whether Starkie 'didn't play up the Irish to pander to Murphy.' Also recognizing the Irishman's ability as an actor, she deemed him 'the sort of person Murphy loved':[66] the Chancellor had a taste for entertainment, dinner parties, while Starkie was always ready to perform either verbally or musically. Ned Kehde, a student of History at Kansas between 1959 and 1963 remembers Starkie on campus, '[seeming] often to have a violin case in his hand'. He also recalls his 'incessantly smoking Mississipi Crooks' and habitually finding [the professor] in the Union playing pool'. He was struck by the story-telling, recalled as 'so outrageous, how could it all [have been] true?' but they were 'great stories' and his listeners were 'enthralled' both by the content and the narrator's 'Churchillian-time way of talking',[67] which rang awesome in the 1950s mid-west. Then members of staff at Kansas, Seymour Menton and Vernon Chamberlin, remembered Starkie as 'the garrulous Irishman'[68] and 'a colourful old guy',[69] respectively, the latter not being struck by Starkie as a scholar in 'a book-digging, foot-noting way'[70] but aware that he found popularity among the student body.

Between 15 June and 10 August 1960, Starkie taught at the Summer Institute of the Modern Languages Department at Purdue University, Lafayette, Indiana, an experience he was to repeat in 1961 and 1962. The course was run under the auspices of the State Department and Starkie was scheduled to deliver 'a course of lectures on Spanish civilization ... for French and Spanish college and school teachers'.[71] He described the Purdue period as 'very methodical', providing the detail of his day in correspondence addressed to Enid:

> I get up at 6a.m. and we breakfast at 6:45a.m. My day lecture is at 9:50a.m. We all lunch together in hall at 12:15p.m. We dine in the erum at 5:30p.m. I have my one evening lecture at 7:30p.m. in English for the entire Institute, i.e. the teachers

64 M.L. Davis, *The culture broker*, pp 11, 13. **65** Ibid., pp 15–6. See also: *http://www.kuhistory.com/ proto/story.asp?id–51*, accessed 30 Nov. 2011. Murphy resigned on 17 March 1960. **66** Author's interview with M. Stokstad, University of Kansas, Lawrence, 17 Oct. 2000. **67** Author's interview with N. Kehde, University of Kansas, Lawrence, 18 Oct. 2000. **68** Author's telephone conversation with S. Menton, 18 Oct. 2000. **69** Author's telephone conversation with V. Chamberlin, 18 Oct. 2000. **70** Ibid. **71** W. Starkie to J.G. Murray, 7 June 1960 (JMC). Writing to R. Vosper almost a year on, Starkie referred to the institute at Purdue as 'the National Defence Language Institute' (W. Starkie to Dr R. Vosper, 14 April 1961, SRL, UKAN, RVC, Starkie, Walter RG 32/1/4).

of French (there are about 25) and Spanish (there are 50). All the other lectures I give in Spanish.[72]

After completing his commitment at Purdue, Starkie flew to Dublin where he stayed for the second fortnight of August, visiting his mother in the nursing home 'every single afternoon' for some three or four hours and finding her 'sometimes in very good form [and] not [having] lost her interest in the world and international politics.'[73] He travelled to Spain to stay with his daughter Alma and family in Madrid. He also managed to spend some time in London where the Murrays took him to see Terence Rattigan's 'Ross' at the Theatre Royal Haymarket with Alec Guinness playing the role of T.E. Lawrence.[74] The play dated back to 1922, the beginning of Starkie's adult career, and would have appealed to the author and his publisher since, apart from the fascination Lawrence's adventurous life might hold, it deals with the adoption of disguise.[75] By mid-September Starkie was in Boulder, Colorado, ready to take up a Visiting Professorship in Comparative Literature, while Italia had travelled to Toronto to be with Landi. By the 20th, accommodation had been settled. The 'small apartment on campus ... rather stark and austere and not spacious'[76] did not possess the charm of 'the little house' the couple had rented on Lawrence's Alabama Street, which had reminded the ageing but still fairy-struck Starkie of the one 'discovered by Hansel and Gretel in the wood [,] as illustrated by ... uncle Arthur Rackham'.[77] However, the Boulder landscape, 'a paradise in the Rockies',[78] offered compensations.

The 1959–60 academic year was more intense than ever, particularly from the month of January and into the following academic year, 1960–1, when Starkie became Visiting Professor of Romance Languages at UCLA. Apart from the visiting professorships, there were a number of positive developments with regard to postings and publications. In January Starkie delivered six seminars and two auditorium lectures at the Cleveland Museum of Art, for which the Professor was offered a flat fee of $1,000.[79] He covered the literature, art, music and culture of Spain from the sixteenth to the twentieth centuries, introducing slides and music into most of the sessions. The seminars were to be open to members of staff at the museum, 'several neighbouring university professors from Art History and Romance Language Departments and a few museum members'[80] with thirty or forty people expected for the seminars and between one and two hundred for the lectures. In the event, the lecturer defeated all

---

72 W. Starkie to E. Starkie, 21 July 1960 (ES Bodl.). 73 W. Starkie to E. Starkie, 20 Sept. 1960 (ES Bodl.). 74 The theatre outing was on the night of 3 September 1960 (J.G. Murray to W. Starkie, 8 Aug. 1960, JMC). 75 Diana Murray recalled her husband having 'a wonderful false beard and make-up' to hand at 50 Albemarle Street which he would wear if there was someone waiting whom he didn't wish to speak to as he was leaving the building (D. Murray interviewed by S. Bradley, 15 June 2000, BTL, BL, C872/41, F8164–F8165). 76 W. Starkie to E. Starkie, 20 Sept. 1960 (ES Bodl.). 77 W. Starkie to Dr R. Vosper, 7 Oct. 1959 (KSRL, UKAN, RVC, Starkie, Walter. RG 32/1/4). 78 W. Starkie to J.G. Murray, 26 Nov. 1960 (JMC). 79 Edward B. Henning, Curator of Modern Art, to W. Starkie, 14 Mar. 1960 (Archive of the Cleveland Museum of Art (henceforth CMAA). The programme began on 3 January and finished on the 11th. 80 James R. Johnson, Associate Curator of Education, to W. Starkie, 2 Nov. 1960 (CMAA, Records of the Department of Education (no longer available)).

expectations, drawing multitudes: he saw 'enormous audiences'[81] before him and museum records were to reveal attendance by 'over a thousand people'.[82] At the end of the year, Starkie occupied the Sloan Visiting Professorship at the Menninger Institute in Topeka, Kansas, a post which (as Starkie was to inform more than one correspondent) had previously been occupied by Aldous Huxley.[83] June found Starkie and Italia in 'a nice apartment' and 'very busy' at Purdue. On this occasion Italia had been brought in to give daily classes 'under the scheme' while her husband lectured every second day on Spanish civilization with delivery of 'some special public lectures', a timetable which allowed him 'a good deal of time'[84] for his own work. It was already 'very hot' in June in Lafayette but 'plenty of electric fans'[85] brought some relief. Apart from the university appointments, Starkie's own writing at this time was related to his memoirs and essays connected to texts to be brought out by the New American Library: Yeats's *Celtic twilight*, published together with a selection of his early poems, James Stephens's *Deirdre* and at Christmastime he missed the MLA congress at Chicago in order to move forward with his translation of Cervantes' *Novelas ejemplares*; an unabridged *Don Quixote* was also in the pipeline for Weybright's New York enterprise. In England, J.M. Dent brought out Borrow's *The Bible in Spain* and *Lavengro* with introductions by Starkie, a move which led him to challenge the House of Murray for letting his earlier publications slip out of print. As to books in print, the Swiss publication continued to reap returns, the author noting that 8,500 copies had been sold at $50 per copy, a success for which he admitted he had 'never dared to hope'.[86] A more modest publication but one which Starkie was glad to see reappear in November after so many years, albeit abridged, was *Spanish raggle-taggle* in a Penguin paperback.

When protesting to J.G. Murray about his earlier publications being neglected, Starkie claimed that J.M. Dent were '[t]he only people in England' who had remembered him 'as a writer of Gypsy books and a Borrovian'.[87] The GLS were to prove him wrong in the wake of Augustus John's passing, inviting him to become President of the Society. Though surprised that he was remembered, the nomination signified great satisfaction.[88] On the family front too there was good news: Landi had established a new family with whom he was living in Jamaica. Undoubtedly, by the end of the year there was much to be positive about but it had started with a source of profound sadness: the death of May Caroline on 20 February. The mourning filtered into summertime, when her son made his first journey to Dublin following her death. He went out to the cemetery at Glasnevin on Saturday, 19 August, and spent an hour-

---

81 W. Starkie to J.G. Murray, 17 Jan. 1961 (JMC). 82 James R. Johnson to W. Starkie, 16 Jan. 1961 (CMAA, Records of the Department of Education (no longer available)). In this letter Johnson thanked Starkie for 'a most stimulating series of lectures', reporting that everyone he had spoken to had been 'very enthusiastic about them.' 83 For further details of the Menninger Institute, see http://www.menningerclinic.com/about/Menninger-history.htm, accessed 30 Apr. 2012. The visiting professorship took place between 20 November and 20 December 1961. 84 W. Starkie to E. Starkie, 30 June 1961 (ES Bodl.). 85 W. Starkie to J.G. Murray, 26 June 1961 (JMC). 86 W. Starkie to J.G. Murray, 2 Dec. 1961 (JMC). 87 W. Starkie to J.G. Murray, 10 July 1961 (JMC). 88 W. Starkie to E. Starkie, 16 Dec. 1961 (ES Bodl.).

and-a-half by a grave which struck him as looking 'very forlorn', the stone not yet inscribed and 'some withered twigs'[89] carrying a card with her daughter Muriel's name on it. On his mother's former insistence, there was memorabilia to collect: Pater's Shrewsbury rowing cup, the pewter rowing mugs she did not wish to be auctioned and her husband's edition of Aristophanes' *Acharnians*, the only text of the Greek scholar's still in the family, which she had wanted her son to have. Before travelling back to the United States in September, Starkie again stayed with his daughter and her husband in Madrid, flying to London to pick up his transatlantic flight. He flew out on the 12 September and at lunchtime on the 7th met Enid for the first time since the death of their mother. She would have approved of her eldest children's choice of imperial location for the rendezvous: the Athenaeum, majestic Waterloo Place providing a fine setting for commemorating the 'lady'.[90]

By December 1961, the Starkies had settled at UCLA following the appointment of Visiting Professor of Romance Languages for the 1961–62 academic year. The librarian Robert Vopser, whom Murphy had coaxed to Kansas from California during his chancellorship, was now seduced back to UCLA, where tempting opportunities were afforded him.[91] Once the California visiting professorship had been set up, Starkie wrote to Vosper to query him about possible accommodation: 'as near as possible to the campus with a view of the sea ... something very simple and inexpensive, around $100 a month.' The sea was out of reach if distance was a priority (as it was for a man who had never acquired a driving licence), therefore the Starkies took up residence for the following decade at addresses in Ashton and Wellworth Avenues in Westwood Village, just below the university campus. California was appealing on a number of counts: the Starkies had 'many friends'[92] there; on campus there was Italian-inspired architecture, potentially sympathetic to Italia, and the sunny climate of the west coast was ideal for the professor's chronic asthma. Smog hurt the eyes but was only an occasional discomfort.

Starkie's initial appointment at UCLA connected him to Romance Languages but his activity quickly expanded over the decade of the 60s, leading him to deliver seminars and lectures in a number of Departments or divisions: English, Theatre Arts, Spanish and Portuguese, Italian, the Center for Folklore and Mythology and Musicology. Thus he became a familiar figure on campus, some of his lectures drawing such numbers that they were relayed on screen. By May 1962 Starkie knew that he had been reappointed for the 1962–3 academic year and was to receive 'a very good salary.' Already, by this early point in the decade, Starkie was able to speak of 'savings' and had decided to purchase 'a small house and lovely garden' at Chalfont St Peter, just 'one hour from 50 Albemarle Street',[94] as he eagerly pointed out to his London publisher and friend J.G. Murray. The purchase also met with Italia's approval and the couple eventually visited the house in July 1964, but the dream of

---

89 W. Starkie to E. Starkie, 25 Aug. 1961 (ES Bodl.). 90 See the title of E. Starkie's 1941 family memoir and her comment on the part she was groomed for J.F. Larchet, 'Mrs M.C. Starkie. An appreciation', IT, 10 Mar. 1961, p. 7. 91 Author's interview with Loraine Vosper, widow of Robert Vosper, Los Angeles, 20 Nov. 1998. 92 W. Starkie to R. Vosper, 14 Apr. 1961 (KSRL, UKAN, RVC. Starkie, W. RG 32/1/4). 94 W. Starkie to J.G. Murray, 30 May 1962 (JMC).

retirement in England had to be sacrificed, unexpected demands being placed on the Starkies' savings in the wake of the death of Landi's second wife. However, this further sadness occurred towards the end of the decade; the California experience began with great promise and in 1962 the sixty-eight-year-old Starkie seemed unstoppable. He didn't travel to Europe that summer but taught on the course at Purdue as in the previous two years,[95] managing to escape to New Harmony on a flying visit to celebrate the summer solstice. Departing from Purdue in August, he went on to Kansas to stay with friends and work in the university, revising the manuscript of what he continued to conceive of as the first volume of his autobiography before going back to Boulder to pack and travel on to Los Angeles. In May Starkie had written to J.G. Murray, telling him that he felt 'very depressed' on account of the publisher's having been 'so incredibly slow with the first volume of … autobiography'[96] and by November he was again writing to him, anxious to know what stage the publication was at and arguing that he needed to know in order 'to get on with the second volume of my memoirs[,] which cover the main years of my active life'.[97] Murray had responded to Starkie's May plaint in the month of June, pointing out that the 190,000 words Starkie had chalked up was excessive, introducing the notion of 'some gentle prunings' and recommending that the volume end with the author's engagement to be married: 'that splendid natural climax'.[98] As was his wont, Starkie accepted Murray's observations and action ('I always put my ultimate trust in you alone and always accept the verdict')[99] and by November the publisher, who by this time had long pored over the most recent prolix prose and erratic punctuation of the author, had come up with a title, 'Scholars and Gypsies'. With characteristic caution and a consciousness of the cultural echoes in the text of Starkie's life, Murray conveyed his suggestion, adding: 'The echo of Matthew Arnold is perhaps in its favour'.[1] The title was adopted but in the year of the publication the author remained unconvinced: 'I'm still wishing we could find a more effective title'.[2]

If Murray appeared not to be delivering, Weybright certainly was. The edition of Yeats's *Celtic twilight and a selection of early poems* with an introduction by Starkie was published by the New American Library in March and by May was 'doing very well'.[3] It was followed in April by James Stephens's *Deirdre*, with an 'Afterword' by the author's fascinated young follower and fond reader since before the First World War. At the end of the year Starkie's translation of Cervantes' *Novelas Ejemplares* [Exemplary novels] appeared, accompanied by notes and an introduction. The publication of the Cervantes' text coincided with Starkie's delivery of an inaugural lecture at the MLA congress in Washington in late December, where he chose to speak on

---

95 He would have returned to Purdue in the summer of 1963 had he not been awarded the Del Amo Foundation fellowship grant (Del Amo Foundation Collection, California State University (henceforth DAFC, CSU): Grantee Files, Theses and Reports 1927–1979, Starkie, W. 1963, 1965, 1971, 1976, Box 74, Folder 5). See the corpus of the text, above, for further details of the award.   96 W. Starkie to J.G. Murray, 30 May 1962 (JMC).   97 W. Starkie to J.G. Murray, 5 Nov. 1962 (JMC).   98 J.G. Murray to W. Starkie, 19 June 1962 (JMC). On Murray's talent for persuading authors to modify their texts, see D. Murray interviewed by S. Bradley, 15 June 2000, BTL, BL, C872/41, F8164–F8165.   99 W. Starkie to J.G. Murray, 26 June 1962 (JMC).   1 J.G. Murray to W. Starkie, 7 Nov. 1962 (JMC).   2 W. Starkie to J.G. Murray 19 [?] Jan. 1963 (JMC).   3 W. Starkie to J.G. Murray, 30 May 1962 (JMC).

'Cervantes and the English novelists of the eighteenth century', Weybright again promoting the lecturer and boosting his New American Library publications with 'a big exhibition'.[4] In April 1962, Alma gave birth to her second child, a fifth grandson for the Starkies. However, his grandfather was to see little of him before 1964, the summer of 1963 being taken up with the wanderer's longest and most arduous journey to date.

Following delivery of his lecture at the MLA congress in Washington in December 1962, Starkie addressed the Poetry Society of America on James Stephens. At the end of the year, he was back in New York, speaking at the *Herald Tribune* Book and Author luncheon in the Waldorf Astoria, where 'a huge crowd – over 1,200'[5] were gathered. It was also a year of further publications: a translation of *Eight Spanish plays of the Golden Age* for Random House, for which Starkie wrote an introduction, and he also produced 'a long introduction' for a 'special edition'[6] of Francis Hinde Groome's *Gypsy folk tales*. His major publication of 1963 was *Scholars and Gypsies*, dedicated to 'Pater and Mother in loving memory' and launched in London, in his absence, on 21 October. Enid had received an early copy and provided her brother with her views, or her reader's, as she put it, attributing the criticism she expressed by means of a literary conceit. Her approach was initially complimentary before she launched into a tart tirade on the little sympathy her brother had expressed for his family, the neglect of her own achievements (whereas, as she argued, she had been generous in the space and detail she had awarded his in *A lady's child*). She also voiced doubt as to whether John Pentland Mahaffy was her sibling's godfather, as he had claimed, whether Walter's *liaison dangereuse* with Mlle Cora had happened as narrated and whether the many beatings he purported having received from Pater took place.[7] Her brother insisted that all had happened as portrayed.[8]

By January, Starkie was able to report from the States that he had received 'some very good reviews'[9] of his autobiography: in the *New York Times*, *Herald Tribune*, *Saturday Review* and *Los Angeles Times*. Before publication he had also received positive feedback from Weybright as well as from Professor Majl Ewing and other Professors of English who had heard Starkie reading aloud over dinner at the Ewings. However, Starkie's most enriching (if most taxing) experience in 1963 was not the contemplation of the memoir of his childhood and youth in print but the journey he made to Greece, Macedonia, Turkey, Armenia, Iran, Egypt, Burma, India and Pakistan between June and September, courtesy of a $2,000 Del Amo grant. The four-month fellowship grant was awarded to the Visiting Professor 'to enable him to go to Spain and several related Mediterranean and Near Eastern areas to undertake research on "The History and Influence of the Migration, Folklore, Folk Music and Dance of the Spanish Gypsy".'[10] Writing to Enid in October, her brother spoke particularly of

---

4 W. Starkie to J.G. Murray, 30 May 1962 (JMC).   5 W. Starkie to J.G. Murray, 8 Jan. 1963 (JMC).
6 W. Starkie to J.G. Murray, 8 June 1963 (JMC).   7 E. Starkie to W. Starkie, 11 Oct. 1963 (ES Bodl.).
8 W. Starkie to E. Starkie, 24 Oct. 1963 (ES Bodl.).   9 W. Starkie to J.G. Murray, 8 Jan. 1963 (JMC).
10 DAFC, CSU 1: Grantee Files, Theses and Reports 1927–1979, Starkie, W. 1963, 1965, 1971, 1976, Box 74, Folder 5.

24 W.F. Starkie with sisters (left to right) Muriel, Enid
and Nancy, Chalfont St Peter, England, 1964.

the enormous heat he had endured as well as of his enjoyment though the conditions
had been far from ideal for a sixty-nine-year-old:

> I felt very tired at the end of my travelling and was glad to reach the comparative
> peace of Los Angeles. I found the heat very trying in Turkey, Persia and India.
> In Burma [?] the temperature was over 110 with 98% humidity. I enjoyed Greece
> very much this time as I was able to get down to the very south of the
> Peleponnese … I also enjoyed the expedition to Mount Athos, but I found it very
> hard and had a bad attack of asthma there. I had to walk up and down mountains
> carrying my bag: there were no mules for the travellers. The monasteries had
> very little food, just ham in oil and dried bread and resinated wine.

What he found 'most interesting' in India was what became the Lama's final destination with Kim in Kipling's homonymous text, Benares, while he was also captivated
by the Taj Mahal, finding it 'the most beautiful building I have ever seen'.[11]

The demanding summer trip may have contributed to the decline in Starkie's health
from 1964 on. Moreover, he experienced a 'very busy' academic year over 1963–4, with
'a great deal of lecturing',[13] which wouldn't have enabled much rest in the wake of the
previous summer's exhaustion. Bob Zachary at the University of California Press
ironically remarked that Starkie had 'only been doing the work of four to five ordinary
men; he has virtually been having a holiday in other words'.[14] However, the summer
of 1964 was far from relaxing. The Starkies flew to London at the end of July, went to
see their house in Chalfont St Peter and spent five days in Stratford-upon-Avon seeing

11 W. Starkie to E. Starkie, 12 Oct. 1963 (ES Bodl.).   13 W. Starkie to J.G. Murray, 15 July 1964
(JMC).   14 Robert Y. Zachary to J. Boulenger, 19 Aug. 1964 (JMC).

Shakespeare's Chronicle plays before going on to Madrid to stay with their daughter and her family, all in three weeks. Perhaps it is hardly surprising that health should have become an issue. In the autumn of 1964, Starkie found himself at the University of California Hospital, where he was operated on for a hernia and non-malignant tumour, 'found to have been caused by latent T.B.'[15] Furthermore, he suffered a heart attack on the operating table. Any one of these ailments might certainly have slowed down a younger man. Starkie was at home a week on from the operation and by 9 October was telling Enid that he was back at the university:

> with plenty of work ... a number of public lectures as well as ... seminars and classes in Theatre Arts, Folklore-Mythology as well as Spanish [having] just corrected the proofs for the new hard cover third edition of ... *Pirandello* ... and [being] hard at work on the 1,500 page proofs of [the] complete translation of *Don Quixote* for the New American Library.[16]

All this, moreover, while receiving streptomycin injections. Fortunately there was ongoing good news from Landi and his wife and the Starkies had embarked on acquiring a further piece of property, an apartment on the top floor of a skyscraper under construction in Madrid, due to be completed in 1966.

Following the strain on Starkie's system in the summer of 1963 and the decline in health he subsequently experienced, the couple now turned to spending the summers in Los Angeles. 1965 became a relatively quiet year though Starkie's name continued to ring as an author, the University of California Press bringing out an updated *Pirandello* and Weybright the unabridged *Don Quixote*. He also resurfaced as an author in Spain, where the Madrid publishing house Espasa-Calpe produced a reimpression of the 1937 translation of *Spanish raggle-taggle*. The contact forged with Bob Zachary at the university press in California was a promising development, potentially affording Starkie the opportunity of seeing his Alba manuscript in print at last as well as an edition of the Swiss-edited music book in the United States. In London in early August 1964, he had spoken to Murray about the possibility of publication in California while still harbouring the hope that Murray might be involved in the project but the latter was reluctant after the enormous efforts required to adequately shape the volume of autobiography. Murray determined to maintain a low profile, noting the information received and contemplating a pragmatic response:

> [Starkie] says that California Press is reading the typescript of his abortive book on Alba. He still seems to hope that we will publish even though it was commissioned and turned down by Weidenfeld and Harper. Let us let sleeping dogs lie. If California Press were prepared to do all the work of getting it into order [,] we might consider taking sheets.[17]

---

15 W. Starkie to J.G. Murray, a Christmas card for 1964 [no further date] (JMC).   16 W. Starkie to E. Starkie, 9 Oct. 1964 (ES Bodl.).   17 Point 9 on a sheet of 10 headed 'Walter Starkie', initialled JGM and dated 28 Aug. 1964 (JMC).

A year on, Starkie reported having signed a contract for 'The Dukes of Alba' with the University of California Press and was working on reducing the manuscript,[18] understanding by the summer of 1966 that the west coast press would be bringing the book out in the United States and John Murray in London.[19] In 1968 the text had still not gone into galleys, Starkie complaining that the Press had been 'abominably slow and inefficient'.[20] Following his conversation with the author in August 1964, Murray had qualified the book as 'abortive', and so it remained.

By the end of 1965, Starkie was feeling vulnerable. Writing to Albemarle Street, he implored of his old friend: 'Do write to me occasionally, if only to make me feel that I am still a Murray author even though a neglected one.'[21] However, an event at the end of the year may have countered his status anxiety to some extent. Having been elected a Fellow of the Royal Society of Literature, he delivered the Don Carlos Coloma Memorial Lecture on 9 December, His Excellency the Spanish Ambassador, the Marquis of Santa Cruz, presiding. Starkie picked up on the material he had delivered at the MLA congress in Washington, devoting the lecture to 'Miguel de Cervantes and the English novel.'[22] His visit to England also enabled him to visit sister Enid, who had been diagnosed with cancer. By September the following year, her brother was able to report an improvement though the illness was to take her life at the end of the decade.[23] Further recognition for Starkie arrived from Spain in 1966 when he was made a Knight-Commander of the Order of [Queen] Isabel the Catholic (*Comendador de la Orden de Isabel la Católica*). He commented that the distinction was a source of satisfaction as it had been awarded for his writings.[24] A further source of contentment and, no doubt, a degree of relief for a somewhat battered body approaching seventy-two which 'wheeze[d] and gasp[ed]' arrived in 1966 with the concession of a six-month sabbatical, from September to the end of March 1967. Aware of the privilege by early 1966, Starkie reflected in a letter to Enid:

> This is a very nice tribute to me as strictly I'm not elegible for sabbaticals as I am 71 and over age, but the Chairmen of the six Departments in which I have given lectures in the past five years all wrote to the Chancellor and Regents of the University pressing my claims, with the result that they have granted it.[25]

It was fortunate for Starkie that Franklin D. Murphy continued to occupy the chancellorship at UCLA. However, he would not be long in forsaking the institution for the world of business, resigning in 1968 to become Chairman and CEO of the Times

18 W. Starkie to J.G. Murray, 7 Sept. 1965 (JMC). 19 W. Starkie to E. Starkie, 9 Aug. 1966 (ES Bodl.). 20 W. Starkie to E. Starkie, no date [1968] (ES Bodl.). 21 W. Starkie to J.G. Murray, 7 Sept. 1965 (JMC). Murray replied with affection, energy and composure: 'Dearest Walter, It is splendid to get a letter from you, and we were feeling much what you were feeling, because we felt rather neglected, and what recent news we have had been through the University of California Press' (J.G. Murray to W. Starkie, 15 Sept. 1965, JMC). 22 Walter F. Starkie, 'Miguel de Cervantes and the English Novel' in L.P. Hartley (ed.), *Essays by divers hands. Being the transactions of the Royal Society of Literature*, n.s., 34 (London, 1966), pp 159–79. 23 See her obituary in *French Studies*, 24:4 (1970), 439–40, and in TT, 23 Apr. 1970, p. 14. 24 W. Starkie to E. Starkie, 5 July 1966 (ES Bodl.). 25 W. Starkie to E. Starkie, 16 Feb. 1966 (ES Bodl.).

Mirror Company.[26] It was not long after his departure, in 1970, that Starkie's employment at the university was 'terminated ... suddenly'.[27] Starkie appears to have had no inkling of such change as he and Italia set off on 7 October to spend nineteen days at sea on the P&O liner *Georgia*, bound for England. There were many plans. Nancy had been looking after the Starkies' property, 'Bonhay', in Chalfont St Peter and the couple hoped to stay with her there. Enid was to be visited in Oxford, where her brother had not returned since what he described as his 'tragic fiasco in the Spanish Alfonso XIII Chair'.[28] He also hoped to go over to Dublin, albeit briefly, but most of the sabbatical period was to be spent in Madrid, where he intended to attend some of the sessions at the Academy of the Language and the Academy of History. By August of 1966 he had progressed with the second volume of his autobiography and hoped to complete it in Madrid. The top-floor apartment was not yet ready but the couple found comfortable accommodation in Starkie's 1920s haunt, the *Residencia de Estudiantes*. In November, he wrote to Enid to thank her for the 'wonderful day' Italia, Landi and himself had spent with her in Oxford, an occasion on which Starkie finally met Maurice Bowra, whose manoeuvring the candidate had feared when he went for the Chair in Spanish in 1953.[29] The visit to Dublin had also materialized, the occasion providing the opportunity for Starkie to be interviewed at RTÉ.[30]

In the mid-60s, there is a sense of winding-down in relation to the highly intense rhythm Starkie had maintained since his arrival in the United States in the autumn of 1956, afforded, on the one hand, by the sabbatical in 1966 but also a consequence of the decline in his health.[31] He now seemed to be concentrating on seeing the Alba book and his second volume of biography through the press though neither was to materialize. Following Starkie's visit to Albemarle Street in August 1964, it was already clear to Murray that the author's proposed new book should not follow on from 1920, where *Scholars and Gypsies* ended. Murray dangled the carrot of success to bolster his argument: 'I emphasized that [Starkie's proposed new book] must not be thought of as a continuation of his memoirs. To be successful it ought to have a strong overall theme of something like wandering minstrelsy.'[32] The publisher may well have been convinced that more wandering minstrelsy would move the market but he may also have appreciated that in writing of the 1920s and 30s (and Starkie wished to go as far as the Spanish Civil War period), the author would be wading into waters in which, as a supporter of General Franco's cause both throughout the war and subsequently, he might drown. Given the progressive, permissive and pacifist climate of the 1960s,

26 M.L. Davis, *The culture broker*, pp 105–10.   **27** W. Starkie to D.E. Yates, 1 May 1972 (ULL, GLS 39.120).   **28** W. Starkie to E. Starkie, 5 July 1966 (ES Bodl.).   **29** W. Starkie to E. Starkie, 20 Feb. 1953 (ES, Bodl.)   **30** Cathal O'Shannon Snr in conversation with Professor Walter Starkie, 'Seven Days', RTÉ, Tape DLX / 00869.   **31** Jeanne Ross attended an extension course on Joyce, delivered by Starkie in 1967 when, she observed, the professor was 'not in the best of health': he walked with a stick and was noticeably short of breath. Nevertheless, she felt that the class had been 'a very fortunate experience' (author's interview with J. Ross, Los Angeles, 23 Nov. 1998).   **32** Point 1 on a sheet of 10 headed 'Walter Starkie', initialled JGM and dated 28 Aug. 1964 (JMC).   **33** Starkie sent material to Murray and it was acknowledged by the publisher (J.G. Murray to W. Starkie, 8 February 1968, JMC) but the Starkies' family circumstances were radically transformed in the latter part of the 60s, leaving little space and time for focussing on writing.

25 W.F. Starkie lecturing at UCLA, 1967.

there was a risk of ducking if not disaster. On the other hand, Murray could have been anticipating difficulties regarding what could, and could not yet, be told. Starkie wrote on, but no second volume of autobiography ever appeared.[33]

In 1967 a publication revealed that Starkie had returned, albeit briefly, to the author whom he had abandoned for the playwright Benavente in the 1920s. An introduction by him appeared in Princeton University Press's edition of Anthony Kerrigan's translation of works by Unamuno, *Our Lord Don Quixote: the life of Don Quixote and Sancho with related essays*. Having enjoyed the sabbatical period up until March, Starkie was confined to Los Angeles in the summer ('my exile in the Far West'),[34] expressing frustration at not being able to visit London and Dublin, as he had done so often over July or August, but bent on advancing with his Alba and the autobiography. Starkie had commented on son Landi being 'in good form'[35] in 1966 when he stayed with his parents. A year on, Landi rented 'a big house'[36] in Kent, where the Starkies spent Christmas that year, only passing through London as the Madrid apartment was now available and they travelled on to the Spanish capital to take possession of it. Much was good by the end of the year: Landi had passed law exams with honours, was writing articles for the *Manchester Guardian* and other papers while his wife Aideen was working as a psychiatrist. Landi's parents spent Christmas and into the new year with their son and two grandchildren in Kent. However, family fortunes began to falter. Aideen had been taken into hospital in 1967 for what her father-in-law understood at the time was exhaustion.[37] She died in the following year. In a letter to her sister Enid in the summer of 1967, Nancy remarked that their only brother '[would] not face any facts, … never like[d] facing anything unpleasant'.[38] She may have been

34 W. Starkie to E. Starkie, 10 Aug. 1967 (ES Bodl.). 35 W. Starkie to E. Starkie, 5 July 1966 (ES Bodl.). 36 W. Starkie to E. Starkie, 10 Aug. 1967 (ES Bodl.). 37 Ibid. 38 N. Cooper (née Starkie) to E. Starkie, 4 July 1967 (ES Bodl.).

right but he and his wife were to be sorely tried towards the end of the decade, head on, and increasingly afflicted.

In the wake of Aideen's passing, Landi travelled to California with their sons Michael and Patrick. He moved into the Ashton Avenue apartment that his parents had taken on when they first arrived in Los Angeles, just fifty yards away from their current residence. The children went to board at a school in Anaheim run by a French order of Dominican nuns and travelled home every second weekend. Friends of Enid's with whom the Starkies had forged a friendship in Los Angeles, Marianne Eyles and Frances Fowler, responded kindly to the grandparents' unexpected responsibility, taking the couple together with the boys for picnic lunches on the beach at Malibu. Starkie felt that they had been fortunate in placing the grandsons in 'a good school'[39] but the situation was far from easy, creating a drain on the grandparents' savings. Starkie's workload increased. He spoke of 'heavy work at the university', having taken on '[e]xtension lectures as well as [his] regular quota of seminars'[40] and by the end of August 1969, the two families were sharing their living space, Italia experiencing 'a lot of work keeping the house going and looking after the two boys', who had been with them since late June. Starkie spoke with enthusiasm of his grandsons, reporting that they were 'flourishing', having been afforded the opportunity to 'ride and swim, do archery and ... gymnastics' three days a week in the Topanga Canyon but he also spoke of 'a year of terrible anxiety'. He was able to report that Landi seemed to be 'working hard and making his way' although the strain and financial drain continued: 'it has been uphill work, so far I have had to foot the bill.' Another reason for 'working hard all the summer'[41] was with a view to having leave in the autumn to spend time in Madrid. He was also keen to go to Oxford having been invited to become a member of the Advisory Board of the newly formed Beckett Theatre to be erected in St Peter's College. By late October he was there, still projecting the myth of himself as wanderer.[42]

Unexpectedly, Starkie would be back in Oxford in the spring of 1970, to preside at the funeral of his sister Enid, who had died suddenly in April. On his return to Los Angeles, he collapsed in class and was taken into hospital, where he underwent a further operation. Not long after his return home, son Landi had a heart attack, thus beginning a period which Starkie would qualify as 'an eternity of hell for me, my wife and my son',[43] not least on financial grounds as Landi possessed no medical insurance. The turn of the decade brought Starkie an invitation to affiliate with 'the great fraternity of professors emeriti'[44] at UCLA but also brought with it the end of his employment, at a time when the American government had been channelling funds into the Vietnam conflict and Governor Ronald Reagan's programme of 'massive budget cuts'[45] was being implemented in California. Nonetheless, a degree of privilege

39 W. Starkie to E. Starkie, [no date] (ES Bodl.).   40 W. Starkie to E. Starkie, [no date] (ES Bodl.). 41 W. Starkie to E. Starkie, 29 Aug. 1969 (ES Bodl.).   42 'I have always wandered from one country to another' (F. Filson, 'Beckett: a tutor's view', *Oxford Mail*, 31 Oct. 1969, p. 11).   43 W. Starkie to D.E. Yates, 1 May 1972 (ULL, GLS 39.120).   44 W. Starkie to President Lloyd Morrissett, UCLA Emeriti Association, 22 July 1970 (UCLA University Archives Biographical Files (Walter Starkie) (University Archives Record Series 745)).   45 M.L. Davis, *The culture broker*, p. 106.

26 W.F. Starkie with actor Richard Harris on the set of *Camelot*, California, *c.*1967.

remained: he was able to retain an office on campus and carried on with extension lecturing up until 1973 on the Irish Theatre, Pirandello and Gypsies. Students on campus at UCLA as well as a number of younger members of faculty had been calling for change in the humanities curriculum, objecting to 'Western Civilization classes [which] focused on achievements emanating from the European Enlightenment and therefore privileged the values of Western culture.'[46] However, there was still an audience appreciative of the Western paradigm: in Beverly Hills, where ladies of relative leisure resided, such as Billie Heller, wife of celebrity manager Seymour Heller. A group of between thirty and sixty 'homemakers',[47] would gather on Wednesdays between 10:00a.m. and 12 midday at the Heller home, captivated by Starkie's lore of Ireland and Spain and entertained by his taste for gossip. In spite of such appreciation, in early January 1971 Starkie spoke of having felt 'very despondent' over the months since his operation and by May 1972 referred to a 'long lapse of despairing pessimism' which had 'paralyzed'[48] him, preventing progress on the second volume of his memoirs and the publication of the Alba tome. By 1971, the property in Chalfont St Peter, which sister Nancy had 'transformed into a cosy refuge'[49] for her brother and sister-in-law and which Starkie intended to call Undercliffe, 'in memory of the past',[50] had been sacrificed, leaving him 'heartbroken'.[51] Beyond his personal circumstances, Starkie's correspondence from this period reveals a growing alienation from the society around him[52] and a sense of hopelessness in relation to Ireland as he contemplated the development of 'The Troubles' in the north. Writing to his London publisher in 1971, he painted a ubiquitously negative picture of campus life in the United States, contrasting it to the period of his lecture tours in the late 1920s and early 30s when he had been infused, as he recalled, with the optimism of André

46 Ibid., p. 103.   47 Author's interview with Billie Heller, Los Angeles, 1 Feb. 2008.   48 W. Starkie to D.E. Yates, 1 May 1972 (ULL, GLS 39.120).   49 W. Starkie to J.G. Murray, 4 Jan. 1971 (JMC).   50 W. Starkie to E. Starkie, 10 Aug. 1967 (ES Bodl.).   51 W. Starkie to J.G. Murray, 4 Jan. 1971 (JMC).   52 See M.L. Davis, *The culture broker*, pp 82–90, 102–10, 115, for reference to the surrounding society.

Siegfried's *America comes of age*: 'The violent life of today in the American universities with their milling students, bedraggled hippies, indiscriminate sex, dulling opiates, maniacal drugs continually evokes by contrast the continent I wandered through in the years 1929 to 1931.'[53] When corresponding with long-standing Gypsy Lore associate and friend, Dora Yates, in 1972, the negative vision of campus life had come to encompass the whole of the world around him. His ongoing attachment to Ireland and interest in how the country was faring are revealed in a letter to Enid in 1969, where the tone is, notwithstanding, still energetic, alive to what was going on. He was pronouncing on events and eager to engage in discussion:

> What do you think of the Irish fracas? It seemed the other day as we looked at TV as if we were back again in the days of the 'Trouble'. Do you remember the B Specials in the old days? They are just the same as ever, even worse when led by that flaming firebrand Paisley. His voice on TV sounds like Hitler's. The Devlin girl is over here at present: she looks like a little school girl from County Down with her miniskirts and her snappy Belfast accent. I must say that her speech in the House of Commons was a marvel. It took the House by storm – never in the history of Parliament has there been such a 'maiden' speech! The Catholics were lucky to have her for she turned all the sympathy of England in their favour, she is over here raising a million for the Catholics but she is really orating for a Republic for all Ireland. It is ironical to hear this from a Roman Catholic from Ulster.[54]

However, almost three years on, neither Ireland or the world offer any consolation:

> The world today is a sad and sordid place: when I think of my native country, I find no ray of hope: nothing but hatred, bigotry, brutality on all sides! In England you do not seem to be in a much better state, ... Here in USA I have seen hideous chaos on all sides with a hopeless war in Vietnam which has sapped all the energy and good sense [?] of the people. There is nothing but ——— [?] and anarchy everywhere: the streets are no longer safe at nights: several of my friends have been 'mugged', ... The chief danger are the doped people who are so desperate in their craving for heroin that they stop at nothing to get the money to buy it from the 'pushers' and ... it is even dangerous to walk the public streets in the evening and people are even accosted [?] in the approaches to the underground stations.[55]

In spite of finding himself so benighted, Starkie produced a manuscript, dated 23 April 1972, and entitled *The Gypso-Indian trail to El Dorado*.[56] He was perhaps attempting to follow the advice of his London publisher, abandoning the second volume of memoir and creating what Murray had urged in order to guarantee success:

53 W. Starkie to J.G. Murray, 4 Jan. 1971 (JMC). 54 W. Starkie to E. Starkie, 29 Aug. 1969 (ES Bodl.). 55 W. Starkie to D.E. Yates, 1 May 1972 (ULL, GLS 39.120). 56 I am grateful to grandson Michael Starkie for providing me with a copy of the manuscripts of 'The Gypso-Indian trail to El Dorado' and 'The House of Alba, Maecenas of a thousand years'.

a book 'with a strong overall theme of something like wandering minstrelsy'.[57] The text went back to 1930, tracing a journey from Provence to Andalusia, The Fortunate Isles (The Canary Islands), San Antonio, Texas (the Red Indian Festival), Los Angeles, San Diego, Santa Barbara and San Francisco while also referring to 'the myth of the Lost Atlantis'.[58] It was the shortest of projected publications but, like the Alba manuscript and second volume of autobiography, was destined not to appear in print.

In May 1972, the Starkies flew from Los Angeles to Madrid, where Starkie planned to establish his wife in their penthouse apartment. He then intended to travel on to London and hoped to make an 'expedition' to Liverpool to see Dora Yates 'and have a long chat'.[59] It is not clear that he managed to reach London or Liverpool that year. In any event, his wandering days were drawing to a close. He was back in the United States in 1973, delivering Extension Lectures at UCLA. Almost ten years on from the last book of Starkie's published by John Murray, Starkie sent 'a veritable SOS' to Albemarle Street from an apartment on Glendon Avenue in Westwood Village. He explained recent events and the delicate circumstances he and his wife found themselves in as a consequence of debts accrued by his son while also proposing five possible publications, among them 'The house of Alba' and 'The continuation of my Life Story; a much longer book than *Scholars and Gypsies*',[60] projected as covering from 1921 to 1973. On 14 September Starkie travelled to Houston, taken there 'through the generosity of an anonymous Friend',[61] to deliver a lecture entitled 'Scholars and Gypsies' to The Friends of the University of Houston Library. By 1975 he too was settled in Madrid, perched on the fifteenth floor of the skyscraper on calle Princesa from where he could contemplate the nobility and royalty he had shown such deference to: on one side of the building a view of the Alba residence and grounds in the capital, the Liria Palace; on the other, the royal palace. Former *Times* correspondent William Chislett interviewed Starkie there in his eighty-first year, photographing him in and midst Anglo-Irish paraphernalia: a blaizer which carried the seal of TCD and a photograph of Queen Elizabeth II. The professor struck the journalist as a somewhat neglected figure who 'dropped names' (a tendency of Starkie's throughout his life) and who came over, as Chislett recalls, as 'a bundle of contradictions'.[62] Writing to old friend Murray in 1971 and conscious of his advancing years, Starkie himself had remarked that he was 'racked by moments of intense nostalgia', the equivalent, as he noted, of: '"the agenbite of inwit" James Joyce speaks of in *Ulysses*'.[63] The notion in question refers to remorse of conscience[64] rather than, more simply, nostalgia. Starkie may have been unaware of the former meaning but the way in which he exploited the quote from Joyce's *Dubliners* short story, 'The Dead' in *Scholars and Gypsies*, in which he recreated the Miss Ivors and Gabriel Conroy West-Briton encounter in the context of his own youthful Irish experience, suggests regret,

---

57 Point 1 on a sheet of 10 headed 'Walter Starkie', initialled JGM and dated 28 Aug. 1964 (JMC). 58 W. Starkie to D.E. Yates, 1 May 1972 (ULL, GLS 39.120). 59 Ibid. 60 W. Starkie to J.G. Murray, 14 May 1973. I am grateful to Michael Starkie for providing me with a copy of his grandfather's letter. 61 T.J. MacMorran, 'Dr Starkie speaks on "Scholars and Gypsies" to the friends of the library', *Aldus* 2:2 (Nov. 1973), page not numbered. The 'anonymous Friend' was in all probability Jane Blaffer Owen. 62 Author's interview with W. Chislett, Madrid, 9 May 1997. 63 W. Starkie to J.G. Murray, 4 Jan. 1971 (JMC). 64 D. Gifford with R.J. Seidman, *Ulysses annotated* (Berkeley, 2008), p. 22.

27 W.F. Starkie with Italia, celebrating her eightieth birthday, Los Angeles, California, 1971

becoming tantamount to an *apologia pro vita sua*, coupled with the forgiveness (unlike in the case of Miss Ivors) of Mother Ireland towards her prodigal son:

> – What's a West Briton, Maggie? I suppose I'm one myself.
> – Sure of course you are! But we forgive you, for how could you be otherwise? You know less about your country than if you were a foreigner. Your parents have never given you the opportunity of understanding our struggle for our country's right to be free and independent.[65]

Arguably, whatever Starkie's parents never provided him with the opportunity for understanding, he could have moved on. In this connection, it may be worth taking into consideration that the text in question was published in a volume of autobiography which appeared two years after the passing of his mother, the 'lady' who had continued to hold the fort and flown the flag of the Union following her husband's premature death. The volume was devotedly dedicated to the parents but also conveys, through 'Maggie' in Starkie's refashioning of the *Dubliners* episode, a consciousness of their shortcoming as educators of their son while also 'suppos[ing]' his own in failing to embrace the Ireland that the colonizing culture had ignored, at best. Thus, Starkie resolutely remained a Peter Pan, resistent to growing up with the land of his birth on her own terms. In later life, he identified himself as 'a disciple of James Joyce'.[66] Perhaps there was an awareness, too, of having possessed a status not unlike Stephen Dedalus's, as initially identified in Joyce's *magnum opus*: both 'a lovely mummer', even a 'peerless' one,[67] as well as 'the servant of two masters, … an English and an Italian

---

65 W. Starkie, *Scholars*, p. 46. Quoted as epigraph to Part One, above.   66 Dedication on J. Joyce's *The cat and the devil* (London, 1965), given to Georgina Noueiri (née Warner), dated in Oxford, 30 Oct. 1969. I am grateful to G. Noueiri for sharing Starkie's dedication on his gift to her with me. No doubt *Ulysses* would have spoken to Starkie in a number of ways of the Victorian Dublin he grew up in.   67 Not to say a 'poor dogsbody', '[a] jester at the court of his master' (J. Joyce, *Ulysses*, pp 6, 25).

... the Imperial British state and the holy Roman catholic and apostolic church ... [a]nd a third ... who want[ed] him for odd jobs'.[68] Above all, of the first. Indeed, not unlike Alice, eager to participate in the 'great huge game of chess ... being played all over the world', for the 'fun' of it and in spite of the minor status one might have to bear, as long as one might take (play a) part. Alice's desire made Starkie's: 'How I *wish* I was one of them. I wouldn't mind being a Pawn, if only I might join ...'[69]

The sunny climate of southern California had been kind to the asthma sufferer and although the move to Madrid brought the couple close to the warmth of their daughter Alma and her family, the winters in the Spanish capital could be severely cold. In 1976, as October turned into November, Starkie's chronic complaint developed into cardiac asthma and he was taken into the British-American hospital. The first impression was that the patient would rally but he did not. His wife and daughter were with him when the wandering ceased: at 11a.m. on 2 November 1976. Italia soldiered on for six months. Her daughter recalls her continuing to brush her deceased husband's hat and coat, hanging where he had habitually left them; her not eating in Alma's absence.[70] Both are buried in the British Cemetery, situated in the Madrid working-class quarter of Carabanchel, where the capital's patron saint is celebrated in the May festivity of San Isidoro. It is an area of Madrid associated with fierce fighting during the Spanish Civil War, which housed a notorious prison during the Franco regime and is now one of the most ethnically diverse neighbourhoods in Spain.[71]

The remains of Walter Fitwilliam Starkie and Italia Augusta Porchietti Starkie lie in the company of those of British nationals but also alongside the European aristocracy – exiles of lost causes, such as the Bagration dynasty who left Georgia following the 1917 Russian Revolution; the Estonians Tataiana de Korf and her husband; a Polish Count: Zavadowsky Miklazewsk; descendants of Empire like the Austro-Hungarian family of bankers, Bauer; entrepreneurs, such as the Frenchman of Swiss parentage Émile Huguenin-Lhardy, founder of the colonial-façaded Restaurant Lhardy in early nineteenth-century Madrid. There are diplomats too: British Embassy employee Arthur Yencken, whose plane was shot down on a flight to Barcelona in 1944; men of adventure: thus, the pioneering photograper Charles Clifford; women of enterprise: Irishwoman Margaret Mary Kearne Taylor, who founded the Embassy tea-salon in Madrid and a heroine in so far as she risked her life during the Second World War to help the hounded escape;[72] and the world of enter-tainment is also represented: the lion-tamer William Parish, the circus impresario of

---

68 J. Joyce, *Ulysses*, pp 5, 191, 20. As Jeri Johnson has pointed out: 'While Joyce does not name the third, the most obvious candidate is "Mother Ireland".' (J. Johnson, 'Explanatory notes' in J. Joyce, *Ulysses*, p. 767.) Starkie specifically rendered the surrogate Mother service over the years of the Free State government. 69 L. Carroll, *Alice's adventures in Wonderland* and *Through the looking-glass* (Oxford, 2009), p. 144. Linda Hutcheon's definition of the 'ex-centric' may also be considered pertinent here: 'the off-centre: ineluctably identified with the centre it desires but is denied' (L. Hutcheon, *A poetics of postmodernism. History, theory, fiction* (London, 1988), p. 60). 70 Author's telephone conversation with A. Starkie, 1 June 2011. 71 Information about the British cemetery in Madrid can be found at *http://www.britishcemeterymadrid.com*. I am grateful to David Butler for sharing his wealth of knowledge about the cemetery with me. 72 P. Martínez de Vicente, *La clave Embassy* (Madrid, 2010).

28 W.F. Starkie in his penthouse apartment on calle Princesa, Madrid, 1975.

what became widely known in Spain as El Circo Price. The range of nationalities is broad, stretching up into northern climes, to Sweden, across the Atlantic to the United States, on to the Caribbean and Australia, as is that encompassing age, talent and belief: Jews and at least one Muslim grave alongside Christian ones. Ultimately, a sod without segregation of age, ethnicity or creed, one which has incorporated human variety. A place where Walter Fitzwilliam Starkie might rest in peace and feel close to the 'pawnshop'[73] of his birth: a relatively small plot absorbed into a larger territory, haunted by the ghost of time past, not unreminiscent of the paradise lost, the Never [-To-Be-Again] Land of childhood. Having reached 'the Eighth Square',[74] the revels may be continuing as he feasts and feigns alongside the company he sought and culti- vated when not in pursuit of Gypsies and low life, as he had roistered at Lhardy and wherever, whenever the opportunity struck, throughout, and effusively embracing, the time of his life – an existence laced with fictions, riddled by Alice's 'favourite phrase "Let's pretend".'[75] Perhaps the greatest, lifelong pretence and act of (self-) deception, that of believing himself anything other than an Irishman.

73 J. Joyce, *Ulysses*, p. 25.   74 L. Carroll (2009), p. 146. Readers of *Through the looking-glass* will remember that in the Eighth Square 'it's all feasting and fun'.   75 Ibid., p. 126.

Appendix

'Musical notes of the week'. 'Valkyries of the Violin', 13 November 1926, 231–2.
'Royal Dublin Society. Solomon's playing', 20 November 1926, 255.
'The London Symphony Orchestra. Sir Thomas Beecham as conductor', 4 December 1926, 255.
'Music of the week. Mr. Duffy's Recital. Colonel Brass as conductor'. 'RDS. The Recital of Miss Myra Hess', 11 December 1926, 327.

1927
'Youra Guller', 15 January 1927, 455.
'The Rose String Quartet', 22 January 1927, 480–2.
'RDS. The Philharmonic Trio', 29 January 1927, 506–8.
'Bratza's Violin Recitals', 5 February 1927, 530.
'Music of the Week. Friedman Iturbi', 19 February 1927, 576–7.
'The RDS Concerts. Senor [*sic*] Cassado's Recital. Sir Hamilton Harty's Orchestra', 5 March 1927, 624; 626.
'The Dublin Orchestral Society', 19 March 1927, 40.
'Irish composers and Irish players', 26 March 1927, 68; 70.
'The Civil Service Musical Society', 7 May 1927, 212.
'The *Feis Ceoil*', 14 May 1927, 227–9.
'Dublin Wireless Orchestra Concert', 4 June 1927, 310.
'John McCormack', 13 August 1927, 545–6.
'New play at the Abbey. *The Drapier letters*', 27 August 1927, 597.
'"Oedipus at Colonus" at the Abbey Theatre', 17 September 1927, 40–1.
'Literature and life. Beethoven. Legend and reality', 24 September 1927, 62–4.
'Civic Week music notes. John McCormack. Comendatore [*sic*] Esposito', 24 September 1927, 64.
'Civic Week Music. Children's Concert. Dublin Philharmonic Society', 1 October 1927, 86; 86–7.
'The opening of the musical season. "Celebrity Concert" ', 29 October 1927, 185–6.
'RDS.The Hallé Orchestra', 5 November 1927, 206–7.
'RDS. Walter Lieseking', 12 November 1927, 228–30.
'Music of the Week. Elena Gerhardt and Cortot', 19 November 1927, 254–5.
'RDS. The Virtuoso Quartet', 19 November 1927, 255.
'RDS. Senor [*sic*] Cassado and Madame Mendelssohn', 26 November 1927, 280–1.
'RDS. Piano and strings', 3 December 1927, 304.
'"*Mallorca the Magnificent*"', 10 December 1927, 330–1.
'Music Notes: The Dublin Orchestral Society', 10 December 1927, 326.
'RDS. London String Quartet', 17 December 1927, 327.
'Music Notes. Philharmonic Society. "Elijah" (Mendelssohn)', 17 December 1927, 352–3.
'RDS. Segovia', 17 December 1927, 353–4.
Diálogo de las lenguas by Juan de Valdés. Edition with introduction and appendices by Janet H. Perry, MA (University of London Press)', 24 December 1927, 378.
'Literature and life. The spirit of Spain', 24 December 1927, 371–3.

1928
'Music of the week. John McCormack', 7 January 1928, 422.
'Miss Forsyth's Vocal Recital', 21 January 1928, 462–3.
'RDS. Isolde Menges', 21 January 1928, 463–4.

'Literature and life. The fantastic in literature', 28 January 1928, 479.

'Music notes. The Dublin Philharmonic Society', 28 January 1928, 480.

'RDS. Brailowsky', 28 January 1928, 480–2.

'Music notes. Abbey Theatre ballets', 4 February 1928, 501.

'Miss Culwick's Choir', 4 February 1928, 501.

'Johan Strauss. The waltz king', 4 February 1928, 501–2.

'RDS. The Brosa Quartet', 4 February 1928, 502.

'RDS. Madrigals', 11 February 1928, 520.

'The Pirani Trio', 11 February 1928, 520–1.

'RDS. Albert Sammons', 18 February 1928, 540.

'Music Notes. Dublin Orchestral Society', 25 February 1928, 561–2.

'RDS. Catterall Quartet', 25 February 1928, 562.

'RDS. Smeterlin', 3 March 1928, 580.

'Music notes. Dublin Philharmonic Orchestra', 10 March 1928, 12.

'RDS. The Lener [*sic*] Quartet', 10 March 1928, 12.

'Celebrity concert. Sir Thomas Beecham', 17 March 1928, 34.

'Andromaque at the Peacock Theatre', 17 March 1928, 34–5.

'The *Feis Ceoil*', 26 May 1928, 229–30.

'Comendatore [*sic*] Esposito' [signed 'Musician'], 2 June 1928, 253–4.

'RDS. The Halle Orchestra', 27 October 1928, 153.

'Music Notes. The Schubert Centenary Concert', 10 November 1928, 193; 194.

'RDS. Miss Jelly d'Aranyi [*sic*]', 10 November 1928, 194.

'Music notes. Paderewski', 17 November 1928, 213.

'The Dublin Operatic Society', 17 November 1928, 213.

'RDS. The London String Quartet', 17 November 1928, 213–14.

'Literature and life: the evolution of music', 24 November 1928, 231–2.

'Music Notes. Orloff', 24 November 1928, 232–3.

'Miss Rachel Levin's Recital', 24 November 1928, 233.

'Music Notes. Miss Culwick's Concert', 1 December 1928, 253.

'The London String Quartet', 1 December 1928, 253.

'Music notes. Cortot, Thibaud and Casals', 8 December 1928, 275–6.

'RDS. Miss Myra Hess', 8 December 1928, 276–7.

'Music Notes. Dublin Philharmonic Society', 15 December 1928, 300–1.

'RDS. Harp Ensemble', 15 December 1928, 301.

1929

'RDS. Dohnányi', 19 January 1929, 400–1.

'Monsieur Jean Du Chastain', 22 June 1929, 313.

'The eternal dances of Spain', 3 August 1929, 427–8.

'Chaliapine', 9 November 1929, 195–6.

'Music notes. RDS. Philharmonic Society', 9 November 1929, 196.

'RDS. Robert Casadesus', 16 November 1929, 216–17.

'RDS. The Philharmonic Trio', 23 November 1929, 237–8.

'Reviews. Introduction to the method of Leonardo Da Vinci. By Paul Valery. Translated by Thomas Mc Greevy' (London: Rodeker), 28 December 1929, 339–40.

1930

'The Léner String Quartet', 8 February 1930, 458.

'Literature and life. Modern music', 12 April 1930, 113–14.

ARTICLES IN THE *IRISH INDEPENDENT* (1936; 1938)

'An Irishman visits the war front. Experiences on a big troopship', 4 March 1936, p. 11.

'With Dr Starkie in Abyssinia (2). I fly in a "Disperata" bomber', 6 March 1936, p. 6.

'With Dr Starkie in Abyssinia (3). Battle on edges of precipices', 9 March 1936, p. 11.

'With Dr Starkie in Abyssinia (4). Native allies of Italy', 11 March 1936, p. 11.

'With Dr Starkie in Abyssinia (5). Conquest by roads', 13 March 1936, p. 7.

'With Dr Starkie in Abyssinia (6). I watch the Italian doctors at their job', 16 March 1936, p. 6.

'With Dr Starkie in Abyssinia (7). Religion of the people', 17 March 1936, p. 7.

'Behind the scenes in war-torn Spain. The old Spain and the new', 24 January 1938, p. 5.

'Behind the scenes in war-torn Spain. How an Irish hero died in action', 25 January 1938, p. 7.

'Behind the scenes in war-torn Spain. I smoke the Moorish pipe of peace', 26 January 1938, p. 6.

'Behind the scenes in war-torn Spain. Aragon. The pivot of the war', 27 January 1938, p. 6.

'Behind the scenes in war-torn Spain. The Alcazar', 28 January 1938, p. 9.

'Behind the scenes in war-torn Spain. Besieged in a wrecked fortress', 29 January 1938, p. 7.

'Behind the scenes in war-torn Spain. Salamanca. City that became a capital in a hurry', 31 January 1938, p. 7.

'Behind the scenes in war-torn Spain. Irishmen in Franco's capital', 1 February 1938, p. 12.

'Behind the scenes in war-torn Spain. When the reds raided the banks of Spain', 2 February 1938, p. 7.

'Behind the scenes in war-torn Spain. General Franco. The man and his cause', 3 February 1938, p. 6.

'Behind the scenes in war-torn Spain. Tense days that shook the world', 4 February 1938, p. 6.

'Behind the scenes in war-torn Spain. I go up to the northern battlefields', 8 February 1938, p. 7.

'Behind the scenes in war-torn Spain. When red troops encircled Oviedo', 9 February 1938, p. 7.

'Behind the scenes in war-torn Spain. How a gallant Irishwoman died', 10 February 1938, p. 6.

'Behind the scenes in war-torn Spain. Back to the frontier at Irun [*sic*]', 11 February 1936, p. 6.

'Behind the scenes in war-torn Spain. Dr Walter Starkie sums-up', 12 February 1938, p. 7.

'Portugal revisited. The scholar comes to the rescue', 16 February 1938, p. 7.

'Portugal revisited. Centenary of a great university', 17 February 1938, p. 5.

'Portugal revisited. Dr Adolfo [*sic*] Salazar. A dictator in spite of himself', 19 February 1938, p. 7.

'Portugal revisited. Dr Salazar's five fundamental principles', 21 February 1938, p. 7.

'Portugal revisited. Principles of the corporative state', 22 February 1938, p. 8.

'Portugal revisited. Communism has gone bankrupt in the soviets', 23 February 1938, p. 6.

'Portugal revisited. Salazar and fascism', 24 February 1938, p. 9.

'Portugal revisited. From the Tagus to the Douro', 25 February 1938, p. 13.

'Portugal revisited. Where wine chiefs sit and savour their famous port', 26 February 1938, p. 6.

Bibliography

PRIMARY SOURCES

Interviews /Correspondents
María Victoria Alfaro Drake, Charles Aliaga Kelly, Pat Anderson, Ramón Araluce, Juan Arias, Pablo Arribas Briones, Augusto Assia, Pamela Bacon, Manuel Balson, Tibor Bene, Jean François Berdah, Csilla Bertha, Jane Blaffer Owen, Patricia Boylan, Julio Caro Baroja, Vernon Chamberlin, Arthur Chandler, William Chislett, John Cogollado, John Crow, Enrique de Aguinaga, Louis de Goor, Terence de Vere White, John Dew, Elsie Dunnin, Josephine Elliott, John Espy, Norah Fahie, Kevin Flanagan, Bernard Galm, Anthony Garret Anderson, Pilar Gefaell de Valverde, José Luis Gil Aristu, Henry Goodman, David Gordon, Joyce Gordon Rangen, Roger Griffin, Phillip Griffin, Vyvyan Harmsworth, Mary Hawley, Billie Heller, Francis Heller, Michael Holroyd, Rosemary Hone, Muriel Horsford (née Starkie), Claude Hulet, Ned Kehde, Dermot Keogh, Jascha Kessler, Declan Kiberd, Ludmila Klurfain Spyridakis, Teresa Lafita, Corinne Lamont, Mr & Mrs G. J. Larchet, Gillian E. Leonard, Robert Lima, Miklós Lojkó, Edna Longley, Eva López de (Rubia) Barcia, Tomás Mac Anna, Doireann MacDermott, Hilary Mackendrick, Peter Magurean III, Antonio Masip Hidalgo, Alexandra Mason, W.J. McCormack, Seymour Menton, Thomas Middleton, Manuel Muñoz Montón, Christopher Murray, Diana Murray, John G. Murray, Georgina Noueiri, Manus Nunan, Conor Cruise O'Brien, Ulick O'Connor, John O'Keeffe, Patricia O'Malley, Jesús Pardo, S.L. Piggins, Paul Preston, Jaan Puhvel, S. Ramaswamy, José Rey Ximena, Jeanne Ross, Maite Santos Torroella, Joan de Segarra, Delia Salvi, Mercy F. Simms, Allegra Snyder, Alma Starkie, Michael Starkie, Patrick Starkie, Ed Stenton, Marilyn J. Stokstad, María Rosa Suárez-Zuloaga, Averil, Lady Swinfen, Nancy Tornero, Jaime Vandor, Loraine Vosper, Kathleen Walsh, Francis Warner, D.A. Webb, Arnold Weiss, A.J. White, Jenei Zsolt.

Archives and libraries
Abbey Theatre
Alexandra College
Ampleforth Abbey
Archivio Centrale dello Stato
Archivo General de la Administración
Archivo Manuel de Falla
BBC Written Archives Centre
Biblioteca de Catalunya
Biblioteca de Asturias Ramón Pérez de Ayala
Biblioteca de Catalunya
Biblioteca Marucelliana
Biblioteca Nacional de España
Bodleian Library
British Council

Cadbury Research Library: Special Collections, University of Birmingham
California State University, Dominguez Hills
Casa Ignacio Zuloaga
Casa-Museo Unamuno
Churchill College, Cambridge
Cleveland Museum of Art
Fundación Casa de Alba
Fundación Menéndez Pidal
Hemeroteca Municipal de Madrid
Humanities Research Center, University of Texas at Austin
Harvard University
Il Vittoriale degli Italiani
McGill University
Ministerio de Asuntos Exteriores
Monasterio de Santo Domingo de Silos
National Library of Ireland
National University of Ireland Galway
New Harmony, Indiana
Real Academia Española
Real Academia de la Historia
Royal Irish Academy
Royal Irish Academy of Music
Royal Society of Literature
RTÉ Written Archives
Shrewsbury School
Special Collections, University of Houston Libraries
Special Collections Research Center, Southern Illinois University, Carbondale
Special Collections Research Center, University of Chicago Library
Spencer Research Library, University of Kansas
The Athenaeum
The British Institute of Florence
The British Library
The John Murray Collection
The National Archives of Ireland
The National Archives of the UK
The St John's College Robert Graves Trust
The Women's Library, London Metropolitan University
Trinity College Dublin
Trinity College Hartford, Connecticut
Universitat de Barcelona
University College Dublin
University of California Los Angeles
University of Liverpool
University of Reading
Uppsala universitetsbibliothek
Westminster Diocesan Archives

Periodicals

ABC, Aldus, Alexandra College Magazine, Anti-Suffrage Review, APA Magazine, APA News Bulletin, Arriba, Avui, Bibliografía Hispánica, Books of Today, Bulletin and Scotts Pictorial,

Bulletin of Spanish Studies, Canadian Medical Association Journal, Catholic Herald, Chicago Sunday Tribune, Contemporary Review, Cork Examiner, Cuadernos de Historia Contemporánea, Daily Express, Daily Mail, Destino, Diario de Barcelona, Diario de Burgos, Dublin Gazette, Dublin Magazine, El Alcázar, El Correo Catalán, El Correo de Andalucía, El Correo Español – El Pueblo Vasco; El Debate, El País, España, Evening Mail, Evening Herald, Everyman, Fortnightly Review, French Studies, Glasgow Herald, Harvard University Gazette, Hartford Courant, Hermathena, Ideal, Información, Informaciones, International Journal of Iberian Studies, Irish Arts Review, Irish Book Lover, Irish Independent, Irish Press, Irish Statesman, Irish Times, John O'London's Weekly, Journal of Contemporary History, Journal of the Gypsy Lore Society, Keystone Folklore. The Journal of the Pennsylvania Folklore Society, La Época, La Gaceta del Norte, La Vanguardia, Las Provincias, Levante, Luz, Madrid, Misión, Musical Times, News Bulletin of the All Peoples' Association, Oxford Mail, Patria, Presto, Proceedings of the Royal Irish Academy, Pueblo, Quarterly Review, Residencia, Revista de Occidente, Revista Nacional de Educación, Studia Silensia, Studies, Sunday Independent, Sunday Times, The British-Italian Bulletin, The Catholic Bulletin and Book Review, The Gazette, The Listener, The Red Triangle, The Red Triangle Bulletin, The Salopian, The Spectator, The Star, The Times, Time and Tide, TLS, University of Chicago Weekly Calendar, Westminster Gazette, Ya.

Recordings

Walter Starkie interviewed by Bernard Galm, Oral History Program, UCLA, Nov. 1970 – Feb. 1971.

Walter Starkie interviewed by Cathal O'Shannon, Snr., 'Seven Days', RTÉ, DLX / 00869.

Papers

The Papers of Walter Fitzwilliam Starkie, 1894–1976: TCD MSS 9171–9208

Correspondence and Papers of William Joseph Myles Starkie, 1860–1920: TCD MSS 9209–9210

BOOKS AND ARTICLES BY WALTER STARKIE

1. Books

1.1. Books – authored

Starkie, W. (1924) *Jacinto Benavente*. London, Humphrey Milford.

—— (1926) *Luigi Pirandello*. London, J.M. Dent.

—— (1937) *Luigi Pirandello, 1867–1936*. With a prologue by W. Starkie. London, John Murray.

—— (1965) *Luigi Pirandello (1867–1936)*. With an introduction by W. Starkie. Berkeley, University of California Press.

—— (1933) *Raggle-taggle. Adventures with a fiddle in Hungary and Roumania*. London, John Murray.

—— (1934) *Spanish raggle-taggle. Adventures with a fiddle in North Spain*. London, John Murray.

—— (1961) *Spanish raggle-taggle*. London, Penguin.

—— (1936) *Don Gypsy. Adventures with a fiddle in Barbary, Andalusia and La Mancha*. London, John Murray.

—— (1938) *The waveless plain. An Italian autobiography*. London, John Murray.

—— (1940) *Grand inquisitor. Being an account of Cardinal Ximenez [sic] de Cisneros and his times*. London, Hodder and Stoughton.

—— (1953) *In Sara's tents*. London, John Murray.
—— (1957) *The road to Santiago. Pilgrims of St James*. London, John Murray.
—— (1958) *Spain. A musician's journey through time and space*. Geneva, Edisli.
—— (1963) *Scholars and Gypsies*. London, John Murray.

1.2. Books – translated

Cervantes Saavedra, M. de (1954) *Don Quixote of La Mancha* [An abridged version]. Translated and edited with a biographical prelude by W. Starkie. London, Macmillan.
—— (1957) *Don Quixote of La Mancha. An abridged version designed to relate without digressions the principle adventures of the knight and his squire*. Translated and edited with an introduction by W. Starkie. New York, Mentor Books.
—— (1963) *The deceitful marriage and other exemplary novels*. Translated and with a foreword by W. Starkie. New York, New American Library.
—— (1964) *Don Quixote*. Translated and with an introduction by W. Starkie. New York, New American Library.
Fonseca, Rodolfo L. (1954) *Tower of ivory* [*Turris eburnea*]. Translated by W. Starkie. London, Jonathan Cape.
Menéndez Pidal, R. (1950) *The Spaniards in their history* [the introductory essay extracted from *Historia de España*]. Translated and with a prefatory essay on the author's work by W. Starkie. London, Hollis and Carter.
Olagüe, I. (1954) *This is Spain*. Translated and with an introduction by W. Starkie. London, Cohen and West.
Pérez de Ayala, R. (1933) *Tiger Juan* [*Tigre Juan* and *El curandero de su honra*]. Translated by W. Starkie, with an introductory essay. London, Jonathan Cape.
Ruiz, J. et al. (1964) *Eight Spanish Plays of the Golden Age* [Texts by Juan Ruiz, Lope de Rueda, Lope de Vega, M. de Cervantes, Tirso de Molina, Calderón de la Barca and the anonymous *The mystery play of Elche* [*El misterio de Elche*]. Translated, edited and with an introduction by W. Starkie. New York, Random House.

1.3. Books – introductions to, forewords and afterwords

Belloc, H. (1959) *Camino de Roma* [The path to Rome]. Prólogo por W. Starkie. Barcelona, Juventud.
Borrow, G. (1948) *The Romany Rye*. With an introduction by W. Starkie. London, The Cresset Press.
—— (1961) *The Bible in Spain*. With an introduction by W. Starkie. London, J.M. Dent.
—— (1961) *Lavengro*. With an introduction by W. Starkie. London, J.M. Dent.
Crotty, H.D. (1963) *Glimpses of Don Quixote and La Mancha*. With an introductory essay by W. Starkie. Los Angeles, The Zamorano Club.
Groome, F.H. (1963) *Gypsy folk tales*. Foreword by W. Starkie. London: Herbert Jenkins.
James, M.R. [1945?] *Libro de fantasmas* [A book of ghosts]. Prólogo de W. Starkie. Barcelona, Hesperos.
López Cruz, F. [*c*.1967] *La música folklórica de Puerto Rico* [The folkloric music of Puerto Rico]. Prólogo de W. Starkie. Sharon, Conn., Troutman.
Porta, J. (1946) *Bajo los puentes (La vida de los gitanos)* [Under bridges (The life of Gypsies)]. 'Preludio' de W. Starkie. Barcelona [published by the author].
Révesz, A. (1947) *La vida patética de Eleanora Duse* [The pathetic life of Eleonora Duse]. Prólogo de W. Starkie. Barcelona, Iberia.
Rosa-Nieves, C. [1967] *Voz folklórica de Puerto Rico* [The folkloric voice of Puerto Rico]. Prólogo de W. Starkie. Sharon, Conn., Troutman.

Sampson, G. (1953) *Historia de la literatura inglesa* [The concise Cambridge history of English literature]. Prólogo de W. Starkie. Madrid, Pegaso.

Shelley, P.B. (1947) *Adonais*, trans. V. Gaos, Colección Adonais 38. Prólogo de W. Starkie. Madrid, Adonais.

Stephens, J. (1962) *Deirdre*. With an afterword by W. Starkie. New York, New American Library.

Unamuno, Miguel de [1967] *Our Lord Don Quixote. The life of Don Quixote and Sancho with related essays*, trans. A. Kerrigan. With an introduction by W. Starkie. London, Routledge and Kegan Paul.

Yeats, W.B. (1962) *The Celtic Twilight* and *A selection of early poems*. With a foreword by W. Starkie. New York, New American Library.

1.4. Books – contributions to

Starkie, W. (1925) 'Luigi Pirandello and the contemporary drama in Italy' in *Homenaje ofrecido a Menéndez Pidal. Miscelánea de estudios lingüísticos, literarios e históricos*, vol. 3. Madrid, Hernando, pp 157–63.

—— (1928) 'Whither is Ireland heading – is it fascism? Thoughts on the Irish Free State' in *A survey of fascism. The yearbook of the International Centre of Fascist Studies*, 1. London, Ernest Benn, pp 223–34.

—— (1931) 'What the Royal Dublin Society has done for music', *The Royal Dublin Society bicentenary souvenir*, Dublin, pp 60–5.

—— (1933) 'Introductory essay' in R. Pérez de Ayala, *Tiger Juan*, trans. W. Starkie. London, Jonathan Cape, pp 11–38.

—— (1939) 'Sean [*sic*] O'Casey' in L. Robinson (ed.), *The Irish theatre*. London, Macmillan, pp 149–76.

—— (1950) 'Cervantes y la novela inglesa' [Cervantes and the English novel] in F. Sánchez Castañer (ed.), *Homenaje a Cervantes*, vol. 2. Valencia, Mediterráneo, pp 353–64.

—— (1951) 'Sir John Pentland Mahaffy 1839–1919' in *Of one company. Biographical studies of famous Trinity men, 1591–1951*. Dublin, Icarus, pp 89–100.

—— (1953) 'Homenaje a Don Ramón Menéndez Pidal' in *Estudios dedicados a Menéndez Pidal*, vol. 4. Madrid, 1953, pp 535–53.

—— (1955) 'Santiago, Inglaterra e Irlanda' in *Santiago en la historia, la literatura y el arte*, vol. 2. Madrid, Editora Nacional, pp 93–111.

—— (1956) 'Random memories of the Academy 1906–1956' in *The Royal Irish Academy of Music 1856–1956. Centenary souvenir*. Dublin, pp 25–33.

—— (1956) 'Reflejos en Inglaterra de la personalidad del Rey Católico' in *Estudios del Quinto Congreso de Historia de la Corona de Aragón*, 2. Zaragoza, Institución Fernando el Católico, pp 197–220.

—— (1958) 'St James the Apostle' in P. Caraman (ed.), *Saints and ourselves*. Third series. London, Hollis & Carter, pp 1–15.

—— (1966) 'Yeats and the Abbey Theatre' in *Homage to Yeats 1865–1965. Papers read at a Clark Library Seminar, October 16, 1965*. UCLA, William Andrews Clark Memorial Library, pp 3–39.

—— (1966) 'Miguel de Cervantes and the English novel', The Don Carlos Coloma memorial lecture, 1965, in L.P. Hartley (ed.), *Essays by divers hands. Being the transactions of the Royal Society of Literature*, n.s., 34. London, Oxford UP, pp 159–79.

—— (1969) 'The Gypsies of Granada' in J. Jones, *Paintings and drawings of the gypsies of Granada*. London, Athelnay Books, pp 27–48.

1.5. Books – translations of books by W. Starkie

Starkie, W. (1933) *Zigenarfiolen. Vagabondliv på ungerns och Rumäniens landsvägar* [*Raggle-taggle*], trans. A. Eje. Stockholm, Holger Schildts.

—— (1937) *Aventuras de un irlandés en España* [*Spanish raggle-taggle*], trans. A. Espina. Madrid, Espasa-Calpe.

—— (2006) *Aventuras de un irlandés en España* [*Spanish raggle-taggle*], trans. A. Espina; prólogo de I. Gibson. Madrid, Espasa-Calpe.

—— (1944) *Don Gitano. Aventuras de un irlandés con un violín en Marruecos, Andalucía y La Mancha* [*Don Gypsy*], trans. A. Espina. Barcelona, José Janés.

—— [1945?] *Trotamundos y gitanos (Aventuras de un juglar en Hungría y Rumanía)* [*Raggle-taggle*], trans. María Alfaro; prólogo de J. Gómez de la Serna [dated March 1944]. Madrid, Aguilar.

—— (1946) *Pirandello*, trans. C. Álvarez Peña. Barcelona, Juventud.

—— (1946) *La España de Cisneros* [*Grand inquisitor*], trans. A. de Mestas. Barcelona, Juventud.

—— (1956) *Casta gitana* [*In Sara's tents*], trans. Rosa S. de Naveira. Barcelona, José Janés.

—— (1958) *El camino de Santiago: las peregrinaciones al sepúlcro del apóstol* [*The road to Santiago*], trans. Amando Lázaro Ros. Madrid, Aguilar.

—— (2010) *El camino de Santiago. Las peregrinaciones al sepúlcro del apóstol* [*The road to Santiago*], trans. Amando Lázaro Ros; prólogo de I. Gibson. Palencia, Cálamo.

—— (1995) *Les racleurs de vent. Avec les Tsiganes de la puszta et de Translvanie* [*Raggle-taggle*], trans. P. Giuliani. Paris, Éditions Phébus.

2. *Articles*

W[alter]. [F[itzwilliam]. S[tarkie]. (1922) 'With the Fascisti in Italy', *Irish Times* (21 Oct.), p. 9.

—— (1922) 'The New Italy', *Irish Times* (4 Nov.), p. 10.

Starkie, W. (1923) 'Benavente: the winner of the Nobel prize', *The Contemporary Review*, 123 (Jan.), 93–100.

—— (1923) 'Jacinto Benavente and the modern Spanish drama', TLS (11 Jan.), 27.

—— (1924) 'Gregorio Martínez Sierra and the modern Spanish drama', *The Contemporary Review*, 125 (Feb.), 198–205.

—— (1924) 'The *Commedia del Arte* and the Roman comedy', *The Proceedings of the Royal Irish Academy*, 36, Sect. C (April), 333–50.

—— (1924) 'Il teatro grottesco', *Dublin Magazine*, 2 (Aug.), 14–18.

—— (1925) 'Carlo Goldoni and the *Commedia dell'Arte*', *The Proceedings of the Royal Irish Academy*, 37, Sect. C (Aug.), 53–86.

—— (1925) 'Richard Wagner and the music drama', *Quarterly Review*, 485 (July), 115–129.

—— (1925) 'Glorious musical pageant', *Irish Independent* (17 Sept.), pp 7–8.

—— (1926) 'A philosopher of modern Spain', *The Contemporary Review*, 129 (Jan.), 80–6.

—— (1926) 'Galdós and modern Spanish drama', *Bulletin of Spanish Studies*, 3:11 (1 Jan.), 111–17.

—— (1926) 'El teatro inglés contemporáneo' [Contemporary English theatre], *Residencia*, 1:1 (enero – abril), 42–53.

—— (1928) 'Blasco Ibáñez, 1867–1928', *Nineteenth Century and After*, 103, 542–59.

—— (1928) 'Holy Week in Seville, 1. Cathedral ceremonies on Holy Thursday', *Irish Independent* (12 April), p. 6.

—— (1928) 'Holy Week in Seville, 2. The sadness of Good Friday', II (13 April), p. 6.

—— (1928) 'Holy Week in Seville, 3. The processional images', II (14 April), p. 6.

—— (1928) 'Dictator's call to religion', *Daily Express* (14 April), p. 11.

—— (1928) 'Is Spain growing tired of bullfights?', *Daily Express*, (16 April), p. 9.

—— (1929) 'Modern Spain and its literature' ('Personalities of modern Spain'; 'The drama of Spain'; 'A modern Don Quixote'), *The Rice Institute Pamphlet*, 16: 2 (April), 47–110.

—— (1929) 'Den irländska nationalteatern' [The Irish national theatre], translated from the author's manuscript by A.L.W., *Ord och Bild*, 38: 10 (24 Oct.), 529–548.

—— (1929) 'Den irländska nationalteatern. Det psykologiska dramat' [The Irish national theatre. The psychological drama], translated from the author's manuscript by A.L.W., *Ord och Bild*, 38: 11 (22 Nov.), 593–608.

—— (1933) 'The Gypsies as Minstrels', JGLS, 3rd series, 12:2, 65–82.

—— (1934) 'Gypsy music in Hungary', JGLS, 3rd series, 13:1, 49–51.

—— (1934) 'Transylvanian Gypsy musicians', JGLS, 3rd series, 13:3, 133.

—— (1935) 'The Gypsy in Anadalusian folk-lore and folk-music', *The Journal of the Royal Musical Association*, 62:1, 1–20.

—— (1935) 'Gypsy folklore and music. Historical discussion of Gypsy migrations and the characteristics of their music and dance', *English Folk Dance and Song Society*, 2, 83–91.

—— (1936) 'A letter from the Tigre' [*sic*] front', *The British-Italian Bulletin* (18 April), 3.

—— (1936) 'Spanish kaleidoscope: a background', *The Fortnightly*, 140, n.s. (Dec.), 682–88.

—— (1937) 'Hungarian Gypsy fiddlers', JGLS, 3rd series, 16:3, 97–105.

—— (1937) 'An appreciation' [obituary article on Herbert Hughes], II, 3 May, p. 13.

—— (1938) 'Ireland today', *The Quarterly Review*, 271: 538 (Oct.), 343–60.

—— (1939) 'The Gypsies at Saintes-Maries-de-la-Mer, 1938', JGLS, 3rd series, 18:1, 19–24.

—— (1939) 'An appreciation' [obituary article on W.B. Yeats], II, 30 Jan., p. 9.

—— (1946) 'A Spanish ballet company', *Ballet*, 2:7 (Dec.), [12]–18.

—— (1947) 'Cervantes y Shakespeare', *Revista Nacional de Educación*, Año 7, Segunda época, 71, 9–27.

—— (1947) 'Cervantes militar' [Cervantes the soldier], *Ejército*, 8:93, 27–32.

—— (1947–48) 'Cervantes y Toledo', *Arte y Hogar*, número extraordinario, 60–5.

—— (1948) 'The British Council in Spain', *Bulletin of Spanish Studies*, 25:100, 270–5.

—— (1951) 'Obituary Robert Alexander Stewart Macalister', JGLS, 30:1–2 (June–April), 160.

—— (1952) 'El autor en España' [The author in Spain], *Bibliografía Hispánica* (March), 37–39.

—— (1953) 'The Gypsies of southern Spain: being a review of *Gitanos de la Bética* by José Carlos de Luna (Ediciones y Publicaciones Españolas, S.A.), Madrid, 1951', JGLS, 3rd series, 32:1–2 (Jan.–April), 55–66.

—— (1954) 'Cervantes y los gitanos' [Cervantes and the Gypsies], *Anales Cervantinos*, 4, 1–48.

—— (1954) 'The Gypsy Pilgrimage to Saint Sara (1951)' [an excerpt from *In Sara's tents*], JGLS, 3rd series, 33:1–2 (Jan.–Apr.), 14–28.

—— (1957) 'Gypsies on the road to Compostella' [excerpt from a chapter of *The road to Santiago* in a first unabridged form], JGLS, Third series, 36 (Jan–April), 2–8.

—— (1957) 'Jerome Bosch's "The haywain" ', JGLS, 3rd series 36:3–4 (July–Oct.), 83–87.

—— (1959) 'A memoir of Alfonso Reyes', *The Texas Quarterly* 2:1 (Spring), 67–77.

—— (1960) 'Cervantes and the Gypsies', JGLS, 3rd series, 39:1 (Jan.–April), 131–51.

—— (1962) 'Augustus John, O.M.: our past president and his daemon', JGLS, 3rd series, 41: 1–2 (Jan.–April), 82–9.

—— (1964) 'A Gypsy tribe in Italy (1919)', [an extract from *Scholars and Gypsies*], JGLS, Third series, 43:1–2 (Jan.–Apr.), 12–19.

—— (1969) 'W.B. Yeats and the Abbey Theatre', *The Southern Review*, n.s. 5:3 (Summer), 886–921.

Note: See Appendix for a series of articles published in the *Irish Independent* during the Italian occupation of Abyssinia and the Spanish Civil War.

3. *Occasional publications and ephemera*

Starkie, W. (1945) 'Homenaje al Excmo. Sr. D. Ramón Menéndez Pidal. Consejero de la Hispanidad.' Madrid, Instituto Británico en España. [A lecture delivered at a tribute to the scholar R. Menéndez Pidal at the British Institute in Madrid, 24 Nov. 1944.]

—— (1946) 'Cervantes y Shakespeare. Conferencia pronunciada en el Teatro Calderón de Barcelona, la noche del 23 de enero de 1946, con motivo de la extraordinaria representación de *Hamlet* en homenaje a la literatura inglesa.' Barcelona, pp. 3–16. [A lecture delivered at the Calderón Theatre in Barcelona on the night of 23 Jan. 1946 at a special performance of *Hamlet* in Spanish, organised as a tribute to English literature.]

—— (1947) 'El teatro experimental en Inglaterra [Experimental theatre in England]', in the theatre programme for the 'Teatro de Cámara', Cuarta sesión: 'Desde los tiempos de Adán' [Ever since paradise] by J.B. Priestley, no page number. [Performance in Madrid, 10 July 1947.]

—— (1954) 'Conferencia conmemorativa Eugene O'Neill (1888–1953) [A lecture in memory of E. O'Neill]'. Madrid, Colección Estados Unidos, pp 9–37. [A lecture delivered at the Casa Americana in Madrid, 3 Mar. 1954.]

—— (1955) An explanatory note in the programme for a performance in Spanish of Beckett's *Waiting for Godot* in the 'Paraninfo' at the Facultad de Filosofía y Letras, Universidad Complutense de Madrid, directed by Trino Martínez Trives, who also translated the text, 28 May 1955. [Starkie's text is reproduced in J. Guerrero Zamora (1961) *Historia del teatro contemporáneo*, 4 vols (Barcelona, Juan Flors), i, pp 281–2].

4. *RTÉ scripts and recordings*

Starkie, W. (Date?) 'If I were Director of Broadcasting'. Script and recording unavailable.

—— (Date?) 'Do we get too much fresh air?' Script and recording unavailable.

—— (1940) 'Bulgaria and its folk', Schools broadcast (12 April). Typescript remains (uncatalogued); recording unavailable.

5. *Unpublished manuscripts*

Starkie, W. (1972) 'The Gypso-Indian trail to El Dorado.'

—— ([Undated]) 'The House of Alba, Maecenas of a thousand years.'

SECONDARY SOURCES

A catalogue of graduates at the University of Dublin vol. 5, containing the names of those who proceeded to degrees from the September commencements of the year 1917 to the spring commencements of the year 1931 (1931). Dublin, Hodges, Figgis.

A survey of fascism. The year book of the international centre of fascist studies, vol. 1 (1928). London, Ernest Benn.

Abellán, M.L. (1980) *Censura y creación literaria en España*. Barcelona, Península.

Alba, Duque de (1948) 'Walter Starkie' in *Eusayos Hispano-Ingleses. Homenaje a Walter Starkie*, pp 5–6.

Alcalá, J. de (1980) *Alonso, mozo de muchos amos o el donado hablador*. Madrid, Aguilar.

Alemán, M. (1999) *Guzmán de Alfarache*. Barcelona, Planeta.

Alington, C.A. ([no date]) *Fables and fancies*. London, The Religious Book Club.

—— ([no date]) 'A fable' in *Fables and fancies*, pp 1–2.

—— (1914) *A schoolmaster's apology*. London, Longman's Green & Co.

Allen, N. (2003) *George Russell (AE) and the new Ireland, 1905–30*. Dublin, Four Courts.

Althusser, L. (1971) *Lenin and philosophy, and other essays*, trans. B. Brewster. London, NLB.

Álvarez Rosete, A. (2004) ' "¡Bienvenido Mr Beveridge!" El viaje de William Beveridge a España y la previsión social franquista', *International Journal of Iberian Studies*, 17:2 (2004), 105–16.

Annual Report of the British Institute of Florence (1925–6). Florence.

Annual Report of the Institute of International Education (1956). New York.

Anonymous (2011) *Lazarillo de Tormes / 'Lázaro de Tormes'*. Barcelona, Galaxia Gutenberg.

Anonymous ([date unknown]) 'The wraggle-taggle Gypsies' in J.R. Murray, *Old chestnuts warmed up*, pp 101–2.

Anti-Semitism. http://www.yadvashem.org.il, accessed 23 March 2012.

Auden, J.E. (ed.), (1922) *Shrewsbury, Royal School, Old Salopian Club Yearbook*. London.

Auden, J.E. (ed.), (1928) *Shrewsbury school register*. Shrewsbury.

Augusteijn, J. (ed.), (1999) *Ireland in the 1930s. New perspectives*. Dublin, Four Courts.

Backscheider, P. (1999) *Reflections on biography*. Oxford, Oxford UP.

Bailey, K.C. (1947) *A history of Trinity College Dublin 1892–1945*. Dublin, The University Press Trinity College.

Bakhtin, M.M. (1981) *The dialogic imagination. Four essays*, ed. M. Holquist; trans. Caryl Emerson and Michael Holquist. Austin, University of Texas Press.

—— (1981) 'The functions of the rogue, clown and fool in the novel' in *The dialogic imagination*, pp 158–167.

—— (1984) *Rabelais and his world*. Bloomington: Indiana UP.

Baldoli, C. (2003), *Exporting fascism*. Oxford, Berg.

Balfour, S. & P. Preston (eds), (1999) *Spain and the great powers in the twentieth century*. London, Routledge.

Barker, F. & P. Hulme (1988) 'Nymphs and reapers heavily vanish: the discursive con-texts of *The Tempest* in J. Drakakis (ed.), *Alternative Shakespeares*, pp 191–237.

Barreiro, C. '*La Época*, la conciencia de una monarquía liberal', *Arbil*, 74. http://www.arbil.org/(74)epoc.htm, accessed 1 Jan. 2011.

Barry, K. (ed.), (2000) *James Joyce. Occasional critical and political writing*. Oxford, Oxford UP.

Bartlett, C.J. (1978) *A history of postwar Britain 1945–1974*. London, Longman.

Bassnett-McGuire, S. (1983) *Luigi Pirandello*. London, Macmillan.

Baudelaire, C. (1961) *Les fleurs du mal*. Paris, Garnier Frères.

Beevor, A. (2007) *The battle for Spain. The Spanish civil war, 1936–1939*. London, Phoenix.

Bence-Jones, M. (1990) *A guide to Irish country houses*. London, Constable

Benton, M. (2009) *Literary biography. An introduction*. Oxford, Wiley-Blackwell.

Berdah, J.F. (1993) 'La "propaganda" cultural británica en España durante la Segunda Guerra Mundial a través de la acción del "British Council": un aspecto de las relaciones hispano-británicas (1939–1946)' in J. Tusell et al (eds), *El regimen de Franco. Política y relaciones exteriores*, pp 273–86.

Berend, I.T. (1998) *Decades of crisis: Central and Eastern Europe before World War II*. Berkeley, University of California Press.

Bew, P. (1996) *John Redmond*. Dublin, Dundalgan Press.

—— (2009) *Ireland. The politics of enmity 1989–2006*. Oxford, Oxford UP.

Bhabha, H.K. (ed.), (1994) *Nation and narration*. London, Routledge.

—— (1994) 'Introduction: narrating the nation' in H.K. Bhabha (ed.), *Nation and Narration*. London, Routledge.

Bideleux, R. & I. Jeffries (1998) *A history of Eastern Europe. Crisis and change*. London, Routledge.

Billiani, F. (ed.), (2007) *Modes of censorship and translation. National contexts and diverse media*. Manchester, St Jerome.

Boehmer, E. (1995) *Colonial and postcolonial literature*. Oxford, Oxford UP.

Bonsall, P. (1998) *The Irish RMs. The Resident Magistrates in the British administration in Ireland*. Dublin, Four Courts.

Bosworth, R.J.B. (2002) *Mussolini*. London, Arnold.

Bristow, J. (1991) *Empire boys: adventures in a man's world*. London, HarperCollinsAcademic.

British cemetery Madrid. http://www.britishcemeterymadrid.com, accessed 17 June 2012.

The British Institute of Florence. http://www.britishinstitute.it/en/aboutus/asp, accessed 16 Oct. 2010.

Brontë, C. (1985) *Jane Eyre*. London, Penguin.

Brown, T. (2004) *Ireland. A social and cultural history, 1922–2002*. London, Harper Perennial.

Burns, J. (2009) *Papa spy*. London, Bloomsbury.

Burke, M. (2009) *'Tinkers'. Synge and the cultural history of the Irish traveller*. Oxford, Oxford UP.

Burtchaell, G.D. & T.U. Sadleir (eds) (1935) *Alumni Dublinenses. A register of the students, graduates, professors and provosts of Trinity College in the University of Dublin (1593–1860)*. Dublin, Alexander Thom.

Callahan, D. (2005) 'The early reception of Miguel de Unamuno in England, 1907–1939', *Modern Language Review*, 100: Supplement. *http://www.mhra.org.uk/ojs/index.php/MLR/article/viewfile/21/31*, accessed 11 August 2011.

Camps, A., J.A. Hurtley & A. Moya (eds), (2005) *Traducción, (sub)versión, transcreación*. Barcelona, Promociones y Publicaciones Universitarias.

Carr, R. (2001) *Modern Spain, 1875–1980*. Oxford, Oxford UP.

Carroll, L. (2009) *Alice's adventures in Wonderland* and *Through the looking-glass*. Oxford, Oxford UP.

Cervantes, Miguel de (2005) *El ingenioso hidalgo Don Quijote de la Mancha*, ed. J.Jay Allen. Madrid, Cátedra.

——— (2010) *Novelas ejemplares, vol. 1*, ed. F. Sevilla Arroyo & A. Rey Hazas. Madrid, Espasa.

——— (2011) *Novelas ejemplares, vol. 2*, ed. F. Sevilla Arroyo & A. Rey Hazas. Madrid, Espasa.

Chambers, R. (2010) *The last Englishman. The double life of Arthur Ransome*. London, Faber & Faber.

Chiarelli, L. (2005) *La maschera e il volto*. Bari, Palomar.

Christian, W.A., Jr. (1996) *Visionaries. The Spanish Republic and the reign of Christ*. Berkeley, University of California Press.

Coke, D.F.T. (1925) *The bending of a twig*. London, Chapman & Hall.

Coletes Blanco, A. (1984) *Gran Bretaña y los Estados Unidos en la vida de Ramón Pérez de Ayala*. Oviedo, I.D.E.A.

——— (1984) 'Traducciones y selecciones de la obra de Pérez de Ayala publicadas en Gran Bretaña y los Estados Unidos', *Boletín del Instituto de Estudios Asturianos*, pp 41–53.

Collis, R. (1937) *The silver fleece. An autobiography*. London, Thomas Nelson.

Coolahan, J. with P.F. O'Donovan (2009) *A history of Ireland's School Inspectorate, 1831–2008*. Dublin, Four Courts.

Curtis, K. (2010) *P.S. O'Hegarty (1879–1955). Sinn Féin Fenian*. London, Anthem Press.

Davis, M.L. (2007) *The culture broker. Franklin D. Murphy and the transformation of Los Angeles*. Berkeley, University of California Press.

Day, P. (2011) *Franco's friends. How British intelligence helped bring Franco to power in Spain*. London, Biteback.

Deane, S. (ed.), (1991) *The Field Day anthology of Irish writing, vol. 3*. Derry, Field Day.

Deane, S. (1991) 'Autobiography and memoirs, 1890–1988' in S. Deane (ed.), *The Field Day anthology of Irish writing, vol. 3*, pp 380–3.

de Vere White, T. (1965) 'Social life in Ireland 1927–1937', *Studies* (Spring), 75–82.

Dear, I.C.B. & M.R.D. Foot (eds), (1995) *The Oxford companion to the Second World War.* Oxford, Oxford UP.

De la Serna, Fray Clemente (1976) 'Fray Justo Pérez de Urbel' in *Homenaje a Fray Justo Pérez de Urbel, OSB.*, 1, pp 23–32.

Dekker, T. (1648) *English villanies eight severall times prest to death by the printers, but are now the ninth time (as at first) discovered by lanthorne and candle-light, and by the helpe of a new cryer.* London. EEBO Editions.

——— (1648) 'Of Moone-Men' in *English villanies eight severall times prest to death by the printers, but are now the ninth time (as at first) discovered by lanthorne and candle-light, and by the helpe of a new cryer*, Chapter 7 [pages not numbered].

Denzin, N.K. (1989) *Interpretive biography.* Newbury Park, Sage.

De Man, P. (1979) 'Autobiography as de-facement', *Modern Language Notes*, 94:5 (Dec.), 919–30.

Dillon, E.J. (1919) *The peace conference.* London, Hutchinson.

Dodd, L. (ed.), (1999) *Nationalisms. Visions and revisions.* Dublin, Film Institute of Ireland.

Dolan, T.P. (1999) *A dictionary of Hiberno-English.* Dublin, Gill & Macmillan.

Donaldson, F. (1984) *The British Council. The first fifty years.* London, Jonathan Cape.

Drakakis, J. (ed.), (1988) *Alternative Shakespeares.* London, Routledge.

Duff, A. *www.arthurduff.com*, accessed 30 Sept. 2010.

Duque de Alba [Jacobo Fitz-James Stuart y Falcó] (1948) 'Walter Starkie' in *Ensayos hispano-ingleses. Homenaje a Walter Starkie*, pp 5–6.

Durán. (1987) *Libros y manuscritos. Subasta número 210* (enero). Madrid.

Durán. (1996) *Subastas de arte, libros y manuscritos. Subasta número 313* (diciembre). Madrid.

Eaglefield-Hull, A. (ed.), (1924) *A dictionary of modern music and musicians.* London, J.M. Dent.

Ensayos hispano-ingleses. Homenaje a Walter Starkie (1948). Barcelona. José Janés

Erasmus, D. (1976) *Praise of folly*, trans. B. Radice. London, Penguin.

Espinel, V. (1980) *Relaciones de la vida del escudero Marcos de Obregón.* Madrid, Aguilar.

Ferriter, D. (2005) *The transformation of Ireland, 1900–2000.* London, Profile Books.

Fisher, G.W. (1899) *Annals of Shrewsbury School.* [s.l.], Methuen.

Fleischman, A. (ed.), (1952) *Music in Ireland: a symposium.* Cork, Cork UP.

Foley, T. (ed.), (1999) *From Queen's College to National University. Essays on the academic history of QCG/UCG/NUI, Galway.* Dublin, Four Courts.

Foley, T. & F. Bateman (1999) 'English, history and philosophy' in T. Foley (ed.), from Queen's College to National University, pp 384–420.

Frazer, J.G. (1900) *The golden bough: a study in magic and religion.* London, Macmillan.

The French Department, Trinity College Dublin. http://www.tcd.ie/French, accessed 9 May 2012.

Ganivet, Á. (1946) *Spain: an interpretation*, trans. J.A. Carey. London, Eyre & Spottiswoode.

Gaos, V. (1944) *Arcángel de mi noche. Sonetos apasionados, 1939–1943.* Madrid, Adonais.

Gibson, I. (2006) 'Prólogo' in W. Starkie, *Aventuras de un irlandés en España*, pp 9–13.

——— (2010) 'El hispanista andarín y juglar' in W. Starkie, *El camino de Santiago. Las peregrinaciones al sepúlcro del apóstol*, pp 5–8.

Gifford, D. with R.J. Seidman (2008) *Ulysses annotated.* Berkeley, University of California Press.

Gil, A. (2009) *La censura cinematográfica en España.* Barcelona, Ediciones B.

Gissing, G. (2004) *By the Ionian Sea. Notes of a ramble in southern Italy.* Oxford, Signal Books.

Giudice, G. (1975) *Pirandello: a biography*, trans. A. Hamilton. London, Oxford UP.

Goad, H.E. (1929) *What is fascism? An explanation of its essential principles.* Florence, The Italian Mail & Tribune.

Gollancz, I. (ed.), (1916) *A book of homage to Shakespeare*. Oxford, Humphrey Milford.

Gómez de la Serna, J. [1945?] '"Trailer" biográfico del profesor Walter Starkie' in W. Starkie, *Trotamundos y gitanos (Aventuras de un juglar en Hungría y Rumanía)*. Madrid, M. Aguilar, pp 7–24.

González, E. (1990) *La vida y hechos de Estebanillo González: hombre de buen humor compuesto por él mesmo [sic]*, ed. A. Barreiro & J.A. Cid. Madrid, Cátedra.

González Cuevas, P.C. (2003) *Maeztu. Biografía de un nacionalista español*. Madrid, Marcial Pons.

Gordon, D. (2008) 'Walter Starkie and the greatest novel of all', *First principles* (4 Oct.). http://www.firstprinciplesjournal.com/print.aspx?article–579&loc–b&type–cbtp, accessed 26 May 2012.

Gorell, Lord [Ronald Gorell Barnes 3rd Baron] (1927) *Education and the army. An essay in reconstruction*. London, Humphrey Milford.

Graham, H. (2002) *The Spanish republic at war, 1936–1939*. Cambridge, Cambridge UP.

—— (2005) *The Spanish civil war. A very short introduction*. Oxford, Oxford UP.

Grene, N. (ed.), (2009) *J.M. Synge. Travelling Ireland. Essays 1898–1908*. Dublin, Lilliput.

Griffiths, R. (2010) *Fellow travellers of the right. British enthusiasts of Nazi Germany, 1933–1939*. London, Faber & Faber.

Grubgeld, E. (2004) *Anglo-Irish autobiography. Class, gender and the forms of narrative*. New York, Syracuse UP.

Guinness, D. (1988) *Georgian Dublin*. London, Batsford.

Hall, R.C. (2000) *The Balkan wars, 1912–1913: prelude to the First World War*. London, Routledge.

Hamilton, H. (2003) *The speckled people*. London, Harper Perennial.

Hamilton, J. (1990) *Arthur Rackham. A life with illustration*. London, Pavilion.

—— (1991–2) 'Edyth Starkie', *Irish Arts Review Yearbook*, pp 154–64.

Hayes, C.J.H. (1945) *Wartime mission in Spain*. New York, Macmillan.

Hegarty, S. & F. O'Toole (2006) *The Irish Times book of the 1916 rising*. London, Gill & Macmillan.

Hegel, G.W.F. (1910) *The phenomenology of mind*, vol. 1, trans. J.B. Baillie. London, Swan Sonnenschein

—— 'Independence and dependence of self-consciousness. Lordship and bondage' in *The phenomenology of mind*, pp 175–88.

Herlihy, J. (2005) *Royal Irish Constabulary officers. A biographical dictionary and genealogical guide, 1816–1922*. Dublin, Four Courts.

Hindle, W. (ed.), (1939) *Foreign correspondent. Personal adventures abroad in search of the news*. London, George G. Harrap.

Hodgson, R. (1953) *Spain resurgent*. London, Hutchinson.

Hogan, R. & M.J. O'Neill (eds) (1968) *Joseph Holloway's Irish theatre*, vol. 1. Dixon, CA, Proscenium.

Homenaje a Fray Justo Pérez de Urbel, OSB, 1 (1976) *Studia Silensia 3*. Santo Domingo de Silos, Abadía de Silos.

Hone, J.M. (2007) *Memories of W.B. Yeats, Lady Gregory, J.M. Synge and other essays*. Dublin [privately published].

—— (2007) 'Great Householder: Rt. Hon. Laurence Waldron' in J.M. Hone, *Memories of W.B. Yeats, Lady Gregory, J.M. Synge and other essays*, pp 167–74.

Hornby, E. & D. Maw (eds), (2010) *Essays on the history of English music in honour of John Caldwell: sources, style, performance, historiography*. Woodbridge, Boydell.

Howson, H.E. (1919) *Two men: a memoir*. Oxford.

Hulme, P. (1986) *Colonial encounters: Europe and the native Caribbean, 1492–1797*. London, Methuen.

—— & T. Youngs (eds), (2002) *The Cambridge companion to travel writing*. Cambridge, Cambridge UP.

Hunt, H. (1979) *The Abbey. Ireland's national theatre*. Dublin, Gill & Macmillan.

Hurtley, J. (1992) *José Janés: editor de literatura inglesa*. Barcelona, Promociones y Publicaciones Universitarias.

—— (2005) 'Re-writing the road: Walter Starkie on St James's way' in A. Camps, J.A. Hurtley and A. Moya (eds), *Traducción (sub)version, transcreación*, pp 155–63.

—— (2007) 'Tailoring the tale. Inquisitorial discourses, and resistance, in the early Franco period (1940–1959)' in F. Billiani (ed.), *Modes of censorship and translation. National contexts and diverse media*, pp 61–92.

—— (2008) 'The writer, the translator and strategic location: adapting the adventures' in L. Pegenaute et al. (eds), *La traducción del futuro: mediación lingüística y cultural en el siglo 21, vol. I: La traducción y su práctica*, pp 27–34.

Hutcheon, L. (1988) *A poetics of postmodernism. History, theory, fiction*. London, Routledge.

Hyde, D. (1988) 'The necessity for de-Anglicising Ireland' in M. Storey (ed.), *Poetry and Ireland since 1800: a source book*, pp 78–84.

Ilie, P. (1980) *Literature and inner exile: authoritarian Spain, 1939–1945*. Baltimore, Johns Hopkins UP.

The Italian Department, Trinity College Dublin. http://www.tcd.ie/Italian, accessed 9 May 2012.

Jackson, A. (1993) *Sir Edward Carson*. Dublin, Dundalgan Press.

Jefcoate, G. '"A difficult modernity": the library of the Catholic university of Nijmegen, 1923–1968'. http://dare.ubn.kun.nl/dspace/bitstream/2066/90906/1/90906.pdf, accessed 14 March 2012.

John Murray's autumn list 1939 (1939). London, John Murray.

John Murray spring list 1940 (1940). London, John Murray.

Johnson, J. (2008) 'A chronology of James Joyce' in J. Joyce, *Ulysses*, pp lxiii–lxix.

Joyce, J. (1965) *The cat and the devil*. London, Faber & Faber.

Joyce, J. (2000) *A portrait of the artist as a young man*. Oxford, Oxford UP.

Joyce, J. (2008) *Ulysses*. Oxford, Oxford UP.

Kahn, C. (2001) 'Remembering Shakespeare imperially: the 1916 tercentenary', *Shakespeare Quarterly*, 52:4 (Winter), 456–78.

Katz, J. (1980) *From prejudice to destruction: anti-Semitism, 1700–1933*. Cambridge, Harvard UP.

Kearns, K.C. (1994) *Dublin tenement life*. Dublin, Gill & Macmillan.

Keaveney, A. (1999) 'Classics in Victorian Galway' in T. Foley (ed.), *From Queen's College to National University*, pp 326–43.

Keene, J. (2001) *Fighting for Franco. International volunteers in nationalist Spain during the Spanish civil war, 1936–1939*. London, Leicester UP.

Kenneally, I. (2008) *The paper wall. Newspapers and propaganda in Ireland, 1919–1921*. Cork, The Collins Press.

Kennedy, M. (1996) *Ireland and the League of Nations, 1919–1946. International relations, diplomacy and politics*. Dublin, Irish Academic Press.

Kennedy, M. (ed.), (1996) *The concise Oxford dictionary of music*. Oxford, Oxford UP.

Kershaw, I. (2009) *Hitler*. London, Penguin.

Keyserling, Hermann Alexander, Count (1928) *Europe*. [s.l.], Cape.

Kiberd, D. (1995) *Inventing Ireland*. London, Jonathan Cape.

Kipling, R. (2008) *Kim*. Oxford: Oxford UP.

Klemperer, V. (2010) *The language of the third reich*, trans. M. Brady. London, Continuum.

Lamb, R. (1997) *Mussolini and the British*. London, John Murray.

Lancaster, L.W. (1978) *Masters of political thought, vol 3: Hegel to Dewey*. London, Harrap.

Lawrence, T.E. (1939) *Seven pillars of wisdom. A triumph*, 2 vols. London, The Reprint Society by arrangement with Jonathan Cape.

Lecane, P. (2005) *Torpedoed! The RMS Leinster disaster*. Penzance, Periscope.

Lee, Sir S. (1925; 1927) *Edward VII. A biography*, 2 vols. London, Macmillan.

Lendvai, P. (2003) *The Hungarians. A thousand years of victory in defeat*, trans. A. Major. London, Hurst.

Ley, C.D. (1981) *La costanillo de los diablos. (Memorias literarias 1943–1952)*. Madrid, José Esteban.

Liebich, S. 'Educating adult readers: the national home reading union in Australasia, 1892–1898.' *http://ah.brookes.ac.uk/conference/presentation/educating_adult_readers/*, accessed 18 April 2012.

Linehan, T. (2000) *British fascism, 1918–1939. Parties, ideology and culture*. Manchester, Manchester UP.

Llano, S. (2002) 'Walter Starkie y el British Council en España: música, cultura y propaganda' in J. Suárez Pajares (ed.), *Música española entre dos guerras: 1914–1945*, pp 187–217.

Llera, J.A. & P. Canelo (eds), (2003) *60 años de Adonais: una colección de poesía en España (1943–2003)*. Madrid, Juan Pastor.

London, J. (1997) *Reception and renewal in modern Spanish theatre: 1939–1963*. Leeds, W.S. Maney & Son Ltd for the Modern Humanities Research Association..

Lyons, F.S.L. (1985) *Ireland since the famine*. London, Fontana.

Mackay, F. (2002) *Battleground Europe. Touring the Italian front 1917–1918. British, American, French and German forces in northern Italy*. Barnsley, Leo Cooper.

Mackenzie, C. (1960) *Sinister Street*. London, Penguin.

Machiavelli, N. (1975) *The prince*, trans. G. Bull. London, Penguin.

Macran, H.S. (1912) *Hegel's doctrine of formal logic. Being a translation of the first section of the subjective logic*. Oxford, Clarendon Press.

—— (1929) *Hegel's logic of world and idea, being a translation of the second and third parts of the subjective logic, with an introduction on idealism limited and absolute*. Oxford, Clarendon Press.

Madariaga, S. de (1974) *Morning without noon. Memoirs*. Farnborough, Saxon House.

—— (1974) *Españoles de mi tiempo*. Barcelona, Planeta.

—— (1974) 'El marques Merry del Val' in *Españoles de mi tiempo*, pp 37–45.

—— (1974) 'Ignacio Zuloaga' in *Españoles di mi tiempo*, pp 119–25.

Maeztu, R. de (1941) *Defensa de la hispanidad*. Madrid, [no publisher specified].

Mainer, J.-C. (2003) 'Al final del verano de 1943 ...' in J.A. Llera & P. Canelo (eds) *60 años de Adonais*, pp 15–30.

—— (2012) *Pío Baroja*. Madrid, Taurus.

Mansfield, C. ([1975]) *The Aravon story*. Dalkey.

Martínez de Vicente, P. (2010) *La clave Embassy*. Madrid, La Esfera de los Libros.

Matthaei, R. (1973) *Luigi Pirandello*, trans. S. & E. Young. New York, Ungar.

McDowell, R.B. (1970) *The Irish Convention, 1917–18*. London, Routledge and Kegan Paul.

McDowell, R.B. & D.A. Webb (1982) *Trinity College Dublin, 1592–1952. An academic history*. Cambridge, Cambridge UP.

McGarry, F. (2005) *Eoin O'Duffy. A self-made hero*. Oxford, Oxford UP.

McGuire, J. & J. Quinn (eds), *The dictionary of Irish biography*. Cambridge, Cambridge UP.

McIntosh, G. (1999) 'Acts of "national communion": the centenary celebrations for Catholic emancipation, the forerunner of the Eucharistic congress' in J. Augusteijn (ed.), *Ireland in the 1930s. New perspectives*, pp 83–95.

McVeigh, S. '"As the sand on the sea-shore": women violinists in London's concert life around 1900' in E. Hornby & D. Maw (eds), *Essays on the history of English music in honour of John Caldwell: sources, style, performance, historiography*, pp 232–58.

Melvin, P. (1996) 'The Galway tribes as landowners and gentry' in G. Moran (ed.), *Galway: history and society. Interdisciplinary essays on the history of an Irish county*, pp 362–374.

Menéndez Pidal, R. (1924) *Poesia juglaresca y juglares: aspectos de la historia cultural de España*. Madrid, Centro de Estudios Históricos, Junta para Ampliación de Estudios e Investigaciones Científicas.

Menninger Institute http://www.menningerclinic.com/about/Menninger-history.htm, accessed 30 Apr. 2012.

Merendero Antonio Martin. *http://sinalefa5.wordpress.com/2011/07/31/merendero-antonio-martn*, accessed 25 May 2012.

Mintz, J.R. (2004) *The anarchists of Casas Viejas*. Bloomington, Indiana University Press.

Mompou, F. (1948) 'A Walter Starkie' in *Ensayos hispano-ingleses. Homenaje a Walter Starkie*, p. 223.

Michener, J.A. (1968) *Iberia. Spanish travels and reflections*. New York, Random House.

Montoliú, P. (2005) *Madrid en la posguerra, 1939–1946*. Madrid, Sílex.

Moran, G. (ed.), (1996) *Galway: history and society. Interdisciplinary essays on the history of an Irish county*. Dublin, Geography Publications.

More, T. (1976) *Utopia*, trans. P. Turner. London, Penguin.

Moreno Fonseret, R. & F. Sevillano Calero (eds), (1999) *El Franquismo: visiones y balance*. Alicante, Universidad de Alicante.

Murphy, D. (2009) 'Waldron, L.A.' in J. McGuire & J. Quinn (eds), *The dictionary of Irish biography*, pp 697–8.

Murphy, D.J. (ed.), (1987) *Lady Gregory's journals. Vol. 2, Books thirty to forty-four: 21 February 1925–9 May 1932*. Gerrards Cross, Colin Smythe.

Murphy, F.D. http://www.kuhistory.com/proto/story.asp?id–51, accessed 30 Nov. 2011.

Murray, C. (2006) *Seán O'Casey. Writer at work. A biography*. Dublin, Gill & Macmillan.

Murray, J.R. (1997) *Old chestnuts warmed up*. London, John Murray.

Nobel Prize (1922) http://nobelprize.org/nobel_prizes/literature/laureates/1922/press.html, accessed 12 June 2010.

O'Brien, M. (2008) *The Irish Times. A history*. Dublin, Four Courts.

O'Connor, U. (1981) *Oliver St John Gogarty*. London, Granada.

O'Connor, V.L. ([1916]) *A book of caricatures*. Dublin, Tempest.

O'Doherty, C. (1997) 'William Joseph Myles Starkie (1860–1920). The last resident commissioner of national education in Ireland'. DPhil. Thesis, University of Limerick, May 1997.

O'Duffy, E. [1938?] *Crusade in Spain*. Dublin, Browne & Nolan.

O'Dwyer, F. (1997) *The architecture of Deane and Woodward*. Cork, Cork UP.

O'Dwyer, R. (2009) *The Eucharistic Congress*, Dublin, Nonsuch.

O'Halpin, E. (1987) *The decline of the Union. British government in Ireland 1892–1920*. Dublin, Gill & Macmillan.

O'Tuathaigh, G. (1999) 'The age of de Valera and newsreel' in L. Dodd (ed.), *Nationalisms. Visions and revisions*, pp 24–8.

330 *Bibliography*

Orwell, G. (1938) *Homage to Catalonia*. London, Secker & Warburg.

Overy, R. (2010) *1939. Countdown to war*. London, Penguin.

Pardo Sanz, R. (1999) 'La política exterior del Franquismo: aislamiento y alineación internacional' in R. Moreno Fonseret & F. Sevillano Calero (eds), *El Franquismo: visiones y balances*, pp 93–117.

Paris Peace Conference *http://.history.sandiego.edu/GEN/ww1/1919League2.html*, accessed 27 April 2012

Pearson, P. (1998) *Between the mountains and the sea: Dun Laoghaire – Rathdown County*. Dublin, O'Brien Press.

Pegenaute, L. et al. (eds), (2008) *La traducción del futuro: mediación lingüística y cultural en el siglo 21, vol. 1: La traducción y su práctica*. Barcelona, Promociones y Publicaciones Universitarias.

Pellizzi, C. (1924) 'Fascism's problems and realities', trans. M.G. Stampino & J.T. Schnapp, in J.T. Schnapp (ed.), *A primer of Italian fascism*, pp 95–102.

Pérez de Villanueva-Tovar, I. (2011) *La Residencia de Estudiantes 1910–1936. Grupo universitario y residencia de señoritas*. Madrid, Publicaciones de la Residencia de Estudiantes.

Petriella, D. & S. Sosa Miatello *Diccionario biográfico Italo-Argentino*. http://www.dante.edu.ar/web/dic/p.pdf, accessed 25 April 2012.

Phillips, R. (1997) *Mapping men and empire*. A geography of adventure. London, Routledge.

Pihl, L. (ed.), (1994) *Signe Toksvig's Irish diaries, 1926–37*. Dublin, Lilliput.

Pike, D.W. (2008) *Franco and the axis stigma*. Basingstoke, Palgrave Macmillan.

Pine, R. (2002) *2RN and the origins of Irish radio*. Dublin, Four Courts.

Pine, R. & C. Acton (eds), (1998) *To talent alone. The Royal Irish Academy of Music, 1848–1998*. Dublin, Gill & Macmillan.

Portero, F. (1999) 'Spain, Britain and the cold war' in S. Balfour & P. Preston (eds), *Spain and the great powers in the twentieth century*, pp 210–28.

Preston, P. (1995) *Franco. A biography*. London, Fontana Press.

Rankin, I. (2003) *Telegram from Guernica. The extraordinary life of George Steer, war correspondent*. London, Faber & Faber.

Renan, E. (1882) 'What is a nation? [Qu'est-ce qu'une nation?]' in H.K. Bhabha (ed.), *Nation and narration*, pp 8–22.

Report of the British Council 1940–1941 (1941). London, British Council.

Report of the British Council 1947–1948 (1948). London, British Council.

Report on the work of the British Council for the year ended 31 March 1951 (1951). London, British Council.

Rey-Ximena, J. (2008) *El vuelo del Ibis*. Madrid, Facta.

Reynolds, P. (2007) *Modernism, drama, and the audience for Irish spectacle*. Cambridge, Cambridge UP.

Ribagorda, Á. (2008) 'El Comité Hispano-Inglés y la Sociedad de Cursos y conferencias de la Residencia de Estudiantes', *Cuadernos de Historia Contemporánea*, 30, 273–291.

Rice Institute Pamphlets. http://ricehistorycorner.com/2010/12/06/the-rice-institute-pamphlets, accessed 19 May 2012

Richardson, J. (1973) *Enid Starkie*. London, John Murray.

Rivero Taravillo, A. (2011) *Luis Cernuda. Años de exilio (1938–1963)*, vol. 2. Barcelona, Tusquets.

Robinson, L. (ed.), (1939) *The Irish theatre. Lectures delivered during the Abbey theatre festival held in Dublin in August 1938*. London, Macmillan.

Robson, K. (1939) 'With Franco in Spain' in W. Hindle (ed.), *Foreign correspondent. Personal adventures abroad in search of the news*, pp 253–69.

Roche, A. (1994) *Contemporary Irish drama. From Beckett to McGuinness*. Dublin, Gill & Macmillan.

Rodríguez Acosta, J.M. *www.fundacionrodriguezacosta*, accessed 28 March 2012.

Rothermere, Viscount [Harold Sidney Harmsworth] (1939) *My campaign for Hungary*. London, Eyre and Spottiswoode.

The Royal Irish Academy of Music, 1856–1956. Centenary souvenir (October, 1956) Dublin.

Royal Merchant Ship *Leinster, www.rmsleinster.com*, accessed 25 April 2012.

Ruiz, J., Arcipreste de Hita (2002) *Juan Ruiz Arcipreste de Hita, y el libro de buen amor*, ed. F. Toro Ceballos & B. Morros. Alcalá la Real, Ayuntamiento de Alcalá la Real.

Ruiz-Castillo Basala, J. (1972) *El apasionante mundo del libro. Memorias de un editor*. Madrid, Agrupación Nacional del Comercio del Libro.

Ruskin, J. (1894) *Verona and other lectures*. Orpington, G. Allen.

Russell, B. (1984) *A history of western philosophy*. London, Unwin Paperbacks.

Saddlemyer, A. (ed.), (2011) *W.B. Yeats and George Yeats. The letters*. Oxford, Oxford UP.

Saz Campos, I. (1986) *Mussolini contra la Segunda República. Hostilidad, conspiraciones, intervención (1931–1936)*. València, Edicions Alfons el Magnànim.

Schnapp, J.T. (ed.), (2000) *A primer of Italian fascism*. Lincoln, University of Nebraska Press.

Seale, P. & M. McConville (1978) *Philby. The long road to Moscow*. London, Penguin.

Seco Serrano, C. & J. Tusell (1995) *La España de Alfonso XIII: el estado y la política (1902–31). Historia de España Menéndez Pidal, 38, vol. 2*: Del plano inclinado hacia la dictadura al final de la monarquía 1922–31. Madrid, Espasa-Calpe.

Shakespeare, W. (1987) *As you like it*. London: Methuen.

—— (2008) *A midsummer night's dream*. Oxford, Oxford UP.

Shelley, P.B. (1947) *Adonais*, trans. V. Gaos. Madrid.

Shrewsbury, Royal School, Old Salopian Club. Shrewsbury Roll of Service September 1915 (1915). Shrewsbury.

Shrewsbury School prize lists (1910, 1911, 1912). Shrewsbury.

Siggins, B. (2007) *The great white fair. The Herbert Park exhibition of 1907*. Dublin, Nonsuch.

Sinclair, A. (2004) '"Telling it like it was"? The "Residencia de Estudiantes" and its image', *Bulletin of Spanish Studies*, 81:6, 739–63.

Singer, P. (1983) *Hegel. A very short introduction*. Oxford, Oxford UP.

Sissons, M. & P. French (eds), (1986) *Age of austerity*. Oxford, Oxford UP.

Sissons, M. & P. French, 'Introduction' in M. Sissons & P. French (eds), *Age of austerity*, pp xvii–xx.

Skidelsky, R. (1990) *Oswald Mosley*. London, Papermac.

Somerville, E. OE. & M. Ross (2000) *The Irish RM*. London, Abacus.

Somerville, E.OE. (2000) 'Preface' in E.OE. Somerville & M. Ross, *The Irish R.M.*, pages not numbered.

SS *Duchess of York*. http://www.theshipslist.com/ships/lines/cp.html, accessed 29 Dec. 2010.

Stanford, W.B. & R.B. McDowell (1971) *Mahaffy. A biography of an Anglo-Irishman*. London, Routledge & Kegan Paul.

Starkie, E. (1941) *A lady's child*. London, Faber & Faber.

—— (1943) 'Nostalgie de Paris d'une irlandaise', *Aguedal* (May). (Typed manuscript dedicated to Josep Carner by E. Starkie, Biblioteca de Catalunya, Arxiu Josep Carner.)

Starkie, M.C. (1916) *What is patriotism. The teaching of patriotism*. Dublin, HMSO.

Starkie, Mrs W.J.M. (1952) 'The Royal Irish Academy of Music' in A. Fleischman (ed.), *Music in Ireland: a symposium*, pp 104–12.

Starkie, W.J.M. (1913) *Statement of evidence given by W.J.M. Starkie, Resident Commissioner to the [IRELAND] Vice-regal committee on national education*. [s.l.]

—— (1916) 'The wit and humour of Shakespeare' in I. Gollancz (ed.), *A book of homage to Shakespeare*, pp 212–26.

Stephens, J. (1992) *The insurrection in Dublin*. Gerrards Cross, Colin Smythe.

Stevens, J.A. (2007) *The Irish scene in Somerville and Ross*. Dublin, Irish Academic Press.

Storey, M. (ed.), (1988) *Poetry and Ireland since 1800: a source book*. London, Routledge.

Suárez Pajares, J. (ed.), (2002) *Música española entre dos guerras: 1914–1945*, Granada, Publicaciones del Archivo de Manuel de Falla.

Summerfield, H. (1975) *The myriad-minded man: a biography of George William Russell 'AE' 1867–1935*. Gerrards Cross, Colin Smythe.

Synge, J.M. (1952) *Collected plays*. London, Penguin.

—— (1952) 'Deirdre of the Sorrows' in *Collected plays*, pp 211–65.

The Ulster Covenant http://www.proni.gov.uk/index/search_the_archives/ulster:covenant. htm, accessed 20 April 2012.

Thompson, M. (2008) *The white war. Life and death on the Italian front 1915–1919*. London, Faber & Faber.

Thom's official directory of the United Kingdom of Great Britain and Ireland for the year 1893 (1893) Dublin, Alex. Thom & Co.

Thom's official directory of the United Kingdom of Great Britain and Ireland for the year 1903 (1903). Dublin, Alex Thom & Co.

Thom's official directory of the United Kingdom of Great Britain and Ireland for the year 1926 (1926). Dublin, Alex. Thom & Co.

Tracy, R. (2007) 'Foreword' in J.A. Stevens, *The Irish scene in Somerville and Ross*, pp viii–xii.

Trinity College (1931) *A catalogue of graduates of the University of Dublin vol. 5, containing the names of those who proceeded to degrees from the September commencements of the year 1917 to the spring commencements of the year 1931*. Dublin, Hodges, Figgis.

Tusell, J. et al. (eds), (1993) *El regimen de Franco (1936–1975). Política y relaciones exteriores*, tomo 2. Madrid, UNED.

Unamuno, M. de (1912) *Del sentimiento trágico de la vida*. Madrid, Renacimiento.

—— (1998) *Tres novelas ejemplares y un prólogo*. Madrid, Alianza.

Vena, M. (2001) *Italian grotesque theatre*, trans. M. Vena. Madison, Fairleigh Dickinson.

Venn, J.A. (1954) *Alumni Cantabrigienses, Part 2: 1752–1900*, vi. Cambridge.

Ventosa, J. (1948) 'Una gran causa común' in *Ensayos hispano-ingleses. Homenaje a Walter Starkie*, pp 355–7.

Villares, R. & J. Moreno Luzón (2009) *Restauración y dictadura*. Barcelona, Marcial Pons.

Villari, L. (1924) *The awakening of Italy*. London, Faber & Gwyer.

—— (1926) *The Fascist experiment*. London, Methuen.

Von Montë, W.J. & J. Milns West (1932) *Shrewsbury School: the last fifty years*. Shrewsbury, Wilding & Son.

Waugh, E. (1985) *Waugh in Abyssinia*. London, Penguin.

Webb, D.A. (ed.), (1951) *Of one company. Biographical studies of famous Trinity men*. Dublin, Icarus.

Welsford, E. (1935) *The fool: his social and literary history*. London, Faber & Faber.

West, J.M. (1937) *Shrewsbury*. London, Blackie & Son.

Weybright, V. (1967) *The making of a publisher. A life in the twentieth century book revolution*. New York, Reynal in association with William Morrow.

Whiston, J. 'Walter Fitzwilliam Starkie' in the *Oxford dictionary of national biography*. http://www.tcd.ie/HispanicStudies/assets/pdf/Starkie%20DNB%28W%29PDF.pdf, accessed 12 June 2012.

White, A.J.S. (1965) *The British Council. The first twenty-five years*. London, British Council.

Winstone, H.V.F. (1990) *Woolley of Ur. The life of sir Leonard Woolley*. London, Secker & Warburg.

Who was who 1951–1960, 5 (1961). London, Adam & Charles Black.

Wills, C. (2007) *That neutral island*. London, Faber & Faber.

Woodhouse, J. (1998) *Gabriele D'Annunzio. Defiant archangel*. Oxford, Clarendon Press.

Woolf, V. (1998) *Orlando. A biography*, ed. J.H. Stape. Oxford, Blackwell.

Yapp, A. (1927) *In the service of youth*. [s.l.], Nisbet.

Yapp, M.E. (ed.), (1997) *Politics and diplomacy in Egypt. The diaries of Sir Miles Lampson 1935–1937*. Oxford, Oxford UP.

Yates, D.E. (1953) *My gypsy days*. London, Phoenix House.

Yeates, P. (2001) *Lockout: Dublin 1913*. Dublin, Gill & Macmillan.

Yeats, W.B. [& Lady Gregory] (1953) *Cathleen Ni Houlihan* in *The collected plays of W.B. Yeats*. London, Macmillan.

Index